Ripley's Believe It or Not!®

Encyclopedia of the Bizarre

AMAZING, STRANGE, INEXPLICABLE, WEIRD, AND ALL TRUE!

BY JULIE MOONEY AND THE EDITOR'S OF RIPLEY'S BELIEVE IT OR NOT!®

BLACK DOG
& LEVENTHAL
PUBLISHERS
NEW YORK

This edition published in 2005.
Copyright © 2002 Ripley Entertainment Inc.
"Ripley's" and "Believe It or Not!" are registered trademarks of Ripley Entertainment Inc.

Published by
Black Dog & Leventhal Publishers, Inc.
151 West 19th Street
New York, NY 10011

Distributed by
Workman Publishing Company
708 Broadway
New York, NY 10003

Cover design by Andy Taray
Interior design by Edward Miller

Printed in China
Library of Congress Cataloging-in-
Publication Data available upon
request.

h g f e d c b a

ISBN: 1-57912-482-8

Table of Contents

S

T

U

V

Chapter 61

Vacation & Tourism

Lodging • Dining • Museums • Tourist Attractions

W

Chapter 62

Weapons & Warfare

Warfare • War Machines • Weapons and Armor

Chapter 63

Weather

Atypical Weather • Forecasting • Atmospheric Phenomena • Extreme Temperatures
• Thunder and Lightning • Hurricanes • Freak Storms • Floods • Tsunamis and Wild
Seas • Tornadoes • Snow • Rainfall • Odd Rain

Index

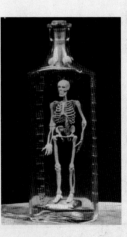

Introduction

Brace yourself—things are about to get weird. You're about to experience your world in a way you've never seen it before.

Before you is a collection of the strangest, wildest, and most bizarre phenomena in nearly every subject you can imagine.

Use this book to expand your own boundaries, to stretch the realm of what's possible. Use it to enrich your knowledge of your favorite subjects—to salt them with a tang of the bizarre.

You can also use this book as a creative resource, as a jumping-off point for the imagination. Writers, artists, musicians, teachers, scientists, creators, and explorers of all types will find inspiration within these pages.

For nearly eighty years, Ripley's Believe It or Not!® has been the trademark of the astonishing but true. Ripley's has amazed generations by presenting us with bizarre facts beyond our own experiences and bringing the extraordinary home. It's a celebration of the amazing and inexplicable within ourselves, the Believe It or Not! inside all of us.

Welcome to your world—it's weirder than you think!

Chapter 1

Abilities & Achievements

Ripley's is known for celebrating astonishing capabilities, from the backward walkers and three-legged racers of the very first Believe It or Not! cartoon in 1918, to the dare-devils and performance artists of the cutting-edge TBS television show. Welcome to Ripley's collection of abilities and achievements: a celebration of unique and astonishing talents.

ABILITIES AND ACHIEVEMENTS OF CHILDREN

• **Helen Riordan** climbed Pikes Peak in 1921—14,018 feet—at the age of three.

Ralph Roland Dowell, of Grand Junction, Colorado, could perform a "wrestler's bridge" at the age of two and a half.

• **Charles White** of Syracuse, New York, at the age of four years, eleven months, could pick up a 150-pound man.

• In July 1927, **George Cowie**, age fourteen, made his way alone without money across the continent in eleven days.

• **Joann Barnes**, age fifteen, of California, once swung sixty-eight hula-hoops on her body at the same time!

• **Elie Gourbeyre**, of Nouara, France, could lure any bird to her shoulder merely by crooking her finger! Her strange powers lasted only six years, until she turned twelve.

• **Dellen Millard** of Brampton, Ontario, Canada, flew solo in both an airplane and a helicopter—at the age of fourteen!

Kathalen Bentley of Mohawk, Oregon, could balance on her mother's hand at the age of $7^1/_2$ weeks.

At the age of three and a half, **Lynwood Ganza**, of Los Angeles, California, could do a "flag."

• **Travis Park**, age nine, could suck in his stomach so far it touched his backbone!

ABILITIES OF INFANTS

• **Gregory Borka**, of Hatboro, Pennsylvania, began walking when he was only thirteen days old!

• **Martha Ann Koop**, of Martin, Tennessee, could talk at the age of six months.

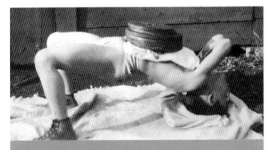

Romeo Lacroix, Jr., seven years old, supported 104 pounds while bridging on his neck.

• **Sandra Sheffield**, of Wainwright, Alberta, Canada, balanced upright on her father's hand at the age of five weeks!

CHILD ARTISTS AND MUSICIANS

• **Wang Yani**, of Gongcheng, China, began painting at the age of two, and had painted over four thousand works by the time she was six! She is the youngest artist to have had a solo show at the Smithsonian Institution.

• **Georgie Pocheptsov**, of Potomac, Maryland, created paintings that hung in major galleries across the United States and sold for up to nine thousand dollars each—when he was only seven years old!

• Little **Joanne Carswell**, of Jacksonville, Florida, at age two, could sing one hundred songs.

• **Scott MacIntyle**, of Redondo Beach, California, blind since birth, taught himself to play the piano at the age of three!

• **Leo Kushner** could play the piano at the age of twenty-seven months.

CHILD ATHLETES

• **Margaret Gestring** won a gold medal in diving at the 1936 Olympic Games, at the age of thirteen years, nine months!

• **Sally Brenner**, at age two, of Chicago, Illinois, was the youngest cyclist in the world.

• British jockey **John Daly** rode ten winning horses when he was only ten years old!

• **Troy Fergus Sharp**, of Ontario, Canada, swam five hundred fifty yards nonstop and unaided at the age of four.

CHILD GENIUSES

• Child prodigy **William Sidis**, of Boston, Massachusetts, could type in English and French at the age of two, and at the age of five wrote a treatise on anatomy!

• **Nicholas MacMahon**, of Surrey, England, taught himself to read at the age of one!

• **Seth Kinast**, of Hutchinson, Kansas, at the age of three, could recite the alphabet in Greek, count in German and Spanish, and had read almost twelve hundred books!

The young genius **LING-YONG KIM** of Seoul, South Korea, could solve mathematical problems based on Einstein's theory of Relativity—like this one to determine the indefinite integral—at the age of 4. $\int \frac{x}{\sqrt{x^2+4}}\,dx$

• **Billy Bracket**, of Hendersonville, North Carolina, at the age of twenty-six months, could recite from memory ninety nursery rhymes.

CHILD HEROES

• **Stephanie Taylor**, age eleven, of Vista, California, established a non-profit organization that has raised over twenty-five thousand dollars to buy bulletproof vests for police dogs!

• **Betty Lane Lindley**, of Chicago, Illinois, was a registered junior lifesaver at the age of six years! In September 1926, at the age of seven, she finished a two-mile marathon swim!

• **James Bliemeister**, age twelve, of West Seneca, New York, stopped a gas pipe from exploding by using a wad of chewing gum to plug the hole until emergency workers arrived!

CHILD INVENTORS

• **Brett Hudspeth**, of Pittsburgh, Pennsylvania, invented a chalk dispenser that distributed loose chalk neatly into a tray—when he was only nine years old!

• Eight-year-old **Brian Berlinski**, of Clifton, New Jersey, invented a silent car horn for hearing impaired drivers. A light on the dashboard flashes at the sound of a honking horn!

• **James Egerer** and **James McNelly**, both age twelve, of Hemlock, Michigan, built a four-and-a-half-foot-tall hot air balloon that actually flies, using a balsa wood frame and thirty-five birthday candles!

• Schoolgirl **Melanie Lamontagne**, of Timmins, Ontario, Canada, invented snowshoes for dogs!

CHILD SCHOLARS

• At age ten **Greg Smith** attended Randolph Macon College in Ashland, Virginia. Only three years before he was in the second grade!

• **Adragon de Millo**, of San Jose, California, earned a college degree at the age of eleven but didn't graduate junior high school until the age of thirteen!

EARLY CAREERS

• **Martin Luther King** was ordained a minister and elected assistant pastor at the age of eighteen.

• The youngest magician, **William Moreno Junior** of New York City, performed magic tricks on the stage in a solo act at the age of three.

• **Henri de Lorraine** (1614-1664) was appointed abbot of the monastery of Mont Saint Michel, one of the largest monasteries in all France, when he was only one year of age. He was abbot of nine monasteries at the age of twelve.

• **Johnny Clem**, of Newark, Ohio, joined the Union Army in 1862 at the age of ten and was wounded twice. He later applied for admission to West Point but was rejected.

• **Ellen Terry** (1847-1928), the English actress, never attended school, yet made her debut in a Shakespearean role before Queen Victoria at the age of nine.

• **Georges Feydeau** (1862-1921), the French dramatist, after his first visit to a play, at the age of six, wrote one himself.

ABILITIES AND ACHIEVEMENTS OF THE DISABLED

• **Joe Engressa**, a blind college student from Florida, could whistle the exact tones needed to place a long distance telephone call!

Musician **Anton Pagani** of La Salle, Illinois, could whistle "The Piccolino" while playing an accordian with his hands and a cello with his feet... and he was blind!

John Martin of Sarasota, Florida, had his head so severely mangled in an elevator accident that it was necessary to remove both his eyes. Yet he went on to build this astonishing house-car (note that the flowers in the window boxes are real!) in which he and his wife toured the country.

CASEY BOEHMER of Jerseyville, Ill., is a one-armed world-champion juggler!

• **Brian Opekan**, of Saint Catherine's, Ontario, Canada, blind since the age of eighteen, has a black belt in jujitsu and teaches self-defense!

• **Sherry Johnson**, age twelve, of Opelika, Alabama, blind since the age of two, is a champion rodeo rider!

• **Helen Keller**, deaf and blind from a young age, had such a well-developed sense of smell that she could identify each of her friends by their scents!

• **Jose Pinto**, ninety-five percent blind, drove seven miles through the city of Madrid to work every day!

• The man who read with his tongue: **William McPherson**, of Kansas City, Missouri, blind and armless, could read with his tongue as rapidly as average-sighted people could read with their eyes.

• Paraplegic **Carl Brinker** made a rapid descent of a 110-foot cliff backwards—in a wheelchair.

• The most amazing tourist in all history: **James Holman** (1786-1857), an Englishman, traveled alone for fifty years to France, Germany, Italy, and Switzerland, and wrote three travel books, although he had become totally blind at the age of twenty-one!

DISABLED ATHLETES

• After breaking his back in a motorcycle accident in 1985, **Jon Franks** of Hollywood, California, has gone on to compete in six triathlons, five marathons, and two biathlons!

• **Pete Gray**, center fielder for the Saint Louis Browns in 1945, had only one arm and caught with an unpadded glove!

• **Tom Dempsey**, born with only half a right foot, shares the National Football League record for the longest field goal, at sixty-three yards! He held the record alone for twenty-eight years.

Bill Irwin, a blind hiker from North Carolina, walked the 2,000-mile-long Appalachian Trail in eight months with only a guide dog to lead him!

EXCLUSIVE MEMBERSHIP

• The entire staff of a fast-food restaurant in Kuala Lumpur, Malaysia, has speech and hearing disabilities!

• All the players on an amateur soccer team in Roehampton, England, are one-legged except for the goalie—who has only one arm!

• In 1992, three blind climbers who had never before encountered snow, scaled 17,220-foot Mount Shitidhar in the western Himalayas!

• In Olney, Texas, there is an annual dove hunt exclusively for one-armed hunters!

ABILITIES AND ACHIEVEMENTS OF SENIORS

• **Joe Walden**, age one hundred and two, of Jacksonville, Florida, joined the Boy Scouts of America after he was fifty years old, and was honored with a merit award after fifty years of distinguished service!

• At the age of ninety, **Viola Krahn** won the three-meter springboard competition at the United States Masters' Indoor Diving Championships in Brown Deer, Wisconsin.

• **Norman Freeman**, an insurance broker of Chicago, Illinois, took up judo at fifty and won his black belt at sixty-five.

LENA STUMPF, a college student of Lepzig, Germany, paralyzed in both legs as the result of diphtheria, spent 2^1/$_2$ years in bed and was told by doctors that her case was hopeless. She devised a set of exercises herself and won the West German Pentathlon Championship (high jump, spear throwing, broad jump, discus, and running) in both of the next two years.

Perry L. Biddle of DeFuniack Springs, Florida, hoists himself up into a Human Flag position on his ninetieth birthday.

FATHER OSWALD McGINN, AGE 77, OF SAN ANTONIO, TEXAS, WAS A CRACK SHOT WITH A REVOLVER AND HE COULD SPLIT A BULLET BALANCED ON A RAZOR BLADE!

HARRY BIB OF GRAHAM, TEXAS, WHO HAS TWO ARTIFICIAL KNEE IMPLANTS, *MADE HIS FIRST PARACHUTE JUMP AT THE AGE OF 77!*

Henry D. Lewis, the oldest person in St. Augustine, Florida (itself the oldest city in the United States), at age ninety-five proved he was still spry. He said his ability spoke well for the Florida climate, where he had wintered for the last twenty-nine years.

• **Lieutenant Gershom Rice I** (1696-1781), of Auburn, Massachusetts, enlisted in the Revolutionary Army in 1776 at the age of eighty!

• **Carobeth Laird**, of Poway, California, wrote her first book at the age of eighty.

• **Elbert Lowenstein** of Nebraska, age sixty-two, once walked one thousand miles across six states to attend his fiftieth high school reunion!

AWARDS AND HONORS

• Actress **Janet Gaynor** won Academy Awards for three different films —*Seventh Heaven*, *Angel Street*, and *Sunrise*—in one year!

• **Ken Riordan,** of Grant's Pass, Oregon, has been an Eagle Scout since 1958 and has nine sons who are all Eagle Scouts!

• The only person in history with the name Oscar to win an Oscar Award was **Oscar Hammerstein II**!

• "The Queen's Scarf": In 1900, **Private Richard Thompson** of Ottawa, Canada, was awarded a scarf hand-knitted by England's Queen Victoria for bravery during the Boer War!

• "**Sandy**," the mongrel dog that starred in the Broadway musical *Annie*, won two Tony awards and performed for two United States Presidents!

"KERMIT THE FROG" —a puppet—was presented with an honorary doctorate from Long Island University! (1996)

• **Mary Babnick Brown**, of Pueblo, Colorado, received an award from the Colorado Aviation Historical Society for donating thirty-four inches of her hair for use in bombsights during World War II!

DEXTERITY AND FLEXIBILITY

• Pianist **Arthur Schultz**, of Hamtrack, Michigan, could play the piano with his hands upside down. He claimed he had to wait five minutes after doing this before he could play with his hands right-side up again.

• Argentine contortionist **Hugo Zamaratte** can fold his five-foot-nine-inch frame into a bottle twenty-six inches high and eighteen inches wide.

• **Moses C. Lanhorn**, Jr., of Monroe, Michigan, can stand facing forward with his feet facing backward—and walk.

• **James A. Garfield**, the twentieth President of the United States, could write Latin with one hand and Greek with the other simultaneously!

• Due to a strange twist of fate, **Avery Tudor** of New York City was able to turn his feet around backwards.

Martin Joe Laurello, "The Human Owl," could turn his head backwards.

Contortionist **F. Velez Campos** could bend his knee in the opposite direction.

Miss Zelma George of Canton, Ohio, could write forwards, backwards, upside down, and upside down backwards, and also write a different sentence with each hand in any combination of upside down, backwards, etc., simultaneously.

Leena Deeter could sign her name with both hands simultaneously—in any combination of backwards, forwards, right-side up, or upside down.

John Leather could move each eye independently of the other.

Robert Aitken, of San Francisco, could take off his hat with a double-back arm.

Julius B. Schuster, card sharp and world's champion "Pickup Artist," held twenty billiard balls in one hand in Jeanette, Pennsylvania. Schuster was one of Ripley's favorite Odditorium performers, and Ripley's frequently featured his manual dexterity skills not only in the cartoon but also on Believe It or Not! radio and television programs. Other stunts included picking up and holding twenty-five tennis balls and twenty baseballs, and most difficult of all, picking up from a flat surface and holding ten billiard balls in each hand in such a way that his hands could be turned in any position, even upside down.

• **Billy Rose**, the flamboyant Broadway showman, could write shorthand backwards with his left hand while writing it forwards with his right hand.

ENDURANCE AND STRENGTH

• **Harry Houdini** (1874-1926), the famed magician, could open cans with his teeth.

Triple view of Master Engineer Junior Grade **Gardner A. Taylor** lifting a 155-pound anvil with his ears, at the Pheasant Hunters Banquet in Winner, South Dakota. Later the sixty-four-year-old war veteran broke his own record by adding a 20-pound weight to the same anvil at the Peacock Café. Sixteen years later he was still going strong, lifting a 110-pound anvil with his ears on his eightieth birthday.

Joseph Green, a.k.a. "The Mighty Atom," could pull three cars weighing twenty-one thousand pounds—with his hair!

THE **MAN** WHO STRANGLED A LEOPARD WITH HIS BARE HANDS!
CARL AKELEY (1864-1926), WHO BECAME A CELEBRATED HUNTER AND EXPLORER, IN HIS FIRST ENCOUNTER WITH A WILD BEAST, WHEN JUMPED BY A FIERCE LEOPARD, IN SOMALILAND, CHOKED IT TO DEATH ... (1896)

Human magnet! **James Garry**, of Denver, Colorado, could lift a 14-pound weight by using only the vacuum created by the palm of his hand!

Paul von Dullack, of Chicago, talked continuously for 82$\frac{1}{2}$ hours on a Chicago radio show. He maintained a minimum of 75 words a minute.

• **James Paul**, "The Greek Titan," of Brooklyn, New York, could lift six people, weighing a total of seven hundred thirty-five pounds, with his teeth!

• **Tim Tufton**, of Tuftonboro, New Hampshire, was so powerful that he could leap out of a deep barrel without touching it with his hands!

• **Eugene Sandow**, a nineteenth-century strongman, could tear a stack of three full decks of cards in half!

• **Moyne Mullin**, of Berkeley, California, could support her entire weight on her elbows.

• **Count Meral**, an Italian nobleman, could part his hair using only the muscles of his scalp!

EXTRAORDINARY MENTAL ABILITIES

• **Johann Gottlieb Fichte** (1762-1814), the German philosopher, could repeat from memory verbatim any sermon he ever heard.

• **Elijah the Gaon**, Chief Rabbi of Lithuania, never forgot a book once he read it. Gaon committed to memory twenty-five hundred volumes. He knew by heart the Bible, Midrash, Mekilta, Sifre Tosedfta, Seder Olam, the Talmud, the Zohar, the Code, Rashi, Rambam, and many other religious texts and could quote any passage at will.

• **Willi Melnikov**, a professor who lived in Moscow, Russia, could speak ninety-three different languages!

• In the 1930s, **Arthur Lloyd**, of Medford, Massachusetts, the "Human Card Index," carried fifteen thousand notecards in a special jacket with forty pockets, and could locate any card in five seconds.

UNUSUAL ABILITIES

• **Roger Reed,** of Columbia, South Carolina, can chew razor blades without cutting his mouth to pieces!

• **Kevin Cole**, of Carlsbad, New Mexico, can blow a piece of spaghetti out of his nose a distance of seven and a half inches!

• **Johnny "Cigars" Connors**, of Roxbury, Massachusetts, rolled a peanut with his nose from Boston to Worchester.

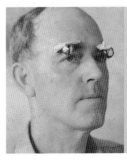

Musical eyebrow! **F. G. Holt**, of Nashville, Arkansas, attaches small bells to his eyebrows and plays various tunes. He has complete control of all the muscles of his face.

• **Paddy Davison**, of Ohio, can spear his cheeks with meat skewers, pierce his neck with a giant pin, and hammer nails through his hands and feet without injury!

• **Jim Purol** can stuff his mouth with one hundred fifty-one drinking straws!

• **Hal Cort**, of Cincinnati, Ohio, can talk with his mouth taped and his nose closed.

• **Thomas MacClure**, of Detroit, Michigan, hypnotizes fish.

• **Hadji Ali**, a vaudeville performer in the early 1900s, could swallow watermelon seeds, jewels, coins, and peach pits—then regurgitate specific items as requested.

• **Jim Chicon** can snort milk through one of his nostrils then eject it from his eye!

MAT PLENDL of Redondo Beach, Calif., CAN SPIN **30 HULA-HOOPS** AROUND HIS BODY ALL AT THE SAME TIME.

Famous Ripley's "girner," J. T. Saylors

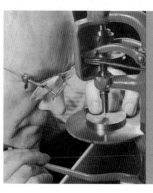

Arthur Benson of Lancaster, Pennsylvania, drilled a hole in a human hair.

- **A. Kimberly Goodman,** of Chicago, Illinois, can pop her eyeballs right out of their sockets!

- **Stephen Woodmore,** of Kent, England, can speak at a rate of over six hundred thirty-seven words a minute!

ALFRED LANGEVIN

Alfred Langevin could smoke a pipe, play a recorder, smoke a cigarette, and even blow up a balloon—through his eye!

H. C. Harris, Sr., played harmonica with his nose while whistling, in Jackson, Mississippi. All of the dozens of Ripley contestants who submitted their simultaneous whistling and harmonica-playing talents believed theirs was a unique skill.

FUTURE TRACK STAR: "BABY FLO JO" OUTRUNS THEM ALL

Sometimes athletic talent is evident at an early age—and in little Kyenishi Jeter's case, a very early age. Apparently born to become a track star, Kyenishi is already leaving seasoned athletes, including grown men, in the dust. And she's only six years old!

Kyenishi's mom and dad, Kieonte and Anthony Jeter, discovered their daughter's astonishing talent for running just over two years ago, when they were out for a jog around Baltimore, Maryland's, Lake Montebello. Little Kyenishi, then only four, wanted out of her stroller. The moment her parents set her down on the two-mile track that circles the lake, she was off like a shot!

After she had been running for several miles, her concerned parents tried to get her to take a break. But the little girl asked, "Why'd you stop me? I'm having fun!" Kyenishi covered an astonishing eight miles on her first run!

Kyenishi's been running ever since. Worried that all this exercise might be harmful to somebody so young, her parents consulted with her pediatrician, Doctor Niru Parekh. The doctor cleared Kyenishi to run as much as she liked, guessing that the preschooler would stop of her own accord whenever she got tired.

Kyenishi now has her own track coach, and a group of fellow athletes, all adults, with whom she trains regularly—and whom she regularly outruns!

Kyenishi has earned the nickname "Baby Flo Jo," after her hero, the late Florence Joyner. There's little doubt that Kyenishi will be a star some day. But for now, her parents are wisely letting her enjoy a mostly ordinary life as an adorable little girl. Kyenishi celebrated her fifth birthday by breaking a ten-minute mile!

Chapter 2
Accidents & Disasters

IN 1972, VESNA VULOVIC, A STEWARDESS ON A FLIGHT OVER CZECHOSLOVAKIA, SURVIVED AN EXPLOSION WHILE INSIDE THE PLANE'S TAIL, THAT THREW HER 33,000 FT. TO THE GROUND!

Welcome to Ripley's grisly gallery of bizarre accidents, tragic deaths, heroic rescues, and survival against astonishing odds. In nearly every case these accidents are freak occurrences, often Believe It or Not! candidates in and of themselves. But even more remarkable are the tenacious individuals who experienced—and survived—these horrifying events. You may find it hard to believe that these survivors, whether through luck, or through their own tenacity, came through their misfortunes alive.

ACCIDENTS

• Accidents are the cause of death of seven out of every one hundred Canadians.

• In the late 1800s, **Charles Bastard,** lessee of the Adelaide City Baths in Adelaide, Australia, had to dive to the bottom of the baths to rescue a man who, with iron plates attached to his feet, claimed he had invented a contraption which would enable a man to walk on water!

• In the summer of 1923, **Delbert C. Hughes,** of Clarinda, Iowa, had his hat pinned to his head with a pitchfork that fell from a hayloft! His father pulled the pitchfork from his skull by hand. Hughes recovered fully and suffered no ill effects.

• In 1990, **Bengt Svensson,** of Trollhattan, Sweden, had an inch-long metal screw removed from the inside of his head forty-eight years after it entered his skull during a handgun accident!

• **Travis Bogumill,** of Stanley, Wisconsin, survived having a 3.2-inch-long nail shot into his brain!

STRANGEST ANNAL OF THE SEA! The sailing ship "ECLIPSE" was struck by a meteor in the mid-Pacific. The masts were carried away, and the vessel was abandoned with a loss of 3 lives. Lifeboats covered the 900 miles to Hawaii in 13 days.

Aimé Grosjean, AGE 72, of Regensdorf, Switzerland, WAS BLOWN OFF A 17TH-FLOOR BALCONY BY A GUST of WIND, BUT LANDED ON A LOWER FLOOR, UNHARMED!

Believe It or Not! IN 1994, in Arenys de Mar, Spain, A DRIVER and PASSENGER *ESCAPED UNHARMED FROM A TRUCK THAT COLLIDED WITH A CAR, FELL ONTO A RAILWAY TRACK* AND WAS CRUSHED BY A TRAIN!

AIRCRAFT ACCIDENTS

• A vulture flying at an elevation of thirty-seven thousand feet collided with an airplane over Africa's Ivory Coast!

• Parachutist **Michael Loeb** got tangled during a jump and spent twenty minutes dangling one thousand feet above the ground from a plane traveling one hundred fifty miles per hour!

• American pilot **Hank Dempsey** fell out of an airplane flying at twenty-five hundred feet and hung for twenty minutes from the plane's stairs until the copilot safely landed the aircraft!

• In 1993, all one hundred sixty-three passengers on an Air India flight that had crashed upside down and burst into flames walked away from the wreckage!

• In 1994, **Ray and Audrey Goldman** discovered a thermometer from an airplane that had crashed into Oregon's Lake Hyatt in 1971. It was still in working condition after twenty-three years underwater!

• **Harry Griffiths** survived being dragged a half-mile at one hundred miles per hour over an ice field while dangling from the belly of a World War II bomber plane!

• Saved by a wedge of cheese: **Frank Emmert Junior** of Superior, Wisconsin, survived a plane crash by holding a foam piece of cheese over his face, which absorbed the force of his fall!

AUTO CRASHES

• Two-year-old **Michael Collins,** of Rochester, Pennsylvania, drove his mother's car over a guard-rail, down a fifty-four-foot embankment, and across a four-lane highway—yet escaped without injury!

• In 1933, seven Japanese acrobats survived a high-way accident by diving out of the windows when their bus skidded off a cliff!

• **Sobhy Iskander,** of Mississauga, Canada, escaped without injury when a lawn-mower blade sliced through his car windshield and pierced the dashboard!

• In 1985, **Robert Lagree,** of Austin, Texas, survived being pinned between two trucks by pushing one—weighing sixty-three thousand pounds—off his chest!

• In 1995, **David Abel,** of Orlando, Florida, had to escape through a broken window when his Jeep™ was rammed from behind, flipped over twice, and totally destroyed—yet he walked away with only a cut on his left pinky!

A GERMAN COUPLE *DROVE THEIR CAR DIRECTLY INTO A RIVER* WHEN THEIR LUXURY CAR'S COMPUTERIZED NAVIGATION SYSTEM FAILED TO TELL THEM THEY WERE SUPPOSED TO TAKE A FERRY!

A sedan driven by Robert Stone was cut in half in a collision yet its windows were not even cracked.

• In 1969, **Miles Lucas,** of New Jersey, fell from his car after it was struck by another car. His vehicle then crashed into the wall of a cemetery and came to rest on a tombstone bearing his name!

• The driver of a two-ton ice cream truck that careened two hundred fifteen feet down a hill and into a tree in Reelsville, Indiana, was a nanny goat!

• **Clarence Wills,** age seventy-seven, of Lincoln, Nebraska, escaped without serious injury after the wheels of his car slipped off their repair blocks, pinning him under the vehicle for forty-five minutes!

• **Peter Karpin,** a German spy, had his money confiscated by French authorities who used the funds to buy a car that was later involved in a fatal accident…in which the victim was Peter Karpin!

• **Richard Topps,** of Derbyshire, England, survived a motorcycle accident that left him impaled on a four-foot-long wooden fence post. His body was pierced from hip to chest, yet the post missed all his vital organs!

• In 1952, a stock car finished first in a race even though its wheels came off. It flipped over and skidded upside down across the finish line!

• A brick mailbox hit by a car flipped in the air and crashed through the roof of the car. No one was injured and not one brick fell off or was damaged!

ELECTRIC SHOCKS

• **Reverend Henry Land** and his daughter **Fay** survived a 7,200-volt electric shock. Although badly burned, fifteen-year-old Fay instructed rescuers in reviving her father!

• Drum major **Steve Harding,** of Ventura, California, threw his baton into the air, tangling two four-thousand-volt power lines, which blacked out ten blocks, put a radio station off the air, and started a fire!

• "Lucky landing": **J. H. Hedley,** a Canadian pilot, on January 6, 1918, was thrown from his plane three miles in the air when it went into a vertical dive to avoid enemy fire—but then landed on the fuselage as the plane leveled off!

• In 1967, seventeen-year-old **Brian Latasa** received a jolt of two hundred thirty thousand volts of electricity while climbing a power tower in Los Angeles, California—yet survived!

• In 1981, **"Sedgewick,"** a cat in Cambridge, England, survived a thirty-thousand-volt electric shock that blacked out part of the city!

EXPLOSIONS

• Acoustic, sound-activated mines set in Tokyo Harbor during World War II were accidentally detonated by the drum-like noise of croaker fish.

• In 1994, a rock blasted from a construction site crashed through the roof of **Helen Walkus'** home in Port Hardy, British Columbia, over two miles away!

FALLS

• **Racine Gomez,** of Denver, Colorado, age two, survived both falling from a three-story apartment window, and a tornado that rolled her over in her mother's car three times, without any injuries!

• **Sergeant Nick Alkemade,** a British bomber pilot, plunged eighteen thousand feet— over three miles—without a parachute and survived, landing in a snow bank only four feet deep!

• **"Barbara,"** a cat, survived a fall of three hundred feet from a thirty-story building in Hong Kong!

• In 1991, skydiver **Jill Shields,** of Euclid, Ohio, survived a 9,500-foot fall after her parachute failed to open!

• **Joshua Beatty,** age two, of Southfield, Michigan, survived a fall from a ninth-floor window when his diaper snagged on a bush!

SARAH ANN HENLEY survived falling 250 feet from the Clifton Suspension Bridge in England when her petticoat opened like a parachute! (1859)

• Skydivers **Mike Hussey** and **Amy Adams,** of Columbus, Ohio, survived after falling 13,500 feet with a torn parachute that had snagged on the plane's tail!

• **Jens Jension,** of Denmark, fell into a spiky barberry bush and had to visit his doctor two hundred forty-eight times to have 32,131 thorns removed from his body!

• **John Scott,** of England, survived several free-fall drops in a mine elevator before safety engineers testing the elevator's emergency brakes realized he was inside!

• "The catch of his life": **Javon Saucier,** age six, of New Haven, Connecticut, caught and saved a falling three-year-old child who accidentally fell from a fifteen-foot-high window!

FIRES

• In 1928, a windmill on a farm in Kaltendorf, Germany, began spinning so fast in high winds that it caught fire and burned to the ground!

• In Tokyo, Japan, in February 1657, a kimono believed to have caused the deaths of its three previous owners was burned by a priest in a fire that destroyed three hundred temples, five hundred palaces, nine thousand bridges, and killed over one hundred thousand people!

• **Michael Rodrigue,** of Sarasota, Florida, used a jug of iced tea to extinguish a car fire in order to rescue a woman from inside the burning car!

• A company in Prairie Village, Kansas, has invented a fire escape device that consists of a hundred-foot-long aluminized elastic tube with exit zippers every seven feet!

• After saving a family from a fire, firefighters in Dudley, England, returned to the house and rescued a pet tarantula spider by carrying it out in a soup ladle!

• **"Jaguar,"** a Siamese cat owned by Joanie and Harry Smith of Charlotte, North Carolina, jumped on her sleeping owners' backs to warn them of a fire burning in their house!

• In 1879, **Benjamin B. Oppenheimer** invented a device for saving people from high-rise hotel fires that consisted of padded shoes and a five-foot parachute fastened to the head!

• In 1931, the Olson McClintock icehouse near Blanca, Colorado, burned to the ground without the ice inside melting!

• The El Rey Theater in Manteca, California, was gutted by fire after a showing of the film *The Towering Inferno!*

• A fire has been burning underground in the town of Centralia, Pennsylvania, for over thirty years!

• In 1994, four restaurant employees in Jeffersonville, Indiana, locked in a freezer by robbers who set a fire, survived after a bucket of spilled pickles extinguished the flames!

An electric refrigerator was found undamaged in a house after a fire had completely destroyed the building. The contents were still fresh and the ice cubes were not melted!

• A chain of bonfires stretching from Britain to Rome was used to signal **Emperor Claudius** to join his army in battle!

• A fire in a coal mine in Straitsville, Ohio, burned continuously for fifty-two years!

• A dog playing with matches started a house fire in Kelso, Washington!

LIGHTNING STRIKES

• In the Xinjiang Uygur, autonomous region of China, there is a one-hundred-mile-long area where freak lightning storms regularly cause trees to burst into flames!

• After becoming blind and deaf in a truck accident, **Edwin Robinson,** of Falmouth, Maine, regained his sight and hearing after being struck by lightning!

• In May 1951, lightning set fire to two houses in Marianna, Florida—one belonging to **C. N. Horne** of North Green Street, and the other to **S. H. Horne** of South Green Street!

• In 1910, **Ray Caldwell,** a pitcher for the Cleveland Indians, was struck by lighting and knocked out, but went on to finish and win the game!

SHIP WRECKS

• The *H.M.S. Eurydice*, a British naval training ship that sank on March 24, 1878, was sketched as it capsized by one of only two survivors of the three hundred twenty-eight seamen aboard.

• In February 1864, the body of **Alfred Goering,** skipper of the German brig *Juno*, was the only survivor when the ship sank in a storm off the island of Islay in the Hebrides, carrying fifteen crewmen to their death. Goering had tied his oilskins with string at the wrists and buttoned his clothes, thus imprisoning a quantity of air, and his boots had filled with water, allowing him to float in an upright position.

• A boat carrying coal to light the newly erected lighthouse of Saint Agnes on the Scilly Isles, England, for the first time, hit that lighthouse in the darkness and was wrecked, October 30, 1680.

THE MOST AMAZING SURVIVALS IN THE ANNALS OF THE SEA! THE HILDA, A SMALL CHANNEL STEAMER, CARRYING 74 PASSENGERS AND CREW, SPLIT IN HALF ON A VOYAGE FROM ENGLAND TO FRANCE ON NOV. 18, 1905-- BUT 26 MEN MANAGED TO CLING TO THE SHIP'S MAST WHICH BROKE AWAY FROM THE VESSEL AND BECAME WEDGED UPRIGHT IN A REEF. THE NEXT DAY, RESCUERS FOUND 20 DEAD MEN WITH THEIR FINGERS FROZEN TO THE MAST--BUT THEIR TIGHTLY PACKED BODIES HAD ENABLED 6 TO SURVIVE

The Dundee Star, a Scottish bark abandoned by its crew in a gale off Midway Island, drifted completely around the earth in 4 years and finally piled up in 1891 on Midway Island— the very spot from which she started her phantom voyage!

• In 1905, the *S.S. Dora*, carrying three passengers and mail, was completely disabled by a storm on a voyage from Valdez, Alaska. It drifted helplessly for sixty-three days, then was blown safely into a harbor in the Strait of San Juan de Fuca, Washington.

• In 1807, the *Union*, a whaling ship commanded by Captain Edmund Gardner, sank off the coast of South America on a voyage from New Bedford, Massachusetts, after colliding with a whale.

• Two Maori women, the only survivors of a shipwreck in Cook Strait, New Zealand, were saved by floating eighty miles to safety on the carcass of a whale!

In 1903, in Lindal, England, a 200-foot-deep hole suddenly opened up and swallowed a locomotive, then buried it under tons of dirt!

• The *Star of the South*, a steamer out of Dunedin, New Zealand, went aground on the coast of New Zealand three times—the third time she was abandoned as a total loss.

TRAIN WRECKS

• **Sara Gillies,** of Perth, Australia, age nine months, survived inside her baby carriage after the carriage was hit and dragged under an oncoming train!

• On July 19, 1991, a runaway train in India carrying twenty-seven wagon loads of cattle, traveled for over two hours and fifty-eight miles through thirteen stations before it could be stopped!

• **Douglas Scandlin,** of Louisville, Kentucky, escaped untouched by a freight train that passed completely over his body!

"PIGGYBACK COLLISION" DURING A SNOWSTORM in 1898 NEAR Fitchburg, Mass., A TWO-CAR MILK TRAIN CRASHED HEAD-ON INTO A LOCOMOTIVE, LANDING ON TOP of IT—WITHOUT SERIOUS INJURY TO ANYONE ONBOARD EITHER TRAIN!

ANIMAL ATTACKS

• **Gail Brooks** saved her boyfriend's life after he was attacked by a shark, by closing off a bleeding artery with dental floss!

• In 1971, **Rodney Fluery,** of Mountain, California, bit a rattlesnake to death after it attacked him and his dog!

• **"Sidney,"** a bulldog owned by Kathy Wood of Laguna Beach, California, frequently knocks down skateboarders and steals their boards!

• In 1924, **Fred Cunningham,** age fourteen, was lifted off a golf course by an eagle with a wingspan of eight feet!

OOOUUFF!

SURFER *JOHN FERREIRA* of Stanford, Calif., SURVIVED A GREAT WHITE SHARK ATTACK BY JAMMING HIS SURFBOARD INTO THE SHARK'S JAWS!

• A pheasant in Tenby, West Wales, brought mail service to a halt for several weeks by repeatedly attacking the postman!

• In 1978, glider pilot **Antonio Beozzi** was attacked by an eagle that broke into the cockpit as his plane soared 4,600 feet over the mountains near Turin, Italy.

• In Niceville, Florida, a red-tailed hawk tried to fly off with Sandy Parks' six-pound Chihuahua, but she managed to save the dog by yanking on its leash until the bird let go!

• **Maddie Mix,** of Baton Rouge, Louisiana, survived after an estimated ten thousand bees invaded her car, by driving through a car wash where she was rescued by a beekeeper who happened to be washing his car at the same time!

• In 1940, on a highway near Rouyn, Quebec, a moose that rammed a ten-ton truck walked away while the truck had to be towed!

• In March 1990, during a family picnic, an eagle in Isfahan, Iran, swooped down and carried away a two-year-old child!

NATURAL DISASTERS

AVALANCHES

• The Notch House, a hotel in New Hampshire's White Mountains, was originally the home of a family that was wiped out trying to flee from an avalanche. Ironically, they would have been safe if they had stayed in the house, which remained undamaged.

FIFTEEN *IGUANAS* THAT WERE SWEPT OUT TO SEA ON A RAFT of WATER-LOGGED TREES *TRAVELED OVER 200 MILES* from Guadeloupe to Anguilla IN THE Caribbean! (1995)

EARTHQUAKES

• **Antonio Morelli** (1739-1814), an opera singer, was only sixteen years of age when he was buried for a week under a demolished church by the great earthquake of November 1755, in Lisbon, Portugal, yet his hair turned snow white.

• Earthquake shock waves travel five miles per second.

IGREJA do CARMA AN EDIFICE BUILT IN LISBON, PORTUGAL, AROUND 1400, WAS ALMOST COMPLETELY DESTROYED BY AN EARTHQUAKE IN 1755--ONLY *ITS SLENDER ARCHES REMAINING UNDAMAGED*

FLOODS

• The church bell that was provided by providence: The Episcopal church of Butteville, Oregon, constructed in 1869, was without a bell for a year for lack of funds. A great flood destroyed a church in neighboring Champoeg, and its bell was washed ashore near the Butteville church, where it is still in use today.

THE WOMAN WHO FLEW ON A FEATHER BED!
ELIZA STATE DURING THE CYCLONE OF 1860 IN MASSAC COUNTY, ILL., WAS LIFTED AS SHE SLEPT ON HER FEATHER BED IN BOAZ AND CARRIED THROUGH THE AIR INTO POPE COUNTY —*LANDING UNHARMED 8 MILES FROM HER HOME!*

AMBER COLVIN, AGE 9, OF SHADYSIDE, OHIO, SURVIVED A FLOOD THAT DESTROYED HER FAMILY'S HOUSE — *BY RIDING INSIDE A BATHTUB DOWN THE OHIO RIVER!*

The AIRBORNE STEEPLE—Honfleur, France. It was blown from its church to the roof of the bell ringer's house across the street, where it has remained for more than 500 years.

• The mountain that drowned a city: Antigua, Guatemala, a flourishing city and a cultural center with universities, was washed away when the side of Mount Agua burst and released its crater full of water on the city below.

LANDSLIDES AND ROCKFALLS

• The Frank Slide in Alberta, Canada: On April 29, 1903, a huge wedge of limestone—four thousand feet wide, 1,300 feet long,

and five hundred feet thick, comprising more than 70,000,000 tons of rock—buried five square miles of the valley of a mining town, and sixty-six bodies, to a depth of one hundred feet.

• The entire village of Runswick, England, slipped into the sea in 1669—yet not a single inhabitant was drowned! All the residents of Runswick were attending a funeral in a neighboring village at the time of the catastrophe.

TORNADOES

• In 1877, a tornado in Mount Carmel, Illinois, carried a church spire a distance of seventeen miles!

TSUNAMIS

• On July 15, 1912, a huge boulder weighing 235 tons was lifted by a wave from the bottom of the sea and flung atop another rock in Waverly, NSW, Australia.

VOLCANIC ERUPTIONS

• The statue of a chained watchdog was molded in A.D. 79 from the impression made by a dog straining

to escape the volcanic destruction of Pompeii.

• A cornu, a musical instrument of ancient Rome, found in the ruins of Pompeii, could still be played nearly two thousand years after the city's destruction.

WEAPON WOUNDS

• **Oliver Anthony,** of Memphis, Tennessee, was shot by a robber while playing golf, but survived when the bullet lodged in a golf ball inside his trousers' pocket.

• "Abs of steel": **Roch Beaudry** was fired at by an assailant at an Ottawa, Ontario, Canada, bus stop, but stopped the bullet with his stomach! It didn't even pierce his skin!

• In 1992 **Elvira Evers,** of Los Angeles, California, accidentally shot in the abdomen while nine months pregnant, gave birth to a healthy baby girl, who was born with a bullet lodged in her right elbow!

• Security guard **Albert Howard,** of Dorset England, survived being shot at when the bullet lodged in his prayer book.

• While on a hunting expedition in 1989, **Lars Invar Carlsson,** of Helas, Sweden, was shot and killed by a dog.

• **Patrick Vaillancourt,** of Montreal, Canada, was stabbed four times during a fight, but survived without any organ damage because a firefighter's badge he keeps in his wallet took the brunt of the blows!

• **Larry Lands,** of Potosi, Missouri, while on a hunting trip, was accidentally shot in the leg by a turkey!

GARY LEE OF LOS ANGELES, CALIF., WAS SHOT IN THE CHEST BY ROBBERS AFTER HIS CAR BROKE DOWN, BUT SURVIVED WITH ONLY MINOR INJURIES BECAUSE THE .25 CALIBER BULLET LODGED IN HIS POCKET RADIO!

• **Joe Petrowski,** of Winnipeg, Canada, was accidentally shot in the back by his pet dog, Vegas, but the dog then dragged the wounded man to safety!

• **Kenneth McCarrol,** of Detroit, Michigan, survived being shot by a burglar after the bullet bounced off his pocket calculator!

• **Kevin Panten**, age fourteen, of Slinger, Wisconsin, accidentally shot by a deer hunter, survived after spitting out the bullet that had entered through his neck!

• Doctors in Bangkok, Thailand, removed the unexploded head of an M-79 grenade from the arm of **Hoang Minh Son**, a farmer who was digging in his field when his hoe struck the shell!

• **Cole Woolner**, of Detroit, Michigan, survived being shot by a robber because the bullets lodged in two deep-dish pizzas he was delivering!

• **Bruce Levon**, of Grosse Pointe, Michigan, was accidentally shot in the head in 1983, and he didn't know it until doctors spotted the slug in an X-ray eight years later!

• **Private William Parker**, a soldier in the United States Army fighting in Vietnam, survived after a shot to his head was deflected by the Bible he wore underneath his helmet!

RESCUES

• **Gene Chaffin**, of Encinitas, California, rescued a pregnant doe after the animal was struck by a car. He delivered two fawns by Caesarian section and saved one by performing mouth-to-mouth resuscitation!

• **Kathie Vaughan**, of Franklin, Indiana, paralyzed from the waist down in an accident, was dragged away from her burning van by her pet Rottweiler!

• **Hamdija Osman**, a bus driver in Yugoslavia, kept his bus from rolling over a cliff by jamming his legs under a wheel, stopping the vehicle and saving thirty passengers!

• In 1940, **Warren Felty** rescued **William Miller** from a snowbank after a car accident; four years later, while a prisoner of war in Germany, he saved the same William Miller from freezing to death!

• In 1942, **Winkie**, a Royal Air Force carrier pigeon, flew one hundred and eighteen miles to alert rescuers of a bomber that had crashed into the North Sea!

THE GIRL WHO WAS SAVED BY HER HAIR!
CAROLINE HOMASSEL
BLOCKED FROM ESCAPE IN A THEATRE FIRE IN RICHMOND, VA. HAD BRAIDS SO LONG THAT A MAN TRAPPED WITH HER USED THE GIRL'S HAIR TO LOWER HER SAFELY TO THE GROUND!
CAROLINE IN TURN SUMMONED HELP FOR HER RESCUER – DR. PHILIP THORNTON – AND LATER MARRIED HIM!
1811

• A group of one hundred monkeys in Assam, India, stopped traffic and rescued a young monkey that had been accidentally hit by a car! The animals blocked cars for half an hour before carrying the injured monkey away.

• **Priscilla**, a pet pig, rescued a drowning boy by swimming out into a lake and towing him safely to shore!

Deep-sea diver J.T.L. POWERS rescued his diving partner from the jaws of a giant grouper by punching the fish in the eye!

HENRIK CARLSEN, A DANISH FISHERMAN, SURVIVED 15 DAYS ON AN ARCTIC ISLAND off Greenland BY LYING UNDER HIS BOAT and EATING SNOW!

SURVIVORS

• Speed skater **Jaqueline Boerner** of Germany, unable to skate for more than a year after a serious car accident in 1990, won a gold medal at the 1992 Olympics!

• **David Hicks**, of Mont Alto, Pennsylvania, who lost both arms in a motorcycle accident, regularly bowls using his feet!

• **Wesley Askins**, of Lake Luzerne, New York, who lost his sight in a car accident, rebuilds car engines for a living and is a champion archer!

• After their car broke down, **Jennifer Stolpa** and her five-month-old son, **Clayton**, survived four days of freezing temperatures without food inside a Nevada cave while her husband, James, walked forty-five miles through a blizzard to get help!

• **Norma Hanson**, while diving off Catalina Island in California, survived an attack by a great white shark by kicking out its teeth with her steel-toed boots!

• **Doug Simonson**, of Sumpter, Oregon, after a crash in his truck, crawled six miles for help with a broken shoulder and neck!

• **Chuck Woulard**, of Vidalia, Georgia, played eighteen holes of golf with a live diamondback rattlesnake inside his golf shoe!

• In 1992, sixteen Americans and sixteen Russians spent four months in a town built on an ice flow set adrift in the Weddel Sea!

THE MAN WHO BORE A CHARMED LIFE! FRANK TOWER AN OILER, SWAM AWAY FROM 3 MAJOR SEA DISASTERS — THE TITANIC, IN 1912 THE EMPRESS OF IRELAND, IN 1914 AND THE LUSITANIA IN 1915

THE HUMAN CORK!

CASIMIR POLEMUS of Ploërmel, France, WAS INVOLVED IN 3 SHIPWRECKS – AND EACH TIME WAS THE SOLE SURVIVOR! HE WAS THE SOLE SURVIVOR OF THE "JEANNE CATHERINE," WRECKED OFF BREST ON JULY 11, 1875, THE "TROIS FRÈRES," WRECKED IN THE BAY OF BISCAY ON SEPT. 4, 1880, AND L'ODEON," WRECKED OFF NEWFOUNDLAND ON JAN. 1, 1882

Michail Lasjuv, of Russia, who lost both hands, his vision, and his hearing during World War II, learned to read braille using his lips!

CHELSEA TAESYA, AGE 3, SURVIVED WITHOUT INJURIES AFTER CLINGING TO THE WINDSHIELD WIPERS ON THE BACK of HER FATHER'S CAR for ALMOST 12 MILES AT SPEEDS of 83 MPH! A PASSING MOTORIST FINALLY NOTIFIED HER FATHER!

• Shipwrecked in the Pacific Ocean, **Lottie Stevens,** of New Caledonia, drifted at sea for thirteen days on the back of a giant manta ray!

• American **Kathy Nelson** survived without serious injury spinning upside down for almost half an hour when a carnival ride that usually took only four minutes got stuck in high gear!

• **John Barkley**, of Paris, Illinois, broke his neck in two places and shattered the vertebrae in his back in three places after diving into a swimming pool—yet he has now been cleared for all sports except football.

• In 1990, a woman in Denver, Colorado, tied up by robbers, was rescued after dialing 911 with her nose!

• **Dirk Steem**, of Germany, survived spending a week in Lake Michigan on an air mattress that had drifted seventeen miles from shore!

• During a fight, a Gilbert Island native had a five-inch knife driven into his forehead. The knife remained in his forehead three days, but he suffered no ill effects!

• In 1989, **William Lamm**, of Vero Beach, California, escaped unhurt after being sucked into a water intake pipe and traveling through it for fifteen hundred feet at fifty miles per hour!

• Four men who spent two days drifting one hundred miles in the Florida Gulf Stream were saved after signaling to a rescue plane with their credit cards!

CAROL MURRAY of BRADFORD, ONT., CANADA, SURVIVED AND IS WALKING AGAIN **AFTER HER PARACHUTE FAILED TO OPEN AND SHE PLUNGED 3,200 ft. TO THE GROUND!**

VALENTIN GRIMALDO of Texas, bitten by a coral snake, killed the poisonous reptile by biting off its head, then he used its body as a torniquet to save his life!

• In 1966, **Victor Surpitski**, of Ipswich, Massachusetts, survived a sixty-foot fall from a sky-walker truck—while holding a running chainsaw!

• In 1993, **Donald Wyman**, of Punxsutawney, Pennsylvania, trapped under a fallen tree while working in the forest, amputated his own leg with a pocketknife, then drove himself two miles to get help!

• **Clara Crosbie**, a girl twelve years of age, was lost in the Australian wilderness near Lilydale for twenty days in the middle of winter without food or shelter yet suffered no ill effects from either exposure or her fast.

ACCIDENT PRONE

• **Anna Hascher**, age eighty-two, was hit and run over by the same car driver in Klosterneuberg, Austria, in 1983 and in

1992, in accidents that occurred just five hundred yards apart!

• "Calamity Mary": **Mary Bergere** survived thirteen automobile accidents in which the cars were demolished each time. She also was thrown from a horse, kicked by a cow, bitten by a dog, and scratched by a wildcat, and survived an Arizona cloudburst, a Florida hurricane, a Kansas cyclone, a Mississippi flood, a California earthquake, and a three-thousand-foot fall from an airplane—all without a single serious injury!

• **Gus Cohen**, of England, survived the sinking of the *Titanic*, a head wound during a World War I bombing, and falling out of moving train into the path of a car!

• In 1994, in Arenyas de Mar, Spain, a driver and passenger escaped unharmed from a truck that collided with a car, fell onto a railway track, and was crushed by a train!

• A woman driving in Reykjavik, Iceland, was hit by the same car twice within twenty-four hours! The remote North Atlantic

island has a population of only two hundred seventy thousand and in some areas people can drive for hours without seeing another vehicle!

Nicholas Fagnani, the "fall guy," fell 20 stories from the Liberty Band Building in Buffalo, New York, and lived. At the age of five he fell 55 feet, at twelve he fell 60 feet and was later hit by a fast train and thrown 300 feet into the air.

A LEAP FROM LION'S BACK—ONE LUCKY COUPLE SURVIVES A FREAK OFF-ROADING ACCIDENT

When Tina and Shawn Hasty set out for a weekend of off-roading in Utah's Moab Desert, they had no idea that their trip would take a nearly fatal turn. Tina and Shawn headed for a rock formation known as Lion's Back, a favorite challenge for off-roaders. Lion's Back, a steep, rising ridge with sharply sloping sides, attracts crowds of off-roaders, who customarily applaud each driver who makes it to the top of the ridge, turns around, and navigates safely back down.

As Tina and Shawn started up the slope in their 1977 Blazer, something seemed terribly wrong. Judy Hewitt, Tina's mom, watching from the crowd, felt a sense of dread the moment Tina got behind the wheel.

Tina and Shawn's journey up Lion's Back was uneventful, as was the turn-around at the top, but moments after they began their descent, their truck's brakes failed. Rolling faster and faster downhill, out of control, Tina and Shawn had no time to think about death. Shawn recalls, "I just told Tina to hang on." Tina says, "I just told him I loved him."

Their truck became airborne, then plowed nose-first into the desert floor, flipped over, and stopped.

The crowd immediately feared the worst, as well they might have. Collision expert Rusty Haight, upon examining the wreck, said "This crash had fatal written all over it." If Tina and Shawn had hit any of the hundreds of nearby boulders, instead of the small patch of softer dirt, it almost certainly would have been.

Miraculously, Tina escaped the crash with only a broken leg; Shawn walked away from it with only minor cuts and bruises—two very lucky off-roaders who somehow managed to cheat death.

EMBARRASSING ACCIDENTS

• **Duane Della,** of Altoona, Pennsylvania, had to be rescued by firefighters after his tongue stuck and froze to the inside of a freezer!

• In 1987, **Mathieu Boya**, of Benin, Africa, while golfing, struck a bird that fell into the cockpit of a fighter plane that in turn crashed and destroyed an entire air force!

• Just moments after **Ryan Newhaus'** mother scolded him to take better care of his car, a single-engine Cessna plane fell from the sky near Englewood, Florida, and crushed it!

• During a concert by composer **Luciano Berio** to promote world peace, a cannon was fired that injured several people and caused a riot to break out in the audience!

• In 1979, a man in Britain who tried to defrost his car door lock by blowing on it got his lips stuck frozen to the metal until he was rescued twenty minutes later!

• The church of Corcuetos, in Spain, which took ninety years to build, collapsed on the very day it was completed!

• **General George Custer** accidentally shot his own horse during a buffalo hunt!

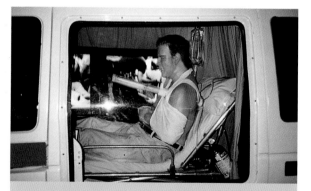

Jack Thompson, as seen here in a wax figure display, survived a car accident in which a metal pole ripped through his torso.

Chapter 3
Agriculture & Sustenance

Purple carrots? Corn cobs as long as your arm? Encounters with freak agricultural products such as these are obvious evidence that something's weird down on the farm. But after you discover the bizarre farming practices we've collected here, you may view that seemingly innocent produce in your fridge with a new respect. . .

FARMING

• You can grow vegetables on the Net without getting your hands dirty! At www.myveggiepatch.com, people can have other people plant, grow, and harvest vegetables for them that are then delivered to their front door!

• In 1993, **Professor Ted Bick**, of Union College, Schenectady, New York, renewed a 198-year-old right that allows professors to graze their farm animals on college land!

• To protect their crops from storms, the ancient Romans buried a frog in the center of their field before they planted, then dug it up at harvest time!

CROPS

• Farmers in Alaska's Matanuska Valley produce ninety-eight-pound cabbages, thirty-two-pound turnips, and sixteen-pound celery stalks!

• **Doctor Leonard Pike**, of A & M University, in College Station, Texas, has developed a carrot that is maroon in color!

• **Mike Dickson**, of Cornell University, has developed orange cauliflowers!

• **Bill Rogerson**, of Greenville, North Carolina, grew a cantaloupe that weighed 72.3 pounds!

S. D. Cornell grew corn 22 feet tall and 62,000 pounds to the acre in Grandview, Washington.

A radish weighing 50 pounds was grown by **Floyd Harris** in Vero Beach, Florida.

Giant squash 4½ feet long raised by **D. Lanson** in San Francisco.

Kenneth Culver, of Sunnyside, Washington, grew a sunflower 19 inches in diameter.

• In northern Japan, apple farmers use turkeys to guard their crops from marauding wild monkeys!

• "Chateau de East 92nd": **Vera Jiji** grew a grapevine four stories up the side of her apartment building in New York City that yields five hundred pounds of grapes every year!

• **Ian Kearns**, of Jersey, England, grows cabbages that stand fifteen feet high, and carves walking sticks from their tree-like stalks!

• A stalk of Mexican corn grown from seeds by **Sion C. Noyes** of Landaff, New Hampshire, was cut down before it had achieved full growth—yet in four months it had reached a height of eleven feet, a circumference of eight and a half inches, and had leaves forty-five inches long.

• **C. L. Spears** has developed cotton that grows in many different colors.

• In 1991, **Daniel Perez** planted one hundred thirty-one stalks of corn along the center divider of Broadway and 153rd Street in upper Manhattan, New York City!

• Grapes with red whiskers are grown in the monastery of Nove Miasto, Bohemia.

PLOWING

• The first contour plowing: The hill of Bubbonia, near Gela, Sicily, retains moisture for its plant life in a maze of ditches that were dug in the seventh century B.C.

• **Bronko Nagurski**, defensive fullback for the Chicago Bears in the 1930s, manually plowed his family's fields without using a horse!

PLANTING

• In 1856, **G. A. Meacham** invented a device that strapped on a farmer's boot to dig holes and plant seeds while he walked!

• The first mechanical planter: A seeder drawn by two oxen and attended by three men was illustrated on a seal excavated at Nippur, Babylon, where it had been buried for 6,000 years.

HARVESTING

• An ancient Egyptian painting indicates that four thousand years ago baboons were trained to harvest figs.

• In Southeast Asia, pig-tailed macaque monkeys are trained to harvest coconuts!

• Women of Honshu, Japan, while harvesting rice, still wear the same style masks they first donned centuries ago to make them unattractive to male supervisors; the masks, however, are used now as protection against insects and sunburn.

MAPLE TREES in Vermont, ARE NOT TAPPED FOR THEIR MAPLE SYRUP UNTIL THEY ARE 40 YEARS OLD, A FOOT IN DIAMETER AND SOME 60 FEET TALL

HAY MOWED BY THE Gujars of Kashmir IS PROTECTED AGAINST RUIN FROM TORRENTIAL RAINS *BY BEING HUNG IN BULKY BRAIDS FROM THE LIMBS OF TREES*

SLOVAKIAN BEEHIVES ARE CARVED TO LOOK LIKE THE BEEKEEPER AND HIS WIFE—*SO THE BEES WILL "RECOGNIZE" THEIR OWNERS*

FARM EQUIPMENT

• A Japanese inventor has designed a gardening tool that contains foldout clippers, shears, and rakes!

• In 1919, **Frederic W. Elleby**, of Modesto, California, invented a mask to be worn while milking cows!

DAIRY FARMING

• A cow must consume over one hundred twenty-five pounds of food and water to produce one pound of butter.

• In order to achieve richer-tasting milk, **Ralph McGregor**, of Dover, Pennsylvania, feeds his dairy cows a diet of hay mixed with chocolate!

• In Missouri, dairy farmers keep their cows warm and milk-producing during periods of freezing weather by using udder supports, towels, and hair dryers!

• In Beverly, England, the farmers put yellow and white leggings on their cows to make them more visible to drivers!

• In order to increase milk production, Polish peasants ritually pour cows' milk through the hole of a wooden charm called a "cow unbewitcher."

• High-tech cattle calls: In Japan, researchers have developed pagers for cows so they can be "beeped" to come back to the barn at milking time!

PIG FARMING

• Scientists in London, Ontario, Canada, have developed a robot called "Robosow" that can feed and soothe sixteen piglets at a time.

• Each year at Thanksgiving time, pig farmers in Philadelphia, Pennsylvania, collect some twenty-four thousand tons of leftover food from curbside trash cans to feed their pigs!

In 1891, the Squire of Flying Hall, North Yorkshire, England, built a GIANT PIG STY in the shape of a Greek temple complete with carved ionic columns!

A World Champion Cow: **"Carnation Ormsby"** averaged 50 quarts of milk and 5 pounds of butter each day for one year.

THE ODDITY FARM: BIG-HEARTED FARMER GIVES MUTANT LIVESTOCK A HOME

Take a closer look at the cattle in Paul Springer's pastures and you might notice something a bit odd. Here and there, you'll find a pig with an extra leg, a pair of donkeys joined at the head, perhaps even a two-headed calf. Paul's Wisconsin farm has become the home of some of the most astonishing livestock oddities in the country. He collects them. You might even say he's fond of them.

Paul first developed his penchant for mutant animals when a steer named Beauregard who sprouted two extra legs from his shoulders, was born on his farm. Beauregard's amicable nature quickly established him as a beloved family pet, and when he passed on, Paul offered his preserved body to Ripley's for future generations to enjoy.

Since then, Paul has actively sought out mutant livestock, animals born with deformities which would otherwise be destroyed because their upkeep would be too costly. Paul keeps his menagerie in a special paddock, free of wires and branches that might snag those delicate extra limbs. His oddities require little special care, except during those first tenuous months of their lives, when their survival is doubtful. Corrective surgery is seldom possible with these animals, because their extra parts are often fused directly to their spinal cords.

In addition to his exotic herd, Paul also keeps one hundred fifty head of normal cattle, as well as miniature burros. He feeds his herd candy in addition to hay, and lavishes great care on them all—whether they have spare parts or not.

FISHING

• Yura Indians of Bolivia fish with bow and arrow.

• Allis shad are so fond of music that German fishermen lure them by attaching bells to their nets.

• A fishing spear invented by Congolese natives has a detachable shaft connected to the barbed head by a cord that floats above the speared fish.

• The hooked spines of the barrel cactus are used in Mexico as fishhooks.

HERDING

• **Mosaku Sakurai**, of Tokyo's University of Agriculture, has designed straw jackets with matching hats to protect cows from insects, disease, and sunburn!

• **Marguerite Hays**, a farmer in Mindemoya, Canada, uses a donkey named Benjamin to guard her sheep from wolves!

SALUKI HOUNDS *WERE CARRIED ON HORSEBACK* BY ARABIAN HORSEMEN HUNTING FOR GAZELLES!

• In Scotland, farmers frequently put braces on the teeth of sheep!

• In the Middle Ages, people used ashes from their Yuletide logs to get rid of vermin in cattle pens, and to cure tooth aches!

• Texas's thirteen-hundred-square-mile King Ranch has 2,730 oil wells and sixty thousand head of cattle that are herded by helicopters!

SHEPHERDS in Mont-de-Marsan, France, TO KEEP THEIR FLOCKS IN VIEW, PATROL ON STILTS FITTED WITH ANTI-FOG LIGHTS

Chapter 4

Animals & Insects

• This dog, owned by **Mrs. W. R. Rhodes** of Shreveport, Louisiana, loved to wear his owner's false teeth!

Welcome to Ripley's menagerie of curious creatures. The animal kingdom offers an endless pageant of bizarre behaviors and unbelievable biological adaptations. In addition to vanished creatures of prehistory, shocking mutations, and life-saving animal heroes, you're about to discover bizarre and little-known facts about many of the everyday animals you thought you knew.

DINOSAURS

• The prehistoric **stegosaurus** had a brain the size of a golf ball, and one or two rows of large bony plates on its back used for defense and to regulate its body temperature.

• A skeleton of the world's longest dinosaur, the one-hundred-fifty-million-year-old **diplodocus** exhibited at the Carnegie Museum of Natural History in Pittsburgh, Pennsylvania, is over eighty-four feet long.

• **Torosaurus** was a horned dinosaur with a frilled bone

at its neck and a head the size of a small car!

The HUMERUS of the 160-foot-long dinosaur *gigantosaurus africanus*, was larger than a 6-foot man—yet its brain was smaller than a man's fist.

THE GIGANTOSAURUS
A HUGE AQUATIC REPTILE OF PREHISTORIC TIMES, WHEN STRETCHED ON ITS BELLY WAS 12 FEET HIGH, WITH A HEAD AND NECK 40 FEET LONG AND A TAIL 80 FEET IN LENGTH !

DOMESTIC ANIMALS

BEASTS OF BURDEN

CAMELS

• **Edward F. Beale** (1822-1893), American diplomat and pioneer settler in California, purchased seventy-seven camels for use on his ranch, then, so that they would understand his commands, learned Arabic.

DONKEYS

• In a Northlea sheep farm near Indian River, Canada, donkeys are used to herd sheep and as bodyguards to keep away coyotes and other predators!

SPOTTED MULE
Owned by Roy E. Head, East St. Louis, Ill.

HORSES

• The **Godolphin Arabian**, one of the three horses from which all thoroughbreds are descended, accidentally kicked to death a cat that shared its stable and shortly afterward died itself—having refused ever again to either eat or drink.

• **"Pat,"** a United States Army horse, now buried beneath a granite headstone at Fort Sam Houston in Texas, lived to the age of forty-five.

TOM WHITE OF Tucson, Ariz., TRAINED A ZEBRA AS A COW PONY

THE DOUBLE-FOOTED HORSE
Owned by R. Van Wert
Cincinnati, Ohio

LIVESTOCK

• The Yokohama, a Japanese fowl, has tail feathers twelve feet long!

CATTLE

• **Christian Leroy,** of Belgium, performed a rock concert for three thousand cows at a local market!

• In Velez, Colombia, a cow stepped on the trigger of a loaded rifle and accidentally shot another cow!

Jeff Drake, of Sedalia, Montana, owned this horse, born without front legs.

A calf with eight legs and two tails, owned by **Alex Harpe** of Buckely, Michigan.

A cow caught a fish and ate it on Bird Island in Corpus Christi, Texas.

A chicken without a beak, owned by **Barney Lederman** of Chicago, Illinois.

CHICKENS

• The flying chicken: **"Shomisha,"** a chicken owned by Morimitzu Neura, of Hammatzu, Japan, flew a distance of three hundred ten feet!

• **"Weirdo,"** the largest California chicken ever recorded, weighed twenty-two pounds! He once killed a rooster, and two cats, injured a dog—and even injured its owner!

DUCKS

• The world's oldest duck: Gryfudd Hughes, of Wales, England, has a pet duck named **"Wil Cwac Cwac"** that is twenty-five years old!

• Twice a day for the past fifty years, five celebrity ducks have been riding the elevator in Memphis' Peabody Hotel from their rooftop home to the hotel's lobby fountain.

PIGS

• The squeal of a pig can reach one hundred fifteen decibels, louder than a Concorde jet!

• The first pig to fly traveled over England with British **pilot J. T. C. Moore-Brabazon,** in 1909!

TURKEYS

• There are no turkeys in Turkey!

• A turkey raised in England in 1989 weighed eighty-six pounds!

PETS

• In 1983, the Shawnee, Kansas *Journal Herald* ran obituary notices of dead pets!

CATS

• **"Myobu No Omoto,"** a cat owned by the Japanese emperor Ichijo, was so well loved that a dog that chased it was exiled and its attendant was put in jail!

• Ted Townsend, of Ormond Beach, Florida, regularly takes his pet cat **"Tobby"** surfing!

• **"Clem,"** the cat, returned to its owner Kurt Helminiak, of Bancroft, Wisconsin, after an absence of eight years!

A CAT DOES NOT USE ITS VOCAL CORDS TO PURR

Larry Heaney, of Annapolis, Maryland, owned this cat with the word "CAT" spelled out in its fur!

"**Frowzy**," a cat owned by Mr. and Mrs. A. W. Mitchell of Vancouver, British Columbia, raised these motherless chicks as her own!

CATS WERE SO SACRED IN ANCIENT EGYPT THAT THEY WERE MUMMIFIED

DOGS

• "**Adjutant**," a black Labrador owned by James Hawkes, lived to be twenty-seven years old!

• "**Ginger**" a spaniel owned by Harold Calvert of Burnt Hills, New York, has her own credit card—with a $10,000 limit—that she uses to buy dog food!

• In 1991, **Robert Wolley**, of New Jersey, paid $1,000 for a birthday party for his dog, "**Jeb**," that included a concert performed by an orchestra and a grooming session with a complimentary bathrobe!

• Nicki Arndt, of Colorado, communicates with her deaf dog "**Annie**" by using sign language!

• "**Gypsie**," a dog owned by Preston Cathcart, asks for food by distinctly saying, "I want some."

• "**Roxie**," dog mascot of the Long Island Railroad for twelve years, had attached to his collar a pass permitting him unlimited riding privileges.

• "**Thisbee**," Marie Antoinette's pet Maltese dog, jumped to its death from the Saint Michel Bridge over the Seine on the day the queen died on the guillotine, October 16, 1793.

• The world's tallest dog: a Great Dane called "**Shamgret Danzal**," of Buckinghamshire, England, stood over forty inches tall!

• The largest, longest, heaviest dog in the world: "**Aicama Zorba**," an old English mastiff owned by Chris Eraclides, of London, England, weighs three hundred forty-three pounds and measures eight feet, three inches from nose to tail!

"**Ginger**," a cocker spaniel, could hold three balls in her mouth at once!

Two-nosed Llewellen setter, raised by **John E. Glenn**, of Benton, Arkansas.

IN 1933, A SETTER NAMED JIM CORRECTLY IDENTIFIED AN ELM TREE, A CAR LICENSE PLATE NUMBER AND THE COLOR BLUE! *IN 1936, THE DOG CORRECTLY PREDICTED THAT THE YANKEES WOULD WIN THE WORLD SERIES!*

Featherless pigeon developed by **Mary A. Summers** of Spokane, Washington.

Mr. and Mrs. E. T. Humphrey, of Sanford, Florida, owned this unusual rabbit, whose tusk grew to a length of one and a half inches.

PET BIRDS

• Former F.B.I. Chief **J. Edgar Hoover** once gave his mother a canary that had been bred by the famous prisoner the "Birdman of Alcatraz"!

• "**Puck**," a budgie owned by Camille Jordan, of Petaluma, California, has a vocabulary of over 1,728 words!

UNUSUAL PETS

• "**Alex**," a pet gibbon, boarded a flight from Phoenix, Arizona, to Minneapolis, Minnesota, and sat in a full-fare seat, undetected until lunch was served!

• "**Lady**," a miniature horse owned by Mary Jelley of Orillia, Canada, stands only thirty-one inches in height, is house-trained, and regularly watches television!

GERARD de NERVAL
(1808- 1855)
PARISIAN POET AND AUTHOR *HAD A PET LOBSTER WHICH HE LED THROUGH THE STREETS OF PARIS ON A LEASH*

The PET RABBIT of Claudia Clerici of Somoma, Ca., grew so fond of spaghetti that it became too fat to keep in the house

• Prairie dogs imported from Texas and Oklahoma are popular pets in Japan!

PET PAMPERING

• The late British singer **Dusty Springfield** bequeathed her cat "Nicholas" to a friend and arranged for the cat's favorite food—canned baby food—to be flown in regularly from the United States!

PERFORMING ANIMALS

• In 1991, an equestrian club in San Francisco, California, celebrated Mozart's bicentennial by training horses to perform ballet to his music!

"Bozo the Mind-Reading Dog," owned by Captain E. C. Lower, could accurately bark out the number, dates, and denominations of coins held in audience members' hands, the number of rings on their fingers, and any number his master was thinking.

• In the 1940s a horse named "**Lady Wonder**" used a typewriter to spell out its psychic predictions, including the reelection of president Truman and America's participation in World War II!

ANIMAL STARS

• In 1978, during an engagement at New York's Radio City Music Hall, the canine movie star "**Lassie**" stayed in a $380-a-night room at the Plaza Hotel!

• Movie star "**Rin Tin Tin**" had his own valet, a personal chef, a limousine, a chauffeur, and a fifty-room dressing facility!

"**TIM**" A COWHORSE OWNED BY J.D. Wilton, of Australia, COULD BALANCE ON A SMALL WOODEN BLOCK

"CHEETAH," the chimpanzee star of over 50 "Tarzan" films is 64 years old and drinks 11 beers a day!

2 ELEPHANTS were trained by a British handler named Cooke to sit at a table and eat a dinner with forks—then finish off their meals with goblets of wine.

LYTAS NALLAS of Cairo, Egypt, TRAINED CAMELS TO WASH WINDOWS BY COATING THE GLASS WITH SUGAR and WATER!

SLURP!

WORKING ANIMALS

• Two bloodhounds owned by **Dr. J. B. Fulton**, of Oneida, Kansas, successfully tracked a horse-and-buggy thief 135 miles!

• "**Ashley Whippet**," a champion Frisbee dog, once leaped so high that he grabbed a Frisbee from the crossbar of a football goal post!

"**Peppy**," a Dalmatian belonging to professional 'birler' Bill Fontana of Fort Frances, Ontario, could roll a log for an entire mile in an hour.

The watchcat tiger used as a "watchdog" at the Des Moines Zoo.

TRES PASSERS
WILL BE
EATEN
SEC. 13   CHAP. 34
CODE 1954

• A ferret named "**Misty**" was used by the United States Space Command in Colorado to help rewire a new computerized command center!

WILD ANIMALS

AMPHIBIANS

FROGS

• The World's Smallest Frog: A new species of frog, "**Eleutherodactylus**," discovered in Cuba, measures less than one inch from its nose to the tip of its tail!

• "The Great Bengal Frog War": In Malaysia, 1970, thousands of frogs staged a bloody fight that lasted over a week!

• Frogs are unaware of changes in body temperature when they occur gradually. So long as the temperature does not change suddenly, they can be frozen to death or roasted without visible discomfort.

• The **arrow-poison frog** (*dendrobates typographus*) secretes venom from its

Six-legged frog, owned by **Glen Lawrence** of Cross Plains, Texas.

back, into which South American Indians dip blowgun darts.

• The **spring peeper**, one of the smallest of all frogs, measures only one inch.

• The **goliath frog**, found only in Cameroon, is a foot long.

• A frog does not drink water. It absorbs it.

• **Wood frogs** can survive below-freezing temperatures in which up to sixty-five percent of their body turns to ice!

TOADS

• Giant South American toads will attack and eat baby alligators!

• The **Colorado River toad** (*bufo alvarius*) is North America's most poisonous toad—its venom can cause paralysis, slurred speech, convulsions, and even death!

• **Couch's spadefoot toad**, found in North America's Sonora Desert, lives underground eleven months each year, surfacing only during the July rainy season.

• The **Cameroon horned toad** is protected from its head to its upper back by a bony calcium shield that resembles a suit of armor.

BIRDS

• Venomous bird: In 1992, scientists discovered that the **hooded pitohui**, a bird found in New Guinea, emits a poisonous toxin from its feathers and skin to ward off predators!

THE **LYRE BIRD** of Australia, MIMICS THE SOUNDS OF OTHER BIRDS, WOOD CHOPPING AND EVEN A BARKING DOG

• Birds must fly at an average speed of eleven miles per hour to stay aloft!

• A group of **larks** is called an "exaltation"!

• A flock of house **sparrows** in Hamilton, New Zealand, learned how to enter a bus station by triggering the light sensors in the automatic doors!

• In 1621, thousands of **starlings** fought a battle in the skies above Cork, Ireland, for two days!

• In Redding, California, a flock of two thousand **Vaux's Swifts** flew down the chimney of Robert Brown's house and into his living room!

• The **white-breasted wren** of Mexico has a song that imitates Beethoven's Fifth Symphony!

• **Crows** in New Caledonia pull twigs from trees, strip the leaves from the twigs, then sharpen one end to a point to use as a probe for bugs!

• **Red-necked phalaropes**, rather than diving, stir up water by spinning in circles to bring food to the surface!

• A **blue jay**'s feathers appear blue, but it is actually an optical illusion, not a real pigment!

• A **red-eyed vireo** bird once sang 22,197 songs in a single day!

• A **woodpecker**'s tongue is attached to a stretchy bone that curls back over the top of the bird's skull and into its nostrils!

• Young **wood swallows**, a species of bird in New Guinea, do not leave the nest when they grow up. They stay and help their parents feed the next brood.

• Baby **robins** eat up to fourteen feet of earthworms every day!

• Baby **yellow-billed cuckoos** are born with leathery black skin that breaks away when the birds are ready to fly!

• A **chickadee** can grow new brain cells!

• Female **wrens** often feed their young up to 1,217 times in sixteen hours!

• **Green herons** catch fish by dropping a feather into the water as a lure!

• After bathing, starlings frequently dry themselves off by using sheep as towels!

BIRDS OF PREY

• "Eagle Lady" **Jean Keene** has fed a flock of over three hundred bald eagles near her home in Homer Spit, Alaska, every morning for the last twenty years!

• **Bald eagles** can swim in the water using their wings in an overhand movement that resembles the butterfly stroke.

• The **bateleur eagle** of Africa, while hunting, flies over a two-hundred-square-mile area every day!

The **CROWNED EAGLE** has crested feathers that resemble a royal crown.

CARRION BIRDS

• A **condor** can cruise for a distance of sixty miles, at thirty miles per hour, without once flapping its wings!

• In 1994, a flock of two hundred **buzzards** terrorized the area of Stafford, Virginia, attacking birds, cats, dogs, and horses!

• In Southern California, **turkey buzzards** are used to detect gas leaks in pipelines!

DUCKS, GEESE, AND SWANS

• **Harlequin ducks** migrate from east to west rather than north to south!

• The **Magellan steamer duck**, found off the coast of Chile, cannot fly, yet swims at speeds of up to 24.8 miles per hour!

• In 1932, an entire flock of fifty-two wild geese were struck by lightning and killed during a thunderstorm over Elgin, Canada!

• **Bar-headed geese** fly over the Himalayas at altitudes of over twenty-five thousand feet!

• The wild geese of the Falkland Islands have a price on their beaks: the authorities pay for each goose killed because a single goose can eat as much grass as a sheep.

HUMMINGBIRDS

• A **hummingbird**'s heartbeat slows down from five hundred beats a minute when active, to less than ten beats a minute when it is asleep!

• Hummingbirds can fly backwards, upside down, and sideways, but they can't walk!

• The **emerald hummingbird** consumes nectar from up to two thousand flowers every day!

OSTRICHES

• During the breeding season, the necks and faces of male ostriches turn crimson!

AN **OSTRICH** IN A SINGLE STRIDE CAN COVER 25 FEET

• In South Africa, ostriches are used to herd sheep!

• An ostrich's eye is bigger than its brain!

• The legs of an ostrich are so powerful they can kill a lion with a single kick!

OWLS

• **"Merlin,"** a great horned owl found near Milton, Canada, underwent cataract surgery at the University of Wisconsin!

• The **Elf Owl** will nest only in a hole made by a woodpecker in the trunk of a cactus.

• Burrowing owls imitate the sounds of rattlesnakes in order to scare off predators!

• North American burrowing owls lay their eggs in abandoned gopher holes and remain underground on the nest for twenty-seven days!

• Barn owls snore when they sleep!

PARROTS AND OTHER JUNGLE BIRDS

• A wild flock of fifty South American **parrots** lives in the middle of the city of San Francisco!

• Blushing bird: The face of the **Australian palm cockatoo** turns bright red when the bird gets excited!

• The male **huia** bird of New Zealand uses his short beak to pry bark from trees, then the female uses her long curved beak to extract larvae. If one of the pair dies, the other will starve to death!

• South claw: All Australian glossy black cockatoos are left-footed!

PENGUINS

• Members of the North Olympic Shuttle and Spindle Guild in Sequim, Washington, knit tiny wool sweaters for penguins who were endangered by a massive oil spill off the coast of Australia!

• A penguin can run as fast as a man!

• Penguins have an organ located just above their eyes that can convert seawater into fresh water!

PIGEONS

• Pigeon nests found in an abandoned steel foundry were made entirely of strips of steel, brass, copper, and aluminum.

• In 1930, a pigeon owned by **J. Stell** and **C. Watson** flew from Hicks Bay to Dunedin, New Zealand—a distance of 1,143 miles—in a single day!

• Pigeons in London hitch rides aboard subway trains!

THE **MALE FRIGATE BIRD** WHEN COURTING PUFFS OUT ITS CHEST UNTIL IT RESEMBLES A GIANT RED HEART

"Peter" A STORK IN GERMANY, WHO LOST HIS BEAK IN A FIGHT, WAS FITTED WITH A RE-PLACEMENT *MADE OF ALUMINUM*

• A pigeon named **"Cher Ami"** that saved an American Battalion during World War I, was fitted with a wooden leg after it was shot while flying over enemy lines!

SEA BIRDS

• A three-month-old baby pelican weighs more than a full-grown adult pelican!

• An albatross can sleep in mid-air while flying at a speed of thirty-five miles per hour.

• The **petrel,** a small sea bird, drinks only seawater. If left inland beside fresh water, it will die of thirst.

• Cormorants on the islands of Albemarle and Narborough, in the Galapagos archipelago of Ecuador, are the only cormorants in the world that cannot fly.

• Pelicans have air-filled pads like bubble packs under their skin that allow them to bounce on the water's surface after diving from heights of over thirty-five feet!

EGGS

• **Sharon Smalling**, of Hampton, Tennessee, has a chicken named "Jinx" that lays eggs with no yolks!

• If you placed all the hens' eggs laid in a year end to end, they would circle the earth one hundred times!

• Jefferson's salamanders die by the thousands in the larva stage because the parents always lay their

An egg was discovered by **Clara Zeitlow** that contained five yolks.

eggs in small puddles of water which dry up before the larvae have had time to develop.

• Turtles in Papua New Guinea, come ashore every December to lay their eggs.

• The Akeyom people count the years and their ages by the number of times the turtles leave the sea for land.

• Hard-shelled turtles lay soft-shelled eggs. Soft-shelled tortoises lay hard-shelled eggs.

• Sea turtles have such a high mortality rate that only one out of every one hundred eggs they lay lives for a year—and only one hatchling out of one thousand eggs reaches adulthood.

INSECTS AND ARACHNIDS

• The **Fulgora**, an insect of South America, frightens off predators with a false face featuring simulated teeth.

ANTS

• The nest of the **bearded Aztec ant** of Brazil consists of thin tubes of a cardboard-like substance that hangs from the branches of a tree like a giant's beard.

• Many types of **desert ant** carry their dead to ant cemeteries.

• To reach underground streams, **desert ants** in Atacama, Chile, dig passages that descend many yards below the surface of the desert.

• **Bulldog ants** bathe every day!

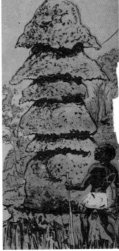

SKYSCRAPERS OF THE JUNGLE
The Pagoda ants of Central Africa build these towering nests, adding another story every year.

APHIDS

• The most fertile bug: In a single year, one cabbage aphid can produce eight hundred twenty-two million tons of offspring—over three times the total weight of the human population of the world!

ARACHNIDS

• The Hawaiian **"Happy Face"** spider has a series of lines and dots on its back that resemble a smiling human face.

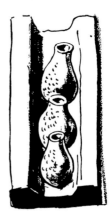

• The European house spider can run three hundred thirty times its own length in ten seconds!

BEES

• A species of bees called the **Royal Mayan** bites its victims instead of stinging them!

BEES in BRAZIL make sour honey.

BEETLES

• **Arctic beetles** and Alaskan flies can survive temperatures of one hundred and forty degrees Fahrenheit!

THE MASON BEE BUILDS FOR EACH OF HER EGGS AN INDIVIDUAL CELL OF CLAY AND SAND, WHICH IS STOCKED WITH POLLEN AND HONEY

• **Goliath beetles** can carry up to eight hundred fifty times their own weight.

BUTTERFLIES

• Male butterflies of the danaidae family attract females with a mixture of fragrances that are stored on their hind legs!

• A monarch butterfly can fly six hundred twenty miles without stopping for food!

THE **DOG-FACE BUTTERFLY**
(Meganostoma Caesonia)
HAS A DOG'S HEAD OUTLINED
ON EACH WING

• The monarch butterfly has a taste sense one hundred twenty times as sensitive to sweets as the human tongue.

• The tongue of a butterfly is as long as its body.

CATERPILLARS

• The nest of a caterpillar of the forests of Guiana, South America, constructed of wood and leaves, is a replica of a snail shell.

1,500,000 different species of insects inhabit the world.

• The **Peruvian caterpillar** places whorls of barbed hair coated with toxic chemicals around a twig in order to keep predators away from its cocoon!

COCKROACHES

• A cockroach can survive for nine days without its head!

LOCUSTS

• A swarm of locusts that ravaged Nebraska in 1875 was made up of an estimated 12.5 trillion locust bugs, weighing a total of 24.6 million tons.

MILLIPEDES

• **Aphiloria corrugata**, an African millipede, sprays its attackers with a deadly cloud of hydrogen cyanide!

MOTHS

• The **sphinx** moth has a tongue so long that it is coiled in a tight spiral.

THE **BENT WING WOOD MOTH**
OF AUSTRALIA
HAS ON EACH WING A RAISED
OUTLINE OF AN EYE--*COMPLETE
EVEN TO A PUPIL*

MAMMALS

ANTELOPE

• Impalas have incisor teeth that move back and forth!

THE **OKAPI** OF AFRICA, CAN WASH ITS OWN EARS WITH ITS 11-INCH TONGUE

BATS

• The Peter's tent-making bat bends leaves with its teeth to shelter itself from the rain.

• The **long-eared bat** of Europe and Africa has hearing so acute it can detect a moth in flight.

• Woolly bats found in West Africa are so small they often live in spider webs!

• In a single night, a colony of bats can eat two hundred fifty tons of insects!

The **FENNEC**, a fox of the Arabian and North African deserts, weights only about 3$\frac{1}{2}$ pounds, but has ears 6 inches long.

BAIRD'S TAPIE (*tapirus bairdii*) is related to the horse and the rhinoceros.

AN ALBINO GIRAFFE PHOTOGRAPHED IN KENYA BY COL. SANDY MACNAB, AN AMERICAN HUNTER -*AND NEVER SEEN AGAIN*

"SNOWFLAKE"
AN ALBINO
GORILLA
CAPTURED IN
AFRICA IN 1967
*HAD WHITE
HAIR, PINK
SKIN AND
BLUE EYES*

The
GOLDEN LION
MARMOSET, of
Brazil, has a mane
like the king of
beasts.

The MARMOSET,
a tiny monkey of
South and Central
America, is worn
in the hair of
Amazonian
Indians to
pick out head
lice.

BEAVERS

• Beavers never stop growing!

CHIMPANZEES

• Kanzi, a pygmy chimpanzee raised at the Language Research Center near Atlanta, Georgia, communicates using over ninety symbols and can understand over six hundred sentences!

• African chimpanzees eat the aspilia plant to relieve upset stomachs!

DEER

• Reindeer are so vital to the Chukchis of Siberia that their language has twenty-six words for reindeer.

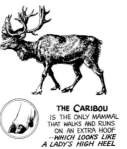

THE CARIBOU
IS THE ONLY MAMMAL
THAT WALKS AND RUNS
ON AN EXTRA HOOF
*--WHICH LOOKS LIKE
A LADY'S HIGH HEEL*

• Reindeer eat over twenty pounds of moss every day!

ELEPHANTS

• In New Delhi, India, a herd of elephants blocked railway tracks and stopped traffic for several hours after an elephant calf was killed by a train!

• "**Moja**," an African elephant at the Miami Metro Zoo, loves to bowl and plays football and softball.

• Elephants can detect underground water!

FERRETS AND WEASELS

• The African linsang, a ferret-like mammal found in West Africa, builds its nest in high tree branches rather than on the ground!

• Ermine in Ireland stage elaborate funerals—often with processions of up to one hundred "mourners" and four "pallbearers" that carry the body of the dead ermine.

HYENAS

• Spotted hyenas are born with a fully developed set of teeth, and siblings fight until only one cub remains!

RATS

• Each year, at the rat Olympics at Michigan's Kalamazoo College, rodents compete in such events as the broad jump, tight rope, and soccer!

• The cloud rat of Mount Pulog, on Luzon Island in the Philippines, barks like a dog, curls up like a rabbit, and climbs trees like a squirrel.

Laboratory mouse
with two tails, owned
by Doctor Reginald
Hewitt, of Pearl
River, New York.

• The kangaroo rat will die unless it takes frequent dust baths.

SHREWS

• The common shrew eats its own weight in food several times each day.

REPTILES

• Diurnal reptiles have eyes with round pupils; nocturnal reptiles have slit-like pupils.

CHAMELEONS

• The sticky tongue of the chameleon extends up to 1 1/2 times its body length to capture an insect and zip it into its mouth all within one-tenth of a second.

JACKSON'S CHAMELEON of E. Africa, CHANGES COLOR BECAUSE ITS SKIN CONTAINS MELANIN *THE SUBSTANCE THAT ENABLES HUMAN SKIN TO TAN*

ALLIGATORS AND CAIMANS

• An alligator can run as fast as a horse!

A **TREE** grew on the dirt-covered back of a very old and very large alligator in British Guiana.

• The alligator, whose brain is about the size of a poker chip, can stay under water without breathing for a full day, and can go a full year without eating.

• Even after a caiman has died it can still slash and bite an attacker!

LIZARDS

• The tuatara, a primitive reptile of New Zealand, has a third eye on top of its head!

• A lizard smells through its forked tongue.

• The gila monster is North America's only poisonous lizard.

• The walking desalinization plant: The chuckwalla of Arizona, during prolonged dry spells, drinks salt water which it can convert into fresh water.

• The thorny devil (*moloch horridus*), of Australia, is protected by its sharp spikes. It eats eighteen hundred ants at a time, and stores water in canals intersecting its scales, which lead to its mouth.

• The helmeted lizard of Central America has twenty-five hundred teeth—when one is lost another replaces it.

SALAMANDERS

• The proteus or cave newt salamander is born with eyes that eventually disappear! It spends the rest of its life living in dark caves!

This extremely rare white alligator was one of a famous brood hatched in 1983 and displayed in numerous aquariums and zoos around the world.

• The tongue of the dwarf four-toed salamander of Georgia is mounted on a stalk growing from its lower jaw.

SNAKES

• The age of a rattlesnake is not computed by the number of its rattles. A rattle may grow two to four buttons a year.

Rattlesnake hibernating in mason jar, Lubbock, Texas.

• A snake sleeps with both eyes open.

• Snakes in the mountains of Valais, Switzerland, lie on the shores of mountain streams and seize trout when they leap above the water.

• The two-headed blind snake of Brazil is neither a snake, nor blind, and is not two-headed—although it is difficult to tell which end is its head. It is a lizard, the same diameter throughout, and can move backward and forward at will.

• A rattlesnake will die if left in the hot sun twenty minutes.

MUSIC

Hath charms to soothe the savage beast? NO! Snakes can't hear!

THE FLAT SNAKE Sea Snake of Malaysia

THE FLYING SNAKE OF JAVA is a rare species that flattens out like a ribbon and sails from tree to tree.

Two-headed snake, photographed in Central Park, New York, by **H. O. Langley** in 1899.

TURTLES AND TORTOISES

• In 1995, a loggerhead turtle fell from the sky onto a highway in Fort Lauderdale, Florida!

• The Kemp's Ridley turtle, the smallest and rarest of sea turtles, is so scarce that the Mexican government sent Marines to guard the only beach on which it nests.

• The heart of a turtle in warm summer water beats up to forty times a minute, but during winter in cold water, when the turtle almost suspends animation in cold water, its heart beats only once every ten minutes.

• Turtle that grew an hourglass figure around a plastic milk jug band.

• A desert tortoise can live for a whole year on what a cow eats in a single day!

• The tortoise has the slowest pulse beat of any animal: thirteen beats a minute.

A HUGE TORTOISE in Port Louis, on the Island of Mauritius, walked with 6 men on its back. (1850)

Julie Hull, of Stuart, Florida, owned this two-headed turtle, both of whose heads operated independently of one another.

• The turtle is the only animal that has its hip bones and shoulder bones inside its rib cage.

SEA CREATURES

• The carrier shell, a New Zealand shellfish, camouflages itself by cementing bits of rock and shell to its back.

• Sea okra looks like a plant but actually consist of hundreds of sea animals, each encased in a tiny vase.

• Sea urchins walk on the tips of their teeth!

• When a hair of its container is touched, the polyp pistol (*hydra virdis*, a sweetwater polyp) fires a poisoned "bullet" that penetrates the skin of its attacker.

CRABS

• Baby sea crabs have eight pairs of jaws, and their teeth are in their stomach.

• Mature robber crabs breathe through lungs, and if kept underwater for more than a few hours, they will drown!

• Over 120 million red crabs cover Australia's Christmas Island once a year, in a migration to the sea that takes up to eighteen days!

Seventeen-pointed starfish.

THE STALK-EYED SQUID HAS ITS EYES AT THE END OF **2** HORN-LIKE EXTENSIONS

The BASKET STAR which, catches the fish on which it feeds by forming itself into the shape of a basket, has 81,920 extremities.

The GURNARD-FISH that walks on its fingers

AN ANIMAL THAT CAN EAT THROUGH METAL. THE *PIDDOCK*, A TYPE OF MOLLUSK, CAN BORE HOLES RIGHT THROUGH CAST IRON.

Robert Ripley with giant Australian man-eating clam at his home in Mamaroneck, New York.

FISH

• A fish called Luther's goby stands guard and warns blind shrimp of any danger, while the shrimp digs an underwater burrow for both species to share!

• A mature sturgeon produces $60,000 worth of eggs!

• After its spine and tail have been severed, the Amazonian black ghost knife fish can simply re-grow the damaged tissue.

• A fur-bearing trout, believed to be a genuine Canadian species, was once exhibited at Edinburgh's Royal Scottish museum!

• Before sleeping, the par-rotfish blows a large bub-ble around itself to hide its scent from predators!

• A catfish forty-six inches long and weighing fifty-six pounds hooked in 1955 by Paul Jones, Enterpir, Kansas, was found to have swallowed an eighteen-inch catfish which in turn had swallowed a sunfish.

• All fish are born without scales!

• The boom boom, a fish of British Guiana, is six feet long, has a mouth a foot wide, and makes a noise like the booming of a drum.

• Catfish smell and taste with every part of their skin, including their whis-kers and fins!

• During times of drought, the African lungfish can survive buried in a dry lake bed for up to four years!

• An eel that lived without eating for four years: It had lost its upper jaw in an accident.

RAYS

• The Coast Guard rescued two boaters near New Smyrna Beach, Florida, after their sixteen-foot boat was dragged in circles for hours by an eighteen-foot-long manta ray!

• Atlantic torpedo rays can emit two-hundred-volt electric shocks—enough to operate a television!

SHARKS

• The stomach of a man-eater, caught near Waikiki, Honolulu, contained the following articles: ten pounds of nuts and bolts, two horseshoes, two soap boxes, a coal shovel, a wristwatch, a mule's hind leg, a nut cracker, a pint of brass buttons, a vanity case, a ten-pound anchor, a cartridge belt, and two bathing suits!

• **Dion Glomoure**, age twenty-one, of Streakley Bay, Australia, landed a record sixteen-and-a-half-foot long white pointer shark weighing 3,351 pounds!

• Embryonic sand tiger sharks battle each other inside the womb until only one shark is left!

• In a ten-year period, the tiger shark produces and sheds over twenty-four thousand teeth!

• The shark is the only fish that can blink its eyes.

SHRIMPS

• The barrel shrimp makes its home inside the hollowed-out skin of a sea quirt.

The FLUTEFISH has a beak shaped like a flute.

THE **MALE BUTTERFISH** PROTECTS THE EGGS DEPOSITED BY THE FEMALE *BY COILING ITS BODY AROUND THE EGGS TO SERVE THEM AS A NEST*

THE**AFRICAN CATFISH** TO FIND ITS FOOD LEAVES THE WATER EACH NIGHT AND *CRAWLS ON LAND*

THE **PELICAN EEL** WHICH HAS BEEN FOUND AT DEPTHS OF 3,000 FEET, CAN STRETCH ITS MOUTH AND GULLET *TO SWALLOW FISH LARGER THAN ITSELF*

THE **SHARK** COMES IN OVER 250 SPECIES-- OF WHICH *ONLY SOME 30 ARE DANGEROUS TO MAN*

THE LEAFY SEADRAGON of Australia LOOKS LIKE DRIFTING SEAWEED and SUCKS UP ITS PREY INTO ITS SNOUT LIKE A VACUUM CLEANER !

SEA MAMMALS

DOLPHINS

• In 1991, three dolphins following a school of fish swam up Italy's polluted Tiber River and spent six hours in the center of Rome!

• A dolphin in the Adriatic Sea off the Italian coast saved the life of a fourteen-year-old boy who'd fallen out of a sailing boat and couldn't swim!

• Dolphins only sleep two hours at a time and always keep one eye open!

WHALES

• For the past five years, **"Humphrey,"** a humpback whale, has had to be rescued by marine biologists after running aground in shallow waters off San Francisco, California!

• At the University of California's Long Marine Laboratory, four sea lions have been trained to videotape gray whales!

• Baby blue whales drink over one ton of milk every day!

• Bull sperm whales can dive to depths of ninety-six hundred feet and hold their breath for up to two hours!

• Humpback whales catch food by swimming in a circle, then blowing a huge tube of tiny bubbles around their prey!

SEALS AND SEA LIONS

• Scientists in Nova Scotia, Canada, have discovered that female seals, even if they are blind, can find their way back to the same eleven-yard square of

beach every year in order to breed!

• **"Hoover,"** a spotted harbor seal in Boston's New England Aquarium, regularly greeted visitors by imitating human voices!

• Sea lions are susceptible to sunburn, and if brought on board a ship, suffer from seasickness!

THE **EMBRYO** OF THE PORPOISE IN ITS 5 STAGES OF DEVELOPMENT REVEALS THAT ITS FLIPPER ORIGINATED AS A **5-FINGERED HAND**

FUR SEALS on St. George and St. Paul, two of the Pribil of Islands in the Bering Sea, between June 20th and July 20th give birth to a total of 360,000 baby seals.

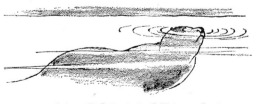

The CALIFORNIA SEA LION uses its nose as bait to capture sea gulls.

A snail killed a snake almost within the shadows of the Empire State Building.

WORMS AND SNAILS

SNAILS

• Snails come in about eighteen thousand species. Snails of the desert sleep for up to four years. The snail's mouth, no larger than the head of a pin, has some 25,600 teeth.

DENDRONOTUS ARBORESCENS
A LONG SNAIL THAT LOOKS LIKE A **MASS OF SEAWEED**

• Snails move at 0.000362005 miles per hour!

WORMS

• **Christopher Hudson** of Brighton, England, trains racing worms!

• The ribbon worm (*lineus gesserensis*) can turn itself completely inside out!

ANIMAL BEHAVIOR

FEEDING

• If people ate like hummingbirds, they would consume the equivalent of two hundred eighty-five pounds of meat every day!

• The king snake does not harm humans but kills and eats rattlesnakes and poisonous copperhead snakes.

• The sea snake, after eating a fish with spines, ejects the spines through its body walls.

• The majority of water turtles eat animals, but land tortoises only eat plants.

• A boa constrictor can go without food for a whole year!

• Leafcutter ants cultivate kohlrabi gardens for food inside their nests.

HUNTING

• Badgers and coyotes frequently hunt together— one digs and flushes out small game, while the other captures the prey when it tries to escape!

MATING

• In South Wales, a male dachshund and a female Great Dane produced a litter of thirteen "great dachshund" puppies.

• The female American alligator, to start a courtship, swims in front of a male to make him swim in the direction she wants.

• "**Bronx**," a Rhodesian Ridgeback and "**Bosse**," a Lhasa Apso, were "married" at a dog day-care center in Los Angeles, California!

MIGRATION

• Every September, mountain quail in California leave their nests at altitudes of ninety-five hundred feet and walk down to the five thousand-foot level for the winter!

NESTING

• Nine nests were started by a European blackbird between the rungs of three ladders—but the bird became so confused that it completed none of them.

• Every year starlings return to the same nest, cleaning them with antiseptic plants such as wild carrots and fleabane!

• Having nasty neighbors pays off: In South America, yellow-rumped cacique birds build their nests right beside wasp nests as protection from predators!

• Ravens mate for life and often line their nest with fur of deer, moose, and musk ox!

• The nest of the bee hummingbird is only the size of a quarter!

RAISING OFFSPRING

• "**Lucky**," a cat owned by Jennifer Anderson of London, Ohio, adopted and nursed a baby rabbit!

The face not even a mother could love.
A baby baboon is born with a pink face but at the age of 4 months its face starts to darken and its mother loses interest in it.

• Two male storks built a nest and hatched a penguin's egg!

• Male aphids change their sex in summer and become mothers.

• When "**Jubalani**," an elephant, was abandoned by its biological mother, it was later adopted by a sheep named "**Skaap**" at a wildlife refuge in South Africa!

ELEPHANT, GORILLA, HIPPOPOTAMUS, GIRAFFE, RHINO, WATER-BUFFALO, MUSK-OX, ETC.

• "**Purdy**," a Dalmatian in Marysville, Washington, adopted a brood of striped kittens!

• A cat owned by the **Gagen** family of Schenectady, New York, adopted and raised two baby chicks!

• "**Tisha**," a spaniel, raised a litter of orphaned baby rabbits!

___

SURVIVAL

• "**Vision**," a cat owned by Barbara Williams, of Lantana, Florida, survived six weeks in a dresser drawer after her owner stored the piece of furniture in a warehouse!

• "**Grover**," a cat owned by the Futino family in St. Catherine, Canada, survived after spending a week buried under a sixty-six foot snow bank!

• "**Sergeant Carter**," a Doberman mix owned by Thomas Lewis, of Cleveland, Ohio, fell two hundred feet from a highway bridge, yet walked away without injury!

• Rob Simmonds', pet dog, "**Higbee**," was buried under an avalanche, yet two weeks later was found wandering along a road.

• A black Labrador that suffered a six-inch gash and torn muscles made its way to a hospital in Hamilton, Canada, and scratched at the emergency entrance for help!

• "**Prince**," a dog owned by Ruben Mojica, of Lodi, California, was struck by a car and believed dead—yet after spending eighteen hours inside the morgue freezer at the local pound, Prince awoke, suffering only from freezer burn!

THE ALLIGATOR TURTLE CATCHES FISH WHEN THEY SEIZE ITS TONGUE--WHICH THEY MISTAKE FOR A WORM

BEAR CUBS ARE REARED BY THEIR MOTHERS UNTIL THEIR SECOND SUMMER —AFTER WHICH THEY ARE ALWAYS DESERTED

• "**Tyro**," a three-month-old Labrador puppy in Richmond, Canada, survived after swallowing a nine-inch knife!

• "**Paco**," a blind Bichon Frise dog owned by Frank Woods, of New Smyrna Beach, Florida, survived accidentally falling from an eleventh-floor balcony!

VOCALIZATIONS

• The voices of fish get deeper with age, except for trout, which are sopranos for their entire lives!

• The gunard fish grunts loudly before thunderstorms!

• The sea raven fish got its nickname, the "**Sally Growler**," because it emits loud grunts.

• Whistling dogs: **Dholes**, wild dogs found in Asia, whistle to each other instead of barking!

• "**Melbourne**," a dog in Kansas City, Kansas, can say the word "pasta" on command!

• The **barking frog**, found in Mexico and Arizona, has a call that sounds like the bark of a fox terrier!

• **Aporoscelis**, a reptile of Somaliland, is called "asherbody" meaning "baby," because when touched it makes a sound like a crying infant!

• The **wood turtle** has a whistle that can be heard forty feet away.

• The **gecko** is the only lizard with a voice—when startled, it says "eek!"

• The **muntjac**, or barking deer, found in tropical Asia, makes a loud barking sound to warn other deer of impending danger!

• A law in Virginia made it illegal for a dog to be put to death for "criminal barking."

JOURNEYS

• After being banished from its Moscow home for eating two canaries, "**Murka**," a cat, returned to its owners—after traveling twelve months and four hundred and fifty miles across the Soviet Union.

• A kitten named "**Postage Due**" fell asleep in a mailbag in Washington State and traveled over four hundred miles before being rescued!

• "**Ranulph**," a tomcat, traveled three hundred miles from the north of England back to the home of his former owner Gil Bray of Archiestown, Scotland, just days before the man was due to move away!

ANIMAL HEROES

• A baby kangaroo rescued by **Nigel Etherington**, of Perth, Australia, later saved Etherington from a fire by banging its tail on a door until he awoke and escaped!

• "**Fizo**," a dog in Sydney, Australia, was awarded the Purple Cross for bravery after saving three children from a deadly snake!

• During the nineteenth century, "**Bummer**" and "**Lazarus**," two stray dogs that roamed San Francisco, California, were given special exemptions from wearing leashes after they helped stop a runaway horse!

• "**Bernard**," a Saint Bernard dog from Eagle, Canada, rescued Jack Grover from a crashed van by pulling him through the windshield and licking his face until help arrived!

• A woman in Hermitage, Tennessee, who fell and cut her head, was rescued after her pet canary "**Bibs**" flew down the road and alerted her niece of the danger by tapping on her window until she rushed to the accident scene!

• "**Trixie**," a dog owned by Jack Fyfe of Sydney, Australia, kept his master alive for nine days after the man suffered a stroke and was paralyzed. He brought water to him in a soaked towel until help arrived!

• **Katherine George**, age three, of Bowie, Maryland, survived twelve hours in near freezing temperatures by being kept warm by her two pet dogs!

• "**Lady**," a husky dog owned by Teresa Martines, of Loveland, Colorado, survived being bitten three times by a rattlesnake while saving an eight-year-old girl!

• A barking dog woke up twenty-five people in Jiangsu Province, China, and saved them from a flood that later destroyed their homes! No one knew who the dog belonged to and after the disaster the animal mysteriously disappeared!

THE **DOG** THAT SAVED **92** LIVES!

THE S.S. ETHIE, A COASTAL STEAMER OF 414 TONS, AGROUND ON MARTIN'S POINT OFF CURLING, NEWFOUNDLAND, AND BREAKING UP IN A VIOLENT STORM AND HEAVY SEAS, WAS UNABLE TO FIRE A LIFELINE OR LAUNCH ITS BOATS, AND *NO MEMBER OF THE CREW DARED ATTEMPT TO SWIM ASHORE.* A NEWFOUNDLAND DOG MADE THE SWIM WITH A LIFELINE GRIPPED IN ITS TEETH AND ALL 92 PASSENGERS AND CREW MEMBERS WERE PULLED TO SAFETY ON A BOATSWAIN'S CHAIR (Dec.10,1919)

• **"Weela,"** a pit bull terrier owned by Lori Watkins, of Imperial Beach, California, saved the lives of thirty people, thirteen horses, twenty-nine dogs, and one cat during a severe flood!

• **"Browny,"** a dog owned by Virgilio de Guzman, of Saudi Arabia, saved the life of its owner's seven-month-old baby sister by killing a snake that had crawled into her crib!

• **Mrs. Candelaria Villanueva**, who was thrown into the sea when an inter-island Philippine passenger ship sank six hundred miles south of Manila, was kept afloat for two days by a giant sea turtle! Mrs. Villanueva was riding the turtle's back when a rescue ship sighted her.

• A dog named **"Roc"** saved its owners from a house fire by ringing the doorbell to wake them!

UTAHRAPTOR: JURASSIC DISCOVERY TURNS FICTION INTO FACT

In 1994, millions of movie-goers thrilled to the dinosaurs brought to life in the film *Jurassic Park*. The movie featured several terrifying prehistoric "bad guys," including a voracious nine-foot-tall man-eater named "Velociraptor."

Velociraptor was loosely based on a real-life dinosaur, a small carnivore that lived millions of years ago. But the filmmakers felt that Velociraptor, who was in reality only the size of a bulldog, wasn't scary enough to terrorize audiences as he needed to. So they embellished him. Taking a bit of paleontological license, they made him four times larger than he actually had been, so that human beings would make the ideal-sized prey.

But amazingly enough, only a few months before the movie opened, a new species of dinosaur was discovered in Utah. Named "Utahraptor," this new and frightful carnivore measured an impressive seventeen feet from nose to tail—and bore an uncanny resemblance to the fictional creatures in the film!

Chapter 5

Anthropology & Archaeology

STONEHENGE
THE ANCIENT MONUMENT IN WILTSHIRE, ENGLAND,
CONSTRUCTED MORE THAN 3,500 YEARS AGO,
REQUIRED 33 MILLION MAN-HOURS TO BUILD

Anthropologists and archaeologists are an odd lot. They seek for clues to the nature of humankind by searching out its furthest extremes: obscure, isolated tribes; the crumbling remnants of vanished civilizations; and human ancestors so ancient that we must stretch to even call them human. The past offers up its tales at a whisper, but those quiet voices of ages past tell remarkable tales of who we are, and what we have been. . .

ANCIENT CIVILIZATIONS

• Homes of Egyptian aristocrats had copper pipes with hot and cold running water as early as 1500 B.C.

• The ancient Incas used the skin of their enemies to make drugs and their shin bones to make flutes!

• The ancient Mayans often filed their front teeth to fine points!

• In three thousand B.C., the average life span was only eighteen years!

• In 1991, archaeologists in Cairo, Egypt, discovered a forty-six-hundred-year-old Egyptian skull that showed evidence of brain surgery!

BATHROOMS
DISCOVERED IN THE ROYAL PALACE OF MARI, IN SYRIA, UNCOVERED AFTER HAVING BEEN BURIED FOR 4,000 YEARS, HAD *MODERN, INSIDE PLUMBING THAT STILL WORKS*

ARCHAEOLOGICAL SITES

• As early as 400 B.C., bamboo pipes were used in China to carry water and natural gas!

• Archaeologists in Ashkelon, Israel, have uncovered a fifth-century-B.C. Phoenician cemetery for dogs, with over twelve hundred skeletons!

SCIENTISTS IN LADBY, DENMARK, *UNCOVERED A 1,000-YEAR-OLD VIKING WARSHIP* THAT HELD THE BODY OF A VIKING WARRIOR, BURIED WITH HIS WEAPONS, HIS FAVORITE HUNTING DOGS, *AND 12 HORSES!*

• British archaeologist **Lord Carnavon** and twelve others associated with King Tut's tomb, were not killed by an ancient curse but from a three-thousand-year-old fungus that grew on buried food!

• Ancient Greek and Egyptian temples dating back as early as 2500 B.C. were found to contain mysterious "talking" idols and hidden doors that opened when a fire was lit on a special altar!

• Archaeologists in Britain have determined that a chunk of stone used by people in Southampton, England, to prop up their bicycles is actually a priceless three-thousand-year-old-statue!

ARTIFACTS

• The ancient Egyptians built pyramids that contained everything the king would need in the afterlife—including a bathroom!

• In 1992, archaeologists discovered a jar in southwestern Iran containing five-thousand-year-old beer!

• In 1986, scientists found a fifteen-hundred-year-old vase near Rio Azul, Guatemala, that held residue from a chocolate drink!

• Recipes for beer—prescribed as medicine—have been found on Sumerian tablets dating back to 2000 B.C.!

THE **FIRST** DOCTOR
A MEDICINE MAN DEPICTED IN A DRAWING ON THE WALLS OF THE Trois Frères Cave, in Southern France, *17,000 YEARS AGO* – THE CAVE MEDICINE MAN IS WEARING A STAG MASK, THE PAWS OF A BEAR, AND THE TAIL OF A WILD HORSE

A HUMAN SKELETON still visible on the wall in Patrishow, Wales, was painted centuries ago in BLOOD.

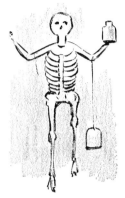

Newgrange, an ANCIENT BURIAL MOUND near Drogeda, Ireland, was built more than 5,000 years ago—predating both Stonehenge and the Great Pyramid of Giza!

A MECHANICAL STATUE DEPICTING 2 WORSHIPERS POURING A LIBATION FOR THE GODS WAS EXHIBITED THROUGHOUT ANCIENT EGYPT 1,900 YEARS AGO

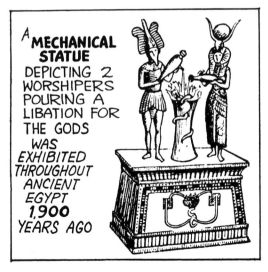

• Archaeologists in Japan have discovered the remains of ovens used twenty-eight thousand years ago to cook prehistoric elephants that once lived on the Japanese plains!

The OLDEST BELL IN THE WORLD It was found near Babylon and first pealed about 1,000 B.C.

The WORLD'S OLDEST PIECE OF ART A carving of a horse 2½ inches long and made from the ivory of an ancient mammoth is 32,000 years old.

• A stand of wheat grew from seeds found in two thousand quarts of wheat stored in a cellar of the palace of Karmir Blur in Soviet Transcaucasia, which was excavated in 1946, after having been buried for twenty-seven hundred years!

• A grain thresher still used in Turkey consists of a wooden board studded with stone "teeth" and was invented 2,000 years ago.

• The world's oldest bakery: In 1991, scientists in Giza Plateau, Egypt, discovered a forty-six-hundred-year-old bakery, with hearth, dough vats, and bread pots that could produce enough food for thirty thousand people!

• A cup with a handle excavated in the Wetterau region of Germany was produced by a skilled potter 4,000 years ago.

• Archaeologists discovered a forty-six-hundred-year-old bone fork in northern China!

HUMAN ANCESTORS

• The brains of Neanderthals were bigger than those of modern humans.

• We're not bigger than all our ancestors! Modern humans, averaging five feet, eight inches in height, actually are one inch shorter than our Stone Age ancestors (400,000 to 8000 B.C.), who averaged five feet, nine inches.

• In 1991, scientists in Japan studying genetics found that humans are more closely related to chimpanzees than chimps are to gorillas.

MUMMIES

• In 1991, scientists discovered the body of a four-thousand-year-old man on a 9,800-foot-high Austrian glacier!

• The mummified feet of wealthy Egyptians were often preserved in special cases on which were modeled the accurate replicas of their sandaled feet.

• In 1994, archaeologists in Zanjan, Iran, uncovered the perfectly preserved body of a man who had been buried in a salt quarry twenty-six hundred years before!

Archaeologists in Peru have found sealed vases filled with still-edible peanuts dating back to 1550 B.C. in the arms of entombed bodies!

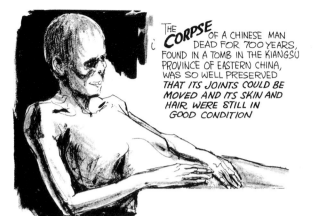

THE **CORPSE** OF A CHINESE MAN DEAD FOR 700 YEARS, FOUND IN A TOMB IN THE KIANGSU PROVINCE OF EASTERN CHINA, WAS SO WELL PRESERVED *THAT ITS JOINTS COULD BE MOVED AND ITS SKIN AND HAIR WERE STILL IN GOOD CONDITION*

• "Pum II," an Egyptian mummy who died twenty-seven hundred years ago, when examined at the Wayne State University School of Medicine in Detroit, Michigan, was found to still have red-painted finger-nails.

ANTHROPOLOGISTS AND ARCHAEOLOGISTS

• **Sir Edward Burnett Tylor** (1832-1917), the famed anthro-pologist who founded cultural anthropology, was an armchair anthropologist who shunned fieldwork.

• **Jane Dieulafoy** (1851-1916), as a reward for her archaeo-logical discoveries in Persia and Iraq, was granted special per-mission by the French govern-ment to wear trousers.

FOR ARCHAEOLOGISTS OF THE FUTURE

• A time capsule at Oglethorpe University, in Atlanta, Georgia, not to be opened until 8113, is the size of a swimming pool and contains thousands of items, including model trains, ashtrays, and cartoon film clips!

THE World's Oldest Chewing Gum!

Archaeologists in Sweden discovered a 9,000-year-old piece of birch resin with teeth marks in it!

DEAD MEN TELL TALES AT GUANAJUANTO'S MUMMY MUSEUM

Sometimes dead men do tell tales, especially when they've been preserved as thoroughly as the mummies at Guanajuanto, Mexico's Mummy Museum. The museum is home to one hundred eight forgotten corpses, so intact that in many cases visitors can easily read from them the stories of their deaths.

The Mummy Museum displays the residents of a "rental graveyard" dug in 1860. At the time it opened, the families of those buried there paid an annual rental for space inside its burial niches. In 1865, the bodies were exhumed. But what came out of the grave sites looked so much like the fresh corpses that had gone in that even the scientific community was baffled. The region's hot, dry air, and the limestone-rich ground had somehow worked together to "cure" the bodies into natural mummies.

Curators at the Mummy Museum show visitors the evidence of each corpse's cause of death: the noose marks around one neck, the bullet hole in another's side, the tumor that ended yet another's life. Grisliest of all, though, is the body of a woman curators know only as "Ignacia," whose raised arms and expression of hor-ror indicate that she had been buried alive.

Whereas most corpses are buried with their hands folded across their chests, Ignacia's arms are raised across her face, with one forearm in her mouth, as though to comfort her crying. Curators theorize that she had suffered an epileptic seizure, and her family, believing her dead, buried her. She later awakened inside her own tomb!

Chapter 6
Architecture

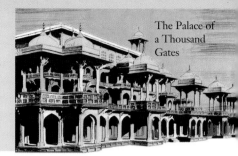

The Palace of a Thousand Gates

Floating churches? Castles built of snow, salt—or wine? Buildings in the shapes of elephants, tractors, pineapples, leaping fish? It seems that we can't content ourselves with four simple walls and a roof. We pour some of our most extraordinary ingenuity into the construction of our architecture, as you're about to discover. . .

ANCIENT STRUCTURES

• The **Parthenon** in Greece has no straight lines and contains no mortar!

• In ancient Mesopotamia so much garbage and soil was dumped into the streets that the street level raised higher than the floors of the houses!

• A Celtic hut near Apt, France, built by merely piling stones atop one another, without mortar of any kind, has been perfectly preserved after twenty-five hundred years.

APARTMENTS

• The **Pontalba** house, built in 1850 in New Orleans, was the first apartment house erected in America.

• A company in Scandinavia outfitted an entire apartment with fur, including a fur-covered shower curtain, mink-covered books, and fur picture frames!

ARENAS

• **Charlie** and **Bill Hume** operate a barbershop in Sandwich, Massachusetts, decorated to look like Boston's Fenway Park baseball stadium, complete with a giant scoreboard!

• Edmonds, Washington, is home to a basketball court with a floor made from recycled tennis shoes!

• Many bullrings in Spain display statues honoring **Sir Alexander Fleming**, the discoverer of penicillin!

• The world's biggest Scrabble game: A giant Scrabble game covered the entire soccer field at Wembley Stadium in London, and had letter pieces that required two men each to lift them!

• The **National Bowling Stadium** in Reno, Nevada, has eighty lanes!

BRIDGES

• The **Old Carr Bridge** over the Dulnan River in Scotland was built by the Romans and has been used for sixteen hundred years.

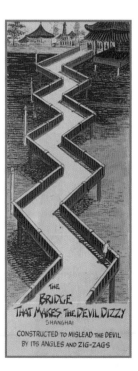

THE BRIDGE THAT MAKES THE DEVIL DIZZY
SHANGHAI
CONSTRUCTED TO MISLEAD THE DEVIL BY ITS ANGLES AND ZIG-ZAGS

THE ONLY BRIDGE IN THE WORLD THAT STEAMSHIPS PASS OVER! Håverud, Sweden --IT CARRIES THE DALSLAND CANAL OVER A WATERFALL AND UNDER ANOTHER BRIDGE

THE **SACRED BRIDGE** AT NIKKO—RESERVED FOR THE GODS ALONE!—WAS DYED RED WITH HUMAN BLOOD!

THE **WORLD'S NARROWEST DRAWBRIDGE** THE SOMERSET BRIDGE IN BERMUDA HAS AN 18-INCH-WIDE WOODEN FLAP TO ALLOW THE MASTS OF SAILBOATS TO GO THROUGH.

LUXURIOUS YACHTS
CRUISING THE EPINAL CANAL IN THE NORTH OF FRANCE, CROSS OVER THE MOSELLE RIVER ON A 100-YEAR-OLD BRIDGE MORE THAN ONE MILE LONG--WITH WATER 7½ FEET DEEP!

• Hamburg, Germany, has 2,556 bridges—more than London, Amsterdam, and Venice put together!

• One of the towers of New York City's **Brooklyn Bridge** is set on sand instead of bedrock!

CASTLES AND PALACES

• **Blonay Castle** in Vaud, Switzerland, has been occupied by the same family for seven hundred ninety-four years!

• The odd-shaped castle tower of Oxford, England, was built in accordance with instructions that it could not be round, square, oval, or oblong.

• The castle of Verres, Italy, was purposely ruined

by having its roof removed because buildings without roofs were not taxable.

• The first Earl of Exeter built **Wothorpe Castle** in England in 1600 as a place to retreat to each morning while his ancestral castle was being swept and dusted.

THE UNCOUNTABLE COLUMNS OF KAIROUAN, TUNISIA

NO MUHAMMADAN IS ALLOWED TO COUNT THE MANY COLUMNS OF THE GREAT MOSQUE OF SIDI-OKHBA UNDER THREAT OF BLINDNESS

ALL OF THE COLUMNS WERE TAKEN FROM THE RUINS OF CARTHAGE
THE EXACT NUMBER IS STILL UNKNOWN

JOHN BISHOP, of Pueblo, Colorado, aided only by members of his own family, using only pick, shovel, wheelbarrow, and machinery built by John and his father, has labored for 13 years building a stone castle that will be 120 ft. high, with towers, a massive gatehouse, drawbridge moat, spiked gate, and a chapel complete with a pipe organ!

• The castle of **La Punta** in Ajaccio, Corsica, was originally part of Napoleon's palace of the Tuileries in Paris, which was burned by a French mob in 1871. Duke Jerome Pozzo Di Orgo, whose family had long feuded with that of Napoleon in Corsica, bought the debris and spent $400,000 and fifteen years rebuilding the castle as a symbol of his victory over his old enemy.

• The palace of the **Sultan of Brunei** has over seventeen hundred rooms, two hundred fifty-seven toilets, and a garage for one hundred ten cars! It would take a visitor over twenty-four hours, spending thirty seconds in each room, to see every room!

THE CASTLE THAT REFUSES TO FALL: Bridgenorth, England. It was blown up in 1651 and has been defying gravity for 305 years.

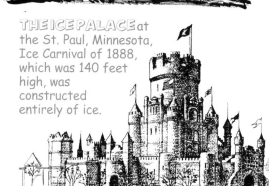

THE ICE PALACE at the St. Paul, Minnesota, Ice Carnival of 1888, which was 140 feet high, was constructed entirely of ice.

CHURCHES AND PLACES OF WORSHIP

• The prescription pagoda: In 1352, a portable marble pagoda was shipped in two sections from Peiping, China, to Seoul, Korea, on the advice of a physician to save the life of Princess Pazla, who was homesick for her native China.

• The **Mount Sung Pagoda** in China, built fourteen hundred years ago, is the only pagoda in the country with twelve sides.

• In Japan, a bear searching for beehives accidentally exposed a rare wooden tablet at the **Nagano Imamiya Daimyojin Shrine** that had been sealed inside the walls since 1527!

• The fragrant minaret: **The Koutoubia**, an eight-hundred-year-old tower in Marrakech, Morocco, was built with mortar mixed with over nine hundred bags of musk so that the holy building would always smell like perfume!

• The bell tower of Carbini, Corsica, originally served as a belfry for two churches, but since one of them was destroyed, the tower itself is now used as the Church of Saint Quilico and at the same time serves as the belfry of Saint John's Church.

• In the fourteenth century, the oak stalls in the **Cathedral of Winchester**, England, were constructed so that an occupant who dozed was pitched forward.

TEMPLE OF BROKEN DISHES
The Wat Arun—242 feet high. Bangkok, Siam. A magnificent and colorful temple built of broken dishes salvaged from a wrecked ship.

UNDERGROUND **CHURCH** CARVED FROM SOLID SALT! — WIELICZKA, Poland
A COMPLETE CITY HAS BEEN BUILT IN THESE SALT MINES WHERE **1500** MEN WORK DAILY.

CHRISTO REY, the floating church.

• The steeple of the parish church of Ecles, England, was buried under sand by a gale in 1605, and then exposed again by high winds blowing in the opposite direction two hundred seventy-five years later!

• The church of Ulrichsteinh, in Germany, holds Catholic and Protestant services alternately.

• The tower of **Saint Peter's Church** in Irthlingborough, England, is separated from the church by the local college, the executives of which used the tower as an apartment house.

• **Saint Elizabeth's Church** in Eureka Springs, Arkansas, built against a mountainside by Richard Kerens to mark the spot where he last saw his mother, can be entered only through an adjoining belfry.

• The great monstrance of the **Cathedral of Toledo**, Spain, originally owned by Queen Isabella, was made from the first gold brought back by Columbus from the New World.

• The **Frederiks' Church** in Copenhagen, Denmark, was started in 1749, but its builders ran out of funds. It was completed one hundred and forty five years later in 1894.

THE CAVE TEMPLES at Yunkang, China, ARE LINED WITH HUNDREDS OF STATUES -WITH BUDDHAS OCCUPYING ELABORATELY CARVED BOXES AND LESSER DISCIPLES RELEGATED SMALL NICHES

THE **PULPIT** of the CATHEDRAL of Freiberg, Germany, IS SHAPED LIKE A TULIP

ALL-GLASS CHURCH Tubize, Beligum. The entire structure consists of glass erected upon a glass foundation.

AN ANCIENT ROCK CHURCH LOCATED IN A MOUNTAIN CAVE NEAR LALIBELA, ETHIOPIA, LOOKS LIKE A BEACHED NOAH'S ARK

THE **RECLINING BUDDHA** IN THE WAT PO TEMPLE OF BANGKOK, THAILAND, IS 160 FEET LONG AND THE SOLES OF ITS FEET ARE COVERED WITH COMPLEX DESIGNS IN *MOTHER-OF-PEARL*

• The Seeing Eye Temple, of Katmandu, Nepal. The ubiquitous eyes painted upon the temple look straight into the heart of a sinner and are the greatest deterrent to crime in the city.

There is a CHURCH in Taitung, Taiwan, bulit in the shape of a sailing ship!

• The steeple of the old church of Keith, Scotland, for a period of two hundred twenty-eight years, was the town jail.

• The **Ardara Church** of Italy, in which services are held regularly, was constructed by carving into solid rock.

THE STRANGEST MINARET IN ALL HISTORY!
The MUEZZIN
OF THE MOORISH ARMY OF KING YACOUB II el MANSUR
AFTER THE BATTLE OF ECIJA IN SPAIN
DELIVERED HIS CALLS TO PRAYER 5 TIMES EACH DAY FROM
ATOP A PILE OF 18,000 HEADS --
HACKED FROM THE BODIES OF DEFEATED SPANISH SOLDIERS!
September, 1275

THE CHURCH BELFRY
OF GRAUN, A VILLAGE IN THE ITALIAN TYROL,
IS THE ONLY VISIBLE TRACE OF THE COMMUNITY --
-- WHICH WAS ENVELOPED YEARS AGO
BY THE WATERS OF LAKE RESCHEN

• The steeple of the **Church of Saint Peter** in Riga, Latvia, leans two feet off center.

• **Mount Mai Chi Shan** in China has one hundred ninety-six temples carved in its solid rock. Pilgrims are able to reach them only by climbing rickety ladders and scaffolding.

• The **Church of Cave**, New Zealand, was built in 1929 without a single nail and without the use of a hammer. Its walls are stone, its roof is slate, and its wooden seats were hewn out of solid lumber with an adze.

• **Saint Anthony's Chapel** in Bosnia, in which services are held daily, is hewn out of rock salt.

CITIES AND TOWNS

• The vertical village of El Arbaa, Algeria: The one hundred homes in this village are built into the face of a high precipice—most of them accessible only by ladders.

• The thirteenth-century village of Fabbriche in Di Careggine, Italy, which lies two hundred fifty feet below the surface of Lake

Vagli, is only visible when a nearby dam is drained and cleaned once every ten years!

• Almost all of the three hundred residents of Whittier, Alaska, live in the same fourteen-story apartment building, and for the first time in history, the town has its own road, opened on June 6, 2000!

• All of the buildings in Jaipur, India, were painted pink in 1865 for a visit by the Prince of Wales!

FARM STRUCTURES

• The first chicken coop, originally built in 1923 with an ocean view, is a protected site under the National Register of Historic Places and is displayed at the Delaware Agriculture Museum in Dover!

PALMANOVA, a town in Italy, to justify that it would resemble a star freshly fallen from the heavens, was developed in the shape of a 9-pointed star.

• A sixteen-sided barn designed and built by **George Washington** was one of the wonders of his time.

• The farm buildings at Voss, Norway, are built against the mountain with their roofs pitched in line with its slope so that the frequent avalanches will roar harmlessly over them.

FOUNTAINS

• A public drinking fountain in Burgas, Spain, gushes forth water at a temperature of one hundred fifty degrees.

• The Indian fountain erected in Mount Kisko, New York, designed for watering horses, bears the inscription, "God's only beverage for man and beast."

THE **PINEAPPLE FOUNTAIN** in Aachen, Germany, SPOUTED WATER FROM **129 POINTS**

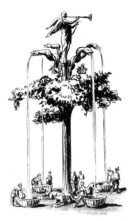

A HUGE SILVER FOUNTAIN BUILT FOR MONGOL PRINCE MANGU KHAN IN THE 13th CENTURY HAD 4 SPOUTS--*EACH DISPENSING A DIFFERENT ALCOHOLIC DRINK*

GARDENS

• Old shredded bank notes are used at the Middleborough Botanic Centre in England as garden compost to grow plants!

• David Jones, of England, invented the world's first portable garden that can be dug up and transported to different locations!

Hospitals

• The **Hospital of the Holy Ghost** in Nuremberg, Germany, was constructed on a bridge over the river Regnitz because there was no room for it on the ancient city's streets.

HOTELS

• The **Madonna Inn** in San Luis Obispo, California, features themed rooms, including the "Caveman," constructed with two-hundred-ton boulders and rock waterfalls!

Atlantic City: New Jersey's famous **Elephant Hotel,** as it appeared in 1933. It has since been rebuilt and is now a popular museum in Margate, New Jersey.

The **UPSIDE-DOWN HOTEL** The Hotel du Lac in Tunis, Tunisia, looks like an upside-down staircase

THE GARDEN of BOMARZA near Viterbo, Italy INSTEAD OF TREES, FLOWERS AND FOUNTAINS, HAS MONSTROUS STATUES CARVED FROM THE SOLID ROCK. *ONE FACE IS SO LARGE IT CAN BE ENTERED THROUGH THE MOUTH*

• The **Hotel Quinta Real** in Zacatecas, Mexico, was formerly a bullfighting ring!

HOUSES

• The tree house of Tillamook, Oregon: In 1851, for two months a hollow spruce tree was the home of **Joe Champion**, the first white man to settle in the Tillamook region.

• Windows were once taxed in Genoa, Italy, so people frequently painted imaginary windows on the sides of their homes!

A house in Truckee, California, was painted in a clean-up drive in 1 minute, 56½ seconds by 104 teenagers.

A HERMIT'S CAVE in Kediri, Java, has its ENTRANCE CARVED TO RESEMBLE A MONSTER WITH A WIDE-OPEN MOUTH

• The stone houses of the Ighchen tribe of Algeria are built with loosely piled stones because a chieftain became mortally ill on a visit to Paris, France, in 1880 and blamed his sickness on the mortar in his hotel's walls.

• The round house in Evanston, Illinois, was built in 1856, by students of a Bible institute, entirely from lumber washed ashore from wrecked ships.

• **Tim** and **Kathy Robertson,** of Baker, Louisiana, dismantled a Victorian cottage board by board and piece by piece, then rebuilt the entire home on their property over a period of four years!

• The old stone house in Morgantown, West Virgina, was built in 1795 as a dwelling but successively served as a pottery, tavern, tailor shop, tannery, church, and junk shop—it is now a thrift shop operated for charity.

• The house in which Mozart composed *The Magic Flute* was moved from Vienna to Salzburg, the composer's birthplace—a distance of one hundred fifty miles.

• **Damien Boyd**, of Toronto, Canada, converted a 1969 fire truck into a mobile home, complete with computer, television, VCR, and sun deck!

• "The Winchester Mystery House": **Sarah Pardee Winchester,** of

The QUEEREST HOUSE IN AUSTRALIA AT BALLARAT
CONSTRUCTED OF AN ENDLESS MEDLEY OF MISCELLANEOUS OBJECTS IN A VAST VARIETY OF COLORS
LAMPS, JUGS, DISHES, PLAQUES, SHELLS, ROCKS, ORNAMENTS, STATUETTES, BROKEN GLASS, ETC.

San Jose, California, had useless stairways and doors that opened into blank walls built into her 160-room mansion in order to appease evil spirits.

• In 1916, a forty-ton brick house was ordered from a catalog company and shipped by mail!

• An entire house was built in Nashville, Tennessee, in four hours, thirty-nine minutes, eight seconds!

• In 1996, the town of Lefors, Texas, gave away parcels of free land to anyone who promised to build a house there!

• **Samrauy Chuenchum,** of Ayudhya, Thailand, a former bus driver, built a two-bedroom, sixty-two foot long house in the shape of a double-decker bus!

• **James McEachem**, of Tulsa, Oklahoma, had his entire house stolen!

• **Marcel** and **Maureen Lauberte**, of Corona, California, have a house that stands fourteen feet high, twenty three feet long and is built in the shape of a shoe.

THE NIGHTCAP HOUSE - New Caledonia

BUILT BY A NATIVE WHO PATTERNED HIS HOME AFTER THE **HEADCOVERING** IN WHICH A FRENCH GOVERNOR OF THE COLONY ALWAYS SLEPT – EVEN TO THE **TASSEL!**

Justo Rosito, of Alcolea del Pinar, Spain, carved this seven-room house out of solid rock over a span of twenty years.

A SIX-STORY PYRAMID
THE HOME OF WAUKEGAN, ILL., CONTRACTOR JIM ONAN AND FAMILY, IS COVERED WITH 24-KARAT GOLD PLATE, SURROUNDED BY A MOAT, HAS 17,000 SQ. FT. OF SPACE AND IS BUILT AT **ONE-NINTH THE SCALE OF EGYPT'S GREAT PYRAMID!**

• Computer wizard **Bill Gates** lives in an automated house and can fill the bathtub in his master bathroom to a desired temperature and depth while he's driving home from work!

• **Felix Famularo** decorated the front porch of his Picayune, Mississippi, home with over seventy-nine thousand metal pop-top tabs!

EVERY DOORWAY
in the village of Mogroum, Chad, Africa IS SHAPED LIKE A KEYHOLE – *IN THE BELIEF **IT WILL KEEP OUT UNWANTED VISITORS***

• The world's biggest log cabin, in Portland, Oregon, is made out of two million feet of lumber and covers a square city block!

• **Jim** and **Aaron Kennedy** of Walker, Louisiana, built a two-story tree house in a one-hundred-twenty-year-old beech tree that includes all the amenities of a real home: electricity, hot and cold water, air-conditioning, and satellite television!

• A dwelling in Airth Stirlingshire, England, built as a summer house in 1761, is shaped like a pineapple.

THE **CROOKED HOUSE**
IN THE DUDLEY AREA OF ENGLAND'S MIDLANDS
LOCATED OVER AN OLD COAL MINE
TILTS 45 DEGREES

• In Spring Green, Wisconsin, a fifty-five-ton boulder stands wedged inside a two-bedroom house!

LANDMARKS

• Seattle, Washington, is home to a famous landmark called "Lincoln's Toe Truck": an advertisement for a towing firm, it consists of a pink truck with a set of giant pink toes on top!

• The cable cars in San Francisco, California, are recognized as moving national landmarks!

• In 1994, a newsstand in Harvard Square, Boston, was designated a national historic landmark!

LIGHTHOUSES

• A house in Eastham, Massachusetts, was built between two old lighthouses.

• In Biloxi, Mississippi, a sixty-five-foot-high iron lighthouse stands in the center of a four-lane highway!

THE **HOMES**
of the NUBAS of Central Africa
ARE BUILT ON HUGE BOULDERS
-BALANCED SO PRECARIOUSLY THAT
THEY TEETER IN THE WIND

THE GENERAL NOBLE REDWOOD TREE HOUSE
LONG A LANDMARK IN WASHINGTON, D.C., WAS BUILT FROM THE STUMP OF A GIANT CALIFORNIA SEQUOIA THAT *TOOK LUMBERJACKS A WEEK TO CUT THROUGH*

THE FLATTEST FLAT IN THE WORLD.

An architectural eccentricity in Alexandria, Egypt. A family of 5 lives in 3 rooms hung on a wall.

• The lighthouse on Tybee Island, Georgia, built in 1648, served without a light of any kind for one hundred forty-two years—it was merely a daytime warning until 1790.

• **Roger Penfold** built a circular island home, including a lighthouse and a tennis court, off Portsmouth, England, out of a fort that had held four hundred men!

MONUMENTS AND STATUES

• **Nek Chand Saini**, of Chandigarh, India, has created over twenty thousand sculptures, waterfalls, and bridges around his home using old car parts, light bulbs, and bicycle frames!

• The memorial tower of Mohonk, New York, marks the border of three townships and overlooks six states: New York, Connecticut, Massachusetts, Vermont, New Jersey, and Pennsylvania.

• Statues in ancient Rome were often made with detachable heads so the heads could be replaced by more popular personalities if desired!

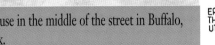

A lighthouse in the middle of the street in Buffalo, New York.

MEMORIAL TO A TALKING RABBIT Falkenburg, Germany ERECTED BY TOWNSFOLK, WHO CLAIMED THEY HEARD THE BUNNY DISTINCTLY UTTER THE WORDS *"GOOD MORNING"*

THE GREAT DAIBUTSU A 50-FOOT-HIGH BUDDHA IN KAMAKRA, JAPAN, HAS IN THE CENTER OF ITS FOREHEAD A BLOCK OF PURE SILVER MORE THAN A FOOT WIDE.

THE STATUE OF BUDDHA near Nonsan, Korea, HAS A SHRINE ON TOP OF IT -TO PROVIDE THE BUDDHA WITH A HAT

ODD STRUCTURES

• A giant coffeepot located atop a tower in Stanton, Iowa, is thirty six feet high, twenty feet wide, six feet deep and could hold 640,000 cups of coffee.

• The tower of Ulm, Germany, which has been standing since 1578, leans four feet, eight inches off center.

Gigantic marble statue 27½ feet high erected to CAPTAIN HANSON GREGORY, inventor of the hole in the doughnut!

THE BEGGAR'S MEMORIAL
Yunnan Sen, China
FOR **73** YEARS
HUN LIANG PLEADED FOR ALMS—
BUT BEFORE HIS DEATH HE
DIRECTED THAT THE COINS HE HAD
COLLECTED BE MELTED TO
ERECT A **SOLID BRONZE**
PAGODA – AS A MONUMENT
TO THE **GENEROSITY** OF HIS
BENEFACTORS!
HE HAD NOT SPENT A SINGLE
ONE OF THE COINS

• The magnetic observatory at Trinity College in Dublin, now used as a weather bureau, was built in 1837 entirely without the use of iron.

• People in Berlin celebrated the fiftieth anniversary of the East German Communist state by erecting a 39.6-foot-long replica of the Berlin Wall using twenty-six four-pound chocolate bricks!

A **TOWER**, EXHIBITED IN OSAKA, JAPAN, **CREATED OUT OF 5,000,000 POSTCARDS**— THEY WERE PART OF 93,000,000 CARDS MAILED IN A CONTEST TO SELECT THE **8** MOST BEAUTIFUL SIGHTS IN JAPAN

A PARK MONOLITH IN OSLO, NORWAY, 55 FEET HIGH, ON WHICH A SCULPTOR HAS CARVED **121** HUMAN FIGURES IN THE **SOLID ROCK**

• A two-room fisherman's cottage in North Wales is only six feet wide and stands ten feet high!

• **Captain John Waite** (1700-1769), of Peak Island, Maine, built two fireplaces in his parlor— one for himself, and the other for his servant.

OFFICE BUILDINGS

• Lamara, Colorado, is home to an office building made completely of petrified wood!

THE LEANING "TOWER" OF JAPAN
A HOUSE IN SHIZUOKA CITY, WHICH SEEMS TO HAVE BEEN GOBBLED UP BY THE EARTH, WAS DESIGNED SPECIFICALLY TO ALERT RESIDENTS TO A PREDICTED EARTHQUAKE

A PRIVATE CLINIC
in Geneva, Switzerland, IS SHAPED LIKE A *FLYING SAUCER*

An office building in Turlock, California, was designed to look like a GIANT BULLDOZER.

An office building in Tokyo, Japan, has a giant RED BALL embedded in its side.

PLUMBING

• **John A. Kostopoulos**, of Boron, California, hung over four hundred toilet seats on a fence around his home! John hand-painted each one with portraits and scenes.

• The courthouse in King County, Texas, did not install indoor plumbing until 1982!

• Homes of Egyptian aristocrats had copper pipes with hot and cold running water as early as 1500 B.C.

PRISONS

• The debtor's prison of Accoma, Virginia, built in exchange for twenty-five thousand pounds of tobacco in 1731, is still in use as a library after two hundred twenty-nine years.

NEWGATE PRISON
IN WHICH LOYALISTS WERE CONFINED IN CONNECTICUT DURING THE REVOLUTION, WAS A FORMER COPPER MINE *120 FEET BELOW THE SURFACE*

PUBLIC BUILDINGS

• The town hall of Pevensey is the smallest in all of England, yet it also served as the courthouse and local jail.

• The Bryan cabin in Dallas, Texas, was the first house built in Dallas, its first courthouse and post office, and the founding place of the orphanage.

• The Kaiserhaus of Goslar, built before 1050, is the oldest non-religious structure in all of Germany.

RESTAURANTS

• A 690-foot-high television tower in Suttgart, Germany, features a restaurant at a height of four hundred ninety feet.

• Lincoln's Silver Restaurant in Haugan, Montana, has over twenty-six thousand silver dollars mounted on its walls!

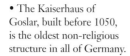

A FIST GRIPPING A STAFF STILL ADORNS THE ANCIENT GOVERNMENT PALACE OF Dubrovnik, Yugoslavia —THE EMBLEM OF ITS AUTHORITY TO PUNISH EVILDOERS

THE FACADE OF AN EDIFICE HIDING A GIANT ELECTRICAL TRANSFORMER NEAR BONN, W. GERMANY, *RESEMBLES A CARICATURE OF A HUMAN FACE!*

A restaurant in a suburb of Los Angeles, California, in the 1930s was shaped like a **BULLDOG**.

THE NATIONAL FRESHWATER FISHING HALL OF FAME IN HAYWARD, WIS., HALF A CITY BLOCK LONG AND 4½ STORIES HIGH, *WAS CONSTRUCTED TO LOOK LIKE A LEAPING MUSKIE*

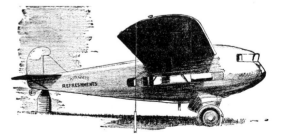

A $320,000 Hot Dog Stand, built from a twin-motored cabin plane.

ROADS AND PARKING STRUCTURES

• America's most crooked road: Colorado's Broadmoore-Cheyenne highway, seven miles long, traverses an area of one and a half square miles.

• The town of East Longmeadow, Massachusetts, has a seven-street intersection with no traffic lights!

• The main street of Barbotan, France, runs right through the town's church.

• In 1895, workers at a sugar factory in Chino, California, created a surface for paving roads made out of leftover molasses!

HIGH PARKING A garage in an attic! House built on a hillside—the living quarters are below the garage. Sausalito, California.

The Hotel Clark garage has a street-level entrance on every floor.

• Engineers in Milan, Italy, have designed a completely automated parking garage in which cars can be parked eight stories underground using elevators and horizontal conveyors!

• A busy intersection in Albuquerque, New Mexico, sports a twenty-five-foot-high tile-covered archway with a 1954 Chevy on top!

• Interstate highway 84 near Hermiston, Oregon, has designated rest areas for horses.

• The world's shortest highway: The Wanganui motorway in New Zealand is less than a half mile in length and takes only forty-five seconds to traverse!

PARKING GARAGES in Chicago, Illinois, owned by Myron Washaver, feature different musical themes on each floor so that people can remember where they parked.

• The world's oldest paved road: A road near Giza, Egypt, measuring seven and a half miles long, was built forty-six hundred years ago!

STAIRS

• The steepest stairway: The stairs between High Town and Lower Town in Bar-Le-Duc, France, rise so abruptly that they zigzag from one street to another so the climber won't suffer vertigo.

• The long stairway on a century-old house in Mobile, Alabama, originally led directly to the sidewalk but it was switched to the porch side by a mother who feared passing gentlemen would glimpse her daughter's ankles.

• The longest staircase: A power station in western Norway has a stairway with 3,875 wooden steps that rise 4,101 feet!

THEATERS AND OPERA HOUSES

• The **Theater of the Independents** in Rome, Italy, is located at an ancient Roman bath.

• Honey is harvested on the roof of the **Paris Opera House**!

TUNNELS AND SEWERS

• A person shouting inside a tunnel at **Villa Simonetta**, near Milan, Italy, can hear his own echo sixty times!

• Sewer tours: Visitors to Paris, France, can take guided tours of the city's thirteen-hundred-mile-long underground sewer system!

WALLS AND GATES

• **The Lion's Gate** in Harrar, Ethiopia, is shaped like a lion's head because the king of beasts is the country's emblem.

• A marble slab in the wall of **Saint Joseph's Old Cathedral** in Buffalo, New York, was the tombstone of an early Christian martyr buried in the catacombs of Rome 1,900 years ago.

• Rip Collins, a first baseman with the Chicago Cubs and the Saint Louis Cardinals in the 1930s, used broken baseball bats to make a fence around his Albany, New York, home!

WATER STRUCTURES

• An aqueduct built by the ancient Romans in the second century in Merida, Spain, is still in use!

• A swimming pool in Casablanca, Morocco, measures 1,574 feet in length!

• The arches surmounting Town Hall Street in Bonifacio, Corsica, also serve as aqueducts through which rainwater from the roofs is carried to a cistern as a reserve against drought.

• A well in Greensburg, Kansas, in 1887, measuring one hundred nine feet deep and thirty-two feet in diameter, was dug completely by hand!

WINDMILLS

• The Devil's Windmill near Guerande, France, is so called because its owner **Yves Kerbic** insisted that in exchange for his soul the devil helped him build it in a single night.

• **John Lorenzen** of Woodward, Iowa, who has never paid for electricity, has run his one-hundred-acre farm using the power from windmills for over sixty years!

• In 1928, a windmill on a farm in Kaltendorf, Germany, began spinning so fast in high winds that it caught fire and burned to the ground!

• **Bill Dalley** of Portales, New Mexico, has a collection of sixty antique windmills!

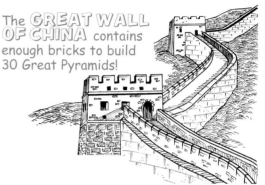

The **GREAT WALL OF CHINA** contains enough bricks to build 30 Great Pyramids!

THE FAMOUS "BIRD ROOST" MIYAJIMA - INLAND SEA OF JAPAN -
TORIIS - MEANING BIRD RESTS - ARE PLACED BEFORE ALL SHINTO SHRINES AND SACRED SPOTS.
THE TORII WAS ORIGINALLY A PERCH FOR SACRED FOWL THAT HERALDED THE RISING SUN

The HORSESHOE GATE

A gateway in Toledo, Spain, featuring this inscription: "I am the finest and best preserved gateway in the city. The Moors built me eight centuries ago, shaping the passageway in the likeness of their horses' hooves. The kings fortified me, the sun is my lover, greeting me every morning and taking leave of me every evening with a kiss; therefore I am known as Puerta Del Sol—the Gateway of the Sun."

The archway at the entrance to City Center Park in Jackson, Wyoming, is constructed entirely of elk antlers.

THE MISSILE SILO HOUSE—TURNING A SYMBOL OF WAR INTO A PLACE OF PEACE

If you visited the spacious home of Kansas couple Edward and Diane Peden, you'd likely be impressed with its warmth and coziness. The Peden's unique dwelling place, however, was not always as charming as it is today. Only a handful of years ago, it was home to a four-megaton warhead. Edward and Diane have made their home underground—in a former missile silo.

When Edward and Diane first took a tour of their new home-to-be, many of the eighteen thousand square feet were under eight and a half feet of water. Renovation would be no easy task, but this piece of real estate came at a bargain price: a mere $40,000, even though it had cost taxpayers $25 million to construct.

After the formidable job of renovating their new home, Edward and Diane were faced with yet another task: transforming the negative energy, left over from the structure's days as an instrument of war, into the positive, life-affirming energy of a peaceful home. Edward and Diane regularly meditate, drum, and perform various other healing rituals. Their efforts are paying off: what was once a symbol of death and destruction has become a warm, inviting home.

Chapter 7

Art

Denise Sansevera, of Dobbs Ferry, New York, creates and sells pictures of "faeries" etched into tree fungi.

Welcome to Ripley's art gallery, a collection of some of the strangest and most creative works in the world. Artistic expression is fertile ground for the bizarre. It is boundless exploration. It is forever challenging limits, pushing the edges of technique, material, and subject. And the sheer act of creation, by its nature, expands the creator. If we're truly expressing ourselves, with all our uniqueness and individuality, we can't help but seem a little bizarre. When it comes to artistic expression, the weirder the better!

• Britain's "Living Paintings Trust" uses molded plastic thermoform reproductions to help the visually impaired experience fine art!

ARTISTS

• A woman bought a book for one dollar at a flea market in Amsterdam, the Netherlands, that turned out to be a sketch book containing original drawings by Rembrandt worth over $50,000!

• **Leonardo da Vinci,** Italy's most celebrated painter, could paint with equal dexterity with either hand.

• In the fifteenth century, Leonardo da Vinci designed a pile driver with an automatic release.

• A practical helicopter was designed by Leonardo da Vinci more than 400 years ago.

• Leonardo da Vinci designed multi-tiered superhighways centuries before their advent!

• California artist **Tim Hawkinson** frequently models his sculptures using parts of his own body, including a two-inch-tall piece called "*Bird*" that was made entirely from his own fingernails!

• French artist **Claude Monet** frequently worked on six paintings at the same time!

• **David Hammons,** an artist in Harlem, New York, once sold autographed snowballs!

Ernie and **Dot Lind,** photographed in 1939, while creating bullet-hole art.

Jeff de Boer, of Calgary, Canada, makes authentic medieval armor for cats and mice.

• Michelangelo created a still-life drawing of wine, fruit, bread, and spaghetti as a shopping list for his cook who didn't know how to read!

• **Peter Paul Reubens**, the famed Flemish painter, was knighted by King Charles I of England because the monarch could not pay his $15,000 fee for painting a ceiling.

• **James McNeill Whistler**, the American artist whose painting of his mother immortalized him, had repeatedly insisted that no fine art could become popular.

• **George Washington Whistler**, the engineer who built the first mile of passenger railroad track in the United States, considered a genius in his time, is now virtually forgotten—yet his wife, Ana, a nonentity in her lifetime, is immortalized in the painting *Whistler's Mother*.

• The "Peanuts" cartoon creator **Charles Schulz** took a correspondence course called "Drawing of Children" when he was a nineteen-year-old student, and received a grade of only C+!

• Cartoonist **Charles Schulz** drew every single "Peanuts" comic strip by hand for almost half a century!

• **Pablo Picasso**, creator of a painting that recently sold for forty-eight million dollars, was so poor early in his career that he burned some of his drawings to keep warm.

• **Paul Warhol,** of Pittsburgh, Pennsylvania, the sixty-seven-year-old brother of pop artist Andy Warhol, had an exhibit of paintings he created using chicken feet as brushes!

• Spanish artist **Salvador Dali** once held a party at which every guest came dressed as a bad dream!

• The French painter **Marc Chagall** paid for everything by check, yet his signature was considered so valuable that few were ever cashed!

• **Gord Hamilton**, of Richmond Hill, Ontario, Canada, creates paintings with hidden electrical elements that act as room heaters.

• **Morris Katz**, of New York City, is the world's

• **Cesar Ducornet**, a nineteenth-century artist, drew with his feet!

• German artist **Adolph Menzel** paid local police to wake him whenever a large fire broke out in the city so he could paint the scene!

• Artist **Henri Matisse** frequently drew on his bedroom walls using a piece of charcoal fixed to a long cane!

• **Paul Cezanne**'s parrot could say "Cezanne is a great painter."

most prolific painter: he can paint at a rate of 2.64 feet of canvas per minute and has sold more than one hundred fifty thousand paintings.

• **Anne Brenner**, of Paris, France, creates works of art by placing canvasses in the mud at animal watering holes on Africa's Ivory Coast so that hippos and rhinos can walk across them.

• British sculptor **Henry Moore** created a fourteen and-a-half-foot-high monument called *Sheep Piece* for the sheep that wandered across his farm in Herefordshire, England!

• "Thick paintings": For the past ten years, Canadian artist **Eric Cameron** has been applying one hundred seventy coats of gesso undercoating a year to twenty-seven cherished objects including a chair, a head of lettuce, and a lobster!

• French artist **Chantal Cottet** creates "blast art" by sculpting with dynamite, hand grenades, and artillery shells!

• **Deborah Lacayo** of Cottage Grove, Oregon,

carves and paints miniature people on the ends of toothpicks!

• American sculptor **J. Seward Johnson** creates such lifelike sculptures that one of his figures was once shot at!

• **Evelyn Rosenberg** creates works of art by sculpting patterns onto plaster molds that are then imprinted on metal sheets using explosives!

• **Linda Montano** and **Tehching Hsieh**, performance artists in New York City, created a work of art by spending a year tied together at the waist by an eight-foot rope!

• French artist **Cesar** created a sculpture in the shape of a thumb that sold for $1 million!

• **Kent Twitchell**, of Los Angeles, California, paints wall murals on buildings in downtown Los Angeles that take up to nine years to complete and stand six stories tall!

• Sculptor **Roberto Moriconi**, of Brazil, once carved a door in exchange for a car, and created a sculpture to trade for a sofa!

• Art Deco designer **Erté** frequently attended Paris balls wearing a gold lamé suit studded with diamonds and a long cape trimmed with fresh roses!

• **Denny Dent**, a United States artist, pays tribute to musical artists by painting a portrait of them faster than the time it takes to play one of their songs!

• In the 1920s, **Huang Erh-nan**, a Chinese artist, created elaborate paintings on silk by using his tongue instead of a brush!

ANIMAL ARTISTS

• In 1977, **Raphael Boronali** exhibited paintings in Paris that were created by a donkey with a paintbrush tied to its tail!

SUNSET SAM, a dolphin at the Clearwater Marine Science Center in Florida, creates watercolor paintings holding the paintbrush in his mouth.

• "Bud D. Holly," a cat in Mendocino, California, who creates paintings by walking across paper, sold two works of art at a one-cat show!

EXHIBITIONS, GALLERIES, AND MUSEUMS

• In 1991, an art gallery in Nova Scotia, Canada, held an exhibition of "refrigerator art" drawn by children!

• In 1992, an art gallery in New York City displayed two hundred paint-by-number creations collected by writer Michael O'Donoghue!

• The National Portrait Gallery in Washington, D.C., displays a portrait of former President George Bush painted inside a three-and-a-half-inch-high bottle!

• **Bruce Johnson**, of Halifax, Canada, exhibits the work of local artists by displaying them in laundromats around the city!

• In 1992, an art gallery in Alexandria, Virginia, had a display of trash art, including a cityscape made out of cereal boxes, radio tubes, and toothpicks, and a chair made out of an old water heater!

• In 1991, an exhibition of working drawings of computer chips and circuitry was shown at New York's Museum of Modern Art!

• In 1991, at Rotterdam's Museum of Fine Arts, an exhibition of modern art included live models displayed in glass cases!

• The creators of the works of art in the Anonymous Museum in Chicago are never identified!

MATERIALS

• In 1970, Swiss artist **Dieter Roth** created works of art from food and currently has an exhibit of forty suitcases filled with different kinds of cheese that have been on display for nineteen years.

• **Ken Kirby**, of Toronto, Ontario, Canada, has created a 12-foot-by-152-foot landscape painting of the Canadian Arctic using two

thousand feet of lumber, five liters of glue, and fourteen thousand staples.

• **Bob Hoke** of Scottsdale, Arizona, uses a high-speed drill to create delicate filigree patterns on ostrich eggs that take up to four hundred hours to complete!

• **Laurie Palmer**, an artist in Springfield, Illinois, created an art exhibit of sweat that featured sweaty T-shirts spread on wooden shelves!

• **George Gutarra**, of New York City, creates sculptures from pieces of stainless steel cutlery!

• California artist **Buzz Spector** has created a sculpture called *Toward a Theory of Universal Causality*, using sixty-five hundred books arranged in one hundred sixty-eight steps!

• French artist **Armand Pierre Arman** created a work of art in a fifty-foot grotto using twelve tons of telephone parts.

• **Andy Goldsworthy**, an artist in England, creates works of art out of icicles, goose feathers, snowballs, and reeds!

TYREE GUYTON OF DETROIT, MICH., TURNS ABANDONED BUILDINGS INTO *WORKS OF ART* BY COVERING THEM WITH EVERYTHING FROM OLD BICYCLE PARTS TO PHONE BOOTHS AND BATHTUBS!

Jim Gary, of Farmingdale, New Jersey, creates colorful life-size dinosaurs from used car parts.

AN ELEPHANT
CARVED IN NEW DELHI, INDIA, FROM *A SINGLE PIECE OF IVORY—* ALL THE DECORATIVE FEATURES INCLUDING THE BLANKET, CHAIN, PENDANT AND BELLS' SWING FREELY *-YET ARE STILL ATTACHED TO THE BODY OF THE ELEPHANT*

Slater Barron, of Long Beach, California, creates life-size sculptures, portraits, and murals out of laundry lint.

• Artist **Rob Mulholland** created a three-hundred-foot-long human figure in a Glasgow, Scotland, park using three hundred thousand aluminum cans.

• **Dominique Bordenave**, a French artist, creates sculpture characters using old shoes!

TO CELEBRATE *MIDSUMMER'S DAY,* ARTIST Andy Goldsworthy DISPLAYED 13 ONE-TON SNOWBALLS ON THE STREETS of London, England.

HE COLLECTED SNOW OVER TWO WINTERS AND KEPT IT IN COLD STORAGE!

MARY LOUISE LYNCH OF DELL CITY, TX, CREATES SCULPTURES OUT OF GIANT TUMBLEWEEDS!

• Commercial artist **Peter Rocha**, of San Francisco, California, created a four-foot-by-six-foot mosaic of the Statue of Liberty using fourteen thousand jellybeans!

• **Nicki Nickerson** of Lisle, Canada, paints wildlife scenes on the bones of cattle and pigs!

This replica sailing ship was made from chicken bones.

• "The Iron Zoo": **Jean Dakessian,** an artist in Coalinga, California, has painted fifty oil pumps to look like insects and animals!

• **William Wardham**, the official artist-in-residence at San Francisco's garbage dump, creates sculptures out of metal scraps that are displayed at the dump!

• **Franco Ricardo**, of Warwick, Rhode Island, carved a life-size sculpture of United States President Bill Clinton, his wife, Hillary, and daughter Chelsea—out of brownies—about fifty-seven million calories worth!

• **Harry Kalenberg**, of Dallas, Texas, paints popcorn kernels to resemble animals and people, and sells the figures for up to $300 per kernel!

• **B. W. Crawford**, of Denton, Texas, creates sculptures of such famous figures as Elvis, Dolly Parton, and Miss Piggy, using pecan shells!

• **Tommie Godwin** uses chain saws and chisels to create sculptures out of cypress stumps in Dead Lake, Florida!

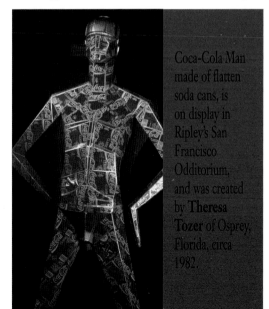

• **George Vlosich**, of Lakewood, Ohio, takes up to fifty hours to create portraits of famous people such as Mickey Mantle, Mike Piazza, and the Chicago Bulls on an "Etch a Sketch" toy! Then he sells them for up to $3,000 each!

• **Harold Dalton**, a nine-teenth-century American artist, using butterfly scales and the skeletons of marine organisms, created detailed pictures on glass slides that were smaller than a postage stamp!

• **Donna Hensley**, of Texas, is an artist and furniture maker who creates tables and chairs out of the bones of animals that have been accidentally run over on local highways!

• **Elvira Ballard** of Salmon, Idaho, creates sculptures out of masking tape!

• In the 1960s, American artist **Joe Veno** created full-sized sculptures of animals, including lions, roosters, and owls, out of old computer chips and wire!

• Artist **Simon English**, by raking and burning hay into strategic positions, created a three-hundred-foot-long image of a zebra in a field in Warwickshire, England!

• "Balloon art": **Bruce Walden** of Toronto, Canada, creates giant sculptures, including an eighteen-foot-high Pinocchio, out of balloons!

• **Gilbert Tim Sit**, of France, carves delicate sculptures from ordinary chicken eggs!

H.L. CHEW of Toronto, paints portraits on cobs of corn—including Robert Ripley, the Mona Lisa, and U.S. President Bill Clinton

Italian sculptor **Livio di Marchi** carves clothing including shirts, jackets, and ties out of pine wood. His carved-wood Mercedes-Benz 1953 gull-wing boat/car is shown here.

Coca-Cola Man made of flatten soda cans, is on display in Ripley's San Francisco Odditorium, and was created by **Theresa Tozer** of Osprey, Florida, circa 1982.

COSIMO CAVALLARO COVERED AN ENTIRE ROOM of New York City's WASHINGTON JEFFERSON HOTEL **WITH THOUSANDS of POUNDS of MELTED CHEESE!**

ARTIST MARY ENGEL MADE A SCULPTURE of AN ELEPHANT OUT of HUNDREDS of **BULLETS!**

ARGENTINE DANCER GUILLERMO ALIO and HIS PARTNER, PASCAL COQUIGNY, CREATED A PAINTING WHILE **DANCING THE TANGO** WITH PAINT THAT HAD BEEN SPLASHED ON THE SOLES of THEIR SHOES!

• In 1990, **Jaques Tokar** carved a four-foot-high bust of Soviet leader Mikhail Gorbachev out of an eight-hundred-pound block of ice cream.

• Artist **David Krepfle**, of Dubuque, Iowa, creates sculptures using living trees in their natural forest setting.

• "Edible art": **Roland Winbeckler**, of Kent, Washington, creates life-size sculptures—including Marilyn Monroe, King Tut, and huge lions and tigers—out of sugar, flour, shortening, and buttercream!

• **William Hilderbrand, Senior**, of Frederick, Maryland, decorates furniture, including lamp stands, clothes trees, and wall plaques, with walnut and hickory shells!

• **Anne Vasjo**, of Kamloops, Canada, creates sculptures in the Canadian Arctic made from ice and snow!

• **Jana Sterback**, an artist from Montreal, Canada, created a sculptured dress, using fifty pounds of raw steaks, that now hangs in Canada's National Gallery!

• "A furniture forest": **Chris Castle**, a furniture designer, grows trees in the shapes he needs to make tables and chairs.

• **Bill Coyne**, an artist in Richmondville, New York, created a work of art by "planting" dozens of old bicycles into a hillside near his home!

• **P. J. Roths**, of Maurice, Louisiana, carves elaborate scenes of helicopters, ships, and animals out of styrofoam coffee cups!

• In Houston, Texas, there is an annual "can castle competition" in which contestants create spacecraft, Viking ships, and bald eagles out of beer cans!

• Scottish artist **David Mach** spends hours creating bust sculptures out of thousands of matchsticks that he then sets on fire!

• Artist **Janice Krangle**, of Ontario, Canada, creates sculptures of animals using welded steel and chicken wire.

• Artist **Rick Ladd**, of New York City, makes chairs and light fixtures using discarded bottlecaps!

• The International Society of Copier Artists, that creates art using photocopiers, is based in New York City and has over one hundred fifty members!

• In 1928, biochemist **Alexander Fleming**, of Scotland, created living paintings using penicillin and bacillus molds on blotting paper!

• "Wearable art": A fashion show in New Zealand featured clothing made from coffee filters, moss, and popcorn, and an outfit made entirely of licorice!

• Artist **Vik Muniz**, of New York City, creates portraits of children using white sugar sprinkled on black paper!

• **Miguel Lopez Tulsa**, of Lemon Grove, California, paints landscapes on spoons, glass, and tiles, using the fingernail of his index finger as a paintbrush!

• **Louis Zelko**, of Toronto, Canada, carves portraits of famous people on eggs!

• Artist **Art Grant** created a model of the San Francisco skyline using over five thousand containers of "Rice-a-Roni"!

• The ancient Polynesians used a "mattang," or web of interlocking sticks, to study the patterns that waves form when deflected by land!

• **Jamy Verheylewegen**, of Belgium, creates oil paintings while underwater and exhibits his canvasses in swimming pools!

• American artist **Robert Sullivan** creates animal sculptures out of hundreds of used computer parts!

• Artists **Steven Lowy** and **Pascal Giraudon**, of New York, sell prints of manhole covers using steamrollers to imprint the designs on paper!

• **Steve Tobin**, of Pleasant Valley, Pennsylvania, makes rubber casts of giant African termite mounds, then dips them in bronze and sells the sculptures for $60,000!

• Dental technician **Ron Grant**, of Los Angeles, California, paints cartoon characters, team logos, and animal portraits on his patients' teeth!

REPRODUCTIONS

• **Theodore Conibear**, of Los Angeles, California, created a replica of *The Last Supper* using three tons of sand!

• **Scott McCrindle**, of Oakville, Ontario, Canada, created a ten-by-seven-foot replica of the *Mona Lisa* out of sixteen thousand Smarties!

• The Reverend **Marian Paskowics**, of Reading, Pennsylvania, has rendered reproductions of the fifty state capitols, every President of the United States, and *The Last Supper*—in straw.

• Artist **Terry Niedzialek** sculpted Tim Bowman's shoulder-length hair into a replica of the Three Mile Island nuclear towers!

• **Gerry Kirk**, of California, a full-time sand sculptor, is the creator of a three-hundred-thirty-ton sand replica of the United States Capitol, a fifty-six-foot-high castle, and a giant triceratops dinosaur!

• **Art Grant**, of San Francisco, California, sculpted a giant replica of the *Venus de Milo* out of twelve thousand pounds of soap!

• Lester Gaba recreated *The Thinker* in soap.

A life-sized replica of Da Vinci's *Last Supper*, created from paper grocery bags by **Anton Schiavone**, of Bangor, Pennsylvania.

• Fifteen villagers of D'Albi, France, spent twenty-four hours arranging 24,800 glasses of wine, beer, and juice into a forty-nine-foot-by-twenty-six-foot copy of a painting by Toulouse-Lautrec!

WORKS OF ART

• Tibetan Buddhist monks often use up to seventeen different shades of sand to create intricate mandala paintings that are ritually dismantled shortly after they are completed!

Tadhiko Okawa recreated Da Vinci's *Mona Lisa* and other classic works of art from pieces of strategically burnt toast.

• A long-lost sculpture created by Michelangelo in 1494 was discovered in the lobby of an apartment building in New York City!

• A fiberglass cow set in the middle of a major intersection has been a local fixture in Harvard, Ilinois, for twenty-five years!

• A famous portrait of the Duke of Monmouth, who was beheaded in 1685, was painted after his death—his body was disinterred and his head sewn back on!

• Artist **Peter Lewis** of Edmonton, Canada, created a waterfall that is thirty feet higher than Niagara Falls, in the middle of a dry Canadian prairie!

• **Paul Dawkins**, of London, Canada, created the "Temples of Time," a sculpture that stands sixty-seven feet high, and contains seventy thousand tons of sand!

• A company in Santa Rosa, California, creates intricate lace-like designs on paper using a ten-thousand-watt laser!

• **Fabio Rodriguez** of Van Nuys, California, has a

1979 Honda Civic covered with 25,171 dimes and one quarter!

• In the Fitzroy Gardens of Melbourne, Australia, artist **Ola Cohn** carved a six-hundred-fifty-year-old blue gum tree with fairies, kangaroos, and koalas!

• In 1991, Americans **Chico MacMurtie** and **Rick Sayre** created a robotic sculpture that can contort into several different positions!

• **Robert Berks**, a Long Island artist, began working in 1991 on a herd of one thousand copper buffaloes to be displayed near the Oregon Trail!

• A key element in French artist **Marcel Duchamp**'s 1915 work called *The Large Glass* was dust affixed to a pane of glass with varnish!

• German artist **Joseph Beuys** created a work of art by drilling a hole in the wall of a Dusseldorf art gallery—the hole was insured for $20,000!

• In 1517, **King Francis I** of France bought the *Mona Lisa* to display in his bathroom!

• Hungarian sculptor **Jozsef Horvat** carved a stone grandfather clock that stands fourteen feet high and weighs 1.4 tons!

• While standing twelve hundred feet away, using binoculars and walkie-talkies, French artist **Jean-Marie Pierret** directed a team of painters applying sixteen tons of paint to a nuclear power plant in Cruas, France!

• A museum in Braunschweig, Germany, displayed a "painting" by **Till Eulenspiegel** that was a totally blank canvas with a frame!

• A painting by **Albert Bierstadt**, a nineteenth-century landscape artist, measured over one hundred fifty square feet and was so large that a house had to be built around it!

• "Luminous earth grid": San Francisco artist **Stuart Williams** covered the hills around Benicia, California, with 1,680 interconnected fluorescent tubes of light!

• "Cynthia," a mannequin created by American artist **Lester Gaba** for a New York City department store, was so life-like that

he took her to nightclubs and parties as his guest!

• In 1831, American artist **William Henry Brown** created a silhouette portrait of the sixty-five members of the Saint Louis fire engine company that measured over twenty feet in length!

• Artist **Manuel Andrada**, of Ecuador, painted a microscopic version of *The Last Supper* on a grain of rice using hairs from the back of his hand for paintbrushes!

• Artist **Tyree Guyton** has decorated his car and a block-long section of Heidelberg Street in Detroit, Michigan, with thousands of polka dots!

• British artist **Tracey Emin** sold a work of art that consisted of her old unmade bed—complete with dirty sheets, a vodka bottle, and old tissues—for $225,000!

• Artist **Alexander Calder** created a fountain for the Paris Exposition of 1937 that contained mercury instead of water! Whenever tourist tossed in coins to make a wish, the coins floated!

The famous painting of a FIFE PLAYER AND TWO DRUMMERS was not painted during the American Revolution and originally showed 3 Civil War recruits in civilian clothes.

• **Claudine Masson**, a French neurobiologist, has invented a method of protecting fine art with perfume scents that can only be detected by specially trained dogs!

• **Alan Whitworth** has spent the past thirteen years sketching every one of the 800,000 bricks in the thirteen-mile long, sixteen-hundred-year-old Hadrian's Wall in northern England! He sketches at a rate of five-eighths of a mile in sixteen months!

• Inside Poland's seven-hundred-year-old Wieliczka salt mine, miners have carved hundreds of sculptures of saints out of salt!

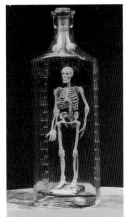

• **Clarence W. Pearson**, of Mt. Vernon, Illinois, whittled each bone of this skeleton out of maple wood, then painstakingly assembled them inside the bottle.

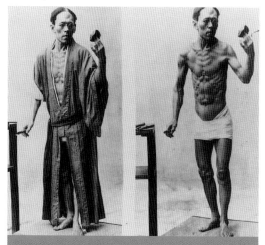

• Master sculptor **Hananuma Masakichi**, believing himself to be dying of consumption, created this life-like self-portrait, complete with his own nails, teeth, and hair, as a farewell gift to his beloved. He later regained his health, but lost his lover. The artist is pictured on the left; his creation appears on the right.

• **Wanda Bell**, of Bell Buckle, Tennessee, bought a painting for $25, then discovered a rare portrait by Sheldon Peck underneath worth $250,000!

• In 1775, **Martin Van Butchell**, a dentist and surgeon in London, England, painted different-colored spots on his white pony—a different color every day.

• A nine-story-high mural designed and constructed on the outside wall of Santa Rosa's Children's Hospital in San Antonio, Texas, by artist **Jesse Trevino**, has over 150,000 pieces of hand-cut tile!

• American artist **Beriah Waall**, during the 1980s, created and circulated over five hundred thousand handmade clay coins that had been cut with cookie cutters and baked in a kiln!

• In 1513, **Raphael** was commissioned by Pope Leone I to paint a life-size portrait of "Annone," his dancing elephant!

• French sculptor **Frederic Auguste Bartholdi** created the Statue of Liberty by using his mother Charlotte for the face and his mistress Jeanne-Emilie Baheux de Puysieux for the body!

• Mexican artists **Jose Ferez Kuri** and **Andrea di Castro** created an aerial heart-shaped drawing over Ireland that measured nine hundred miles in length! They've also made aerial art over Canada, Spain, Rumania, and Britain!

• Jouy-en-josas, France, is home to a two-hundred-foot-high sculpture consisting of fifty-eight wrecked cars embedded in an upright rectangle of cement!

• In 1991, a sculpture erected in Toulouse, France, consisted of a giant fork embedded in a bus!

• "The tempest prognosticator": **George Merryweather**, of England, created an instrument to forecast the weather made of a carousel with twelve pint bottles, twelve hammers, bells, and live leeches!

• In March 1990, residents of a village in north Moravi, Czechoslovakia, sold their twelve-foot statue of Josef Stalin to a Miami Beach resident for $50,000!

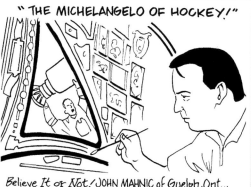

"THE MICHELANGELO OF HOCKEY!"

Believe It or Not! JOHN MAHNIC of Guelph, Ont., Canada, SPENT **2,300 HOURS** PAINTING AN 89ft. by 3.7ft. CANVAS MURAL CALLED "THE CANADIAN GAME" WHICH FEATURES IMAGES of 162 NATIONAL HOCKEY LEAGUE PLAYERS AS WELL AS LOGOS, TROPHIES AND MASKS.

- In Glendon, Canada, there is a twenty-seven-foot-high, six-thousand-pound steel and fiberglass sculpture of a perogy speared through the middle with a giant fork!

- **Art Grant** of San Francisco, California, created a two dimensional sculpture of a stagecoach using one million pennies!

- Artist **Heinz Gaugel** spent eight hours a day for five years creating an oil painting in Berlin, Ohio, that measures ten feet by two hundred sixty-five feet, almost the length of a football field!

- **Ed Massey** sculpted a wedding dress for his bride, Dawn Harris. He created 1,060 flowers out of fabric and modeling paste and attached them to a steel frame that formed the body of the dress. The dress weighed two hundred pounds, and the bride had to be wheeled down the aisle!

- A woman in Toronto, Canada, had a sculpture her father bought for $2 at a garage sale forty years ago appraised by art experts:—they said it is now worth $150,000!

- *Spindle*, a sculpture in Berwyn, Illinois, consists of eight cars on a steel spike!

- A single half-hour cartoon show for kids may contain as many as eighteen thousand drawings, called "cels"!

- A man in Berkeley, California, who bought a painting by artist **Richard Diebenkorn** at a garage sale, sold it in an online auction for $135,805!

- Artist **Tadashi Kawamata**'s sculpture called *Favela* (or "Shelter") erected on the lawn of the National Gallery of Canada consists of thirty-five rough-hewn wooden shacks!

- **Carly Johnson**, age four, of Manchester, England, painted a watercolor that was exhibited at the Manchester Academy of Fine Arts!

- "Spouting bowls": During the fifth century B.C., Chinese artisans made bronze bowls that, when filled with water and rubbed rhythmically, produced standing waves that rose up to three feet high.

- Mount Rushmore was originally designed to feature the faces of Western heroes Kit Carson, Jim Bridger, and John Colter!

- In 1890, when a statue of Apollo was unveiled at a college in Ada, Ohio, it was dressed in velvet knee britches so as not to offend the public!

- **Marcia Green** and **Ann Dunbar** of New Mexico glued two hundred twenty pounds of pinto beans on a 1964 Mercury car!

MAMMARY MASTERPIECES— ARTIST ANGEL TOLENTINO KEEPS ABREAST OF NEW PAINTING TECHNIQUES

Angel Tolentino's whimsical paintings are wildly popular. Their subject matter is not extraordinary: fruit, flowers, fish, martini olives, and hurricanes, but it's not her subjects that have art connoisseurs lining up to purchase her works; it's her technique. You won't believe what Angel uses as her brushes, and no, you can't watch her while she paints in order to find out.

Angel uses her breasts to apply paint to her masterpieces. She loves the rounded shapes they produce on the canvas: "When you look around, it does seem as if everything is in a circular pattern."

Angel experimented with several techniques for applying the paint to her breasts before she settled on what she calls the "stamp pad technique": Angel spreads the colors she desires on a metal cookie sheet, holds it to her breasts, then presses her breasts onto the canvas. The results are whimsical, sensual recreations of everyday objects. For example, an application of yellow and black stripes, from breast to canvas—with a few added legs and antennae—yields a work which Angel calls her "Boob bee."

Friends and family are not the least bit embarrassed by Angel's revealing artwork. They're supportive, viewing it as a wholesome form of self-expression. Angel's boyfriend Woody Coker says, "She's actually very shy and modest."

Angel sells prints of her artwork on the Internet, and donates thirty percent of her profits to breast cancer research.

Chapter 8
Beauty, Grooming, & Hygiene

A body is a costly luxury, as anyone who owns one can attest. We spend an astonishingly large chunk of our lives cleaning the thing, grooming it, feeding it, tending its health, and beautifying it in all manner of ways to make it appealing and acceptable to others. We pierce it, tattoo it, pluck away its hair—and these activities are tame compared to some others. Herein you'll discover many of the astonishing lengths to which we're willing to go to achieve the body beautiful.

BARBERING AND HAIRSTYLING

HAIR CARE

• **Samuel Rubin**, of Missouri, invented a scalp massager that consists of a platform on which a person balances upside down and puts his head on a circular moving disk!

• In the United States, the week of October 20th is celebrated as National Shampoo Week!

• Navajo Indians brushed their hair with bundles of grass.

• If the electrons that flow through an electric hair dryer in one second were grains of sand, there would be enough sand to build a twenty-foot-wide beach to the sun!

• **Alva Dawson**, of Jacksonville, Florida, invented a hat with a built-in comb!

HAIR STYLING

• **Benjamin Franklin** was so popular in Paris, France, that women in 1776 wore their hair in a curly mass that resembled his beaver cap!

• In ancient Greece, woman wore live cicadas held on golden threads as ornaments for their hair.

• During the reign of England's Elizabeth I, men kept their beards in place by clamping them into small wooden presses while they slept.

• Turkana tribesman of Africa adorned their own hair with that from some of their ancestors.

• Actress **Marlene Dietrich** frequently highlighted her hair with twenty-four-carat gold dust!

FRENCHWOMEN IN THE 17TH CENTURY CREATED ELABORATE HAIRDOS WITH SCENES FROM LITERATURE, MODELS OF THE CITY OF PARIS, WINDMILLS AND WATERFALLS!

THE ANCIENT ASSYRIANS CUT THEIR **HAIR** IN THE SHAPE of TIERED PYRAMIDS! (1500 B.C.)

Anthony Silvestri, a hair stylist of Plainsboro, New Jersey, cut the hair of his scuba-diving instructor, Bill Pasternick, under water!

Robert Armel, of Front Royal, Virginia, can cut women's hair and give them flattering airwaves while blindfolded.

• In ancient Rome, men frequently painted hair onto their bald heads!

Unzie, an albino, had snow-white hair that measured eight feet in circumference.

• A lady's hairstyle popular in France in the 1830s featured an arrow.

• **Pietro Santoro**, a barber in Washington, D.C., uses a lighted candle to trim, style, and dry hair!

SHAVING AND BEARD CARE

• The average man has thirty thousand hairs on his face that, left unshaved, could grow to a length of thirty feet!

• In 1900, **Samuel Bligh** invented a device with a roller covered in emery for grinding away whiskers!

• Composer and pianist **Frederic Chopin** (1810-1849) often wore a beard on only one side of his face—the side facing the audience!

BATHING

• Bathrooms in British Ramada Inns are stocked with plastic ducks called "Reggies" that can be taken home in special boxes with air holes!

• In the State of Pennsylvania, it was once against the law for anyone to bathe more than once a month!

• France's **King Louis XIV** took only three baths during his entire lifetime—all against his will!

• Clients at bathhouses in Japan can soak in bathtubs full of milk or red wine with scented herbs!

• Beer bath: **The Kloster Brewery** near Berlin, Germany, sells quart bottles of dark beer concentrate that are mixed with water for bathing!

Eastman Smiley, of Hartford, Connecticut, had a mustache twenty-five inches long.

• **Queen Isabella**, of Castile, took only two baths during her lifetime— one at birth, and the other just before her wedding!

• **Joachim Patinier** (1475-1524), a leading Flemish painter, went through his entire life without ever taking a bath.

• Physicians in England in 1797 attacked barbers who still called themselves "surgeons," demanding to know why the "pitiful, paltry, shaving, soaping, beggarly barbers go under the denomination of barber surgeons."

BEAUTY REGIMENS

• In the fourteenth century, **Queen Isabeau** of Bavaria used a mixture of boar's brains, crocodile glands, and wolf blood as a skin lotion.

MALAITAN TRIBESMEN of the Solomon Islands WORE FLOWERS IN THEIR EARS AND ALSO STRUNG THROUGH A HOLE IN THE END OF THEIR NOSE

• Austria's **Empress Elizabeth** (1837-1897) kept her skin smooth by wearing a mask of raw veal!

• **Catherine de Medici** (1529-1589), of Italy, regularly washed her face with a mixture of dew-covered peach blossoms gathered at dawn, and almonds crushed into a paste in the moonlight!

QUEEN ELIZABETH I (1533-1603) of England BATHED REGULARLY *ONCE A MONTH*

• **Diane de Poitiers** (1499-1566), a famed French beauty noted for her complexion, used no cosmetics except rainwater.

• Englishmen used tiny ivory combs to groom their eyebrows!

• In the Middle Ages, women used the juice of the poisonous belladonna plant to enlarge the pupils of their eyes.

COSMETICS AND TOILETRIES

MAKEUP

• In Morrisville, Pennsylvania, it was once against the law for women to wear makeup— including rouge, lipstick, and eye shadow—without a special permit!

• Makeup boxes used by women in Ancient Egypt were often six inches high, and the "kohl," or eye makeup, was applied with wood, bronze, or glass sticks.

• Fingernail polish was first worn in the year 600 B.C.!

• Fashionable women in ancient Egypt used the dust from ground pearls as eye shadow.

• In China during the Han Dynasty, noblemen painted dark rings around their eyes to enhance their beauty.

• The Broadway cast of *Cats* has used two hundred twenty-five gallons of makeup remover since the show opened in 1982!

• One tube of Maybelline's "Great Lash" mascara is sold every 1.9 seconds in the United States!

• A plague of flies caused women to use makeup! The ancient Egyptians made up their eyes not to beautify themselves but as protection against flies!

NAIL CARE

• **Oliver Heaviside**, a nineteenth-century British scientist, regularly wore pink nail polish and furnished his house with nothing but granite blocks!

• **Dalas Tomkins**, of Hawthorne, California, invented artificial fingernails with built-in clocks that display the date and time!

• Ancient Chinese nobles grew their fingernails to great lengths to show their rank, and protected them with carved gold nail guards!

• A company in Japan makes stick-on nail attachments that are made out of edible seaweed!

• A popular new fashion experience is the "cash tip" manicure in which pieces of money are cut up and applied directly to fingernails!

PERFUMES

• In London, England, passengers on the "East Line" of the city subway are issued perfume to help combat the smells in the underground!

• **Wayne Avellanet**, of Dallas, Texas, has invented an aerosol spray that captures the smell of a crowded subway!

• "La Pooch" Canine Caterers, Incorporated, a company in Philadelphia, Pennsylvania, sells perfumes for dogs!

• The ancient Egyptians, in place of perfumes, wore large cones of scented fat on their heads that slowly melted and dribbled all over their bodies.

• During the Elizabethan era, gentlemen in London, England, in order to neutralize the smell of garbage in the streets, carried walking sticks that released perfumes into the air!

• Froggy perfume: Male tree frogs use a dab of perfume that they produce themselves in order to attract females!

• A company in Japan has developed women's gloves that are embedded with capsules of perfume!

HYGIENE

• In the sixteenth and seventeenth centuries, Germans wore a flea trap suspended from a string around their necks.

MOUTH CARE

• The ancient Romans used toothpaste made from honey, salt, and ground glass!

• In 1961, **Bird A. Eyer**, of Seattle, Washington, designed and patented a toothbrush for dogs!

Miss Marie Idah Brunozzy of Wanamie, Pennsylvania, spent three years and eight months growing these attractive fingernails—the longest of which was $5^3/_8$ inches. Employed in a children's toy store, she claimed the children admired her nails and would stop in the shop just to see how things were growing.

• People lose about 4.5 pounds of hair and skin every year.

• Early toothbrushes have been found in Egyptian tombs dating back to the year 3000 B.C.!

MAYAN INDIANS FREQUENTLY SHARPENED THEIR TEETH TO A FINE POINT AND INSERTED JEWELS INTO THEM.

PATENT# 4,748,709 "MOUTHBRUSH" IN 1988, Dennis Oates of California INVENTED A BRISTLE TOOTHBRUSH THAT IS INSERTED INTO THE MOUTH and "CHEWED" LIKE GUM.

The Great Omi, the world's most tattooed man.

- A toothpaste in China called "S.O.D.," or "super-oxide dismutase," promises to brush away senility.

TATTOOING, BODY PIERCING, AND COSMETIC SURGERY

TATTOOING

- **Bernard Moeller**, of Bristol, Pennsylvania, has over fourteen thousand tattoos covering his entire body, except on his head and face!

- Eskimo girls once tattooed their faces by lacing wet sinew blackened with carbon through holes in their skin.

- **Walter Stiglitz**, of North Plainfield, New Jersey, has 5,552 tattoos covering his body.

- The faces of Maori tribal leaders of New Zealand are elaborately tattooed in a painful process in which the skin is broken with a chisel made of human or albatross bone. A dye made of juices is then injected into the wound. The price for their pain is posterity: after their deaths, their tattooed heads are removed and preserved!

BODY PIERCING

- **The Gauntlet**, a shop in Los Angeles, California, specializes in piercing customers' tongues, noses, and eyebrows!

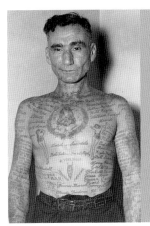

Dick Hyland, "The Human Autograph Album," was "signed" by over six hundred celebrities—including Robert Ripley!

A PAINFUL SAMOAN BEAUTIFICATION RITUAL CALLS FOR THE UTMOST ENDURANCE

In the Polynesian nation of Samoa, native men willingly submit to a five-day ritual of tattooing so painful that it has cost some individuals their lives.

Samoans consider the procedure a rite of passage and a test of manhood, as well as a great honor, as they are marked with the traditional symbols of their ancestors. The tattoos are believed to imbue the wearer with great spiritual strength, but the process of applying them calls for near-superhuman endurance. For five consecutive days, men undergoing the procedure must submit to five hours of pure torture. Those who complete the process are celebrated as heroes; those who do not complete it bring shame to themselves and their families.

Twenty-five-year-old Samoan native Ailani Alo has dreamed of undergoing the ritual since boyhood.

When he chose to have the procedure done, he was supported by friends and family, especially his sister, Saine Alo Vaii, a medical doctor.

Ailani put himself in the hands of a traditional Samoan tattooist, who worked with tools made from boar's tusks, in a procedure which implanted a permanent ink, made from kerosene and ash, under Ailani's skin.

On the first day of the ritual Ailani stoically endured five hours of the procedure, after which his wounds were scrubbed with salt water. But that night, Ailani began running a high fever, and was rushed to the hospital with a serious infection. Yet rather than dishonor his family, Ailani reported to the tattooist the next day, even though he was still feverish and taking a prescribed dose of antibiotics.

On the third agonizing day, Ailani had lost a great deal of his stoicism. "So much pain...," he described. "It's like a needle goes into the skin and plays inside your flesh." By the fourth day, Ailani needed help to walk. But on the fifth day, Ailani's tattoos, from torso to knees, were at last complete. And the minute the tattooist struck his last blow, Ailani became the celebrated guest at a feast in his honor.

Chapter 9
Beliefs & Superstitions

THE DEMON OF THE SOUTH-WEST WIND WAS ONE OF MANY EVIL SPIRITS WHICH ANCIENT BABYLON-IANS FOUGHT BY A SPECIAL BRANCH OF MEDICINE

You're not superstitious, are you? You've never owned a lucky baseball cap? You've never named—maybe even talked to—your car, with the idea that something friendly is less likely to break down on you, or involve you in an accident? Do you put on your clothes in a certain order each morning, to make sure the day turns out right? Have you ever chastised yourself for wishing misfortune on someone, lest your thought cause it to happen? Consciously, we know that such things aren't so, but—why take chances?

BELIEFS

• A chalice in the **Chapel of the Chalice** in the Cathedral of Toledo, Spain, is believed to be the actual Holy Grail.

• A mummified hand cut from the body of a hanged man was carried by burglars in ancient England in the belief it could open locked doors.

• Indian sentinels still are posted on mountain tops in Mexico each June to watch for the return of Emperor Moctezuma II, last Aztec ruler of Mexico, who died four hundred and eighty-two years ago.

• During the Middle Ages, it was believed that the ringing of church bells could dispel lightning.

• In East Africa, tribesmen fed bits of lion heart to their sons to increase their bravery!

• The Puritans objected to soft music on the grounds that it could lead to depravity among the young.

The BLOOD SPRING Glastonbury, Eng. It is believed that St. Joseph of Arimathea brought the holy grail to England 1,900 years ago and buried it here. Red water issues forth continuously from this spring—although the cup is not visible to any but the pure and holy.

A **GREEK MAGIC DIAL** created 1,700 years ago was believed capable of giving the proper answer to questions on any subject.

• The ancient Egyptians believed that eating cabbage prevented drunkenness, and they actually built temples to honor the vegetable!

• Divining rods were made of hazel wood because hazel smells "wet," and it was considered mystic because it blooms in the fall.

• In ancient England it was believed holy wells could reveal if an ill person would live or die, by observing whether one of his garments floated on the water or sank.

• Paying off a debt on New Year's Day in Portugal is avoided in the belief that if anyone pays a debt on that day he will be paying creditors throughout the coming year.

BELIEFS ASSOCIATED WITH ANIMALS

• Crows in Java are believed to carry the souls of suicides.

YAK TAILS ARE HUNG OVER TEMPLES BY KIRGHIZ TRIBESMEN OF THE HIMALAYAS *TO WARD OFF EVIL SPIRITS!*

• In some parts of Scotland, the killing of a butterfly is banned in the belief that they harbor the souls of lonely persons.

• The ibis was venerated as sacred in ancient Egypt because its appearance always coincided with the rising of the Nile, on which the life of the country depended.

• Members of Karachi, Pakistan's Shidi community, present offerings of fresh meat to the crocodiles in a nearby lake in order to obtain blessings and good luck.

• The ancient Egyptians believed that the blood of a black bull, cooked in oil, could turn gray hair black.

THE **WORLD** as conceived by the ancient Hindus was supported on the backs of four elephants— standing on top **A GIANT TURTLE.**

BELIEFS IN CURATIVE POWERS

• The Well of Doon, in Donegal, Ireland, is surrounded with bandages and crutches abandoned by visitors convinced that they were cured merely by drinking its waters.

MISTLETOE WAS CONSIDERED SO SACRED BY THE ANCIENT DRUIDS, THAT IT WAS CUT WITH A GOLDEN SICKLE AND CAUGHT IN A CLOTH SO IT WOULD NOT BE DEFILED BY THE EARTH

BAGWANI TEMPLE— HOME OF INDIA'S SACRED RATS

Each year, thousands of faithful Hindus from around the world journey to Bagwani Temple in Rajasthan, India, home of India's sacred rats. The ornate temple is virtually crawling with the rodents, yet rather than being repulsed, believers flock to the temple for a chance to pray to them, to worship them, and—if they are extremely lucky—to touch them.

Bagwani Temple was built six hundred years ago, and is today maintained by a single family that lives among the rats and cares for them. They are often bitten by their charges, but none of the caretakers has ever contracted an illness. Unlike ordinary street rats, the temple rats are clean, and possess no odor. As one temple worker explains, "Rats within the temple don't go outside, the ones outside don't come in."

Many Hindus believe that the sacred rats possess healing powers. Followers often strain for a glimpse of one of four pure-white rats, believed to be the most powerful of all. Anyone who touches one of the white rats is said to be protected for life.

• Patients slept in the temples of Asclepius in ancient Greece in the belief that the god of medicine would cure them, coming to them in a dream.

• A stalagmite in the cave of Eleithya, on the island of Crete, was worshipped by ancient Greeks as a goddess and prayed to by expectant mothers, because it resembles a woman holding a child.

BELIEFS IN EVIL FORCES

• "Old Granny Kempoch," a stone in Gourock, Scotland, was regarded with such fear in the seventeenth century that nine persons suspected of plotting to throw it into the sea were burned at the stake.

• The red seal stamped on documents by the head of the Taoist sect of China is believed capable of protecting them from evil spirits.

• In the National Museum of Antiquities in Edinburgh, Scotland, there is a collection of pebbles and "fairy coffins" to ward off nightmares and evil spirits!

BELIEVED TO BE LUCKY

• In 1992, a company in Hangzhou, China, paid twenty-eight thousand dollars for a mobile telephone number it considered to be lucky!

• Seeds of the "lucky nut" plant are carried by natives of the West Indies and placed in the hands of newborn babies, in the belief that it will assure good fortune.

THE DARUMA DOLLS OF JAPAN
NATIVES BELIEVE THAT ANY WISH MADE WHILE PAINTING IN THE EYES OF ONE OF THESE DOLLS IS BOUND TO BE FULFILLED

GOOD LUCK CHARMS WERE WRITTEN BY TAOIST PRIESTS IN CHINA, AS A MEANS OF CURING ALL DISEASES-- THEN THE FORMULA WAS BURNED BY THE PATIENT AND SWALLOWED

Chapter 10

Birth

CRYSTAL CORNICK of Baltimore, Md., defied odds of about 1 in 50 million to give birth to her second set of triplets in under two years!

"Better never to have been born at all," a Jewish proverb tells us, "but of all those among us, not one is so lucky." Those of us who have been through it can attest, being born is not easy, though some of us come into this world under particularly difficult and bizarre circumstances. Welcome to the tenuous and often amazing world of neonates—and the dramatic entrances they sometimes make into the world.

• The world's population increases by 237,748 people every twenty-four hours!

PREGNANCY

• Clock-makers in Basel, Switzerland, have developed a watch that can tell when the best time is to conceive boys versus girls!

• In Bangkok, Thailand, women of childbearing age perform a fertility ritual in which they walk under an elephant!

• "Maternity Rock" of Locronan, France, is a stone on which childless women sit, in the belief that it will assure them a son or daughter within a year.

BIRTH

DELIVERY

• **Rose Morrison**, of Portland, Maine, gave birth to a healthy baby boy just hours after running 7.2 miles and finishing second in a 2.4-mile race!

• The entire court of Louis XIV and XV had to be present during the delivery of a baby to verify that the offspring was indeed royal and not a commoner smuggled in from a village mother.

MULTIPLE BIRTHS

• **Christine McDonnell**, of Ireland, gave birth to one set of twins on

The HOLY CANNON of Batavia, Java— to which Javanese women pray for babies. They come from all parts of the island to worship—bringing gifts of incense and flowers

February 29, 1956, and another set of twins on February 29, 1960!

• **Charles** and **Gladys Benoit**, of Eunice, Louisiana, are the parents of five sets of twins—Wilda and Wilma, Jeanette and Jeanelle, Joe and Joanne, Gerald and Darrel, Brenda and Linda!

- **Donna Krasenics**, of Atlanta, Georgia, gave birth to a child in April 1990, and delivered its twin in July!

- **Santos Mora-Rivas**, of Wenatchee, Washington, was born at 10:06 A.M. on December 31, 1999, and his twin brother, Orlando, was born at 12:16 A.M., January 1, 2000!

- **Sandy Charles**, of Cuba, New Mexico, gave birth to twin daughters—one in Cuba, New Mexico, and the other in Albuquerque, New Mexico—eighty-four miles away.

- Twin sisters **Ilene Stokes** and **Irene Carey** gave birth to baby girls on the same day, in the same hospital, in the same room, with the same doctor!

RARE BIRTHS

- **Skylar Dae Westerholm**, born in 1992, was the first female to be born in the Westerholm family of North Dakota in one hundred ten years!

- In the "Chronique Publique Dans la Revue Retrospective Sous la Regne de Louis XV" (1642-1743) there appears an account of La Belle Paule Fieschi of Rue de la Perle, Paris, who became a mother at the age of ninety. The child, a boy, was born on December 1, 1742.

"THE WORLD'S SMALLEST MOTHER" GUDDI, A WOMAN FROM AGRA, INDIA, *WHO STANDS ONLY* 38 *INCHES TALL, GAVE BIRTH TO A* 19.6 IN. *BABY!*

- In 1956, **Ruth Kistler**, of Glendale, California, gave birth to a daughter at the age of fifty-seven.

STRANGE BIRTHPLACES

- Until January 1978, no human had ever been born in Antarctica!

- **Amal Ahmed Farran** gave birth to a baby girl in a courtroom in Damietta, Egypt, and named the child "Ginaya," the Arabic word for "felony"!

BIRTHDATES

- People of the Ashanti tribe of West Africa name their children after the day on which they were born!

- A girl born in 1978 in Britain was named "Friday, February Eleven."

- **Deborah** and **Raymond Krystofik**, of West Seneca, New York, both born on September 9, had twin daughters born on their birthday!

- **Katrina Marie Barker**, of Saint Louis, Missouri, born on the third day of the third month at 3:37 A.M., is the third child of a third child!

- All five children of **Mr. & Mrs. Ralph Cummings**, of Clintwood, Vermont, were born on February 20th, but in five different years!

BABIES

- A baby born to the Amharas of Ethiopia is given as a name the first word uttered by the mother after the infant's birth.

BABY BOTTLES in 17th-century Europe often were made from cow's horns.

CHILDREN of the Babendzere Tribe - Africa ARE DIAPERED WITH **LEAVES**

- Baby bonuses were first introduced by **King Louis XIV** of France in 1669!

- A baby that is born among the Akha tribe in Thailand cannot be touched until it has cried three times!

- The obligatory gifts a godmother bestows on a baby in the Yahgan tribe of Tierra del Fuego, South America, are two hollow bird bones, to be used as a drinking tube, and a back scratcher.

- Portuguese women in the 1920s often carried their children in large baskets on their heads.

- Among the Thais of Vietnam, a baby boy must decide his future vocation on his first birthday. Symbols of various occupations are put in front of him, and the object he first grasps will determine his life's work.

- Your teeth start growing six months before you're born!

MOTHERS in Old China often carried their children in baskets suspended from a pole balanced on their shoulders.

ABORIGINE MOTHERS of Northwestern Australia CARRY THEIR CHILDREN *HORIZONTALLY ACROSS THEIR BACKS*

HIGH-TECH IMAGERY CREATES 3-D PICTURES INSIDE THE WOMB

Every expectant couple wonders what their new baby will look like. Now, cutting-edge technology is offering parents-to-be a chance to take a three-dimensional peek at their child.

Until today, the only prenatal imaging available came in the form of blurry, disorienting ultrasound. A new device, however, takes pictures of the fetus from three different angles, then combines them to form a remarkably detailed image.

The technology allows doctors to more readily discover defects, and in addition to its use in obstetrics, it may eventually make traditional X-rays obsolete. But its most heart-warming application is the opportunity it gives new parents to begin bonding with their baby even before its birth. As one mother-to-be told us, "I feel like we've met. . .almost."

Chapter 11

Body & Mind

• **Marguerite Russell** could fold her tongue.

Ripley's fans are familiar with anatomical oddities. Generations of Ripley's aficionados have marveled at individuals with horns, multiple tongues, breasts in unusual places, or hair that stands up on command. But some of the most astonishing anatomical features are the ones you contain within your own body, even if you happen to have been born with a more conventional configuration of body parts. Did you know, for example, that you can be identified by your tongue prints? Would you believe that your toenails are miniature gold mines? Or that your bones are four times stronger than concrete? Do you know what your brain has in common with a bowl of Jell-O? Within these next few pages, we may very well convince you that, just by being human, you're a walking Believe It or Not!

BODY

BODY CHEMISTRY

• The average human being sweats two and a half quarts of moisture and produces a quart of saliva every day!

• The human body has a net worth of about $4.50! That's the monetary value of its elements—including oxygen, carbon, hydrogen, and calcium, as well as the value of the average person's skin!

• The average human body contains enough potassium to fire a small cannon and enough carbon to fill nine hundred pencils!

BLOOD

• If all the blood vessels in a human body were placed end to end, they would stretch twelve thousand miles!

• Researchers at Illinois' Northwestern University have developed a blood substitute similar to "Teflon," a non-stick cookware coating!

• Scientists in Minnesota have developed a wristwatch that can measure blood sugar levels from the perspiration of diabetics.

BONES

• An adult's body contains two hundred bones—fifty-two of them are located in the feet!

• The hyoid, found at the base of the tongue, is the only bone in the human body that is not connected to another!

• The smallest bone in the human body, the stapes, located in the ear, measures only 1.02 inches in length and weighs 0.00015 ounces!

BREASTS

• **Magdalena Strumarczuk**, of Tobolsk, Russia, had her breasts on her back. In spite of their unusual placement, they appear to have functioned normally—Strumarczuk successfully breast-fed all three of her children.

CELLS

• Every minute three hundred million body cells die and are replaced by new healthy cells!

"Slim the Shadow," of Baltimore, Maryland, was 7 feet tall and weighed 90 pounds. He was the same weight for 16 years.

• If the DNA elements comprising a single human cell were written in twelve-point type, the letter string would stretch over ten thousand miles.

EARS

• Empress **Marie Louise** could wiggle her ears.

• **Roy Phillips**, of Sedgley, England, can blow bubbles through his ears! He also inhales smoke through his mouth, then blows it out his ears!

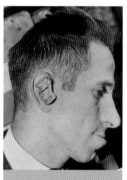

Brooklyn's **Max Calvin** never needed to fish for change. He could hold twenty-five quarters in his ear!

The **VUANYAS** of East Africa can tie their ears into knots.

EYES

• Humans and elephants are the only land mammals that shed tears during times of crisis!

Leopard "Popeye" Perry, of Richland, Georgia, could "dislocate" his eyes at will.

Mrs. Shirley Santos of New Bedford, Massachusetts, has an arrowhead-shaped birthmark in the iris of her right eye and her twin brother has an identical marking in his left eye.

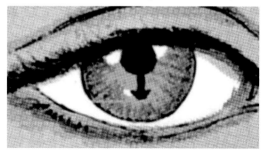

• The human eye can detect five hundred different shades of gray, and can distinguish up to seven million different shades of color!

• It takes one fortieth of a second to blink!

• The lenses in your eyes continue to grow throughout your entire life!

• During a lifetime, a person blinks three hundred thirty million times.

• The retina of the human eye has one hundred thirty-seven million cells— one hundred thirty million for seeing black and white, and seven million more to see colors!

FACE

• It is possible to make over one thousand different facial expressions!

FEET

• Your toenails contain traces of gold!

• The scent left on a human footprint is strong enough for another person to follow!

FINGERS

• In an average lifetime, a person flexes his finger joints over twenty-five million times!

• **Lorenz Geer**, a strongman from Munich, Germany, once lifted five hundred fifty-seven pounds using only his middle fingers!

• A baby boy born in 1921 in London, England, had fourteen fingers and fifteen toes!

• **Godfrey Hill**, of England, has twelve fingers instead of ten! He got his first pair of six-fingered gloves from a glove maker in Dorset, England!

• **Hermann Gorner**, a German strongman, could write his name on a wall while a one-hundred-ten-pound weight hung from his thumb.

HAIR

• In an average lifetime, the human body produces three hundred fifty miles of hair, or about seven miles a year!

• The average person loses about sixteen hundred eyelashes a year!

Lydia McPherson, who had a 7'4"— long mane of hair, once held the record for the longest red hair in the world.

YOUNG ABORIGINES OF CENTRAL AUSTRALIA PLEAT THE HAIRS OF THEIR BEARD AROUND *THE CURVED TAIL OF A THALGOO -- AN AUSTRALIAN MAMMAL*

The MAN WHOSE HAIR TURNED WHITE IN 30 SECONDS! A planter named Harris was attacked by a tiger. Help arrived within half a minute and Harris was rescued—but his hair had turned white. Singapore-1925

"The Whisker Prince" (left), with his eleven foot beard, greets "The Whisker King" (right), who sports a whopping seventeen-foot-long beard!

The monarch whose ailment started a fashion! KING CHRISTIAN IV (1588-1648) of Denmark wore his hair long and in a pigtail tied with ribbons because he suffered from a scalp condition that made it impossible for him to get a haircut. His courtiers all adopted the king's hair style.

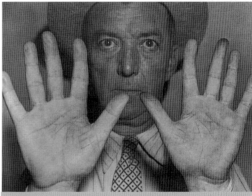

The hands of **Jerome W. Baker** have the word "thee" grown into the palms.

HANDS

• Every male in the **Colombiere** family of Nancy, France, was born with two left hands: both their hands had thumbs on the right side. They were perfectly normal in every other way. This trait only appeared in Colombiere males; females of the Colombiere family had normal hands.

Miss **Melba Mueller**, of Texas, can tie her arms behind her back at will.

• **Chou Kung**, the inventor of the compass, had a swivel wrist and could turn his hand completely around.

Wang, a Manchurian farmer, had a thirteen-inch-horn growing from the back of his head.

Charles Cheer, a.k.a. "the man with the xylophone head," had a musical cranium upon which tunes could be played.

HEAD

• In 1668, **Mary Davis**, of Chester, England, had two four-inch horns growing from her head.

HEART

• An astronaut's heart actually shrinks in the weightless atmosphere of space!

• In seventy-five years the human heart pumps 3,122,000,000 gallons of blood—enough to fill an oil tanker over forty-six times!

• A person's heartbeat cannot be heard! The sound you hear is the sound of the opening and closing of the heart's valves!

KIDNEYS

• Kidneys contain over one million tiny tubes, with a total length of over forty miles!

• **Denna Sayles**, of Fairfield, California, has four kidneys!

LEGS

• **Herb Tanner**, age ninety-two, of Cleveland,

Ohio, the world's oldest skydiver, has two artificial knees!

• Diver **Henri Bource** has lost his left leg to a great white shark—twice!

LUNGS

• The total surface area of a pair of human lungs is equal to that of a tennis court!

• Every day the average person circulates twelve cubic meters of air through his lungs—that's one trillion particles of air!

• Human lungs have three hundred thousand capillaries that, if stretched, would measure fifteen hundred miles in length!

• The average adult breathes 23,040 times each day!

MOUTH

• **Mandy McMichael**, of Florence, Italy, can fit a whole baseball into her mouth.

• Tongue prints are as unique as fingerprints.

Edward Bovington, of Burnham, England, had three tongues.

MUSCLES

• It takes fifty-four muscles for a person to take a single step forward!

• It takes seventy-two different muscles to talk!

• Human eye muscles move ten thousand times a day!

• It takes twenty different muscles to form a kiss!

• In order to turn your foot outward, you must use thirteen muscles in your leg and twenty in your foot!

NAILS

• **Louise Hollis**, of Compton, California, requires ten hours a week to care for her twenty-one-inch fingernails and her six-inch toenails!

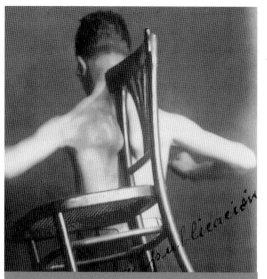

Feria Mundial of Mexico City lifted a chair his shoulder blades.

• Fingernails grow faster than toenails!

• If you never cut your fingernails, by the time you reached the age of eighty, they would be thirteen feet long!

NOSE

• The olfactory nerves found in the nose are the only nerves in the human body that can regenerate themselves!

THOMAS WEDDERS, an 18th-century Englishman, had a nose that measured 7¹/₂ inches in length.

• The drops of moisture in a sneeze can travel up to one hundred fifty feet per second—that's one hundred two miles per hour!

SKIN

• A square inch of skin on the human hand has seventy-two feet of nerves!

• A person's skin weighs twice as much as his brain!

• By the age of seventy, the human body has shed forty pounds of skin!

• Each square inch of human skin contains six hundred twenty-five sweat glands!

• Many residents of Troublesome Creek, Kentucky, have blue skin!

STOMACH

• If unraveled, the human esophagus, stomach, and large and small intestines would reach the height of a three-story building!

• David Hale, of Pulaski, Virginia, can suck in his stomach to reveal his ribs and clavicle!

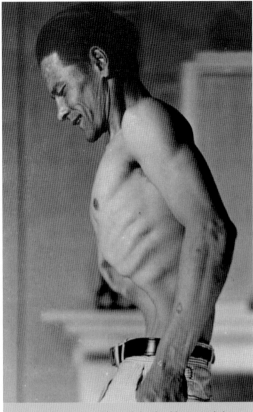

Anato Hayes could touch his backbone with his stomach.

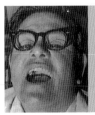

Antonio José Herrera, of Alburquerque, New Mexico grew a third set of teeth. All of his teeth were kicked out by a horse when he was 10 years old.

• **Alfred Hitchcock** (1899-1980) did not have a bellybutton!

TEETH

• **Richard Hofmann,** of Lake City, Florida, has a bite strength of nine hundred seventy-five pounds per square inch—more than six times the human average!

• **Ma Yonghan,** of Ningxia, China, grew a new set of molars at the age of one hundred one!

VOICE

• **Ellen Matthews,** of Collingwood, Australia, lost the use of her voice in an accident. She recovered it seven and a half years later, but thereafter spoke with a Scottish accent.

HEIGHT

• **Igor Ladan,** of the Soviet Union, stood six feet tall at the age of seven!

• **Andy Charlton,** of Redlands, California, at age seventeen, stood seven feet, three inches tall, wore a size twenty-one shoe, and was still growing.

• **Haji Channa,** the world's tallest man, stands eight feet, three inches tall, weighs three hundred sixty-five pounds, and wears a size twenty-two shoe!

JEAN BIHIN of La Reid, Belgium, WHO GREW TO A HEIGHT OF 8'5" AND A WEIGHT OF 316 POUNDS WAS SUCH A TINY INFANT AT BIRTH THAT HE WAS NOT EXPECTED TO LIVE AS AN ADULT HE OFTEN ATE AN ENTIRE CALF IN A SINGLE MEAL

ALEXANDER POPE (1688-1744) The English poet was only 4'6" tall and so frail that he wore a corset to remain upright and 3 pairs of stockings to make his legs appear thicker.

LONGEVITY

• **David Kendrick**, of Berkshire, New York, has invented a "life expectancy timepiece" that gauges how-long the wearer has to live based on his lifestyle!

SLEEP

• The average seventy-five-year-old person has spent two hundred twenty thousand hours, or almost twenty-five years of his life, asleep!

• In 1934, **D. C. Fraser**, of Gladwin, Michigan, age fifty-seven, while sleep walking, climbed a seven-foot barbed-wire fence without waking or tearing his nightgown!

MIND

BRAIN

• The human brain can produce enough electricity to power a toy train!

• The human brain has a storage capacity of one hundred trillion bits of information—equal to the information contained in five hundred thousand sets of the *Encyclopedia Britannica!*

• By the age of sixty, the human brain contains four times as much information as it did at age twenty-one! However, short-term memory diminishes after the age of thirty!

• In computer terms, the memory capacity of the human brain is ten trillion bytes, or one thousand times bigger than a one-gigabyte hard drive!

INTELLIGENCE

• **Mary Dunn**, of Bonne Terre, Missouri, had a vocabulary of thirty-eight hundred words, a repertoire of one hundred songs, and an I.Q. of one hundred eighty-five— forty-five points above the genius level—at the age of twenty-eight months.

• **John Suart Mill**, the English writer and economist, is estimated to have had an I.Q. of one hundred ninety.

• **Stephan Gelach** (1546-1612), Dean of the University of Tubingen in Germany, could remember almost every line he ever read—yet he constantly forgot his own name.

"NO DIFFERENT THAN ANYONE ELSE"— ROSEMARIE SIGGINS LIVES A FULL LIFE WITH ONLY HALF A BODY

Don't you dare feel sorry for Rosemarie Siggins. She lives a happier, more fulfilling, and yes, more normal life, than many of us who were born anatomically complete. It's only if you haven't had a chance to get to know her that you might think something's missing.

Rosemarie was born with a rare genetic birth defect known as sacral agenosis, which left her without legs, a pelvis, or any spinal cord below her ribcage. Rosemarie explains her condition with what she calls the "Barbie doll" analogy: "If you pop the legs off a Barbie doll, what you have left is me."

Rosemarie's parents, however, never for a moment let her think her condition was going to limit her. "Growing up, I was never allowed to use the words 'no' or 'I can't.' If I couldn't keep up with the other kids, my dad would say, 'Why don't you get on a skateboard?' It was the way they supported me and built up my confidence that made me who I am today."

Rosemarie Siggins also has found what many would give half their bodies for: her soul mate. She and her husband, Dave, came together over their mutual love of cars. Dave admired Rosemarie's can-do attitude, and especially loved the fact that she shunned a wheelchair for her preferred method of transportation: a skateboard. "I thought that was the neatest way to get around."

Only once has Rosemarie ever felt that something was missing in her life. A few years after she met Dave, Rosemarie realized that she wanted to have a child. She had to go to several doctors before she found one that would support her in attempting to bring a baby to term. Nobody knew whether Rosemarie's body could accommodate a growing fetus, whether there would be enough room for the two of them inside her abbreviated torso.

But Rosemarie, who will never say the word "can't," managed just fine. On January 6, 1999, she gave birth to a healthy baby boy, whom she named Luke. Now, with supportive parents, an adoring husband, and a wonderful son, Rosemarie feels that her life is complete: "God dealt me a pretty good hand."

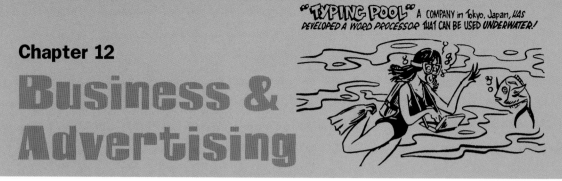

Chapter 12

Business & Advertising

The world of business is a kaleidoscope of constant change. Competing for sales, companies must continually reinvent themselves and reach for new ways to capture their customers' attention. As you're about to discover, some business innovations go to unusual extremes.

ADVERTISEMENTS

• **Charles Wilkinson**, a dairy farmer in Kemblesville, Pennsylvania, has turned his cows into mobile road signs because signs are prohibited along Route 696!

A SHOE COMPANY IN FRANCE ADVERTISED ITS PRODUCT BY USING A CAR SHAPED LIKE A LACE-UP BOOT!

• When the song "How Much Is That Doggie In The Window?" was popular in the early 1950s, a pet shop and a record store in Sydney, Australia, teamed up to cash in on the hit. The record store displayed a sign reading: "If you want the record, come in here. If you want the dog, he's around the corner." The pet shop put up a similar notice, in reverse order.

• In the 1920s, an American candy company, as an advertising stunt, chartered a biplane to drop candy bars—each fitted with a parachute—over forty different cities!

• Computerized cardboard cutouts that speak when someone stands in front of them are being used to promote Hollywood films!

• **Marc Halberstadt**, of New York, wrote a book-length advertisement about himself in order to attract a wife!

• In 1985 a Parisian inventor devised a mobile printing press that consisted of a tricycle with rubber tires embossed with type that left advertising messages on the streets!

• United States President **Theodore Roosevelt** was responsible for the Maxwell House coffee slogan, "Good to the Last Drop"!

SIGNS

• The legend beneath the figure of a dog in an ancient floor mosaic in Pompeii, Italy, reads "Beware of dog."

• A road sign near a creek on Big Jack Mountain, New South Wales, Australia, reads "When this sign is under water, the crossing is dangerous."

• A sign in Mossyrock, Washington: "Dead End: Swofford Cemetery."

BUSINESS CARDS

• **Bill Fink**, a graphic artist in Hollywood, California, uses a business card that is a signed plaster cast of his own size-ten foot!

No Parking Signs in Randoph, Vermont.

BUSINESS PROCEDURES

• In China, during the third century B.C., businessmen used fingerprints as personal seals on documents!

• A Baltimore company that manufactures seasonings issues its annual report with a different scent each year—including curry, nutmeg, and cinnamon!

• **Albert Tangora**, former world's typewriting champion, could type 160 words a minute and add a column of figures five wide and six deep at the same time! He once wrote 265 words in one minute without an error, making 14 strokes per second!

Sign on the way to Markle, Indiana.

Welcome to... **MARKLE** HOME OF '902' HAPPY PEOPLE AND '4' GROUCHES

• In 1991, new beverages with sugar and vitamin C supplements, called "Hard Work" and "After Work," were introduced to Japanese workers to increase productivity!

• **Alexander Bain**, a Scottish clockmaker, invented the fax machine in 1842!

• Researchers at the University of Cincinnati, Ohio have discovered that certain scents, including peppermint, can improve the concentration of office workers!

• A company in Nantick, Massachusetts, trains salespeople to break boards with their hands and walk over hot coals—to boost their self-confidence!

• **Anthony Rossi**, head of a multi-million dollar company headquartered in Bradenton, Florida, works eight hours a day, six days a week at the office, and several hours more at home almost every night—at the age of seventy-seven.

• At a public relations company in Edison, New Jersey, the staff dresses up, not down, on Fridays by wearing ball gowns and tuxedos to work!

```
FAITHN
OTEXER
CISEDSO
ONWA
XETHSI
CKE
ANOD
OMINI
1578
```

INSCRIPTION IN WENDOVER CHURCH, England, WHICH, WHEN DECIPHERED, READS: *FAITH NOT EXERCISED SOON WAXETH SICKE YEAR OF THE LORD 1578*

IN JAPAN, BUSINESS EXECUTIVES ARE SENT TO A COLLEGE FOR **CIRCUS CLOWNS** WHERE THEY LEARN STILT-WALKING AND PANTOMIME.

Believe It or Not! A HIEROGLYPH DISCOVERED ON THE SIDE OF THE GREAT PYRAMID **GIZA** in Egypt READS: "*THIS END UP*"!

SIGN ON AN OLD MOONSHINERS' ROAD, NEAR MONTREAT, N.C., DEPICTING A JUG, AND INTENDED TO READ: "*IT'S JUST 1 MILE*"

A **SIGN** HANGING ON THE HOSPITAL OF ROTHENBURG, GERMANY, SINCE 1704 STILL WARNS: "It is forbidden to quarrel, fight or brawl here. Guilty parties will have their right hand chopped off"

"OFFICE ON THE ARM" BRITISH TELECOM HAS DEVELOPED A **PORTABLE OFFICE** CONSISTING of A DISPLAY SCREEN, A MICROPROCESSOR KEYPAD, AND A MOBILE PHONE THAT ALL ATTACH TO A PERSON'S ARM!

Chapter 13

Clothing, Jewelry, & Fashion

HUGE GOLDEN GLOVES A PRODUCT OF THE ANCIENT CULTURE OF PERU MORE THAN 2,000 YEARS OLD

It's often said that what we wear reveals who we are. But fashion isn't always that simple a matter. A business suit might, in most circumstances, give the wearer a professional air—but what does it say about him if the suit is made of live grass? Or of human hair? Then, too, there are parts of the world in which, no matter how smartly you think you're dressed, you might as well be naked if your wardrobe doesn't include, for example, an antelope's tail. Welcome to Ripley's fashion show, a celebration of all that's weird to wear. What do these unusual garments say about their wearers? We'll let you decide.

ACCESSORIES

• **Dick Dumas**, an American designer, bought hundreds of glass animal eyes from a local taxidermist, then made them into cufflinks, buttons, and shoe buckles!

• Suspenders were invented in 1799 by **Orange Webb**, a shipping merchant, to pay off debts.

• A company in Buckinghamshire, England, has developed a solar-powered backpack!

GLOVES

• **Terence David King**, of Britain, has invented gloves that fit two hands so courting couples can hold hands while keeping warm!

• **Prince Philip**, of Calabria, the son of Charles III of Spain (1716-1788), always wore sixteen pairs of gloves at the same time!

HANDKERCHIEFS

• The ancient Romans always carried two handkerchiefs—one on the left wrist and another tucked at the waist or around the neck!

• In the eighteenth century, France's **King Louis XVI** passed a law making it illegal to carry a handkerchief that wasn't exactly sixteen inches by sixteen inches!

PURSES AND HANDBAGS

• In 1556, **Charles IX** of France made it a crime for anyone to carry a purse!

THE CLOAK THAT WAS WORN FOR 885 YEARS
KING CHARLES of Hungary WAS CROWNED ON DEC. 20, 1916 IN THE MANTLE OF ST. STEPHEN —WHICH HAD BEEN WORN AT THE CORONATION OF EVERY HUNGARIAN MONARCH SINCE 1031 !

• **Ava de Marco** and **Rob Brandgee**, of Pittsburgh, Pennsylvania, make ladies purses from license plates, street signs, and aluminum cans!

• **Laurie Carter**, of Vancouver, Canada, creates handbags out of recycled paper that will not disintegrate even when wet!

SCARVES

• In 1988, residents of Potter's Bar, in Hertz, England, knitted the world's longest scarf, measuring twenty miles, thirteen feet in length!

• A company in New York City has developed microwaveable scarves that give off warmth for up to sixty minutes!

UMBRELLAS

• French composer **Erik Satie** (1866-1925) had a collection of over two hundred umbrellas and always wore one of his twelve identical gray velvet suits!

• Full-body umbrella: A Japanese inventor has devised an umbrella equipped with a three-hundred-sixty-degree sheet of clear vinyl that covers the entire body!

JEWELRY

• Canadian jewelry designer **Danny Pollack** creates brooches out of used dentures!

• Designer **Christopher Roule** uses real braille symbols on his necklaces!

• A company in Mountain View, California, makes bracelets, key chains, and earrings out of used microprocessor chips!

• Inca noblemen wore solid-gold ear spools in their ear lobes that were as large as eggs!

• A jeweler in New York City designed a diamond-studded brassiere that sells for $3 million!

• **Jay Mosier**, of Charlton, New Jersey, creates jewelry out of discarded aluminum beverage cans!

• **Irene Neal**, of Wilton, Connecticut, uses plastic waste—including six-pack rings and yogurt containers—to make jewelry!

• The re-cycle line: **Carolyn Forsman**, of New York City, designs jewelry out of bicycle chains and locks!

• **Kathy Richard**, of Abbeville, Louisiana, creates jewelry out of alligator bones and teeth!

• **Janet Cooper** makes jewelry out of recycled bottle caps!

• Woman notables in the Bhil tribe of India never remove their nose rings or brass ornaments.

EYEWEAR

• The ancient Inuit ten thousand years ago wore hand-carved eyeglasses to reduce the effects of snow glare!

• **David Pollack**, of Potomac, Maryland, invented golfing bifocals with a bifocal section that allows the wearer to see things close up at the corner of the lens instead of at the bottom!

• In the eighteenth century, eyeglasses were often fitted with tiny mirrors for looking in all directions!

HATS

• Swiss peasant women in the mid-seventeenth century wrapped their braids around the crown of their hat.

FALCONERS in medieval times wore special hats to keep their birds dry.

TEENAGERS IN THE SUDAN wear a headdress with three shells dangling in front of their face. They have to walk in a dignified manner or the shells will bounce against their nose.

• Special hats to lend distinction to clergymen were the sole offerings in **Mr. Thomas Cole**'s shop in nineteenth-century England.

HATS DESIGNED TO BE UNFLATTERING

WOMEN of Banjermasin, Borneo, FOR 100 YEARS HAVE WORN HUGE HATS **WHICH HIDE THEIR BEAUTY—** THE CUSTOM STARTED WHEN THE SULTAN OF BORNEO WOULD SEIZE ANY WOMAN WHOSE FACE APPEALED TO HIM

• The curious academic cap worn at English and American colleges is Chinese in origin and was designed two thousand years ago!

• Footmen at the Royal Castle of Ameliaborg, Denmark, wear as part of their ornate headgear, pots filled with artificial flowers.

• A patent for a mechanical hat that salutes when the person wearing it bows to greet someone was filed at the United States patent office in 1895.

• At birth, children in Kweilin, China, are given a hat which is expected to last the rest of their lives.

• **James Hetherington**, of London, England, invented the stovepipe hat—and was fined two hundred fifty dollars for wearing it.

• Women in ancient Greece wore sun hats of plaited straw atop their regular headgear.

• Girls of the Damara tribe of Rhodesia, Africa, wear three-pronged leather hats copied from the helmets used by the ancient Vandals when they invaded Africa under King Genseric more than fifteen hundred years ago.

• Native women of Bolivia wear tribal tall hats made of white cardboard.

• A lady's bonnet in the South during the Civil War could cost as much as $250, so resourceful women created their own headgear— from corn husks, palmetto leaves, and straw.

• The "boater" hat, adopted by adults in the mid 1800s, was originally designed for children.

JACKETS AND COATS

• In Spain during the sixteenth century, men wore jackets which were artificially padded in front with horsehair, rags, or wool!

• In the sixteenth century, upper-class European women often wore "flea furs" around their shoulders to attract and trap fleas!

• In 1954, American **Howard C. Ross** invented a raincoat that expands to fit two people at the same time!

• Japan's **Toray Industries Inc.** has designed winter jackets for children that change color when the temperature drops!

• A fashion show in New York City featured such high-tech clothing as a temperature-regulated coat made with electrophoretic ink that changes color to blend into the surrounding landscape!

• Raincoats in the first century A.D.: Romans in adverse weather wore a "cucullus," a hood with a short cape attached to it.

SHIRTS AND BLOUSES

• The detachable shirt collar for men, once the height of fashion, was invented in 1825 by a woman—**Hannah Lord Montagu**—who tired of washing the entire shirt when only the collar was dirty.

• A man's shirt made in Bombay, India, measured forty-nine and a half feet in length!

• It takes six hundred and thirty silkworm cocoons to make a single silk blouse!

ENGLISH SAILORS in the 18th century—even the toughest of them—wore skirts.

SWEATERS

• Japanese clothing designer **Yohji Yamamoto** created a sweater with four arms that sells for $800.

• **Liz Kusak**, of Canoga Park, California, knits sweaters from dog hair!

TROUSERS

• In 1874, riveted jeans sold for $13.70 per dozen—that's $1.14 a pair!

• During the Norwegian civil war in the thirteenth century, military scouts were called "birchlegs" because they wrapped their calves and feet in layers of bark to keep warm.

• Overalls in the nineteenth century were advertised as sturdy enough to withstand attacking dogs.

SKIRTS

• Girls in Fano, Denmark, wear six petticoats.

• Men in ancient Egypt often wore one skirt over another.

• Early trendsetters: Women in New France (now Quebec) were wearing miniskirts in the streets as early as 1749!

DRESSES

• British designer **Christine Hughes** has created a dress and hat using old car parts including reflectors, headlights, and air filters!

• **Jennifer Calder**, of Denver, Colorado, created a two-piece dress using three thousand tin-can tabs and seventy-five hundred safety pins!

THE **FIRST** SEE-THROUGH FASHIONS

DANCERS IN THE NEW HEBRIDES, IN THE SOUTH SEAS, WEAR WEB COSTUMES *WOVEN BY SPIDERS ON SPECIAL CONICAL FORMS*

• Korean women in the 1930s, instead of sewing their dresses, usually pasted them together at the seams.

• In the 1940s, American **Dorothy Rodgers** invented a "try-on" dress pattern that could be washed, ironed, and altered!

• For over one hundred years, fashion shows in Paris have traditionally ended with the appearance of a model dressed in an unusual wedding gown!

• The world's first dress-form mannequin was discovered in King Tut's tomb!

• In 1396, **Charles VI** of France sent a life-size doll dressed in the current fashions to the wife of England's King Richard II as part of a proposal for peace!

• **Pauline**, sister of Napoleon Bonaparte, wore gowns made of muslin so thin that the material had to be sewn underwater to prevent the threads from breaking.

THE MOST EXPENSIVE DRESS OF ALL TIME
Marie de Medici QUEEN of FRANCE WORE A DRESS COSTING $19,000,000.00 IT WAS EMBROIDERED WITH 39,000 PEARLS AND 3,000 DIAMONDS

SHE WORE IT ONLY ONCE Sept. 14, 1606

SHOES

• Workers repairing drains at a cobbler's shop in Monmouth, Britain, discovered hundreds of shoes and sandals believed to be seven hundred years old!

• In 1877, **W. T. Steiger** patented an automatic foot warmer, consisting of a long rubber tube with a funnel for breathing into, that was worn around the neck and inserted into each shoe!

The SILVER SLIPPERS made for a twelve-year-old bride of the sultan of Zanzibar were attached to the foot by clamping the big toe around a knob.

• In the twelfth century, European men wore soft leather shoes with long, stiff, pointed toes. To keep from tripping, they fastened the points to their knees!

• "Exerlopers," invented by **Gregory** and **David Lekhtman**, of Montreal, Canada, are spring-loaded shoes designed to improve balance and muscle tone!

• A shoe owned by **Darrel Grenfell**, of Australia, weighs one hundred sixty-seven pounds and is almost five feet long.

• In 1904, **Percy Adolphus Vaile**, of New Zealand, invented shoes with a metal lining and a reinforced toe that could be fitted with dumbbells and weights!

• The first running shoes: Native people of Brazil developed the first slip free soles by covering the bottoms of their feet with rubber sap then drying them by the fire.

• During the 1930s, several American shoe stores installed X-ray machines to determine whether their customers' shoes fit properly!

• Japanese women in the 1800s wore sandals with air-filled bellows in their heels that produced musical notes when worn!

• A Japanese company has invented tiny wheels that attach to women's high heels for improved balance when walking!

• In 1992, a United States company created a running shoe with a heel light generated by a computer chip for jogging at night!

• In 1935, a patent was filed for shoes that filled with air at the touch of a button. It added up to five inches to the wearer's height!

BOOTS MADE FROM THE LEGS OF A BEAR WERE WORN BY AMERICAN INDIANS TO CONFUSE TRACKING PURSUERS

• In Tibet, it's against the law to wear white shoes!

• A woman wearing stiletto heels exerts an average of five hundred fifty-two pounds of pressure per square inch!

• In the 1920s, New York designer **Yanturni** molded lightweight shoes out of lace, velvet, and gold!

SOCKS AND STOCKINGS

• A child's sock found in a grave in Egypt had been knitted fifteen hundred years ago.

• **Bill R. Clark**, of Jonesboro, Arkansas, filed a patent for a device that embosses numbers on socks to assist in sorting them when they come out of the dryer!

• Sweet socks: A company in Dodgeville, Wisconsin, has developed socks with silver coated fibers that prevent the growth of bacteria that causes foot odor!

• In Fort Payne, Alabama, one hundred mills produce sixty million pairs of socks every year! The town also has a museum dedicated to hosiery!

• The ancient Romans wore socks with toes!

• Researchers at the University of California at Davis have developed socks that stay fresh and odorless even after they've been worn for several days!

UNDERGARMENTS

• Japanese inventor **Katsu Katugoru**, whose greatest fear is drowning, has invented inflatable underwear! Unfortunately, the garment accidentally inflated to thirty times its original size in a crowded subway!

"UNDO VISION"
NICHOLAS GRAHAM OF SAN FRANCISCO, CALIF., HAS INVENTED 3-D UNDERWEAR— BOXER SHORTS AND T-SHIRTS *WITH IMAGES OF FISH, DUCKS AND GODZILLA!*

• In honor of Mozart's bicentennial, a lingerie company in Japan designed a musical brassiere!

• Astronauts wear underwear lined with tubes of water to keep cool!

SLEEPWEAR

• The ancient Greeks always wore white nightgowns in the belief that they warded off bad dreams!

• Five-star general **Dwight David Eisenhower** had five stars sewn on the lapels of his pajamas!

SWIMWEAR

• The bikini bathing suit, invented in 1946 in Paris, was named after **Bikini Atoll**, the islands used in the 1940s to test atom bombs!

• In the 1920s, women on American beaches could be arrested for wearing bathing suits that revealed the thigh or upper arm!

• A new type of swimsuit premiered at the 2000 Summer Olympics, called "fastskin," compresses the body, and is covered in tiny ridges like a shark's skin for increased speed!

ENSEMBLES

• **Marine Gall**, of Burlington, Canada, has developed a line of "anti-sun" clothing that filters out harmful ultraviolet rays!

• "Electric clothing": **Captain Maurice Seddon**, of Berkshire, England, has invented a track suit, a dressing gown, and gloves heated by twelve volts of electricity!

MATERIALS

• **Peter Tully**, an artist in Sydney, Australia, created a suit and vest out of stitched-together holographic images!

• Scottish artist **Joe Pilgrim** creates earrings, clothing and hats out of salmon skin!

• **Alison Bailey-Smith**, an English artist, makes hats, shoes, and jewelry from recycled industrial wire mesh, television wire, and vegetable netting!

• British artist **Cas Holmes** created a kimono out of used tea bags!

• Scientists in Australia have developed a breed of self-shearing sheep with wool that can be removed by hand!

• **Doanne Tinker**, a student in Birmingham, England, creates clothing out of recycled aluminum cans!

• **Bill Black**, a hairdresser in Austin, Texas, creates clothing out of human hair, including a bikini that sold for $350! He is shown wearing a human-hair vest.

• It takes 663,522 spiders to make one pound of silk!

• A company in Japan creates sportswear using chitin extracted from crab and lobster shells!

• **Janet Groenert**, of Minneapolis, Minnesota, creates clothing out of recycled garbage—including coats from paper bags, suits from old magazines, and dresses from plastic bubble wrap!

EDIBLE GARMENTS

• Designer **Olivier Lapidus** designed a ball gown made out of chocolate, and **Jean-Louis Sherrer** made a chocolate handbag, jewels, and a hand-warmer for a fashion show in New York City!

• **Alicia Rios**, of Spain, makes edible hats using fresh vegetables, seafood, and bread!

COSTUMES

• Over 1.25 tons of yak hair have been used for costumes in the Broadway production of *Cats* since it opened in 1981!

TRADITIONAL COSTUME

• Clothing worn by children in many areas of Holland reveal whether they are from the city or country—and even their religion.

• The traditional Scottish kilt was, in fact, invented by an Englishman—**Thomas Rawlinson**—in the eighteenth century!

• The first Scottish kilts measured over fifteen feet in length.

THE **LAKALAI** of New Britain in the Pacific, WHO WEAR IN CEREMONIES, MASKS IN THE SHAPE OF A BLUE REEF FISH, ARE CONVINCED THAT IF THEY SHOULD EAT SUCH A FISH THEY WOULD *DIE IN A FEW DAYS*

HARA-KIRI is performed in Japan in a special costume, and the suicide must grasp the sword by the blade instead of the handle.

A **WIDOW** in the VUGUSSU TRIBE, So. Africa AS MOURNING GARB WEARS HER *DECEASED HUSBAND'S CLOTHING*

TRICK RIDERS
OF THE BRITISH ARMY
WHO CALLED THEMSELVES
"THE DEATH OR
GLORY BOYS,"
DRESSED AS SKELETONS

THE **TALL** FEATHERED HEADDRESS
WORN BY THE BOYS
of the Booli Tribe, in the Congo,
IS ANCHORED AGAINST THE HIGH WINDS
*BY A STRING ATTACHED TO
ONE OF ITS WEARER'S TEETH*
THE WIND EVENTUALLY CAUSES THE
STRING TO WEAR A GROOVE IN THE
YOUTH'S UPPER LIP—WHICH IS BELIEVED
TO ENHANCE HIS MANLY APPEARANCE

• The blue people of Morocco: Berbers of the Draa Valley use a blue indigo dye on their clothing which gradually turns their entire bodies an indelible blue!

• The most dazzling soldiers of all time: The army uniform of the Matabele tribe of Africa included a headdress and cape made with $500 worth of ostrich feathers.

• **Sultan Medangba** Chief of the Ituri tribe of Africa, wears an antelope tail as his ceremonial garb.

• The attire Southern women wore to church in the United States during the 1700s determined how much their husbands were required to put into the church collection plate: the most elegant clothing required the highest payments.

CLOTHING TRENDS

• In Italy during the sixteenth century, **Catherine de Medici** ruled that women should have a waist that measured no more than thirteen inches, and she designed a steel-hinged corset to help them achieve the goal!

• **Paul I**, Emperor of Russia (1754-1801), issued proclamations and orders dictating how his subjects should dress, and issued fines to people wearing pantaloons, trousers, tail coats, boots, or waistcoats!

• China's Ming Emperors (1368-1644) decreed that the color green was a royal color, and anyone other than the Emperor who was caught wearing anything green would be put to death!

• When France's **Marie Antoinette** became pregnant, she started a fashion trend among the ladies of the French court, who began wearing pillows under their clothes to imitate her!

• A Swiss company has developed a line of clothing called "skim" that features personal e-mail addresses stitched right on the clothing for easy-access dating!

• In Bangkok, Thailand, it is acceptable to wear red only on Sundays!

LAUNDERING

• In the early 1900s, the soap that people in the U.S. used to wash their clothes turned the fabrics yellow, so the clothes had to be dyed blue to make them appear to be white again!

• The average family of four washes one ton of laundry every year!

• Finnish women, in the bitter cold of the northern winters, wash their laundry by chopping a hole in the ice.

• A company in Japan has developed a "washing machine" that straps to a person's legs and allows the wearer to do his laundry while walking!

WELL-DRESSED

• The emperor of the ancient Incan Empire wore a different vicuña wool robe every day of the year!

• **Archduke Ferdinand** of Austria was so concerned with his appearance that he frequently had himself sewn into his uniforms!

• During the eighteenth century, **Comte D'Artois**, of France, wore a suit with a set of diamond buttons, each containing a tiny clock!

- Actor **Yul Brynner** only wore black clothes for the last forty-five years of his life!

- United States millionaire **Jim Brady** owned a different matching set of shirt studs, stick pins, cuff links, vest buttons, and diamond-encrusted belt buckles for every day of the month!

- **Albert Einstein** never memorized his telephone number and bought several sets of identical clothing to avoid wasting time having to match his clothing every day.

- **Grantley Berkeley** (1800-1881) was the last Englishman to wear a cocked hat—he wore three different colored vests simultaneously and always sported four gaudy silk cravats.

- In 1992, an orangutan in Borneo mugged a French tourist, then fled into the jungle with the man's clothes!

- **King Francis I** (1494-1547), of France, had a black velvet suit with 13,400 solid-gold buttons!

Owen Totten, of Mt. Erie, Illinois, wore a 5,600-button suit—no two buttons are alike!

"TECHNO-BRA"—WITH THIS CUTTING-EDGE SATELLITE TECHNOLOGY, YOUR UNDERWEAR MAY LITERALLY SAVE YOUR LIFE

Within a couple of years, a revolutionary new personal safety device will hit the market. Using state-of-the-art cellular and satellite technology, this new instrument can tell police precisely who you are, where you are, and whether or not you're being attacked.

And the whole thing fits inside women's underwear. In fact, it is women's underwear.

The "Techno-bra" is the brainchild of Kirstie Falconer, an industrial-design engineering student who developed the bra after many frightening nighttime trips alone across her isolated school campus.

Kirstie designed the bra with a miniature global positioning system, just like the "Lojack" devices installed in cars. The system is activated by a sudden jump in the wearer's heart rate. Exercise doesn't trigger it, because an exercising person's heart rate climbs slowly, whereas a sudden fright, as in an attack, causes the heart rate to leap suddenly. When the mechanism is triggered, it begins beeping softly. If it's a false alarm, the wearer can press a button and turn it off. If she doesn't press the button, the bra calls the police!

The "Techno-bra" runs off a three-volt battery hidden in the front clasp that lasts up to seven years. Unless you know just where to look, the bra appears to be a normal undergarment. The "Techno-bra" will retail for about fifty dollars. Kirstie hopes that her invention will offer women a feeling of safety and peace of mind.

Chapter 14
Coincidences

There are those who believe that nothing happens by chance. Cultures and peoples across time and space have considered bizarre coincidences to be signs or omens, and have altered their behavior accordingly. Some say these highly improbable occurrences offer us a rare, behind-the-scenes peek at a master plan seldom visible to us mortals. Others may suggest they're a glitch in the vastly complex "program" we call reality. Some calculate the infinitesimal odds of a given coincidence occurring within our lifetimes, and insist that if it does occur, there must be some meaning behind it. But, however some may explain it, there are many among us who do not believe in chance. After reading the following unlikely occurrences, you may count yourself among them.

COIN TOSS

• A tossed coin, to fall heads up fifty times in a row, would require one million people tossing ten coins a minute for forty hours a week—and then it would occur only once in every nine centuries.

IMPROBABLE FINDS

• The five children of **Mr. and Mrs. Paul Early**, of Salem, West Virginia— Stephen, Michelle, Jim, Cindy, and Cheri—found one six-leaf, twenty five-leaf, and sixty-five four-leaf clovers in an area measuring only one square yard.

IMPROBABLE OUTCOMES

• The **S. S. Lufra** and the **Wagoola** raced from Hobart, Tasmania, Australia, to London, England—a distance of eleven thousand miles— and finished in a dead heat! They sailed from Hobart on July 26, 1876, and reached London on October 25th, just seven minutes apart—so the ninety-one day race was officially pronounced a tie!

IMPROBABLE SHOTS

• **Fred J. Simon**, of Lincoln, Illinois, made a slide for a bolo tie from two thirty-caliber bullets— one of which had pierced the other in the air.

• **Newton Smith**, of Cuero, Texas, killed three deer with one shot! Smith had seen only one deer, but his bullet passed though a second standing behind it, then through a third deer

These Union and Confederate bullets met and fused in mid-air!

standing in the brush fifteen feet away.

The STRANGEST GUNFIGHT IN HISTORY! City Marshal Jeff Packard, of Bakersfield, California, and a fugitive named "Outlaw" McKinney drew and fired simultaneously—and each bullet entered and plugged the other man's gun!

IMPROBABLE WINNERS

• The odds: 15 trillion to one! **Evelyn Marie Adams**, of Point Pleasant, New Jersey, won her state's Pick-6 game twice, collecting $3.9 million in 1985, and $1.5 million in 1986! Between her two big prizes, she also won $500 in the lottery's daily game.

• The Lions Club of Nevada, Iowa, in a drawing for door prizes, successively called on the Reverend James Dendler, Henry Scudder, and William Dial to draw the winning stubs, and each drew his own number.

CLOSE CALLS

BABIES

• The baby that was blown seventy feet by gunpowder and lived: On January 4, 1649, an infant sleeping in its cradle on Great Tower Street, London, England, was hurtled to the roof of a nearby church by an explosion that demolished his home—yet the baby was found slumbering peacefully in its undamaged cradle! The child's parents were among those killed, and its identity was never discovered.

• After a cyclone swept through Marshfield, Missouri, on April 8, 1880, a baby girl was found sleeping peacefully in the branches of a tall elm. The child was never identified and was later adopted by a local family.

• On December 2, 1927, little **Marie Finster** jumped from the roof of a building in Vienna and was saved from death by falling into the arms of her mother—who happened to be passing along the street below that very minute!

BULLETS

• **Angel Santana**, of New York City, escaped unharmed when a robber's bullet bounced off his pants zipper!

• Detective **Melvin G. Lobbett** of Buffalo, New York, shot by a .38 caliber revolver at close range, was saved when the bullet hit his badge, which he had dropped into his coat pocket only a moment before the shooting.

• The general who saved his life by buying the wrong-sized hat! **General Henry Heth** (1825-1888), leading a Confederate division in the Battle of Gettysburg, was hit in the head by a Union bullet, but his life was saved because he was wearing a hat two sizes too large, with newspaper folded inside the sweatband! The paper deflected the bullet, and the general, unconscious for thirty hours, recovered and lived another twenty-five years.

FALLS

• When his plane caught fire over England, **Sergeant Jim Webb** of Geneva, Nebraska, bailed out at twenty-three thousand feet—and landed astride a grazing horse in a field in Surrey, England.

• In 1942, **Lieutenant I. M. Chisov**, a Russian pilot, fell 21,980 feet from his fighter plane—and survived!

NEAR MISSES

• Special Delivery: **Sergeant Joseph Charles** was in a foxhole in New Guinea when the mail boys called him to come out for a letter. He had crawled out about ten feet when a Japanese plane flew over and dropped a bomb that completely destroyed the foxhole he had just left.

• In 1915 the U-35, a German submarine, escaped a direct hit by a British torpedo in the Atlantic when the projectile suddenly hurtled over the sub, merely damaging its guardrail.

• On January 14, 1858, three bombs thrown at the carriage of **Emperor Napoleon III** of France killed or wounded every one of the one hundred fifty-six men in his honor guard—yet the Emperor and his Empress escaped unharmed.

PRECISION WAVES

• Bumped off: A sailor was sleeping on the deck of an Italian destroyer when it accidentally collided with an American rocket carrier ship. The impact bumped the sailor off the Italian ship and onto the deck of the American ship! Both ships continued on their respective ways.

• **Captain Brisco**, master of the *Grace Harwar*, washed overboard by a gigantic wave en route

from Delaga Bay, East Africa, to Gisbourne, New Zealand, was saved from certain death when a second wave flung him back to his original position on the ship's bridge.

• **Lieutenant Commander Robert W. Goehring** was swept off the Coast Guard cutter *U.S.S. Duane* by a gigantic wave during a storm. The ship was turned around to rescue him, when suddenly another huge wave tossed him back on board to safety!

SAVED BY STRANGE CIRCUMSTANCES

• The composer who was saved by an apparition: **Christopher Gluck** (1714-1787), the German composer, refused to sleep in his room one night after seeing an apparition of himself enter it. The next morning he found that the ceiling had collapsed on his bed and would have killed him if he had been laying in it!

• The man whose life was saved by a ghoulish jest: **Sir Hugh Acland**, of Killerton, England, was pronounced dead in 1770, but was revived when a

footman sitting with the "body" poured a drink of brandy down Acland's throat. He lived another eighteen years.

• In Nicosia, Cyprus, an Omani woman who was being prepared for burial was revived after her son, following traditional Muslim funeral rites, splashed her with water!

COINCIDENTAL DATES

BIRTHDAYS

• **Stanley Caleb McKee**, of Orange, Texas, was born on the morning of January 1, 1981—the first baby of the year in his community.

His father, Keith McKee, was born on January 1, 1955—the first baby of that year in his community!

• Happy, happy, happy birthday! Mr. and Mrs. E. H. Bisch of Santa Rosa, California, have three children, all with the same birthday: Peggy, born May 28, 1954; Scott, born May 28, 1958; Kristine, born May 28, 1959. The odds against three children in the same family being born on the same date are twenty-eight million to one.

• **Stuart B. Grayson**, of Springfield, New Jersey, was born on April 4, 1927. His sister Rhonda was

THE MAN WHO WAS SAVED BY A RAILROAD WRECK!
In 1886, Jerry Simpson, working on a railroad in the Cascade Range, in Washington, saw a runaway North Pacific engine bearing down on him, and preferring instant death to a crippling injury, threw himself across one of the rails. The careening engine's wheels rose from the rails a moment before he would have been killed—and the engine cleared his body and crashed into the gully below.

born on April 4, 1922. His wife, Helen, was born on April 4, 1932, and their first child, Jan, was born on April 4, 1956.

THE ONLY SEVEN-MASTED SCHOONER ever was named after Thomas W. Lawson, author of *Friday the Thirteenth*. She was wrecked on Friday the 13th, 1907.

DEATH DATES

• Historically, September 1 is not a good date to be in Japan. Severe earthquakes devastated Japanese cities on September 1, 259; September 1, 827; September 1, 867; September 1, 1185; September 1, 1649; and September 1, 1923.

• "If I died this hour, I should die happy," said English comedian **John Liston**, on Sunday, March 22, 1807, at 10:30 A.M. as he was married in the Church of St. Martin-in-the-Fields to Miss Tyrer, an Irish balladeer. Thirty-nine years later, as the clock struck

10:30 A.M. on Sunday, March 22, 1846, Liston died in his wife's arms.

• **Emmett Kelley** and **Karl Wallenda**, the famed clown and the renowned aerialist, both of whom had starred in the Ringling Brothers and Barnum and Bailey Circus in New York, both died on the day that the circus opened in New York— Wallenda on March 22, 1978, and Kelley on March 28, 1979.

COINCIDENTAL DEATHS

• A falling stone that killed two men inside Victoria State Coal Mine, Wonthaggi, Australia, was in the shape of a coffin, with the outline of a white cross on top!

• An ambulance in Nykroppa, Sweden, sent to pick up **Lars Elam**, a patient with a high fever, returned to the hospital with the patient driving it and the regular driver lying dead in the back from a heart attack.

DEATH FORESHADOWED

• The man who challenged fate—and lost: **Moses**

Carlton, a ship magnate of Wiscasset, Maine, in 1800 threw his gold ring into the Sheepscot River and boasted, "There's as much chance of my dying a poor man as there is of ever finding that ring again." Only a few days later, Carlton found his ring in a fish served at his table, and when President Madison embargoed American ships because of the British impressment of American seamen, Carlton died a poor man.

THE TRAGEDIAN WHO COULD NOT ESCAPE TRAGEDY
AESCHYLUS (525–456 B.C.) AUTHOR OF 70 GREEK TRAGEDIES. NEVER WENT OUTDOORS DURING STORMS BECAUSE AN ORACLE HAD WARNED HIM HE WOULD DIE BY *A BLOW FROM HEAVEN*— SITTING OUTDOORS IN GELA, SICILY, ON A SUNNY DAY, HE WAS KILLED WHEN AN EAGLE MISTOOK HIS BALD HEAD FOR A ROCK AND *DROPPED A HUGE TORTOISE ON HIM TO BREAK ITS SHELL*

THE PORTRAIT THAT DIED WITH NERO!
A MAMMOTH PAINTING OF NERO
120 FEET HIGH – IN THE GARDENS OF MAIUS IN ROME WAS DESTROYED BY A BOLT OF LIGHTNING ON THE VERY DAY NERO TOOK HIS OWN LIFE IN A VILLA 4 MILES AWAY

A few years after the death of **SMITH TREADWELL**, an exact likeness of him appeared on his gravestone.

• The jest that proved prophetic: **Edward Moore** (1712-1757), the English dramatist, although apparently in perfect health, sent his own obituary to the newspapers on February 27, 1757, giving the next day as his date of death. He suddenly became ill—and died on February 28, 1757.

GRISLY COMEUPPANCE

• When **Vera Czermak** learned that her husband had betrayed her, she jumped out of her third-story window. She survived, but she landed on her husband, who was killed.

• **Sheriff Henry Plummer**, of Bannack, Montana, was found guilty of moonlighting as a highwayman, and was hanged on a gallows he had built himself for the execution of a horse thief.

WEDDED DEATH

• **Francesco delle Barche**, fourteenth-century Venetian inventor of a catapult that could hurl a three-thousand-pound missile, became entangled in his war machine during the siege of Zara, Dalmatia, and was hurled into the center of the beleaguered town. His body struck his own wife, who had entered Zara without her husband's knowledge, killing them both!

• On July 30, 1984, **Florence Graziano**, of Chicago, Illinois, hospitalized with a minor heart attack, visited her mortally ill husband, Salvatore, who was in the same hospital, then returned to her own room and died—at the exact same moment as her husband!

UNLIKELY OBITUARIES

• The trunk that delivered a dead bride's trousseau: The schooner *Susan and Eliza* was wrecked in a storm off Cape Ann, Massachusetts, as it was carrying Susan Hinchborn, one of its owner's daughters, to her wedding in Boston. All thirty-three persons on board perished, and no trace of the ship was ever found—except for a trunk bearing Susan's initials that contained her trousseau, which was cast ashore at the feet of her waiting fiancé!

• In New Zealand, a grieving widow whose husband had died two days earlier, was shocked to receive a telegram addressed to her, which read: "Arrived in Paradise today. Everything lovely." The telegram was signed with her dead husband's initials! It turned out that the telegram had been sent to her in error, and was actually meant for a woman of the same name at a different address. The other woman's daughter, whose initials were the same as the dead husband's, was writing to tell her mother that she had arrived at the town of Paradise, on Lake Wakatipu.

COINCIDENTAL NAMES

• Actor **Sean Connery**, who played the film character James Bond, was once stopped for a traffic offense by a policeman called sergeant James Bond!

APPROPRIATELY NAMED

• Don't drink and run! A horse scratched (not fit to run) in the ninth race at Belmont Park racetrack in Queens, New York, on July 11, 1985, was named "Too Much to Drink."

• Two automobiles that collided in Ajax, Ontario, on a slippery winter day were owned by motorists named Snow and Blizzard.

• A boat hurled onto the beach at Westport Point, Massachusetts, in the New England hurricane of 1954, was named "Last Fling".

SAME NAME, DIFFERENT PERSON

• On May 3, 1972, **Patrick Donnelly**, of Belfast, Ireland, stopped to pick up a wallet he saw lying in the road. In order to find the name of its owner, Donnelly leafed through the wallet, only to discover that the owner's name was. . .Patrick Donnelly! The wallet belonged to another Patrick

• Meet **Lorraine** and **Loretta Szymanski**, of Pittsburgh, Pennsylvania—and **Lorraine** and **Loretta Szymanski** of Pittsburgh, Pennsylvania! Both sets of twins attended the same school, in the same classroom, and lived in the same neighborhood, but were not related in any way!

Donnelly who lived in the nearby town of Augher. The first Patrick Donnelly contacted the second, and returned the lost wallet.

• A briefcase containing $5,000 worth of bonds registered in the name of **Paul Devries** of San Francisco, California, was found on a golf course by Paul Devries of Daly City, California. They were not related and had never met.

COINCIDENTAL OCCURRENCES

• The man who was cleared of a murder charge by a classified ad: **Jesse Boorn**, of Manchester, Vermont, who was convicted of murdering his brother-in-law, Russel Colvin, was freed from jail when an ad in the *Rutland Herald* on November 29, 1819, resulted in the discovery that the supposedly slain man was living in Dover, New Jersey.

• **Mr.** and **Mrs. L.B. Willsey**, of Sacramento, California, read an advertisement describing just the kind of home they wanted, and called the agent, only to learn that it was an ad for their own house, put on the market a month earlier!

COINCIDENCES ACROSS TIME

• A pocket guide to New York City issued in 1864 was found by **German**

Suarez, of Medellin, Columbia, in the Brazilian jungle—more than a century after its printing!

• Two of America's greatest and best-loved presidents are linked by an eerie set of coincidences. Both Kennedy and Lincoln were deeply involved in civil rights issues—slavery in Lincoln's day, and segregation in Kennedy's. Lincoln's assassin, John Wilkes Booth, was born in 1839. Kennedy's assassin, Lee Harvey Oswald, was born in 1939. Lincoln had a secretary named Kennedy who warned him not to go to the theater that night. Kennedy had a secretary named Lincoln who warned him not to go to Dallas. Both were shot on a Friday, from behind, with their wives present. Booth shot Lincoln in a theater and ran into a warehouse; Oswald shot Kennedy from a warehouse and ran into a theater. Both were succeeded by men named Johnson. The Johnson who succeeded Lincoln was born in 1808; the Johnson who succeeded Kennedy was born in 1908.

COINCIDENCES IN FAMILIES

• **Mrs. Anna Harahuess**, of Coaldale, Pennsylvania, on her seventy-seventh

THE GHOST SHIP THAT SAILED HOME 13,000 MILES WITHOUT A CREW!

THE MINERVA - WRECKED IN THE INDIAN OCEAN ON A VOYAGE FROM ELY'S HARBOR, BERMUDA TO AFRICA -- WAS RETURNED TO THE PORT FROM WHICH IT SAILED BY THE WINDS AND TIDE!

THE LAST ENTRY IN THE VESSEL'S LOG BOOK WAS 14 MONTHS OLD --, AND NO CLUE TO THE FATE OF THE CREW HAS EVER BEEN FOUND.

• Identical twins **Max** and **Bernard Friedman** bought identical coats without the knowledge of the other brother in stores 350 miles apart. Bernard lived in East Chicago, Indiana, and Max lived in Des Moines, Iowa, but both purchased light plaid topcoats with the serial number 17343, only discovering the coincidence months later.

ABRAHAM LINCOLN

ABRAHAM LINCOLN was the 2nd member of his family to die by an assassin's bullet. The other was his grandfather. Both victims were named Abraham; both had wives named Mary; both had a son named Thomas. The name Abraham has never again been given to any member of the family.

ONE SNAKE BITE KILLED 3 GENERATIONS OF THE SAME FAMILY.

The Kingswald Family—Austria 1928: A viper bit the grandfather and the fang remained in his boot. His son and grandson wore the boots and were poisoned also.

birthday in November, 1982, received birthday cards from three grandchildren, one posted in Boston, Massachusetts, a second from Honolulu, Hawaii, and the third from Falls Church, Virginia—and all three had by chance sent the identical card!

• A bottle of nerve pills was swept out of the bedroom of Mrs. Lena McCovey when a flood destroyed her home on the Klamath River. It was found two hundred miles away at Coos Bay, Oregon, by Mrs. McCovey's sister!

FAMILY MISHAPS

• Captain **Edward Ladner**, Master of the schooner *Dewdrop*, was thrown overboard in a storm in 1919, six hundred miles off the coast of Brest, France, His body was never recovered. His father, Captain Edward Ladner, was lost from the schooner *Arethusa* in 1900, and his grandfather, Captain Edward Ladner, vanished from the schooner *Cairns* in 1881, in storms at the same spot!

• In Bermuda, brothers **Erskine L. Ebbin** and **Neville Ebbin** both died one year apart after being struck by the same taxi, driven by the same driver, and carrying the same passenger!

• **Jabez Spicer**, of Leyden, Massachusetts, killed by two bullets on January 25, 1787, in Shays' Rebellion at Springfield Arsenal, was wearing the coat in which his brother Daniel had been slain by two bullets on March 5, 1784. The bullets that killed Jabez passed through the same two holes in the cloak that had been made when Daniel was slain three years earlier.

• **Mrs. Rudolph Brown**, of Lawrence, New York, became the mother of twins on March 4, 1958. Her mother became the mother of twins on March 4, 1935; and her sister became the mother of twins on March 4, 1949.

DOPPLEGANGERS

• **Pauline Taylor** and **Pauline Taylor**, both of Detroit, Michigan, were born within two hours of each other, were almost identical lookalikes, and developed the same tastes in dress, food, clothes, and hobbies—yet were in no way related.

• The monarchs who looked like identical twins: **Czar Nicholas II** of Russia and **George**, the Prince of Wales, who later became King George V of England, delighted in passing themselves off as each other when the Czar visited England in 1893.

• **Judge James Barlow** and **Judge John Benavides**—total strangers—were each married in San Antonio, Texas, on December 22, 1951. Both honeymooned in Monterrey, Mexico, and the wife of each man gave birth to a daughter on the same day—January 11, 1953—and in the same hospital. Both men became district judges in San Antonio and both had courtrooms on the second floor of the Bexar County courthouse.

LOST AND FOUND

• A needle embedded in the knee of **Mrs. Helen Jensen**, of Seattle, Washington, when she was a small child was removed from her baby thirty years later.

• **Ellen Rice**, of Borger, Texas, in February 1984, sent her great-grandson James H. Green, resident of Oklahoma City, Oklahoma, a one-dollar bill inscribed with his name. He spent it, and in June the same bill was tendered at a concession stand operated by Mrs. Rice in Texas!

• **Mrs. Maggie Jacobs**, of St. Joseph, Missouri, found her great-granddaughter's ring, which had been lost for six years, when she discovered two radishes in her garden had grown together—with the ring encircling them!

FOUND AFTER DECADES

• After her marriage in 1924, **Judit Jacobstam**, of Moja, Sweden, lost her wedding ring in a hayfield. It was found buried under a lilac bush sixty-five years later!

• **Bob Prenosil**, of Cedar Rapids, Michigan, reported his 1937 Ford Tudor stolen in 1961, and found it at a swap meet thirty years later!

• **Bill Linscott** of Adams, Massachusetts, lost a U.S. Army canteen cup with his name scratched on it when he was wounded in Italy in 1945. It was found and returned to him when he toured Italy with his army buddies in 1985, forty years later!

RETRIEVED FROM WATER

• **Stephen Law** of Markham, Ontario, Canada, hunting for a ring lost by his father in five feet of water in Muskoka Lake, found a topaz ring lost by his grandmother forty-one years before!

• A key chain with several keys lost by **C. Dornqwast** in the Wolf River of Wisconsin, was recovered a year later inside a six-pound walleye pike.

• **Ralph Rigdon**, on a fishing trip from Mystic, Connecticut, lost his worker identification badge in thirty feet of water off the shore of Fisher's Island in Long Island Sound, and hooked it in the same spot two months later!

CURSED

• The music with the most tragic score in operatic history! **Eugene Massol**, tenor star of the Paris Opera, at the performance of *Charles VI* on February 9, 1849, sang in French the line, "Oh God, crush him," with a finger pointing at the vaulted ceiling—from which at that very moment a stagehand fell to his death! The following night, Massol pointed to an empty loge as he sang the line, but a patron entered it and dropped dead! On the third night, the tenor gestured at the orchestra pit and a musician collapsed and died! The opera was not revived until 1858, when it was to honor Emperor Napoleon III, but assassins bombed the emperor's party, causing one hundred fifty-six casualties.

• Since its first performance in 1606, Shakespeare's *Macbeth* has brought bad luck to many involved with it.

In recent times, Lawrence Olivier was almost killed during a performance. Charlton Heston was badly injured during rehearsals, and President Lincoln read it to friends the day before his assassination.

LUCK, BAD

• **Stuart Carter**, a graduating senior at Rosenburg High School in Oregon, was scheduled to receive a special award for perfect attendance, but he was absent on the day the honors were given out!

• Busted! **Yusuke Shikauchi** of Tokyo, Japan, who had sneaked away from his job to attend a baseball game, won an automobile raffled off at the stadium—and found his picture on newspaper front pages.

• **John Howard Payne**, author of "Home, Sweet Home," never had a home! He wandered the globe all his life, until he died penniless in Tunisia.

• **Paul Hubert**, of Bordeaux, France, was convicted in 1863 of murdering himself! He served twenty-one years in solitary confinement before it was discovered that his supposed victim was none other than himself!

REVERSAL OF FORTUNE

• **Peter Barr** of Saint Faiths, England, totally blind for ten years, suddenly regained his sight when he pounded his hands together in an argument.

DWIGHT D. EISENHOWER Who became one of the most successful commanders in history, was admitted to West Point in 1911, only because the applicant who ranked ahead of him in his entry test flunked the physical.

THE CURSE OF THE ROMANOV EMERALD

CZAR PETER III (1728-1762)

WAS GIVEN AN EMERALD - BY THE CZARINA ELIZABETH - AND WAS DEPOSED AND SLAIN

HIS SON - PAUL I - WORE THE EMERALD ONCE - AND WAS ASSASSINATED

ALEXANDER II DISCOVERED THE EMERALD 80 YEARS LATER - AND WAS BLOWN UP BY A BOMB

HIS GRANDSON - NICHOLAS II - LAST OF THE ROMANOVS TO WEAR THE EMERALD - WAS EXECUTED BY THE BOLSHEVIKS

NO ONE KNOWS WHO HAS THE EMERALD IN HIS POSSESSION TODAY

• She gets "credit" for catching a thief! **Diane Klos**, cashier in an Irvington, New Jersey store, was given her own stolen credit card for a purchase by a customer who claimed to be her!

• Mr. and **Mrs. Albert F. Briles**, of Cedar Rapids, Iowa, driving to a convention in New Orleans, had their new station wagon stolen eighteen hours after they bought it. Luckily the vehicle was recovered, and they won a second station wagon in a drawing at the convention!

MESSAGES IN BOTTLES

• **James Jarvis**, of Stratford, Ontario, Canada, received a $47,000 piano as a gift for answering a note he found inside a bottle!

• A bottle containing a note describing the fatal injury of **Chunosuke Matsuyama** and the death of forty-four shipmates on a hunt for buried treasure in 1784, was washed ashore at Matsuyama's own village in Japan—one hundred fifty-one years later!

NATURAL COINCIDENCES

STRANGE OCCURRENCES IN FAUNA

• A lost donkey wandering aimlessly over the Idaho hills near what is now the town of Kellogg, accidentally discovered a mine worth $100 million. The animal was found standing on an outcropping of ore over what became the famous Bunker Hill & Sullivan Mine.

"Ginger," a ten-month-old fox terrier with two hearts, was owned by Edna Markham of Hollywood, California.

The **Jordan** family, of East Falls, Pennsylvania, owned this black dog with a perfect five-pointed white star on his chest!

"Vickie," a black cat with a natural white "V" on her chest, was born on V-Day!

• All the books on insects in the junior high school library in Moultrie, Georgia, were destroyed by termites.

• Three frogs were found in a potato by **Mrs. Ed Hansen** of Foley, Minnesota.

STRANGE OCCURRENCES IN FLORA

• A blackthorn tree in Bra, Italy, burst into bloom on the coldest day of winter

annually for six hundred thirty-nine years.

• Over a century ago, twelve sycamore trees were planted beside the Grace Episcopal Church in Plymouth, North Carolina. Each tree was named after one of Christ's apostles. The tree called Judas was hit by lightning and destroyed.

• The Peace Poplar planted in Jena, Germany, in 1815, to celebrate the end of the Napoleonic

• **Mrs. Henry G. Hesslink** found "God" in her eggplant! The seeds of the eggplant Mrs. Hesslink sliced for dinner on Sunday, August 15, 1948, spelled out the name of its creator: 'G-O-D.'

• **William H. Rainey,** of Fort Worth, Texas, holds his four-foot-eleven-inch Snake Cucumber.

Spiro Agnew Eggplant: **Johnny Brenner** discovered this eggplant bearing the silhouette of former Vice President Spiro Agnew.

This peculiarly hand-shaped carrot was found by **Tommy Andrews** at the Palace Café in Redlands, California.

• Potato plane, grown by **J. J. Brophy** and submitted by **Charles A. Shinn** of Hines, Oregon. The aerodynamic spud grew all in one piece and weighed three pounds. Only the paper propeller was added.

War with France, toppled suddenly, ninety-nine years later, on August 1, 1914—the day World War I started.

STRANGE ENCOUNTERS WITH SEA LIFE

• The jet that collided with a fish: a mid-air collision between a fish and a jet liner in Juneau, Alaska, delayed the plane's flight for an hour. The fish had been dropped by an eagle flying above the jet.

• **E. H. Eadie**, of Charleston, South Carolina, caught two fish—each one with a natural number marking on its tail: "1" was caught first; "2" second.

• When **James Price**, of Locust Grove, Arkansas, accidentally dropped his dentures into Bull Shoal Lake, he wrote them off as a loss. But 10 days later, he got them back—when he caught a 20-pound catfish that had swallowed them!

A RAILWAY TRAIN was stalled by thousands of crabs that made the rails so slippery the train was unable to move. Manzanillo, Mexico.

Crab with a bonus claw, caught in Barnaget Bay, New Jersey.

STRANGE OCCURRENCES IN WEATHER

• A statue of **Tlaloc**, the Mexican rain god, was moved to the new archaeological museum in Mexico City in 1964 during the dry season—yet on that day there was a torrential rain.

• In 1916, the city of San Diego hired rainmaker **Charles Mallory Hatfield** to fill its drought-stricken reservoirs. After Hatfield performed his service, over fifteen inches of rain fell, causing billions of gallons of water to flood the city! When Hatfield tried to

collect his $10,000 fee, the city fathers agreed to pay it—as long as Hatfield was willing to pay $3,500,000 in damage suits filed against the city!

• An obelisk erected by the French historian **Raynal** on the island of Alstad, Switzerland, to honor Swiss liberty, aroused a fierce controversy which ended dramatically on March 6, 1796, when Raynal died in Paris—on that same day, the obelisk was destroyed by lightning!

STRANGE PHYSICS

• A fire hose set on fire by cold water! F. R. Daniel, Chief Engineer of the Milwaukee Fire Insurance Rating Bureau, reported that high pressure had created enough friction heat to set a hose on fire.

• In Columbus, Nebraska, a bullet was shot through another—fired from the same gun—in mid-air! The gun was pointed directly skyward and fired twice— the ascending bullet struck the descending bullet!

• An antique clock owned by **Mrs. Mary O'Connor**, of Lancaster, California, that had not worked for months, was started again on February 9, 1971, by an earthquake.

REUNIONS

• **Diego Quiroga**, a Spanish aristocrat who had become separated from his wife while fleeing Madrid during the French invasion of 1811, heard a newborn infant whimpering in a snow-covered field. He wrapped the baby girl in a blanket and carried her on his horse to the village of Venta de Pinar, where he learned the infant was his own daughter, born to Mrs. Quiroga only a few hours earlier and abandoned by a nursemaid in the confusion of flight! The infant suffered no ill effects, and lived to the age of eighty!

• Identical twins **Mark Newman** and **Jerry Levey**, adopted by different families five days after their birth in 1954, did not meet again until 1986—thirty-two years later. Both are volunteer New Jersey firemen. A friend had spotted their resemblance at a firefighters' convention.

• When **Jack B. Miller**, an insurance adjuster of Coral Springs, Florida, made a business call to **Jack R. Miller**, a security firm operator in North Miami, Florida, he learned that he was talking with his father whom he hadn't seen for thirty-one years.

NUMERIC COINCIDENCES

• **Bismarck**, first Chancellor of the German Empire, studied in three schools, was ambassador to three countries, served three kings, fought in three wars, had three horses killed under him, signed three peace treaties, and established the Triple Alliance. He had three names (Bismarck, Schoenhausen, and Lauenburg), three titles (Count, Duke, Prince), and three attempts were made on his life. He resigned three times, was the father of three children, and his coat of arms consisted of a three-leaf clover intertwined with three oak leaves.

• "Cancer Crusader," the seventh dog in the seventh race run at Mobile Greyhound Park, Mobile,

BROTHERS REUNITED AFTER 30 YEARS BY THE SMELL OF AN APPLE

A TRAVELER STANDING IN THE R.R. DEPOT IN STILLWATER, OKLA. WAS EATING AN APPLE, WHEN A STRANGER APPROACHED AND SAID, "THAT SMELLS LIKE A NORTH CAROLINA APPLE." "IT IS", SAID THE TRAVELER, "I'M FROM NORTH CAROLINA." "SO AM I", SAID THE STRANGER — AND THEY TURNED OUT TO BE BROTHERS WHO HAD NOT MET IN 30 YEARS!

BROTHERS MEET HUNTING EACH OTHER'S GRAVE. Grant and Karl Winegar—marines—hadn't seen each other for 20 months but knew that each was in the Pacific area. When fighting on Iwo Jima, each thinking that the other might have been killed, they went prowling through a cemetery reading the inscriptions on the grave markers—when suddenly they met face to face.

Alabama, on the seventh day of the seventh month of 1977, weighed seventy-seven pounds and finished seventh.

RECURRING COINCIDENCES

• Lightning strikes thrice: In 1991, lightning destroyed a house in Maleville, France, for the third time.

• The Vermont State Fair held in White River Junction, Vermont, was plagued by rain annually for thirty years. The opening date was changed repeatedly in an attempt to get good weather, but in 1928 the fair was abandoned.

• Each of the five husbands of **Frau Irmgard Bruns** of Berlin committed suicide.

IN 1943 M/SGT. JOHN HASSEBROCK of Buffalo Center, Iowa, received a 3-day pass to marry a WAC corporal when he went overseas. They lost track of each other until, one night in France, he made a convoy to the front lines and went to a farmhouse to spend the night. THERE HE MET HIS WIFE! ON THE EXACT DAY AND HOUR OF THEIR FIRST WEDDING ANNIVERSARY!

A PERFECT MATCH— INTERNET ROMANCE SAVES A LIFE, DEFYING ODDS

Lonely hearts throughout the ages lament the overwhelming odds lovers must beat in order to find their true soul mates. So what are the odds that your one true love is also the one person in a million who can save your life? This incredible coincidence is the reason Theresa Dravek is alive today.

Theresa was diagnosed with kidney failure in 1981, and received a transplant. The new kidney failed only a year later, and Theresa was sent home from the hospital with a grim prognosis. Over the years, as her health gradually waned, Theresa occupied herself by chatting on the Internet. She became cyber-friends with a British cyclist named Ian Fleming. Their friendship quickly blossomed into something more profound, even though Theresa made no secret of the fact that she was far from healthy.

In 1997, Ian traveled four thousand miles to spend Christmas with Theresa, and on New Year's Eve, he asked her to marry him. Just as the happy couple was making wedding plans, however, doctors found a tumor growing on Theresa's one healthy kidney. Doctors held out little hope of finding a kidney donor that was a proper genetic match for Theresa in time to save her life. Ian insisted that he be tested. Against all odds, he was a perfect match.

Two months after their wedding, Theresa and Ian were wheeled into surgery. It took two hours to remove Ian's kidney, and another three hours to transplant it into Theresa. Just a few days after the successful surgery, Ian and Theresa were up and walking.

Theresa's prognosis is excellent. She and Ian are enjoying a happy life together. Theresa has now taken up her husband's favorite sport, cycling. It's her second great passion in life—Ian, of course, is the first.

Chapter 15

Communication

Today's generation has the great fortune to be explorers of a new communication frontier: the Internet. Still too new to be reined in by excess regulation, communication in cyberspace is as bold, as boundless, and in some ways as risky as were journeys into uncharted territories in centuries past. So it was, as you'll discover, with other communication media in their early days. As an accomplished veteran of newspaper, radio, television, and the Internet, Ripley's is the ideal guide through the weirdest realms in the communication world. Let us now take you on an exploration of the extremes to which we humans will go to get our message across.

THE **SKYTALE** USED IN ancient Sparta **FOR SECRET MESSAGES** A STRIP OF PARCHMENT WAS WRAPPED SPIRALLY AROUND A STICK AND THE MESSAGE WRITTEN ON ITS FOLDS COULD LATER BE READ **ONLY WHEN IT WAS WOUND IN THE SAME WAY ON AN IDENTICAL STICK**

• The @ sign used in email addresses is five centuries old! Professor **Giorgio Stabile,** of Italy's La Sapienza University, found the symbol in a letter dated May 4, 1536!

ANTIQUATED

• A relay team of ancient Inca messengers called Chasquis carried messages 1,250 miles from Quito to Cuzco, Peru, in five days, running at an average of ten miles per hour!

• The couriers whose messages could never be secret: Aztec messengers carrying news of a victory to the Mexican emperor ran hundreds of miles in ceremonial garb waving a sword joyously and roaring victoriously. If the news was bad they ran silently and in humble garb.

EMAIL AND INTERNET

• Russian **Victor Yazykov,** sailing alone in the South Atlantic, performed surgery on his own arm by following instructions from Doctor Daniel Carlin of Boston, relayed via email from halfway across the world.

• "Cyberstalking": A man identified only as "Roger" was the prey in the world's first live game of human hunting on the web! It took a week to find him in a Berlin library, counting books!

• In 1997, 67 million computer email users in North America sent 2.7 billion messages!

• In June 1999, between fifty and one hundred thousand people logged on to hear a concert from Verona, Italy, of Verdi's *Aida,* the first opera to be broadcast via the Internet!

• In 1999, a NASA expedition set up the first Internet link to the North Pole and made the very first North Pole to South Pole conversation ever!

• "**Rattie**," a white rat owned by teacher Judy Reavis of California, helps to hook up classrooms to the Internet by carrying a string attached to wires through the walls of one room into another!

• The Virtual College of Texas offers academic courses online to students but doesn't issue any degrees.

• When a computer glitch occurred in Sydney, Australia, hundreds of programmed soda pop machines began dialing ambulance and fire emergency lines.

• A company in San Francisco, California, has developed Internet software that is scented with a plug-in device for web surfers called "Smell-O-Vision"!

• The Vatican may consider recognizing **Saint Isodore of Seville** as the Patron Saint of the Internet! A clergyman during the sixth century, Saint Isodore created a twenty-volume encyclopedia—one of the earliest databases.

• A ferret named "**Misty**" was used by the U.S. Space Command in Colorado to help rewire a new computerized command center!

• A company called NCR has developed the "M-Bracelet," an electronic device worn on the wrist that allows the user to send and receive messages and link up with websites and automated teller machines!

• A man who works as a computer systems manager in Dallas, Texas, legally changed his name to "Dotcomguy" and has vowed to stay inside his apartment for a year, ordering everything from groceries to clothing via computer!

RADIO

• The first radio program presenting the human voice and music was broadcast from a remote coastal station at Brant Rock, Massachusetts, on Christmas Eve, 1906.

• "Around the World with Ripley": In 1934, **Robert**

"WIND-POWERED RADIO"
BBC RADIO 4 in Dorset, England, ON July 19, 1992, BROADCAST *THE WORLD'S FIRST RADIO PROGRAM POWERED BY A WINDMILL!*

Ripley, a pioneer radio personality, was the first man to broadcast a radio program to every country in the world simultaneously!

• When the racehorse "**Man O' War**" died in 1947, its body lay in state for three days: the funeral was attended by one thousand people and broadcast on the radio!

• During the Vietnam War, American soldiers tossed "Slinky" toys over tree branches to serve as radio antennas!

• American gossip columnist Walter Winchell spoke up to two hundred words a minute during his weekly radio broadcasts!

TELEPHONE

• A company in Japan has developed false fingernails that glow when the wearer is talking on a cell phone!

• At England's Chester Zoo, "**George A. Giraffe**," who stood a record eighteen feet tall, frequently chewed the telephone wires near his pen, scrambling local phone service!

IN TAKASAKI, JAPAN, THERE IS A PHONE BOOTH BUILT IN THE SHAPE OF A GIANT BASS FIDDLE!

• Spanish artist **Salvador Dali** designed a lobster-shaped telephone.

• **Bob Prosser**, of Turtle Lake, Wisconsin, has a collection of five hundred thousand telephones, including an explosion-proof military phone, a fourteen-carat gold Swedish phone, and a crank model used by the last Sultan of Turkey!

• In Shoup, Idaho, there are no power lines, televisions, or stereos!

• The first phone book was published in New Haven, Connecticut, in 1878, and contained only fifty names!

• An answering machine in San Diego, California, created to take calls from "Elvis Spotters," has already received over fifty thousand calls!

• **John Paul Getty**, one of the richest men who ever lived, had a pay telephone in one of his mansions!

• Italian film director **Franco Zeffirelli** phones his pet dogs every day whenever he is working in a foreign country!

• The Lazy E Ranch in Gutherie, Oklahoma, has pay telephones that are six and a half feet above the ground, for use by cowboys on horseback!

• At the University of Guelph, in Ontario, old phone books are used as bedding for cattle and sheep!

• In Ghana, West Africa, people often have to wait up to thirty years for a telephone to be installed in their homes!

• **Albert Einstein** never memorized his own telephone number!

• American Stephen Roberts has pedaled over sixteen thousand miles on a bicycle equipped with a cellular phone, a fax machine, and seven on-board computers!

• In 1878, in Connecticut, telephone operators answered the phone by saying "ahoy!" instead of "hello."

• **Tom Morton**, who memorized the entire phone book of his hometown of Blackpool, England, offers free directory assistance to city residents!

• The world's smallest police station in Carabelle, Florida, is actually a phone booth!

TELEVISION

• In Ust, Kamchatka, a town in the former Soviet Union, the reward for catching fifty stray dogs is a new fridge, and one hundred dogs are worth a color television!

• In December 1990, **King Taufa Ahav Tupon IV** of Tonga, celebrated his twenty-five years of rule by bringing television to the islands for the first time!

IN 1993, ISRAEL'S PHONE COMPANY OFFERED A SERVICE *FOR PEOPLE TO FAX MESSAGES TO GOD* TO BE PLACED IN Jerusalem's Wailing Wall!

• **Janet Richardson**, of Overland Park, Kansas, emerged from a coma after hearing the theme song of her favorite television show playing in her hospital room!

VERBAL AND NONVERBAL COMMUNICATION

• **Joseph W. Charles**, of Berkeley, California, waved to motorists who passed his home each morning for thirty years!

• Scientists at the Almaden Research Laboratory in San Jose, California, have developed transmitters and receivers that transfer electronic data via handshakes!

UNUSUAL FORMS OF COMMUNICATION

• Residents of Bird Village, Turkey, use whistling to communicate with others for distances of up to five miles away!

• A baby monitor, consisting of a Dictaphone and a loud-speaking amplifier in the receiver, was invented in the United States in 1919!

A phone booth in the middle of nowhere! Believe It or Not! There's a phone booth located in the Mojave Desert 14.26 miles from the nearest paved road! Rick Karr of Texas spent 32 days camping out at the booth answering calls from around the world!

CYBER-SCAMS: SHYSTERS ON THE INTERNET

The Internet has been called a frontier, and like all frontiers, it's a haven for shysters. Con artists, hoaxers, and the just plain annoying have taken up residence online, preying on unsuspecting web-surfers. We often make ourselves a convenient target because we seldom realize how simple it is for them to invade our privacy. Internet cons and hoaxes come in a variety of types. Here are just a few:

Scammers will send you an email offering a phone number you can call to get free U.S. Treasury money. The 809 area code you'll dial is outside the U.S., and those minutes you spend on hold, or talking to an operator who barely speaks English, will cost you $5 to $25 per minute!

Shysters pretend they're with your Internet service provider, and email you with the news that the system has experienced an error, and they need your password so that they can reenter it. Don't believe it! They'll access your mail, send mail to others pretending they're you, or worst of all, access your private online accounts and charge up your credit cards!

Urban myths spread like wildfire via email. You might have read the ones about the poodle (Chihuahua, hamster) in the microwave, the AIDS-infected needle in the movie theater seat (ball crawl, sandbox), or the fictitious Microsoft bid to buy the Catholic church. The major tip-off? Somewhere in the email it will probably say, "Send this to everyone you know!"

Not all Internet bugaboos are as dangerous as they seem. All those warnings about emails that eat your hard drive if you open them? Another hoax! No harm will come to you, your computer, or your data simply by opening and reading an email. Not so, however, for attachments that may come from unknown senders. These can contain "Trojan Horses" that will access or erase your data. Just don't open attachments unless you know what you're getting and who sent it, and you'll be fine.

Chapter 16
Contests & Prizes

AT THE KENTUCKY STATE COUNTY FAIR, THERE IS AN ANNUAL CONTEST for POULTRY DRESSED IN FANCY CLOTHING!

Are you the kind of person who never wins anything? Maybe you just haven't yet discovered your medium. Perhaps you've got a latent talent for franks-and-beans diving, or spaghetti sculpture. Or maybe worm charming is your cup of tea. Who knows? Perhaps you'll uncover a hidden talent as you peruse Ripley's gallery of bizarre contests.

CONTESTS

• In Toronto, Canada, there is an annual contest in which secretaries throw typewriters from a rooftop at a bull's-eye on the ground!

In Sonkajarvi, Finland, there is an annual "WIFE CARRYING RACE" in which husbands carry their wives over an 835-ft. obstacle course!

• In England there is an annual championship pie-throwing contest in which contestants heave cream pies at people standing eight feet away!

• The annual Eskimo Olympics, held in Alaska, include ear weight lifting, raw whale-blubber eating, and people-tossing events!

• Winners of the International Rotten Sneaker Challenge, held in Montpelier, Vermont, have their smelly running shoes put on display at the Odor Eaters Hall of Fumes!

• In Crisfield, Maryland, there is an annual National Hard Crab Derby in which crustaceans race down a wet twenty-foot ramp!

• In 1991, biology students at Indiana's Purdue University staged the Giganteus Stakes, a race for cockroaches!

• For one hundred sixty-nine years, residents of Peters Hollow and Rome Hollow, Tennessee, have held an annual Easter egg fight in which contestants sit in a circle and tap eggs together—the last one with an uncracked egg wins!

"RACING CHAIRS" IN Manlius, N.Y., THERE IS AN ANNUAL RACE IN WHICH CONTESTANTS RUN ¼ MILE DOWN THE TOWN'S MAIN STREET WHILE PUSHING SOMEONE IN A CHAIR!

• In Caroga Lake, New York, there is an annual outhouse race, in which competitors pull wooden outhouses through snow and ice!

• In Caryville, Florida, there is an annual International Worm Fiddling Contest in which contestants play music to draw earthworms out of the soil!

• Drivers at the Annual B.F.I. International Truck and Heavy Equipment Rodeo compete in an event to crack an egg set atop a traffic cone using the tip of a bulldozer's seven-ton steel blade!

• **Vinnie Gorman**, of Victoria, Canada, organized a Meatloaf Derby in which drivers cooked eighteen-ounce meat loaves on their car engines while driving ten laps around a race track!

• At an annual bridge-building contest in Kelowna, Canada, contestants use pasta to build bridges that can support up to two hundred sixty-five pounds!

• Ear pulling, one of the events at the World Indian-Eskimo Olympics, involves stretching a twine tied between two men's ears until one man yells "Uncle"!

• The annual Lineman's Rodeo in Saint Louis, Missouri, features a race in which linemen climb up and down utility poles carrying raw, unbroken eggs in their mouths!

• In Yellville, Arkansas, there is an annual wild turkey calling contest in which entrants compete in three categories: the mating call, the lost call, and the cluck assembly!

• A popular game show in Japan called *The Ultra Quiz* tests up to five thousand contestants at one time inside a sports stadium, offering such top prizes as helicopters!

• In Fremont, Nebraska, the winners of a spelling bee were given trophies that had a spelling mistake in the inscription!

• In 1992, balloonists from Belgium, Britain, Germany, the Netherlands, and the United States competed in the world's first balloon race across the Atlantic Ocean!

IN ALICE SPRINGS, AUSTRALIA, PARTICIPANTS IN THE ANNUAL **HENLEY-ON-TODD** REGATTA RACE CROSS DRY RIVER BEDS CARRYING **BOTTOMLESS BOATS!**

• In 1992, in Tokyo, Japan, sixty infants competed in a contest to determine which child could cry the loudest!

• Since 1936, the town of Coalinga, California, has held an annual horned toad derby!

IN Whitehorse, The Yukon, THERE IS AN ANNUAL **"CHAIN SAW CHUCK"** IN WHICH COMPETITORS HURL CHAIN SAWS UP TO 55 ft.!

Believe It or Not! IN Lake City, Colo., THERE IS AN ANNUAL COFFIN RACE.

AT THE ALL-JAPAN ROBOT SUMO WRESTLING TOURNAMENT IN TOKYO, JAPAN, 6-LB. ROBOTS "WRESTLED" INSIDE A 5-FT.-WIDE SUMO RING!

Believe It or Not! IN Seattle, Wash., THERE IS AN ANNUAL "SPAM CARVING CONTEST" IN WHICH CONTESTANTS CREATE SCULPTURES OUT OF LUNCHEON MEAT!

• In Reedpoint, Montana, there is an annual race in which hundreds of sheep charge down Main Street, and a contest is held to determine the prettiest ewe and the ugliest sheep!

• A contest to find the World's Greatest Liar is held annually in West Lakeland, England!

• One of the entries at the Paper Airplane Flying Classic held at the University of California in 1973 was a plane made of Passover matzos!

• The annual world pillow fighting championship in Kenwood, California, features contestants battling with pillows while sitting on a greased pole placed over a mud pit!

• In Clute, Texas, there is an annual Mosquito Festival with a "Mr. and Mrs. Mosquito Legs" contest!

• In Baton Rouge, Louisiana, there is an annual guitar-throwing contest!

• At the annual crabapple fair in Egremont, England, prizes are awarded for "gurning through a braffin"—the art of making the ugliest face while wearing a horse collar!

• In Lewes, Delaware, there is an annual "World Championship Punkin Chunkin" contest, in which contestants fire a pumpkin with devices that use centrifugal force!

• In Coulterville, California, there is an annual "Coyote Howl" festival with prizes awarded for the most authentic-sounding howl!

• A prize-winning egg laid by a hen at the annual "World's Largest Egg" contest held in Maine measured 6.4 inches!

• In 1993, the first annual Custodial Olympics took place at the University of Kansas, with events including buffing, sweeping, and sponge tossing!

• In Cooper's Hill, Brockworth, England, there is an annual cheese rolling race in which competitors run downhill while rolling large disks of cheese!

• In Folkestone, England, there is an annual snail race!

PRIZES

• When he won his first professional match in 1989, **Yasokichi Konishiki,** a Samoan-American Sumo wrestler, received a prize of four tons of rice, five thousand eels, and a huge silver Coca-Cola bottle!

IN Pelican Rapids, Mich., THERE IS AN ANNUAL "UGLY TRUCK CONTEST" WITH CATEGORIES INCLUDING WORST PAINT JOB, MOST RUST and MOST EXHAUST SMOKE!

• In order to attract new fans, the Kansas City Blades hockey team offered free tickets to fans who could throw a thirty-gallon garbage can the farthest!

• A clothing store in Vienna, Austria, offered 5,000 shillings worth of merchandise to the first five customers daring enough to enter the store completely naked!

• In Grand Prairie, Texas, there is an annual "World Championship Pickled Quail Egg Eating" contest, and a "Stewed Prune Pit Spitting" contest!

• Immortality contest: In 1993, a United States company ran an essay contest for which the grand prize was "Cryonic Suspension After Death"!

• In 1955, the Quaker Oats Company of Canada placed legal deeds to one square inch of land in the Canadian Yukon inside their boxes of puffed rice and puffed wheat.

• **Emperor Yu** of China once offered a prize of $1,500,000 to any person who could make his wife smile!

• Space Travel Services of Houston, Texas, recently ran a sweepstakes in which the winner got five hundred thousand dollars and a trip into space aboard a Soviet rocket ship!

• **Lisa Burton** of Midland, Michigan, won a new truck by standing next to the vehicle with her lips pressed against it for seventeen hours!

• In 1852, "**Black Swan**," a racehorse that won a nine-mile endurance race in California, collected a prize of $25,000 in gold, five hundred mares, five hundred stallions, five hundred calves, five hundred heifers, and five hundred sheep!

• **Rubin Susteras**, of Brampton, Canada, won a car in a contest by standing and touching it for ninety-six hours without ever removing his hand from the vehicle!

• Ukrainian **Alexei Antonovich Brazhnik** won a two-week trip to Britain but could not get permission to leave his country until 1993, when he finally made the trip—twenty-eight years after winning it!

• An Internet company in Shanghai held a competition for computer hackers: the first prize of $600 went to the person who could break into their computer system.

• In 1993, **Margaret Davis**, of Consett, County Durham, England, won the first Scottish Sheep Counting Championship by counting two hundred eighty-three animals as they ran by!

• **Andy Boorman**, of San Luis Obispo, California, won first prize in a contest as Wells Fargo's one-millionth Internet customer. He received six shopping carts full of pennies, weighing three and a half tons—worth $10,000!

• Contestants at the annual "Birdman" competition in Eastbourne, England, leap off the town's pier in an attempt to fly!

• **David Huard** of Toronto, Ontario, won a $3,500 prize of a La-Z-Boy recliner with a built-in cooler, speakerphone, heated padding, and a massage system, after he sat and watched four consecutive screenings of the movie *Love Story*!

"LOVE ME, LOVE MY COUCH" Elma Jean Donnelly of New Castle, Penn., WON THE $2,000 FIRST PRIZE, BEATING OUT 1,200 OTHER CONTESTANTS, for HAVING THE UGLIEST COUCH IN AMERICA!

• In 1992, at a Boston, Massachusetts charity auction, people bid on a chance to swim with the sharks and moray eels at the New England Aquarium.

• **Dennis L. Wheat** of Malvern, Arkansas, in 1964, won a used car in a raffle, and discovered he had been awarded the very same sedan he had traded in six years earlier!

• **Thomas Lucas** and the **Earl of Oxford** in Colchester, England, played a game of dice in 1543 for the guardianship of a six-month-old heiress. Lucas became the infant girl's guardian and later arranged her marriage to his son John.

WINNERS

• **D.C. Nix**, of San Antonio, Texas, won the first annual "Texas Laugh" contest with a laugh described by judges as sounding like a pig with asthma!

• On February 10, 1995, **Suzanne Sherman**, of Holland, won a chocolate eating contest in Hollywood, California, by consuming 1.09 pounds of chocolate in five minutes!

• **Hiroyuki Saito**, behind in his rent, won the "Halls' Year-end Loud Voice" contest by shouting, "Hey, landlord, wait three days for the rent!" at one hundred twenty decibels!

Aileene Aalbu won a beauty pageant and a funny-face contest on the same day.

• **Christl Cranz**, of Germany, competed in the 1936 Winter Games and won a gold medal for downhill skiing—with one arm in a sling!

• **Dave Griffiths** of Kitchener, Ontario, won ten thousand dollars in a contest by coating himself in honey and feathers and diving for an apple in a vat of pig fertilizer.

• **George Gibson**, of Hay River, Northwest Territory, won a new pickup truck by finding the truck's key amongst one hundred forty others while swimming in a pool of lime green Jell-O!

Gus Simmons was declared the winner of this ice-sitting contest at White City Casino, Chicago, on July 31, 1933—until judges discovered he was running a 102 degree fever and disqualified him!

- In 1989, **Peter Roman**, of Brooklyn, New York, won a first prize of one thousand dollars in the "World's Largest Roach" contest, with a cockroach that measured 1.88 inches!

- In 1990, **Flora Mackay** of West Covina, California, won first prize in the "Great American Snail Festival" with her two snails dressed as a bride and groom!

- At the annual German Oktoberfest in Kitchener, Canada, **Kevin Roberts** shaved his head, covered himself in molasses, and ate a worm—all to win ten thousand dollars!

- **Steve Sacco**, of Toronto, Ontario, won a trip to Miami after diving into a vat of wieners and beans and finding a videotape of the film *There's Something About Mary*!

- **Liz Fernandez**, while a student at the University of California at Berkeley, won first prize in a contest for the messiest room in the state of California!

- In 1993, United States Senator **Paul Wellstone** won a watermelon-seed spitting contest in Owatonna, Minnesota, by sending a seed thirty-two feet, two inches!

- **Ed Burman**, of Fallston, Maryland, won first place over one hundred thousand other contestants in the first annual United States Mooing Contest!

- **"Lucky,"** a cocker spaniel in Shanklin, England, won first prize in a raffle—the prize was a turkey dinner served in a local restaurant!

- **Tex Tyrell** won a "tall tale" contest in Alice Springs, Australia, by telling incredible stories continuously for eight hours!

- **Chris McCarron**, of California, entered a contest sponsored by the United States music video network MTV, and won first prize—a thousand-watt radio station in South Georgia!

LOSERS

- French runner **Alain Lacouture**, in 1992, won a $2,500 prize for finishing last in the Boston Marathon— three hours behind the winner!

- **Asanokiri**, a Sumo wrestler in Japan, lost a match after his loincloth fell off—the first time in eighty-three years of wrestling that this obscure rule had ever been enforced!

BIG TEXAS STEAKHOUSE— HOME OF THE PLATE-CLEANING CHALLENGE

Amarillo's Big Texas Steakhouse offers a challenge to its customers: eat everything on your plate, and your meal is free. If you leave anything behind, you pay $50.

Sound easy? Think again. Your dinner comes with a set of rules: you must eat it all without getting up, you can't have help, and you have to eat everything within one hour. And if you get sick, the whole bet is off. And you'd better bring a hearty appetite, because at the Big Texas Steakhouse, the steaks are a whopping seventy-two ounces—that's more than seventeen quarter-pounders!

Owner Bobby Lee recalls that a number of customers have managed the challenge over the years. Some have set records. The fastest steak eater was Frank Pastone, pitcher for the Cincinnati Reds, who polished off his steak in nine and a half minutes. The youngest steak-chawing champ was an eleven-year-old boy. The fastest woman did it in thirty-two minutes. But the all time record was held by a six-hundred-fifty-pound wrestler who, within the hour time limit, finished not one but two of the Texas-sized steaks.

Chapter 17
Customs & Etiquette

THE Masai Tribe of Tanzania, WHO REGARD SPITTING AS A SIGN of RESPECT and GOODWILL, SPIT AT EACH OTHER WHEN THEY MEET and AGAIN WHEN THEY SAY GOODBYE!

If there's one thing any world traveler can tell you, it's that there's more than one way of doing just about everything. We've brought together a collection of some of the world's most unusual customs, rituals, roles, ceremonies, and folkways, many of which may not appear to make sense to us, yet all of which, in their own cultural context, serve their purpose.

CUSTOMS

• The guard that protects the hut of an African witch doctor against burglaries is a huge image of its owner.

• East Indians on Nias Island, located off the coast of Sumatra, demonstrate their jumping prowess by leaping over six-foot-high pillars placed in the middle of the street.

• The land that is made more sacred by a bolt of lightning: Natives inhabiting the shores of Lake Titicaca, in South America, mark each spot where lightning has struck by erecting a mound surmounted by a cross.

THE **MUDMEN** of the Asaro Valley, Eastern Highlands, New Guinea, CAKE THEIR BODIES WITH MUD AND WEAR GROTESQUE MASKS FASHIONED FROM MUD

• It was once customary for the people of the Ozark Mountains to squash the first louse they found on a child's head with a tin cup if they wanted that child to be a dancer!

• Headhunting was practiced by the Montenegrins of Yugoslavia until 1913!

• In ancient Rome, people showed their appreciation by flapping the edges of their togas instead of clapping.

• People of the Easter Islands tell stories using string images called "Kai Kai" that they shape with their fingers, like in the children's game "cat's cradle."

• People on the island of Nauru in the Pacific Ocean practice a custom called "Bubutsi" in which anyone who admires anything automatically receives it as a gift!

• Women in Madagascar gather the webs of the nephila orb-weaving spider and spin the threads into textiles!

• In eighteenth-century France, it was customary for a gentleman to greet a lady he met in the street by kissing her on the neck!

• People of the Torres Strait Islands place the heads of corpses on ant hills until they are picked clean, then paint them red and display them in baskets!

CEREMONIES

• Lake Guatavita, in Colombia, South America, was once used by the Chibcha Indians for a ceremony in which they threw emeralds, gold, and other treasures into the lake.

• In Burgos, Spain, people perform an annual ceremony, commemorating King Herod and the Slaughter of the Innocents, in which a man leaps over male babies on a mattress, symbolizing evil passing overhead!

• Japanese children participate in a special ceremony in which they ask the pardon of fish they have eaten.

ORDEALS

• In India each spring, during the feast of Holi, blazing fires are lit in each of the Bhil villages, and in every town some fifty natives walk through the flames—barefoot and wearing flimsy garments! More than five thousand annually perform the fire walk to assure speedy recovery of sick relatives—yet not one person has ever suffered burns.

• The most hazardous safe-conduct pass in history: Any Turkish subject with a grievance against the Grand Vizier could win an immediate audience with the ruler by laying upon his head a blazing fire pot. But it was only a one-way pass: if he failed to prove his complaint he was immediately beheaded.

RITUALS

• Dormice were so revered by the ancient Romans that they were weighed before guests as a sign of hospitality.

• In Albania, friends greet each other by touching temples—symbolizing that their thoughts of each other are sincere.

RITES OF PASSAGE

• Young men and women in Bali are initiated into adulthood by having their teeth filed!

• In ancient Greece, when children reached the age of twelve or thirteen they had to dedicate their toys to the god Apollo as a sign that their childhood was over!

A **SADDLED HORSE** TO ENABLE EACH CALIPH OF BAGHDAD TO ESCAPE IN THE EVENT OF REVOLT WAS KEPT IN CONSTANT READINESS FROM **760** TO **1258** —A PERIOD OF **498 YEARS!**

STATUS

• Children of the Hidatsa Indian tribe of North America, upon reaching maturity, adopted the name of another member of the family, who was then required to take a different name.

STONE KNIVES were used by the Aztec Indians to cut out the hearts of 50,000 sacrificial victims a year.

A CEREMONIAL STRANGLING CORD used on the Marquesas Islands in the Pacific has a carved sacred figure made of human bone at each end.

● The social status of the early Romans was indicated by the stripe bordering their togas.

● Shoe shines originated with the Spanish caballeros, who polished their boots so everyone would recognize they were gentlemen who rode horseback instead of walking on dusty roads.

● Malatian tribesmen of the Solomon Islands once advertised the fact that they had killed and eaten many enemies by drilling a hole in the tip of their own nose.

ETIQUETTE

● **Lady Gough**, distinguished blue-nose of England, wrote a book on etiquette in 1863, on page 80 of which appears this passage: "The perfect hostess will see to it that the works of male and female authors are properly separated on her bookshelves. Their proximity, unless they happen to be married, should not be tolerated."

● The first book of etiquette and table manners, entitled *The Instructions of Ptahhotep*, was written in Egypt in 2500 B.C.!

● A book on etiquette, written five hundred years ago, urged diners not to grab their food with both hands and to use three fingers only.

FOLK WAYS

● Many American Indian tribes visited saunas before hunting trips in the belief that it would so cleanse them that animals would be unable to discern their scent.

● Kitchen floors in rural areas of the district of Engadine, Switzerland, are still paved with cobblestones in the belief

THE **SWINGING BRAHMINS OF BANGKOK** Thailand— PARTICIPANTS IN A COMPETITION HELD AT A HARVEST FESTIVAL, RIDE A GIANT SWING AND ATTEMPT TO CATCH A BAG OF MONEY SUSPENDED FROM A POLE WITH *THEIR TEETH*

THE **BLOODIEST** SPOT ON EARTH! THE SACRIFICIAL STONE OF THE AZTECS, MEXICO D.F. *MORE THAN 1,000,000 HUMAN BEINGS HAD THEIR HEARTS CUT OUT ON THIS STONE!*

that walking on them barefooted will strengthen the feet.

• Schoolgirls in Guinea, Africa, balance their schoolbags on their heads because they consider it improper to carry anything in their hands.

• The men who chip rocks with their teeth! The aborigines of the Gibson Desert of Australia are the only people on Earth who create stone tools and weapons by shaping rocks with their teeth!

THE ANCIENT INCAS USED THE SKIN of THEIR ENEMIES TO MAKE DRUMS AND THEIR SHIN BONES TO MAKE FLUTES!

GIRLS on the island of Crete 3,500 years ago practiced the dangerous sport of bull jumping—grabbing a charging bull by the horns and allowing the enraged animal to toss them onto its back!

• Men attending meetings in colonial Boston's cold halls often rented dogs to serve as foot-warmers at a charge of sixpence per dog.

• The ancient Romans always carried two handkerchiefs: one on the left wrist and the other tucked at the waist or around the neck.

THE DINNER THAT MUST BE EATEN UNDERWATER
Hatta, India

A SACRED POOL IN WHICH ONCE EACH YEAR 5,000 PILGRIMS EAT A FULL MEAL WHILE SWIMMING BENEATH ITS SURFACE

THE DEATH-DEFYING LAND DIVERS OF VANUATU

Every spring, the natives of the Pentecost Islands in the nation of Vanuatu carry out a bizarre and hazardous custom: they dive to the ground from tall platforms, with nothing but slender vines tied around their ankles to break their fall.

The Pentecost Islanders have been performing this ritual for more than a hundred years—long before the first European bungee jumper. Known as "land diving," the custom has its origin in an ancient tribal myth. The legend has it that a husband and wife once quarreled, and the woman fled into the jungle. The husband followed, and discovered his wife high up in the branches of a tall tree. When he climbed towards her, she leapt from the tree. The husband leapt after her, not realizing that she had tied strong vines around her ankles. She survived; he did not.

Every spring, the Islanders begin preparing for the ritual weeks in advance. It takes nearly five weeks to construct the tower, which may stand as high as eighty feet. The men also turn up the soil at the base of the tower to provide a softer landing. Next, the vines are prepared. The chief cuts the first vine, then other vines are cut to match each diver's height.

Boys as young as eight make the jump, and men are under pressure to jump higher as a show of their bravery. The men take every precaution they can, but these are seldom enough—the Islanders sustain a number of serious injuries every year. Yet despite the risks, the hazardous custom of land diving may well continue for another hundred years.

TABOOS

• Churches on the Faeroe Islands, off Denmark, stand in yards overgrown with lush grass. There is a severe shortage of grass for the island's animals but the churchyard grass, when harvested, is always thrown into the sea.

• Cattle in India cannot be worked on Mondays—yet thier masters are not granted a day of rest.

• Farmers in the Maprik territory of New Guinea are forbidden to eat produce from their own land. Each farmer exhibits his crops in the marketplace, then exchanges his produce for that grown by another farmer.

• The Chief of the M'Betou tribe of the African Congo is forbidden to lay aside his uniform, hat, or spear—even in his sleep!

• The leaders who are forbidden to have a natural death! A chief of the Dinka tribe of Sudan, Africa, when he becomes fatally ill or so old that death appears near, is always buried alive!

Chapter 18

Death

A COMPANY IN WINDSOR, MASS., MAKES "LIFE COFFINS" — CUSTOM MADE CASKETS THAT CAN BE USED AS BOOKCASES or WINE CABINETS UNTIL THEY ARE NEEDED FOR BURIAL!

Death is the one frontier that we're all destined to explore. As you're about to read, some of us cross over into that uncharted territory by dramatic and extraordinary means. But while we might not be able to do much about the time, place or manner of our exits from this world, with a little fore-thought, we may be able to choose the legacies we leave behind. What epitaph, for example, best commemorates our lives? What type of tombstone suits us? Need we settle for staid granite, when we could go with, say, plate glass? Would a simple upright slab do the trick, or could our headstone be in the shape of. . .a pool table? A playing card? Or a cellular phone? Should we secret away the fragile vessels of flesh we abandon at the end of our lives, or display them, in their ever-changing states of decay, for the world to see? Ripley's offers here a glimpse into a world we're all one day fated to know: the secret lives of the dead.

• Every ten seconds, sixteen people die on earth—and forty-five more are born!

BRUSHES WITH DEATH

• **Bill Goss**, who wrote the book *The Luckiest Unlucky Man Alive*, has nearly died thirty times in the past forty-four years, including nearly drowning in the kitchen sink when his head became lodged between two running faucets!

• In 1960, writer **Ernest Hemingway** read his own obituary published in newspapers around the world after his plane crashed in Africa!

DEATH DEFERRED

• The bullet that found its mark after twenty years! In 1893, **Henry Ziegland**, of Honey Grove, Texas, jilted his sweetheart, who then killed herself. Her brother tried to avenge her by shooting Ziegland, but the

bullet only grazed his face and buried itself in a tree. The brother, thinking he had killed Ziegland, committed suicide. In 1913, Ziegland was cutting down the tree with the bullet in it—it was a tough job so he used dynamite—and the explosion sent the old bullet through Ziegland's head, killing him!

• **Nicola Baillot** (1791-1896), a Napoleonic sol-dier captured in the battle of Waterloo, was freed in

ON Borneo, IN THE 19TH CENTURY, WHEN A PERSON DIED, HIS BODY WAS SQUEEZED INTO A JAR AND KEPT IN THE HOUSE of HIS RELATIVES for A YEAR, PRIOR TO BURIAL!

1815 on a doctor's verdict that he was near death from tuberculosis—yet he lived for another eighty-one years.

CAUSES OF DEATH

• **Will Rogers**, America's most beloved humorist in the 1930s, unwittingly wrote his own obituary. Before he was killed in a plane crash in 1935, he had been working on what was to be his last newspaper column. The last word he wrote was "death."

• **Louis Le Debonnaire**, of France, was frightened to death by an eclipse.

• The man who was seen to death: **Wei Chieh**, son of Wei Huan (286-312), was popularly known as "The Jewel" on account of his great beauty. At the age of five, his handsome face and graceful form caused the populace to regard him as a supernatural being. He became the heir-apparent of China, but during political troubles it was necessary for him to flee to

the city of Nanking, where people crowded around him in such numbers and stared at him so hard that he was literally "seen to death."

• Author **Sholom Aleichem** disliked the number thirteen so much that none of his manuscripts had a page thirteen, and when he died on May 13, 1916, his epitaph was changed to read May 12!

• English philosopher **Francis Bacon** caught a cold and died after conducting an experiment on preserving meat in which he stuffed a dead chicken with snow!

• British novelist **Arnold Bennett** (1867-1931) died of typhoid fever during a demonstration to prove that the water in Paris was safe to drink!

• **Calchas**, an ancient soothsayer, died laughing after hearing he had outlived the predicted hour of his death!

• **Bat Masterson**, Dodge City's legendary lawman, died sitting at his desk at the *New York Morning Telegraph* where he worked as the sports editor!

• In 1923, a horse named "**Sweet Kiss**," ridden by Frank Hayes, won a race at Belmont Park in New York even though Hayes died in the saddle coming down the home stretch!

• In 1911, **Bobby Leech** survived going over Niagara Falls in a wooden barrel, but died several months later after slipping on a banana peel!

• So that composer **Giuseppe Verdi** (1813-1901) would not be disturbed as he lay dying, city officials in Milan, Italy, had the surrounding streets covered in straw to muffle the noise!

• French playwright **Molière** became ill and died while playing the role of the hypochondriac in his play *The Imaginary Invalid*!

• **George E. Spillman**, of Austin, Texas, died at 8:00 P.M. on the 8th day of the 8th month in 1988 at the age of 88!

• In 1931, an oil worker at a well site in Mexico drowned while suspended sixty feet in the air, even though he was two miles from the nearest pool of water!

AN ELABORATE BOAT OF BAMBOO, COVERED WITH SILK PAPER AND INTRICATE CARVINGS, WAS BUILT IN 1909 TO CARRY THE SPIRIT OF THE DECEASED DOWAGER EMPRESS OF CHINA TO HEAVEN *AND WAS BURNED ON THE DAY IT WAS LAUNCHED*

SUICIDE

• Wealthy people comprise eight percent of all suicides in the United States.

• **Baron Gros** (1771-1835), a French painter, was so hurt by criticism of his last painting that he drowned himself in three feet of water.

• The Roman epicure **Apicius**, first century A.D., financially ruined by his own elaborate banquets, poisoned himself in fear of starvation!

• **Charles Boothby Skrymshire** (1740-1800) was known as the prince of England's dandies—yet he ultimately committed suicide because he was tired of the trouble of donning his fancy dress.

• **Jean-Marie Roland** (1734-1793), a French financier, was sentenced to death by the French Revolutionary tribunal while he was in Normandy, far from the Parisian executioners. Knowing that if he went to the guillotine his estate would be confiscated, he assured his daughter an inheritance by taking his own life.

• **Jean Ciffer** committed suicide by eating his entire fortune. He died, but an autopsy was performed and the money was recovered.

DYING

• On his deathbed, the venerable **Bede** (673-735), an English monk, carefully divided up his most valued possession—a handful of pepper.

• Cards from beyond: **Donald Mir**, of Rochester, New York, created a line of greeting cards designed to be sent to the deceased's loved ones after the sender dies!

• In 1909, **Cesare Lombroso**, an Italian criminologist, who had a collection of human heads preserved in beeswax in glass bottles, left instructions for his own head to be added to the collection!

LAST WISHES

• **Pope Pius X**, unable during his lifetime to keep a promise to visit Venice, was borne there in a special gondola car forty-five years after his death.

• In his will, **Bill Johnson**, of Pasadena, California, asked that his ashes be loaded into two dozen fireworks shells and set off in the sky!

• When **Hazel Moore** of Melbourne, Australia, died, she left her estate of $20,000 to Michael O'Connor, who had kissed her once ten years before!

• **Napoleon's** last wish was to have his head shaved and his hair divided equally amongst his friends!

THE COSTLIEST FUNERAL IN HISTORY—$600,000,000 WAS SPENT ON THE FUNERAL OF ALEXANDER THE GREAT! 1000 miles of road were hewed through the wilderness so that the jewel-studded hearse—drawn by 64 horses—could travel from Babylon to Alexandria.

LAST WORDS

• The last words of the eighteenth-century French grammarian **Dominique Bounhours** were, "I am about to—or I am going to—die. Either expression is used."

• The last words whispered by **Charles Gussman**, a television writer who wrote for the soap opera *Days of Our Lives*, were, ". . .and now for a final word from our sponsor…"!

FUNERALS

• In past years, death notices in North Carolina were delivered to each home in the community pinned to palm leaf fans.

PREPARING THE BODY

• The jade funeral suit of **Princess Tou Wan** of China, who died in the first century B.C., is composed of two thousand pieces of jade sewn together with gold and silk-covered wire.

• A tribe in Malaysia observes a waiting period of twenty years between the time a man dies and when he's buried!

FUNERAL ON SKATES

IN THE LAND OF THE WENDS, ON THE RIVER SPREE IN GERMANY, A NETWORK OF LAKES AND STREAMS TAKES THE PLACE OF ROADS — MOURNERS IN FUNERAL PROCESSIONS *WEAR ICE SKATES IN WINTER — USE BOATS IN SUMMER*

TRANSPORTING THE BODY

• In some parts of Britain some thoroughfares were designated "corpse roads," to be used only by mourners going to the local cemetery!

• "The Universe Hearse": **Todd** and **Kiaralinda Ramquist**, of Safety Harbor, Florida, drive a hearse that is covered with thirty thousand tiny Plexiglas pieces that have been engraved with words to live by!

• Seminole Indians used a pole as a bier from which the deceased was suspended by cloth loops.

FUNERAL RITES

• During the funeral of Roman Emperor Nero's wife, **Poppea**, more perfume was sprinkled than the country of Arabia could produce in a year!

• In China, packets of "joss" money, in denominations up to fifty million, are burned in honor of dead ancestors and to guard against evil!

• The Batak warriors of northern Sumatra carried life-size wooden puppets, carved in the likeness of the deceased and fitted with sponges in the eyes, to ward off evil spirits at funerals!

CREMATIONS OF NOBLE TRIBESMEN ON BALI WERE CARRIED OUT BY PLACING THEIR BODIES IN HOLLOWED-OUT TREE TRUNKS CARVED TO LOOK LIKE COWS.

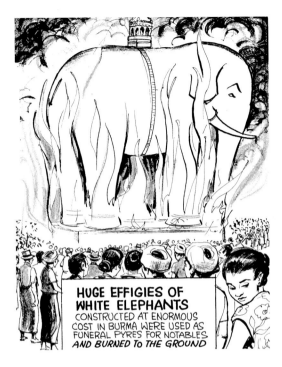

HUGE EFFIGIES OF WHITE ELEPHANTS CONSTRUCTED AT ENORMOUS COST IN BURMA WERE USED AS FUNERAL PYRES FOR NOTABLES *AND BURNED TO THE GROUND*

THE DANCING CORPSES

A wealthy native of the Kapsiki Tribe of Africa is prepared after death for the gay life a person of standing is expected to lead in the next world by being hoisted out on the shoulders of the village blacksmith— and getting a dancing lesson that lasts for hours!

• **Bill Roberts**, of Madison, Wisconsin, staged his own funeral while he was still alive! He even walked ahead of the coffin and its six pallbearers to the reception!

• A nineteenth-century Dutch merchant named **Kales** left instructions in his will that his coffin be lined with cigar boxes and tobacco and that every smoker in the Netherlands be invited to his funeral!

• Cunard Line, owners of the *Queen Elizabeth II*, has started a special service that allows next-of-kin to book passage for a deceased person who wishes to be buried at sea!

• A company in Des Moines, Iowa, offers a service in which the ashes of hunters are loaded into shotgun shells and fired during memorial services!

• In November 1989, **Polly Ketron** arranged and attended her own funeral, then celebrated her seventy-sixth birthday two days later.

THE FUNERAL THAT LASTED A WHOLE YEAR!

The body of **General Yi Chun** was carried in a funeral procession from Peking to Kashgar Sinklang 2,300 miles away. The funeral lasted from June 1, 1912, to June 1, 1913.

A COMPANY in Osaka, Japan, OFFERS ELABORATE, HIGH-TECH FUNERALS COMPLETE WITH A MOTORIZED COFFIN, SPOTLIGHTS, DRY ICE and A LASER SHOW!

HANNAH BESWICK of Lancashire, England, LEFT INSTRUCTIONS IN HER WILL THAT HER BODY BE REGULARLY INSPECTED for SIGNS of LIFE, SO HER DOCTOR HAD IT PLACED INSIDE A HOLLOW GRANDFATHER CLOCK FOR EASY VIEWING!

• The Point Coupe Funeral Home in Louisiana offers mourners a chance to view their deceased relatives through a picture window without leaving their cars!

• The remains of an Egyptian prince were given a Christian burial in Middlebury, Vermont— 3,828 years after his death!

• The feast of the dead: The Igorots of the Philippines, upon the death of a family member, stage a month-long banquet with the corpse propped in a chair as the guest of honor.

• **Stonewall Jackson's** amputated left arm was given its own formal military funeral near Chancellorsville, Virginia, while his body was burned over one hundred miles away in Lexington!

• The world's first space funeral: The ashes of *Star Trek* creator **Gene Roddenberry** were blasted into space on board a Pegasus rocket that will circle the Earth for years!

• The Uape Indians of the Upper Amazon drink the ashes of their dead mixed with casiri, a local beverage, in the belief they will absorb all the good qualities of the deceased!

EULOGIES

• Eulogy given in the western Australian town of Sandstone in 1908, by a Jewish prospector: "There lies the body of the first Jew to die in Sandstone. Please God may he be the last, because I'm the only other one in this district, and I'd hate to die in a place like this."

• When English beekeeper **Margaret Bell** died, hundreds of bees swarmed around her house and stayed for over an hour!

• A four-faced clock displayed outside of a San Francisco, California, jewelry store stopped working when the proprietor, **Rocco Matteuci**, died!

• The well that mourned **Columbus**: A well in Palos, Spain, that supplied the water for the three ships with which Columbus discovered the New World dried up suddenly on May 20, 1506, the day on which Columbus died!

BURIAL AND CREMATION

• **Patty Kramp**, of Edmonton, Alberta, Canada, makes coffins out of logs that are lined with leather and have horseshoes for handles!

• **Marquis Yi**, a fifth-century b.c. Chinese ruler, was buried with a three-ton set of sixty-four bronze bells and twenty-one young female attendants to play them for him in the afterlife!

• Actor **Errol Flynn** was buried with six bottles of whiskey in his coffin!

• A headstone in Ruidoso, New Mexico, reads: "Here lies John Yeast, pardon me for not rising."

• The skeletons of natives of Goulburn Island, Australia, are always buried in hollowed-out tree trunks.

WHEN HE DIED IN 1683, RELIGIOUS LEADER ROGER WILLIAMS WAS BURIED BESIDE AN APPLE TREE IN PROVIDENCE, R.I. — THE ROOTS OF THE TREE SLOWLY ABSORBED HIS BODY AND ASSUMED A HUMAN SHAPE!

• The **Tlingit Tribe** of Alaska cremated all their dead except shamans, whom they believed would not burn. Shamans were embalmed and placed in primitive shelters along with a slave, sacrificed to serve them in the afterlife.

• **Willie Stokes**, of Chicago, Illinois, was buried in a car-shaped coffin fitted with Illinois license plates!

• In 1991, a company in Sydney, Australia, began making "ecologically safe" coffins out of recycled newspapers!

• **Blackbird**, a chief of the Omaha Indian tribe, was buried on the back of his horse!

• **Gianna Lahainer**, of Palm Beach, Florida, delayed her husband's burial during the high-society party season by having him embalmed and put on ice for forty days!

• **Alice Whitfield** was buried sitting upright in her favorite rocking chair!

• When **Jimmy Dale Struble**, of Grand Junction, Colorado, died in 1992, he was buried standing up, with his boots on!

• When **Grover McIntyre**, of Chester, Pennsylvania, died, he was buried in a custom-made casket decorated with parts from his Mercedes-Benz car, including the grille and hood ornament!

• For over twenty years, a Tibetan monk lived in a walled-up tomb with only a small peephole to receive his daily food!

• When **Aurora Schuck**, of Aurora, Indiana, died in 1989, her body was buried inside her 1976 Cadillac.

• The sarcophagus containing the body of **Cardinal Guglielmo Fieschi** in the church of San Lorenzo Fuori Le Mura in Rome, Italy, was originally a pagan coffin and is adorned with the likenesses of pagan gods.

• In ancient Siam, when a member of royalty died, a Siamese cat was placed in the same tomb, which had tunnels that allowed the cat to escape to a temple, where it would be protected for life!

• **Dennis Hoegh**, of Gladstone, Michigan, makes coffins for dogs, cats, hamsters, and turkeys!

• **Sir Walter Raleigh** requested that his coffin be lined with old cigar boxes!

• In 1991, **Connie Scramlin**, a Detroit Tigers fan from Flint, Michigan, was buried in a team uniform in a casket bearing the team colors and covered in tiger lilies!

• The American Funeral Service Museum, in Houston, Texas, has a 1925 solid-glass casket on display, as well as a funeral bus in which the family, pallbearers, and the deceased all rode to the cemetery together!

• Composer **Frederic Chopin** requested that his body be cut open before burial—to make sure he was not alive!

Kane Quaye Soneth of Accra, Ghana, CREATES COFFINS IN UNUSUAL SHAPES— INCLUDING GIANT LOBSTERS, COCOA PODS, CARS and CHICKENS — THAT REFLECT THE OCCUPATION of the DECEASED!

REST IN PEACE   IN MEMORY

• The **Earl of Antrim**, Ireland, requested that he be buried upright on a hill so that he could look down on his castle, but drunken gravediggers buried him upside down by mistake!

CREMATION

• Be an astronaut in the afterlife! A company in Houston, Texas, will fly a person's cremated remains into deep space for $4,800!

• When **Dean Goddin**, of Farmington, Illinois, died, he requested that his best friend Everett Staffeldt place his ashes inside a pair of carved duck decoys and take them with him hunting every season!

Soul Pots— In Cameroon, Africa, pots are sculptured to resemble a native's departed parents, and in the belief the pots are a refuge for their souls, a dutiful son daily provides nourishment by dropping in meat and beer.

CLAY FUNERAL URNS were made by the ancient Mayans in the shape of animals.

• In 1998, **Jose Fernandez**, a weather researcher, had his ashes scattered in the eye of Hurricane Danielle, four hundred miles off the coast of Miami, Florida!

• The ashes of astronomer **Eugene Shoemaker**—who had always wanted to go to the moon—were carried aboard the 1999 Lunar Prospector flight! The vehicle landed in a moon crater as part of a controlled crash!

• Cremation urns used to hold the ashes of the ancient Etruscans were kept in tombs shaped to resemble the houses in which the deseased had lived.

BURIED ALIVE

• Writer **Hans Christian Andersen** was so afraid of being buried alive that he kept a letter on his nightstand that read, "I'm not really dead, I only look as if I am!"

• In 1968, **Emma Smith** spent one hundred and one days buried alive in Skegness, England, setting a world record at the time.

DEPARTED

• **Hallie Broadribb**, of Valleyview, Alberta, Canada, who had her leg amputated due to cancer, kept the limb in a freezer for a year, then held a funeral and buried it in its own casket!

• The wax-embalmed bodies of the late Hapsburg emperors are held in crypts in a monastery in Vienna, Austria, while their mummified intestines are in Saint Stephan's Cathedral, and their hearts are kept in the Augustiner Church!

MOURNING AND REMEMBERING

• During the Edwardian Era, it was customary for mourners in Sussex, England, to decorate a beehive in black ribbon as a means of notifying the bees of a death in the family!

• When his owner died in 1858, a Skye terrier named **"Bobby"** stayed at his master's grave in Edinburgh, Scotland, for fourteen years.

• In 1990, 5,271 tap dancers performed a choreographed routine in New York City as a tribute to the late **Sammy Davis, Junior**!

• In China, people place winter clothing and paper money on the graves of their ancestors for them to use in the afterlife!

THE HEAD-STONE on the grave of Platt R. Spencer whose style of writing was adopted throughout America bears his name in his own spencerian hand. Ashtabula County, Ohio.

GRAVESTONES in Corwen, Wales OFTEN HAD WAVY TOPS —SO MOURNERS COULD KNEEL CONVENIENTLY WITHOUT GETTING THEIR KNEES WET IN THE GRASS

• "**Shep**," a sheepdog, after seeing the casket of its owner loaded onto a train in 1936, watched every passenger train for five years at the Great Northern Railway depot in Fort Benton, Montana!

• Every year since 1717 in Wotton, Surrey, England, five boys receive forty shillings each for laying their hands on the tombstone of **William Glanville** while reciting verses from the Bible!

• In Guruayur, India, elephants and their drivers pay homage to an elephant that died in 1977 by placing garlands on a statue erected in its honor!

• Every four years in Anambanzana, Madagascar, there is a ceremony in which relatives buy new clothes for deceased ancestors whose bones are dug up and then paraded around the village!

• A clock in the palace of **King Louis XIV** of France stopped at 7:45 A.M., the precise time of the king's death!

• It is customary in Japan for the family of a deceased person to hand out small packets of salt to mourners to protect them from the dead!

• When an Asmat warrior of New Guinea dies, his eldest son inherits his skull, and uses it as a pillow at night!

• In 1971, after the death of a friend, **John Francis** took a vow of silence that lasted seventeen years!

• Women of the Warramunga tribe of Australia do not speak for a year after the death of their husbands—instead communicating only with hand and arm gestures!

• The mourning clock: The astronomical clock of Hampton Court, London, which was constructed in 1540, always stopped when any long-time resident of the palace died.

• A mail service to the grave: Natives of the Suki tribe in Africa write letters

to their dead relatives for a full year after their death.

• The faithful mourner: **Ludwig Devrient**, actor friend of E. T. A. Hoffmann, originator of *The Tales of Hoffmann*, visited the latter's grave and drank countless champagne toasts to his departed companion three days a week for ten years.

• A widow in Tikarland, Africa, as a gesture of mourning, must wear two buttons from her deceased husband's clothing, in her nostrils!

• Dani tribesmen of New Guinea, to mourn a relative or repent a misdeed, amputate one of their fingers.

• An aborigine widow of the Murray River tribe of Australia must mourn her dead husband for three months, adding an additional layer of clay to her head each day. At the end of the mourning period the fourteen-pound coating of clay and all her hair are removed together and placed in the husband's grave—to assure him his widow has truly mourned him.

TOMBSTONE OF A.D. HULING, A BLACKSMITH, *DISPLAYING HIS ANVIL, HAMMER AND TONGS* Brownell, Kans.

GRAVES

GRAVE SITES

• The ashes of "The Great Lafayette," a British illusionist, were buried with the embalmed body of his dog, "Beauty," in a glass coffin!

• In Torajaland, South Sulawesi, Indonesia, painted wooden effigies of the dead are ritually placed in cliff-side graves!

• When opera great **Enrico Caruso** died, his body was placed in a transparent coffin in Del Planto Cemetery in Naples, Italy. His clothes were regularly changed for his adoring fans!

- Astronomer **James Lick** is buried at the base of the telescope at the Lick Observatory, located on Mount Hamilton in San Jose, California.

- **Sir Nicholas Crispe**, a courtier of England's King Charles I, had his heart buried at the foot of the King's throne!

- **Richard Slyhoff** left instructions that he was to be buried under a leaning rock in Jefferson County, Pennsylvania, because he believed that on Judgment Day the rock would fall and hide him from the devil! Unfortunately for Mr. Slyhoff, soil erosion eventually moved the rock ten feet!

- **Count Carl Von Cosel**, of Key West, Florida, left a telephone at the grave of his beloved **Maria Elena De Hoyos** after she died in 1931, so that he could continue to speak with her!

- **Jim Tipton** documents and photographs the graves of celebrities and puts them on the World Wide Web!

- Singer **Steve Goodman** had his ashes buried under home plate at Chicago's Wrigley Field.

- The embalmed body of the sixteenth-century Spanish conquistador **Francisco Pizarro** is still on display in a glass casket in Lima, Peru!

- The preserved body of a man who worked as a gardener, and later as a footman, at the Maharajah of Mysore's palace in Bangalore, India, is on display in a glass case!

- "Grave Line," a company in Los Angeles, California, takes tourists on a tour of the graves of such Hollywood stars as Marilyn Monroe, Montgomery Clift, and Douglas Fairbanks—in a hearse!

- In New Guinea, the mummified bodies of dozens of Kukukuku tribemen, who died defending their village eighty years ago, are displayed on scaffolding to honor their bravery!

- The remains of **Henry Trigg**, a farmer in Hartfordshire, England, were placed in the rafters of a barn that is now used as a bank!

- Built in 1493, the door to the tomb of Holy Man Seyif Ghazi in Turkish Anatolia is solid silver.

- In Sabina, Ohio, the embalmed body of a man was on public display for thirty-six years, in the hopes that someone would be able to identify him!

- The tomb of the thirteenth Dalai Lama of Tibet, Lhasa, is covered with 30,000 ounces of solid gold—valued at $9,000,000.

- Scientist in Ladby, Denmark, uncovered a one-thousand-year-old Viking war ship that held the body of a Viking warrior buried with his weapons, his favorite hunting dogs, and twelve horses.

- The monument in Graceland Cemetery, Chicago, Illinois, over the grave of **William A. Hulbert**, the first president of the National Baseball League, is a stone baseball.

- A tombstone in Fairplay, Colorado, marks the grave of a burro. The burro, named "**Prunes**," died in 1930 at the age of sixty-three, after having worked in all the mines of the district for a continuous period of sixty-two years.

ROSE MARTIN of Fall River, Mass., was buried in her 1962 Corvette. (1998)

THE **GRAVE** of MANFRED ASHO A WEALTHY NATIVE OF THE CAMEROONS, WHO DIED IN 1933, IS TOPPED BY A HUGE STATUE AND BESIDE IT IS A TABLE *ON WHICH A MEAL IS SERVED FOR HIS SOUL EACH VISITING DAY*

Concert pianist **Madge Ward's** gravestone is a 25-ton black granite grand piano! (Tyler, Texas)

THE **GRAVE** of **EDGAR ALLAN POE** in Baltimore, Md., HAS BEEN VISITED BY AN UNKNOWN PERSON FOR OVER **35** YEARS ON JANUARY 19th, POE'S BIRTHDAY, WHO PLACES ON THE FAMED 19th CENTURY MYSTERY WRITER'S TOMBSTONE *A BOTTLE OF COGNAC AND A BOUQUET OF ROSES.*

• The graves of Chukche natives of Siberia are decorated with reindeer antlers, with an additional set being added each year.

• In Nara, Japan, a lantern in the tomb of the Buddhist priest **Kobo Daishi** in the monastery of Koya San has been burning continuously for 1,126 years.

• The tomb of the Queen's little finger in Seoul, South Korea: When **Queen Min** of Korea was murdered and her body burned by the Japanese in 1895, the Koreans searched the ruins, but all they could find was a bone of her little finger. An entire city was then destroyed to make a beautiful burial ground for her finger.

• The sarcophagus of the first Tashi Lama of Tibet, in the monastery of Tashi, Lhumpo, twenty-five feet high and twenty-five feet wide, is studded with precious stones, and contains a ton of gold.

• The grave of a chief of the Saturiwa Indians of sixteenth-century Florida was topped by the large ornamental shell he had used in life as a drinking cup.

• The Tomb of the Horse: A magnificent temple was erected in Baroda, India, over the grave of a horse that belonged to Sayed, a Hindu saint.

TOMBSTONES

• A headstone in a cemetery at Saint Kilda, Victoria, Australia, depicts a hand holding an overflowing jug of beer. The stone was the result of a threat often made by the widow to her thirsty husband!

• A stone caboose in Union Cemetery, Uhrichsville, Ohio, marks the grave of a railway worker who was killed by a runaway caboose!

• Dairy magnate **Gail Borden** had a tomb built in the shape of a milk can!

Mr. and **Mrs. Vieira's** headstone is shaped like a set of playing cards and a pair of dice.

R. E. Bahm's grave in Husser, Louisiana, is decorated with the collection of Native American arrowheads he cherished since boyhood.

CEMETERY LOTS SIDE BY SIDE
Beloit, Wis.

SHOES   STOCKINGS

"The Tomb of the Unknown Plumber"
A gravestone covered in pipes and faucets in the Main Street Cemetery in Plaquemine, La., belongs to an unknown man who died in 1904 and worked as a plumber!

The Grave of **Guy Akrish** of Ashkelon, Israel, has a head-stone shaped like a giant cellular phone!

GRAVESTONE IN COOPERSTOWN, N.Y.
SUPPOSED TO READ "OH LORD SHE IS THINE"
BUT THE STONE CUTTER FOUND THE STONE TOO NARROW

OH LORD
SHE IS THIN

• A company in California makes solar-powered gravestones that greet visitors with recorded messages!

• In the early 1900s, tombstones were sold through the Sears catalog!

• The gravestone in Laurel Grove Cemetery in New Jersey of electrician **Sal Giardino** is shaped like a giant light bulb!

• A child's school slate in a wooden frame, erected as a tombstone in Glancourse Scotland, stood for ninety-one years.

EPITAPHS

• "Here stands old Britt Bailey." —Epitaph to James Britton Bailey, who was buried standing up because he refused to look up to any man.

• "Husband: I am anxiously awaiting you, 1827." "Wife: here I am, 1867." —Gravestones in a Paris, France, cemetery.

• "Here lies an atheist: All dressed up and no place to go."—Epitaph in Thurmont, Maryland.

• "Here lies, cut down like unripe fruit, the wife of Deacon Amos Shute. She died of drinking too much coffee, Anny Dominy Eighteen Forty." —Epitaph in Canaan, New Hampshire.

• The tomb in Salona, Yugoslavia, of **Monsignor Franc Builc**, a celebrated archaeologist, is a replica of an ancient Roman dwelling and bears this epitaph which he wrote himself: "Here lies a sinner."

• A tombstone erected by disappointed heirs in the new church at Amsterdam, Holland: "Effen Nyt" (exactly nothing.)

• "Here lies the body of Emily White: she signaled left and then turned right." —A gravestone in a cemetery in Huddersfield, England!

• The epitaph of the late **Shirley Pitts** of London, England, dubbed "The Queen of Shoplifters" reads, "Gone shopping"!

• "Tim: A good dog." —Grave marker in Cottonwood Spring, Coachella Valley, California, for a canine that saved its master's life by intercepting the deadly strike of a rattlesnake.

Epitaph ON THE TOMBSTONE OF AN UNKNOWN MAN near the Molyneux River, N.Z.

• A tombstone in Oak Woods Cemetery, Chicago, Illinois, reads, "See, I told you I was sick."

• A tombstone in Iowa of a traveling salesman reads, "My trip is ended, send my samples home."

• The tombstone of an attorney in Willwood Cemetery, Rockford, Illinois: "Goembel, John E. 1867-1946: the defense rests."

• The gravestone of American actress **Joan Hackett** reads, "Joan Hackett: 1934-1983. Go away—I'm asleep."

• A tombstone in Weather Hill, New England, reads: "Here lies the body of Samuel Proctor, who lived and died without a doctor."

GRAVESTONES in New England, IN THE 1600s OFTEN FEATURED CARVED SKELETONS

• The epitaph of **Thomas Windell** of New Albany, Indiana, the inventor of glass tombstones, reads: "T. Windell: A curious fact it has sometimes been said that he made it while living but enjoys it while dead."

• "Here lies Lester Moore, four slugs from a forty-four, no Les, no Moore" —Epitaph in Boot Hill Cemetery, Tombstone, Arizona.

• A gravestone near Uniontown, Pennsylvania: "Here lies the body of Johnathon Blake, stepped on the gas instead of the brake."

• "Some mother's son." —Epitaph on the grave of an unknown sailor in Patrick Churchyard, Isle of Man, England.

• A tombstone in a cemetery in Medway, Massachusetts, reads, "Beneath this stone, this lump of clay, lies Uncle Peter Daniels, who too early in the month of May, took off his winter flannels."

• At the Colon Cemetery in Colon, Michigan, the "Magic Capitol of the World," the headstone of **John Jones** reads, "Now I have to go and fool Saint Peter"!

• "If I was so soon to be done for, what was I ever begun for?"—Old Hill Cemetery, Plymouth, Massachusetts.

• A tombstone in Lee's Summit, Missouri, reads, "1909—died whenever. Guess who—Me."

• "Here lies John Phillips, accidentally shot as a mark of affection by his brother." —Epitaph in a cemetery, Bath, Maine.

• "Owen Moore
Is gone away
Owin' more
Than he could pay."
—Epitaph in Surrey, England.

• "In memory of Elizabeth, who should have been the wife of Simeon Palmer." —Gravestone in Little Compton, Rhode Island.

• Someone who did not think much of the local brew at Kissing Point, Australia, penned the following words for a dead friend's gravestone: "Ye who wish to lie here, drink Squire's Beer."

• "In memory of Ellen Shannon, aged twenty-six, fatally burned 1870 by the explosion of a lamp filled with Danforth's Non-explosive fluid." —Epitaph in a cemetery at Guard, Pennsylvania.

• "Here lies the body of Solomon Peas under the daisies and under the trees Peas is not here—only the pod; Peas shelled out; went home to God." —Gravestone in Wetumpka, Alabama.

The JOHNSON FAMILY PLOT in London Cemetery, London, Kentucky. The center grave is that of E. H. Johnson. The gravestone to Johnson's left reads: "Molly R., wife of E. H. Johnson. 1878-1917. No Better Woman Ever Lived." The gravestone to the right: "Sarah E., wife of E. H. Johnson. 1874-1906. No Better Woman Ever Lived."

VERNA RICHARDSON of Madison, Wisc., makes caskets that look like houses!

• "Here lies the father of twenty-nine, He would have had more but he didn't have time."—Gravestone in Moultrie, Georgia.

• "Here lies Fred. . .
Who was alive
And is dead
there's no more to be said"
—Grave of Frederick, Prince of Wales.

• "Here lies A. P. Sisson: God only knows what will become of him in the future."—Gravestone in Red Oak, Louisiana.

MEMORIALS AND MONUMENTS

• At Japan's Asahi Breweries Company, deceased workers are honored on a marble memorial at which executives regularly report on company business!

• The names of thirty-eight living people—originally presumed dead—are on the Vietnam Veteran's Memorial in Washington, D.C.!

• The statue erected in Vienna, Austria, to commemorate **Franz Schubert** cost more than the composer made in his entire life!

• In Temple Yard, Shimoda, Japan, a monument to a cow, erected by the butchers of Tokyo in 1931, marks the spot where in 1858 the first cow in Japan was slaughtered for human consumption.

GRAVEYARDS

• During the Victorian era, visitors to New York cemeteries were charged admission for guided tours of the grave sites!

• The Saint Joseph Cemetery in Rayne, Louisiana, is the only cemetery in the United States that faces north and south!

• Yokohama Chuo Cemetery in Japan features a lifelike robotic replica of a Buddhist priest with blinking eyes that chants over the dead each morning!

• At the Illinois Pet Cemetery in Hanover Park, Illinois, pet owners can be buried alongside their pets!

• The Hamilton Mausoleum near Glasgow, Scotland, has a fifteen-second echo in which a single voice can sound like a choir!

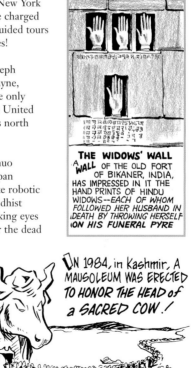

THE WIDOWS' WALL A WALL OF THE OLD FORT OF BIKANER, INDIA, HAS IMPRESSED IN IT THE HAND PRINTS OF HINDU WIDOWS--EACH OF WHOM FOLLOWED HER HUSBAND IN DEATH BY THROWING HERSELF ON HIS FUNERAL PYRE

IN 1984, in Kashmir, A MAUSOLEUM WAS ERECTED TO HONOR THE HEAD of a SACRED COW!

THE SKELETON THAT IS A MEMORIAL TO A SCIENTIST **DR. FRIEDRICH THEODOR MECKEL** (1756-1803) PROFESSOR OF SURGERY AT THE UNIVERSITY OF HALLE, GERMANY, WAS THE FIRST MAN TO BEQUEATH HIS BODY TO SCIENCE—AND HIS SKELETON HAS BEEN PRESERVED AS A MONUMENT TO HIM FOR 199 YEARS.

• The Key Underwood Coon Dog Memorial Graveyard near Tuscumbia, Alabama, is a cemetery dedicated to just one breed of dog—the coon hound!

• A cemetery in Memphis, the ancient capital of Egypt, contains over sixty tombs holding mummified bulls buried in stone sarcophagi!

AFTER DEATH

• **William Frederick Heitmuller**, a right fielder for the Los Angeles Angels, won the 1912 Pacific coast batting championship with a .335 average—twenty days after he died!

• **Charles Tomlinson**, a retired funeral home director in Florida, has read his own published obituary

• At the Paco Cemetery in Manila, the Philippines, remains are cached in chambers in the cemetery's wall for an annual rental fee. If families fail to pay the fee, the remains are removed and burned. Ripley's Believe It or Not! founder, Robert Ripley, is shown here inspecting the graves (1932.)

twice, once in 1995, and once in 1996!

• When he died in 1832, British philosopher **Jeremy Bentham** left his body to the London hospital—on the condition his skeleton and a wax likeness of his face are present at all board meetings! The tradition has been maintained for over 170 years.

CORPSES THAT DON'T DECAY

• When he died, the body of **Chih Hang**, a Buddhist monk, was placed in an urn for five years. The body did not decay, so his followers in Taiwan had it gilded in pure gold and turned into a shrine.

• The body of **Sir Friedrich Von Kahlbutz**, on display in Neustadt, Germany, has been naturally mummified without any preservatives!

MOBILE CORPSES

• When he died in 1928, writer **Thomas Hardy's** ashes were buried in Westminster Abbey in England—but the family cat stole his heart. It was later recovered and buried in Stinson, England.

TEMPORARY CORPSES

• **Sam Pearce**, of Glanville, South Australia, was officially pronounced dead on two occasions. The first time was in 1906, when he was admitted to a hospital, pronounced dead, and sealed in a coffin. Just as he was being lowered into his grave, he revived and hollered to be released! He was driven back to the hospital in his hearse. Thirteen years later, a police officer was called to guard Pearce's house to guard his body after an Adelaide newspaper reported him dead. The officer excused himself later that morning when the "corpse" got up and made breakfast!

• A native of Thursday Island, Australia, was badly mauled while pearl diving and pronounced dead by friends who pulled his bloody body from the sea. They wrapped him in canvas for burial, but just as the "body" was about to be lowered into its grave, it sat up and emitted a loud groan. Those who didn't run away in terror unwrapped the man. Six months later he was diving for pearls again!

• Two-year-old **Christopher Falcon**, son of David Falcon and Beatriz Templa of Cebu, Philippines, was pronounced dead on the morning of Good Friday, March 26, 1948. He had "died" of whooping cough. Friends and neighbors gathered to hold vigil over his tiny white coffin. Six hours had passed when, to the amazement of those gathered around him, Christopher suddenly revived! The incident created a widespread sensation, and young Christopher went on to live a normal, healthy life.

• The man whose life was saved because he was bitterly hated! **Davit Beck** (1621-1656), famed Dutch court painter who would never permit wine to touch his lips, was pronounced dead in 1647. His servants, bitter against their tyrannical master, poured wine into the corpse's mouth which unwittingly revived their master!

• Old Man's Day is celebrated on October 2 in Hertfordshire, England, to commemorate **Matthew Hall**, a sixteenth-century farmer, presumed dead, who was revived when pallbearers accidentally dropped his coffin onto the road!

• **Musyoka Mutata**, of Kitui, Kenya, was pronounced dead three times during his life, but he revived the first two times his body was placed in a coffin!

• The fourteenth-century Italian poet **Petrarch** was declared dead in 1344, yet twenty hours later he suddenly sat up in bed! He lived for another thirty years.

UNBURIED CORPSES

• The corpse that found its way home: **Ann Gourlay**, a passenger on the schooner *Claire Clarendon* when it was wrecked off the Isle of Wight in 1836, was drowned, but her body was carried fifty miles by the tides, and deposited on the beach in front of her father's cottage.

• Coughlan's Come Home Again! **Charles Coughlan**, of Prince Edward Island, died in 1899 and was buried in Galveston, Texas. His coffin was washed out to sea, floated two thousand miles, and finally washed ashore—on Prince Edward Island, Coughlan's home!

• When England's **Sir Walter Raleigh** was beheaded in 1618, his wife Elizabeth buried his body but kept his embalmed head in a bag for the last thirty years of her life.

GRISLY HARVEST ON THE BODY FARM; DECAYING CORPSES YIELD A BUMPER CROP OF FORENSIC EVIDENCE

Wander too close to an obscure padlocked enclosure on the wooded grounds of the University of Tennessee, and you're sure to get a whiff of something unpleasant. Death, decay, rotting flesh—human flesh.

No, this is not a crime scene, although it could easily be mistaken for one. It's the Body Farm, the only forensic lab of its kind. Inside this three acre lot, more than two hundred bodies are decaying, in various simulated scenarios of murder: in the trunks of cars, under tarps, and under piles of leaves.

Half of the world's forensic anthropologists have studied here, under the tutelage of forensic anthropologist Doctor William Bass. Bass created the Body Farm in 1971, after police asked him to identify several badly decomposed bodies, some of which were no more than piles of bones. Bass recognized the need to study more closely the processes human bodies go through as they decay under various conditions.

The more he and his pupils learned about the effects of time, weather, and other factors in the deterioration process, the more they would be able to tell police about the circumstances of a given crime.

Where do the Body Farm's corpses come from? Many are unclaimed bodies; others were donated by those who wished to have their bodies willed to science—a gift of forensic knowledge to future generations. After all, as Doctor Bass puts it, "Why, when you die, should you stop helping people?"

Chapter 19

Entertainment

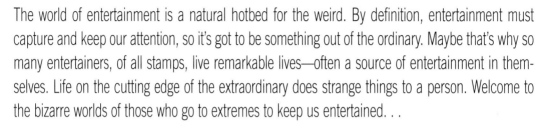

Believe *It* or *Not.*/ OLIVER HARDY WAS A FAMOUS **MOVIE VILLAIN** *BEFORE* HE *TEAMED UP* WITH COMIC PARTNER STAN LAUREL./

The world of entertainment is a natural hotbed for the weird. By definition, entertainment must capture and keep our attention, so it's got to be something out of the ordinary. Maybe that's why so many entertainers, of all stamps, live remarkable lives—often a source of entertainment in themselves. Life on the cutting edge of the extraordinary does strange things to a person. Welcome to the bizarre worlds of those who go to extremes to keep us entertained. . .

ACTORS AND ACTRESSES

CLASSIC STARS

• The first movie star! In 1893, **Fred Ott**, an aide in Thomas Alva Edison's lab in West Orange, New Jersey, gave the first performance in film history: a sneeze!

• **Mickey Mouse** was so popular during the 1930s that he was billed on movie marquees as prominently as Greta Garbo.

• Actress **Lillian Gish** played Lionel Barrymore's daughter in an early silent film, his wife in a 1930s film, and his mother in the 1947 film *Duel in the Sun*!

• Charlie Chan, the fictional Chinese detective created by **Earl Derr Biggers**, was never portrayed in the movies by a Chinese actor!

• Actress **Sarah Bernhardt** frequently slept in a coffin and once consulted a doctor to have the tail of a tiger grafted to the base of her spine!

• Actor **George Raft** turned down the lead roles in *High Sierra*, *The Maltese Falcon*, and *Casablanca*, roles that made Humphrey Bogart famous.

• Actress **Helen Hayes**, whose career spanned eight decades, won three Tonys, two Oscars, an Emmy, and even a Grammy for a recorded reading of the Bill of Rights!

• A Tony medallion stolen from actress **Jessica Tandy** in the 1950s was found in a riverbed by Jack Willemse of Parkhill, Ontario, Canada, and returned to her forty years later!

• American actress **Joan Crawford** had a contract with MGM Studios that stipulated the time she had to be in bed each night!

• During the 1940s, nylon stockings belonging to movie actress **Betty Grable** were sold at auction for $40,000 and later made into parachutes!

LON CHANEY TO ACHIEVE HIS TERRIFYING CHARACTER IN "THE PHANTOM OF THE OPERA" IN 1925, *INSERTED HOOKS IN HIS NOSTRILS TO STRETCH HIS NOSE*

• American film star **John Wayne** began his career by playing "Singing Sam," the first singing cowboy!

• In 1964, an African Masai chief tried to "buy" actress Carroll Baker as a wife for one hundred fifty cows, two hundred goats, and $750 cash!

• Actor **Sir Lawrence Olivier** tripped over a doorway and fell into the footlights during his first professional stage performance!

• The sound effects for actor Gene Kelley's dancing feet in the film *Singin' in the Rain* were made by two women tap dancing in buckets of water!

• In the film *Gold Diggers of 1933*, actress **Ginger Rogers** sang the song "We're in the Money" in pig Latin!

• **Spencer Tracy's** 1937 Oscar for Best Actor was mistakenly engraved with the name "Dick Tracy"!

• Hollywood actress **Ava Gardner** left a trust fund of several million dollars, her mansion, and a personal maid to her dog, "Morgan"!

• Film star **Erroll Flynn**, while visiting Cuba in the 1930s, hired an orchestra to follow him wherever he went!

• Actor **Maurice Chevalier's** movie contract had a clause that rendered the agreement void if he lost his French accent!

• *Tarzan* star **Johnny Weissmuller** had a contract that stipulated he had to weigh one hundred ninety pounds or less, and for every pound over one hundred ninety he was docked $5,000—up to $50,000 a day!

• Movie star **Edmund Low** (1890-1971) once had a $35,000 insurance policy on his nose!

• Actress **Greta Garbo** had six safes installed in her Duesenberg car!

• Western movie star **Roy Rogers** once received 78,852 letters from fans in a single month!

• Actor **James Dean** was still receiving fan mail two years after his death!

• At age eighty-two, actor **Kirk Douglas** made his eighty-second film!

BEN TURPIN, the cross-eyed silent-screen comedian who earned $3,000 a week, invested his money in apartment houses—and served as his own janitor in all of them.

HORROR FILM STAR BELA LUGOSI WAS BURIED IN HIS FAVORITE 'DRACULA' CAPE!

THE STRANGEST DRAMATIC SCHOOL IN HISTORY
CHARLES DULLIN (1885-1949)
the brilliant French actor
RECEIVED HIS DRAMATIC TRAINING
RECITING POETRY DAILY FOR SEVERAL YEARS
IN A CAGE FULL OF LIONS

• Actor **George Reeves** needed three people to help him in and out of his Superman costume!

• When actor **Anthony Quinn** shaved his head for a role in the 1968 film *The Magus*, the studio took out insurance in case his hair failed to grow back in!

CONTEMPORARY STARS

• World champion body-builder **Arnold Schwarze-negger**, who won his first Mr. Universe title at the age of twenty, has won a record thirteen world bodybuilding titles!

• In 1991, American actor **Telly Savalas** received a medal for winning a spelling bee as a school boy in 1934!

• In 1993, a new species of spider was named "calponia Harrisonfordi" after actor **Harrison Ford**!

• Japanese-American actor **Pat Morita**, star of the *Karate Kid*, suffered from spinal tuberculosis as a child and spent nine years confined to bed!

ACTOR JAMES EARL JONES, THE VOICE OF DARTH VADER IN "STAR WARS," STUTTERED SO BADLY AS A CHILD THAT HE HAD TO COMMUNICATE BY WRITING NOTES!

ACTOR ORSON WELLES, AFTER BREAKING HIS ANKLE, PLAYED THE LEAD ROLE in Shakespeare's KING LEAR— IN A WHEELCHAIR! (1956)

• The white polyester suit worn by actor **John Travolta** in the film *Saturday Night Fever* sold at auction for $145,000!

CHILD STARS

• Actress **Margaret O'Brien**, who won an Academy Award at the age of seven, had it stolen in 1955, and then returned to her forty years later by two men who found it at a flea market!

• Twenty thousand people on the island of Bali in Indonesia once gathered on a hill to pray for the recovery of child movie star **Shirley Temple** when she had fallen ill!

• Child star **Shirley Temple** received one hundred thirty-five thou-sand gifts on her eighth birthday!

SILENT-FILM STARS

• **Charlie Chaplin** made thirty-five films in a single year!

• **Charlie Chaplin**, long after he became a million-aire, continued to live in a shabby hotel room, and kept his studio checks in a trunk for months.

• One scene of **Charlie Chaplin's** 1932 film *City Lights* took three hundred forty-two hours to film!

• Comedian **Charlie Chaplin** once took part in a Charlie Chaplin look-alike contest—and lost!

WILLIAM S. HART (1872–1946) The Western star of the silent screen began his career as a Shakespearean actor.

Believe It or Not! SILENT SCREEN COMIC BUSTER KEATON HAD A CONTRACT WHICH FORBADE HIM from SMILING IN HIS FILMS!

• The boots that **Charlie Chaplin** ate in the 1924 film *The Gold Rush* were made of licorice!

PRIOR CAREERS

• **Mack Sennett**, producer of *The Keystone Cops* and other famous films, began his career playing the hind legs of a stage horse.

• **Warner Oland**, the actor who became famous playing the Chinese detective Charlie Chan in the 1930s, was at one time an opera singer.

• Actor **Walter Brennan** (1894-1974) started his career in Hollywood by doing a voice-over for a donkey.

• **Cliff Gorman**, the movie actor, once worked for a

scientific supply company as a frog embalmer.

• Comedian **W. C. Fields** once worked as a professional drowner, pretending to drown in order to draw crowds to the beach in Atlantic City.

CINEMA

• The first motion picture studio, created by Thomas Alva Edison in East Orange, New Jersey, in 1893, was mounted on a pivot so that its stage could be turned to the sun—and cost only $637!

• American film producer **Darryl F. Zanuck** rented the entire country of San Marino, the world's oldest republic, as the medieval setting for his film *The Prince of Foxes*.

When Harold Lloyd's film *Safety Last* premiered in 1923, theaters hired nurses to care for moviegoers who fainted while watching the scene where Lloyd actually dangled from a skyscraper's clock!

In 1940, New York City's Globe Theatre accepted firearms instead of cash as admission to the film *Contraband: U.S. Blackout!*

ONE, ADULT.

IN 1908, THE FILM *"Macbeth"* WAS BANNED in *Chicago, Ill.*, BECAUSE of THE SCENE IN WHICH *King Duncan* IS STABBED TO DEATH!

GONE WITH THE WIND
THE MONUMENTAL MOVIE MADE IN 1939, RESULTED IN THE SHOOTING OF 449,512 FEET OF FILM -- OF WHICH ONLY ABOUT 20,300 FEET APPEAR IN THE FINAL PICTURE

• The film *The Execution of Mary, Queen of Scots*, made in 1895, was the first film to use trained actors!

• The first Western, *Cripple Creek Barroom*, was made in 1898, lasted but one minute, had no action, and the role of a barmaid was played by a man.

• **George Melies'** *Cinderella*, made in 1899, was the first movie to tell a complete story.

• In the 1956 film *The Ten Commandments*, a blind man is shown wearing a modern wristwatch!

• In Malta, all patrons attending the premiere of the American film *Broadway Melody* were asked to wear tennis shoes!

• A fifteen-second kiss by **May Irwin** and **John C. Rice** in the movie *The Kiss* in 1896, brought the first demand for film censorship.

• The director who found fame is fleeting: **Erich von Stroheim** (1885-1957), the motion picture director, was named one of Hollywood's ten best directors in 1926, but was not even given an honorable mention in 1927, and was a has-been by 1928.

• In 1914, Mexican general **Pancho Villa** signed a contract with Mutual Films of New York for the screen rights to his guerrilla war.

• The "blood" used during the shower scene in the movie *Psycho* was actually chocolate sauce!

• The premier screening of the **Howard Hughes** film *Underwater* took place in a Florida lake with all of the guests wearing scuba gear!

• In the early 1900s, some hotels posted signs that barred dogs and actors!

• Stunt men who risked their lives in the early movies were paid $5 a day.

• **Carl Laemmle**, owner of Universal Pictures between 1915 and 1920, hired and fired sixteen studio managers—each lasting about four months.

• In 1933, the word "filthy" could not be used in Hollywood films!

• **Joseph Farnham** won an Academy Award for the 1927 film *Wings*—for the title writing!

• During World War II, the Oscar Awards were made of wood due to a shortage of metal!

• Employees of the State of Georgia were given a paid holiday in 1939 to view the premiere of the film *Gone with the Wind*!

• Movie producer **David O. Selznick** was fined five thousand dollars by the Motion Picture Association of America for allowing the word "damn" to be said in the film *Gone with the Wind!*

COMEDY

• **Ora Bayes** (1880-1928) became a comedienne because she forgot the lines of a song. In desperation she made motions with her hands and did the chorus in pantomime—and the audience's roars of laughter launched her on a new career.

Comedian **W.C. FIELDS** cured his insomnia by sleeping under a beach umbrella sprinkled with water from a garden hose!

• **Edward Everett Horton**, the comedian, was a hypochondriac who refused to kiss on stage or screen—and he called his Hollywood estate *Belleigh Acres*.

• **Rich Little**, the impressionist, has a repertoire of one hundred sixty-four voices.

MAGICIANS

• **Richard Valentine Pitchford**, a magician from Wales, was a failure when successively billed as "Valentine Professor Thomas" and "Val Raymond," but became a star as "Cardini."

• **Seamus Burke**, a professional magician, bound from head to foot and carrying a sealed tissue bag over his shoulder, after two minutes behind a screen would reappear to his audience inside the sealed bag.

RADIO

• *The Easy Aces*, one of the most popular radio programs in the United States during the 1920s and 1930s, was created when **Goodman** and **Jane Ace** had to substitute for performers who failed to appear.

• The only animal to star in its own radio show was the dog "**Lassie**"! She whined, growled, and barked at the appropriate times.

STAGE

• In the 1600s, acting was considered to be such an evil occupation that actors from England were forbidden by law from emigrating to America!

• "No" actors are talented: Actors at the "No" theater in Japan—which has a 500-year tradition—are extremely talented; "no" in Japan means talent.

• **George Jones**, a nineteenth-century Shakespearean actor known as Count Johannes, was so often pelted with cabbages at New York theaters that he had to be protected from the audience by a net.

IN Germany ESCAPE ARTIST *HARRY HOUDINI* WAS LASHED TO RAILWAY TRACKS and NARROWLY ESCAPED DEATH WHEN THE Berlin-Dresden Express ARRIVED EARLY and SEVERED HIS ALREADY LOOSENED BONDS!

• **William MacDonald**, an eighteenth-century Scottish actor, for years never walked without his cane, and kept it beside him when he slept. After his death it was discovered that it was a hollow whiskey container.

• Punch and Judy puppet shows were staged in England as early as the 1600s.

• **Ellen Terry** (1847-1928), the English actress, played Shakespeare's Lady Macbeth in a costume adorned with real beetle wings.

TELEVISION

• A nursery school in Reigate, England, changed its name from "South Park" to "The Orchids" in order to distance itself from the popular United States television show and movie! The film alone contains at least three hundred ninety-nine swear words and one hundred twenty-eight crude gestures!

• By the age of fifteen, the average young television viewer has seen shows in which over thirteen thousand persons have died violently.

TELEVISION STAR VANNA WHITE of THE SHOW "WHEEL of FORTUNE" CLAPS AN AVERAGE of 720 TIMES PER SHOW AND HAS WALKED MORE THAN 443 MILES ON THE SHOW SINCE 1982.

• The palomino horse that played "Mister Ed" on the popular television show of the 1960s was frequently given his favorite treat of peanut butter so his mouth would move to simulate talking!

• During most of the time that actor **Raymond Burr** played "Perry Mason," he never owned a television set!

• *Wheel of Fortune* television star **Vanna White** was a spelling champion in high school!

THEATERS

• In 1927, **Norma Talmadge** became the first actress to leave her footprints outside Grauman's Chinese Theater in Hollywood—by accidentally stepping in wet concrete.

• Imax movies are projected onto a six-story-high screen using a fifteen-thousand-watt lamp that gets as hot as the surface of the sun!

• The Royal Theater of Drottingsholm Palace, Stockholm, Sweden, is the only eighteenth-century playhouse in which performances are still staged regularly—and still use the original decor, props, and stage machinery.

• The Greek theater of Aspendos, Turkey, constructed two thousand years ago, was so acoustically perfect that every

word spoken on its stage could be heard with clarity in any of its thirteen thousand seats.

ACTORS in ancient Rome, when they died, always were buried wearing the masks of their stage roles. This was to make certain they would be judged in the hereafter by their acting ability rather than their private conduct.

The ORIGINAL *"BATMAN"* WAS INSPIRED by *Leonardo da Vinci's* "ORNITHOPTER," **A ONE-MAN FLYING MACHINE** *DESIGNED IN THE EARLY 1500s!*

Entertainer **Judith "Sparky" Roberts** of Eugene, Oregon, could manipulate puppets with her feet while standing on her head and whistling.

THE **MASKS**
WORN BY ACTORS ON THE ANCIENT GREEK STAGE WERE SO CONSTRUCTED *THAT THEY MAGNIFIED THE WEARER'S VOICE*

ACROBATS at the French court in the 18th century played a bass drum while walking a tightrope.

VAUDEVILLE AND VARIETY

• Vaudeville performers in the United States had to provide photos of themselves for use by the theater. Performers knew they were fired if their photos were removed after a performance.

• In the 1930s, a vaudeville contortionist named **Brawerman**, or "King Brawn," could pass his entire body through a gutted tennis racket.

CIRCUSES, FAIRS AND EXHIBITIONS

• "The Iron House," an exhibit that toured London, England in the 1750s, featured a cage in which hawks, owls, and pigeons—natural enemies—lived together amicably.

• Every Wednesday night, actors **Katie Massa**, **Nicholas Foster**, and **Cece Pleasant** perform an episode of their "Subway Soap Opera" on the Number One subway line in New York City!

ONE-OF-A-KIND PERFORMANCE ARTIST: A CANCER SURVIVOR TURNS TRAGEDY INTO ENTERTAINMENT

Performance artist Scott Sabala is a living testament to humankind's ability to triumph over tragedy. In 1987, at the age of twenty-three, Scott's relatively normal life was turned upside down when he was diagnosed with a brain tumor.

The cancerous growth, as big as a man's fist, filled an entire side of Scott's upper jaw. Scott underwent surgery to remove the tumor, but it reappeared in 1992, this time worse than before. In order to save Scott's life, doctors had to remove a huge portion of his face, leaving him with a gaping cavity where his left eye had once been, and an open channel from his eye socket to his throat.

When the bandages came off, and Scott finally got up the courage to look in the mirror, the results were worse than he could possibly imagine: "I was crushed. I was devastated."

As he was recovering, however, Scott made a decision. He was going to adopt the most positive attitude he could about his condition. He was going to find a way to turn his tragedy into a triumph. Rather than hide behind a prosthetic, Scott decided to turn his unique anatomy into a show.

Today, Scott's act features a number of stunts that only he can accomplish, such as drinking water through his eye, and a feat he calls "the human jack-o-lantern," in which a flashlight inserted in his mouth lights up his eye socket. He also passes a tiny video camera on a cable though the cavity in his head, giving audiences a closeup tour of the inside of his unique anatomy. At the end of the act, he waves goodbye to the crowds in his own inimitable fashion: waggling the tip of his tongue inside his eye socket!

Scott explains, "The point of my act is not to gross people out but to show them how you can get by and go on with your life and make light of it. I want to make them laugh."

Chapter 20
Environment

BY THE TIME IT IS COMPLETE IN THE YEAR 2005, NEW YORK CITY'S MOUNTAIN OF GARBAGE ON STATEN ISLAND WILL BE 505 FT. TALL— 24 FT. HIGHER THAN EGYPT'S GREAT PYRAMID AT GIZA!

Americans are a trashy lot. We generate a mind-boggling amount of garbage each day. But over the past several decades, we've slowly been learning that there's only so much room to stow all that junk. We're gradually coming to understand that our environment can only take so much abuse, and we've begun to come up with some pretty clever solutions to our pollution. Herein, we'll introduce you to a number of outrageously creative ways to reincarnate our garbage into something environmentally friendly.

RECYCLING

• **Susan Lake**, of Toluca, California, created a wedding dress and bouquet out of recycled trash, including plastic bags, egg cartons, and cotton balls!

• Tetra Pak, Inc. of Sweden, makes briefcases, luggage, and furniture from recycled garbage.

• In 1990, Proctor and Gamble began recycling four tons of dirty disposable diapers to make them into park benches and building supplies!

• European car manufacturers including BMW and Mercedes-Benz are now producing cars made with recycled plastic parts!

• A company in Lake Oswego, Oregon, makes shoes out of recycled diapers, tires, paper bags, and coffee filters!

• One ton of recycled paper saves seventeen trees, up to twenty-four thousand gallons of water, and forty-one thousand kilowatt hours of energy—enough to power a house for six months!

• A recycling machine built in Wausau, Wisconsin, digs up chunks of old highway concrete, grinds them into powdered concrete, and then pours new pavement!

SHIRLEY GREEN of CAPE MAY COURT HOUSE, N.J., CREATES MINIATURE HOUSES OUT of RECYCLED MATERIALS, INCLUDING **PLASTIC CASSETTE BOXES, TWIST TIES and PLASTIC CAPS!**

Andrea Burke of Portland, Ore., *LIVES IN A HOUSE MADE from RECYCLED NEWSPAPERS, RYEGRASS STRAW and FLUORESCENT LIGHT BULBS!*

"BOVINE BEER"

A BREWERY in Edmonton, Alta, Canada, RECYCLES ITS OUTDATED BEER BY DELIVERING IT TO FARMS WHERE IT IS MIXED *INTO THE FEED!*

Believe It or Not! SCULPTOR JANET MORTON of Toronto, Ont., Canada, MADE A GIANT COZY TO COVER AN ENTIRE HOUSE — *USING 700 RECYCLED SWEATERS!*

ARTIST Rick Ladd of New York City MAKES CHAIRS and LIGHT FIXTURES USING DISCARDED BOTTLECAPS!

RESOURCES

• The United States uses more steel to make bottle caps than to make car bodies!

• The average American home uses over one hundred thousand gallons of water every year! It takes seven gallons to flush a toilet, about fifty gallons for a shower, two gallons to brush teeth, and twenty gallons to wash dishes per day!

THREATS TO THE ENVIRONMENT

• In 1978, harmful insects throughout the world were combated with four billion pounds of insecticides—one pound for every person on earth.

• Every year seventeen thousand species of plants and animals unique to tropical rain forests disappear due to deforestation!

• A day's garbage from New York City could easily fill the Empire State Building!

IN 1991, SIDEWALK VENDORS IN MEXICO CITY BEGAN SELLING OXYGEN AT A COST OF 5,000 PESOS TO HELP COUNTERACT THE SMOG!

COMMODIOUS TALENT: TOILET SEAT ARTIST IS PRIVY TO A CREATIVE FORM OF RECYCLING

Plumber Barney Smith can give you the straight poop on recycling. For the past thirty years, he's practiced an unusual form of self-expression: creating works of art on discarded toilet seats!

Smith's unusual hobby began thirty years ago with a visit to a plumbing supply store, where he discovered a huge stack of discarded toilet seats waiting for disposal. On an impulse, he asked if he could keep them. That first batch of oval canvases has today grown into a private museum of over five hundred works of art!

Just about anything can become material for Smith's one-of-a-kind creations. He has toilet seats covered with eyeglasses, pill bottles, World War II ration notes, beehives—even a piece of the Space Shuttle. "When my wife said, 'Have you lost your marbles?' I told her, "No, I got 'em on a toilet seat!"

TRASH INTO ART

• Artist **Rob Mulholland** created a three-hundred-foot long human figure in a Glasgow, Scotland park using three hundred thousand cans!

• **P. J. Roths**, of Maurice, Louisiana, carves elaborate scenes of helicopters, ships, and animals out of Styrofoam coffee cups!

• British artist **Jud Shadbolt** creates chairs from recycled objects, including brass taps, keys, and farm machinery!

• **Jose Martin Pacheo,** of New York City creates elaborate colorful masks out of recycled plastic bottles!

• **Rosa Patoine**, of Hardwick, Vermont, created a braided rug using five hundred and forty-five plastic bread bags!

• "Cyclestone": Artists **Wallace Brighton** and **Maggie Rodman**, of Pickering, Ontario, have invented a sculpting material made out of recycled plastic and glass that is similar to soapstone!

• **Gaston Marticorena,** of New York City, makes chairs out of clear vinyl stuffed with shredded income-tax receipts!

• American artist **Jon Bok** makes furniture decorated with bottle caps, olive oil cans, and discarded padlocks!

RUSSELL ZEID of TORONTO, ONT, CANADA, CREATES GIANT SCULPTURES of DINOSAURS – INCLUDING A 2½ TON DINOSAUR HE'S DUBBED "ALBERTOSAURUS" – USING RECYCLED JUNK AND CAR PARTS!

"TRASH-O-SAURUS" At the Children's Garbage Museum of Southwest, Connecticut, there is a 24-ft. long, 11-ft. tall sculpture of a dinosaur made out of trash—the one-ton work of art equals the amount of garbage each person in the U.S. generates every year!

Chapter 21
Exploration & Discovery

What do Michael Jordan, Gary Larson, and Harrison Ford have in common? They've all lent their names to newly discovered life forms! In spite of all the creatures we've studied and named, there are still hundreds of thousands yet to be discovered. Just when we think we've seen it all, new horizons are forever opening before us, beckoning to the willing adventurer. Whoever said there's nothing new under the sun has obviously not yet toured Ripley's collection of bizarre discoveries and amazing explorations!

DISCOVERIES

BIOLOGICAL DISCOVERIES

• A giant eyeball, the size of a baseball, found floating twenty-six miles off Key West, Florida, is believed to have belonged to a five hundred pound octopus!

• The world's fastest bacteria: *Bdellovibrio bacteriovorus*, a microscopic bacterium, jumps fifty times its own length using a propeller that spins one hundred times a second!

• Marine biologists estimate that as many as five million marine species have yet to be discovered!

• A new strain of bacteria discovered in 1933 was named "Salmonella Mjordan" after basketball star Michael Jordan.

• In 1991, scientists discovered a new species of beaked whale in the Pacific Ocean off Peru—the first new species of whale to be found in twenty-eight years!

• In 1993, scientists identified a new species of mammal in central Vietnam (*Psudoryx nghetinhensis*) that looks like a cross between a goat and a cow!

• The world's smallest frog! A new species of frog, *Eleutherodactylus*, recently discovered in Cuba, measures less than twenty-five millimeters from its nose to the tip of its tail!

• In 1990, biologists discovered a previously unknown species of tamarin, just ouside Brazil's capital city of São Paulo, which they named the "blackfaced lion tamarin."

A **BALLOON** IN WHICH SWEDISH EXPLORER S.A. ANDREE AND 2 COMPANIONS TOOK OFF FROM SPITZBERGEN TO THE NORTH POLE IN 1897, WAS FOUND 33 YEARS LATER PERFECTLY PRESERVED BENEATH THE ARCTIC ICE --*EVEN WITH PHOTOGRAPHS TAKEN BY THE EXPEDITION INTACT*

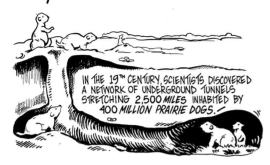

IN THE 19TH CENTURY, SCIENTISTS DISCOVERED A NETWORK OF UNDERGROUND TUNNELS STRETCHING 2,500 MILES INHABITED BY 400 MILLION PRAIRIE DOGS.

A CONSTRUCTION CREW TUNNELING INTO NEW YORK'S FIRST SUBWAY FOUND A 120-FT. WAITING ROOM WITH PAINTINGS, A FOUNTAIN AND A GRAND PIANO!

ALLEN AND ANNETTE CLAUSEN OF TAMPA, FLA., NOTICED HONEY OOZING FROM THEIR FLOORS AND FIREPLACE AND THEN FOUND A 300 LB. BEEHIVE BEHIND ONE OF THE WALLS OF THEIR NEW HOME!

• **Doctor Russell Vreeland** and **Doctor William Rosenzweig**, of West Chester University in Pennsylvania, have discovered a bacteria called *Bacillus permians* that has been dormant inside a salt crystal for two hundred fifty million years!

• The Maues marmoset of Brazil, a zebra-striped primate, was not discovered until 1992!

• In 1996, a monkey the size of a mouse, weighing two hundred grams, was discovered in Fujian Province, China!

• The black-headed sagui dwarf monkey, discovered in 1997, is only five inches long!

HISTORIC DISCOVERIES

• A copy of the first printing of the United States Declaration of Independence was discovered in 1991 behind a painting that was bought for four dollars at a flea market!

PROFITABLE DISCOVERIES

• **Lawrence Shields**, age ten, discovered a 1,061-carat sapphire worth over thirty-five thousand dollars—in a bucket of dirt!

• **Ramiz Uzum**, of Istanbul, Turkey, survived the devastating earthquake that struck the city in August 1999, and returned to his ruined home to discover a winning lottery ticket worth $365,000!

• Dairy farmer **Kevin Elliott**, of Britain, trying out a metal detector for the first time, discovered a hoard of 9,377 Roman coins—the largest ever found in Britain—worth hundreds of thousands of dollars!

• A new signature of **William Shakespeare**, if one were to be discovered, would be worth one million dollars!

BIZARRE DISCOVERIES

• In 1999, archaeologists from Britain's Museum of London discovered a five-hundred-year-old banana peel while digging in a Tudor-era rubbish pit!

• Divers searching the wreck of the *Amsterdam*, a Dutch ship that sank in the English Channel in 1749, found a bottle of red wine on board that still tasted fine after two hundred thirty-six years underwater.

• In 1971, **Ed Stainer**, of Blaydon, England, pulled up a floorboard in his living room and discovered a hole one thousand feet deep!

EXPEDITIONS

• In 1991, to commemorate the millennium of the discovery of America, Gaia, a seventy-eight-foot replica of a Viking ship, retraced the voyage of Viking explorer Leif Eriksson to North America from Norway!

• Vinland, the Viking name for New England, is mentioned in a Viking writing carved in 1065 on a stone found in Hoenen, Norway, that reports a Viking journey to Vinland in 985.

EXPLORERS

• **Nathaniel Brown Palmer** (1799-1877), as captain of a United States sealing ship in 1820, discovered the continent of Antarctica—at the age of twenty-one.

In 1989, nine members of the Ansett Social Climbers of Sydney, Australia, dined with table, chairs, wine, and a three-course meal at the summit of the 22,205-ft. Mt. Huascaran.

• **Christopher Columbus**, when he discovered the New World, was receiving a salary of two thousand maravedis a month, the equivalent of $13.90!

• The man who organized the voyage that discovered America: Spanish navigator **Martin Pinzon** (1440-1493) secured the crew for the expedition of 1492 after Columbus failed to do so, helped finance it, and commanded the *Pinta*, the ship that first sighted

land. Pinzon was the man the crews looked to for direction because they distrusted Columbus because he was a foreigner!

• **Captain Finn Ronne**, the American explorer, on his journey to chart the South Pole, traveled thirty-six hundred miles by ski and dog sled—a greater distance by that means than any other man in history.

• England's King Henry VII rewarded explorer **John Cabot** for his discovery of Cape Breton Island in Canada with a gift of ten pounds!

• **Louis Antoine de Bougainville** (1729-1811) soldier, navigator, and explorer, commanded the first French circumnavigation of the world only

three years after transferring to the navy from the French army.

• **William Damier** (1652-1715), the first Englishman to visit Australia, was a buccaneer who complained that he found nothing worth plundering.

• **Richard Burton** (1821-1890), the British explorer who discovered Lake Tanganyika in Africa, could read and speak twenty-nine languages.

• Captain **Charles Francis Hall** (1821-1871), an American Arctic explorer, memorized every word in Bowditch's *New American Practical Navigator*, and all its calculations and tables—a total of four hundred sixty pages.

THOMAS SIMPSON of Scotland
ON HIS 1839 EXPEDITION TO THE FAR NORTH TRAVELED 1,400 MILES IN KAYAKS LASHED TOGETHER-- THE *LONGEST JOURNEY EVER NEGOTIATED IN THE HIGH ARCTIC IN SMALL BOATS*

IN 1993, 38 people reached the 28,028-ft, summit of Mt. Everest –ALL AT THE SAME TIME!

THE SEARCH FOR THE LOST ARK OF THE COVENANT:
A REAL-LIFE INDIANA JONES BELIEVES HE'S FOUND IT

Mention the Ark of the Covenant, and movie-lovers immediately identify this sacred relic with the fictional adventurer Indiana Jones in the 1981 film *Raiders of the Lost Ark*. But many movie fans may not realize that the Ark is not fiction but fact. It exists. Or at least, according to the Bible, it existed. And explorer Bob Cornuke, a real-life Indiana Jones, is determined to find it.

Cornuke has traveled the globe in search of ancient Biblical artifacts. But he reverently admits that the Ark of the Covenant, the gilded receptacle of the original Ten Commandments, would be the ultimate discovery: "People have given their lives in search of the Ark."

For several years, Cornuke has been researching biblical clues to the Ark's whereabouts, which he has published in a recent book titled *The Sign and the Seal*. Cornuke's book describes a controversial theory that suggests that the Ark traveled from Jerusalem to Ethiopia.

Although numerous theories exist as to the Ark's location, Cornuke subscribes to the Ethiopian theory, particularly because Ethiopia possesses the only living legend of its whereabouts. Approximately fifteen thousand people believe that the Ark was removed to an obscure island in the Nile River. A Biblical basis does exist for this belief, as the island is described in scripture. Cornuke searched the Nile for such an island, and amazingly, he found it.

The island matches the Biblical description exactly. Cornuke discovered a group of monks living on the island, guarding a number of relics they claim belonged to the Ark. They even showed Cornuke a set of four holes in the ground where the Ark was believed to have rested. The Ark, however, is no longer on the island. The monks told Cornuke he was sixteen hundred years too late.

According to the monks' story, the Ark was stolen in A.D. 400 and removed to a city by the name of Axun. Cornuke researched the ancient city, and was astonished to discover that it still exists.

Upon journeying to Axun, Ethiopia, Cornuke discovered an ancient temple surrounded by a tall iron gate, protected by an armed guard. Residents of Axun believe that the Ark rests inside this temple. The entire village has pledged itself to protect the Ark—if anyone tries to enter the temple, the guards will sound the alarm, and every resident will come running, armed with everything from kitchen knives to machine guns.

Cornuke met with the Ark's caretaker—a man more than one hundred years old—who is one of only two individuals alive who have seen the Ark. The Ark is believed to be so sacred that no one else is even allowed to look upon it, let alone touch the relic.

Cornuke, however, has not given up hope. He still dreams of one day seeing with his own eyes whether the Ark really does reside within Axun's temple, but when asked whether he would touch the Ark if given the chance, Cornuke replies reverently, "I don't know."

- **Zebulon Pike** (1779-1813), who discovered Pike's Peak in Colorado, never was within fifteen miles of the mountain peak.

- In a period of fifty years, **Christian Klucker** (1853-1928), one of Switzerland's most famous mountain guides, climbed more than three thousand of the tallest peaks in France, Switzerland, and Austria— one hundred of them had never been climbed before.

- Mountain guide **Johann Ostler** climbed Germany's highest peak, the 9,728-foot Zugspitze, five hundred times, and yet he died after hurting himself chopping wood.

- **Jean-Baptiste Maquinaz**, a famous alpine mountain guide, lost all ten toes and the soles of both feet after they froze in 1893—yet he continued to lead alpine climbs for another thirty years.

- In 1823, **John Cleves Symmes** of Saint Louis, Missouri, tried to gain government funds to finance a trip to the center of the Earth via holes in the ice at the North Pole!

Chapter 22
Family Life

An old proverb states that home is the one place you can go where they have to take you in. But a homecoming can become a tricky proposition if you have, as one father did, more than three hundred children. Or, as one mother had, seven sons—all of whom became executioners. Family get-togethers might get downright odd if your two siblings were born in different centuries. And if the luck of the draw presents you with twins, you'd better hope you don't live among the Tumbukas, who will banish you into the woods for a month. Better to pack up your twosome and take up residence with the Yorubas, who present the mother of twins with a gift whenever they meet her. But despite the variations, family is one of the few concepts we share in common with all human societies—no matter how weird the folks down home might be.

FAMILIES

• The **Grix** family, of Toronto, Canada, has produced five living generations in seventy-three years!

• **Morgan Ford**, of Tecumseh, Michigan, has a one-hundred-twenty-four-year-old fruitcake that has been in his family since it was baked in 1878!

• A family in Alameda, California, has thirteen men named **Frank J. Manibusan**!

FATHERHOOD

• **Colonel William Cobbe** (1613-1665), of Sandringham, England, was the father of two priests and four nuns.

• **Doctor Jahial Parmly**, a dentist of Peryr, Ohio, was the brother of three dentists and the uncle, brother-in-law, and cousin of fourteen dentists.

CHILDREN in Thurø, Denmark, for OVER 25 YEARS HAVE TIED THEIR PACIFIERS ONTO THE "PACIFIER TREE" WHEN THEY KICK THE HABIT.!

• American boxer **George Foreman** named all five of his sons George!

• **Jose Garcia**, of Cordoba, Mexico, became a father and a great-grandfather the same day.

• **Stephen Pozdzioch** was the father of seven children—each born in a different country.

• **Pierre Defournel**, of Barjac, Vivarais, was the father of three children, each born in a different century! The first boy was born in 1699, the second was born in 1738, and the third was born in 1801. Each son was born to a different wife. Defournel married his third wife when he was one hundred twenty and she was nineteen. He died in 1809 at the robust old age of one hundred twenty-nine. The "Magasin Pittoresque," a document written in 1877, has a reprint of the original birth certificates of the three children.

• **John Hammond**, of Rushford, New York, was the father of ten schoolteachers.

• **Phillipe Antoine de Claris** (1707-1767), whose wife was a niece of Voltaire, was the father of seven nuns.

• **Ugo Fieschi**, of Genoa, Italy, founded a family that included two popes, seventy-two cardinals, and one hundred archbishops!

• **Samuel Foreman** (1714-1792), of Matawan, New Jersey, was the father of a general and two majors, and the father-in-law of two other majors—all of whom served in the Continental Army during the American Revolution.

MOTHERHOOD

• **Marie-Laetitia Ramolino**, born on the island of Corsica in 1750, was the mother of four kings, two queens, a duchess, and a prince. Of her thirteen children, the most famous was her second child, Napoleon, who became Emperor of France. Joseph, her eldest son, became the King of Spain. Jerome was crowned King of Westphalia; Louis was the King of Holland. Her daughters, Maria Annunciata and Caroline Elisa, became Queen of Naples and Queen of Toscana. Of her other famous children, Lucien became the Prince of Canino, and Marie Pauline was the Duchess of Guastalla. She outlived them all by more than twenty years and died in 1836.

• Ninety-six-year-old **Vashti Risdall**, of Minnesota, has been a foster mother to one hundred sixty-two children since 1948!

"THE WORLD'S OLDEST TWINS"

KIN NARIA and GIN KANIE of Tokyo ARE **107 YEARS OLD**! AT THE AGE of 100, THEY RECORDED A **RAP RECORD** WHICH MADE THE POP CHARTS in Japan!

- **Merret Lassen** (1789-1869), of Rantum, Germany, was the mother of twenty-one children, eleven of whom went to sea—seven as captains of their own ships.

- **Ann Clark** (1727-1799), of Virginia, was the mother of five officers in the American Revolution—two of them generals—and the mother-in-law of four officers.

SIBLINGS

- In 1935, **Ruth Barrett Benedict**, of Shenandoah, Illinois, became a sister-in-law to her own sisters!

- In southern India, among the Brahmans, it was once customary for an unmarried eldest son to be "married" to a tree to allow his younger siblings to wed before him!

TWINS

- Twins in the Yoruba tribe of Africa are held in such respect that a mother carrying twins must be given a gift by every passerby to greet her.

- A woman of the Tumbuka tribe in central Africa who becomes the mother of twins is expelled to live with her husband in the forest, existing for two months without salt or cooked food.

- Lincoln Elementary School, in Saint Louis, Missouri, has twelve sets of twins out of a total of three hundred fifty students!

GRANDPARENTS

- **Dick Hoty**, of Holland, Massachusetts, and his son Rick, who has cerebral palsey, traveled thirty-seven hundred miles from Santa Monica, California, to Boston, Massachusetts, in forty-seven days on a specially built bicycle!

- In 1992, **Tom Dickey**, an eighty-two-year-old blind cyclist, and Stirling Thomas, his grand-nephew, pedaled a tandem bicycle over 3,700 miles from Los Angeles, California, to Boston, Massachusetts.

GENEALOGY & HEREDITY

- **Adrian Targett**, of Cheddar, England, has traced his family tree back to a nine-thousand-year-old skeleton of an ancient hunter that was found only half a mile from his home!

- **Hugh Frerrand**, appointed hereditary janitor of Skipton Castle in England, bequeathed his post to twelve successive generations. The same family held the job for four hundred thirty-eight years, from 1189 to 1627.

WOLF FAMILY WALKS TALL

The Wolf family, of Marshfield, Wisconsin, enjoys an uncommon pastime: stilt walking! Ed Wolf, known in stilt-walking circles as "Steady Eddie," has been walking on stilts since he was a boy, and once held the height record for walking on forty-foot-tall stilts. When Ed Wolf started a family, he was thrilled to find that his children all shared his passion for stilt walking. When Ed's first son, Travis, was born, Ed was ready with a tiny custom-made set of stilts. Just after Travis took his first step, Ed made sure his second step was on stilts!

Travis was soon followed by Tony, Ashley, and Jordan, all of whom have adopted their father's favorite pastime. The children share a playful rivalry, their stilts gradually becoming higher and higher. In fact, in 1998, Travis broke his father's record, walking on a pair of fifty-seven-pound stilts that stood a full nine inches higher than his father's! To accomplish this feat, Travis had practiced on the stilts for months inside the safety of the family's grain silo.

Travis is likely to have some competition from his youngest brother, Jordan, in the near future as Jordan has his eye on his big brother's record. In the meantime, "Steady Eddie" Wolf enjoys watching the close camaraderie his children share over their mutual passion. It's enough to make any father walk tall!

Chapter 23

Feats & Stunts

Astonishing feats and death-defying stunts have always been a mainstay at Ripley's. And almost as amazing as the stunts themselves are the extraordinary lengths these performers go to, to achieve them. Performers may spend years in practice, endure excruciating pain, and challenge themselves in unbelievable ways—all to make a single stunt look easy.

FEATS

• Can you top this? At age thirty-six, **Roy Robert Smith,** of Denver, Colorado, had never tasted an ice cream soda, Coca-Cola, ginger ale, wine, beer, or whiskey; never used tobacco in any form, never dipped snuff; never gone swimming, hunting, fishing,

hiking, or ice-skating; never played football, billiards, poker, cards, baseball, basketball, tennis, golf, hockey, or polo; never pitched a horseshoe; never driven a car, or ridden a bicycle, motorcycle, or horse; never seen an earthquake, flood, or tornado, nor witnessed a fatal accident; never seen a race of any kind; never been inside a saloon or speakeasy; never been struck or stunned by lightning or bitten by any kind of animal, reptile, or poisonous insect; never had a surgical operation; never shot a gun, pistol, rifle, or cannon; never been robbed or burglarized; never participated in a fight; never gambled nor bet; never been aboard a steamship or yacht; never ridden in a balloon or airplane; never milked a cow or goat; never been underground in a cave or mine; never joined a club, lodge, church, or organization; never seen a bullfight or duel; never harnessed a horse; never attended a rodeo; never been in a lumber camp, sawmill, granary, or foundry; never studied a foreign language; never been outside the United States; never been convicted of a crime; never fainted; never been inside a penitentiary, nor been a patient in a hospital or sanatorium; never kissed a girl; and never been engaged to marry.

• **Naomi Thorne,** a.k.a. "Santa Fe Kate," expertly played the piano while blindfolded and wearing thick gloves—even with a thick blanket covering the keyboard!

93 strands of thread through an ordinary sewing needle, by **Harold Blahnik,** of Kewannee, Wisconsin.

THE MAN WHO COULD LEAP ON EGGS WITHOUT BREAKING THEM!
JOSEPH DARBY of Dudley, England, COULD JUMP UPON AN OPEN BASKET OF EGGS AND THEN LEAP OFF AGAIN WITH SUCH LIGHTNING RAPIDITY *THAT HE WOULD NOT CRACK EVEN A SINGLE SHELL !*

To BOOST ATTENDANCE, IN 1984, SPANISH MIME ALBERT VIDAL SPENT THREE DAYS *INSIDE A CAGE* AT MIAMI'S METRO ZOO.!

PLEASE DON'T FEED THE **MIME!**

• **Francis Johnson**, of Darwin, Minnesota, collected this enormous ball of twine single-handedly. The ball required a railroad jack to lift, and sat chained to a tree in Johnson's yard for more than forty years. It is now sheltered by the top of Johnson's own silo, and sits across the street from the Stringball Café, where visitors can purchase their very own Stringball T-shirt.

• **Connie Phares**, of Marion, Indiana—the world's first toe-skater!

• **Catherine Hopper**, of Cincinnati, skipped rope 499 times on roller skates without a miss!

FEATS OF BALANCE

• **Anis S. Cementwala**, age twelve, of Bombay, India, built a tower of playing cards fourteen stories high, using only jokers!

• In 1992, **Brian Berg**, of Spirit Lake, Iowa, using two hundred decks of playing cards, built a seventy-five-floor house of cards that stood over fourteen feet high!

School teacher **Bob Dotzauer,** of Cedar Rapids, Iowa, although disabled in one leg, could perform numerous remarkable feats of balance.

• A magnetic pulley held a man by the iron nails in his shoes (with co-workers dangling from an iron bar) at Dings Magnetic Separator Company in Milwaukee.

"Breezy" Anneberg, of Kansas University, walked up five flights of stairs on his hands.

The **Great Johnson**, a.k.a. "The Silent Entertainer," could still place his entire weight on a single small glass even when he was in his sixties.

In 1993, **John Evans,** of Giltbrook, England, balanced a car on his head for two minutes!

• **Doctor A. C. Johnson** of Detroit, Michigan, could balance an egg on the back of a spoon!

• Fourteen men rocked on a single motorcycle, Colorado Springs, Colorado.

• **Joe Horowitz,** of Los Angeles, California, "The Man with the Iron Nose," balanced an eighteen-pound sword on the tip of his nose.

• One hundred and eleven dominoes were balanced on one domino by **Edwards Woodward**. The structure stood for $10^1/_2$ hours.

This performing stack of musicians performed regularly in a New York City club during the 1940s.

FEATS OF DISCIPLINE

• A statue carved out of a mountain by one man! In Kiating, China, a 204 foot high image of **Mi Lo**, the future Buddha, was created by a monk named Yuan K'ai, who chiseled it out of solid rock, laboring alone for seventy-two years.

^ HOUSE OF CARDS CONSTRUCTED BY PAUL WARSHAUER AND PAUL ADLER, STUDENTS AT THE NORRIS UNIVERSITY CENTER AT NORTHWESTERN UNIV., Evanston, Ill., *50 "STORIES" HIGH AND CONTAINING 7,725 PLAYING CARDS.*

EDWARD TER KAZARIAN of ARMENIA CARVED 300 ELEPHANTS ON A SINGLE HUMAN HAIR!

• **Leuben**, the famous German lunatic, bet that he could turn up an entire pack of cards in a certain order. He turned the cards ten hours a day for twenty years—exactly 4,246,028 times—before he succeeded.

• **Dipak Syal**, of Yumuna Negar, India, wrote eight hundred thirteen letters on a single grain of rice!

JAMES ZAHAREE of Long Beach, Calif., wrote Lincoln's Gettyburg Address on a single human hair!

• **Pan Xixing**, of Wuxi, China, engraved this message on a grain of rice: "True friendship is like sound health, the value of which is seldom known until it be lost."

• **Doctor John Mason Neale** (1818-1866), of Cambridge, England, in a period of twenty-two years, wrote hundreds of hymns, countless newspaper articles, and one hundred forty books.

• **Alan Foreman**, of New Barn, England, wrote a 1,402,344-word letter to his wife that took two years to complete!

• **Acqueline Jones**, of Lindale, Texas, sent his sister Jean Stewart of Springfield, Maine, a letter that took eight months to write and had 1,113,747 words!

FEATS OF ENDURANCE

• **Baldasaire Forestiere** (1879-1946), an Italian immigrant who once worked as a "sand hog" building New York City's subways, built himself a new house in Fresno, California, using only a pick and shovel! Without

• U.S. Navy wrestling champion **Joe Reno**, hypnotized by Rajah Yogi in Dallas, Texas, slept buried in a coffin for nearly seventeen days in June 1930 without food or water to set a new world record for hypnotic sleep. Within fifteen minutes after being reawakened by Rajah Yogi, Reno wrestled Shreveport, Louisiana, middleweight champion Red Lindsey to a ten-minute draw!

blueprints of any kind, Forestiere dug single-handedly over a thirty-seven-year period a thirty-five-room home, with a mile of connecting tunnels—all underground.

• **Bobby Walthour**, a marathon bicycle racer, was twice pronounced dead during a sixty-day race—but he recovered each time and continued to compete!

DORIS MAGER OF THE FLORIDA AUDUBON SOC., TO RAISE MONEY TO AID INJURED BIRDS, SPENT 7 DAYS IN A NEST *ABANDONED BY EAGLES*

• The most astounding climbing feat in all of history! **Billie Quill** climbed Sutherland Falls in New Zealand, 1,904 feet high, and then descended again through the torrent of water—both in the same day, March 9, 1890.

• In 1991, **Stephane Wuttunee**, a Cree Indian, paddled solo in a canoe for over two thousand miles, following the path of his ancestors along rivers and lakes from Edmonton to Quebec City, Canada!

• In 1981, **Bill Neal**, of Britain, crossed the English Channel from Dover to Cape Gris in Nez, France, in thirty hours, twenty-nine minutes—in a bathtub!

• **Barbara Rickard**, of West Sussex, England, ran a mile in eight minutes, 14.80 seconds wearing Wellington boots filled with custard!

• **Matt Frondor**, of San Antonio, Texas, drove across the United States, from New York City to San Francisco, California, taking a photograph every mile along the way!

• The perfect host: **Cornelius White**, of Pembroke, Massachusetts, entertaining friends at the Bunch of Grapes in Pembroke, rode on horseback to Boston and back—seventy-five miles in six hours—to buy a bag of lemons for punch.

• **Jose Ordonez**, of Colombia, South America, on the air at a radio station, told four thousand jokes in thirty-six consecutive hours!

• **John Slater**, of Melvaig, Scotland, walked the entire length of Britain—six hundred miles—from Scotland to Land's End, England, in his bare feet and wearing striped pajamas!

• To Yates on Skates! In 1979, **Ted Coombs**, of Hermosa Beach, California, traveled from Los Angeles, California, to New York City, and back to Yates Center, Kansas: fifty-two hundred miles—on roller skates.

• On July 19, 1955, nineteen-year-old **Giuseppe de Ponti,** of Melzo, Italy, arrived in Venice—after floating in an inner tube for one hundred twenty-two hours, paddling two hundred ten miles with only his hands. Ten miles of his journey was on the open ocean.

• **Kenichi Horie**, of Japan, traveled ten thousand miles across the Pacific Ocean, from Ecuador to Tokyo, in one hundred thirty-eight days, in a thirty-one-foot boat made from recycled aluminum and powered by solar panels!

• In 1990, **Kevin Foster**, of California, rode thirty-seven hundred miles along the Great Wall of China—on a bicycle!

FEATS OF HEIGHT

• In 1982, **Larry Walters**, of Los Angeles, California, flew in a lawn chair held up by twenty-four helium-filled balloons—to a height of three miles!

• Four year old **Billy Crawford**, harnessed to a gigantic balloon that rendered him virtually weightless, spent several hours in 1934 making gigantic leaps over and around Cleveland, Ohio.

• **Larry Frakes**, of Fort Worth, Texas, flew a home-made box kite to a height of twenty-five hundred feet! The kite interfered with air traffic control and a police helicopter located it by tracking its flight!

FEATS OF MEMORY

• **Rachael MacCrimmon**, of Saint Kilda, Hebrides, Scotland, memorized the entire Bible.

• **Professor John Bagnell Bury** (1861-1927), of Cambridge University in England, prepared himself to edit Gibbon's *Decline and Fall of the Roman Empire* by mastering nine languages.

FEATS OF PAIN

• A juggler performing on the streets of Bombay, India, in the 1940s would, for a small handful of coins, lift a snake with his eyeballs. The juggler placed a python in a basket, wrapped the basket in cloth, then tied the cloth to a strong, thin rope, at the end of which were two hollow leaden cups. The juggler would place the cups over his eyeballs to create suction, then shut his eyelids over the cups, and lift the basket. Afterwards, the juggler

removed the cups from his eyes, accompanied by a horrible sucking sound. The feat seemed to cause

• Richmond, Virginia's own Peruvian fakir, **Jose Fernandez**, could swallow safety razor blades and drive a 20-penny nail into his head up to the hilt.

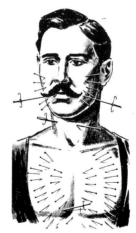

• **Rosa Barthelme**— The Human Slate.

him great discomfort—his bloodshot eyes streamed tears and he appeared to have difficulty seeing for several minutes after he preformed the stunt.

• **Kajuku Kodai**, a Buddhist priest in Japan, regularly performs a feat in which he sits inside a steaming wok filled with boiling water!

• **August L. Schmolt** smacked himself on the bicep with a four-pound hammer every day for forty years, yet even severe blows would not bruise his skin.

THE HUMAN PINCUSHION
EDWARD H. GIBSON
A VAUDEVILLE PERFORMER IN THE EARLY 1900'S, PERMITTED AN ASSISTANT AT EACH PERFORMANCE *TO STICK 60 PINS INTO HIS FACE AND BODY*

FEATS OF SPEED

• **Roy Dean** completed a London *Times* newspaper crossword puzzle—considered the world's most difficult puzzle—in three minutes, forty-five seconds!

FEATS OF STRENGTH

• **Chuck Burger**, a professional wrestler, with a mooring line around his neck, pulled a four-hundred-ton, 165-foot-long cruise boat into its slips.

Rasmus Nielsen, of Angel's Camp, California, lifted a two-hundred-pound anvil with a metal bar skewered through both nipples.

Joseph Ponder, of Love Valley, North Carolina, smashes cement blocks with a 20-pound sledge hammer moving at 66 miles per hour—held in his teeth.

Singlee, the "Fireproof Man," a popular Ripley's Odditorium performer in the 1930s.

"Professor" **Leo Kongee** could sew buttons to his tongue.

Leona Young, of Norwich, New York, a.k.a. "The Devil's Daughter," felt no pain when applying a plumber's torch directly to her tongue.

• **Harry McGregor** could pull his wife, Lillian, in a wagon, using only his eyelids!

• **Bill Phillips, Junior,** of Dublin, New Hampshire, a boy fourteen years of age, bit a ten-penny nail in half.

• **Gardner A. Taylor**, of Winner, South Dakota, lifted a 155-pound anvil with his ears.

• In 1957, strongman **Paul Anderson** lifted a table with a steel safe and auto parts on top that weighed a total of 6,270 pounds!

• **H. Paolias**, of Birmingham, England, once performed a feat of strength in which he balanced a sofa, upon which his wife was reclining, on his head!

STUNTS

• Trick-Riding Grandmother! **Tad Lucas**, world champion trick rider, rode in the same rodeo at Madison Square Garden, in New York, as her daughter and granddaughter!

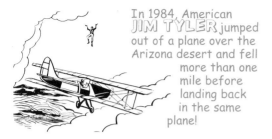

In 1984, American **JIM TYLER** jumped out of a plane over the Arizona desert and fell more than one mile before landing back in the same plane!

"The MONSTER COLLISION"

ON Sept. 15, 1856, THE MISSOURI, KANSAS and TEXAS RAILROAD STAGED A **CRASH** *BETWEEN TWO LOCOMOTIVES* ON A LINE NEAR Waco, Texas, BEFORE A CROWD of 40,000 PEOPLE.

Jo Ann Summer, of Decatur, Alabama, tap-danced on top of two milk bottles.

• **Chester Cable**, of Hossapple, Pennsylvania, spun a ten-foot-long table thirty times in sixty seconds—using only his feet!

• Daredevil **Alain Robert** scaled the exterior of the forty-eight-story Elf Aquitaine Building in Paris, France, in twenty-five minutes—without safety ropes!

• In 1919, **Edith Clifford**, an English circus performer, had a twenty-three-inch bayonet fired from a cannon and shot into his mouth.

• **Giovin Sondrio**, in appearances throughout Europe in the 1920s, repeatedly shot his initials into a playing card at a distance of twenty-two feet—blindfolded!

• In May 1918, **Willy Coppens**, a Belgian flying ace in World War I, safely landed on a German balloon—and then took off again.

• **Lillian Boyer**, a stunt flyer of the 1920s, to demonstrate that she could equal the daring of any man, hung from the wing of a plane by one hand.

• **Annie Oakley** (1860-1926), the famed American sharp-shooter, using a .22 caliber rifle, once shot 4,772 glass balls tossed into the air.

Wally Parker, of Cheswick, Pennsylvania, hit a four-inch target with one hand while balancing on the other.

• **William Elsworth Robinson**, a nineteenth-century conjuror, performed a trick in which he caught bullets in a plate!

• **Vasili Mochanou**, of Ottawa, created a replica of the Canadian flag using twenty-seven thousand snowballs!

The warrior monarch who had legs like steel springs. **King Teutobod**, who ruled the Teutonse from 125 to 101 B.C. could vault over the backs of 6 horses.

Mighty-jawed **Jackie Del Rio,** of Chicago, Illinois, could lift two tables and six chairs using only his teeth!

COUNT MORIC SANDOR

(1805-1878) A Hungarian daredevil horseman, drove a coach-and-four horses down the steep stairway of Bada Castle.

IN 1992, in New York City, **6,008 PEOPLE TAP-DANCED TOGETHER DOWN West 34TH STREET!**

Even walking can be hazardous: a 46-year-old Junkers bomber, piloted by **Martin Caidin**, flew at 9,000 feet over Palatka, Florida, with 19 wing walkers on its left wing.

GROUP STUNTS

• In September 1999, two thousand seventy-one students at the University of Guelph in Ontario, Canada, all blew bubbles with bubble wands at the same time!

• In Greenburgh, Pennsylvania, twelve people pushed a hospital bed a distance of 1,776 miles in seventeen days!

STUNT EATING

• **Krishana Muniandy**, of Seremban, Malaysia, swallowed a twelve-inch-long snake moments after the reptile had bit him!

• In 1988, a man from San Antonio, Texas, ate twenty-nine jalapeño peppers in two minutes!

• **Doctor William Buckland**, the first professor of geology at England's Oxford University, ate the heart of France's King Louis XIV at a dinner party!

• In 1968, **Paul Shaw**, of Wiltshire, England, ate sixteen ounces of grass clippings with a knife and fork in fifteen minutes, 0.05 seconds!

ON 1987, A TEAM OF 90 SCHOOLCHILDREN in Japan SKIPPED IN UNISON OVER A SINGLE JUMPROPE 160 TIMES!

- **Michel Lotito**, of Grenoble, France, who eats two pounds of metal each day—once ate a supermarket cart, seven television sets, and a Cessna light plane!

- In 1991, **Llewellyn Diamond**, a British fisherman, raised $1,100 for a charity by eating a bucket of live worms!

- In 1990, **Phil Turco**, of Madison, Wisconsin, swallowed three hundred thirty-nine goldfish in two hours!

- In 1991, **Michael Christopher Rice**, of San Diego, California, ate ninety-one large fishing worms in ninety-one minutes!

- **Kerry White** ate 12,547 baked beans, one at a time with a cocktail stick, in twenty-four hours!

- **Hadji Ali**, a vaudeville performer in the early 1900s, could swallow watermelon seeds, jewels, coins, and peach pits, then regurgitate specific items as requested.

AN 18TH-CENTURY FRENCH ENTERTAINER NAMED **DUFOUR** ONCE ATE A MEAL OF SNAKES, RATS, AND TOADS GARNISHED WITH THISTLES, SPIDERWEBS, AND BUTTERFLY WINGS! HE LATER DRANK FLAMING BRANDY AND ATE FOUR LARGE CANDLES FOR DESSERT!

DEADLY SPIN—CYCLE CHALLENGE
ESCAPE ARTIST CONFRONTS HIS FEARS INSIDE A WASHING MACHINE

Escape artist Rick Maisel has been challenging death throughout his career, yet he had to admit to himself that he still had a few phobias to conquer. He was afraid of water, of tight spaces, and, of course, of death itself. Maisel also knew that the best way to conquer a fear is to meet it head-on. So he decided to develop a stunt that would force him to confront the things he feared the most: he would handcuff himself and attempt to escape from a washing machine—a running washing machine.

To perform the stunt, Maisel shackles himself with five pairs of handcuffs and two pairs of leg irons. Then he carefully folds himself inside the round barrel of the washer. Just stuffing himself inside the machine is a formidable feat.

Timing is everything in this stunt. It is crucial that Maisel free himself before the machine begins its deadly spin cycle: "With seventy-two G forces, and four hundred fifty RPMs, it could literally extract my insides."

With Maisel inside, the washer is sealed and the wash cycle begins. Revolving at one hundred thirty-five times a minute, the machine forces water and soap into Maisel's nose and eyes. As seconds tick by, the machine fills with water, depriving Maisel of oxygen.

Moments later, Maisel knocks—with an unshackled hand—on the door of the washer. Attendants open the machine, and Maisel pours out, along with several gallons of soapy water. He's dizzy and gasping for breath, but he's free of his shackles—and of his fears.

Chapter 24
Food & Drink

• **Mr. Hugo**, an employee of Brown's restaurant in New York City, here shown carrying eight cups of coffee with one hand. Hugo later topped his own feat by toting ten cups in one hand. He was also able to take orders for twenty-five sandwiches at one time without writing them down and serve them all correctly.

The best things in life are. . .edible. Humankind has taken the art of eating far beyond mere sustenance and into the realm of recreation. Eating is fun, plain and simple—ask anyone who grew up in the seventies. (Remember Pop Rocks? Atomic Fireballs? Chomping wintergreen Lifesavers in front of a bathroom mirror with the lights off, to see the sparks?) A wise anthropology professor once said, "If you're strictly a meat and potatoes man, you're going to miss a lot of joy in the world." There's endless pleasure to be had if you see eating as an adventure. And if you plan on getting through this next section with your appetite intact, we certainly hope you do.

• The average person eats 66,133 pounds of food in a lifetime—equal to the weight of six elephants!

• In an average lifetime, an American consumes: four tons of beef, four tons of potatoes, two tons of chicken, twenty thousand eggs, three and a half tons of sugar, one hundred eight thousand slices of bread, two thousand gallons of milk, eighteen hundred gallons of beer, and eighty thousand cups of coffee!

COOKBOOKS AND RECIPES

COOKBOOKS

• The first cookbook: In the fourth century B.C., **Archestratus** of Gela, a Greek poet, published *The Art of Cooking*, containing several hundred recipes written in rhyme.

• **Ronald Taylor** has written two cooking books that use bugs as the main ingredients:

Butterflies in My Stomach and *Entertaining Insects*!

RECIPES

• A new recipe perfected in ancient Greece was considered as important as the creation of a poem.

• The original recipe for Peking duck contained fifteen thousand words!

• The enzymes in a pineapple have always made it impossible to gel, but chef **Heston Blumenthal**, of Bray, England, worked with physicist **Nicholas Kurti** to create pepper and pineapple jelly, and crab ice cream—both considered impossible combinations!

COOKING AND SERVING

COOKING METHODS

• The hot seat: Cooks in native restaurants in Indian supervise the preparation of meals while sitting on the hot stove.

The RIJSTTAFEL, a popular Javanese dish, requires 20 waiters to serve it! Hotel des Indes BATAVIA-1924

STORED FOOD is safeguarded by the Maori natives of New Zealand by perching it on top of an upended war canoe.

• **Frank Antonievich** won a bronze medal, a diploma, and a ten-dollar goldpiece when he cooked 100 pancakes in $22\frac{1}{2}$ minutes at the Grand Central Palace in New York. He was as fancy as he was productive, tossing the flapjacks in six different pans behind him from between his legs and catching them in the same pans in front of him.

THE FIRST PIZZA WAS MADE MORE THAN 2,000 YEARS AGO BY ROMAN SOLDIERS WHO ADDED OLIVE OIL AND CHEESE TO MATZOS --THE TRADITIONAL JEWISH PASSOVER BISCUITS

IN FURNAS, ON THE ISLAND OF Sao Miguel, VILLAGERS REGULARLY COOK THEIR FOOD IN HUGE POTS SET INTO THE GROUND AND HEATED BY A NEARBY VOLCANO!

• Clayton's Café in Tyler, Texas, boasted that waitress **Blanche Lowe** could carry twenty-three coffee cups in one hand.

• World-champion chicken picker "**Buck**" **Fulford,** of Port Arthur, Texas, could kill, pick clean, cut up, cook, and eat a chicken in one minute and fifty seconds. Elaborating on his technique, he explained that it took forty seconds to cut off the chicken's head and allow it to die, ten seconds for scalding, three or four seconds to pick and clean the chicken, three seconds to cut it up into four portions and drop it into boiling grease,

thirty seconds to cook it, followed by cooling it in cracked ice, and the rest of the time was for savoring and eating the fowl. Fulford's other accomplishments included plucking and picking as many as twelve chickens in one minute.

Ripley's — BELIEVE IT OR NOT!

IN England DURING THE 1400s, TERRIERS WERE TRAINED TO RUN INSIDE REVOLVING CAGES TO TURN A CRANK TO FIRE A SPIT!

IN Davie, Fla., THERE IS A FAST-FOOD RESTAURANT WHICH CATERS TO COWBOYS ON HORSEBACK WITH A "TROT-THROUGH" WINDOW and a CORRAL PARKING LOT!

...AND A SIDE OF HAY.

pie, chocolate, cigars, and peanuts—all existed in America before the coming of the white man.

SPECIALTIES

• "Balutes"—eggs cooked just before they are ready to hatch—are regarded as a great delicacy in the Philippines.

• Pearl duck, a specialty of the Three Provençal Brothers restaurant in Paris, France, in 1791, was always garnished with a $1,000 string of pearls—the diner had to return the pearls.

• Pickled flamingo tongues served on gold plates were a delicacy at banquets in ancient Rome!

• In Japan, noodles and coffee sprinkled with flakes of fourteen-karat gold are popular taste treats.

• A favorite delicacy among many residents of Nuoro, Sardinia, is "casu marzu"—brown lumps of rotting cheese that are crawling with maggots!

DINING CUSTOMS

• The ancient Fijians ate their regular meals using

• Standing wheat was cut, threshed, ground into flour, and baked into biscuits in Carrolton, Missouri, 1878, in four minutes, thirty-seven seconds.

• A Hindu named **Shalkla** cooked his dinner on his head in a coal-burning brazier!

FOOD SERVICE

• Pizza deliveries were first made in Italy during the nineteenth century by

boys balancing tin stoves on their heads to keep the pies warm!

MENUS

• Locusts, lizards, ants, and deep-fried scorpions are all on the menu at the Imperial Restaurant in Singapore!

• Menu for an all-American meal: tomato soup, turkey, potatoes, squash, sweet potatoes, succotash, corn bread, pineapple salad, tapioca pudding, pumpkin

• "Physical Perfectionist" **Charles Russell** received quite a bit of mail after his appearance in Ripley's cartoon on May 18th 1939, prompting him to try even harder for another claim to fame. Russell saw the Believe It Or Not® cartoon about Mr. Hugo, who was able to carry eight cups of coffee with one hand, and figured if he hoisted his sister in one hand and twelve cups of coffee in the other—on ice skates—he, too, could achieve another entry in Ripley's feature. His logic proved infallible.

FILM DIRECTOR *ALFRED HITCHCOCK* ONCE THREW A DINNER PARTY *for* ACTRESS *Gertrude Lawrence* WITH ALL THE FOOD—INCLUDING PEACHES, TROUT and ICE CREAM—**DYED BLUE.**

Ed Kottwitz poses with the thirty cobs of sweet corn he gnawed clean in order to win the title of World Champion Corn Eater. Kottwitz held the corn-eating record from 1931-1934.

their hands, but when eating human flesh, they used special wooden forks!

• At the turn of the century in Morocco, diners could only lick their fingers in strict order: fourth, second, thumb, third, and first!

FEASTS

GIGANTIC CONCOCTIONS

• Pat Burns, Canadian cattle king, received a birthday cake weighing three thousand pounds.

• Roman Emperor **Heliogabalus** (A.D. 204-222) once hosted a state banquet featuring a menu consisting of peas mixed with gold, rice with pearls, and lentils garnished with jewels!

• The Orleans County Fair at Albion, New York, featured a pie twelve feet across, weighing three tons. The pie required one hundred twenty-five bushels of apples, six hundred pounds of flour, and five hundred pounds of sugar.

• The tower of butter ("tour de beurre") at the Cathedral of Rouen, in France, in the fifteenth century, was so named because it was built with money from the sale of indulgences, permitting the parishioners to eat butter during Lent.

• The largest cake ever baked: The army of **Frederick William I** baked a cake eighteen yards long and eight yards wide, requiring thirty-six bushels

of flour, one ton of butter, one ton of yeast, and five thousand eggs.

• In Pittsburgh, Pennsylvania, a cake six feet high was made with a concrete mixer.

HELMUT MOELK, A NEW YORK CITY CHEF, MADE A 101-YARD LONG APPLE STRUDEL USING 250 LBS. OF APPLES AND OVER 200 LBS. OF DOUGH!

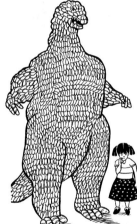

"MONSTER-LOAF"
SIX CHEFS AT A HOTEL IN TOKYO CREATED A 10-FT.-TALL, 1,100 LB. REPLICA OF GODZILLA USING 14,000 PIECES OF BREAD!

GIGANTIC MEALS

• Can you eat a bale of hay in ten minutes? Yes! First burn the hay, then dissolve the ashes in a beverage.

GIGANTIC COCKTAILS

• The seventy-five thousand dollar toast: **Sir Thomas Gresham** drank to the health of Queen Elizabeth with a glass of wine containing a large pearl that had been crushed to dust.

ENGLAND'S **K**ING HENRY VIII (1509-1547) ONCE ORDERED A **165-LB.** **PLUM PIE** THAT MEASURED **9 ft.** IN LENGTH AND HAD TO BE CARRIED ON A CART.

"BIGGEST KEBAB"

In 1993, in Windhoek, Namibia, 70 people using 1,320 lbs. of meat, 760 onions, and 400 lbs. of apricots created a half-mile-long kebab!

A FOOD COMPANY in Belgium CREATED A SINGLE STRAND of SPAGHETTI THAT MEASURED 468 FEET IN LENGTH!

"THE BIGGEST CAESAR SALAD IN THE WORLD"

Believe It or Not! 10 CHEFS in Tijuana, Mexico, MADE A GIANT CAESAR SALAD IN A 30-YARD LONG TROUGH USING 1,200 HEADS of LETTUCE, 1,200 BOILED EGGS, 75 LITERS of OLIVE OIL, 53 Kg. of LEMONS and 99 kg. of PARMESAN CHEESE!

AN **EGGSAGGERATION**

HUGE OMELETTE COMPOSED OF **7,200** EGGS WAS FRIED IN A PAN **8** FEET ACROSS. *IT WEIGHED HALF A TON !* THE PAN WAS GREASED BY ATTACHING SLABS OF BACON TO THE FEET OF GIRLS WHO TURNED IT INTO A SKATING RINK

• In 1991, at a bar in Sun City, South Africa, bartenders created a giant cocktail with 2,150 liters of tequila, grenadine, and pineapple juice!

BEVERAGES

ALCOHOL

• *Every Boy's Book of Sports and Amusements*, published in 1856, recommended beer over tea for children, stating: "Tea we believe to be undesirable, and a pint of really sound bitter will be found to agree much better."

• A company in Washington has developed a coffee-flavored beer!

• Aztec priests were the first people to place worms in the bottom of mescal, believing that it instilled the drink with a life spirit!

• Germans drink more beer than anyone else in the world—yet in 1979 the nation's biggest brewery derived most of its profits from bottled water.

• Only five people in the world know the secret formula for making Angostura aromatic bitters, an ingredient in cocktails that was invented one hundred seventy-five years ago!

• In 1993, in an experiment to create beer in a weightless atmosphere, a German company placed a tube of fermenting yeast aboard the Space Shuttle *Columbia!*

• In Gricova, Moldova, under the intersection of Riesling Street and Cabernet Boulevard, lies a maze of tunnels containing 9.2 million gallons of champagne and wine!

Ripley's — BELIEVE IT OR NOT!

CHRIS WARDEN, a pub owner in Cornwall, England, to discourage drinking and driving, provides customers with walkers equipped with bicycle bells and reflectors!

• In 1935, eighteen-year-old **Edd Woolf** drank five gallons and thirty ounces of water, then had a sandwich and a malt at Cheque's Confectionery in Duncan, Oklahoma. All this in less than thirty minutes! Woolf performed this amazing feat to win six dollars.

• Researchers in Australia have determined that some bubbles in a pint of Guinness stout actually do travel downwards, thereby defying the laws of nature!

• "The angel's share": Every year in France, twenty-three million bottles of cognac evaporate during the liquor's aging process!

• A bottle of champagne contains an average of fifty-six million bubbles!

COFFEE

• Coffee is a fruit juice.

• Coffee will cool quicker if the cream is added last.

• In the seventeenth century, people frequently added butter to their coffee before drinking it!

• Coffee made in a percolator is not percolated but decocted.

A winery in France sank 10,000 bottles of wine in the Bay of Biscay in the belief that sea water would help it age better!

• **"Scuba" Osborne,** of Myrtle Beach, South Carolina's, famous Bowery Tavern, could carry 34 mugs of beer at once! Scuba was one mug shy of Pittsfield, New York's, Clement Piehl's 35-mug record, featured in Ripley's on February 23, 1935.

HMMMM... CHATEAU DE SEAWEED.

F · 216

• The value of a good cup of coffee: **Osman**, an innkeeper, was made King of Tripoli in 1701 solely because he brewed the best coffee in the country.

• It takes all the beans from twelve coffee trees to make two cups of coffee!

• Coffee was originally used as a medicine.

• **King Frederick the Great** (1712-1786), of Prussia, drank coffee brewed with champagne instead of water.

• The first man to put milk in his coffee! **Johan Nieuof**, of the West India Company, in Brazil, was the first to mix coffee and milk. A monument was erected in his honor in Pernambuco.

• **William Harvey** (15788-1657), the seventeenth-century English doctor who discovered how blood circulates, believed coffee was "the source of happiness and wit." He willed fifty-six pounds of coffee to the London College of Physicians to be brewed once a month for his surviving friends.

LEMONADE

• In 1857, **Pete Conklin** created pink lemonade when he unwittingly used a bucket of water in which a circus performer had soaked his red tights.

MILK

• A quart of milk is heavier than a quart of cream.

• In India, milk is sold in frozen blocks and strung together.

• In 1940, a dollar could buy nine quarts of milk!

• Milk is sold in sheets in Denmark: the dehydrated milk is restored to liquid form by dissolving it in hot water.

• The "Milk Girls," who peddled milk in nineteenth-century England, were allowed to add one third water to each container of milk, by an act of Parliament.

• A jug of milk submerged in a well for nine years was still wholesome.

SODA

• **Joseph Priestley** (1733-1804), an English chemist, created soda water after he became interested in the formation of gases during fermentation when he moved next door to a brewery.

U.S. COMPANY CALLED "EXCUSE ME INC." MAKES A SODA POP CALLED "BELCHER" THAT DELIVERS THE LOUDEST AND MOST EXPLOSIVE BELCH AFTER DRINKING IT!

• A glass of soda water can be detected by all five senses: sight, taste, touch, smell, and hearing.

TEA

• Tea was so sought after in the 1600s that royalty paid $40 a pound for it.

• Tea in Tibet, Mongolia, and parts of China, is taken with salt instead of sugar.

• The Burmese eat tea instead of drinking it.

• If you use milk in your tea you are drinking leather. Milk contains fibrin and albumen. Tea contains tannin. The mixing of the two make a turbid liquid—the turbidity thus caused is tannate of fibrin, or leather.

WATER

• The average person drinks sixteen thousand gallons of water during his lifetime!

• Fifty percent of the world's population does not have an adequate supply of fresh water.

• Drinking water in the United States has been found to contain more than three hundred different chemicals.

• Glacial ice, originally brought back from Greenland by polar explorer **Doctor William Baker**, was one hundred thousand years old and free of bacteria. A trendy New York City department store imported four thousand pounds of it and charged $7 for thirty-five ounces.

FOODS

• A gallon of vinegar weighs more in the winter than in the summer: it expands in warm weather, thus the jug will hold less.

• The sandwich was invented by the **Earl of Sandwich**.

• The first pizzeria in the United States opened in New York City in 1895.

• Sauerkraut is an old Chinese dish, called "kumshi," invented twenty-five centuries ago.

• Chop Suey is unknown in China. It was created by an Irishman in San Francisco.

BREAD

• Brazilian Indians make bread from poisonous roots! The roots of the manioc or cassava plant are highly poisonous—but Brazilian natives discovered a method of removing the poison by squeezing the sap out of the roots.

• The oldest loaf of bread in the world was found in the ruins of Pompeii, where it had lain buried for nearly two thousand years.

• A loaf of bread contains 13,165,434,288 layers of dough.

• In Damascus, a loaf of bread is three feet in diameter.

• The wheat needed to make a one-pound loaf of bread requires two tons of water to grow.

• White bread was originally used exclusively for church services.

• In 1924, a loaf of bread cost three hundred billion marks in Germany. A loaf of stale bread sold for $118.

• **Jacob Schudnaggies**, of Spring Valley, New York, owns a piece of military-issue hard tack that was made in 1896—and is still "fresh."

A **SPECIAL CAKE** BAKED IN HESSEN, GERMANY, ONLY FOR A CHILD ENTERING SCHOOL FOR THE FIRST TIME

• **Mrs. M. K. Bills**, of Cleveland, Ohio, found a $20 bill in a loaf of bread.

George Gotsis, of Chicago, cut a 16-inch loaf of bread in perfect slices in 40 seconds—blindfolded!

BUGS

• In Africa, the mopane worm caterpillar is a favorite delicacy. It can be stewed, fried, or eaten fresh from the tree!

• A popular dish in Burma is pork-stuffed cricket.

•The adult daily requirement of phosphorus, calcium, riboflavin, and iron can be obtained by eating twenty caterpillars.

• The ancient Aztecs frequently ate bee maggots, mixed with wild honey and grasshoppers, cooked in a stew!

• Hungry for something different? Try the Australian witchetty grub, a moth larva found among the roots of the witchetty bush. The chubby grub is lightly crunchy when baked, soft and buttery when eaten raw.

• In Oaxaca, Mexico, grasshoppers fried in garlic and lemon are a favorite food!

• In Australia, moths toasted on a stick are a favorite food!

• Termites cooked in vegetable oil and salt are a delicacy among the Bantu tribe of South Africa!

CANDIES

• The man who introduced chewing gum to the United States: **General Antonio Lopez de Santa Anna**, President of Mexico and the one responsible for the massacre at the Alamo, chewed chicle while being escorted through the United States in 1837 as a prisoner of war. John Adams, his secretary, later obtained some chicle from trees in the Mexican jungle, flavored it, and founded the chewing gum industry.

SKULLS MADE OF CANDY AND SOLD ON A FIESTA DAY IN MEXICO, ARE GIVEN BY YOUTHS TO GIRLFRIENDS AS A SIGN OF THEIR HIGH REGARD

• "Hotlix," tequila-flavored lollipops with worms embedded in them, are a popular treat in California.

CHEESE

• The name of a cheese made in Oberammergau, Germany, is oberammergau erpassionsfesspielalpenkrauterklostedelikatfruhstuckskase.

• Billiard balls are made of cheese! Common cottage cheese, when moistened with forty percent formaldehyde, becomes so hard that pool and billiard balls can be made from it.

• A dull knife can slice cheese thinner than a sharp knife can.

• Can you increase the number of holes in a cheese without reducing its weight? Sure, just cut it in half!

CHOCOLATE

• Chocolate was a drink only, until the middle 1800s, when an English firm developed a process to produce the first solid eating chocolate.

• In Central America, during the eighteenth century, no one under the age of sixty was allowed to drink chocolate!

DESSERTS

• Cake placed in an atmosphere of helium will keep fresh indefinitely.

• Boston cream pie served in Washington is the same dessert as Washington cream pie served in Boston.

• An upside-down cake is right-side up when it is upside down.

• A coconut cake has remained on **Cad Harrell's** Tarboro, North Carolina dining room table for seventeen years.

• The average American eats thirty-five thousand cookies during his lifetime!

• The best kind of gingerbread does not contain ginger.

• **Mrs. C. B. Osborne**, of Runnels, Iowa, can make a glass of jelly in a minute—even in winter!

• Americans eat eight hundred eleven million gallons of ice cream annually—equal to twenty-six billion scoops.

- **Dolly Madison**, wife of President Madison, invented ice cream, and was the first hostess to serve it in this country.

EGGS

- You can spin a boiled egg, but not a raw one.

- An egg is warmer at the broad end than at the other.

- Place an egg in a glass of fresh water, add two tablespoons of salt, and the egg will float.

- You can stand an egg on end without breaking the shell! Shake it violently until you break the yolk, which will settle to the bottom.

- The whites of eggs and the deadly venom of a rattlesnake contain the same chemical constituents, in the same proportion.

FISH

- The term hundred herring in the English herring trade actually refers to one hundred thirty-two fish.

- The more sardines packed in a can, the greater the profit to the packer—the oil is more costly than the fish.

- Sardines are sold one at a time from an open can in China.

- There is no such fish as a sardine. The fish may be pilchards, herring, or anchovies.

FRUITS

- The apple is a member of the rose family.

- Apricot pits are more valuable than apricots.

- There are about five hundred different types of bananas!

- The banana is not a fruit and it grows upside down! They are picked when green and are not good if allowed to ripen on the plant.

- Coco-de-mer, the double coconut of the Seychelles—the largest nut in the world—can weigh fifty pounds. The fruit is an aphrodisiac.

- The Romans used lemons as mothballs.

- A lemon is a berry, not a fruit!

- Momordica, a fruit of Mexico, tastes like roast veal.

GARLIC

- Inspiration by the bowl: **Jean-Toussaint Merle** (1783-1852), the French playwright, insisted that he was able to turn out one hundred twenty plays only because he drank garlic soup every night for fifty-nine years.

- Garlic belongs to the lily family.

GRAINS

- A sack of flour will keep indefinitely under water.

- In 1840, Alaskan wheat sold for $5 a head in South Carolina.

HONEY

- To make a pound of clover honey, bees must take the nectar from sixty-two thousand blossoms, requiring 2,750,000 visits to the clover fields.

MEAT

- Meat was often sold door-to-door in the United States in the 1890s, in unrefrigerated wagons.

- Baloney is unknown in Bologna, Italy. There it is called mortadella. Baloney comes from the Spanish word "bolonio," meaning foolish.

- A can of bully beef eighty-one years old was found to still be in perfect condition.

- **Sam Rosenbaum**, a butcher in Hollywood, California, can examine a cubic inch of meat and tell from exactly which part of the animal it was cut.

- **P. D. Gwaltney, Junior** had a pet Smithfield ham, which, although never introduced to cold storage, remained tender and sweet and fit to eat after thirty years!

- A Chicago, Illinois company has developed hot dogs with edible ink messages on them!

- The left ham is more tender than the right ham because pigs use only their right leg to scratch themselves.

- Saucissenkartoffel-biersauerkrautkranzwurst is a Cologne sausage—and was a favorite dish of Mark Twain.

Petrified ham, owned by **George Kern**, of Columbus City, Iowa.

• A steak is made up of nearly seventy-five percent water.

MUSHROOMS

• The mushroom is a fruit.

• **G. F. Brazier**, of Silverton, Oregon, grew a mushroom weighing twenty-six pounds.

PASTA

• Spaghetti is a Chinese dish, invented one thousand years before Italy knew of it.

• American **Nicholas A. Ruggieri** has invented a sealed cup of wound spaghetti that can be eaten with a straw!

POULTRY

• A chicken without feathers is "dressed."

• The bird that was too good-looking for its own good: The swan, although its meat is tough and oily, was often served in medieval times because it looked so attractive on the banquet table.

REPTILES

• In Hong Kong, snakes are the chief ingredient in both a popular broth and in a potent wine.

SALT

• Salt is composed of two poisons: sodium and chlorine.

• Salt added to a grapefruit will make it sweet.

SEAFOOD

• The first American settlers used lobsters to fertilize their gardens, and fed them only to widows, orphans, and servants!

• One Tridacna gigas, the giant clam of the South Seas, will make one hundred gallons of chowder.

• A clam is meat, is Latin not English, and means "secretly thou goest."

SUGAR

• Sugar was once so rare in Europe that is was as valuable as precious gems and considered a suitable wedding present for a queen!

• If you break a lump of sugar in the dark it will show a flare of bluish light.

• A teaspoonful of sugar can be dissolved in a glass full of water to the brim without spilling a drop.

• Sugar was used only as a medicine in the fourteenth century.

VEGETABLES

• **John Rimmer** of Cadishead, England, grew a cabbage weighing seventy-four pounds.

• **Tom Fisher** of Grand Haven, Michigan, grew a cucumber six feet, two inches long.

• The Vidalia onion, grown in rural Georgia, contains more sugar than some popular soft drinks.

SALT IN THE WESTERN SUDAN, AFRICA, IS SOLD "BY THE STRAW"— THE SALT IS CRYSTALLIZED AROUND THE STRAW AND SOLD A DOZEN AT A TIME

LOW FAT, HIGH PROTEIN, CRUNCHY—SO WHAT IF THE ANTENNAS TICKLE ON THE WAY DOWN?

The students of the Iowa State University Entomology Club really love bugs—especially toasted ones, with a little Cajun seasoning. These bug aficionados not only like studying the six-legged members of the animal kingdom, they also enjoy them as a tasty snack.

And why not? They're high in protein, low in fat and, according to Entomology Club members, quite tasty. For the novice bug-chugger, club member Gretchen Schultz recommends crickets in Jell-O. She recommends lemon: "Yellow really pronounces the color of the crickets!" With crickets in Jell-O safely tucked under your belt, you may want to move onto more adventurous fare, say, candy apples coated with mealworms.

But once you're a seasoned connoisseur of the crawly, you simply must try the bug-lovers favorite: Chocolate-Covered Grasshoppers:

- 6 to 8 large grasshoppers
- Brown sugar
- Corn syrup
- Butter
- Melted chocolate
- Candy molds

Cut off the grasshoppers' legs. Simmer butter, brown sugar, and corn syrup together to make a candy sauce. Dip grasshoppers in sauce to form a candy coating. Fill chocolate molds half way. Add grasshoppers. Fill molds the rest of the way. Bake. Enjoy!

• The world's hottest chili registers eight hundred fifty-five thousand Scoville units—that's almost twice as strong as the Mexican habanero!

• The famous voyage that owes its success to chopped cabbage! When **Captain Cook** (1728-1779), set sail around the world with two ships in 1776, he expected to lose sixty percent of his crew to scurvy, but his four-year expedition did not lose a single man to that scourge because Cook prescribed a steady diet of sauerkraut. The only deaths were the captain himself, who was killed by natives, and the ship's cook, who succumbed to tuberculosis.

• In India, Assam tribesmen eat the "naga jolokia" chili at every meal—and regularly use it as a weapon!

• To keep horseradish hot, you must keep it cool!

• A potato is neither a fruit nor a vegetable.

OTHER FOODS

• Ambrosia, the food of the immortal gods, is a ragweed causing hay fever. It is inedible by man or beast.

• **Constantin Boym** and **Laurene Leon**, of New York City, invented edible almond- and hazelnut-flavored pencils!

• Arabs regularly gather the Biblical manna from heaven. It is a resinous gum from the twigs of the tamarisk, an evergreen shrub, found in the mid-Sinai.

• In a village near Accra, Ghana, five thousand tons of rock are mined every year, then crushed and mixed with water and turned into an edible dough!

Chapter 25
Games & Pastimes

IN THE 1800s, IT WAS POPULAR TO RACE BICYCLES AGAINST ICE SKATERS ON THE FROZEN DELAWARE RIVER FROM PHILADELPHIA TO TRENTON, N.J.!

Board games, card games, shuffleboard, horseshoes—games are part of the tapestry of our lives. We've grown up with them; we've made some of our most cherished memories with family and friends over them. Yet few of us have given them much thought. You probably grew up playing hopscotch in the park, for example, but do you know who first invented it, and when? The answer may surprise you. Likewise with that church hall favorite, bingo: there's a reason the game is so popular—do you know how many ways you can make bingo on a standard ninety-number board? Hint: the answer's got eight digits. Then, in addition to those tried and true favorites, we've added a few new and unusual pastimes. Where else, for example, will you learn what equipment is required for "Whiff-whaff"? Read on, if you're game.

• The 1900 Olympics in Paris featured competitions in billiards, checkers, and fishing!

• The old shell game: The Japanese carrier snail camouflages itself by covering its back with smaller shells.

• **John Winslow**, of Gloucester, Virginia, played with a yo-yo for five days straight—one hundred twenty consecutive hours!

BILLIARDS AND POOL

• **Mike Hammer** and **Richard Becker**, of New York City, played a game of pool that lasted one hundred ten hours!

• In 1987, **Rob McKenna**, of Blackpool, England,

James Evans, a pocket billiard star, ran the entire rack of 15 balls from an open break without missing or allowing the cue ball to touch a cushion on any shot!

sunk fifteen pool balls in only 37.9 seconds!

• In 1995, **Larry Grindinger**, of Duluth, Georgia, balanced four billiard balls on top of a beer bottle, then shot out the bottom three balls with his cue ball, leaving only the fourth ball balanced on the bottle! He has other extraordinary skills. While blindfolded, he can spit a cue ball out of his mouth onto a nine-foot pool table. He bounces it over five rows of balls and sinks four balls in two pockets! He has also trained his dog "Jake" to shoot pool with his nose!

BINGO

• There are forty-four million ways to make bingo on a ninety-number bingo card.

• Bingo was originally called "beano"!

BOARD GAMES

• In July 1989, twelve hundred people played Monopoly continuously for fifty days while submerged in an eight-thousand-gallon tank of water.

• **Rick Polizzi**, of Los Angeles, California, has a

collection of over four hundred board games, including "The Great Escape," in which handcuffed players must find the keys.

GREGORY R. BROTZ of Sheboygan, Wisc., INVENTED A COMPETITIVE BOARD GAME THAT IS OPERATED BY **BRAIN WAVES!**

• A new board game called "Infection" pits players against each other playing on a board infected with such diseases as smallpox and athlete's foot! The first player to be cured completely wins!

BOWLING

• There is a bowling alley in Tokyo, Japan, with five hundred and four lanes!

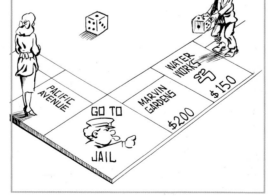

STUDENTS IN BURNT LAKE, N.Y., RAISE MONEY FOR CHARITY BY PLAYING MONOPOLY ON A LIFE-SIZE BOARD!

• **Stanley Flasser**, of Wilkes Barre, Pennsylvania, bowling on his twenty-first wedding anniversary, rolled twenty-one consecutive strikes.

• **Don Newport**, of Fort Lauderdale, Florida, bowled one thousand games in succession in a period of one hundred eleven hours.

CARD GAMES

• Playing cards, until the invention of printing in the fifteenth century, were hand-painted works of art, and could be afforded only by the wealthy.

• In 1990, the United States Playing Card Company began reproducing decks of cards with

A 5,000-YEAR-OLD BOARD GAME WITH PYRAMID-SHAPED DICE WAS FOUND IN THE ANCIENT CITY OF UR IN IRAQ.

escape maps drawn on them that were used by prisoners of war during World War II!

• Playing cards used in India are round!

• There are fifty-four octillion (54,000,000,000, 000,000,000,000,000) possible hands that can be played in a game of bridge!

CHECKERS AND CHESS

• **Doctor Reuben Fine** of New York City played and won four time-limit chess games simultaneously—while blindfolded!

• The living pawns: The **Emperor of Annam**, now Vietnam, celebrated each New Year's Day by competing with his Prime Minister in a chess game in which the chess pieces were living men. The winning pieces were rewarded, but the losers were jailed.

• Once every two years, in Marostica, Italy, a chess game is played on a huge board with people dressed in fifteenth-century costumes acting as the chess pieces!

• There are 170,000,000, 000,000,000,000,000,000 ways to play the first ten moves in a game of chess!

EIGHTEENTH-CENTURY FRENCH COMPOSER AND CHESS MASTER *FRANCIS ANDRÉ DANICAN* WAS THE FIRST MAN TO WIN A GAME OF CHESS WHILE *BLINDFOLDED!*

JIM and RUTH BUTLER of Oakville, Ont., Canada, HAVE A BACKYARD GARDEN THAT FEATURES A GIANT CHESSBOARD WITH 33-ft.-HIGH CHESS PIECES!

• **Greg Davis** and **Mark Schumacher**, of Nunawading, Austria, played checkers in a restaurant for one hundred thirty-eight hours and twenty-eight minutes (August 26 to September 1, 1985).

• **Judit Polgar**, of Hungary, age seventeen, was the world's top female chess player in 1993.

• **T. J. Eisenbraun**, of Boardman, Ohio, and his brother Mike, of Portland, Tennessee, have been playing the same chess game by mail for over three years!

• "Deep Blue," the computer that beat world chess champion **Garry Kasparov** in a recent rematch, can analyze two hundred million chess moves per second!

DARTS

• In 1993, Boca Raton, Florida dart player **Johnny Mielcarer** hit twelve hundred bull's-eyes in ten hours!

• **David P. Engvall**, of Baldwin Lake, California, fired a dart from a fifty-inch slingshot a distance of 1,565 feet!

DICE

• The first dice used in gambling were actually the ankle bones of sheep.

• Dice used by gamblers in ancient Rome had fourteen sides.

HORSESHOES

• **Ted Allen**, of Boulder Colorado, pitched two hundred two-pound horseshoes in 1955 and made one hundred eighty-seven ringers.

IN NOVEMBER, 1989, THE FIRST WORLD CHAMPIONSHIP OF *NUN-SNOOKER* WAS HELD AT THE TYBURN CONVENT IN LONDON, ENGLAND!

VIDEO AND ARCADE GAMES

• **Billy Mitchell,** of Florida, playing at an arcade, became the world's first recorded master of the video game Pac Man by scoring 3,333,360 points—a perfect score!

• **Terry Smith**, of Hul, in Humberside, England, playing pinball on two straight machines for seventy straight hours, scored 490,397,440 points!

UNCOMMON GAMES

• British Prime Minister **Neville Chamberlain** (1869-1940) invented the game of snooker!

• He who gets slapped! In the Philippines there is a game in which each player takes his turn at slapping the other on the thigh with all his might. The first one to draw blood wins.

• Snapdragon, a popular game played in the early 1900s, challenged players to snatch pieces of fruit and nuts from a dish of flaming brandy!

• In 1923, **Anton Hulsman,** of San Francisco, California, invented an arcade game in which players pitch a ball at a human target!

• A company in Vernon Hill, Illinois, has developed a table tennis game that uses no ball! Players hit a glowing red projection!

The ANCIENT AZTECS in Peru played "Tlachtli," a basketball-like game in which players who scored **were allowed to grab clothing and jewelry** from spectators!

IN Pátzcuaro, Mexico, RESIDENTS CELEBRATE THE NEW YEAR BY PLAYING A HOCKEY-LIKE GAME USING A BURNING BALL OF RAGS FOR A PUCK!

"BIMITI" A GAME PLAYED in South America, REQUIRES COMPETITORS TO RUN ALONG A TRACK TOWARDS A TROUGH FILLED WITH BEER WHILE BYSTANDERS THROW HANDFULS OF HOT PEPPER and ASHES AT THEM!

"SWING YOUR TRACTOR..."

Believe It or Not! **TRACTOR SQUARE-DANCING** IS A POPULAR PASTIME AMONG FARMERS IN IOWA! THEY TOUR THE COUNTRYSIDE PROMENADING AND DO-SI-DO-ING ON VINTAGE TRACTORS!

UNUSUAL PASTIMES

• In New Zealand, a popular pastime involves riding inner tubes through underground caves that are teeming with eels!

• "Nagasaki Hata": Japanese fighting kites that fly at high speeds have strings that are covered with ground glass in order to sever the lines of opponents' kites!

• In "pok-ol-pok," an ancient children's game in which the players tried to put a rubber ball through a stone ring, winners were allowed to take the losing team's jewelry and clothing!

"ICY MERRY-GO-ROUND" THE INUIT CARVE HUGE TOPS OUT OF ICE FOR CHILDREN TO RIDE ON!

Believe It or Not! IN ITALY, STRESSED OUT EXECUTIVES RELIEVE THEIR ANXIETY BY DRESSING UP AS GLADIATORS AND FIGHTING EACH OTHER WITH WOODEN CLUBS AND SPEARS IN PUBLIC TOURNAMENTS!

BUGGY ROLLIN'—WHY JUST SKATE ON YOUR FEET WHEN YOU CAN HAVE WHEELS ALL OVER!

Something weird is roaming the streets of Paris at night. It's shiny, silver-black, has two legs, two arms—and too many wheels to count. It's Roller Man, and despite the otherworldly appearance of his costume, he's quite human. He's a twenty-eight-year-old inventor named Jean Yves Boudeau, and he's created what may become the hottest new pastime: Buggy Rollin'!

Jean's futuristic Buggy Rollin' suit took nearly a year to create: six months of research, a month to construct the prototype, and more than two months of testing and adjustment. The form-fitting suit with the bug-like helmet features wheels on its back, chest, stomach, bottom, knees, and hands. Its boots feature regular inline skates, but this is the only part of the Buggy Rollin' suit that could be described as ordinary.

Once inside the Buggy Rollin' suit, Jean can skate in any one of twenty positions, at speeds of more than thirty miles per hour.

Buggy Rollin' requires the agility of a hockey player, and the balance of a gymnast. It's nowhere near as easy as Jean makes it look. Why does he do it? "To make people smile. That's the purpose of Buggy Rollin'."

The Buggy Rollin' Suits will soon be available for purchase, but will retail for approximately $750.

Chapter 26

Geography

Welcome to Ripley's international tour of some of the world's most peculiar places. We'll explore unusual borders and territories; uncover little-known facts about a few of your favorite cities, countries and states; journey to obscure sovereign nations; and visit some of the most unusual destinations on earth.

Vinievier Simpson, the boy "spell" binder of Kentucky, could spell the names of the principal states and cities of the world at age four.

BORDERS AND TERRITORIES

• A European border that is crossed without a passport! Travelers can cross the border between Germany and Austria in a salt mine at Hallein, Austria. Traversing a series of slides at up to forty miles per hour—sitting astride a hardwood rail—it is possible to visit Germany without presenting a passport.

• The Cape of Good Hope is not the most southern part of Africa!

• Prior to the revolution of 1917, **Czar Nicholas II** of Russia planned to build an electric fence around Russia's borders, and bridges across the Bering Strait!

ISLANDS

• The fastest-moving place on Earth: The Tonga Islands in the South Pacific move ten inches each year!

• Barbara Airport in the Outer Hebrides Islands, of Scotland, is just a stretch of shell beach accessible only twice a day!

• "The most remote island in the world": Tristan da Cunha, a thirty-eight-square-mile island in the South Atlantic with two hundred residents, is seventeen hundred miles away from the nearest continent!

• The first place to be illuminated by the first sunrise of the twenty-first century was Kao, an island in the South Pacific!

NATIONS

• Every year about forty-three million tons of dust settles over the United States!

• Canada's coastline equals a distance more than twice the circumference of the Earth!

• Indonesia has thirteen thousand separate islands that cover three different time zones!

• A plot of land in Ireland has a lease signed on December 3, 1888, that doesn't expire for ten million years!

• South Africa is the only country in the world with three national capital cities!

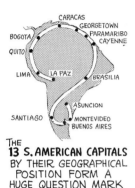

THE 13 S. AMERICAN CAPITALS BY THEIR GEOGRAPHICAL POSITION FORM A HUGE QUESTION MARK

STATES

• In 1991, the Colorado Senate approved a bill making it illegal to bad-mouth meat, fruits, and vegetables!

• Washington is the only state to have an official dance, the square dance!

• Alaska was bought by the United States for two cents an acre.

• Alaska has a coastline larger than that of all the other coastal states in the U.S. combined.

STREETS

• "Gum Alley," an alleyway in San Luis Obispo, California, is covered with thousands of pieces of used bubble gum that have been left by visitors!

• Kitty Witches' Row, a street in Great Yarmouth, England, is so narrow that at one point it is only one foot and eleven and a half inches wide!

• Lombard Street in San Francisco, California, often called "the crookedest street in the world," was a two-way thoroughfare in the 1920s.

CITIES, TOWNS AND VILLAGES

• The town of Wethersfield, Connecticut, is the only place to have ever been struck twice by meteorites—once in April 1971, and again in November 1982!

• Lynchburg, Tennessee, where Jack Daniel's Tennessee Whiskey is distilled, is a "dry" town, where the drinking of alcohol has been illegal since 1933!

• Llivia, a town in France, is part of Spain, although it is located four miles from the Spanish border.

• The City of Salt: An underground city in Wieliczka, Poland, is carved completely out of solid salt!

• Abbotsham, England, hosts daily races of sheep dressed in knitted sweaters running along a six-hundred-sixty-foot track!

• Josefsberg, a village in South Tyrol, Italy, is in perpetual shadow for ninety-one days each year. Mountains cut off the sun from November 3 until February 2.

• Montana is home to a town officially designated for prairie dogs!

• Saint Agnes National Park, in Los Angeles, California, created by American newspaperman Gene Fowler, is only six feet in size!

• Atrani, a village of twenty-six hundred in Italy, consisting of houses jammed together between a rocky mountain and the sea, does not have a single street traversing it.

• Ganvie, in Benin, West Africa, was built on bamboo stilts in the center of a lake to escape French tax collectors.

THE **CITY** OF **NO CHILDREN!** (1816)
WHEN THE SOVEREIGN CITY OF RAGUSA, Dalmatia, WAS CONQUERED BY THE AUSTRIANS — IT DECIDED *NOT* TO BEAR THE ALIEN YOKE.
SO SECRETLY THEY VOWED NOT TO HAVE CHILDREN — WITH THE RESULT THAT THEY DIED OUT COMPLETELY IN 2 GENERATIONS

- There's more than one Empire State Building in New York City!

- Atlanta, Georgia, is home to thirty-two streets named "Peachtree."

- Locke, a town in California near Sacramento, is the only town in the world outside China built entirely for Chinese immigrants by Chinese immigrants.

- The rainbow that founded a town: Akreijit, a community in Mauritania, was constructed at the end of a rainbow that had remained visible in the sky in 1840 for a full month.

- The town that lost a generation! Every girl in Corte, on the island of Corsica, vowed in 1729 to remain single until children born in the town would no longer be enslaved by the people of Genoa. They kept their pledge until the Genoese were driven out of Corsica—thirty-nine years later.

- **Captain Thomas P. Leathers** (1816-1889), a native of Kentucky, was so fond of his adopted town of Natchez, Mississippi, that he named seven successive steamboats *The Natchez*. He was a huge man and had many narrow escapes from death, but he was finally killed in New Orleans by a hit-and-run bicycle.

- **Samuel L. Tilley** (1818-1896), a Canadian statesman, first suggested calling his country a dominion because of a quotation in the Bible, Psalm 72: Verse 8—"He shall have dominion from sea to sea and from the river unto the ends of the earth."

- Seattle, Washington, is home to four hundred forty-eight coffee houses—and even the waters of Puget Sound are full of caffeine!

- Goslar, a city in Germany, is one thousand years old.

- Coos Bay, Oregon, is the largest shipping port for lumber in the world.

- Rockhall, a seventy-foot-high rock in the Atlantic, west of Scotland, is inhabited only by sea birds. In 1955, it was formally annexed by Great Britain as a territory.

- Peking, China, when invaded for the first time in history by a European army, was defended only by a few Chinese who attempted to frighten off the enemy by waving paper tigers and dragons.

CITY OF THE DEAD

MESHED — IRAN

A PERSIAN CITY PAVED WITH TOMBSTONES

THE SPACE AROUND THE SHRINE IS ONE VAST GRAVEYARD
PEOPLE PAY FROM $50 TO $500 FOR THE PRIVILEGE OF
INTERMENT WITHIN ITS SACRED PRECINCTS

• **Lowell Davis** has relocated the gas station, general store, and blacksmith shop of Red Oak, Missouri, to his farm twenty-three miles away!

• **King Seleucus** (358-281 B.C.) of Syria, founded thirty two cities, each of which became a center of Greek culture. He named sixteen of the cities after his father, Antioch.

• The town that never sees the winter sun: Rjukan, a community of six thousand persons in Norway, is surrounded by mountains so high that throughout the winter its inhabitants never see the sun

• Trevelez, a village in Spain, is celebrated for producing hams and other meat products—yet its inhabitants are strict vegetarians.

• Yellow Pine, Idaho, deep in the mountains of Boise National Forest, is fifty-two miles from the closest town and can be reached only by ski plane—yet its residents so value their isolation and independence that they have refused to install a single telephone!

• More dead than alive! Colma, California, with fourteen cemeteries, has a dead population of over one million, while the living population totals only seven hundred fifty. The town has no funeral homes.

• Real de Catorce, a former mining town in Mexico, is the only community in the western hemisphere that can be entered only through a tunnel.

• **John Harris English**, military surgeon in Parramatta, Australia, escaped a court martial and changed the name of a large section of the city of Sydney by discovering in the military charges against him a one-word error. Harris's offense occurred on the 19th "instant" (meaning the 19th of the present month), but the charge stated it took place on the 19th "ultimo" (the past month)—and today a large section of Sydney is named "Ultimo."

• During the 1830s, hordes of pigs roamed the streets of Cincinnati, keeping the city clean of garbage!

• Dede, a village along the bed of the Yangtze River, China, is inhabited for only three winter months because it is underwater the other nine months of the year.

• Every building in Ochiltree, Texas, when the railroad bypassed it in the 1920s, was hitched to huge tractors and moved to a new site along the railroad.

• The town of Duirat, in Southern Tunisia, is located entirely inside a single mountain.

• Baarle-Nassau and Baarle-Hertog are actually just one village with six thousand Belgian and Dutch residents, served by two mayors, two police forces, two flags, and two income tax rates!

• The town on wheels: Lakewood, in western Australia, a community in the heart of a lumber and gold-mining area, has its homes, shops, post office, and police station mounted on railroad cars.

• A city gate in Ayassoluk, Turkey, built by the Greeks sixteen hundred years ago, was constructed out of tombstones and coffin lids.

• Indian **King Kusinaba** was the father of one hundred daughters, all of them hunchbacks. To commemorate his great family tragedy, the King founded a city and named it Kanyakubja, "The City of the Deformed Maidens." The city remains today, although its name has been shortened to Kanauj.

IN THE TOWN of Culembourg, the Netherlands, SIX SHEEP ARE LET LOOSE IN THE STREETS TO CONTROL THE SPEED of RUSH-HOUR TRAFFIC.

COOBER PEDY—AUSTRALIA'S UNDERGROUND CITY

Drive the lonely Outback highway that passes by Coober Pedy, and all you're likely to see are several slate-colored mounds rising from the desert floor. But, believe it or not, beneath those mounds is a comfortable community of homes, offices, churches, hotels, and shops—a veritable underground city.

The city of Coober Pedy began as an opal mine in 1915. When the region experienced an opal boom in the 1960s, miners decided to build their homes inside the mine in order to escape the desert's blistering one hundred twenty degree heat. Below ground, the temperature remains a cool seventy degrees.

Many of Coober Pedy's residents find life underground so comfortable, they seldom venture topside. They have everything they need below the ground. There's plenty to attract tourists, too. Visitors to Coober Pedy often stay in Elsa Gladwin's underground hotel, although they complain that there's no light to wake them up in the mornings.

At first, life underground in Coober Pedy was nearly as harsh as life topside. But today's Coober Pedy homes have electricity, running water pumped directly from underground pools, and gravity-fed sewage disposal. A three-bedroom home can be dug to order in as little as three weeks, at a cost of approximately $12,000. But there's a bonus—if the homeowner finds opals during the dig, the construction may pay for itself!

- In Turkey, there is a secluded village called Polonezkoy where the residents are all of Polish descent and speak in an ancient Polish dialect!

- New York City has 12,187 taxis, but in Silsbee, Texas, there's only one—owned and operated by **Wand Reynolds**. She usually gets one or two fares a week!

- After four years of drought, the town of Monticello, California has reemerged from the man-made lake that had covered it since the 1950s!

- Since 1986, **Bob Carlson** has walked every single street and alley in San Francisco, California.

- The breakfast capital of the world: Battle Creek, Michigan, has an annual festival in which breakfast is served for the entire town on a half-mile-long table!

- Houses in Mezhirich, a town in the Soviet Ukraine, were built fifteen thousand years ago made entirely of mammoth bones!

- Juneau, Alaska, is the largest city in the United States!

- In 146 B.C., the ancient Romans destroyed the city of Carthage. In 1985, 2,131 years later, descendants of both sides met in Tunis to make peace.

SOVEREIGN NATIONS

- The Sovrano Internazionale Militare Ordine de Malta, a nine-hundred-thirty-year-old principality with one hundred citizens, is only the size of a football field!

- Malta is the only country in the world so small that it has its own street address.

- **Leonard** and **Shirley Caset**, in 1970 turned their twenty-nine-square-mile farm in western Australia into an independent principality!

- For three days out of every year, a fifteen-hundred-square-mile section of Colorado is officially independent from the United States!

- Cars, planes, income tax, and divorce are prohibited on the Channel Island of Sark—the last remaining feudal state in Europe!

- "The Kingdom of Humanity": In the 1960s, American **Morton F. Meads** claimed ownership of a group of islands in the South China Sea, declaring them to be an independent republic, and made Beethoven's Fifth Symphony its national anthem!

Chapter 27
Geology & Natural Phenomena

Psst—want to know where you can go to see a "moonbow"? Care to go skydiving—underground? Would you believe us if we told you there's a river that flows vinegar, and another that explodes during thunderstorms? Before you is a collection of vanishing lakes, glowing caves, tropical glaciers, and other unbelievable geological phenomena, some of the Earth's most extraordinary natural wonders.

• The amount of underground water in the United States is fifty times greater than that of all its rivers and streams combined.

• The ghostly forest: Dead trees buried for centuries in the forest of Tutira, New Zealand, reappear on the ground after every fire like images on a photographic plate.

CANYONS

• The Grand Canyon could hold the entire population of the world!

• The Grand Canyon is not the deepest canyon in the United States!

Hell's Canyon on the Idaho/Oregon border is twenty-two hundred feet deeper!

CAVES

• A pipe organ in the Luray Caverns in Virginia was built using the caverns' natural stalactites instead of metal pipes!

• The Beckham Creek Cavern in Jasper, Arkansas, is a deep mountain crevasse that was once used as a bomb shelter but is now a bed and breakfast inn!

• The Caves of the Thousand Buddhas near Tunhwang, China, comprise five hundred caves hollowed out of a sheer cliff—an area ten stories high and a mile in length, constructed by Buddhist monks over a period of one thousand years.

• The grotto of the two flags in the cave of Holl Loch, in Switzerland, has two huge stalactites on its wall shaped like fluttering flags.

DESERTS

• The singing sands of the Gobi Desert: Wind blowing over the sand dunes causes a constant sound that varies from a roll of drums to a deep chant.

THE **STANDLEY CHASM** IN THE MacDonnell Mountains of Australia, **20** FEET WIDE AND **500** FEET DEEP, IS A CLEFT SO DARK THAT A MAN STANDING AT THE BOTTOM OF IT *CAN SEE STARS IN THE DAYTIME*

THE MAN WHO WAS
IN LOVE WITH HIS
SHADOW
WILLIE BEYER,
a businessman of
Halberstadt, Germany,
to view the brocken
specter, an enormously
magnified shadow cast
upon the clouds from
Mount Brocken when the
sun is low, climbed 3,733
feet to the top of the
mountain 650 times.

• Fifteen hundred of the oases in the Sahara Desert of a total of two thousand oases in the area were artificially created—they comprise irrigated valleys in which palm trees were planted to provide shade.

EARTHQUAKES

• The deep-sea oarfish helps scientists in Japan predict earthquakes by swimming to the surface from depths of over two hundred meters!

• During the 1994 California Earthquake, only one egg broke at the largest egg farm in the United States, located only five miles from the earthquake's epicenter!

• Earthquake shock waves travel five miles in one second!

• Hundreds of hibernating snakes mysteriously emerged from below ground just before an earthquake struck China in 1975.

• The great Alaskan earthquake of March 1964 shook the ground for over four minutes!

FALLS

• Cumberland Falls in Kentucky, one hundred fifty feet wide and sixty-eight feet high, forms a moonbow (a nocturnal rainbow) each time there is a full moon. The only other waterfall in the world that displays a moonbow is Africa's Victoria Falls.

• Niagara Falls has a water flow of three hundred seventy-nine thousand tons per minute yet it would require two million years for all the waters of the earth to flow over Niagara.

• Niagara Falls stopped flowing on March 29, 1849!

• The amazing waterfall of Kapilatirtham, India: its flow always increases during periods of drought!

• The frozen waterfall of Mount Beardmore in the Antarctic has a height of more than ten thousand feet—sixty times that of Niagara Falls.

TREES AND FIELDS in Delburne, Alta., Canada, **BEGAN SPONTANEOUSLY BURSTING INTO FLAMES** IN 1998 DUE TO AN UNDERGROUND FIRE IN A COAL BED THAT HAS BEEN BURNING STEADILY for **140 YEARS!**

THE **SEVEN RAINBOWS OF GULLFOSS**
Iceland
THE **SUN** SHINING ON A BLANKET OF SPRAY
ALWAYS CREATES THIS AMAZING BRIDGE OF COLOR
650 FEET WIDE!
COPR. 1951, KING FEATURES SYNDICATE, Inc., WORLD RIGHTS RESERVED.   4-15

GLACIERS AND ICE FORMATIONS

• In the Swiss Alps there is an ice hall with a stove, table, and piano inside—all carved from the ice of a glacier!

• "B-9," an iceberg that broke away from the Ross ice shelf in 1987, measured ninety-six miles long, twenty-two miles wide, seven hundred fifty feet deep, and contained two hundred eighty-seven cubic miles of fresh water—enough for every person on Earth to drink two glasses a day for 1,977 years!

• There is a glacier located on the equator!

• An iceberg contains more heat than a match!

• An iceberg is ninety percent underwater—and that portion often melts faster than the part above the surface.

ISLANDS

• The island of Surtsey rose from the sea off Iceland after a volcanic explosion! Two years later it measured two and a half square miles and had plants growing on it!

• The ship that became an island: A sailing ship abandoned in the Maroni River between French and Dutch Guiana filled with soil and sprouted trees and plants—all in a period of thirty-six years.

• The island created by throwing rocks: Chisel Island in the Gulf of Kotor, Yugoslavia, originally was only a small rock projecting above the water. To enlarge it to accommodate a church, natives threw stones at the water for one hundred fifty years.

LAKES AND BAYS

• The lake that yields fish and crops: In the fall, Popovo Field, near Trebinye, Yugoslavia, is a lake twenty miles long and two hundred feet deep, teeming with millions of food fish. But each spring the water drains out through funnel-like holes and its bed becomes a fertile field harvested by twenty villagers.

• The waters of death! The crew of the ship *Carnegie* discovered an area of the South Seas one hundred miles wide and one thousand feet deep where no life can exist!

• The lake of poison: For centuries criminals near Naliabganj, India, were executed by being forced to drink its water.

THE GREAT LAKE of SODA
EAST AFRICA
MYSTERIOUS LAKE 22 MILES LONG AND 10 MILES WIDE WITH A CRUST 8FT. THICK OF PURE BAKING SODA - THE SAME AS USED BY HOUSEWIVES. THE SODA IS REPLACED FASTER THAN MACHINERY CAN REMOVE IT!

• Lake Mashu in Japan has the clearest water in all nature. It is transparent to a depth of one hundred thirty-six and a half feet.

• Polynya, a lake discovered by a joint team of American and Russian explorers in the heart of the Antarctic ice pack, appears and disappears, and sometimes covers an area of one hundred thousand square miles—yet it is completely free of ice.

MOUNTAINS

• A person standing on top of the 11,200-foot-high Mount Izaru in Costa Rica, can see both the Pacific and Atlantic Oceans at the same time!

• The Andes are not the world's longest mountain chain! The Mid-Ocean Ridge stretches 52,080 miles beneath the waters of the Arctic, Atlantic, Indian, and Pacific Oceans!

• Ruapehu Mountain in New Zealand, nine thousand feet high, has a boiling-hot lake in its center—yet its peak is covered with ice, blocks of ice that are melted by the heat and carried away by subterranean channels for the source of the Whangehu River.

• Borneo's Sarawik Cavern is a hollow mountain range big enough to hold forty Boeing 747 airplanes!

OCEANS AND SHORES

• The tide of Chepstow, England—the highest in all Europe—measures seventy feet high.

RIVERS AND STREAMS

• During lightning storms, the Powder River in Wyoming actually explodes like gunpowder! The Indians gave the river its name because they thought it contained gun-powder, but the explosions are caused by lightning touching off bubbles of natural gas in the water.

• The Amazon River flows into the ocean at a rate of 23,543 cubic yards per second!

• The bed of the Kruk-Dayra River in central Asia was bone-dry for sixteen hundred years—but its waters returned in 1934 and the river has flowed normally ever since.

THE LOOP-THE-LOOP RIVER
THE RIVER JORDAN, NEAR ITS MOUTH IN PALESTINE MEANDERS THROUGH AN AMAZING SERIES OF TIGHT TWISTS AND TURNS

BLACK SANDS OF KALAPANA
One of the strangest and most beautiful beaches in the world is this unusual jet-black beach made of **disintegrated lava**: truly a long-to-be-remembered sight as the foaming turquoise sea crashes and withdraws, leaving the sands glistening.

SACRED SOURCE! of the Platania River. This famous river of Olympia, Greece, flows out of the heart of a tree! Inside of its trunk is a chapel lighted by a lantern which has been burning for the past 2,000 years.

ROCK FORMATIONS

• As the result of alternate freezing and thawing, Arctic land near Spitzbergen, Norway, often forms amazing symmetrical sections, each separated by a border of stones.

• Nature's lighthouse: Mount Pelee's eruption on Martinique in the West Indies in 1902 ejected a stream of lava that hardened immediately to form a great cone sixteen hundred feet above the crater. The tower of lava glowed so brilliantly that it lit up the area for months!

• The ringing rocks: In Pottstown, Pennsylvania, there is a huge pile of boulders on which tunes can be played by hitting stones of different pitch with a hammer.

The Goblet of Venus in San Juan County, Utah, was 15 feet high and stood on a base 10 inches wide, marvelously wrought in stone by the lathe work action of the wind.

THE **THREE-WAY ROCKING STONES** near Salisbury, Rhodesia. Each of the 3 stones is so delicately balanced that frequently they rock simultaneously in different directions.

THE **SLEEPING GIANT** Serra dos Orgaos Mountains, at the entrance to the harbor of Rio de Janeiro, Brazil.

THE WOMAN OF STONE WHO WEEPS
The Seated Woman a natural sculpture in rock near Manisa, Turkey, BECAUSE OF HIDDEN SPRINGS OF WATER HAS APPEARED TO BE SHEDDING TEARS FOR 2,000 YEARS

A NATURAL TEMPLE
Comprising white coral limestone columns and a granite roof carved by the waters of the Werb River in Ethiopia.

The
PHANTOM SHIP
A natural rock formation in Crater Lake, Oregon, that appears to be a full-rigged ship and its crew. An optical illusion, it vanishes from time to time by blending with the cliff behind it, then suddenly reappears.

THE WATERFALL STONE NEAR HYDEN, AUSTRALIA, A ROCK THAT GIVES THE APPEARANCE OF A POWERFUL WATERFALL.

THE GAADA STACK on Foula, Shetland Islands, a natural rock rising from the water, forms four separate archways—one in each direction

• The Bell Tower of Val Montanaia in Italy is a natural rock formation in which a daring mountain climber suspended a real church bell to heighten the rock formation's amazing illusion.

• A giant boulder miraculously balanced on the top of a three-thousand-foot-high mountain near Kyakito, Burma, is a holy shrine worshipped by Buddhist monks.

• The bridge that turned to stone: A petrified tree, thousands of years old, bridges a chasm in the petrified forest of Arizona.

SINKHOLES

• In 1980, a half-mile-wide crater opened in Louisiana's Lake Peigner, swallowing the thirteen-hundred-acre lake, five

HALEMAUMAU
The "HOUSE OF EVERLASTING FIRE"
3000 FEET WIDE — 1000 FEET DEEP
THE FIRE PIT OF KILAUEA VOLCANO, HAWAII —— ONE OF THE MOST STUPENDOUS SPECTACLES ON EARTH
ALTHOUGH KILAUEA IS THE LARGEST ACTIVE VOLCANO IN THE WORLD— ITS CRATER CONTAINS A HOTEL, U.S. MILITARY CAMP AND LANDING FIELD

houses, nine boats, two oil rigs, and a mobile home!

• A pothole measuring forty-two feet wide and fifty feet deep was discovered in a hillside in Archibold, Pennsylvania, in 1881!

In 1981, a 400-ft. SINKHOLE in Winter Park, Fla., swallowed a house, five cars and a swimming pool!

TECTONICS

• Residents of southern California are moving to Alaska! The tectonic plate beneath the region is headed north, and will collide with Alaska in approximately one hundred fifty million years!

VOLCANOES

• Mount Erebus, an active volcano found in Antarctica, spews pieces of pure gold when it erupts!

• Mount Galeras, a fourteen-thousand-foot volcano located in Colombia, South America, produces one pound of gold a day!

• Scientists have discovered a volcano thirty-nine hundred feet underwater in the Bismark Sea off the coast of Papua New Guinea, that emits molten gold and silver!

• The youngest volcano: Showa Shinzai, in Japan, which began to form in December 1943, erupted six months later when it reached a height of 656 feet. It is now 1,337 feet high—and is still growing.

• Rainbow Lake, a volcanic crater lake on the west coast of Lanzarote, in the Canary Islands, because of layers of lava, constantly displays six different colors.

CAVE OF THE SWALLOWS— SKYDIVING UNDERGROUND

A seven-hour trek from Mexico City, Mexico, brings travelers to one of the most bizarre caves in the world: the Cave of the Swallows, a deep vertical chasm, so named for the tens of thousands of swallows that circle inside its hollow chamber.

The Cave of the Swallows is deep enough to hold the Empire State Building. Its floor can be reached by rappelling, but many spelunkers prefer a more thrilling means of reaching the bottom— by parachute.

Jumpers who take the express route down literally risk life and limb. If they get too close to the cave's jagged walls, their parachute could be shredded. If one of the cave's hundred thousand birds gets tangled in the parachute's lines, the chute could buckle.

But most spelunkers say the journey to the bottom is well worthwhile. The landscape at the base of the cave is like that of another planet. No direct sunlight reaches the ground here, but glossy green moss covers the cave's floor and walls. When it's time to return to the surface, spelunkers are hauled up by a winch, two at a time.

IN 1943, A NEW VOLCANO BURST OUT of a FARMER'S FIELD in Paricutin, Mexico!

• For the past fifteen years, many visitors to Hawaii's Kilauea volcano have been returning pieces of volcanic rock they have picked up at the site to release the goddess "Pele's" legendary curse on souvenir takers!

• The chapel of Saint Michel D'Aguiche, in Le Puy, France, was built on top of a two hundred sixty-foot-high pillar of rock that was once an active volcano!

• Vulcan Island, in the harbor of Rabaul, New Britain Island, erupted from the sea in a single night in 1870, and a few years later, after exploding into the air, became a six-hundred-foot-high volcano.

• After the eruption of the volcano "Krakatoa," in Sumatra in 1886, the Dutch gunboat *Berouw* was torn from its moorings by a tidal wave that tossed it almost two miles inland!

• In 1994, scientists discovered a volcano near the South Pole under 1.2 miles of ice!

WATERHOLES AND GEYSERS

• The geyser that gushes on demand! An artificial geyser in Soda Springs, Idaho, created in 1937 when drillers tapped a subterranean chamber containing carbon dioxide gas and water, can be turned on at will to send water one hundred seventy-five feet in the air!

• The Ullboennalenna waterhole in northwest Australia is a reservoir of water in solid rock, and because of its bottleneck opening, natives can get at its water by inserting a glass plunger at the end of a rod.

• Holes on the rocky coast of Mauritius in the Indian Ocean spout water high into the air with a roar that can be heard three miles away.

Chapter 28
Government & Politics

Thomas Jefferson KEPT TWO GRIZZLY BEARS AS PETS!

Think the Election 2000 mess in Florida was an aberration? Think your vote can't make a difference? You'll be amazed to discover how many elections have been decided by a single vote. Have you bought the old line about the inevitability of death and taxes? Wait until you read how many generations got by without paying a penny in income tax! You're about to meet politicians who aren't human—and a few that aren't even alive! You're on your way to witnessing elections decided by body lice, and inaugurations attended by goldfish. Our collection of bizarre political facts may challenge your notions of who our political figures are, and how governments must be run.

ANCIENT GOVERNMENTS

• The Roman Senate had members whose duty it was to watch the weather and predict storms in order to ensure a good day for voting!

• The Althing of Iceland is the world's oldest parliament—founded in A.D. 930!

FOREIGN GOVERNMENTS

• In 1990, the French government created a new cabinet position called the Ministry of Rock and Roll!

• In nineteenth-century Sweden, a new Burgomaster was chosen by placing a louse in the center of the table: the man whose beard the insect jumped into held the office for the next year!

TRIBAL GOVERNMENT

• Tribal councils ruled ancient German communities, and to assure weighty consideration of all legislation, each proposal had to be discussed at two successive sessions—the first while the council members were drunk, and the second when they were sober.

UNITED STATES GOVERNMENT

• *The United States Congressional Record*, printed and published every day, contains over four million words!

• In 1914, the United States State Department sent an invitation to the opening of the Panama Canal to the nonexistent Swiss Navy!

AMBASSADORS AND DIPLOMATS

• Chinese ambassador **Li Hung Chang**, when he visited the United States in 1896, brought forty aides and servants, three hundred pieces of luggage, a golden sedan chair, songbirds, parrots, chickens, and a supply of one-hundred-year-old eggs.

POLITICAL CUSTOMS

• The strangest political custom in all the world: The mayor of Grammot, Belgium, and every member of his town council, once each year for the last six hundred seventy-two years, have been required to drain a cup of wine containing a live goldfish.

POLITICAL LEADERS

• Cuban leader **Fidel Castro** appeared as an extra in the Hollywood film *Bathing Beauty*, starring Esther Williams!

• In 1960, **Fidel Castro** of Cuba gave a speech at the United Nations that lasted over four and a half hours!

• **Sir Winston Churchill**, former Prime Minister of Great Britain, once worked as a greeting card designer for Hallmark!

• **Lord Monteagle of Brandon**, a member of the British House of Lords since 1947, gave his first speech in 1992.

• The **Dalai Lama**, ruler of Tibet and a prisoner of the Red Chinese in his own palace, announced that he would escape on the afternoon of March 17, 1959. That afternoon, although Red troops surrounded the palace and huge searchlights were trained on the building, the Dalai Lama and eighty companions escaped—under cover of a sudden sandstorm.

CONGRESS PEOPLE

• **Hubert Humphrey**, who later became a United States senator, as a youth completed a two-year course at the Denver College of Pharmacy in six months—memorizing the English and Latin names and proper dosages of all the drugs in the pharmacist's pharmacopoeia.

• **Sam Houston** (1793-1863), the founder of Texas, as a United States senator for his state, at times became so bored by debates that he whittled on the senate floor.

• Former United States senator **Barry Goldwater** recommended peanut butter as a shaving cream.

GOVERNORS

• The governor who tried to upstage a United States President: **John Hancock**, as governor of Massachusetts, maintained that as a state's chief executive he had official precedence over President George Washington within his own state, but finally capitulated when Washington refused to make the first courtesy call.

• **John Quitman** (1799-1858) was elected president of Mississippi's senate in 1835 so that he could serve as the state's governor. The term of Mississippi's governor had expired on November 20, 1835 and his successor would not be inaugurated until January 7, 1836. Every state official eligible to succeed to the post had been elected to another office.

• When **Peter Stuyvesant**, governor of New York, lost his leg in a battle in 1644, his amputated leg was given a Christian burial with full military honors!

• Until 1968, the governor of New Hampshire could declare war on any other country without permission from Washington!

MAYORS

• A can of foot powder, called "Palvapies," was elected mayor of Picoaza, in Ecuador!

• Mayor **Fiorello H. LaGuardia** (1882-1947), of New York, once ordered his police to arrest all known gangsters on sight.

• **Baron Anton Ulrich von Holzhausen** (1754-1832) was the thirty-sixth member of his family to serve as mayor of Frankfurt on the Main, in Germany.

• **Brian Zimmerman**, age eleven, was elected mayor of Crabb, Texas!

"GO AHEAD, MAKE MY SUNDAE" ACTOR CLINT EASTWOOD'S FIRST ACTION AS MAYOR of Carmel, Calif., **WAS TO LEGALIZE ICE CREAM PARLORS.**

THE MAYOR OF HIGH WYCOMBE, ENGLAND, IS PUBLICLY WEIGHED AT THE BEGINNING AND END OF HIS TERM TO DETERMINE IF HIS *MUNICIPAL DUTIES HAVE WEIGHED HEAVILY UPON HIM*

FRANCO RICARDO of Warwick, R.I. carved a life-size sculpture of U.S. President Bill Clinton, his wife, Hillary, and daughter Chelsea—out of brownies—about 57 million calories worth!

THE AMERICAN PATRIOT WHO LED THE COLONIALS IN THEIR REVOLUTION AGAINST ENGLAND WAS GEORGE de HERTBURN

GEORGE WASHINGTON'S ORIGINAL NAME WAS DE HERTBURN, BUT WHEN HIS ANCESTOR, WILLIAM DE HERTBURN, EXCHANGED HIS VILLAGE FOR ONE NAMED WESSYNGTON, THE FAMILY CHANGED ITS SUR-NAME-- *LATER ANGLICIZED TO WASHINGTON*

• In 1693, **Jacques Daude** purchased for himself and his successors the office of mayor of Le Vigan, France, for perpetuity for $2,373. Jacques, his son, and his grandson, filled the post successively until 1774, when the city ended its contract by refunding the original payment.

RELUCTANT LEADERS

• **Captain Sir Henry Paulet**, to avoid a threatened fine of $2,500 for refusing to serve as sheriff of Hampshire, England, had himself committed to an insane asylum for six months.

PRESIDENTS

• The man who refused to be President! **Doctor Jose Maria Vargas** (1786-1854), elected President of Venezuela against his will, resigned three times—and finally fled his country rather than fill its highest office!

• **Ignacio Camonfort**, President of Mexico, headed a revolution—against himself! On February 5, 1858, he deposed himself and drove himself into exile.

AMERICAN PRESIDENTS AND FIRST LADIES

• United States President **George Washington** gave an inaugural address that contained only one hundred thirty-five words!

• **Mary Washington** (1708-1789), the mother of George Washington, who lived to see him become the first President of the United States, had refused to let him join the British Navy as a boy.

• **George Washington** carried a sundial instead of a watch to tell time!

• American artist **Charles Wilson Peale** painted George Washington's portrait seven times, and once made him a set of false teeth out of lead and elks' teeth!

UNTIL 1929, THE PRESIDENTS of THE United States DID NOT HAVE A PRIVATE PHONE AND HAD TO USE A PHONE BOOTH IN THE WHITE HOUSE LOBBY!

During his Presidency, **RONALD REAGAN** received over seventy-five thousand gifts, including three hundred seventy-two belt buckles, a dog house, a six-foot-tall pencil, and a four-square-foot portrait made out of ten thousand jelly beans!

EDITH WILSON, THE WIFE OF U.S. PRESIDENT *WOODROW WILSON*, OFTEN RODE A *BICYCLE IN THE CORRIDORS OF THE WHITE HOUSE!*

ROUND AND ROUND SHE GOES...

Believe It or Not! U.S. PRESIDENT *Richard Nixon* ONCE WORKED AS A **CARNIVAL BARKER!**

• President **John Quincy Adams** kept an alligator in the East Room of the White House!

• **Mason L. Weems** (1760-1825), who sold Bibles in colonial taverns, was the first person to record the famous story of George Washington and the cherry tree.

• **Thomas Jefferson** had a pet mockingbird that followed him upstairs to bed every night!

• **William Henry Harrison** (1773-1841), ninth President of the United States, was the first to campaign actively for the office, and the first to die in office.

• **John Tyler** (1790-1862), tenth President of the United States, unable to get a decent job after leaving that office, worked at a village pound tending horses and cow.

• United States President **Millard Fillmore** (1800-1874) was so straight-laced that throughout his life he avoided any hotel that served liquor, and gambled only once—on a turkey raffle at the age of fifteen.

• **James Knox Polk** (1795-1849), the eleventh President of the United States, was the first chief executive whose election was flashed across the country by telegraph.

• First Lady **Abigail Adams**, wife of United States President John Adams, used to hang the family laundry in the White House East Room to dry!

• **John Quincy Adams** (1767-1848) was a foreign diplomat at the age of fourteen!

• A man among men! **Theodore Roosevelt** (1858–1919), once delivered a one-hour speech in spite of being shot moments before by a would-be assassin!

• United States President **Andrew Jackson**, during his term in the White House, made all of his own clothes!

• **Zachary Taylor**, the twelfth President of the United States, never voted in an election.

• United States President **John F. Kennedy** was the first president born in the twentieth century.

• When **Zachary Taylor** became President of the United States in 1849, he kept his horse "Old Whitey" on the front lawn of the White House!

• The man who almost fought a duel with Abraham Lincoln: **James Shields** (1806-1879), a state officer in Illinois, challenged Abraham Lincoln to a duel in 1842, and the two actually met on the field of honor, but were reconciled at the last moment.

• President **Millard Fillmore**, in 1851, became the first chief executive to use a bathtub in the White House.

• United States President **Ulysses S. Grant** was once arrested near the White House and fined twenty dollars for driving a team of horses too fast!

• **Eliza Johnson**, wife of President Andrew Johnson, regularly spent hours tutoring her husband, who had no formal education!

• The middle initial "S" in United States President **Harry S Truman**'s name didn't stand for anything!

• **David Rice Atchison**, a state senator from Missouri (1843-1855), was President of the United States for one day!

• United States President **Grover Cleveland** had his upper jaw removed and replaced with one made of vulcanized rubber!

• **Theodore Roosevelt** concerned about the over-cutting of forests, banned Christmas trees from the White House!

• **Calvin Coolidge**, President of the United States from 1923 to 1929, was the last President to write his own speeches!

• During his entire forty-seven year government career, **Herbert Hoover** turned over every one of his salary checks to charity!

• United States President **Franklin Delano Roosevelt** was related to eleven different United States presidents!

• United States President **Ronald Reagan** was once given an honorary doctorate in professional football!

• United States President **Jimmy Carter** was the first president born in a hospital!

• **James Abraham Garfield**, twentieth President of the United States, was the first Presidential candidate to make political speeches in a foreign language, German.

• **Richard Nixon** was the only United States President to visit all fifty states while in office!

• After **President George H.W. Bush** banned broccoli from the White House in March 1990, California broccoli growers delivered nine tons of the vegetable to Washington!

• United States President **Bill Clinton** is the most widely traveled of any President in history!

PRESIDENTIAL PETS

• United States President **Theodore Roosevelt** once had a pet hyena!

• United States President **Calvin Coolidge** kept a pygmy hippopotamus as a pet!

Believe It or Not!
Former U.S. President
ABRAHAM
LINCOLN
had a pet turkey at
the White House!

• *Millie's Book*, the autobiography of Unites States President **George H.W. Bush**'s pet dog, when it was first published, outsold the memoirs of former President Ronald Reagan!

• **"Socks,"** United States President Bill Clinton's family cat, received boxes full of mail every day from cat fanciers across the United States!

NONHUMAN POLITICIANS

• In 1936, a mule named **"Boston Curtis"** ran for a Republican precinct seat and won by a unanimous vote of fifty-two

• For ten years the mayor of Sunol, California, was a black dog named "**Bosco.**"

• "**Clay Henry,**" a twenty-two year old beer-guzzling goat, served as the mayor of Lajitas, Texas.

BUREAUCRACY

• In 1993, the United States debt reached an estimated $322 billion—a sum that would take a single person 61.2 years to spend at $10,000 a minute!

• In 1993, **Joanna Gurn**, of West Palm Beach, Florida, received a refund from the United States government for a total of one cent!

POLITICAL PARTIES

• In 1797, the President and Vice President of the United States were from two different political parties!

• In 1990, beer drinkers in Czechoslovakia formed their own political party, "The Friends of Beer," to run in the country's first free election in forty years!

TAXES

• An income tax of two percent on all earnings above four thousand dollars a year was imposed by Congress in the 1894—but the Supreme Court banned it as unconstitutional.

• The United States Income Tax, on the eve of World War II, affected fewer than five million people.

• A slave revolt in Rome in 102-101 B.C. led General **Gaius Marius** to appeal to Bithynia, a Roman protectorate, for army recruits—but Roman tax collectors had seized so many of its subjects as slaves it had no able-bodied men.

TAX COLLECTOR *Ludwig Dobermann* of Apolda, Germany, IN THE 1880s DEVELOPED A BREED OF DOG TO HELP HIM COLLECT TAXES!

VOTING

• The election for Republican Presidential ticket of 1892, with **Benjamin Harrison** and **Whitelaw Reid**, is the only election in American history in which both candidates graduated from the same university, Miami University of Ohio.

• In 1990, in Appenzell, Switzerland, twenty-five hundred men armed with swords voted to reject a motion granting women the right to vote on local issues!

• A polling station in Tulsa, Oklahoma's, twenty-fifth precinct is opened for every city council election even though no one has lived in the area for twenty years!

• In Saint Thomas, North Dakota, the outcome of the 1998 municipal elections was decided by the toss of a coin!

• In ancient Greece, if a man was not married by the time he was thirty, he lost his right to vote!

• The entire cost of **Abraham Lincoln's** nomination for the Presidency of the United States—including even the travel expenses of the delegates—was less than $700.

• Dry for over one hundred forty years: In 1992, residents of Ephraim, Wisconsin, voted to retain a ban on liquor in the town that dates back to the 1850s.

• A Swiss voter, casting his ballot at a citizen's assembly, carries a sword as a symbol of his citizenship.

• **Sam Houston** (1793-1863), running for governor of the cattle-raising state of Texas, once campaigned against an opponent by denouncing him as a vegetarian.

• In a November 1994 election in Rice, Minnesota, two men who tied for a seat on the city council settled the race by cutting cards!

• **James Farrington** and **Joann Carlson**, two candidates locked in a tie for the office of mayor of Estancia, New Mexico, settled the vote by playing a hand of five-card stud poker!

• Loving County, Texas is the only county in the United States that has more registered voters than it has residents!

• **Arthur Lang** of Chicago, Illinois, registered to vote for the first time in February 1990—at the age of one hundred twelve!

• The man whose vote changed history: Senator **Edmund G. Ross** (1826-1907), of Kansas, at the impeachment trial of President Andrew Johnson, cast the decisive vote that enabled Johnson to serve out his term—this action ruined Ross politically, financially, and socially.

• Out of over three thousand United States counties, only the voters in Crook County, Oregon, have chosen every winning United States presidential candidate since 1884!

• San Marino, the smallest republic in the world, pays its citizens who live abroad to return home to vote in local elections!

CANDIDATES

• At age one hundred two, **Nathalie Vanloock**, of Belgium, ran for a six-year-term municipal office.

• A man in Carson City, Nevada, ran for office in the 1992 Democratic primary as "God Almighty"!

• **James Schoolcraft Sherman**, of Utica, New York, a Vice Presidential candidate, died six days before election day, yet still received 3,484,780 votes!

• **Peter Cooper**, who invented the gelatin dessert now known as Jell-O, once ran for President!

• **Luther Devine Knox** legally changed his name to "None of the Above" in order to run in a Louisiana gubernatorial election!

• A man named "Zero Population Growth" ran in a state election in Australia on a platform against overpopulation!

• **Hitler, Stalin,** and **Frankenstein** were the names of candidates in an election in Meghalaya, India, in 1993!

THE FIRST PRESIDENTIAL POLLS
INFORMAL POLLS DETERMINING THE POPULARITY OF PRESIDENTIAL CANDIDATES WERE CONDUCTED BETWEEN 1880 AND THE 1900s BY PUTTING THEIR PICTURES ON CIGAR BOXES--AND THEN NOTING WHICH SOLD THE BEST.

• At the 1972 United States Democratic Party Convention, the fictional television character "**Archie Bunker**" received a vote for President!

• In 1986, Morris the Cat of television commercial fame set out to gain the Democratic nomination for President of the United States!

• **Derrick Sever** of Gayton, Ohio, at the age of seventeen was too young to vote but ran for office as the sole Democrat in a race for a seat in the Ohio legislature!

WITH ONE VOTE

• **John D. Bilotti**, after a recount, was elected mayor of Kenosha, Wisconsin, by one vote.

• One vote elected **John Quincy Adams** President.

• One vote elected **Thomas Jefferson** President.

• A single vote beheaded **Charles I** of England.

• One vote elected **Rutherford Hayes** President.

• A single vote enacted military conscription in 1941.

• Texas, California, Washington, Oregon, and Idaho all became states because of a single vote.

• One vote elected Governor **Morton** of Massachusetts.

• One vote elected **Oliver Cromwell.**

• A single vote made France a Republic in 1875—and ended France's status as a Republic in 1940.

Chapter 29

Habits & Eccentricities

If we're truly being ourselves, we can't help but seem at least a little weird. Individuality is bound to take some odd turns from time to time, and as you're about to read, some of us develop our eccentricities to unbelievable extremes. We've put together a concordance of bizarre habits of sleep, eating, home decor, dress, and more—and we'll introduce you to some of the world's most colorful and eccentric characters, in all their glory.

DINING HABITS

• French writer **Honoré de Balzac** frequently ate one hundred oysters, twelve lamb cutlets, a whole duckling, and two partridges, followed by wine and coffee for dinner!

• English Lord **Gerald Tyrwhitt-Wilson** frequently brought his horse into the drawing room for tea!

• **Chand Mal Mali**, of Kanwab, India, eats over two pounds of charcoal every day!

• **Hajara Amma**, at age seventy, of Jamnagar, India, has been eating two pounds of sand every day since the age of twelve.

• **Czar Peter the Great** of Russia (1672-1725) drank twenty-one glasses of water and ate twelve figs and six pounds of cherries every morning!

• **Alan Fairweather**, of Edinburgh, Scotland, eats five pounds of potatoes every day and likes to vacation at the International Potato Centre in Lima, Peru!

• **Francis Henry Egerton**, the eighth Earl of Bridgewater, England, regularly dined with twelve dressed dogs—each dog attended by its own servant!

• **Charles Kazan**, of Los Angeles, California, age eighty-one, has eaten over 102,200 slices of bologna and over 58,400 hot dogs during his lifetime!

• **Pat Crowther** of Sheffield, England, drank seventy cups of tea a day with five spoonfuls of sugar in every cup!

DR. SANCTORIUS SANCTORIUS (1561-1636), professor of medicine at the University of Padua, Italy, and inventor of the clinical thermometer, to study variations in his body weight ate all his meals for a period of 13 years while seated on a scale.

DRESSING HABITS

• General **Stonewall Jackson**, while serving as a cadet, wore his army winter coat for an entire summer because he never received orders to take it off!

• Prince **Philip of Calabria**, the son of Charles III of Spain (1716-88), always wore sixteen pairs of gloves at the same time!

• **Donald** and **Nancy Featherstone**, of Irthburg, Massachusetts, dressed exactly alike every day for seventeen years straight!

• Sir **Humphrey Davy**, an eighteenth-century British gentleman who hated to do laundry, wore layers of clean clothes over his dirty ones—up to five shirts and five pairs of socks at a time.

SLEEP HABITS

• **Mark Van Eeghen**, an NFL running back for the Los Angeles Raiders, dived from his television set into his bed every night before a game in order to bring good luck!

• **Charles Taylor**, of Etruria, England, sang himself to sleep every night for eighty years.

Camillo Russo, of Melbourne, Australia, decorated the walls of his home with over 1 million seashells and regularly wears a suit decorated with seashells.

PERSONAL HABITS

• In 2000, **Danielle Tobar**, of Santiago, Chile, slept, ate, read, and talked on the telephone from inside a one-room transparent house!

• Billionaire **John D. Rockefeller** frequently entertained guests by balancing crackers on his nose!

• **Matthew Robinson**, an eighteenth-century Englishman, regularly spent his entire day, including mealtimes, submerged up to his neck in the ocean.

• **Shridhar Chillal**, of Pune, India, has not cut the fingernails on his left hand since 1952, and each nail now measures over forty inches in length!

• **Sam Youd**, a gardener, regularly hugs the two hundred fifty thousand trees he tends in Tatton Park, Cheshire, England!

• American playwright **Maxwell Anderson** did all of his best writing when it rained, so he had a sprinkler system installed over his studio to mimic the sound of rain on the roof!

• **Geoff Allison**, of Boston, Massachusetts, keeps fifty giant Madagascar hissing cockroaches in his apartment as pets.

C. A. Traff, of Galesburg, Illinois, used crutches 11 feet long.

- **Charles Darwin** frequently played music to earthworms!

- The great English lexicographer Doctor **Samuel Johnson** always crossed through a doorway with his right foot first, never walked on sidewalk cracks, and believed it was good luck to touch every wooden post he passed!

- **Jacob Acosta, Junior**, of Austin, Texas, for twenty-six consecutive years grew a bushy mustache in September, then shaved it in April. He kept each one, dated them, and mounted them on paper!

- **Ernie Edwards**, of Built Wells, England, had his knee cap preserved inside a glass paperweight!

- In the sixteenth century, England's **Cardinal Wolsey** (1475-1530) regularly took his cats to church and to state dinners!

- **James Slater,** of Scotland, lived in a cave for years even though it flooded every night at high tide!

- **Florence Nightingale** (1820-1910) always carried a pet owl in her pocket!

ECCENTRICS AND ODD CHARACTERS

- The most eccentric host in history! **Lord Dunsay** (1878-1957), celebrated Irish playwright and owner of Dunsay Castle in County Meath, Ireland, has a dining room as large as a ballroom. The bell to summon his butler was located so far from the host's seat at the table that he rang it by firing at it with a pistol.

- In November 1989, **Polly Ketron** arranged and attended her own funeral—then celebrated her seventy-sixth birthday two days later.

- **Julia Hill** spent an entire year living ninety-nine feet above the ground in a redwood tree!

- After the death of her husband, **King Philip**, in 1506, Queen Juana of Spain had his body embalmed and placed in a jeweled coffin that she kept with her during meals, and even when she slept!

- **Pierre** and **Helene Naudin**, of Choisy, France, use seven-hundred-year-old recipes for cooking, eat with their hands, and wear medieval costumes every day!

- The green man: **Henry Cope**, of Brighton, England, always wore green clothing, lived in a green house furnished with green furniture, and ate only green fruits and vegetables!

- Austro-Hungarian Emperor **Franz Josef**, who died in 1916, steadfastly refused to use such modern devices as a car, a telephone, or a lavatory!

- **Bonaventure van Overbeek** (1660-1706), a celebrated Dutch painter, had such an aversion to stairways that each home he occupied could be entered only by a ladder which he would pull up when he wanted to be alone.

William C. Bostwick, of Philadelphia, Pennsylvania, at age eighty, did his daily shopping on roller skates.

TING CHENG
holy man of Macao, Portuguese China
PLANTED **2** PALM BRANCHES
IN HOLES BORED IN HIS SKULL!
NOURISHMENT FROM CHENG'S BODY KEPT THEM GREEN FOR **10** YEARS
(1851 - 1860)

IN "The New Forest," Hampshire, England, THERE IS A WOMAN NAMED "*ROBINA HOOD*" WHO LIVES IN A CAMOUFLAGE TENT AND ALWAYS DRESSES IN LINCOLN GREEN!

• **Jean Rath**, of Orcutt, California, lives in a purple house with purple appliances, wears only purple clothes, and owns a lilac-point Siamese cat!

• **Jucka Ammondt** of Finland has translated Elvis Presley's hit song "Blue Suede Shoes" into the ancient Sumerian language of Babylon, which died out around 2000 B.C.!

• Open but empty: **Richard George Wild** runs an empty shop in Brisbane, Australia. Although he has nothing to sell he keeps the shop open for sentimental reasons.

• British philosopher **Jeremy Bentham** (1748-1832), who claimed that music was essential to good health, had pianos placed in every room of his house, including the bathroom!

• During the eighteenth century, **Charles Hamilton**, a wealthy eccentric, paid a hermit $700 to live in a cave in his garden!

• During the 1800s, **George Jessop**, of Kenilworth, Maryland, believed that mice and groundhogs would leave a garden if they were politely asked with letters left in their burrows!

• After the death of her husband in 1675, **Madame Magurite-Therese** of France carried his embalmed heart around with her in a tiny glass case!

• Mexican film star **Ramon Novarro** (1899-1968) gave orders to all of his house guests to wear only black, white or silver clothing to match his mansion!

• Argentine writer **Omar Vignole**, author of "My Cow and I" and "What My Cow Thinks" frequently walked a pet cow through the streets of Buenos Aires, Argentina!

• A man named Old Spit-in-the-Sea walked six miles twice a day to spit in the sea.

• A vagabond known as **Dead Eye Jack** was often spotted on the roads of Victoria, Australia, in the early 1900s carrying a coffin on his back, which he used as a home. At night he slept in it, and when it rained he stood it upright against a tree, and slept standing up inside it. As many predicted, one day he never came out!

LIZARD MAN PUSHING THE BOUNDARIES OF WHAT'S HUMAN

Twenty-six-year-old Erik Sprague is becoming a lizard. To date, the full-time bartender and part-time performance artist has spent over one hundred hours in a tattooist's chair, having reptilian scales imprinted all over his body. He has also endured painful surgery to have his tongue forked, his teeth chiseled into points, and knobby, lizard-like ridges surgically implanted over each eye.

It's a long-term transformation. Even Erik has no idea how far it will go. Once a month, Erik places himself in the hands of tattoo artist David "Mad Pup" Brown, who adds more scales to various parts of Erik's body. Brown estimates that in order to cover all of Erik in scales, he's looking at another thousand hours of painful tattoos.

Why is Erik doing this to himself? "It's a fulfillment of who I am," he explains. He says he wants to challenge people's perceptions, "to expand their definition of what's human." Trust us—one look at Erik is all it takes.

• **Ernest Dittemore** owns an eighty-acre farm in Troy, Missouri, yet he lives in a four-foot-by-ten foot hole in the ground!

• A man in Rushmore, England, legally changed his name to "King Arthur" and has a permit to carry his "Excalibur" in public!

• Eighteenth century English eccentric **Jimmy Hirst** wore a lambskin hat that measured nine feet in circumference!

• **Mrs. Thomas Seaman**, of Deer Park, New York, never once left her house throughout the entire twenty-eight years of her married life.

• Eccentric **Jake Manglewurzel**, of Yorkshire, England, regularly lectures from a pulpit on top of his farmhouse about the evils of conformity—to a flock of sheep!

• Surgeon **Angelo Noannoi** (1715-1790), of Florence, Italy, slept fully dressed every night for the last fifteen years of his life because he was afraid that sudden death would find him not looking his best.

• In 1775, **Martin Van Butchell**, a dentist and surgeon in London, England, painted colored spots on his white pony—a different color every day!

JEREMY HIRST OF YORKSHIRE, ENGLAND, TRAVELED THE COUNTRYSIDE *IN A SAILBOAT* MOUNTED ON WHEELS, *WEARING A HAT THAT HAD A 9-FT. BRIM.*

Chapter 30
Hobbies & Crafts

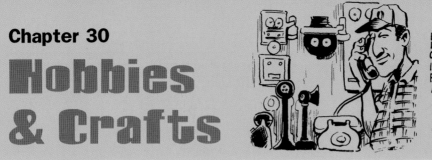

Our hungry minds are one of the features that mark us as distinctly human. No matter how hard we work, there's always leftover brain-space that craves exercise. Perhaps there's something in us that needs to play. Whatever the reason, nearly all of us indulge in some form of hobby. Many of us settle for more traditional pastimes such as whittling and bird watching; others collect any manner of object, from airline barf bags to Pez candy dispensers. Herein, we've indulged our own hobby of collecting weird facts: this time, about the extremes to which we're willing to go to amuse ourselves.

BIRD WATCHING

• Bird watching in the United States is a one-billion-dollar-a-year industry.

• The average bird-watcher can burn up to four hundred seventy-five calories an hour looking for birds!

CARVING, WHITTLING, AND WOODWORK

• **Allen Johnson**, of Lubbock, Texas, blind since 1977, uses power tools to create intricate carved wooden toys!

• **Ralph Threthewey**, of Corvallis, Montana, carves miniature deer and elk antlers the size of a thumbnail, from pecan and walnut shells!

CHAINS

• **Mark Lefont**, of Hollywood, California, carved a twenty-foot-long chain from a tree! It consisted of eleven links, each measuring two feet by three feet. The entire chain weighed fifteen hundred pounds!

• **Gary Duschl**, of Waterdown, Ontario, began making a gum-wrapper chain on March 11, 1965, that now measures 26,503 feet long!

COLLECTIONS

• **Harold Swauger**, of New Philadelphia, Ohio, has a collection of over two thousand coffee mugs!

FLORENCE LAT-MARTON of Kailua, Hawaii, HAS A COLLECTION of OVER 5,000 BARBIE DOLLS IN HER HOME!

• **Norman Wayne Bright** of Heber Springs, Arkansas, has a collection of over seven thousand four-leaf clovers and holds an official license from the Arkansas State Game and Fish Commission to hunt four-leaf clovers!

• **Frank Damek**, of Chicago, Illinois, compiled a complete deck of cards by picking individual cards up from time to time in the street. After ten years he had 37, but it took twenty more years before he finally completed his deck, in 1890.

• The Mouse House! **S. Beagle**, of Toledo, Ohio, has a collection of over seven thousand toy mice, including one on her front porch that stands four feet tall!

• **Sue Sternfeld**, of Queens, New York, has a collection of over seven hundred Pez candy dispensers!

• **Jo Jo Allison**, of New Braunfels, Texas, has a collection of one hundred ten chimney sweep figurines and pictures!

• **Norma Hazelton**, of Van Nuys, California, has a collection of over fifty thousand swizzle sticks!

• **Dory Vanderhoof** and **Margaret Genovese**, of Toronto, Ontario, have a collection of over five hundred potato chip bags from twenty-two different countries.

• **Larry Aikens**, of Athens, Texas, has a collection of over three thousand lunch boxes!

• **Leopold Fechtner**, of Queens, New York, has a collection of over two and a half million written jokes!

• **Lotta Solja**, of Solna, Sweden, has a collection of over two hundred seventy-five parking meters from around the world!

• **Clara Scroggins**, of Tampa, Florida, has a collection of over two hundred thousand Christmas ornaments.

• **Robert Opie**, of Bristol, England, owns a collection of over three hundred thousand product packages—including fifty-eight hundred yogurt containers!

• **Rene Martin**, of Terrebonne, Quebec, has a collection of over eighteen thousand spoons!

• In 1991, the United States Customs Service issued over two million collectors' cards of dogs used in drug-busting operations!

• **Barbara Braun**, of Gnadenhutten, Ohio, has a collection of over ten thousand cookie cutters!

MODELING

• **Bob Haifley**, of Covina, California, created a life-size figure of Jesus Christ using sixty-five thousand toothpicks!

• **Vince Nalbone**, of Los Angeles, California, created a life-size sculpture of a surfer from thousands of toothpicks!

COLLECTING DEATH MASKS IN THE EARLY 1800s WAS A FASHIONABLE HOBBY

- **Norman Kautz**, a machinist in Texas City, Texas, builds model ships inside light bulbs.

UNUSUAL HOBBIES AND CRAFTS

- **Aric Obrosey**, of New York City, uses a knife and a hole punch to create lace-like rubber portraits of famous people.

- **Stephen Engle**, of Hazleton, Pennsylvania, spent twenty years building a fourteen-foot-high wood and plaster clock that has forty-eight moving figurines, including Father Time, Satan, and Molly Pitcher!

- For over forty years, residents of Cawker City, Kansas, have been winding hay twine into a ball that now measures forty feet, three inches in diameter, and weighs 14,984 pounds!

- **Chauncey Shea**, of Saint Catherine's, Ontario, practices forgery as a hobby! He has completed over two thousand forgeries of famous signatures, including William Shakespeare and several Presidents of the United States.

- **Morris Karelefsky**, of Tamarac, Florida, has made more than five hundred chairs—some only one-sixteenth of an inch high—from tin cans.

ED HABERMAN of Tama, Iowa, HAS OVER 1,300 OIL RAGS COLLECTED from SERVICE STATIONS AROUND THE UNITED STATES!

- Brother **Brian Thomas**, of Sydney, Australia, created over four hundred boomerangs, and once threw and caught a boomerang one hundred twenty-nine times in a row!

- **Bill Brownlee**, of Prairie Village, Kansas, is a member of the International Brick Collectors Association, whose three hundred seventy-five members are dedicated to "stimulating interest in the collection of bricks"!

- **Bob Hoke**, of Scottsdale, Arizona, uses high-speed drills to carve delicate filigree patterns on ostrich eggs, which can take up to four hundred hours to complete!

JAMIE BUCHBAUM OF CINCINNATI, OHIO, CREATES COSTUMES FOR COCKROACHES— INCLUDING ONE BUG CALLED "ELVIS PROACHLEY" THAT HAS ITS OWN GUITAR, MICROPHONE AND BLUE SUEDE SHOES!

SERENDIPITOUS SIGHTSEERS— JAMES HARTMAN'S GLOBE-TROTTING SHEEP

The next time you visit a famous landmark, take a closer look around. Peer into an unlikely cranny, and you may discover an unusual fellow sightseer—in the form of a miniature hand-painted sheep. These tiny travelers can be discovered at just about every famous tourist attraction in the world: atop the Saint Louis Arch, beside the Taj Mahal, on the Eiffel Tower, even in Lincoln's lap at the Memorial in Washington, D.C.

These globe-trotting sheep are the work of San Francisco artist James Hartman. He discovered the original sheep in a curiosity shop, and found the little ceramic beast so charming that he made a mold of it and turned out hundreds of copies, each of which he meticulously hand-painted. Hartman gave a sheep to each member of his family, some of whom decided to take them traveling. They set Hartman's sheep up at various travel destinations, snapped pictures, and sent the photos back to Hartman.

And thus, a movement was born.

To date, hundreds of Hartman's ceramic beasts have traveled the globe. But unlike their human shepherds, the sheep never come home. No destination is too outrageous: Hartman says, "We'd like to get a sheep on the moon." Although, he admits, he would settle for sneaking one aboard the space shuttle.

Chapter 31
Holidays, Festivals, & Celebrations

Tired of celebrating the same old holidays year in and year out? Let us help you put a new spin on your annual calendar of events. Have you ever celebrated Lumpy Rug Day, Bald Head Day—or attended the annual Slug Festival? Have you experienced the thrill of the International Pillow Fight Championship? Or sampled any of the savory dishes in the annual Mosquito Cook-off? But don't give up on those traditional holidays just yet. Did you know that Santa Claus has a brother? Or that Mother's Day is celebrated for two days in Mexico? Welcome to Ripley's calendar of holidays, festivals, and celebrations—everything from odd facts about your favorite holidays to bizarre annual events you may have to see to believe.

BIRTHDAYS

• Every day three million people in the United States buy presents for the 673,693 Americans who are celebrating their birthdays!

• In 1990, **Imelda Marcos** of the Philippines threw a party on her late husband's seventy-third birthday. The former president attended—in a frozen casket!

• In Belgium, children celebrating a birthday are given a prick with a needle when they wake up on their special day!

• To celebrate the two hundredth anniversary of the United States Constitution, **Devon Smith** of Wampum, Pennsylvania, traveled around the world collecting over forty-six thousand signatures on a 2,000-foot-long birthday card!

To CELEBRATE THE 72nd BIRTHDAY of Thailand's KING BHUMIBOL ADULYADEJ, A RECORD 572 PARACHUTISTS TOOK PART IN A MASSIVE FREE-FALL OVER BANGKOK!

RESIDENTS of Oak Park, Ill., BIRTHPLACE of AUTHOR *Ernest Hemingway*, CELEBRATE HIS BIRTHDAY WITH A CEREMONIAL *"RUNNING of the BULLS"* USING WHEELBARROWS *INSTEAD of ANIMALS!*

IN 1991, AN EQUESTRIAN CLUB IN *SAN FRANCISCO, CALIF.,* CELEBRATED *MOZART'S BICENTENNIAL BY TRAINING HORSES TO PERFORM BALLET TO HIS MUSIC!*

THE **STRUCTURE** IN WHICH ARAKANESE CHIEFS, IN EASTERN PAKISTAN, CELEBRATE THEIR BIRTHDAYS IS AN ELABORATE BAMBOO MAZE **330** FEET HIGH, THE LUMBER FOR WHICH IS FLOATED DOWN THE SANGU RIVER *ON A RAFT 260 FEET LONG*— THE HUGE MAZE IS NEVER USED AGAIN

• In 1990, 115 people with the surname "Shakespeare" celebrated William Shakespeare's four hundredth birthday at England's New Globe Theater!

VALENTINE'S DAY

• Saint Valentine's Day has been celebrated in much the same manner as it is today since the fourteenth century.

• The world's biggest love-in! In Minsk, Belorussia, six thousand people took part in a simultaneous Valentine's Day kiss!

EASTER

• In April 1998, 322,003 people took part in an Easter egg hunt conducted on the World Wide Web!

• In Germany during the 1880s, Easter eggs that were dyed and inscribed with a person's name and birth date were honored in courts of law as birth certificates!

• An Easter egg hunt held in Homex, Georgia, features 152,125 eggs hidden in a local pasture!

MOTHER'S DAY

• Mother's Day in Mexico is celebrated for two days.

• Mother's Day, originated by **Miss Anna Jarvis** of Philadelphia, Pennsylvania, was celebrated for the first time on May 10, 1908.

INDEPENDENCE DAY

• In 1991, during the annual July 4 celebrations on Coney Island, New York, **Frank Dellaros** of Queens, New York, ate twenty-one hot dogs in twelve minutes, breaking a thirty-two year old record!

• In Denmark, people celebrate July 4 as United States Independence Day!

HALLOWEEN

• Halloween was once known as Nutcracker Night because nuts were thrown into fires to determine if a lover was fickle. If the nuts burst, it was not true love!

THANKSGIVING

• Thanksgiving Day was celebrated in Canada in 1578 by **Martin Frobisher**, forty-five years before the first Pilgrim celebration!

• The first Thanksgiving celebrated by colonists of the United States did not take place in Plymouth, Massachusetts!

• The first Thanksgiving: Berkeley Hundred, a tobacco plantation located near Jamestown, Virginia, was the scene of the first Thanksgiving feast in America on December 3, 1619. Thirty-eight men landed here and held a Thanksgiving Day celebration almost a year before the Pilgrims landed at Plymouth Rock.

CHRISTMAS

• Christmas was banned in England from 1644 to 1681—and outlawed in Massachusetts from 1659 to 1681!

• During the reign of England's King Henry VIII, commoners were allowed to play tennis only during the twelve days of Christmas!

TOMB OF SANTA CLAUS

SANTA CLAUS REALLY *LIVED* — HE WAS THE BISHOP OF MYRA — IN ASIA MINOR. HE DIED DEC. 6, 342 A.D. AND IS BURIED IN THE CHURCH OF ST. NICHOLAS, BARI, ITALY. ST. NICHOLAS WAS NOT ONLY THE PATRON SAINT OF CHILDREN - BUT OF THIEVES AND PAWNBROKERS

• The man who set the date for Christmas: **Julius Sextus Africanus**, a historian in Alexandria, Egypt, established December 25 as the date of the nativity in his "Chronicon from the Creation of the World to the Year 221".

• Christmas, widely celebrated only since the third century, has been observed on January 6 and March 25, as well as on December 25.

Ed Matoukis, of Forty Fort, Pennsylvania, created this Christmas tree, complete with lights, from approximately seven hundred elk antlers.

• The first Christmas in America! Fort Christmas in Haiti was built by Christopher Columbus from the wreckage of the *Santa Maria*. His crew celebrated the New World's first Christmas there in 1492.

• The first artificial Christmas trees were made with dyed goose feathers attached to wire branches!

• In the nineteenth century, the Saint Nicholas National Bank of New York City issued three-dollar bills with the image of Santa Claus on them!

• In 1993, town elders in Assen, the Netherlands, posted signs banning a commercial Christmas!

• In Greece it is customary for people to burn their old shoes during the Christmas season to prevent misfortune in the coming year!

• The world's strangest nativity scene! A nativity scene, complete with replicas of the Holy Child, Mary, Joseph, and stable animals, is presented annually in Amalfi, Italy, at the base of the Grotta Smeralda, thirty feet below the surface of the Mediterranean Sea—where it can only be reached by divers.

• American inventor **Thomas Edison** (1847-1931) created the world's first Christmas tree lights in 1882—just three years after he invented the incandescent light bulb!

• It was once customary for people in Newfoundland, Canada, to throw a burning stick over their house on Christmas Eve to protect it from fire in the coming year!

Believe It or Not!
SANTA CLAUS HAS A BROTHER! ACCORDING TO PENNSYLVANIA DUTCH TRADITION, "BELLS NICHOLS" VISITS CHILDREN ON New Year's Eve AND LEAVES THEM CAKE and COOKIES!

THE STEAUA, a large wood "star" mounted on a broomstick, is carried by boys of Romania as they sing Christmas carols.

THE TASMANIAN SNOW GUM TREE of the Australian Alps is the Down Under Christmas tree. Blizzards twist the gum trees into unusual shapes and, near Mount Stirling, in Tasmania, 2 rows of snow gums have been bent to form a natural arch over the highway.

IN Australia, SANTA'S CHRISTMAS SLEIGH IS PULLED BY KANGAROOS INSTEAD of REINDEER.

• Candles burned during Christmas dinners in England and France for centuries were so large that deep holes were chiseled in the stone floors to contain them.

CHRISTMAS CARDS

• The first Christmas card was created for **Sir Henry Cole** of England, who had one thousand printed for sale in his shop in 1843, but they didn't sell well enough to repeat the effort the following year.

• **Werner Erhard**, of San Francisco, California, sent out 68,824 Christmas cards in December, 1975!

• **Jarrod Booth**, of Salt Spring Island, British Columbia, has a collection of over 205,120 Christmas cards!

SANTA CLAUS

• **Santa Claus** really lived! His body is buried in the Cathedral of Saint Nicholas, Bari, Italy!

• **Saint Nicholas** of Myria, the original Santa Claus, was the patron saint of thieves!

• The only church **Santa Claus** ever attended was the church of Saint Nicholas in Myria, Asia Minor—Santa's hometown!

• Santa Claus's workshop was first depicted by cartoonist **Thomas Nast** in 1866.

• Based on a 1999 estimated population count of North America and Europe, on December 24 of that year Santa Claus had to visit 42,466,666 homes in a twelve-hour period—that's nine hundred eighty-three homes per second!

NEW YEAR

• New Year's Day, until September 1752, was celebrated in England and America on March 25.

• The Puritans in New England refused to celebrate New Year's Day because January was named for the Roman god Janus, whom the Puritans considered a wicked heathen god.

• The Yi people of southwestern China celebrate New Years' twice a year—once in winter and again in summer!

• In January 1990, **James Lawlor**, of Fairfield, Iowa, sent an eight-hundred-foot-long Happy New Year card signed by five hundred thousand people to Soviet President Mikhail Gorbachev!

THE NEW MILLENNIUM

• The Ritz-Carlton Hotel chain offered a special millennium package at a cost of $100,000 per couple that included a private butler, a chauffeur-driven Jaguar, eighteen-carat gold watches, and champagne!

• An American lingerie company offered the ultimate gift to celebrate the millennium—a satin bra and panties encrusted with over two thousand diamonds and diamond-cut sapphires set in platinum, priced at $10 million!

FESTIVALS AND CELEBRATIONS

• In Morgan City, Louisiana, there is an annual festival dedicated to shrimp and petroleum!

• In Bertram, Texas, there is an annual festival devoted to oatmeal—including an oatmeal barbecue!

• In Kewanee, Illinois, the "Hog Capital of the World," there is an annual pork chop barbecue that serves up to thirty thousand pork chops!

• In Fulton, Kentucky, there is an annual banana festival that includes a one-ton banana pudding!

• In Oaxaca, Mexico, there is an annual Feast of Radishes, held every December 23!

• In Japan, during the Hina Matsuri, or Girl's Doll Festival, dolls made of paper and cloth are placed in straw baskets and set afloat to be swept away to another world!

• In Austin, Texas, there is an annual "Butt-Numb-A-Thon" film festival where the audience sits and watches films for twenty-four hours nonstop!

• Laugh-A-Thon: In January 1999, two thousand people in Bombay, India, all members of Laughter Clubs, celebrated World Laughter Day by laughing out loud in a city park!

• Marysville, Kansas, known as the "Home of the Black Squirrels," has selected the black squirrel as its official mascot. It has an official anthem called "Black Squirrel Song," and holds an annual Black Squirrel Celebration!

• In Willow, Alaska, there is an annual potato festival featuring a contest to create the largest sculpture made from whole potatoes!

• In Carpenteria, California, to celebrate the annual avocado festival, the world's largest bowl of guacamole was created, using fifteen hundred avocados, five hundred tomatoes, one thousand chilies, and five hundred cloves of garlic!

• In the United States, the week of October 20 is celebrated as National Shampoo Week!

• Ping-pong Festival: City officials in Chicago, Illinois, set up five hundred ping-pong tables equipped with thirty thousand paddles and balls all around the city for the summer of 2000!

In New Orleans, La., there is an annual MARDI GRAS COSTUME PARADE just for dogs!

The 1946 celebrants of National Laugh Week.

In 1995, at the annual HARVEST FESTIVAL in Keen, New Hampshire, there were 10,540 carved and lit pumpkins on display!

In Seymour, Wisconsin, there is a Hamburger Hall of Fame with an annual "BURGER FEST," featuring a bun toss, a ketchup slide, and a hamburger parade!

THE ANNUAL *DRAGON RACE BOAT FESTIVAL* IN HONG KONG COMMEMORATES THE SEARCH FOR *QU YUAN*, A 3ʳᵈ CENTURY POET *WHO THREW HIMSELF INTO THE RIVER. HE WAS SO ADMIRED, PEOPLE SEARCHED FOR HIS BODY FOR DAYS!!*

• In Green River, Utah, there is a twenty-five-foot-long wooden building shaped like a watermelon that is the center point of the annual Watermelon Day festival!

• To celebrate Midsummer's Day, artist **Andy Goldsworthy** displayed thirteen one-ton snowballs on the streets of London, England! He collected the snow over two winters and had it kept in cold storage!

• To celebrate the annual spring invasion of the banana slug, residents of Monte Rio, California, hold an annual slug festival featuring slug recipes and a crowning of the biggest slug!

• Every March 15 since 1885, the town of Hinckley, Ohio, has celebrated the return of hundreds of migrating turkey vultures to their nests.

• In Macksburg, Iowa, there is an International Skillet Throw, in which competitors heave cast-iron skillets at the head of a stuffed dummy!

• Turtle Days: Every July,

people in Churubusco, Indiana, celebrate the 1948 sighting of the "Beast of Busco," a legendary six-foot-long snapping turtle that appeared in a local lake!

• In 1977, **Stan Boris**, of Petoskey, Michigan, picked nine hundred fifteen morel mushrooms in one hour at the annual National Mushroom Hunting Championship in Boyne City, Michigan!

• Every July, residents of Otisfield, Maine, hold a picnic to honor the memory of **Joe Holden** (1816-1900), a local professor who tried to convince the nation that the Earth was flat!

• October 12 is known as International Moment of Frustration Scream Day!

• In Worthington, Minnesota, there is an annual King Turkey Day, featuring a "Great Gobbler Gallop" turkey race!

• At Cowley's Ridge State Park, Arkansas, there is an annual Mosquito Cook-Off in which mosquitoes are the main ingredient used in all the entries!

In Miami Shores, Florida, there is an annual "MARSHMALLOW DROP," in which 30,000 marshmallows are dropped from a helicopter for children to collect!

• In Portland, Oregon, there is an annual Weiner Dog Summer Nationals race for dachshunds!

• In Carbondale, Illinois, there is an annual sailing regatta featuring unusually shaped boats made out of cardboard!

• In Pasadena, California, there is an annual Doo Dah Parade, featuring garbage-can drum corps, mutant queens, and a synchronized briefcase drill team!

• Lumpy Rug Day is celebrated in Falls Church, Virginia on May 6.

• In Portugal, there is an annual all-night celebration of Saint Joao, in which participants feast on sardines and strike each other on the head with plastic hammers!

• In the United States, March 13 is designated as National Blame It on Somebody Else Day!

• In Westland, Michigan, there is an annual Mud Day celebration featuring a Mr. and Mrs. Mud beauty competition!

• In Baker, Oregon, there is an annual Porcupine Race!

• The town of Metropolis, Illinois, has a twenty-five-foot-high statue of Superman and holds an annual festival to celebrate the super-hero!

• In Banner Elk, North Carolina, there is an annual Wooly Worm Festival and Race devoted to black and brown striped caterpillars!

• The annual World Pillow Fighting Championships are held in Kenwood, California!

• National Sarcastic Awareness Month is celebrated during October in the United States!

• In Wayne, Nebraska, there is an annual Chicken Show and Egg Drop Competition, in which contestants must catch an egg dropped from a height of fifty-four feet, four inches without it breaking!

• National Relaxation Day is celebrated in the United States every August 15!

• Welcome Nerds! In Dallas, Texas, there is an annual Nerd Weekend, held for computer lovers from twenty-seven countries!

• **Randy Ober**, competing at the annual Tobacco Chewing and Spitting Championship in Barstow, California, set a new world record by spitting a wad of tobacco forty-seven feet, seven inches!

• In Virginia City, Nevada, there is an annual International Camel and Ostrich Race!

In Millington, Tennessee, there is an annual INTERNATIONAL GOAT DAY celebration, with prizes awarded to the goat with the longest horns, the goat that gives the most milk, and the best-dressed goat!

AT THAILAND'S ANNUAL VEGETARIAN FESTIVAL, PARTICIPANTS SKEWER THEMSELVES INSTEAD OF MEAT

Phuket, Thailand, is home to an astonishing annual celebration which lasts a total of nine days. During the festival, participants eat no meat, and deny themselves all manner of corporeal pleasures and comforts. They spend the days in deep meditation, often entering trance states, during which they call upon the aid of their deities.

The pinnacle of the festival is the part that visitors find the most shocking: at the height of the festivities, participants grab whatever objects they can and thrust them through their cheeks. Knives, beads, broom handles, even light fixtures are passed through disfiguring slits in their faces.

The tradition began in 1825, as a supplication to the deities who saved the village from a malaria outbreak. Descendants have recreated their sacrifice every year since to express their gratitude.

Participants show little pain. Amazingly, when the ritual is concluded and the objects are removed, bleeding is minimal and wounds heal swiftly, without complications.

• March 15 is celebrated as Ice Bowling Day in Sheboygen, Wisconsin!

• The fishless fishing derby! In Cottonwood, Minnesota, there is an annual ice fishing competition in which only people who don't catch fish win prizes!

• In Pomona, California, there is an annual turkey festival featuring a queen who wears a dress made from seventy-two hundred turkey feathers!

• In Minneapolis, Minnesota, there is an annual International Unicycle Race!

• In Cape May, New Jersey, there is an annual clam-pitching tournament!

• In Aiken, South Carolina, there is an annual Lobster Race and Oyster Parade!

• In Fort Wayne, Indiana, residents celebrate Backwards Day by wearing their clothes backward and walking backward!

• In Myerstown, Pennsylvania, October 24 is celebrated as Bald Head Day!

• In McGregor, Minnesota, there is a festival dedicated to wild rice!

• Sneak Some Zucchini Onto Your Neighbor's Porch Night is officially celebrated on August 8!

• Ocean City, New Jersey, celebrates an annual Quiet Festival, with a Yawn-Along, mimes, and yo-yo competitions!

• January 16—National Nothing Day—was created by newspaperman **Harold Pullman Coffin** so that people could just sit around without observing or honoring anything!

• In Gibsland, Louisiana, there is an annual Bonnie and Clyde festival dedicated to the famous bank robbers, featuring reenactments of a bank robbery and the ambush that ended their lives!

• A crate of strawberries sold for $7,500 at the fiftieth anniversary of the Poteet, Texas, Strawberry Festival.

• No Socks Day is celebrated annually in Pennsylvania!

• In Ligonier, Indiana, there is an annual marshmallow festival.

• In Malvern, Arkansas, there is an annual brick-throwing contest!

BELIEVE IT OR NOT! IN CARYVILLE, FLA., THERE IS AN ANNUAL INTERNATIONAL WORM FIDDLING CONTEST IN WHICH CONTESTANTS PLAY MUSIC TO DRAW EARTHWORMS OUT OF THE SOIL!

Chapter 32

Illusions

OPTICAL ILLUSION
This is not a spiral. All circles are separate and concentric.

Things are not always as they seem. Our eyes can deceive us. Our senses can be fooled, and relatively easily. Once you enter our gallery of human-made and naturally occurring illusions, you may never trust your senses again.

HUMAN-MADE ILLUSIONS

TROMPE L'OEIL

• The house that's not a house! Twenty three Leinster Gardens, in the Bayswater section of London, England, appears to be a handsome four-story apartment building, but actually is a dummy facade painted on a cement wall to conceal the entrance to a subway tunnel!

• In New York City, abandoned slum tenements are camouflaged by having their cemented-up fronts painted to indicate doorways, patios, and windows displaying plants.

THE ILLUSION OF DEATH
AN OPTICAL ILLUSION CREATED BY THE ITALIAN ARTIST GALLIENI... VIEWED FROM A DISTANCE IT APPEARS TO BE A SKULL -- *BUT CLOSE UP IT SHOWS TWO CHILDREN PLAYING IN A WINDOW*

How'd he do that? Both the arrrow heads and arrow tails are bigger than the holes in the glass. **Joseph Shagena,** of Sebring, Florida, created this seemingly impossible artifact.

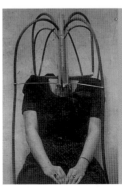

The amazing headless woman, a popular Ripley Odditorium illusion in 1933. Visitors were shown the secret of how the woman was kept alive and were asked never to reveal the secret.

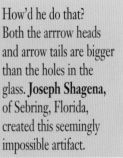

FILIPPO IOCO'S COLORFUL SWIMSUITS ARE SKIN-TIGHT—LITERALLY

Viewing Filippo Ioco's bathing suit creations as they're modeled on the runway, you might not notice anything unusual. In fact, you would probably assume that the colorful fashions you're looking at are some new, skin-tight fabric. But Ioco's swimsuits are, in fact, illusions. The models aren't wearing anything at all—except a thin layer of paint!

Puerto Rican artist Filippo Ioco began his painting career, as most artists do, painting on canvas, but his canvas works failed to inspire the kinds of reactions he was looking for. He wanted people to be amazed by what they saw, and to remember them for more than just a few weeks. So he translated his colorful works from canvas to skin.

At first, Filippo's living human canvases were splashed with a variety of bright abstract patterns, however, Filippo soon segued to realism, painting on "bathing suits" so realistic that they fool just about everybody. Filippo even adds bits of real ribbon and lace, to further the illusion.

At his art shows, some of the models walking the runway are wearing actual swimwear, others are wearing only paint. The audience is encouraged to guess which is which. It's all tastefully done, of course. Filippo explains, "I don't want it to come across as pornographic. I want it to be known as 'artistic nudity.'"

NATURALLY OCCURRING ILLUSIONS

• A sensory illusion: Vanilla has a pleasant aroma but no taste.

• The only place on Earth where everybody wears a halo! In Veithyleisa Fjord, Iceland, a person peering into the fog sees his reflection surrounded by a concentric rainbow of brilliant colors.

OPTICAL ILLUSION
The square is perfect.

TOYAMA BAY in Uozo, Japan, is the site of natural mirages every spring where the images of ships, buildings, and trees are seen floating upside-down over the water!

LUNAR HALO
A double halo framing a cross seen over McMurdo Sound, in the Antarctic. (Jan. 15, 1911)

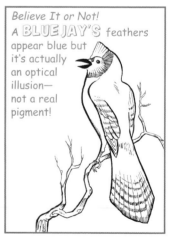

Believe It or Not!
A **BLUE JAY'S** feathers appear blue but it's actually an optical illusion—not a real pigment!

Chapter 33
Inventions

THE TAITO CORP. OF JAPAN HAS DEVELOPED THE *FIRST ROBOTIC ORCHESTRA* WITH AN ELECTRONICALLY CONTROLLED VIOLIN, PIANO *AND* FLUTE!

Got a knack for coming up with outrageous new product ideas? You're in good company. Herein you'll find a compendium of amazing inventions of yesterday, tomorrow, and today—perhaps a few which, once you've discovered them, you may find impossible to do without!

SCHOOLGIRL MELANIE LAMONTAGNE of Timmins, Ont., Canada, INVENTED SNOW SHOES for DOGS!

• The United States Patent Office has issued over four thousand patents for mousetrap designs! The office has thirty-nine different categories, including "choking," "impaling," and "explosive devices"!

• In 1897, **John Sievers, Junior,** of Ammes, Nebraska, patented a hunter's decoy in the shape of a cow that held two men with rifles.

• In 1987, **David Kiner** used eleven-foot-long water shoes called ski jacks to walk on the Hudson River from Albany to Battery Park, New York—a distance of one hundred and fifty-five miles!

• In 1903, **John S. Barnes,** of Payette, Idaho, to keep coyotes away from his farm, designed a scarecrow alarm that fired a blank cartridge every fifteen minutes all night long.

STELLA VIDAL, A FASHION DESIGNER in Argentina, HAS DESIGNED DISPOSABLE DIAPERS for DOGS!

• **Randal Wise,** of Natick, Massachusetts, has designed contact lenses for chickens—and over one hundred thousand birds are already wearing them!

• In 1961, **Bird A. Eyer,** of Seattle, Washington, designed and patented a toothbrush for dogs!

• In 1949, **Rafael A. Gonzales,** of Dayton, Ohio, patented an indoor air-conditioner in the shape of a palm tree!

• A design for a car megaphone for warning pedestrians was filed at the United States Patent Office in 1930!

• Taunton, England, has "talking" trash cans that say "thank you" when garbage is deposited.

• "Shoes for moos": **Jim Wells,** of Elmira, Ontario, has created boots for cows with injured hoofs!

"These boots are made for power-walking!" Scientists in Ufa, Russia, have invented gasoline-powered BOOTS! A person wearing them can cover 13 feet in a single stride!

Believe It or Not! Youssef Bakhos of California INVENTED A SINGING ELECTRIC RAZOR!

IN 1992, A COMPANY in Japan DEVELOPED COMPUTERS THAT CAN BE WORN ON THE HEAD and SHOULDERS of the USER!

CAROL BELL HAWKINS of Benton, Tenn., INVENTED THE "DRIVE CLEANER," A PROTECTIVE BIB FOR DRIVERS WHO EAT THEIR LUNCH ON THE GO!

• In 1972, **Lewis Toppel**, of Madison, Wisconsin, filed a patent for a cigarette package that coughed when opened.

• Six-year-old **Collin Hazen**, of Fargo, North Dakota, has designed a battery-powered dog collar that glows in the dark!

• In 1954, **John La Marr**, of Torrance, California, invented a mechanical doll for practicing dance steps that was set on a pole attached to a rolling ball.

• **Jean Pomerance**, of Los Angeles, California, designs bibs for adults that are to be worn when out in public!

• **Auguste Raymond Despland**, of Switzerland, designed and built a bicycle lawn mower that tilts to cut grass on hills!

• An appliance company in Germany has designed a voice-activated alarm clock that can only be shut off by shouting at it!

• The "autopod," invented by a British company, is a device disguised as a patch of grass in which a car is parked and lowered into the ground!

• In 1953, **George Troutman Jenks**, of Saint Petersburg, Florida, patented a strap-on golfing apparatus that controlled the movements of the hands, arms, head, and shoulders!

• In 1972, **Robert Lamar**, of Houston, Texas, patented a design for a truck that would automatically throw newspapers onto subscribers' lawns!

• **Samuel Rubin**, of Missouri, invented a scalp massager that rubbed a person's scalp across a small platform while it stood on his or her head!

• **Gerald Ollivier**, of Quebec, Canada, has invented an anti-hail cannon that can turn hail into rain or sleet!

• In the nineteenth century, **Professor Mayer**, of France, invented a hearing aid for traffic policemen, which muffled all noise except for the traffic sounds directly ahead!

• **Andre Gamonet**, of Lyons, France, invented a swimming device made of inflatable rubber that featured a hand-operated propeller!

• **David Sideris** and **Michael Ivezic**, of Mississauga, Ontario, Canada, have invented a computerized golf bag called the "Lektronic Kaddy" that can be programmed to follow a golfer around the course!

• **Mabel Yee**, of Emeryville, California, designs products for car travelers, including a massaging car seat and a portable car fridge and stove!

• **Mark Woehrer**, of Nebraska, invented "Tag-a-long," a robotic suitcase carrier that follows its owner wherever he goes!

• **Shimon Sandhaus** has patented a soothing cassette for insomniacs that comes with a two-hundred-fifty-page booklet containing sixty-five thousand hand-drawn sheep inside to count!

• "The Snoozer": **Dan Jagdat**, of Toronto, Canada, invented a nose-shaped pillow that sticks to windows for travelers and commuters!

• **Clarence Birdseye**, the inventor of processed frozen food, once tried to freeze a whole alligator!

• In 1977, **Joe Martino**, of Brooklyn, New York, invented a training baseball bat with a hole in it to be used by trainers and coaches to study bat-ball contact!

• In 1990, **Reginald Claerhout**, of Belgium, invented "Magic Ears"—earplugs that block out background noise yet still allow the wearer to hear human voices!

• **Tom Woods**, of Falls Church, Virginia, invented an anti-snoring device that prevents sleepers from breathing through their mouths!

• "Vertipark" in Munich, Germany, is a parking lot that resembles a Ferris wheel in which cars are vertically parked up to seven stories high!

• Scientists in Japan have developed a paint that is "exothermic" or heat-releasing, which can be used for melting ice on roads or on aircraft!

• At the "Kids Only" Theater in Evergreen Park, Illinois, parents who drop off their children receive a matching bar-coded I.D. card, which they must show in order to reclaim their children!

• In 1991, inventors in Japan designed a roll-away sidewalk!

• **Emily Peters**, age twelve, of Richmond, Virginia, invented an umbrella with a cooling fan inside that is activated by solar rays!

• The "Sinclair C5" tricycle, invented by **Sir Clive Sinclair** of Britain, runs on electricity and can accelerate as fast as a sports car!

• Invented in Philadelphia, a device called "Off Limits," transmits radio signals through a collar whenever the animal wearing it strays onto a carpet!

• **Dr. Hinrich L. Bohn**, a soil scientist at the University of Arizona, uses dirt-filled car bumpers to help filter car fumes!

• In 1991, scientists in Sweden invented a paint that can absorb odors including onions and tobacco!

• **Domingo Tan**, of Alexandria, Virginia, invented a spray that cools the inside of a parked car up to forty degrees Fahrenheit in one minute!

• In 1991, American researchers developed a new car that parks itself using an automated push-button system!

• A company in Japan has developed fire-proof paper that can withstand heat up to fifteen hundred degrees Celsius!

"**CLEANUP SLIPPERS**" A COMPANY in Japan MAKES SLIPPERS WITH A TINY BROOM ATTACHED TO THE TOE of ONE FOOT AND A DUSTPAN TO THE OTHER.

Believe It or Not! Angus MacLellan of Scotland INVENTED THE WORLD'S FIRST **AUTOMATIC BAGPIPE** THAT RUNS ON A BATTERY and REQUIRES NO BLOWING.

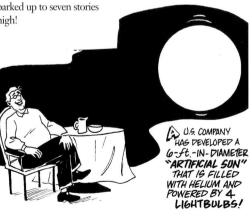

A U.S. COMPANY HAS DEVELOPED A 6-ft.-IN-DIAMETER "ARTIFICIAL SUN" THAT IS FILLED WITH HELIUM AND POWERED BY 4 LIGHTBULBS!

"GAME EAR" A COMPANY in Pennsylvania HAS DEVELOPED A DEVICE for HUNTERS THAT MAGNIFIES THE SOUNDS ANIMALS MAKE WHILE WALKING IN THE WOODS!

"HAPPY SNOOZE" A COMPANY in Tokyo, Japan, MAKES HARD HATS WITH SUCTION CUPS TO ENABLE SLEEPING SUBWAY PASSENGERS TO KEEP THEIR BALANCE.

JAMES D. WILLIAMS of Britain, HAS INVENTED EAR PROTECTORS THAT FIT OVER THE EARS of LONG-EARED DOGS AND KEEP THEM from GETTING COVERED WITH FOOD WHILE EATING!

• A company in Spain has invented a push button device that can rotate a house three hundred sixty degrees in order to take advantage of the position of the sun.

• **David Kendrick**, of Berkshire, New York, has invented a "life expectancy time piece" that actually gauges how long the wearer has to live based on his current lifestyle!

• **Doctor Borne Petruson**, of Sweden, invented an anti-snoring device that can even silence **Mel Switzer**, of Toronto, Canada, whose snores—at 87.5 decibels—are louder than a subway train!

• **Paul Mankiewicz,** of New York City, has invented artificial planting soil made out of recycled polystyrene!

• **Casey Golden**, age thirteen, of Evergreen, Colorado, invented a biodegradable golf tee that dissolves in thirty-six hours!

• In 1879, **Benjamin B. Oppenheimer** invented a device for saving people from high-rise hotel fires that consisted of padded shoes and a five-foot para-chute fastened to the head!

• In 1992, a Canadian patent was issued for shock absorbers for hoofed animals!

STEPHEN HOY of the U.S. HAS INVENTED EDIBLE GREETING CARDS for ANIMALS!

• In 1992, Japanese engineers developed a car cooling system that measures the driver's skin temperature!

• **James Jemtrud**, age six, of North Dakota, in 1992, invented "sucker tucker," a device to keep half-eaten lollipops fresh!

"BRAINSTORM," A U.S. COMPANY, SELLS KITS for MAKING GELATIN DESSERTS from MOLDS of PEOPLE'S FACES!

• **Hayward G. Spangler** and **Eric H. Erickson**, of Tucson, Arizona, filed a patent for a device that determines the temperament of bees in a hive!

• In 1991, British inventor **John Ward** created a self-propelling wheelbarrow!

• A company in Britain has developed an electronic pet door that opens only when approached by an animal wearing a collar key that contains the correct code!

• "Dog Gone," invented by **Gay Balfour**, is a device that sucks gophers and prairie dogs out of the ground so they can be moved to other areas!

• In 1992, researchers at the Japan Bicycle Technical Center built a prototype bicycle with a frame made out of epoxy resin and handmade paper!

• The Ainus of Japan, who pride themselves on their long moustaches, use carved wooden moustache lifters while eating and drinking!

• In 1992, a bicycle designed for riding on water was displayed at the international exhibit of inventions in Geneva, Switzerland!

• A company in Japan has invented a method of attaching false teeth to the inside of the mouth using a magnet and a stainless steel plate!

HIGH-TECH INVENTIONS

• **David Kime**, of Memphis, Tennessee, stages indoor horse races using "super jocks"—remote-controlled robotic jockeys that can ride hackney horses.

• Scientists at Bell Communications Research, in New Jersey, have created a credit card that is imprinted with the cardholder's voice!

• Designed by car engineers in Japan, "The Screamer" is a single-seat vehicle with speed controls operated by the volume of the driver's voice!

• A Japanese electronics company has invented a computerized robotic waiter to take orders in fast-food restaurants!

• Researchers at the Massachusetts Institute of Technology have developed a tiny robotic cockroach named "Squirt" that measures one cubic inch in size and is programmed to react to light and noise!

• **Ted Skup**, of Merrillville, Indiana, has invented "high-tech spitballs"—quarter-ounce squares of putty that are rolled and tossed!

• "Anti-Nap Man": In 1992 a company in Japan invented a device that contains a sensor in a ring which sets off an alarm if a worker dozes off!

• An electronics company in the United States has developed a voice-activated car stereo that plays cassettes or switches stations on command!

A COMPANY IN BRITAIN HAS DEVELOPED A HANDHELD COMPUTER SHAPED LIKE A PEN! INSTEAD OF USING A KEYBOARD, YOU SIMPLY WRITE ON A SURFACE OR EVEN IN MID-AIR!

"MOON SHOES"
LeRoy Hart of Palm Springs, Calif., A FORMER ACROBAT, INVENTED 6-INCH-HIGH TRAMPOLINES THAT STRAP ONTO THE FEET!

D'YA FEEL LUCKY, PUNK?!

YIKES!

Patent # 1,468,373

A PATENT for A "FLY SWATTING DEVICE" SHAPED LIKE A GUN THAT FIRED A SWATTER WAS FILED at the U.S. Patent Office in 1923!

DON'T HAVE A NICE DAY

"PIZZABOT" INVENTED BY AMERICAN DESIGNER *K.G. ENGELHARDT*, IS A ROBOT THAT MAKES PIZZAS WITH TOPPINGS *AND* PLACES THEM IN THE OVEN BY RESPONDING TO VOICE COMMANDS!

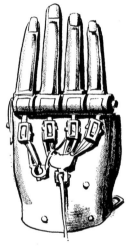

The "**GREEN LADY**" A robot at the Franklin Institute in Philadelphia, Pa., that can write 3 poems and draw 4 pictures was made in 1805.

• **Krishna Persaud**, of Manchester, England, invented an electronic device to locate wild black truffles, a rare fungus that is considered a delicacy and costs up to $90 an ounce!

• In 1991, the United States Army built a high-speed miniature rocket that weighs less than twelve pounds and is powered by thrusters less than one inch long!

• In 1991, scientists invented car headlights as small as a credit card!

YESTERYEAR'S INVENTIONS

• In 1877, **W. T. Steiger** patented an automatic foot warmer that consisted of a long rubber tube, with a funnel for breathing into, that was worn around the neck and inserted into each shoe!

• The first manufactured bubble gum, called "Blibber-blubber," was so sticky that it could only be removed from skin with turpentine!

• A device to exterminate bed bugs using electricity was patented in 1898.

• A device that served as a combination grater-slicer and mouse and flytrap was registered at the United States Patent Office in 1897.

• In 1760, **Joseph Merlin**, a Belgian musician, invented roller skates and first demonstrated them at a ball by skating across the room while playing the violin.

• A method for preserving a dead body in a transparent block of glass was registered at the United States Patent Office in 1903.

INVENTION FOR MAKING DIMPLES Patented May 19, 1896, by M. Goetze.

The first **ARTIFICIAL LIMB** An iron hand ordered by King Robert the Bruce of Scotland for a knight named De Clephanes more than 650 years ago. Each finger could be moved by pressing a button.

• In 1786, **Barbeu de Bourg**, of France, invented a "lightning-conductor umbrella"!

• The first passenger elevator was designed in 1743 for **King Louis XV** of France. The flying chair ran up the outside of the palace at Versailles and was raised and lowered by hand.

• In 1874, **Mr. Von Scheidt**, of Buffalo, New York, invented a bicycle that could safely transport an adult and four children!

• **David Hutton**, a nine-teenth-century Scottish inventor, created a mill for twisting twine that was operated by mouse power!

• In 1907, **Ignatius Nathaniel Soares**, of Framinham, Massachusetts, patented a device that altered the shape of the wearer's nose by applying continuous pressure!

The POLLUTION SOLUTION that was achieved 101 years ago. Anti-pollution costumes with "gas masks," designed for motor-ists of the future were illustrated in a magazine in 1901.

The Missile Launcher invented 10,000 years ago. The ATLATL used by Aztec Indian hunters enabled them to hurl a spear hard enough to kill big game from a considerable distance.

DURING THE REVOLUTION OF 1830 THE NATIONAL GUARD OF PARIS WAS ARMED WITH UMBRELLA GUNS TO PROTECT THEM AGAINST SUN AND RAIN

GETTING UP WITH A BANG
A 17th-century pistol with a built-in alarm clock!

"Knee action" wheels are not new. The idea was used 98 years ago! **John F. Murphy**, of Louisville, Kentucky, patented this idea in 1904.

THE **FIRST** ENVELOPES WERE **MADE OF MUD!** ANCIENT STONE WRITINGS WERE COVERED WITH MUD TO ASSURE PRIVACY

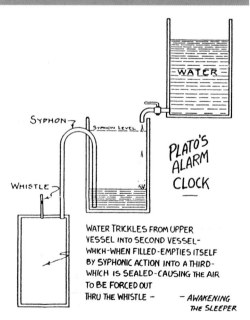

PLATO'S ALARM CLOCK

WATER TRICKLES FROM UPPER VESSEL INTO SECOND VESSEL-WHICH-WHEN FILLED-EMPTIES ITSELF BY SYPHONIC ACTION INTO A THIRD-WHICH IS SEALED-CAUSING THE AIR TO BE FORCED OUT THRU THE WHISTLE –

– AWAKENING THE SLEEPER

• A sewing machine invented in the nineteenth century was powered by a dog running on a disc!

• In 1883, Professor **Baranowski**, of Saint Petersburg, Russia, designed a steam-driven flying machine that was shaped like a bird!

• A hand-cranked calculator designed by **Charles Babbage** in 1849 weighed three tons!

• In 1889, **Christopher W. Robertson**, of Tennessee, invented a locket with an anti-corrosive lining to hold a person's chewed gum!

• A moustache protector devised by **Eli J. F. Randolph**, of New York, in 1872, was a hard rubber device with prongs that fitted into the nostrils to keep the wearer's moustache dry while eating and drinking.

• In 1895, **Francois Baratlon** invented a one-man pedal-powered life buoy to be used by shipwrecked passengers.

• In 1885, American inventor **W. O. Ayres** designed a flying bedstead—with propellers—that could take off vertically!

• In the 1880s, vacuum cleaners required two persons to operate them, one pushing the machinery, the other treading a bellows that sucked up the dust.

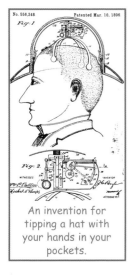

An invention for tipping a hat with your hands in your pockets.

• In 1897, an English manufacturer invented a device that was a combination bicycle and shower-bath!

INDISPENSABLE INVENTIONS

• **Samuel J. Bens**, of New York, patented an exploding golf ball that glows and gives off an odor so it can be found easily !

• "Walking TV": **Brian Elliot**, of Pasadena, California, invented a robotic television that walks from room to room!

• "Give Me a Brake," a $30 device created for nervous passengers, looks like a car floor mat with a pedal, which when pressed makes a sound like screeching brakes!

U.S. PATENT #5,966,743 RANDY FLANN of Milwaukee, Wisc., HAS INVENTED HEADGEAR THAT COMES IN THE SHAPES OF BASEBALLS, FOOTBALLS, BASKETBALLS, SOCCERBALLS, OR HOCKEY PUCKS AND IS ALSO A KEG THAT CONTAINS BEER!

• **John Gruberg**, of Fresno, California, has invented tennis rackets and golf clubs with toothbrushes mounted on their handles so players can practice their swing while brushing!

• In 1986, **Friedrick Winert** filed a patent with the United States Patent Office for a self-lighting cigar.

• **Sarah Cole Racine**, age eight, and her brother Brett, age six, invented edible "Food Tape," tape which, when stuck to sloppy food, makes it easier to eat!

INVENTORS

• **Thomas A. Edison**, the famous inventor, believed that taking off one's clothing caused insomnia. He often slept in his clothes on newspapers beneath a stairway in his laboratory.

• American photographic inventor **George Eastman** lived alone in a mansion with twenty-one telephones, fifteen bathrooms, and an enormous pipe organ that was played every morning by his private organist!

A MILITARY TANK WAS DESIGNED BY LEONARDO DA VINCI IN THE 15th CENTURY

THE ROBOT BARTENDER—
A HIGH-TECH MISSILE GUIDANCE SYSTEM RETIRES TO A PEACEFUL CIVILIAN CAREER

London, England, is home to some of the oldest pubs in the world. But one pub, located just beneath the city's famous landmark, London Bridge, is home to an astonishingly futuristic invention: a robotic bartender!

When customers approach the bar, a slick silver machine with glowing red eyes greets them in a measured British tone: "What can I do for you?" Upon request, the bartender can mix any of seventy-five different drinks, including several exotic cocktails with names like "Plasma" and "Nuclear Synthesis." Customers remark that the robotic bartender's drinks are as tasty as anything mixed by a human being.

How was the technology for this remarkable invention developed? The robotic bartender is actually an ingenious bit of recycling: its operating system was originally built to control a guided missile! The system was purchased in Canada and brought to England to be outfitted with arms, torso, and head, and reprogrammed to manage martinis in lieu of missiles. Most customers agree, the robot bartender is well suited to its new line of work!

- **Benjamin Franklin** (1706-1790), who invented the Franklin stove, also invented a remote-control door lock!

- The great Russian dancer **Vaslav Nijinsky** invented a windshield wiper and a pencil that never needed sharpening!

- **Zeppo Marx**, of the Marx Brothers comedy team, invented an alarm device to be worn on the wrist that measured heartbeats!

- **Alexander Graham Bell**, inventor of the telephone, first answered the device by saying "hoy, hoy" instead of "hello"!

- **Charles Goodyear** (1800-1860), who was instrumental in establishing the rubber industry in the United States, carried out his first experiments in jail—where he had been imprisoned for inability to pay his debts.

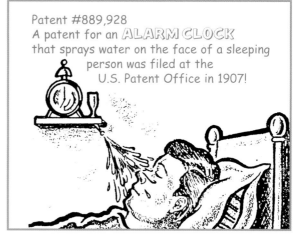

Patent #889,928
A patent for an ALARM CLOCK that sprays water on the face of a sleeping person was filed at the U.S. Patent Office in 1907!

Chapter 34

Labor

JON SATO of Tokyo, Japan, WORKS AS A HUMAN PUNCHING BAG! HE WEARS A FACE MASK AND BODY PADDING AND CHARGES PEOPLE $14 TO PUMMEL HIM for UP TO 3 MINUTES AT A TIME!

Career stuck in a rut? Expand your options! Why resort to a desk job when you could become a professional town drunk, snake milker, or Statue of Liberty? Why settle for stock options and a 401(K) when you could collect your wages in top-of-the-line coffins? In any case, don't make your next career move until you've read Ripley's collection of tales from the world of work. . .

FAMILY TRADES

• **John Beattie** and his father were schoolmasters of Yarrow, Scotland, for a continuous period of one hundred one years.

FIRST IN THEIR FIELD

• **Emma M. Nutt**, of Boston, Massachusetts, who started work for the telephone dispatch company on September 1, 1878, was the first woman telephone operator.

• The first woman typist, **Lillian Sholes** (1856-1941), the forerunner of millions of typists, mastered a typewriter invented by her father in 1872.

• The first professional mourner: The drummer of the Grenadier Guard Regiment of Prussia, by order of King Frederick the Great, throughout the Seven Years' War against Austria and Russia (1756-1763), was severely whipped whenever a grenadier was killed. This made certain that at least one man would cry for each fallen comrade!

HAZARDOUS OCCUPATIONS

• Deep-sea diving from oil rigs is the world's most dangerous occupation: There is an annual death rate of one out of every one hundred divers.

• Itinerant masseurs in ancient Japan were required by law to be totally blind.

• The strangest safety campaign in industrial history: The workman in Ardeer, Scotland, who supervised the machinery in the first British nitro-glycerine factory was prevented from dozing on the job by having him sit on a one-legged stool—this was the only major dynamite factory in the world that never had a serious accident.

Believe It or Not! JESUS LEMO CALVO IS ONE of ONLY 23 LICENSED BARNACLE FISHERMEN IN THE WORLD WHO RISK THEIR LIVES COLLECTING GOOSE BARNACLES AT LOW TIDES from THE ROCKY CLIFFS of THE SISARGAS ISLANDS in Spain!

A **WITCH DOCTOR** in Angola, Africa, to resign his profession must attain an entirely new identity by wearing a mask day and night for a whole year.

LENGTH OF OCCUPATION

• **Ann Nesbit** worked as a governess for the William Robinson family of Cheviot, New Zealand, for seventy years.

• **Archbishop Gaspare Ricciulli** (1496-1592), of Reggio Calabria, Italy, served the church for a period of seventy-one years.

• **Joseph Jefferson** (1820-1905), celebrated American actor, had a stage career of seventy-one years.

• **Charles G. Abbot**, of Hyattsville, Maryland, was still active at the Smithsonian Institute at the age of ninety-seven—after seventy-two years of continuous service.

• **Dominick Falini**, of Westchester, Pennsylvania, at the age of eighty-six, has been a shoemaker for eighty years.

ODD OCCUPATIONS

• **Jennifer Stewart**, of New York City, makes her living by painting herself green and posing as the Statue of Liberty!

• **Mike Pixley** works as a chair tester for La-Z-Boy recliners, averaging twenty-eight hundred rocks per day!

• **Mrs. Mary Ann Smith**, of London, England, earned money by shooting peas at the house windows of families who hired her to wake them up!

• **Jack Black** was, by appointment of Her Majesty Queen Victoria, the Royal Rat Catcher.

• The official town drunk: An elected official in ancient Sparta was required to get intoxicated every day and reel through the streets as an object lesson for the young citizenry.

DEDICATED PROFESSIONALS

• **Henry R. Meyers**, of Chicago, Illinois, worked for a powder company for over twenty-nine and a half years without missing a day for illness.

• **Sidney Wigfall**, of Clearwater, Florida, a taxi driver for forty-six years, wore out twenty cabs—yet never had an accident, and never received a traffic ticket.

Edwin Rose of Hayes, England, A PROFESSIONAL **FOOD TASTER**, TESTS CAT and DOG FOODS! "NICE BOUQUET"

Barney Garland, a veteran elevator operator at the Waldorf-Astoria Hotel in New York, traveled 400,000 miles up and down! Almost the distance to the moon and back.

"ROYAL HEAD HOLDER" Britain's King John (1199-1216) HAD A SERVANT WHOSE OFFICIAL JOB WAS TO HOLD THE KING'S HEAD IF THE MONARCH BECAME SEASICK! URP!

SUCCESSFUL CAREERS

• **Sonja Henje**, the Norwegian skater who appeared in movies and her own ice shows, made over forty-five million dollars skating.

• **A. C. Hobbs**, a locksmith from Boston, Massachusetts, was honored in London, England, in the 1850s when he demonstrated his ability to pick the most intricate locks in English banks.

UNIONS, STRIKES, AND LAYOFFS

• In Thunder Bay, Ontario, one hundred longshoremen went on strike to protest a foreman's swearing!

• **Uriah S. Stephens** (1821-1882), founder of the Noble Order of the Knights of Labor, the first great labor organization in the United States, barred liquor dealers, lawyers, bankers, gamblers, stockbrokers, and physicians from membership.

WAGES

• Dogs working as extras in Hollywood films in the 1930s received $7.50 a day—the same salary as people.

• Roman soldiers in the fifth century A.D. were required to serve for twenty years for a salary of less than a penny a day.

• The Brooklyn Bridge, constructed in 1883, was built by sandhogs who risked their lives for a salary of $2.25 for an eight-hour work day.

• Employers in Uruguay, South America in the 1960s were required by law to pay their workers thirteen months salary for each twelve months of work.

• A cowboy of the old west on a three month cattle drive was paid as little as one hundred dollars and at the end of the trail often spent it all in one night on the town.

Willie Boular, of Atchison, Kansas, deaf, dumb, and legless, laid 46,000 paving bricks in less than eight hours.

BENITO

BENITO OF THE "BLOODY SWORD"

BECAME A PIRATE BECAUSE HE COULDN'T SING

FRUSTRATED IN HIS AMBITION TO BE A CROONER - HE SOUGHT REVENGE ON THE HIGH SEAS AND BECAME THE GREATEST SCOUNDREL OF ALL TIMES - HE LOOTED THE SHIP "MARY DIER" OF TREASURE WORTH $300,000,000 AND BURIED IT ON COCOS ISLAND NEAR PANAMA IN 1820

OCCUPATIONAL HAZARD— A PROFESSIONAL SNAKE MILKER'S SURVIVAL SECRET

Eighty-year-old Bill Haast faces death for a living every day. As the founder of the Miami Serpentarium, Bill milks poisonous snakes, producing venom under laboratory conditions for medical research. The Serpentarium is a leading producer of antivenin. By tempting death, Bill Haast is saving lives.

Since he began his work with poisonous snakes in the 1940s, Bill has been bitten one hundred sixty-eight times— by snakes so poisonous that a single bite could have proven fatal. What's the secret to Bill's survival? Early in his snake-handling career, Bill injected himself with cobra venom. This self-inflicted poison has made him virtually immune to the reptile's bites. Since he built up his immunity, venomous snake bites have put him in a coma, stopped his heart for several terrifying moments, and affected his nervous system—yet he has survived each time. Bill's blood is now so resistant to venom that it has been used in more than twenty transfusions to other snake bite victims.

The experience has made Bill fearless. At the age of eighty, he shows no signs of retiring from his lifelong passion: "As long as I have the use of my hands and can still see and think, I'll keep at it."

• **Mathilde Leblond** worked as a servant for a household in Les Trois Pistoles, Quebec, for fifteen years for a daily wage of four cents—yet she still was able to save enough to loan money to friends and always insisted she was being overpaid.

• Posters displaying a frowning woman were used by Japanese labor unions to protest inflation during a period when Leonardo Da Vinci's famed smiling *Mona Lisa* was being exhibited in that country.

• Female shoe workers in Lynn, Massachusetts, in 1860 became the first women in the United States to stage a strike. They formed the Daughters of Saint Crispin, the first national women's labor union in the country.

• Female teachers in the United States in 1854 were paid an average of $19 a month.

• The church of Saint Mary of Loretto in Sarnen, Switzerland, one of the largest in the country, was built in 1866 under the supervision of an architect named Maria Eltin whose total fee was $10.20.

Albert J. Smith, a one-armed paper hanger from Dedham, Massachusetts, worked on Robert Ripley's office in the Empire State Building.

Believe It or Not! IT TOOK 100,000 MEN 20 YEARS TO BUILD THE GREAT PYRAMID AND THEY WERE PAID WITH GARLIC and RADISHES!

Chapter 35

Language

Believe It or Not! IN BOTSWANA, THE WORD "PULA" MEANS BOTH "RAIN" and "MONEY"!

Welcome to Ripley's lexicon of language facts. Herein, you'll encounter sentences that are grammatically correct in two different languages—with two different meanings. You'll discover what you're really saying when you tell someone to "mind their Ps and Qs." You'll compare the Taki language's three hundred forty active words to English's four hundred fifty-five thousand, all of which can be made with a mere twenty-six letters—as opposed to the seven thousand characters necessary to read the average Chinese newspaper! When you're through, you may find your vocabulary just a bit weirder than it was before!

ALPHABETS

• The oldest known alphabet, found in Ras Shamra, Syria, was carved into rock in the fourteenth century B.C.

OUR ALPHABET

• The twenty-six letters of the alphabet can make 403,290,000,000,000,000,000,000,000 different combinations!

• Can you name the letters of the alphabet in their relative order of frequency of use? E T A I S O N H R D L U C M F W Y P G V B K J Q X Z!

• The oldest record of the Latin alphabet is a gold pin four and a half inches long engraved in the seventh century B.C.

• "Blowzy frumps had quit vexing Jack" is the shortest sentence in the English language that contains all the letters of the alphabet!

BELIEVE IT OR NOT! THE FIRST CARTOONS WITH SPEECH BALLOONS WERE DRAWN BY THE EARLY AZTECS!

OTHER ALPHABETS

• The oldest known Hebrew writing is the name "Tobias"—misspelled on a gravestone erected at Araq el Emir, Jordan, twenty-six hundred years ago.

• There are no vowels in the Arabic alphabet.

• Rotokas, a South Pacific language, has an alphabet with only eleven letters—six consonants and five vowels!

• The alphabet used by the Eskimos of the Canadian Arctic consists of only four vowels and ten consonants—which can be written four different ways.

EXPRESSIONS

• Brass tables in Bristol, England, used by the ancient money changers were called "the nails"—which gave rise to the expression "paying on the nail head."

• The term "wearing your heart on your sleeve" originated with the festival of Lupercalia, held every February 15 in ancient Rome, in which men pinned the name of their beloved on their sleeves!

• The inscription on a painting nearly thirty-six hundred years old, on the tomb of Nakht in Thebes, Egypt, reads, "Celebrate this happy day, for no one has been able to take away what he has with him." This is the origin of the modern phrase, "You can't take it with you."

• The expression "in the nick of time" derives from the ancient practice of recording financial transactions by scoring a stick with a knife!

• To be "unstrung," meaning a state of nerves, originated among the archers of old England, who found it unsettling to meet a foe while carrying a weapon with a loosened bowstring.

• The expression "getting off on the right foot" dates back to the ancient Romans, who believed good spirits always stood by a person's right foot!

• The origin of the term "the whole nine yards" comes from the amount of cloth it took to make a monk's habit!

• The term "penny-pincher" dates back to 1412!

• The term "well-heeled" originated in the seventeenth century, when only the aristocracy were allowed to wear shoes with heels.

• The expression "making ends meet" comes from the sixteenth century, when napkins were first tied around the neck to protect the ruffed collars of noblemen!

• The expression "pin money" dates back to the court of England's Queen Elizabeth I, whose ladies-in-waiting went on an annual shopping spree to buy the latest invention—metal pins!

The phrase "A PARTING SHOT" originally was "a parthian shot"—a backward shot with bow and arrow by which the Parthians of Asia killed their enemies after having pretended to flee.

LANGUAGES

• Aramaic, the ancient language spoken by Jesus Christ, today is spoken in only three remote villages near Damascus, Syria!

COMPLEX LANGUAGES

• English contains the most words of any language, including four hundred fifty-five thousand active words and seven hundred thousand dead ones!

• Reading an average Chinese newspaper requires a knowledge of seven thousand Chinese characters!

• The *Chung-wen ta tzu-tien*, a Chinese language dictionary, is forty volumes long and contains fifty thousand characters, including one character that requires sixty-four different brush strokes!

10 DIFFERENT SIGNS MEANING "WOMAN" ARE USED BY THE KEITA TRIBE OF AFRICA —DEPENDING UPON HER AGE

SIMPLE LANGUAGES

• Taki, a language spoken in French Guinea, has only three hundred forty words!

• Uoiauai, the name of a language in Para State, Brazil, has only seven letters, all of which are vowels!

RARE LANGUAGES

• Women of the ancient Carib tribe, on the island of Dominica, founded their own language that could not be understood by men!

• In 1991, researchers in China uncovered a one-thousand-year-old language called "Nushu" that was created and used only by women!

• Australian Aborigines normally speak a language called "Guwal," but when a man talks to his mother-in-law he speaks in a special tongue called "Dyalnguy"!

CREATIVE LANGUAGES

• English translator **Sir Thomas Urquhart** (1611-1660) devised a universal language in which every word could be read forward and backward!

• "Solresol," a language invented by **Jean-François Sudre** of France in 1827, is the only language that is "spoken" by playing a kazoo!

EXOTIC VOCALIZATIONS

• The Karaya Indians of the Amazon Valley, South America, talk through their nostrils instead of their lips!

• Men of the Mazateco tribe of Mexico use a language of whistles to carry on conversations!

• On the island of La Gomera, in the Canary Islands, residents communicate by using a language of whistles that can take over five years to learn!

• The Zulus of South Africa speak a language that includes fifteen different clicking sounds as consonants!

MISNAMED

• An alligator pear is not a pear, nor is it an alligator. It is a berry.

• The English horn is not English, nor is it a horn. It is French and it is a woodwind.

• What do the Battle of Bunker Hill, the Woodstock Festival, and *Whistler's Mother* have in common? They're all misnamed! The battle took place on Breed's Hill; the festival happened at Bethel, New York; and the painting is called *Arrangement in Gray and Black*.

• Peanuts are not nuts. They are beans.

• The Belgian hare is not a hare. It is a rabbit. An American rabbit is not a rabbit. It is a hare.

• The oyster catcher, a bird, feeds on marine worms, crustaceans, and mollusks, but it neither catches nor eats oysters.

• Rice paper is not made from rice. It is made from a pithy plant called "tung-tsau."

• The Egyptian sphinx is not a sphinx. It is the statue of the god Armachis.

• The mulberry is not a berry. It is a multiple-stone fruit.

PLURALS

• A group of jellyfish is called a "smuck"!

• A group of ferrets is called a "business."

• A group of rhinoceroses is called a "crash."

• A group of elk is called a "gang."

• A group of kangaroos is called a "mob"!

• The plural of octopus is "octopodes"!

• A group of eight of anything is called an "ogdoad."

PRONUNCIATION

• How do you pronounce the name Phtholognyrrh? Believe it or not, it's "Turner."

Phth as in phythsic = T
olo as in colonel = ur
gn as in gnat = n
yrrh as in myrrh = er

PUNCTUATION

• Punctuation can be a matter of life or death! Maria Feodorewna accidentally caught sight of the following note appended to the bottom of a death warrant. It was written in the handwriting of her husband, Alexander III, and read as follows: "Pardon impossible, to be sent to Siberia." Maria transposed the comma so that it read: "Pardon, impossible to be sent to Siberia." The convict was released a free man.

• The comma, because it indicated a sentence has been cut into parts, originally was shaped like a small dagger. The past participle of the Greek word "koptein," meaning "to cut," is "komma."

• The Chinese language does not require punctuation!

SYMBOLS

• Hotels in China rarely have a fourth floor because the character for the number four is the same as the character for death!

"TO LOOK" IN CHINESE, IS WRITTEN BY PLACING THE CHARACTER FOR "HAND" – 手 OVER THAT FOR "EYE" – 目

看

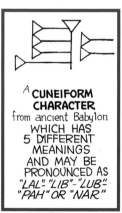

A **CUNEIFORM CHARACTER** from ancient Babylon WHICH HAS 5 DIFFERENT MEANINGS AND MAY BE PRONOUNCED AS "LAL"- "LIB"-"LUB"- "PAH" OR "NAR"

TRANSLATIONS

• Universal word? "Taxi" is spelled exactly the same in English, French, German, Swedish, and Portuguese.

• "Chi chi chi chi chi chi chi chi chi chi" in Chinese means, "When your hunger is keen remember that there are fowls to be had and make arrangements by which you may eat them."

MISTRANSLATIONS

• The Cypriotes, on the Island of Cyprus, say "goodbye" when they mean "hello," due to a printing error in an English textbook introduced to the island.

MULTIPLE TRANSLATIONS

• "Esposa" in Spanish means both "wife" and "handcuffs."

• The term "kemo sabe," or "faithful friend," as used on the radio version of the *Lone Ranger*, actually means "white shirt" in the Apache language, and "soggy shrub" in Navajo!

UNFORTUNATE TRANSLATIONS

• An Estée Lauder perfume called "Country Mist" had disappointing sales in Germany where the word "Mist" is slang for manure!

KUNG FU A TERM USED IN AMERICA TO DESCRIBE A CHINESE FORM OF FIGHTING, IS A MISNOMER AND ACTUALLY MEANS *"TO HAVE A SKILL" IN ANYTHING*

WORDS

• Only three words in the English language end in "ceed": "proceed," "exceed," and "succeed."

THE SYMBOL IN W. Africa FOR ETERNITY IS A SNAKE *BITING ITS OWN TAIL*

A GROUP of PRAIRIE DOGS IS CALLED A "COTERIE"!

• Twenty-five hundred words in *Webster's Dictionary* can be made from the letters in the name of its author, **Noah Webster**!

• Of all the eight-letter words in the English language, only one has only one vowel: "strength."

• The word "set" can be used fifty-eight different ways as a noun, one hundred twenty-six ways as a verb, and ten as an adjective.

ABBREVIATIONS AND ACRONYMS

• "Pumcodoxpursaxomlopar" is the acronym used by the Hughes Aircraft Company for pulse-modulated coherent doppler effect X-band pulse-repetition synthetic-array pulse compression side lobe planar array."

ETYMOLOGY

• The term "pharaoh" originally referred to a palace, not a person!

• The term "bigwig" originated in seventeenth century Europe when only the wealthy could afford to wear wigs!

• The term "honeymoon" originated from an old custom requiring newlyweds to drink honey wine every day for the first thirty days after their wedding!

• The word "candidate" is derived from the Latin "candidates," meaning "a person dressed in white." Roman politicians, to make a good impression, always campaigned in white togas.

• "Agony" comes from "agon," the Greek word for "an athletic contest."

• The word "coach" comes from the Hungarian town of Kocks, where a horse-drawn carriage was designed and built in A.D. 150.

• The word "jinx" comes from the name of jynx torquilla, a woodpecker that some people believe has magical powers!

• The term "windfall" originally referred to wind-blown branches collected for firewood by peasants who were banned by law from cutting down trees!

• The slang word "booze" has been in use since 1325!

• The term "sabotage" originally referred to the wooden shoes, "sabots," tossed by revolting peasants into factory machinery during the French Revolution!

• Why is a turkey called a turkey? In the land of Turkey it is known as the American bird. It is an outgrowth of the Hebrew word "tocki," a peacock. Columbus' Hebrew interpreter called it thus and it's been known as a "turkey" ever since.

• The word "curfew" is derived from a metal shield used in Europe during the Middle Ages to put out the fire in a hearth at the end of the day!

• Author **Mark Twain** was the first writer to use the terms "Wild West," "ex-convict," and "cussword."

• The old English word for spider is "cob."

• The booby, a species of gannet, gave the English language a synonym for stupid—it was called a booby by Portuguese seamen because of its habit of alighting on ships and allowing itself to be captured.

• "Grog," the sailors' drink, is so called from the Grogham Coat worn by Admiral Vernon, commander of the English fleet in the West Indies, who first issued the sailors' rations of one quart of water mixed with a half pint of rum.

• The term "hijack" comes from the Prohibition era when gunmen would approach a truck full of illegal liquor and say, "high, Jack!" a warning to the driver to raise his hands and surrender!

• The words "flammable" and "inflammable" mean the same. "Inflammable" is grammatically correct, but it was feared that safety hazards would result when people mistook "inflammable" to mean "not capable of producing flames."

• The word "vitamin" was not invented until 1920!

BREAKTHROUGH IN BABY TALK—PRE-LANGUAGE TODDLERS EXPRESS THEMSELVES THROUGH SIGNING

It's tough being a toddler. Toddlers have more complex needs than babies, yet they have not yet developed the verbal skills required to express those needs to grown-ups.

But recently, child-development psychologist Linda Acredlo made an astonishing discovery: she realized that her one-year-old daughter was making signs with her hands and face. At first, these signs were simple, spontaneous symbols: her daughter would sniff to indicate "flower," and would make the crawling motion with her hands that she learned from the song "Itsy Bitsy Spider" to mean "spider." "Those things worked for her just like words," Acredlo explains, "And I thought maybe other babies do this and their parents just don't notice."

From this observation, "Baby Signing" was born. Acredlo developed a system of simple signs for babies of eight months and older. Children are taught simple hand signals for "eat," "noise," "outside," and several other concepts that are big concerns in the toddler world.

"It really enriches their lives," Acredlo says. Signing toddlers appear more confident and less frustrated—as do their parents—and it doesn't harm their verbal development in the least. In fact, it accelerates it; babies who learn sign language tend to begin speaking at an earlier age.

• The onion gets its name form the Latin "unio"—which means "a large pearl."

• The word "walrus" means whale horse.

• The word "Texas" means "we are pals." The name of the state is derived from the Cenide Indians.

IMPRESSIVE WORDS

• The term "hippopoto-monstrousquipedalianism," thirty-two letters long, is the term for the practice of using long words!

• "Floccinaucinihipiliffication" is the act or habit of estimating something as worthless!

• "Mihuiittilmoyoiccuitlantonpicixochitl" is an Aztec word of sixteen syllables.

• "Pneumonoultramicroscopicsilicovolcanoconiosis," the name of a lung disease common to miners, has forty-five letters.

• A single scientific word used to describe a process in a human cell, contains two hundred seven thousand letters!

VOCABULARY STRETCHERS

• The act of opening a milk carton so badly that you have to try the other side is called "lactomangulation"!

• If you frequently use words that are spelled the same way backward and forward, you are a "ciloholic"—a person addicted to palindromes!

• The last word in the *Merriam-Webster Dictionary* is "zyzzva," meaning "the last word"!

• "Syzygy," a favorite word among Scrabble players, is an astronomical word used to describe three bodies, such as the sun, moon, and Earth, when they are in line with each other.

Chapter 36
Law

An old law in New York State required trains to have a courier, either on foot or on horseback, to announce their arrival.

TRAIN!

It's said that there's no such thing as perfect justice. But in the following cases, justice is not only imperfect—it can get downright bizarre. You're about to tour some of the strangest courtrooms in the land, encounter a few of the craftiest and creative lawyers, judges, and juries in the world, and tangle with many of the oddest laws ever to make their way onto the books.

COURTS

• In American courts, the bloodhound is the only animal whose evidence can be used to determine guilt or innocence!

• In San Francisco, California, there is a weekly session of "dog court" held at City Hall where dogs are given sentences ranging from behavior modification to training to even the death penalty!

LAWS

• In Cambridge, Massachusetts, it was once against the law to snore in a bedroom unless the windows were closed and the doors were locked!

• Bachelors in Liverpool, England, in the sixteenth century were required by law to stay indoors after nine P.M.

• Croquet was banned in Boston, Massachusetts, in the 1890s!

• During the fifteenth century, men in England, Scotland, and France who refused a woman's proposal of marriage during a leap year could be punished by law!

• In Morrisville, Pennsylvania, it was once against the law for women to wear makeup—including rouge, lipstick, and eye shadow—without a special permit!

• An old law in the state of Connecticut makes it illegal for beavers to build dams!

• A seventeenth-century law in Massachusetts made it illegal for juveniles to curse or physically attack their parents under penalty of death!

ONE TWO

In Judge Milton Wharton's courtroom in Belleville, Ill., the judge, jurors, lawyers and spectators stay alert by doing 4 minutes of aerobics several times a week!

Believe It or Not! The courtroom of Judge Roberto Portugal in Curitiba, Brazil, features soothing music, aromatherapy scents and walls painted with calming colors!

• It's against the law in Detroit, Michigan, to tie your crocodile to a fire hydrant.

• In Chicago, Illinois, it's against the law to eat in a restaurant that's on fire!

• An old law in Bristol, Tennessee, made it illegal for a woman to stop and adjust the line of her stockings in public!

• A British law called the "Holy Days and Fasting Days Act of 1551" makes it illegal for anyone to drive to church!

• It's against the law in San Francisco, California, for anyone to walk an elephant down Market Street unless it's on a leash!

• In Piqua, Ohio, it is illegal for anyone to take a bath before ten P.M.!

• At one time, men in Pine Island, Minnesota, had to remove their hats in the presence of a cow or risk arrest!

• An old law in Nevada prevented anyone from riding a camel on a public highway!

• An old law in Maine made it illegal for a police officer to arrest a dead man!

• In Memphis, Tennessee, a city ordinance bans frogs from croaking after eleven P.M.!

• It was once against the law to sing out of tune in North Carolina!

• Russian **Czar Paul I** made it a crime punishable by death by flogging for anyone to mention his baldness in his presence.

IT'S AGAINST THE LAW in Roderfield, W. Va., TO RIDE IN A BABY CARRIAGE UNLESS YOU ARE AN INFANT!

• According to the Senchus Mor, a set of ancient Irish laws, it was once illegal for bees to trespass!

• A law in Shawnee, Oklahoma, made it illegal for three or more dogs to meet on private property without the permission of the occupant!

• In 1685, the Japanese ruler **Tokugawa Tsunayoshi**, an animal lover, issued a code of thirty-six laws and punishments relating to animal care that included death to anyone who hit a biting dog!

• In 1519, in Stelvio, Italy, moles accused of damaging crops were tried in a court of law and sentenced to exile!

• The village of Mackinac Island, Michigan, first banned the "horseless carriage" over one hundred years ago, and still to this day does not allow cars on the island!

• An old law in North Carolina made it illegal to plow a field using an elephant!

• The state of Wyoming banned photographing

Believe It or Not! IN THE ENGLISH TOWN of York, IT IS STILL LEGAL for CITIZENS TO USE A BOW and ARROW "TO SHOOT ANY SCOTSMAN DISCOVERED OUT AND ABOUT AFTER SUNSET"!

The City of PORT HENRY, N.Y., has passed a law forbidding anyone from disturbing the sea creature believed to live in Lake Champlain!

rabbits from January to April without written permission.

• In Houston, Texas, it's against the law to make a noise while moving boxes!

• In Greece in 330 B.C., a law called the "Stork's Law," or "Lex Ciconaria," was passed making it mandatory for children to care for their parents in old age!

In Pu'uhonua o Honaunau, Hawaii ancient laws called "KAPU" forbade anyone from landing his canoe on a royal beach or letting his shadow fall on palace grounds!

• It was once against the law for dentists to play checkers during their lunch hour!

• Until 1819, it was against the law to cut down a tree in Britain—those found guilty were sentenced to hang!

• **John Mangefel**, the first governor of the island of Yap, passed a law making it illegal to wear a tie!

• In 1756, **King Frederick I** of Sweden issued a law forbidding the drinking of coffee.

• A law in Babylon circa 200 B.C. required ex-husbands to pay alimony!

• An ordinance passed in 1875 in the District of Columbia declared that owning an ailanthus, or "tree of heaven," was against the law!

• In Carmel, New York, it's against the law for a man to go out wearing a jacket that doesn't match his pants.

• In Berea, Ohio, dogs and cats out after dark were once required to wear taillights!

• Onions were banned in many places in ancient India, and people who ate them were required to do so outside city limits!

• It's against the law in New York City to open an umbrella in front of a horse!

• A law in San Francisco made it illegal to dry a car at a car wash with rags made from old underwear!

• In 1511, the prince of Waldeck, Germany, offered a reward of ten thalers to anyone who reported someone illegally drinking coffee!

• Japan's **Emperor Ichijo** (986-1011) once exiled a dog and imprisoned its owner because the dog chased his favorite cat!

• In Mobile, Alabama, it was once against the law for women to wear high heels on the streets!

• In 1785, **King Louis XVI** of France issued a law stating that the lengths of handkerchiefs must equal their width!

• A law in Gurnee, Illinois, made it illegal for women weighing over two hundred pounds to ride a horse while wearing shorts!

• In 1993, the mayor of Cebreros, Spain, officially banned humans and dogs from running in the city streets.

• In Ohio, an old law makes it illegal to fish for whales on Sunday in any lakes or rivers in the state!

• In Essex Fells, New Jersey, an old law stated that ducks could not quack after ten P.M.

• In medieval England, peasants were fined for sending their children to school instead of making them work in the fields!

BELIEVE IT OR NOT! A CITY ORDINANCE IN FREMONT, CA, FORBIDS THE REPAIRING OF SPACECRAFT IN FAMILY GARAGES!

AT ONE TIME in South Foster, Rhode Island, IF A DENTIST EXTRACTED THE WRONG TOOTH from A PATIENT, HE WAS ORDERED BY LAW TO HAVE ONE of HIS OWN TEETH EXTRACTED BY THE LOCAL **BLACKSMITH**.

STEADY, BOY!

AN OLD LAW in Pittsburgh, Pa., MADE IT ILLEGAL FOR A HOUSEWIFE TO HIDE DUST AND DIRT UNDER A **RUG!**

• The states of Illinois, Montana, and Minnesota all require by law that dentures have their owner's social security number on them.

• **King Amanullah** of Afghanistan tried to pass a law requiring all of his subjects to wear bowler hats.

• **Paul I**, Emperor of Russia (1754-1801), issued proclamations and orders dictating how his subjects should dress, and issued fines to people wearing pantaloons, trousers, tail coats, boots, or waistcoats!

• An old law in Saudi Arabia stated that if a man did not keep his wife well-supplied with coffee, she could legally divorce him!

• In ancient Greece, it was against the law for a person to be idle.

• It was once against the law in Alaska to stick your tongue out at someone who caught a smaller fish than yours!

• In Milwaukee, Wisconsin, it was once against the law to leave a car parked on the street unless it was hitched to a horse!

• An old law in Brooklyn, New York, prevents a horse from sleeping in a bathtub inside its owner's house!

• Until recently, New York state law made it illegal to drive away after striking a horse, dog, or cow—but not a cat!

• England's **Oliver Cromwell** (1599-1658) issued a ban against pies, regarding them as an unnecessary extravagance!

• In Newark, New Jersey, it was once against the law to sell ice cream to a customer unless he had a doctor's prescription.

• A law in Kansas made it illegal to eat rattlesnake meat on Sundays!

• In 1807, Czar **Alexander I** of Russia considered long trousers on men to be subversive! He ordered his troops to stop all carriages, and any man found wearing trousers had his legs immediately cut off at the knee!

• Residents of Beijing, China, are forbidden by law to own dogs, but they can rent them at a rate of twenty-three cents for ten minutes!

• An old law in Great Britain made it illegal for anyone to drive a car from the backseat!

• In Brewton, Alabama, it's against the law to ride down the street in a motorboat!

• All sturgeon fish caught in British waters are the sole property of the queen of England!

• In ancient Greece, anyone caught killing a stork was tried for murder!

• In Kansas, a doctor could legally prescribe beer to a patient, but could not join him in drinking any!

• In Zion, Illinois, it is against the law to give a lighted cigar to a dog or cat!

• At one time in Minnesota, if a man hugged or kissed a young woman in front of her parents, it was considered a binding proposal of marriage!

• "Cityspire," a skyscraper in New York City, was fined by the City Department of Environmental Protection for whistling!

• In Orangeville, Ontario, it's against the law for a farmer, while he's around cattle, to wear socks with holes in the toes!

• It was once illegal in Denver, Colorado, for acrobats to perform on the sidewalks any acrobatics that would frighten the horses!

• A law in Green Bay, Wisconsin, states that owners of cars that drip oil on public roads be fined a dollar per drip!

• In New York State, it's against the law to go fishing in your own backyard on Sundays!

• A law in New York made it illegal for dogs to bark continuously for more than fifteen minutes. First time offenders are fined fifty dollars, second-time offenders one hundred dollars, third-time offenders are jailed for fifteen days!

• It was once against the law in Schenectady, New York, to fill holes in the walls with putty on Sundays!

• In Belt, Montana, it was once against the law to dance the "Angleworm Wiggle"!

• In ancient China, a suspect being questioned in court was forced to chew and spit out a handful of rice powder—if the powder was still dry, the suspect was considered guilty!

• It was once against the law in Houston to buy goose liver, rye bread, or Limburger cheese on Sundays!

• In 1610, a law was passed in Virginia making it illegal—and punishable by death—to miss church more than three times in a row!

• In Waterville, Maine, it was once against the law to blow your nose in public!

• In the ancient city of Amyclae, it was forbidden by law to spread rumors of any kind. Violators faced execution!

• During the eighteenth century, the demand for linen was so great that a law was passed stating that only wool could be used to bury the dead!

• The Roman Emperor **Caligula** (A.D. 12-41) made it against the law for Roman citizens to bathe or laugh!

HORSES ARE NOT ALLOWED IN THE TOWN of Fountain Inn, S.C., UNLESS THEY ARE WEARING PANTS!

• A sign posted on the Greenriver Bridge in Guilford, Vermont, warned of a two-dollar fine issued to anyone who passed through the bridge at a speed faster than a walk!

• Until 1936 it was illegal in New York State for men to go out in public without a shirt.

• It's against the law in Oklahoma to get fish drunk.

• In Idaho Falls, Idaho, it's against the law for anyone over the age of eighty-eight to ride a motorcycle!

• In Illinois, it's against the law for barbers to use their fingers to apply shaving cream to a customer's face.

• An old law in Utah states that the height of a woman's high heels cannot be over one and a half inches.

• In Bhutan, people can fish in streams and rivers, but by law must toss back all that they catch!

• A statute in Bibbenden, in Kent, England, states that "birds wishing to sing or crow at sunrise must be two hundred yards away from human habitation."

In **KANSAS** it's against the law to stack more than 8 dishes!

ON Chicago, Ill., IT'S AGAINST THE LAW TO GO FISHING WHILE WEARING PAJAMAS!

• A California state law passed in 1872 makes it illegal to disturb any birds nesting in cemeteries, except for swallows!

• At one time in Owensboro, Kentucky, a woman could only buy a hat if her husband tried it on first!

• In Nachidoches, Texas, people are prohibited by law from cracking pecan shells while attending church!

• In Broome, Australia, all camels traveling on commercial routes must wear flashing taillights!

• A law in Birmingham, Alabama, made it illegal for anyone to drive a car while blindfolded!

• It was once against the law in California to hunt whales from a car!

• It was once against the law in California to set a mousetrap without a hunting license!

• **Queen Elizabeth I** (1533-1603) had an official uncorker of bottles—it was illegal for anyone else to remove secret messages from bottles!

• A law in Colorado Springs, Colorado, states any dog is allowed to bite one person!

• **Sheila Corbin**, of Huntsville, Texas, was arrested in a hospital emergency room on the charge of having overdue library books!

• **King Henry VIII** of England outlawed bowling!

• In Saskatchewan, Canada, marriage commissioners are required to keep all doors open during marriage ceremonies!

• An old law in Saco, Missouri, prohibits women from wearing hats that might frighten timid persons, children, or animals!

• An old law in Memphis, Tennessee, required that anyone ordering pie in a restaurant had to eat it all on the premises!

• A law in Blyth, California, made it illegal for people to wear cowboy boots unless they owned two cows!

• In ancient China, the punishment for public drunkenness was death by strangulation!

• In Alaska, it's against the law to look at a moose from a flying vehicle!

• In Illinois, it is against the law to fall asleep in a barber's chair!

• In Detroit, Michigan, it's against the law to loiter at the city morgue!

• It was once illegal in Wisconsin to serve apple pie without cheese.

• In ancient Greece, it was illegal for an ordinary citizen to own an olive tree!

• An ancient law stated that all residents of Brussels, Belgium, who allowed rainwater to drain into public sewers would have to pay a special tax.

• In 1951, crossword puzzles were banned by law in Burma!

• A law in New Zealand requires dog owners to take their pets for a walk at least once every twenty-four hours!

• An old law in Boston, Massachusetts, made it illegal for a man to serenade a woman at a window late at night unless he had a license!

• A Swedish court decided that the pet dog of a man sentenced to three months in jail should be cared for under the national welfare plan until the prisoner finished his sentence!

• In the state of Oregon, it was once illegal to wipe dishes!

• China's Ming emperors (1368-1644) decreed that the color green was a royal color, and anyone other than the emperor who was caught wearing anything green would be put to death!

• **King John I** did not sign the Magna Carta in 1215!

• In Melbourne, Australia, there is an eight P.M. curfew for cats—and dogs are kept under house arrest at all times!

• In 1536, England's **King Henry VIII** made it illegal to bake mincemeat pies on Christmas Day—a law that still stands today!

• Dry for over one hundred forty years! In 1992, residents of Ephraim, Wisconsin, voted to retain a ban on liquor in the town that dates back to the 1850s.

• An old law in Halethorpe, Maryland, made it illegal to kiss someone for longer than a minute!

• It's against the law in Connecticut to sell pickles that fall apart when dropped from a height of twelve inches!

• A 1937 law made spring cleaning compulsory for all citizens of Hungary!

• In 1992, the government of Singapore banned chewing gum, imposing a $1,200 fine for selling it, and a year in jail for importing it!

• A law in Kentucky made it illegal to shoot an unloaded gun.

• The House of Representatives, a restaurant in Washington, D.C., is required by a federal law passed in 1904 to serve bean soup every day!

• At one time in Germany, the punishment for damaging a tree was death!

• On a street in Savoy Court, London, England, motorists are required by law to drive on the wrong side of the road!

• In Ashland, Wisconsin, it is against the law to play marbles for keeps.

• In medieval Europe, butchers were not allowed to serve on juries!

• **Louis XIV** of France (1643-1715) decreed that only he could sit in a chair with arms!

• A law in Orlando, Florida, states that if an elephant is left tied to a parking meter, a parking fee must be charged!

• In Paoli, Indiana, it's against the law to keep a noisy rooster—the penalty is a $500 fine.

• In the United States in 1919, it was illegal for people to play radios in private homes!

• It's against the law to eat peanuts in church in Massachusetts!

• In the fifteenth century, women in Florence, Italy, were forbidden by law to wear buttons!

• Until 1994, owners of carrier pigeons in France had to register their birds with the Department of National Defense.

• In Reykjavik, Iceland, it's against the law to keep a dog as a pet.

• In Hanford, California, it's against the law to stop a child from jumping in mud puddles!

• It's against the law in Miriam, South Dakota, to "smoke" candy cigarettes while at school!

• An old law in International Falls, Minnesota, stated that cats were prohibited from chasing dogs up telephone poles!

DONALD DUCK comics were once banned in Finland because the character doesn't wear pants!

• In Arkansas, it's against the law to blindfold a bull and lead the animal down a public road!

• A law in Britain makes it illegal for trucks to get stuck under bridges that are too low for them to go under!

• An old nineteenth-century law in Missouri stated that "when two trains approach a crossing at the same time, both must stop and neither may proceed until the other has passed"!

• A law in Cleveland, Ohio, made it illegal to catch mice without a hunting license!

• A 1975 city ordinance in Council Bluffs, Iowa, made it illegal to "worry" black squirrels!

• A law in New Orleans stated that biting someone with natural teeth was "simple assault," but biting someone with false teeth was "aggravated assault"!

• An old law in Hammond, Indiana, made it illegal to throw watermelon seeds into the streets!

• It's against the law to store snowballs in a refrigerator in Scottsbluff, Nebraska!

• It was once illegal in the state of Alabama to call anyone a skunk, or by the name Adolf Hitler!

• In 1993, Representative **Robert Spear** introduced a bill in the Maine Legislature to allow undersized lobsters that are caught to be kept as pets!

ON THE ISLAND of **SARK** in the English Channel, WOMEN WERE GRANTED THE RIGHT TO INHERIT PROPERTY from THEIR FATHERS IN 1999 - AFTER THE ISLAND'S 400-YEAR-OLD LAWS WERE STRUCK DOWN!

YAHOO!

• In England, in 1865, a law was passed setting the speed limit for steam-driven coaches at four miles per hour!

• An old law in Norfolk, Virginia, made it illegal for a woman to appear in public without a corset!

• A plague of fleas was exiled from seventeenth-century Munster, Germany, for a period of ten years!

• It was once against the law for anyone to bathe more than once a month in the state of Pennsylvania!

• In Normal, Oklahoma, people could be arrested, fined, or put in jail for making an ugly face at a dog!

• In Sadieville, Kentucky, property owners are banned by law from mowing their lawns—but fishing in the nude is legal!

• In ancient China, imperial law decreed that anyone who revealed the secret of making silk would be put to death!

• A law in Tylertown, Missouri, made it illegal for a man to shave in the middle of Main Street!

A LAW in Chicago, Ill., MADE IT ILLEGAL TO TAKE A FRENCH POODLE TO THE OPERA!

• A law in Idaho made it illegal to present someone with a box of candy that weighed over fifty pounds!

• In 1986, California District Judge **Samuel King** issued an order for it to stop raining. The state endured five years of drought until the day in 1991 when he rescinded the motion!

• A law in Santa Ana, California makes it illegal for a person to swim on dry land!

• In Coral Gables, Florida, it is against the law to swim in a private pool near a church on a Sunday morning!

• A city ordinance in Baltimore, Maryland, makes it against the law to mistreat an oyster!

• A court in Germany made it illegal to name any hot dog product a "frankfurter" unless it was made in the region around Frankfurt, Germany!

• In England during the fourteenth century, it was against the law for a man who earned fewer than twenty dollars a year to wear a silk nightcap to bed!

LAWYERS

• The first lawyer to use fingerprints in a criminal case was Pudd'nhead Wilson—a character created by Mark Twain in 1894!

• **Nick Jacques**, a lawyer in Helena, Montana, frequently accepts haircuts, sculpture, and goat meat in lieu of cash payments!

• Doctor **John Morton-Finney**, the son of a slave, had twelve college degrees, was fluent in seven languages, and was a practicing lawyer at age one hundred!

• **Marcy Filer**, of Compton, California, finally passed the California Bar Exam after failing the test forty-seven times in twenty-five years!

• **Bill Schlussel**, a lawyer in Huntington Woods, Michigan, operated a law office in the kitchen of a Chinese take-out restaurant!

• In 1993, **Curtis D. Mortenson** got a job as a state attorney in South Dakota by winning a game of poker!

• "Law Dogs": **Kim Pearman**, an attorney in Los Angeles, California, dispenses free legal advice while selling hot dogs at a hot dog stand!

JUDGMENTS

• The ship that became a legal headache! The *Ouzel*, a three-masted galley sailing out of Dublin, was captured by Algerian pirates in 1695, and used as a pirate ship for five years until she was recaptured by her former crew. When the ship sailed home her crew found insurance had been paid on the vessel's cargo and no one could decide who owned the pirate booty—so the money became a philanthropic fund.

• In the first century B.C. during the reign of **Julius Caesar** in Rome, matters relating to property, marriage, and criminal guilt were often decided by the flip of a coin!

• In 1451, in Lausanne, Switzerland, a handful of leeches were brought before a court and ordered to leave the area!

Attorney **Carl Harper**, of Bedias, Texas, won most of his cases because of his secret weapon: a handkerchief filled with chopped onions! More often than not, his flowing tears won the sympathy of the jury!

• In 1991, an appeals court in New York State declared a house in Nyack, New York, to be officially haunted!

• A ruling by the United States Supreme Court in 1893 determined that the tomato was a vegetable and not a fruit!

JUDGES

• In 1991, a judge in Birmingham, Alabama, set bond for a man arrested for theft at $9 trillion—three times higher than the national debt!

• In 1991, in Santa Ana, California Orange County Superior Court, Judge **Robert Fitzgerald** delivered a sentence of life in prison using rhyming verse!

In 1521, French lawyer BARTHOLOMEW CHASSENEE successfully defended some rats charged with unlawfully destroying a crop of barley!

• In 1992, a judge in Newark, New Jersey, sentenced a landlord to live in his own rundown apartment building!

• "Burglarizing the burglar": In 1992, Judge **Brown**, of Memphis, Tennessee, allowed victims of robberies to take anything they wanted from the home of the thief who robbed them!

• In 1992, a judge in Los Osos, California, ordered the owners of three basset hounds to restrict the dogs' barking to once an hour, and no more than two minutes at a time!

• In ancient China, judges wore tinted spectacles to hide their eyes and any reactions to evidence!

• He's judge and jury! Superior Court Judge **John E. Morse, Junior**, of Savannah, Georgia, was called for jury duty and served as a jury member over a land dispute!

• Lancaster County District Court Judge **Donald Endacott** found himself guilty of falling asleep during a court proceeding and declared an official mistrial!

• In 1992, the Oklahoma Supreme Court upheld the election of a judge even though the candidate had recently died!

JURORS

• No justice in Y2K! In 1999 in Philadelphia, Pennsylvania, five hundred people received notices to report for jury duty in 1900!

• Eleven-month-old **Tyler Morey**, of Pittsfield, Massachusetts, was summoned for jury duty!

• **William Woods,** of Ottawa, Ontario, was selected from a random pool of two hundred fifty people for jury selection for his own trial!

LEGISLATION

• The mayor of Grand Lemps, France, a prohibitionist, issued an ordinance that any inhabitant may enter a saloon and drink his fill and then leave without paying.

TRIALS

• A criminal trial in New Delhi, India, lasted thirty-three years and cost the state $677,000!

TRIAL OF THE FLEAS

IN MÜNSTER, GERMANY, IN 1670 AFTER A PLAGUE OF FLEAS THE HIGH COURT *SUMMONED THE INSECTS* TO APPEAR BEFORE IT ALL THE FLEAS DISOBEYED BUT ONE — AND WERE THEREFORE *DISFRANCHISED* AND *BANISHED* FOR *10 YEARS!*

• In 1474 in Basel, Switzerland, a rooster that laid an egg was put on trial and burned at the stake!

• In ancient Egypt, trials were held in the dark so that hearings would be impartial!

• In Oviedo, Spain, a clothes moth was brought before a judge and charged with damaging a tapestry—the moth was sentenced to death and all its offspring were to be banished!

WILLS

• **Anetta Duel**, of London, England, wrote her will on the side of the London *Telegraph* newspaper crossword puzzle, and a judge declared the will valid!

• **G. Clifford Prout, Junior**, president of the Society Against Indecency to Naked Animals, left $400,000 in his will to be spent on clothes for animals.

• United States President **Calvin Coolidge**'s will was only one sentence long!

• After the release of the film *Frankenstein* in 1931, several people tried to sue the production company for frightening them out of their wits!

• In 1709, in Maranhao, Brazil, a nest of termites was put on trial and later given a conditional discharge binding them to keep the peace!

• A stolen parrot in New Delhi, India, brought to court as a witness, identified its real owner by repeating the names of her children!

Chapter 37
Lies, Scams, & Hoaxes

People were more gullible back in Ripley's day. Well, weren't they? Today's techno-savvy, information-hip generation would never fall prey to the chicanery of, say, the Fiji Mermaid, the Fur-Bearing Trout, or Orson Welles' "War of the Worlds" broadcast.

LIES

• *Titanic* Disaster Averted! The ocean liner *Titanic*'s sinking was considered so improbable that every New York newspaper except the *Times* carried headlines on April 15, 1912, stating that all hands had been saved!

• To thwart efforts by fanatics to steal his body, **John Wilkes Booth**, the assassin of Abraham Lincoln, was falsely reported to have been hurled into the Potomac River. Actually his body was buried beneath the floor of a penitentiary cell.

• The statue of field marshal **Blucher** of Prussia, in his hometown of Rostock, was erected during his lifetime because Blucher sent a letter to city officials thanking them for their plan to honor him, even though he knew they had no such intention. After receiving his letter they felt obliged to construct the statue.

SCAMS

• The war council that was ruled for eight years by an empty chair! **General Eumenes**, secretary to Alexander the Great, dominated the other generals after Alexander's death by convincing them that the monarch appeared in a dream and ordered the council to hold all future meetings in the royal tent in the presence of Alexander's throne, crown, and scepter.

Eumenes was obeyed as spokesman for the royal ghost from 323 B.C., the year of Alexander's death, until 315 B.C., when the general himself was slain.

• **Mrs. Theresa Vaughn**, age 24, was arraigned in the police court of Sheffield, England, on December 19, 1922, on a charge of bigamy. In the course of the hearing Mrs. Vaughn confessed to 61 bigamous marriages, which she contracted without obtaining a legal divorce from her first husband. Her husbands were scattered all over the British Isles, Germany, and South Africa, and all her marriages took place within the span of five years.

Photographs of "FAIRIES" taken by Elsie Wright and Frances Griffiths of England in 1917, were regarded as proof by many that fairies existed. But in 1983 Frances and Elsie, now 75 and 81, admitted the "fairies" were actually drawings fastened to photos by hatpins!

THE TABLETS of HISTORY

EMPEROR CHIN SHI HUANG TI (BUILDER OF THE GREAT WALL OF CHINA) ORDERED THE DESTRUCTION OF ALL LITERATURE AND THE EXECUTION OF ALL HISTORIANS SO THAT HISTORY MIGHT BEGIN WITH HIM!

HOWEVER—HE WAS UNSUCCESSFUL..BECAUSE HE OVERLOOKED THE STONE TABLETS OF PEIPING, ON WHICH CHINESE HISTORY WAS ENGRAVED.

WILLIAM CROCKFORD A 19th CENTURY BRITISH GAMBLER, DIED BEFORE HE COULD COLLECT HIS WINNINGS ON THE DERBY OF 1844 — SO CRONIES PROPPED HIS BODY UP IN AN ARMCHAIR IN HIS WINDOW UNTIL ALL HIS BETS HAD BEEN PAID

• The ruins of Ross Castle at Cleethorpes, England, were actually mock ruins constructed in 1885 by a railroad company as a tourist attraction and named for R. Ross, one of its officials.

HOAXES

• It is illegal to "molest, kill, or trample" a legendary sea monster in the White River Monster Sanctuary in Newport, Arkansas.

• The Persian general **Zopyros** literally cut off his nose to spite his enemy! His king, Darius the Great, had laid siege to the city of Babylon, but after twenty months, the city showed no sign of surrender. Zopyros decided

An example of the legendary Fiji Mermaids first made famous by P. T. Barnum. These were merely the front halves of dessicated monkey corpses attached to the back ends of fish, and sold in the South Sea Islands to gullible tourists.

^ **MONUMENT TO A LIAR** A FOUNTAIN IN BODENWERDER, W. GERMANY, DEPICTS BARON KARL von MUNCHAUSEN RIDING HALF A HORSE--A MEMORIAL TO HIS TALL TALE THAT DURING THE TURKISH WARS **HE RODE HALF A HORSE TO VICTORY...**

FINAL CURTAIN—THE MACABRE THEME PARK THAT NEVER WAS

Plug the words "Final Curtain" into your web browser and you may still receive the following website description: "Death Got You Down? At last an alternative! At The Final Curtain, we're throwing away all the rules!" In early 1999, reports of a proposed cemetery theme park chain appeared in numerous newspapers across the country, including the *L.A. Times* and the New York *Daily News*.

Visitors to the Final Curtain site could read a detailed business plan for an international series of death-related theme parks, complete with restaurants such as Heaven's Gate Café and Dante's Grill, gift shops, and "family" entertainment. For a fee, the departed could have their remains on display at a Final Curtain memorial park in the manner of their choosing. The website also announced a Monument Design Scholarship Program, sample entries of which listed such options as:

–a live video feed of the decaying body
–the ashes of the departed mixed with iron filings and placed in a giant Etch-A-Sketch
–a dance floor with a working jukebox placed over the grave site
–the deceased's ashes placed in an electric blender so that visitors could whip him into a frenzy.

Approximately one year and numerous media articles later, the truth came out: Final Curtain was just an elaborate hoax, masterminded by veteran hoaxter Joey Skaggs. Skaggs is a self-styled performance artist and the creative mind behind numerous high-profile hoaxes. Skaggs and his associates reportedly created the hoax to protest the commercialization of the mortuary industry!

that enough was enough. He cut off his own nose and ears, and had himself delivered to Babylon's commanding general. The general believed Zopyros's story that he was a victim of Darius's inhumanity, and that he was thirsting for vengeance. He appointed Zopyros the Chief Defender of Babylon. Zopyros's first deed in his new position was to surrender Babylon to Darius. When Darius beheld Zopyros's mangled features, he shuddered and exclaimed that he would have preferred Zopyros intact to twenty Babylons.

"THE SCIENTIFIC NAME of Scotland's *LOCH NESS MONSTER* IS: NESSITERAS RHOMBOPTERYX" PUBLISHED IN *NATURE MAGAZINE* BY SIR PETER SCOTT and ALAN WILKINS! THE NAME IS ALSO AN ANAGRAM for "MONSTER HOAX BY SIR PETER S."!

Chapter 38
Literature

You probably recall the tales of Mother Goose from early childhood, but did you know that she was not a fictional goose but a real human being? We'll introduce you to her. Great writers such as Victor Hugo and Edgar Allan Poe may be forever remembered for their talent as wordsmiths, but wait until you discover just how dreadfully untalented they were at other pursuits! Millions have thrilled to Bram Stoker's Dracula, but do you know what dish Stoker dined upon the night before he suffered the horrifying nightmare that inspired the book? As we take you through the amazing realm of the published word, we'll offer little known facts about your favorite authors, we'll recount the bizarre circumstances surrounding some of literature's great works, and we'll also introduce you to some lesser-known, but no less extraordinary, literary masterpieces.

THEODOR SEUSS GEISEL CREATED HIS FIRST "DR. SEUSS" BOOK WHILE CROSSING THE ATLANTIC ON THE LINER KUNGSHOLM, SETTING THE METER OF HIS RHYME TO THE RHYTHM OF THE SHIP'S ENGINE!

FOLK TALES AND CHILDREN'S STORIES

• "Old King Cole," the nursery-rhyme king, was an actual monarch who ruled Britain in A.D. 200!

• The original "Winnie the Pooh" was a bear from White River, Canada, named after the city of Winnipeg.

• The Cinderella story first appeared in a Chinese book in A.D. 850!

• Cinderella's slipper was made of fur—not glass!

• Danish children's writer **Hans Christian Andersen** (1805-1875) was so ashamed of his thin body that whenever he went outside he stuffed his clothes with newspaper!

MAGAZINES AND NEWSPAPERS

• **Moloy Kundu** and his wife, **Tapati**, of Calcutta, India, each sold one of their kidneys for a total of $13,716 in order to keep their newspaper in business!

• In 1875 the *Etheridge Courier*, a newspaper in Queensland, Australia, was printed on handkerchiefs because of a paper shortage!

• Dodge City's legendary lawman, **Bat Masterson**, died sitting at his desk at the New York *Morning Telegraph*, where he worked as the sports editor!

• A Paris newspaper was printed in the 1850s on rubber for people who enjoyed reading in the bath!

• During the eighteenth century in London, England, newspaper vendors were held responsible for the contents of the papers they sold, and could be arrested and jailed if stories were false or libelous!

• In 1991, the *Observer*, a newspaper in London, England, corrected a report on the death of composer Wolfgang Amadeus Mozart that they had originally printed in 1791!

• A daily issue of the *New York Times* contains more information than the average person in the sixteenth century would have read during his entire life!

• **Jim** and **Amy Dacycsyn**, of Leeds, Maine, publish a monthly newspaper that promotes thrifty living, called the *Tightwad Gazette*!

• In 1991, a three-foot-high model of the rocket that carried the fictional cartoon character "Tin Tin" to the moon was fired into the sky over the author's home in Welkenraedt, Belgium!

• "Acta Diurna," the first public news bulletin, was created in 59 b.c. by Roman emperor **Julius Caesar**!

• **Fred Crouter**, of Council Bluffs, Iowa, has a collection of seventy-seven thousand newspapers, including a 1669 edition of the London *Chronicle*.

NOVELS

• In early drafts of **Charles Dickens'** *A Christmas Carol*, the character "Tiny Tim" was originally called "Small Sam," then "Puny Pete"!

• The longest novel written in the English language, *Clarissa*, by **Samuel Richardson**, has nearly one million words!

• There are over one thousand literary works in the English language attributed to "By a Lady"!

• The longest novel ever written, *Les Hommes de Bonne Volonte*, by **Jules Romains**, fills twenty-seven volumes!

• A work of science fiction published in 1703 envisions a giant spring mounted atop a mountain used to catapult a man to the moon.

NONFICTION WORKS

• **Alphosine Martin**, of Lafayette, Louisiana, didn't learn to read until the age of eighty, but wrote a cookbook when she was eighty-three!

A **DRAWING** of ALICE LIDDELL, THE HEROINE OF ALICE IN WONDERLAND, WAS MADE BY ITS WRITER, LEWIS CARROLL, FOR A HANDWRITTEN COPY WHICH HE GAVE THE GIRL—BUT HE COVERED IT WITH A PHOTOGRAPH THAT *CONCEALED IT FOR 113 YEARS*

SHERLOCK HOLMES
THE FICTIONAL DETECTIVE EACH YEAR IS SENT HUNDREDS OF LETTERS TO HIS NONEXISTING ADDRESS OF 221 B BAKER STREET

ELBERT HUBBARD'S BOOK "AN ESSAY ON SILENCE" CONTAINS NO WORDS!

- The world's oldest continuously published book: *The T'ung Shu, or Book of Myriad Things*, has been printed annually in China for over four thousand years!

- Englishman **Timothy Dexter**'s autobiography, *A Pickle for the Knowing Ones*, has no punctuation!

- **Charles J. Givens**, whose first book spent two and a half years on the best-seller list, is the author of the three best-selling financial books in history!

PLAYS

- The most famous balcony in history is the balcony in Verona, Italy, from which Juliet listened to Romeo's serenade.

- In **William Shakespeare**'s play *Antony and Cleopatra*, there is mention of the game of billiards—long before the game was even invented!

- **Shakespeare** was once considered too vulgar for England's young ladies. Thomas Bowdler, a nineteenth-century English physician and author, published a ten volume *Family Shakespeare* in which he rewrote the master's works to make his plays fit for mixed company.

- In 1990, **Sean Shannon**, of Oxford, England, recited Hamlet's famous "To be or not to be" soliloquy in a record twenty-four seconds!

PLAYWRIGHTS

- **Shakespeare** wore earrings!

- **William Shakespeare**'s father, mother, and daughter could not read or write!

- **Marcel Steiner** performs a ten-minute version of Shakespeare's *The Tempest* on a stage mounted on the sidecar of a motorbike!

- The English playwright **Ben Johnson** killed an actor in a duel, yet was spared the death penalty because he could read!

- When it was constructed in the sixteenth century, the Lincoln Inn in London, England, had as one of its bricklayers **Ben Johnson**, who became the great dramatist.

POETRY

- Catching the poetry bug: **Mary** and **Christa Armenter**, of Madison, Wisconsin, drove a Volkswagen Beetle covered with magnetic poetry strips across America, stopping at over one hundred schools in thirty cities in the United States to allow children to create poems right on the car!

- In 1902, **Dana Estes** of Boston, Massachusetts, published a book of eighty-three poems, all on the subject of ping-pong!

- A book of poems by English poet **John Milton** (1608-1678), printed in 1852, was bound in the skin of George Cudmore, who had been executed for murder in 1830.

- Poetry in Motion: **Ian McMillan**, a British poet, spent ten days traveling on trains, writing poetry and giving readings on the trains and in stations to cheer up passengers!

POETS

- Poet **Robert Frost** often wrote lines of verse on the soles of his shoes.

- The annual Dragon Race Boat Festival in Hong Kong commemorates the search for **Qu Yuan**, a third-century poet who threw himself into the river. He was so admired that people searched for his body for days!

- English poet **John Milton** memorized all of Homer's *Iliad* and *Odyssey*, *The Aeneid*, by Virgil, and every line of his own poetry!

EMILY DICKINSON
(1830-1886)
THE FAMED AMERICAN POET PUBLISHED ONLY SEVEN OF HER 1,775 POEMS DURING HER LIFETIME--AND *THOSE SEVEN WERE PUBLISHED ANONYMOUSLY*

American poet
EMILY
DICKINSON was
so shy she would often
only talk to guests from
an adjacent room!

• **Virgil** (70-19 B.C.), the Roman poet, once paid the equivalent of $100,000 to provide a lavish funeral for a house fly—including burying it in a special mausoleum on his estate!

• In 1840, New York dentist **Solyman Brown** wrote and published a long poem called "Dentologica: A Poem of the Teeth in Five Cantos" that included a list of three hundred dentists.

• **Emily Brontë** wrote most of her poems on a natural stone chair near Harworth, England, including the lines: "Come, sit down on this sunny stone; 'tis wintry light o'er flow'rless moors...."

• American poet **Amy Lowell** (1874-1925) created a scandal by smoking Manila cigars in public—and once ordered a supply of ten thousand cigars from the Philippines!

• A statue erected in Gyayaquil, Ecuador, to poet **Olmedo** is actually a statue of English poet Lord Byron, bought second-hand!

• To mark the one hundredth anniversary of the death of French poet **Arthur Rimbaud**, runners in a two-hundred-twenty-mile relay passed poems instead of batons!

WRITERS

• **Scott French**, of Foster City, California, has created a computer program that writes fiction in the style of several famous authors, including Jacqueline Susann!

• American author **Erle Stanley Gardner** once worked on seven novels at the same time!

• Fiction writer **Stephen King** has published over ten thousand pages (thirty-one novels) in twenty-three years!

CYRANO de BERGERAC
FAMOUS 17TH CENTURY WRITER & ROMANTIC HERO
FIRST SUGGESTED THE ROCKETSHIP TO THE MOON MORE THAN 300 YEARS AGO! ⬤
IN **1640** HE WROTE A BOOK CALLED *"VOYAGE TO THE MOON AND SUN"* IN WHICH HE EXPLAINED THE POSSIBILITIES OF TRAVEL TO THE MOON BY ROCKETSHIP

• Author **Juan Castillejos** published a book in 1969 that had nothing but the letter "I" on every page!

• Author **Ray Bradbury** wrote *Fahrenheit 451* in the basement of the University of California Library, on a pay type-writer that cost ten cents per half hour of use.

• **Dame Barbara Cartland**, a British romance novelist, dictated six thousand words a day, twenty-six novels a year, to five secretaries!

• British writer **John Creasy**, author of five hundred sixty-four published books, was first published only after receiving seven hundred seventy-four rejection slips!

• **William T. Adams**, in a period of forty-two years, wrote one hundred twenty-six books and more than one thousand short stories—yet he never signed his real name to a single one of them. His most often used pseudonym was Oliver Optic.

• **Jessie Lee Brown** became a best-selling author at the age of ninety-eight!

• **Mark Twain** was the first writer to send a typewritten manuscript to a publisher!

• The first published work of the famous German author **Goethe** was a wine label.

• **Charles Dickens** conceived *Pickwick Papers* as a picture book with abbreviated text, but the artist committed suicide and Dickens was forced to enlarge his text—which made him famous at the age of twenty-four.

• **Charles Dickens**, famed English novelist, always carried a compass

to make certain he would sleep with his head pointing north and "sold" his first short story for a bag of marbles!

• Author **Sylvester Hassel**'s book *The History of the Church* (c. 1884) contains a single sentence of 3,153 words, with 360 commas and 86 semicolons!

• Archdeacon **William North**, of Llangoedmor, Wales, wrote poetry in seven different languages.

• **Georges Simenon** wrote two hundred eleven novels in forty years. He once wrote a full-length novel on the terrace of a cafe in Paris in a single morning.

• To provide a dowry for his daughter, **Denis Diderot**, a French author, sold his library to Empress Catherine II of Russia for $3,000, and contracted to serve as custodian of the library for fifty years at an annual salary of $200. The Empress insisted that the entire salary be paid to him in advance.

• The author who never wasted a sheet of paper: **Abul ala Zohir**, of Seville, Spain, wrote fifty books

on medicine and botany— writing each on the narrow margins of pages in previously published books.

• After losing his fortune, **William Combe**, English author of eighty-six books and two thousand biographies, served as a cook, soldier, and waiter, yet he was so humiliated at finding it necessary to write for a living that he never permitted publishers to use his name.

• **Pierre Nicole**, French author of religious tracts, was so secretive about his work that whenever a visitor entered his study, his writing desk was dropped from sight through a trapdoor.

• **Countess Sofya Tolstoy**, wife and secretary of the famed Russian author Leo Tolstoy, wrote out the 1,216 pages of *War and Peace* in longhand seven times—a total of 4,256,000 words.

• **Honoré de Balzac**, the celebrated French author who worked sixteen hours a day, often drank as many as sixty cups of strong Turkish coffee in a single session of writing.

• **Frederick V. R. Dey**, creator of one thousand Nick Caret novels, often dictated three complete stories, totaling one hundred thousand words, in a single week.

• **Alex Haley**, the author of *Roots*, while in the United States Coast Guard, was its chief journalist—a position created especially for him.

• **Graham Greene**, the English author of *The Quiet American* and other books, relieved his boredom by playing Russian Roulette with a loaded revolver at the age of seventeen!

• **Ernest Hemingway**, the American author who often wrote about wars, never served as a soldier or officer in an army.

"A LICENSE TO READ" DANIEL NUSSBAUM of Los Angeles, Calif., WRITES SHORT STORIES USING ONLY WORDS COMPILED from PERSONALIZED LICENSE PLATES.✓

LONG AGO...

• **Sir Arthur Conan Doyle**, author of the Sherlock Holmes stories, was an eye doctor.

• **Edgar Allan Poe**, the famed poet and writer, was expelled from West Point Military Academy in 1831 for "Gross neglect of duty and disobedience of orders."

• **Victor Hugo**, the great French novelist, was also a politician, but he was such an inept orator that the National Assembly finally barred him from speaking.

VICTOR HUGO (1802-1885), THE FAMED FRENCH AUTHOR, ALWAYS DID HIS WRITING STANDING UP.

• **Jerzy Kosinski**, the Polish-born writer who leaned English as an adult in New York City, revealed that he obtained guidance in grammar and syntax hundreds of times by dialing the telephone operator.

• Writer **Mary Shelley** kept the heart of her husband, poet Percy Bysshe Shelley, in a bottle on her desk!

• **Noah Webster**, the lexicographer, was instrumental in securing the enactment of the copyright law, yet his own name went into the public domain, and can be used on reference works he did not edit.

• **Royall Tyler**, author of America's first successful play, *The Contrast*, always wrote anonymously because he was a noted jurist who became Chief Justice of the Supreme Court of Vermont.

• **Gilbert Patten**, who wrote the famed Frank Merriwell books under the name Burt L. Standish, produced a novel a week for nearly eighteen years—nearly one thousand volumes.

Author **ALEXANDER DUMAS** had a pet vulture that he walked on a leash through the streets of Paris!

• The Wayside, a house in Concord, Massachusetts, has been occupied by three successful authors, **Louisa May Alcott**, who wrote *Little Women*; **Nathaniel Hawthorne**, author of *The Scarlet Letter*; and **Margaret Sidney**, who wrote *Five Little Peppers*.

• **Helen MacInnes**, author of eighteen best-sellers on espionage, was not aware during World War II that her own husband was involved in British espionage.

• **Bram Stoker**, the author of *Dracula*, was inspired to write the vampire story by a nightmare suffered after eating too many crabs at supper.

• **Henry Ward Beecher** once said that he wrote the novel *Norwood* to dispel rumors that he had been the actual author of his sister Harriet Beecher Stowe's vastly superior *Uncle Tom's Cabin*.

LIBRARIES

• In 1991, **Virginia Mayes**, of Richmond, Virginia, returned a library book inscribed by Mark Twain that was sixty-seven years overdue!

• Hairy library: **Abul Kassem Ismael** "Saheb" (938-995), the scholarly Grand Vizier of Persia, had a library of one hundred seventeen thousand books that went with him wherever he went. When the great warrior-statesman traveled, his library followed him on the backs of four hundred camels. The beasts that carried this huge portable collection were specially trained to travel in alphabetical order, and were attended by a host of camel-driver librarians, who could locate any book their master desired in a short span of time.

Chapter 39

Love & Marriage

ZAK DAVIS of Eugene, Ore., INVITED EVYNNE SMITH AND TEN of HER CLOSEST FRIENDS TO THE Sheldon High School HOMECOMING DANCE!

Social science tells us that matrimony is one of the few true human universals, found in all societies. But the form marriage takes, and the manner by which it's brought about, varies astonishingly from culture to culture. Even within our own society, couples occasionally tie the knot in daringly creative ways. As we romance our way through the world of love and marriage, we'll regale you with some of the most amazing courtship rituals in the world, shower you with strange engagement customs, invite you to a few of the most unique wedding ceremonies, and offer you a candid peek into the weirder side of married life. And finally, lest you believe it can't last, we'll celebrate some of the world's longest anniversaries.

• In the third century A.D., **Emperor Claudius II** of Rome banned marriage!

BACHELORS AND SPINSTERS

• The fear of marriage is called "gamophobia"!

• Members of the Punan tribe in Borneo believe that a woman is born without a soul and doesn't acquire one until she marries!

• A Banda girl is not ready for marriage until she has eaten a whole chicken raw.

• In Bihar State, in eastern India, eligible bachelors are frequently kidnapped and forced into marriage!

• In Britain during the seventeenth century, bachelors over twenty-five-years-old were taxed a sum of one shilling a year until they married!

LOVE

• The first love letter: In 1993, Russian historian **Valentin Yanin** discovered a love letter over nine hundred years old written on birch bark!

• **Aiyaruk**, a thirteenth-century Tartar princess, and a champion wrestler, made suitors give up one hundred horses if she could pin them to the mat!

• During the Middle Ages, as a sign of affection, women gave men a present of an apple that they had held overnight in their armpit!

• **Bhupindar Singh**, of Richmond, Canada, created a twenty-three-foot replica of the Golden Temple in Amritsar, India, that took fifteen thousand hours to build, to show his love for a woman he had never met!

• In Japan, men celebrate "White Day" on March 14 by sending gifts, including white candles and lingerie, to women who gave them valentines in February!

OVER 4 MILLION WOMEN in Ravenna, Italy, HAVE KISSED the STATUE of GUIDARELLO GUIDARELLI, A 16th Century ITALIAN SOLDIER!

An AKWABA DOLL is tied to the waist of a girl in Ghana, as a sign that she is still single.

• At the Hitachi Corporation in Japan, there is a company executive who acts as an official company matchmaker!

• In 1562, kissing was banned in Naples, Italy, under punishment of death!

• The fourth **Earl of Harringon** (1780-1851) always wore brown clothing, dressed his servants in brown livery, painted his carriage brown, and insisted on brown horses—all as a tribute to a widow named Mary Brown whom he courted all his adult life.

• Natives of the Zulu tribe in South Africa exchange jewelry that contains coded love messages displayed in the color of the beads!

• In 1991, **Tommy Klyczek**, of Aurora, Illinois, received a love letter from his sweetheart, declaring her love, forty-four years after it was mailed!

• The 1926 film *Don Juan*, starring **John Barrymore**, featured a total of one hundred ninety-one kisses—one

every fifty-three seconds!

LONELY HEARTS

• **Marc Halberstadt**, of New York City, wrote a book-length advertisement about himself in order to attract a wife!

• At the Internet website www.marrytom.com, interested women can e-mail photos and proposals of marriage to actor **Tom Arnold!**

BROKEN HEARTS

• In January 1999, a man in Verona, Italy, sent 1,480 roses to his beloved—one flower for every day of the four years they were together. The young woman, however, turned down his marriage proposal!

• **Eliza Donnithorne**, of Sydney, Australia, jilted at the altar by her fiancé, stopped all the clocks in her house and wore her wedding gown for the next thirty years!

• The Hammond Harwood House in Anne Arundel County, Maryland, was built in the 1770s by **Matthias Hammond** for his fiancée—but she

refused to marry him because she felt neglected while he was spending all of his time supervising its construction.

• **Theodora Cooper** (1734-1824), forbidden to marry her cousin, poet **William Cowper,** when they were both youngsters, insisted on her deathbed sixty-eight years later that her tombstone proclaim that she had died of a broken heart.

COURTSHIP

• American novelist **Jack London** once fought—and lost—a sword duel with his future wife, **Charmian Kittredge**!

• **Chris Sanders** and **Kris Sanders**, of Burbank, California, met, fell in love, and married as a result of forwarding misdirected letters and phone calls to each other!

SPOONING SPOONS ELABORATE WOODEN SPOONS WERE CUSTOMARILY CARVED IN THE 18th CENTURY BY YOUTHS CALLING ON THEIR SWEETHEARTS IN WALES— *TO KEEP THEIR HANDS OCCUPIED*

• To win the hand of the daughter of Maximilian II of Germany, two noble suitors held a wrestling match, with the winner being the one who was the first to stuff his opponent into a muslin bag!

• **Paolina** and **Ake Viking** were married as a result of Paolina's father picking up a bottle with a message inside off the coast of Sicily! The message asked any pretty girl to write! Paolina wrote back, and she and Ake eventually met and married!

LONG COURTSHIPS

• **Beverly Redman**, of London, England, finally agreed to marry her husband, **Keith**, after he made eighty-five hundred proposals in twenty-four years!

• In 1969, **Octavio Guillen** and **Adriana Martinez** were married in Mexico City—after being engaged for sixty-seven years!

The **STRANGEST COURTSHIP IN THE WORLD**!

A **GIRL** of the Mututsi Tribe Africa CARRIES HER FUTURE **HUSBAND** AROUND IN A SLING ON HER BACK!

A WIFE IS USUALLY **10** YEARS OLDER THAN HER HUSBAND, AND THEY BECOME ENGAGED WHILE HE IS STILL AN **INFANT**

• Where the young men never marry in haste: Masai tribesmen of Africa undergo rigorous military training from age eighteen to thirty—and may not marry until after its completion.

PROPOSALS

• **Neil Nathanson**, of San Francisco, California, proposed to **Leslie Hamilton** in a specially designed magazine crossword puzzle!

• Canadian **Kevin Deck** met **Heidi Thomas** via the Internet, romanced her via e-mail, and proposed to her using a giant outdoor video screen!

• Bearded lady **Helena Antonia**, at age eighteen, received eight marriage proposals in a single day but she rejected all of them, and never received another proposal during her entire lifetime!

• **Tone Soerensen**, of Oslo, Norway, proposed to her fiancé, **Frode Jonassen**, by using the public address system of a local supermarket while he was shopping for vegetables!

• **Thomas Edison** proposed marriage to his future wife by tapping out his proposal in Morse code in the palm of her hand!

• When former United States President **Lyndon Johnson** proposed to **Lady Bird Johnson**, he dispatched an aide to find a wedding ring, which was bought for $2.98 at a Sears Roebuck store!

• In East Java, a young man proposes marriage by carrying a model house to the home of the woman's parents—she shows her acceptance by making windows in the hut!

In England and France it was customary for a man to ask for a woman's hand in marriage by giving her a pair of GLOVES on Valentine's Day!

THE ISLAND WHERE EVERY MARRIAGE PROPOSAL WAS AN INVITATION TO DEATH!

A YOUNG MAN ON St. Kilda, in the Hebrides, Scotland WAS NOT PERMITTED TO MARRY UNTIL HE HAD PROVED HIS COURAGE BY STANDING ON THE TIP OF LOVER'S ROCK ON ONE LEG--**AND LEANING OFF BALANCE 850 FEET ABOVE THE SEA!**

• **Johnny Tanyous**, of Lebanon, proposed to his Canadian sweetheart, **Marie-eve Rabath**, while scuba diving sixty-six feet underwater in the Mediterranean Sea!

• **Darold Holcomb** proposed to **Laura Brook** by mowing a giant message into a hillside off United States Route 10 in Farewell, Michigan!

ENGAGEMENTS

• The first engagement ring was a Greek ring dated from twenty-four hundred years ago, engraved with the word "honey"!

• In 1991, in some parts of Papua New Guinea, a bride could still be bought for twenty pigs!

• **Vittoria Chillema**, of Sicily, age sixty-four, was engaged for over forty years, during which time she saved $29,000 for her wedding!

• In France during the seventeenth century, tulips were so highly prized that one bride's dowry consisted of a single bulb from a species called "Mariage de ma fille"!

• In Mallaig, Scotland, couples planning to be married are dragged through the streets in a bathtub, then pelted with flour and eggs!

• In the city of Northfield, New Jersey, marriage licenses can only be obtained at the insane asylum.

• In Yugoslavia, bridegrooms are shaved in public before their wedding, and the hair is wrapped in a towel and sent to the future bride!

• In the nineteenth century, a six-hundred-foot string of diwarra shells could buy a native of New Britain a canoe or a wife!

• Natives of the Kei islands near New Guinea keep records carved in wood of payments made toward the purchase of wives!

THE MARRIAGE ANNOUNCEMENT OF 2 GERMAN CHESS PLAYERS

AFTER INVOLVED COMBINATIONS PETER WEISS WAS CHECKMATED BY ROSIE BLUME

• In Gorazde, Yugoslavia, when a marriage is announced, the new groom is dragged outside by his friends and family, tied to a stake near a bonfire, and released after the bride's mother throws a party!

• Among the pygmy tribes of Africa, a male cannot marry unless he compensates the bride's family by trading a sister or other female for his bride-to-be!

WEDDINGS

WEDDING OUTFITS

• Brides in ancient Rome carried sheaves of wheat during their weddings as symbols of fertility!

• Brides once carried bouquets of garlic, chives, and rosemary as protection against witches and demons.

• During the Tudor period, in England, bridal bouquets were made with marigolds—which were eaten after the ceremony to ensure fertility!

• On her wedding day, **Claudia Armillei**, of Ascoli Piceno, Italy, wore a lace and ribbon veil that was 1,320 feet long!

THE MOST DAZZLING PROCESSION IN HISTORY!
India
THE WEDDING PARTY at the marriage of the daughter of King Deva Raya I of Vijayanagar to Sultan Firoz Shah of Kulbarga WALKED FROM THE CITY GATE TO THE ROYAL PALACE - A DISTANCE OF 6 MILES - *ON A CARPET OF GOLD CLOTH* (1406)

• Wealthy brides in nineteenth-century Syria wore wooden platform sandals that were ten inches high!

• **Leigh Westbrook**, of New York City, wore a gown imprinted with paw prints at her wedding—and had six dogs for bridesmaids!

• Bridal veils were first worn in ancient times to protect the wearer against the "evil eye" of jealous rivals.

• World's longest veil: In 1993, at her wedding in Brive-la-Gaillarde, France, **Corinne Chaminade** wore a bridal veil 910 feet in length, which required six hundred people to carry it up the aisle!

• When **Lola Chestnut**, who worked at the Owens Lighting Center in Myrtle Beach, South Carolina, married **Phillip Watts**, she carried a bouquet of flowers and light bulbs!

• **Yumi Katsura** of Japan designed a wedding gown using twenty-four carat gold leaf and pure gold brocade worth $ 322,000!

• Brides during the American Revolution frequently wore red instead of white as a sign of rebellion!

• **Evan Barton** married **Joanne Etherson** in Sheffield, England, in 1992, wearing a full suit of armor!

WEDDING PARTIES

• **Patty Sullivan**, of Dallas, Texas, has been a bridesmaid twenty-two times, but has never been a bride!

• **Miss Myrtice Roberts**, of Sunnyside, Long Island, New York, was a bridesmaid sixty-two times in two years.

The lace on QUEEN VICTORIA'S wedding dress took **200** women **8 months** to make! It was valued at $50,000.⁰⁰

RINGS

• **Ted Kipperman**, of Houston, Texas, a pawn-broker and chaplain, performs free wedding ceremonies for couples who buy wedding rings in his store!

• A sperm whale's tooth is used in Fiji as an engage-ment ring. It is hung by a rope from the rafters of the woman's house.

CEREMONIES

• The world's first drive-in wedding chapel opened in Las Vegas, Nevada, in 1992!

• In 1888, a wedding with more than six thousand guests was held in Saint Paul, Minnesota, in an ice palace made from fifty-five thousand blocks of ice and lit by electric lamps!

• **Dave Lawrence** and **Jane Harland** were mar-ried over Gloucestershire, England, while standing on the wings of two sepa-rate planes flying eighty miles per hour!

• In 1993, **Linda Baker**, of Santa Monica, California, "married" herself!

• In 1993, **Sam Bradshaw**, of Phoenix, Arizona, and **Kathy Smith**, of Albuquerque, New Mexico, were mar-ried aboard a plane flying at an elevation of thirty-five thousand feet!

• **Dee Bennett** and **Pat Wilhems**, a sanitation worker, were married on the back of a garbage truck: the bride wore a veil made out of one hundred thirty white trash bags!

• **Lora Fowler** and **Vic Fasolino** were married on the roof of a house!

• **Fenton Blagrove** and **Darlene Casey**, of New York City, both confined to wheelchairs after suf-fering strokes, used an electronic keyboard at the hospital where they met to exchange marriage vows!

• **James** and **Julie Cox**, of Des Moines, Iowa, wear-ing black outfits, were wed in a haunted house com-plete with spider webs, caskets, and mummies!

• Cartoonist **Charles Addams**, creator of the television show the *Addams Family*, was married in a pet cemetery!

JERRY ANDERSON and JENNIFER KOOTENAY of Edmonton, Alta., Canada, who meet while playing slow-pitch baseball, were married in team uniforms at home plate!

MARISSA YOUNG and MAX RICHARDSON, a circus clown, were married before an audience of 7,000 people in Charleston, W.Va., in a ceremony with 18 dancers, 5 elephants, and 17 other clowns!

VERONIQUE and PASCAL DRAGATTO of FRANCE CELEBRATED THEIR MARRIAGE BY BEING PULLED AROUND A RACETRACK **BEHIND A CAR** AT 75 M.P.H.!

• **Tom Anderson** and **Sabrina Root**, of Philadelphia, Pennsylvania, paid for their $34,000 wedding by selling advertising at the wedding ceremony and reception!

After exchanging wedding vows, newlyweds Lorenzo Iameo and Sandra Censorio, of Vancouver, B.C., Canada, took their entire wedding party on a roller coaster ride!

• Cliffhangers: **Susan** and **Nigel Longmore** were married dangling from ropes on the side of a mountain near Leek, England!

• **Geoff** and **Catherine Williams** were married in Cornwall, England, at the bottom of an old tin mine. The bride wore a white miner's hat with her wedding gown!

• In 1991, ten couples in Lafayette, Louisiana, were married simultaneously while on a Ferris wheel!

• **Becca Webster** and **Dustin Kielty** were married beside a swimming pool in Valencia, California, then plunged in from a seventy-foot-high tower to celebrate!

• In 1990, in Patan, India, two Hindu brides married the wrong men in a double wedding, due to the brides' heavy veils, but the marriages were declared final by village elders!

• **Rick Rothgeb** and **Diana Barnes** were married while riding the roller coaster at Edmonton, Alberta's "West Edmonton Mall"!

• "Flushed with happiness": In 1996, eight couples were married in the bathroom of a public garden in Taichung, Taiwan!

• **Scott Wallace** and **Tami Weis**, of Chicago, Illinois, were married in the aisle of the supermarket where they first met!

• **Jennifer Beck** and **Toby Miller**, of Shasta, California, were married in 1997 in the kindergarten classroom where they first met as children!

• In 1953, **Frank Dyslin Junior** and **Betty Joy Anderson** were married in Miami, Florida, while waterskiing!

• In 1991, baseball fans **Bill Stoutle** and **Wendy Colton** were married at home plate at Toronto's Skydome Stadium!

• **John** and **J. Len Lauersdorf**, who met while working for a tree-care company in Ravenna, Ohio, were married while hanging from the branches of a tree!

• In Gretna Green, Scotland, couples can exchange wedding vows at the old blacksmith shop—over an anvil!

Allen Roulston and Linda MacLaggan, dressed as Frankstein and the Bride of Frankenstein for their Halloween wedding in Toronto, Canada!

The bride who didn't have a stitch to wear. **MRS. HANNAH WARD**, a widow, at her marriage to **MAJOR MOSES JOY** in Newfane, Vt., wore as a bridal gown a wooden box! In early New England a widow's second husband became legally responsible for all the first husband's debts if the bride brought any of her previous possessions to the wedding—even clothing! Feb. 22, 1789

• **Kay Pippert** and **Steven Smelser**, of Lawrence, Kansas, were married on bus #62—the one the groom drives every day for a living!

• "Underground weddings": Weddings are regularly held one

MOKWAI-MAI AND LO CHI-FAI OF HONG KONG WERE MARRIED UNDERWATER IN A SWIMMING POOL!

DURING HIS REIGN, King Mongkut (Rama IV) of Siam, MARRIED **3,016 WOMEN,** EACH IN A **SEPARATE** CEREMONY!

"I'M GETTING MARRIED EVERY MORNING"

hundred fifty feet below ground at the Dan Yr Ogof Caves in the Swansea Valley in Wales!

• They got her to the church on time! **Anita Hudson**, of York, England, arrived at her wedding on time after

she called in the British army to ferry her across floodwaters!

• "Lover's leap": **Julie Massicott** and **Mike Dearins** were married on board an airplane while flying over Lafayette, Louisiana, then parachuted to their reception!

• **Sven Weitel** and **Anna Steffen** were married sixteen thousand feet in the air over Kruger National Park in South Africa after jumping with the minister from an airplane!

• In 1992, **Lyle Hall** and **Carol Luther** were married on a frozen lake near Merrifield, Minnesota, beneath a fourteen-foot cross made of ice.

• A travel company in Loch Ness, Scotland, offers couples the chance to get married in a submarine with "Nessie" as a possible witness!

NUPTIALS FOR NEONATES

• When **Anne Mowbraw**, daughter of the Duke of Norfolk, married in 1478, she was five years old and her husband, the Duke of York, was only four!

BY THE POWER VESTED IN ME...

In Massachusetts anyone who wants to officiate at a wedding can do so with a special one-day appointment by the governor!

• In Bangladesh, in 1986, an eleven-month-old boy married a three-month-old girl!

• **Isabelle**, the daughter of France's Charles VI, became the second wife of England's King Richard II at the age of seven years, and was a widow at the age of ten!

NUPTIALS FOR NONHUMANS

• In Bangkok, Thailand, two cats were "married" in a $28,000 wedding ceremony that included matching gold rings!

• In 1952, **Mahabat Khan Babi Pathan**, the Maharajah of Junagadh, India, held a state wedding with fifty thousand guests for his golden retrievers!

• **Julie Hims** of London, England, had her golden retriever "Brownie" walk her down the aisle as her bridesmaid!

• A man once married a statue! **Lord Orseley** fell in love with the Venus di Medici and legally married it. He gave the statue a ring costing one hundred thousand dollars.

NUPTIALS FOR THE DEAD

• **Patricia Montenez**, of Marseille, France, married her fiancé, **Claude Darcy**, in a government ceremony even though the groom had been dead for over two years!

• In rural China, weddings are often performed in which deceased single girls and boys are wed in gravesite ceremonies so that the girl can serve her "husband" in the afterlife!

• **Foo Ah Heoh**, of Kuala Lumpur, Malaysia, tormented by dreams of her dead son asking to marry his beloved, contacted the family of **Saw Bee Hong** and learned that she, too, had died. The two families arranged for the dead couple to be wed. Three-foot-high paper effigies of the couple were married, with eighty people attending the nuptials.

WEDDING CEREMONIES IN OTHER CULTURES

• The marriage ceremony among the ancient Aztecs was completed by tying the cloaks of the bride and groom together.

• Turkish bridegrooms were once required to make a promise during their wedding ceremonies to always provide their new wives with coffee. If they failed to do so it was grounds for divorce!

• An old marriage custom in Poland required that the bride and groom both send a surrogate to their wedding: if no evil befell the surrogate couple in fourteen days, then the real bride and groom would go through with their wedding!

• At ancient Anglo-Saxon weddings, it was customary for the father of the bride to symbolically pass his daughter to her future husband by handing over one of her shoes!

THE **BRIDE** AT A GYPSY WEDDING IN ITALY TRADITIONALLY SMASHES A POTTERY JAR OVER THE GROOM'S HEAD

THE BRIDE WHO MARRIED A SEVERED HEAD! Prince Khalid of Multan, India, sent to war on his wedding day, committed suicide after directing that his head be cut off and sent to his fiancée. The wedding was performed with the groom's head on a pillow.

• In medieval Sweden, weddings took place at night and were lit with torches carried by "bridal knights" whose role was to guard the bride!

• In Russia, the best man at a wedding must sign the marriage register guaranteeing that the union will last at least six months or he'll personally pay a fine of one hundred fifty rubles!

• A marriage in Swaziland is not valid until the couple kiss in public two hundred fifty times, matching the number of wives the king has!

• At Jewish weddings in Morocco, it was once customary to toss eggs at the bride!

• To be assured of good fortune, a bride in old England had to be kissed at her wedding by a chimney sweep.

• The Lahlas of Africa have the most "picturesque" wedding ceremony on earth. The marriage rites consist of painting the bride's portrait on a framed canvas which the groom then wears on his nuptial headdress.

The divorce proceedings are even simpler. The husband erases his wife's features from the wedding frame and she passes out of his life.

WEDDING FEASTS

• A traditional wedding feast in ancient Ceram, Indonesia, included two baked possums—female for the bride and a male for the groom.

• In Bali, the groom helps his bride cook the entire wedding feast.

• A Bedouin wedding feast includes egg-filled fish placed inside a chicken, which in turn is put inside a whole sheep—then roasted inside a camel.

WEDDING GIFTS

• Paradise palace in Ferrara, Italy, was built in 1388 by **Duke Albert V** as a gift to his father-in-law. The duke married his valet's daughter and gave her father the palace to induce him to attend the wedding.

• In 1840, **Queen Victoria** received a half-ton slab of cheese as a wedding present that was over nine feet in diameter!

THE WOMEN WHO TREAT THEIR MEN LIKE KINGS! The bridegroom at a wedding in the Muria Tribe of India is adorned with a crown of leaves, carried to the ceremony in a woman's arms, and sits on the lap of a female attendant.

HONEYMOONS

• In Britain, in 1918, a World War I soldier was executed for overstaying his seven-day honeymoon leave!

• **Quincy** and **Ella Scott** spent their honeymoon on horseback riding over two thousand miles.

MARRIED LIFE

• Married women live about sixteen hundred days longer than single women. Married men live thirty-five hundred days longer than single men.

• **Uichi Noda**, of Japan, wrote 1,307 letters to his wife, **Mitsu**, that contained five million characters and were later published in twenty-five volumes, filling 12,404 pages!

• A rare form of marriage called "fraternal polyandry," practiced in Limi, Tibet, allows four brothers to share the same wife.

• Women in ancient Greece counted their age from the date of their marriage, not from the day they were born!

In Japan, married couples practice an ancient ritual called "SHINDAI" in which they settle arguments by slugging it out with pillows!

• Women in Croatia, Yugoslavia, wear a cape to indicate they are single, and a white kerchief if they are married.

• **Prince Urussof**, of Russia, spent over $40 million to buy both shorelines of the Black Sea after his young bride lost her wedding ring in the water!

• **Virginia Cohimia**, of Tulsa, Oklahoma, received fifty dozen roses from her husband Charlie for her fiftieth birthday!

• In seventeenth-century Boston, it was against the law for a man to kiss his wife in public on the Sabbath!

• At one time in Scotland, two people clasping hands signified a temporary marriage that allowed the couple to live together for a year and a day before considering a permanent relationship!

• Husband and wife **Jesse** and **Beryl Tweedle** discovered after they were married that they were born on the same day, in the same hospital, and in the same room!

• In a Chinese proxy wedding, the bridegroom can be represented by a rooster!

• **Jack** and **Blanche Passa**, of Grand Forks, North Dakota, married for forty-nine years, live next door to each other, in "his" and "hers" matching houses!

• The fittest couple in the world: **Peter Reid** and **Lori Bowden**, a.k.a. Mr. and Mrs. Ironman, of Victoria, British Columbia, Canada, are the first married couple to win the Australian Ironman competition!

• Married men in the Akela tribe of Africa always cut their meat into small chunks with a knife held between their toes and before their wedding are required to knock out all their own teeth!

MULTIPLE MARRIAGES

• **Glynn "Scotty" Wolfe**, of Redlands, California, was married twenty-nine times—yet not one of his wives attended his funeral!

• **Adrienne Cuyot**, of Belgium, was married fifty-three times and engaged six hundred fifty-two times in twenty-three years!

• **Giovanni Vigliotto**, of New York City, was married one hundred four times between 1949 and 1981—an average of three new brides every year!

• **King Mongkut** of Siam married 9,016 women, each in a separate ceremony!

• The man who married his own wife and didn't know it! **Humphrey Kynaston**, an English outlaw, divorced a noblewoman named **Isabel of Aston** after ten years of marriage. Fifteen years later, he married a woman named **Marion of Oswestry**. Not until he was on his deathbed, thirteen years later, did he learn that Isabel and Marion were the same woman!

• The man who matched his wives to his initials: **Jethro Alexander Cummings**, of London, England, was married three times. His wives maiden names were **Jane Jethro**, **Alice Alexander**, and **Clara Cummings**.

• **King Rama V** of Siam had three thousand wives and three hundred seventy children: one hundred thirty-four sons, and two hundred thirty-six daughters!

• **Kehna**, Algerian Queen of the Berbers, had a harem of four hundred husbands!

• **Linda Essex Chandler**, the world's most-married woman, has legally been married twenty-two times!

MARITAL SPATS

• **Guilhen da Cabestan**, a thirteenth-century French poet, was killed by a jealous husband who then had the poet's heart cooked and served to his unfaithful wife.

• The waters of a certain spring in Keijo, Korea, are believed to endow a deserted husband with exact knowledge of his wife's whereabouts. Korean husbands must consult this spring before going to court.

DIVORCE

• A wife in ancient China could be divorced for talking too much.

• **Rudolph Valentino**, billed as "The World's Greatest Screen Lover," was married to **Jean Acker** for only one day!

• A hotel in Norwich, England, offers an "amicable divorce weekend" package for couples to spend one last night together and hopefully make up—a lawyer is on call if they don't.

• A woman in the Babira tribe, Africa, is divorced if her husband places a jug of oil, a stick, and two pots on her threshold. The stick symbolizes being driven out with a rod.

• The marriages that lasted beyond the grave! The divorce laws of the Byzantine Empire made it easy to get rid of a living spouse—but there was no way of ending a marriage to a dead wife or husband.

• **Aaron Burr** (1756-1836), a Vice President of the United States and the man who killed Alexander Hamilton in a duel, was divorced by his second wife, Madame Juel, on the day of his death.

• A husband in the Gaira Forest, Colombia, can divorce his wife only by wearing a mask day and night for a full year—so he will emerge as a stranger!

• A wife in Togoland, Africa, can legally divorce her husband by donning a skirt made from the leaves of the shea butter tree. Normally, skirts made of those leaves are worn only by widows.

• Famed Himalayan mountaineers, the Sherpas consider a husband and wife divorced when they break a string.

WIDOWHOOD

• A woman in France who has borne children to a man can be legally married to him after his death.

2,000 WOMEN COMMITTED SUICIDE FOR THIS MAN! Hari Hari II, Maharajah of Vijanyajar, India, had 12,000 wives— when he died in 1378, 2,000 of them sacrificed their lives on his funeral pyre.

- **Sir John Pryce** kept the embalmed bodies of his first two wives in grandfather clocks.

- Widows of Africa's Kavati tribe have a "sound" way of acquiring a new husband. Custom requires a widow to remain near her departed husband's grave, screaming at the top of her lungs and drumming ceaselessly on the walls of the grave with a cudgel until some eligible male offers to marry her, thereby restoring peace and quiet.

- If a warrior of the Masai tribe of East Africa dies before marrying, a bride is frequently chosen to inherit his property and his name!

ANNIVERSARIES

ANNIVERSARY CELEBRATIONS

- In rural Saskatchewan, Canada, "mock weddings" are staged to celebrate anniversaries—with the husband and wife assuming each other's role and clothing while reenacting the marriage ceremony!

- **Mike** and **Laura Dieken**, of Portland, Oregon, celebrate their marriage by renewing their vows every year in a different state! So far they have been married thirteen times!

ANNIVERSARY GIFTS

- **Joe Ashenbrener**, of Nashville, Tennessee, paid $109 for an airline seat for a cake he was taking to his sister's fiftieth wedding anniversary in Las Vegas, Nevada!

SILVER ANNIVERSARIES AND BEYOND

- **Anna** and **Antin Nakonecznyj**, separated for forty-seven years due to a World War II internment, reunited in 1992, just in time to celebrate their fiftieth wedding anniversary!

- **Edmund Sobieski**, age one hundred three, and his wife, **Genevieve**, age one hundred, were married for eighty years!

- Brothers **Robert, Joe, Richard**, and **Fred Hill**, of Ohio, and their wives **Mable, Irene, Mildred**, and **Vesta** have all been married over fifty years!

- **Mr.** and **Mrs. Michael Coughlan**, of Tullamore, Kings County, Ireland, have been married eighty years and have never had a quarrel.

- At Chicago's Holy Name Cathedral, a gathering of seven hundred twenty couples celebrated their fiftieth anniversaries by renewing their vows together!

- Five generations of the Grayson family have celebrated fiftieth wedding anniversaries!

- **Mr.** and **Mrs. Jonathan Graber**, of Freeman, South Dakota, celebrated their fiftieth wedding anniversary with every member of the original ceremony in attendance.

THE MAN WHO MARRIED BARBIE

In 1999, in a solemn ceremony attended by friends and family, Cheng Si Sung of Taiwan married a Barbie doll.

Actually, the doll itself was a stand-in for his real bride, who had been dead for two decades and attended her wedding in a funeral urn.

Twenty years earlier, Sung had been engaged to a woman named Tsai. The two had been very much in love, but Tsai's family had refused to consent to their marriage. Consumed with grief, Tsai committed suicide.

Twenty years later, Sung approached Tsai's family again, claiming to be tormented by her restless spirit. Although Sung had married another woman, he asked to wed Tsai by proxy, so that her spirit could be at rest. Tsai's family consented, as did Sung's present wife.

The Barbie doll, chosen to be the receptacle of Tsai's spirit, was arrayed in traditional Taiwanese wedding regalia and placed in an ornate basket. The man and doll were wed in the presence of both families, then husband, wife, ashes, and doll returned home to begin a new life together.

Chapter 40

Mail & Postage

Believe It or Not! MAIL IS DELIVERED TO THE HAVASUPAI INDIAN RESERVATION 2,400 ft. BELOW THE SOUTH RIM of THE GRAND CANYON BY MULE!

In his heyday, Robert Ripley received so much mail that he earned the nickname "the human post-office." After decades of mail in all shapes and sizes (letters written on animal bones, grains of rice, glass) the postal service refused to deliver any nonstandard Ripley mail. But as you're about to discover, when the bizarre and unusual chooses its destination, no postal regulation can keep it from its appointed rounds.

• Americans send about 7 billion greeting cards every year, including 2.6 billion Christmas cards, 900 million Valentines, and 150 million cards for Mother's Day!

"UNBELIEVABLE MAIL" AT THE HEIGHT of HIS POPULARITY, ROBERT RIPLEY, WHO DIED in 1949 of a HEART ATTACK, RECEIVED A GREATER AMOUNT of MAIL THAN ANYONE ELSE IN THE WORLD — AN AVERAGE of 3,000 LETTERS A DAY — AND HE ONCE RECEIVED 1,750,000 LETTERS DURING A TWO-WEEK CONTEST!

• **Corinne Robinson**, of Scarborough, Ontario, and **Edith Gibbons**, of Northumberland, England, pen pals since the end of World War II, met for the first time in 1993—forty-seven years after they first started corresponding!

ADDRESSES

• The White House, in Washington, D.C., is the only home in the United States that has its own Zip Code: 20500, which is also the only Zip Code in the country ending in two zeros!

DELIVERY METHODS

• Tin Can Island, in the South Pacific Kingdom of Tonga, was given that name because a swimmer once delivered mail between the island and passing ships in a tin can.

• Until 1931, letters sent from the island of Saint Kilda, in the Hebrides, to the mainland, were dispatched in a bottle that was cast into the sea in a wooden box attached to an inflated sheep bladder.

MAIL IS DELIVERED TO ANDADO, AUSTRALIA, ACROSS THE DEAD HEART DESERT IN AN ENGINELESS AUTOMOBILE DRAWN BY A TEAM OF CAMELS

ITEMS MAILED

• The United States Postal Service didn't make it illegal to mail children by Parcel Post until June 1920!

• "**Owney**," a dog with no owner, was mailed a total of forty-three thousand miles, including a trip around the world!

PACKAGING

• Cheaper by the kernel: **Cork Foster**, of Saint Thomas, Canada, uses popcorn instead of Styrofoam as packing material for his mail-order farm equipment!

POSTAGE

• In 1990, pictures of **Eddie Murphy**, **Sammy Davis Junior**, and **Gladys Knight** were featured on seventy-five-cent stamps in Tanzania!

• In 1991, two rare blocks of 1918 United States stamps, printed upside down, sold for $1.21 million at an auction in New York City.

• Albania once issued a stamp commemorating the world's greatest smoker, **Ahmed Zagu**, who smoked two hundred forty cigarettes a day!

OLD SHOES and BOOTS HUNG from A LARGE TREE WERE USED AS POSTBOXES in Olifants Bay, South Africa!

MAIL COURIERS
TRAVELING BETWEEN ARGENTINA AND CHILE IN ANCIENT TIMES SWAM RIVERS, PULLING BEHIND THEM A FLOATING POUCH *THAT CONTAINED THE MAIL - AND THEIR CLOTHING*

"STONE-A-GRAMS" CALIFORNIA ARTIST *NICK AGID* SENDS GIANT LETTERS TO POLITICIANS AND MOVIE STARS *CARVED ON SLABS OF STONE!*

THERE IS AN **UNDERWATER MAILBOX** LOCATED OFF THE COAST OF Susami, Japan, WHERE SCUBA DIVERS CAN MAIL A WATERPROOF CARD!

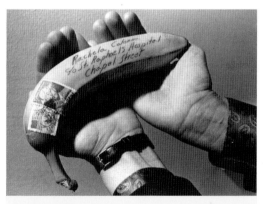

A banana sent by her niece and delivered by mail to **Rachela Colonna**, of New Haven, Connecticut, at the hospital of St. Raphael had on it two stamps and the words "I love you."

• Stamps are the principal export of the Cook Islands in the South Pacific, producing $1.5 million annually: one-fifth of the government's income.

• The most valuable stamp: a one-cent stamp issued in British Guiana in 1873 was sold on April 5, 1980, for $850,000.

SLOW DELIVERIES

• **Johan Wetche**, of Agersted, Denmark, received a letter addressed to his long-deceased aunt that had been mailed eighty-seven years ago from Copenhagen—a distance of only one hundred sixty miles!

• A letter sent from an office in the Federal Building in Eureka, California, took forty-two years to reach a post office box in the same building!

• **Page R. Dye**, of James County, Virginia, received a glove in the mail fifty-three years after he dropped it in Belgium during World War II!

UNLIKELY DELIVERIES

• The smallest postcard ever mailed: A message of forty words written on the back of a two-cent stamp was delivered promptly.

• **Robert Dingle**, of Yucca, Arizona, received a Christmas card through the mail with no address except for: "To Crazy Bob"!

CAMELS WERE ONCE USED TO CARRY MAIL BETWEEN U.S. ARMY POSTS AND SMALL WESTERN TOWNS DURING THE 1850s!

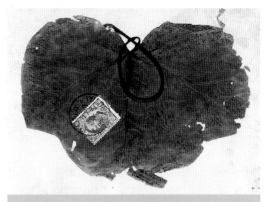

• **Mario L. Previtali**, of Pittsfield, Massachusetts, received a letter from his cousin in Rome, Italy, written on a sycamore leaf. It arrived in perfect condition, without wrapping or protection of any kind.

• You can't get rid of the durned things! Soldier **Leroy Gibson** was followed home by a fruitcake! The cake was mailed from his hometown of Monongahela, Pennsylvania, in 1943 while he was away at war and followed him, always a stop or two behind, as he was transferred to various locales across the Pacific. It finally caught up with him back home in Pennsylvania, 12 years later!

Chapter 41
Manufacturing, Retail, & Products

Until today, if you wanted to grow a tomato in the shape of Elvis, the only option available was to plant your seeds and trust to fate. But one of a vast array of hot new products offers a vegetable mold that will do the trick. In these miraculous days of monumental marketing and colossal capitalism, there's a product for every need—even for those needs you didn't know you had! As you peruse our collection of manufacturing and retailing Believe It or Nots!, you'll discover the amazing tales behind the creation of everyday consumer goods, you'll have the opportunity to browse a gallery of alluring products and indispensable services, and you'll witness some of the most bizarre lengths to which retailers are willing to go to part you from your dollar!

MANUFACTURING

• By the start of 1980, the automobile industry provided one out of six jobs in the United States.

• The Campbell's Soup Plant in Napoleon, Ohio, produces fifteen million cans of soup every day!

• Dijon mustard grinders who cried on the job were often given bonuses because tears meant they were grinding a finer and better product!

• If the grains contained in a one-hundred-and-ten-pound bag of Portland Cement were placed in a row, they would encircle the earth one and a half times!

• Rope makers in Kiangsi, China, work in a wooden tower thirty feet high in the belief that ropes plaited vertically are stronger than those made horizontally.

• It takes two hundred fifty pounds of ore to manufacture a two-and-a-half-pound brass trumpet!

• It takes thirty-two hundred tons of rose petals to make 2.2 pounds of rose oil!

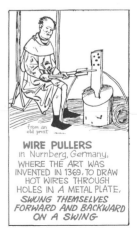

from an old print

WIRE PULLERS
in Nürnberg, Germany, WHERE THE ART WAS INVENTED IN 1369, TO DRAW HOT WIRES THROUGH HOLES IN A METAL PLATE, *SWUNG THEMSELVES FORWARD AND BACKWARD ON A SWING*

PRODUCTS

• In 1955, the Quaker Oats Company of Canada placed legal deeds to one square inch of land in the Canadian Yukon inside their boxes of puffed rice and puffed wheat.

• **Tony Lozano**, of Manteca, California, sells used houses, cut in half and mounted on flatbed trucks, for between $29,000 and $40,000, including transportation!

• In 1856, the sewing machine became the first item offered for sale on the installment plan.

• A sewing machine sold in the nineteenth century was operated by a kitchen-stove steam engine.

A SEWING MACHINE patented in 1858, was built in the form of cherubs.

• A tire manufactured in Akron, Ohio, that sells for over $50,000 is eleven and a half feet high, five and a half feet wide, and weighs twelve thousand five hundred pounds.

• A popular item among new parents in Shanghai, China, is a writing brush made with the hair of newborn babies!

• Vegiforms: **Rick Tweddell**, of Cincinnati, Ohio, has invented plastic molds that change the shape of growing vegetables into likenesses of such famous people as Elvis, Ronald Reagan, and Linda Evans.

• Lucifers: Box matches sold in England in 1829 carried a warning that persons with weak lungs should avoid the fumes.

• Old bottles are the only stock of a store in New York City, which sells them for as much as $350 each.

• Victorinox Cutlery Corporation, manufacturers of the original Swiss Army knife, makes a knife that includes a curved surgical blade for performing tracheotomies!

• **Jim Rogers**, of West Hartford, Connecticut, sells "Invisible Fences" that prevent dogs from escaping their yards!

• Scientists at the Rochester Institute of Technology in New York are working on creating edible packaging for cereal and pasta!

• In 1963, **Henry George O'Hare** patented an anti-fly guard for a cow's eyes!

• Japan's Toray Industries, Incorporated has designed winter jackets for children that change color when the temperature drops!

• A company in New York City makes a plastic and steel wallet that can only be opened with a four-digit code and self-destructs when forced open!

• The Desktech Fun Phone comes equipped with sound effects, including a baby crying and animal noises!

• **Brian Woodward** and **Bob Pine**, of Houston, Texas, make artistic gifts by covering jewelry, clothing, and furniture with macaroni!

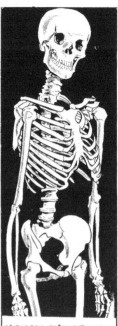

HUMAN SKELETONS WERE ADVERTISED FOR SALE IN 1943 BY A N.Y. CITY FIRM WHICH OFFERED BARGAINS FOR *THOSE WITH BONE DISCOLORATIONS*

• A wristwatch on sale in the United States warns the wearers when they are in danger of getting a sunburn!

• Scientists in Edmonton, Canada, use fake cows smeared with a mixture of cow odors to test insect repellents!

• A company in California makes fireproof roof shingles out of shredded money!

• A popular sports drink sold in Japan is called "Pocari Sweat"!

• A vending machine in Zurich, Switzerland, called "Lucky Can," dispenses prizes when cans are inserted for recycling!

• **Shindy** and **Marshall Rosen**, of Toronto, Canada, sell clear plastic cubes and clocks filled with shredded money!

• **Wayne Avellanet**, of Dallas, Texas, has invented an aerosol spray that replicates the smell of a crowded subway!

• The "Parkulator": A company in Arkansas has developed pocket-calculator–size parking meters that fit onto a car's dashboard.

• A company in Seattle, Washington, makes drive-ways that turn cars on a revolving disk!

• A company in Kyoto, Japan, makes waterproof books for students who like to study in the bath!

• Kanebo, a cosmetics company in Japan, has developed a line of panty-hose that are embedded with vitamins and special scents that are released when worn!

• **Harold Odom, Junior**, of Missouri City, Texas, invented an intravenous watering system for Christmas trees!

• A company in South Glamorgan, Wales, has developed a battery-powered burglar alarm for installation in coffins and graves!

• A disaster-relief organization in London, England, sells pens and pencils made out of metal melted down from dis-mantled war missiles!

• **Hayward G. Spangler** and **Eric H. Erikson**, of Tucson, Arizona, filed a patent for a device that determines the tempera-ture of bees in a hive!

• "Genuflex": A company in Venice, Italy, has devel-oped a confessional with leather seats that is sound-proof, air-conditioned, and has red and green lights to signal those waiting!

• A company in Japan has developed a global satel-lite tracking device to help find elderly patients who have a history of wander-ing off!

• A store in Taiwan that sells bulletproof vests offers a free pair of bullet-proof underpants to every customer!

• In 1991, **Celia Clarke**, of Goleta, California, filed a patent for perfume-scented embroidery thread.

• A spray containing capsaicin, a substance found in hot peppers, is used to ward off grizzly bears!

• In Tokyo, Japan, there are vending machines that dispense frozen meat, jewelry, and even dating information!

• A company was awarded a patent to make snow for indoor skiing and snowboarding.

• A research company in London, England, has developed a "smart" gar-bage can that can read bar codes and sort waste into separate recycling com-partments! The bin can also record which items the household has run out of and needs to replace!

• A company in Japan has developed a robotic cat that interacts with its owner, purrs when stroked, and responds to the sound of the human voice!

• A company in New York City markets cassette tapes for insomniacs that feature someone counting sheep!

COUNTER SPY, A store in Washington, D.C., sells cigarette lighters with tiny cameras, flash guns that cause temporary blindness, and rain-coats with hidden tape recorders that are activated by writing with a special pen!

• A company in Switzerland created a rideable bicycle that is covered with over 1,188 grams of gold and platinum and studded with thirteen thousand carats of emeralds, rubies, diamonds, and sapphires, worth one million dollars!

• A company in Buckinghamshire, England, has developed a solar-powered backpack!

• A company in Tucson, Arizona, sells a piece of software that warns the user when a cat has crossed the computer keyboard and utters a screeching harmonica sound to scare the animal away!

• A company in Vancouver, British Columbia, sells cases of soda decorated with labels that feature photos of the buyer that have been scanned and sent via the Internet to the manufacturer.

• Horse bread! A bakery that opened in Melbourne, Australia, in the 1850s made bread exclusively for horses! Unfortunately, because the bread was cheaper than loaves made for humans, many of the bakery's human customers consumed the five-pound loaves. When many of the human customers complained of stomach ailments, the bakery was forced to shut down.

JOHN SWEENEY of Darien, Conn., WILL BLANKET A HOMEOWNER'S BARE FRONT LAWN WITH REAL SNOWFLAKES for A FEE of $1,000!

Snow Guy

THE WORLD'S FIRST RETAIL STORE MANNED BY ROBOTS IN MINNEAPOLIS, MINN., SELLS COMPACT DISCS!

• A company in Japan has developed a can of noodles that can heat itself to the boiling point!

CATALOG SHOPPING

• In the early 1900s, tombstones, dynamite, and gold toothpicks were all sold through the Sears catalog!

FOR KIDS

• Motorola, Incorporated and Timex Corporation have designed wristwatch pagers for parents and kids based on the one worn by Dick Tracy!

• A store in Toronto, Ontario, sells teddy bears equipped with hidden video cameras designed to help keep watch over children!

FOR PETS

• **Stephen Hoy**, of the United States, has invented edible greeting cards for animals!

• A soft drink for dogs called "Cock-Dog," which has the flavor of meat juice, is being marketed in France, Holland, and the United States!

• "Animal Manors": A company in New York builds custom-made pet houses including a French Chateau for $8,947, and an Egyptian temple decorated with precious gems for $124,000!

• In 1992, **Kenji Kawakami**, of Japan, invented padded booties for cats to dust the floor!

FOR EXPENSIVE TASTES

• In 1989, department stores in Japan offered such items as an electric Persian carpet, a bronze and gold set of golf clubs, and a twenty-four-carat gold fridge!

STORES

• **J. C. Penney** (1875-1971), founder of a chain of stores bearing his name, was told by his father at the age of eight that from that time on he had to buy his own clothing.

• All forty-two residents of Sentinel Butte, North Dakota, had keys to Albert Oldon's gas pump so they could pump their own gas when he wasn't working!

A clothing store in Vienna, Austria, offered the first five customers 5,000 schillings worth of merchandise if they were daring enough to enter the store completely naked!

• **Walter Swan**, owner of The One Book Store in Brisbee, Arizona, sells only one book in his shop—his own memoirs!

• Where music is man's best friend: Bow Wow Records, a music store in Albuquerque, New Mexico, is painted to look like a Dalmatian!

• In the 1950s, Chicago's Marshall Field's department store began closing an hour earlier on Mondays so that the staff and customers could be home in time to watch "I Love Lucy."

• "**Cynthia**," a mannequin created by American artist Lester Gaba for a New York City department store was so lifelike that he took her to nightclubs and parties as his guest!

• In Japan, department stores play "Auld Lang Syne" to warn customers when the store is closing!

• In 1994, a department store in Amsterdam, the Netherlands, used four rattlesnakes to guard a display of diamonds!

• A used bookstore in Tadami, Japan, gave away over twenty-five acres of forestland in exchange for old books!

• In 1991, **Allan Dempsey** received word that a book he had ordered from the Goodspeed Book shop in Boston, Massachusetts, in 1960 had finally arrived—thirty-one years later!

SERVICES

• American Express has a special nine hundred phone number that tells people the weather in six hundred places around the world—including the moon!

• A company in Illinois offers people a chance to have a star in the universe named after them!

ROBERT YOUNG of London, Canada OPERATES A SERVICE CALLED "RENT-A-NERD" for PARTIES, BIRTHDAYS and WEDDINGS!

THRILLS, CHILLS, AND KOSHER DILLS—AN ENTERPRISING SUPERMARKET LIVENS UP A TIRED CHORE

A supermarket in Shen Yeng City, China, has come up with a novel way to attract customers: they've installed a roller coaster on all five floors of their store! As shoppers enter, they're ushered into shiny red and yellow coaster cars, which carry them on a thrilling express ride through the store!

The ride is complete with dips and turns, but it slows to a crawl through each of the store's aisles, allowing riders to browse and select their merchandise. The only drawback is that if customers miss an item, they must repeat the entire ride to get back to the proper aisle!

The store owners hope that the idea catches on, as they'd like to open branches elsewhere. So far, customers' responses have been overwhelmingly positive. Shoppers say it adds a thrill to an otherwise mundane chore!

Chapter 42

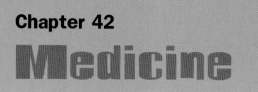

MIKE and LINDA LOYNES of White Rock, B.C., Canada, OPERATE The Llama Therapeutic Group, A COUNSELING CENTER WHERE STRESSED OUT CLIENTS SPEND TIME LIVING AND WORKING WITH LLAMAS!

How sick would you have to be before you tried dosing yourself with horse calluses in warm ale? Would you eat a donkey-hair sandwich to get rid of a stubborn cough, or would you prefer snail tea? Perhaps a little hog lice wine will cure what ails you—it was a popular prescription in medieval Europe.

• During a seventy-six-year life span, the average American citizen is sick about 4,483 days—that's more than twelve years!

ANTIQUATED MEDICINE

• At one time in South Foster, Rhode Island, if a dentist extracted the wrong tooth from a patient, he was ordered by law to have one of his own teeth extracted by the local blacksmith!

• In China, cow gallstones used in traditional herbal medicines sell for over $7,000 a pound!

• Recipes for medicinal beer have been found on Sumerian tablets dating back to 2000 B.C.!

• The world's first drug-store opened in A.D. 754!

• To heal wounds, surgeons in Munich, Germany, use a four-thousand-year-old Egyptian remedy which calls for packing infected areas with sugar!

• Ketchup was originally a medicine and was patented under the name "Doctor Miles' Compound Extract of Tomato!"

• Dentists in medieval England, known as "tooth drawers," wore pointed caps and necklaces made from extracted teeth to signify their occupation!

• The ancient Egyptians used pumice and vinegar to whiten their teeth!

• Ground-up narwhal tusks, sold in British pharmacies until 1746 as unicorn horns, were used to relieve heartburn, sore eyes, and "evil vapours"!

• During World War II, doctors in Fiji used coconut milk as a blood substitute and coconut fibers for stitches!

• In the 1850s, a French doctor named **François Brossais** treated his indigestion by applying leeches to his body fifteen times in eighteen days.

• Ancient Egyptian pharaohs had personal physicians to treat individual parts of their bodies, including separate doctors for the right and left eye!

• The ancient Etruscans made removable dentures and bridges out of gold and animal teeth twenty-six hundred years ago!

FOLK REMEDIES

• Two early treatments for skin diseases were to eat a lizard or to roll in the grass on the morning of Saint John's Day!

Believe It or Not!
THE ANCIENT EGYPTIANS REGULARLY PERFORMED BRAIN SURGERY— 1,500 YEARS BEFORE ANTIBIOTICS WERE DISCOVERED!

• The ancient Greeks believed that eating lettuce could induce sleep!

• Bald people in Trier, Germany, who wanted to stimulate hair growth, paid farmers to have their heads licked by cows!

• Mistletoe was once used to control epilepsy, to counteract poisons, and to relieve hypertension!

• In South Carolina, wearing necklaces of crushed onions was once a form of treatment for children suffering from diphtheria!

• An early technique for reviving a drowning person was to drape him over a horse or across a barrel.

• An early remedy for treating freckles, boils, and croup was to wear a necklace of nutmeg!

• In 1588, **Jean Nicot**, France's ambassador to Portugal, sent tobacco plants to his homeland in the belief that tobacco was a cure for cancer!

• In England, in the 1850s, a remedy for dysentery and epilepsy was to drink powdered human bones mixed with red wine!

• Guests at the Kallawaya adventure spa in Bolivia, South America, are treated by native healers who rub live guinea pigs over their patients' bodies to diagnose ailments!

• In Europe during the twelfth century, ancient Egyptian mummy skin was boiled and ground up for use as a medicine!

• The word "abracadabra" was once used in incantations to cure people of hay fever!

• An early remedy for reviving people hit by lightning was to douse them with cold water and salt for three hours!

• In sixteenth-century Europe, a recommended cure for fainting spells was to take fur from the belly of a live bear, boil it in alcohol, and place it on the soles of the ailing person's feet!

• A restaurant in Guangzhou, China, has nothing on its menu but snake, including snake wine—which locals believe will cure insomnia, glaucoma, and arthritis!

Patients suffering from a STIFF NECK in the 19th century wore a metallic collar equipped with thumb-screws.

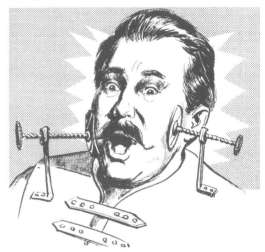

THE ANCIENT BABYLONIANS OFTEN PLACED BEDS WITH SICK PEOPLE IN THE STREET SO PASSERSBY COULD OFFER MEDICAL ADVICE.

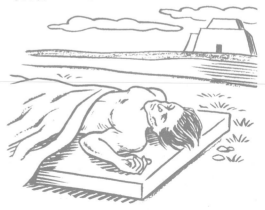

APHRODISIACS

• When potatoes were first brought to Spain in the sixteenth century, they were sold as an aphrodisiac at $1,250 a pound!

• In Europe, during the Middle Ages, chicken soup was considered an aphrodisiac!

CHICKEN POX

• Pioneers believed chicken pox could be cured by having a patient lie down in a henhouse after dark until a black hen flew overhead!

• In North Carolina, an old remedy for chicken pox called for the patient to roll three times on the floor of a hog barn then walk backwards for thirty-three steps!

COLDS

• In Sri Lanka, red ants were once used as smelling salts and as a cure for the common cold!

• In Indiana during the nineteenth century, a folk remedy for a head cold consisted of inhaling the smell from a dirty sock nine times!

COUGHS

• During the Colonial era, a remedy for people suffering from whooping cough was to put garlic in their shoes!

• The Roman scholar **Pliny the Elder** (A.D. 23-79) believed that kissing a mouse could cure a cough!

EAR COMPLAINTS

• Mouse ashes mixed with honey was once used as a remedy for earaches!

• An early treatment in France for deafness was to pour the blood of a mole into the patient's ear!

EYE COMPLAINTS

• An old remedy for curing a sty was to rub a cat's tail gently across the eyelid!

• An ancient Babylonian cure for sore eyes was to drink beer mixed with onions.

HEADACHE

• Headaches are treated by natives of the Barrancas, of Mexico's Sierra Madre Mountains, by stroking the patient's head with a live toad.

IN 1991, THE Albany, N.Y., MEDICAL COLLEGE ORGANIZED AN EXHIBITION of OVER 200 WORKS of ART DEPICTING HEADACHE PAIN.!

• An early folk remedy for headaches was to tie a piece of rope, from a hangman's noose, around the patient's head!

• An early remedy for curing a headache was to have the patient lean his head against a tree while another person drove a nail in the opposite side of the tree!

• One early remedy prescribed for a headache required running around a house three times!

• An old Scottish cure for headaches was to inhale dried moss taken from a human skull!

HICCUPS

• An early method for curing hiccups was to wet a piece of red thread, place it on the patient's forehead, and have him stare at it until he was cured!

SORE THROAT

• In Texas, necklaces of limes were once worn as a cure for sore throats!

• An old remedy for curing a sore throat called for the patients to wear sliced, baked potatoes in a sock around their neck!

STOMACH AILMENTS

• **Stonewall Jackson** frequently sucked on lemons in the belief that it would help cure his indigestion and improve circulation to his cold feet!

• The people of ancient Carthage, in Africa, placed a cow's tail on their stomach in order to cure indigestion!

TOOTHACHE

• In the Middle Ages, it was believed that toothaches could be cured by scratching the patient's gums with a splinter of wood from a tree that had been struck by lightning, then hammering the splinter back into the tree!

- An early remedy for toothaches was to rub a molar from a murdered man on the aching tooth at midnight, while in a graveyard under a full moon!

- The ancient Mayans relieved the pain from a toothache by rubbing their gums with chili peppers!

- Georgia Sea Island residents tie a necklace of alligator teeth around the neck of teething babies in the belief it will ease the pain!

WARTS

- Burnt cobwebs were once used as a remedy for curing warts!

- An early American cure for warts was to rub the wart on a grain of barley and then feed the barley to a chicken!

- Wart biters, grasshopper-like insects, are so-named because Swedish peasants once used the insects to remove warts!

CURE-ALLS

- Sick people in the Middle Ages believed they could be cured of virtually any disease if they cut their hair, then placed the hair between two slices of bread and fed it to a dog!

- The Seneca Indians, of western Pennsylvania, used crude oil to treat everything from sprains to toothaches!

- In 1995, thousands of people flocked to Cikarang, Indonesia, to be licked by a cow believed to possess healing power!

- In ancient Rome, many temples had resident "healing" dogs that were believed to have the power to cure illnesses!

UNCOMFORTABLE CURES

- In eighteenth-century London, England, wine made from hog lice was prescribed as a medicine for jaundice and dropsy!

- During the Middle Ages, one treatment for stuttering was to apply hot irons and spices to the patient's tongue!

- In Louisiana, in the 1800s, a tea made of cockroaches was used as a remedy for tetanus, and cockroaches fried in oil with garlic were used to cure indigestion!

- In eighteenth-century England, snails were boiled in tea water as a remedy for chest congestion.

- An early folk remedy for whooping cough was to put a live frog in the patient's mouth!

- Swallowing a spider and its web was once thought to be a cure for jaundice!

- Boiled toads were once used as a cure for dropsy!

- In Britain, eating fried mice was once considered a treatment for smallpox!

MEDICAL INNOVATIONS

- In 1999, researcher **Judy Siegel Itzkovich** published a study in the *British Medical Journal* that proved that the drug Viagra made flowers stand up tall in a vase and last up to a week longer than normal!

- In 1991, researchers in Beijing, China, developed a cigarette that stops toothaches!

- In 1990, scientists at Cambridge University, working on a cure for baldness, successfully grew human hair in a test tube!

- **Kirk Anzai**, of Ripley, Ontario, Canada, invented the "phone sock," a stretchy sock that fits over the mouthpiece of a telephone to deter the spread of germs!

- A patent for a device that fits between the teeth and helps curb the craving for food or cigarettes was filed at the United States Patent Office in 1965!

- **Tom Woods**, of Falls Church, Virginia, invented an anti-snoring device that prevents sleepers from breathing through their mouths!

- In 1992 **Barry Mersky**, of Bethesda, Maryland, invented a hearing aid that fits inside a tooth!

- **Doctor Crawford Long** of Jefferson, Georgia, was the first physician to use ether as an anesthetic during surgery, after studying guests at an ether party who tumbled and fell without feeling any pain!

• Twenty-three hundred years ago, the ancient Greek scholar **Hippocrates** discovered that chewing willow leaves—the source of aspirin—relieved pain!

• University of Washington researchers have invented a hearing aid that is worn around the stomach instead of the ear!

• **Kenneth L. Pagden**, of Leeton, Australia, invented a "headache treatment apparatus" which consists of an electrically heated cap that raises the temperature at the top of the head through refrigeration coils circling the brow!

• Dried and salted jellyfish are used in China, Japan, and Korea to cure bronchitis and high blood pressure!

HIGH-TECH MEDICINE

• Researchers at the University of California's Crumb Institute for Medical Engineering have designed a toy teddy bear that monitors a baby's sleep patterns and vital signs.

• In 1990, "Robodoc," the world's first robotic device to perform surgery, assisted veterinary surgeons during seven operations in Sacramento, California!

• In 2000, a robot from Da Vinci Surgical Systems performed operations to repair the mitral valves in the hearts of ten patients.

ALTERNATIVE MEDICINE

• In 1991, doctors in American clinics and hospitals began using seaweed to treat patients with skin ulcers!

• In 1992, American biochemists developed a painkiller two hundred times stronger than morphine, from the skin of a frog found in Ecuador!

• **Doctor Michael A. Zasloff** discovered that "Magainin," a substance found in the skin of frogs, helps fight post-operative infection!

ILLNESSES

• Werewolves—fact or fiction? A rare blood disease called congenital erythropoietic porphyria causes leathery skin and the growth of excessive hair on the face and hands.

• **Victor Herbert**, of New York City, sets off metal security detectors due to a condition called hemochromatosis which caused thirty grams of iron—equal to a handful of nails—to build up inside his body!

HOSPITALS, CLINICS, AND DOCTORS' OFFICES

• In 1993, a blood bank in Oslo, Norway offered donors free tickets to see *Bram Stoker's Dracula*!

• The Stanford University Medical Center in California has rooms with computerized window scenes of sunrises and sunsets that simulate the passage of time for recovering patients!

• In the eighteenth century, Saint Bartholomew's hospital in London, England, charged incoming patients a burial fee. It was refundable if they recovered.

DENTISTRY

• Doctor **Jerry Oksiuta**, a dentist in Racine, Wisconsin, removed a tooth from an infant who was only two days old!

• Researchers at the University of Melbourne, Australia, have developed a new additive for candy that helps prevent tooth decay!

• The states of Illinois, Montana, and Minnesota all require by law that dentures have the owner's Social Security number on them.

• "Dentacam", invented by Fuji Optical Systems, Incorporated of California, is a tiny video camera used by dentists that fits into a patient's mouth!

DENTISTS

• **Hannah Hutchison**, the baby daughter of dentist Douglas Hutchison of Des Moines, Iowa, was born with a single tooth!

• **Doctor Justin Altshuler**, a dentist in Boston, Massachusetts, has a pet terrier named "Charlie" that sits in patients' laps to keep them calm while the doctor works on their teeth!

DENTURES

• **Phil Parsons**, of Hull, England, has a collection of over one hundred different sets of broken dentures!

• In July 1990, **Anita Persson**, of Mississauga, Ontario, sent her old dentures to the bank as partial payment on her mortgage!

OPTOMETRY

• The first contact lenses that covered the entire surface of the eye were made by **A. E. Flick** in 1887!

• In 1947, **Doctor Milton Freidwald**, an eye surgeon in Philadelphia, Pennsylvania, removed a machine-gun spring and a steel rod from a soldier's eye, restoring his vision to 20/20!

• Doctors in India performed the first cataract operations over three thousand years ago!

PSYCHIATRY

• **Sigmund Freud** always traveled with a companion because he never learned to read a railroad time-table!

• "Counseling by Mail" offers therapy through the mail for shy or busy New Yorkers!

PHOBIAS

• "Anemophobia" is the fear of wind!

• "Anthophobia" is the fear of flowers!

• "Arachibutyrophobia" is the fear of peanut butter sticking to the roof of your mouth!

• "Chionophobia" is the fear of snow!

• "Genuphobia" is the fear of knees!

• "Lachanophobia" is the fear of vegetables!

• "Linophobia" is the fear of string!

• "Nephophobia" is the fear of clouds!

• "Ombrophobia" is the fear of rain!

• "Pogonophobia" is the fear of beards!

• "Pteronophobia" is the fear of feathers!

• "Pupaphobia" is the fear of puppets!

• "Sesquipedalophobia" is the fear of long words!

• American aviator **Charles Lindbergh**, the first man to fly solo across the Atlantic, had a morbid fear of heights!

• **King Henry III** of France (1574-1589) suffered from "ailurophobia"—a terrible fear of cats!

SURGERY

• **"Monk,"** the dog that performed a delicate eye surgery: Thomas F. Hayne of Fleeton, Virginia, had a tumor in his left eye which needed an operation. His dog accidentally scratched the tumor out and saved his sight!

• The longest operation: In 1979, **James Boydston**, of Des Moines, Iowa, underwent an operation on his arteries that started on June 15 and ended forty-seven hours later on June 17!

• **Hugh Perkins**, of Summerville, West Virginia, while recovering in a hospital, was visited by his pet homing pigeon. The bird flew one hundred five miles and landed on the ledge of its owner's hospital window!

• "Bionic eye": **Harold Churchey**, of Baltimore, Maryland, was able to see for the first time in fifteen years thanks to a miniature video camera, attached to his eyeglasses, that beams electrical impulses to a surgically implanted microchip.

BRITISH SURGEONS, IN AN ATTEMPT TO REGENERATE A SEVERED EAR, GRAFTED PATRICK NEARY'S RIGHT EAR ONTO HIS THIGH!

EXTRACTIONS

• A seven-year-old girl in Istanbul, Turkey, suffering from sore throats for most of her life, had a 1.6-inch nail removed from her esophagus.

• A kidney stone removed from a patient in Georgia in 1937 measured nearly six inches long and weighed 3.25 pounds.

• **Tracy McIntyre**, age sixteen, of Stockton, California, had removed from her right lung a sliver of wood that she had swallowed fourteen years earlier!

• To correct a breathing problem, doctors removed a plastic Tiddlywinks disk from the nose of **Ruth Clarke**, of London, England. The disk had lodged there when she was a child!

• In 1997, **Silvio Jimenez**, age sixty-seven, of Bogota, Colombia, had surgical tweezers removed from his stomach that had been left there forty-seven years earlier!

PROSTHETICS

• **Jane Bahor**, of Duke University in Durham, North Carolina, uses the plastic knee joints of Barbie dolls to make knuckles for prosthetic fingers!

SUBSTITUTIONS

• In 1992, doctors at the University of South Florida Medical Center began using coral in reconstructive surgery to replace human bone!

• **Peter Morris**, of Kingswinford, England, lost his thumb in an accident, but doctors replaced it with his big toe!

TRANSPLANTS

• In 1991, **Sarah Kelton**, of Pittsburgh, Pennsylvania, age nine hours, became the youngest patient to undergo a heart transplant!

• In 1990, doctors at the University of Wisconsin hospital in Madison implanted a second heart in **William Rammer**'s chest!

HEROIC SURGERIES

• **Nichlas Sanchez**, a Colombian soldier, arrived at Bogota's military hospital with a live grenade embedded in his leg! Doctor Richardo Uribe donned a bulletproof vest, then surgically removed the grenade!

• **Penny Pellito** of Miramar, Florida, has undergone six surgical operations—including removing a lesion and a cyst on her wrist—without the benefit of anesthesia!

• **Doctor Heather Clark** saved the life of a man in London, England, by performing emergency heart surgery on him on the floor of a pub!

SELF-SURGERY

• **Doctor Ira Kahn**, of Beirut, Lebanon, while stuck in a traffic jam, successfully performed surgery on himself to remove his inflamed appendix!

• Russian **Victor Yazykoz**, sailing alone in the South Atlantic, performed surgery on his own arm by following instructions from Doctor Daniel Carlin of Boston, relayed via email from halfway around the world!

• Seventy-year-old "Chief" Couzzingo, of Oxford, Ohio, repaired his own broken rib using a piece of metal, an ice pick, a screwdriver, two screws—and no anesthesia!

• The men who sew up their own feet! The Sherpas of Nepal, who climb the Himalayas barefooted, patch the soles of their feet with darning needles and string!

Jan Doot A DUTCH LOCKSMITH, *OPERATED ON HIMSELF WITH A KITCHEN KNIFE IN 1651--REMOVING A 4-OZ. KIDNEY STONE*

• **Colonel J. Hunter Reinburg**, of Wabasso, Florida, claimed that he cured his own failing eyesight with primitive do-it-yourself acupuncture! He was originally rejected as a midshipman because of his poor eyesight, but went on to a distinguished flying career after improving his eyesight by piercing his ears and nose with paper clips!

RECOVERIES

• **Connie Munro**, of Juneau, Alaska, underwent knee surgery but did not regain the full use of her leg until she was charged by a bear and forced to run for her life!

• In 1991, **Wendy McGarr**, of Guelph, Canada, while undergoing dental surgery, regained her ability to hear!

• **Janet Richardson**, of Overland Park, Kansas, emerged from a coma after hearing the theme song of her favorite television show playing in her hospital room!

• **Frederic Green**, age eighty-two, of San Leandro, California, pronounced dead, was revived by the flashbulb of a coroner's camera!

HEALTH AND FITNESS

• Every dish listed on the twenty-five-page menu at Hong Kong's Yat Chau health restaurant is a prescription dispensed by a doctor!

DIETING

• In 1989, **Nick Russo**, of Miami, Florida, went on a diet and placed posters in his favorite restaurants offering a reward of $25,000 to anyone who caught him eating!

In California, fitness buffs keep in shape by strapping themselves into an "ORBOTRON," a 9¹/₂-ft. gyroscope that weighs 1,000 lbs. and rotates 360 degrees!

• In their effort to lose pounds, overweight Americans spend more than $100 million a year.

STRESS MANAGEMENT

• **Cheryle Mary Russel** invented a tear-apart doll used to relieve stress! The doll's head, torso, and limbs are all attached with Velcro!

I'M GETTIN' MARRIED IN THE MORNING...

BUSINESS EXECUTIVES AND BRIDEGROOMS IN Germany RELIEVE STRESS BY SITTING NEARLY NAKED IN FREEZERS WITH TEMPERATURES THAT MEASURE −110°C!

• Stores in New York City during World War II sold mass-produced sculptures called "Wackeroos" designed to be smashed in times of stress!

• In 1991 a company in Japan introduced a chewing gum that monitors stress levels by changing its color!

Believe It or Not! IN ITALY, STRESSED OUT EXECUTIVES RELIEVE THEIR ANXIETY BY DRESSING UP AS GLADIATORS AND FIGHTING EACH OTHER WITH WOODEN CLUBS AND SPEARS IN PUBLIC TOURNAMENTS!

AT THE *BULLET STOP*, A SHOOTING RANGE IN ATLANTA, GA., CUSTOMERS CAN RENT MACHINE GUNS TO *BLAST APART* THEIR HOUSEHOLD APPLIANCES THAT DON'T WORK PROPERLY.✓

DOCTORS, SURGEONS, AND NURSES

• **Sir James Barrie** bequeathed the copyright of his novel *Peter Pan* to Great Ormond Hospital in London, England!

• **Sofie Herzog**, a pioneer doctor in Texas, wore a necklace made of bullets that she had removed from wounded gunfighters!

• **Doctor Alex Carrel**, a French surgeon, learned how to repair severed blood vessels by studying lace making!

• **Doctor Leila**, of Alpharetta, Georgia was still a practicing pediatrician at the age of one hundred!

• A sealed copy of Dutch physician **Hermann Boerhaave**'s book *The Onliest and Deepest Secrets of the Medical Art* sold for $20,000 at auction—and later was found to have only blank pages!

• After serving in the Crimean War for six hundred thirty-two days, nurse **Florence Nightingale** spent the next fifty-four years sick in bed issuing orders to her followers!

• A single carnation has been displayed in the Berg Room of the New York Public Library every day for sixty-two years in memory of **Doctor Henry Berg**, brother of the room's benefactor, **Doctor Albert Berg**!

• "Little Miss Muffet" was a real person! She was the daughter of doctor Thomas Muffet, a nineteenth-century expert on spiders who treated her illnesses with medicines made from spiders!

• In 1993, **Doctor Anna Perkins**, a ninety-three-year-old practicing physician in Westerloo, New York, charged the same rates she set in 1928—$4 for an office visit, $5 for a house call, and $25 to deliver a baby!

DR. CHARLES DREW
(1904-1950) of Washington, D.C., WHO PIONEERED DISCOVERIES IN PRESERVING BLOOD PLASMA, BLED TO DEATH AFTER INJURIES IN AN AUTOMOBILE ACCIDENT

• **Doctor William Price**, of Llantrisant, Wales, who died in 1893 specified in his will that over six thousand tickets be sold to his public cremation.

• In Dover, Ohio, patients of chiropractor **Dan Eberle** set their own fees for their treatments and pay anonymously by placing their payment in a box in the office waiting room!

PATIENTS

• **Samuel Jessup**, a farmer from Lincolnshire, England, swallowed an average of ten thousand pills a year for over twenty years. In 1815 alone, he swallowed 51,590 pills and drank forty thousand bottles of medicine!

• **Hallie Broadribb**, of Valleyview, Alberta, Canada, had her leg amputated due to cancer and kept the limb in a freezer for a year; she then held a funeral and buried the leg in its own casket!

• **Frank Amadeo** of Orlando, Florida, has not consumed food or drink through his mouth in sixteen years due to throat cancer, yet has gained fifty pounds!

- In 1978, **Doug Pritchard**, age thirteen, of Lenoir, North Carolina, went to his doctor with a sore foot. The doctor found a tooth growing in the bottom of Pritchard's instep!

- Actor **Larry Hagman** wore a ring made from a gallstone that he had surgically removed in 1995!

- **Hannah Beswick**, of Lancashire, England, left instructions in her will that her body be regularly inspected for signs of life, so her doctor had the body placed inside a hollow grandfather clock for easy viewing!

- He literally gave away his heart! **Robert Moss**, after receiving a heart transplant, donated his sixty-one-year-old damaged heart to the Science Museum in London, England!

- **Major General Daniel E. Sickles**, whose leg was shattered by a cannonball at Gettysburg in 1863, donated the leg bone to the Medical Museum of the Armed Forces Institute of Pathology in Washington, D.C., in order to visit his missing leg regularly!

- **Emperor Alexius III** (1170-1210) of Byzance suffered so much pain from gout that his regular means of finding relief was applying a red-hot poker to his feet.

- German poet **Baron Oskar Von Redwitz** (1823-1891) complained of a new illness every day for the last twenty-eight years of his life. He described more than ten thousand ailments.

FLESH-EATING MAGGOTS— NATURE'S MICROSURGEONS

Putrid flesh crawling with maggots, once a scene straight out of a horror novel, is also a venue of modern medicine today. Since World War II, medical researchers in Britain have been developing fly larvae for surgical use.

Doctor Stephen Thomas claims that maggot therapy can accomplish what no other surgical procedure can. In cases where gangrene and chronic infection have set in—often a complication of diabetes and other illnesses—hungry fly larvae can, in many cases, save a limb from amputation. The tiny maggots eat away at dead tissue with a precision finer than any surgical instrument, and because of their voracious appetites, they do an extremely thorough job.

Medical technicians place approximately one hundred writhing young maggots onto sterilized bandages, then wrap the patient's affected area with them. The maggots gorge themselves on rotted flesh, and also dine on the bacteria responsible for the infection. Three days after insertion into the wound, the maggots—now five times the size they were before the procedure—are carefully removed. It's vital to get every last one out of the wound before closing it up; if the maggots aren't removed within seventy-two hours, they turn into flies!

Patients claim there's no pain involved, only a creepy sensation as the maggots work their way under the flesh. To date, maggot therapy has saved many a limb from amputation—which most patients agree is worth a few days of the heebie-jeebies!

Chapter 43

Models, Miniatures, & Replicas

Welcome to another wildly popular Ripley's realm: our collection of models, miniatures, and over-sized objects. Herein are replicas and models created from such unlikely materials as bowling balls, toothpicks, and matchsticks. Additionally, you'll discover objects so grand in scale that their construction was a feat in itself, as well as miniatures painstakingly created in exquisite detail. A word to the wise: If you hanker for a firsthand view, many of these amazing articles are on display in twenty-four Ripley's Odditoriums around the world.

MODELS

• **Sheldon Schafer**, of Peoria, Illinois, created a model of the solar system that covers a distance equal to half the United States!

MINIATURES

• A business card inscribed with all 1,562 pages of the Bible has letters one-fifth the size of a hair that can only be read with the help of a microscope!

• **Barbara Raheb**, of Los Angeles, California, has published over three hundred miniature books, by authors ranging from Charles Dickens to Mark Twain.

• Miniature tea set inside a gold locket, part of an elaborate collection of miniatures formerly owned by **Jules Charbneau.**

• **Manuel Andrada**, of Argentina, recreated the *Crucifixion of Christ* on an ordinary dime.

• This seemingly ordinary penny conceals a tiny slide-out drawer with a photograph of miniature collector **Jules Charbneau.**

Miniature pool table, complete with balls and cue sticks, built by **Harvey Libowitz**.

A miniature wooden replica of the Palace of Seventy-two Gables in China's Forbidden City.

Ed R. Turk, of Allenhurst, Georgia, spent more than 5,000 hours carving this miniature wooden replica of the Cathedral of Milan.

Silver inlaid miniature dueling pistols.

Miniaturist **Harvey Libowitz**, of Brooklyn, New York, built a series of functional miniature cameras.

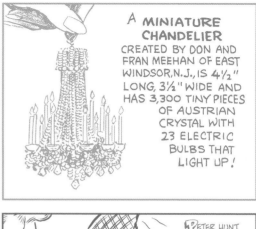

A MINIATURE CHANDELIER CREATED BY DON AND FRAN MEEHAN OF EAST WINDSOR, N.J., IS 4½" LONG, 3½" WIDE AND HAS 3,300 TINY PIECES OF AUSTRIAN CRYSTAL WITH 23 ELECTRIC BULBS THAT LIGHT UP!

• A working scale-model carousel with electric lights and moving horses, created by **Frederick Turner**, of Hounslow, England, as therapy while he recovered from cataract surgery. Built from 1959 to 1967 and requiring 8,000 hours of labor, the carousel stands 6½ feet tall, weighs 450 pounds, and features 32 animals under 400 working lights.

PETER HUNT of Sudbury, England, CREATED A MINIATURE BRASS and SILVER CHESS SET WITH PIECES SO SMALL THAT THEY MUST BE MOVED USING TWEEZERS!

The Lord's Prayer, engraved by **A. Schiller** on the head of a common pin.

The smallest playable violin in the world measures less than one inch long.

OVERSIZED OBJECTS

• Artist **Dick Rivers**, of Schenectady, New York, created a twelve-foot-tall, twelve-hundred-pound replica of a *Tyrannosaurus rex* out of recycled car parts!

• A statue of an oil driller in Tulsa, Oklahoma, stands seventy-six feet high, weighs forty-five thousand pounds and wears a size 112 hard hat.

• Students at the Academy of Science and Technology in Woodlands, Texas, built a reproduction of a 1967 Gibson Flying V guitar that measured forty-three feet long and more than sixteen feet wide!

• A shoe store in New Delhi, India, displays a six-foot-long sandal made from water buffalo hides, which weighs eighty-eight pounds and took sixty days to make!

Arthur K. Ferris, of Ironia, New Jersey, built this fourteen-foot-high bass fiddle.

The Chicago Furniture Mart was home to this fourteen-foot-high pink Naugahyde chair, once the largest chair in the world.

The gigantic Pearl of Lao Tze, valued at several million dollars.

• The largest lobster ever recorded: This gigantic crustacean, caught in 1934 off the Virginia Capes, weighed a whopping forty-two pounds, seven ounces.

"THE WORLD'S LARGEST GLOBE"
DAVID DeLORME of Yarmouth, Maine, CREATED A GLOBE THAT MEASURES 42 ft. in DIAMETER AND TILTS at 23.5°, JUST LIKE THE EARTH!

CHAD WINDHAM SR. of Pendleton, Ore., HAS BUILT A SPARK PLUG THAT MEASURES 8 ft., 8 in. IN LENGTH AND WEIGHS 400 LBS.!

The world's biggest broom, thirteen feet wide and forty feet high, created by the Deshler Broom Factory in Deshler, Nebraska.

• In 1994, residents of Bombay, India, created a necktie that measured 221.1 feet in length!

• It's your move—the International Checker Hall of Fame in Petal, Mississippi, houses a checkerboard measuring sixteen feet by sixteen feet.

• A twelve-foot-tall bronze teddy bear, weighing two tons, was erected outside a store in downtown Boston, Massachusetts!

• **Jim** and **Ruth Butler** of Oakville, Ontario, have a garden in their backyard that features a giant chessboard with thirty-three-foot-high chess pieces!

UNUSUAL MATERIALS

• The American Visionary Art Museum in Baltimore has a sixteen-foot-long model of the ocean liner *Lusitania* on display that is made from one hundred ninety-three thousand toothpicks!

London Tower Bridge, constructed by Englishman **Reg Pollard** from approximately 350,000 matchsticks, featured at Ripley's St. Augustine, Florida, Odditorium.

Six-million-dollar shoe! **Elmer O. Chase**, of Braintree, Massachusetts, built this 10-foot-long, 8-foot-high shoe from 6 million shredded one-dollar bills!

"NORTHLAND"—A MODEL TRAIN BUILDER GOES TO EXTREMES

Plenty of kids grow up playing with model trains. But most kids leave their train sets behind when they enter adulthood. Not so with model train aficionado Bruce Williams Zaccagnino. For Bruce, adulthood is a terrific opportunity—to buy more trains!

Bruce calls his sprawling layout "Northland." His meticulously detailed miniature world is home to eight miles of track and forty scenes, including a medieval castle, a city sky-line complete with skyscrapers, and a thirty-two-foot-long trestle bridge.

"Northland" is now open to the public. Bruce collects a small admission fee to help with expenses. Electricity to run the "Northland" costs a whopping $5,000 a month! On weekends, Bruce lets kids play engineer, guiding the trains through multiple levels of tunnels and tracks.

Bruce describes his model train collection as a passion gone wild. "I believe it was Emerson who said that great things can only be done with enthusiasm—well, I have a lot of enthusiasm!"

Bruce's enthusiasm for miniature trains is obvious. But believe it or not, this model train lover has never ridden on a real train!

• **Joseph Ramsel**, of Savannah, Georgia, built a miniature church complete with pews, altar, baptismal font, confessional, candlesticks, an organ, and a Bible—all out of matchsticks.

• Five hundred children built a sixty-three-foot-tall tower in Saint Louis Park, Minnesota, from two hundred thousand plastic building blocks!

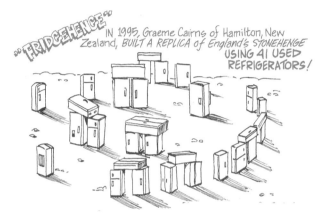

"FRIDGEHENGE"

IN 1995, Graeme Cairns of Hamilton, New Zealand, BUILT A REPLICA of England's STONEHENGE USING 41 USED REFRIGERATORS!

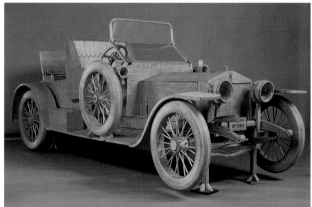

More than one million matchsticks went into **Reg Pollard's** meticulous model of a 1907 Rolls Royce Silver Ghost.

Chapter 44
Money & Finance

Believe It or Not! THE LARGEST COIN EVER STRUCK BY THE *ROYAL CANADIAN MINT* IS A 10 oz. SILVER COIN FEATURING ELVIS PRESLEY.

You're about to cash in on Ripley's wondrous windfall of fabulous financial facts. We've collected below a veritable wealth of what's weird in the worlds of currency, real estate, banking, and wagering. We'll offer you a glimpse into the lives of the wealthy, and regale you with tales of treasures lost and found.

A STACK of ONE TRILLION DOLLAR BILLS WOULD REACH A HEIGHT of 69,000 MILES!

• In 1800, the United States national debt was $83 million, or $16 per person, compared to $13,000 per person in 1990!

CURRENCY

• **Hugh B. McCullough** (1808-1895) opposed federal control over the issuance of currency by state banks, but ironically became the first federal Comptroller of the Currency in charge of all states' issuance of currency.

BILLS

• During the nineteenth century, a three-dollar bill was circulated in Canada!

• A bank robber would have to carry ten tons of money if he stole $1 billion in hundred-dollar bills!

• The United States motto "In God We Trust," according to a federal court, has no religious significance.

• During the nineteenth century, people in New Orleans had to use different bank notes when shopping on opposite sides of Canal Street!

• In 1859, **Joshua Norton** proclaimed himself Norton I, Emperor of the United States, and issued his own five-dollar "imperial" banknotes!

• Over ten thousand different kinds of paper money were in circulation across the United States at the beginning of the Civil War!

• The walls of the Cabbage Key Restaurant in Florida are plastered with thirty thousand American dollar bills, each signed by a customer!

• In 1916, dirty paper money was sent to Washington, D.C., to be washed, ironed—and reissued!

COINS

• It took fifteen tons of steel to make the eighty million Euro coins that began circulating in Europe in 2002!

• In 1999, there was such a serious shortage of pennies in Cape Girardeau, Missouri, that local banks were paying a ten percent premium to customers who brought them in!

• A load of four hundred thousand pennies fell from an armored car turning on an interstate exit ramp near Seattle, Washington!

A $1 COIN ISSUED BY CHINA IN 1928 WAS THE ONLY ONE ISSUED ANYWHERE THAT FEATURED *AN AUTOMOBILE*

A CHINESE SILVER COIN *SHAPED LIKE A SANDAL*

• **Wallis R. Cramond** of Albuquerque, New Mexico, in eighteen years of recreational running, has found over 27,594 coins!

• In ancient Sparta, coins were made out of iron and were so large they could hardly be carried!

• There are no pennies in the United States! The coin known as a penny is officially called "a cent" by the United States government!

• To pay his 1996 taxes, a man in Viarmes, France, rented a convoy of armored vans to transport 3,730,606 one-franc coins weighing twenty tons!

An **ANCIENT COIN** of Naxos, an Island in the Aegean Sea, advertised its excellent wine by featuring a drunken satyr.

COBS, COINS ISSUED IN OLD SPAIN, GOT THEIR NAME FROM THE SPANISH "CABO DE BARRA," MEANING "CUT FROM A BAR," -- *WHICH EXPLAINED THEIR IRREGULAR SHAPE*

• Sculptor **Glenna Goodacre**, who designed the one-dollar coin with the image of Sacagawea, a Shoshone native American girl, was later paid by the director of the United States Mint with five thousand of the coins!

• **Daniel Cherico**, of New Rochelle, New York, in sixty-five years, collected eleven tons of pennies—worth $32,840!

• Coins in Germany after World War I were made out of clay, cardboard, porcelain, and lace-edged pieces of cloth!

• In 1864, the United States introduced a two-cent coin that was in circulation until 1873!

• The Philadelphia Mint established by the United States Congress in 1792, used horse-driven rolling mills to make the country's first coins!

• The Denver Mint in Denver, Colorado, does not make paper money but produces forty-eight million coins a day, including thirty-two million pennies!

• In 1992 near Suffolk, England, **Eric Lawes** used a metal detector to uncover six thousand gold and silver Roman coins worth $15 million!

• From 1859 to 1873, the United States mint issued two-cent, three-cent, and twenty-cent silver coins!

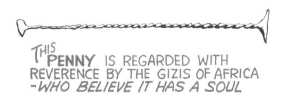

THIS PENNY IS REGARDED WITH REVERENCE BY THE GIZIS OF AFRICA -*WHO BELIEVE IT HAS A SOUL*

• Until 1857, any foreign coins made from precious metals could be used as legal tender in the United States!

• During the American Civil War, coins were so scarce that soldiers used postage stamps to buy supplies and merchants issued their own money!

• **Arnold Batliner**, a professional coin washer, has cleaned over $15.5 million in coins in the last twenty-eight years!

• In the seventeenth century, a coin was issued in Sweden that weighed 38.5 pounds—the heaviest in history!

• During a coin shortage in 1964, a bank in Wisconsin issued wooden nickels that were honored by local merchants!

• In 1994, **Tony Framingham** caught a codfish off the coast of England that had swallowed a Roman coin dated A.D. 200!

• The Trevi fountain in Rome, Italy, takes in an average of $187,400 a year in small change!

• A 1933 British penny sold at auction in London, England, in 1995 for $40,000!

• Paraguay, South America, is the only country in the world that has no metal money!

• In 1992, the United States Mint produced 1.8 billion nickels, 1.5 billion dimes, and 9,324,382,076 pennies!

UNUSUAL TENDER

• Skulls were once used as money in Borneo!

• Bars of salt bound in reeds were used as money in Ethiopia until the 1920s!

• Leather, nails, rice, and musket balls were all once used as money in America!

• In 1977 **Richard Booth** declared himself King of Hay on Wye, England, population twelve hundred, and celebrated by printing his own edible money!

• In the nineteenth century, a Russian fur-trading company in Alaska issued its own banknotes printed on tanned seal skin!

• In April 2000, the government of Brazil issued plastic banknotes!

• "Big money": The one-Kwan note used in China during the fourteenth century measured nine by thirteen inches!

• In 1932, the town of Tenino, Washington, issued money printed on spruce wood!

• Chocolate money: The Aztecs and Mayans used cacao beans for money—ten beans could buy a rabbit, and one hundred beans could buy a slave!

• Indians of the Pacific Northwest used three-foot-high copper plates with carved faces on them as money! The most valuable were worth seven thousand blankets!

LARGE PIECES OF METAL SHAPED TO RESEMBLE OX HIDES WERE USED AS MONEY IN MEDITERRANEAN COUNTRIES 3,000 YEARS AGO!

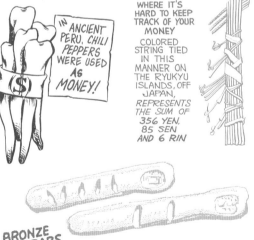

IN ANCIENT PERU, CHILI PEPPERS WERE USED AS MONEY!

WHERE IT'S HARD TO KEEP TRACK OF YOUR MONEY COLORED STRING TIED IN THIS MANNER ON THE RYUKYU ISLANDS, OFF JAPAN, REPRESENTS THE SUM OF 356 YEN, 85 SEN AND 6 RIN

BRONZE BARS WERE USED AS MONEY IN OLD LITHUANIA — *WITH NOTCHES INDICATING THE VARIOUS DENOMINATIONS*

• At one time merchants in eastern China used bricks made of dried tea and animal blood as money!

• In Ethiopia in the late nineteenth century, gun cartridges were exchanged as money and spent shells worn as jewelry.

• Needles were once legal tender in Nigeria.

• In 1685, the first money printed in Canada was in the form of playing cards.

• Nails were once legal tender in the United States—one hundred nails were worth ten pence.

COUNTERFEITING

• **Victor Smith** of Toronto, Canada, found a fake twenty-five-cent piece stamped "counterfeit" in a roll of coins issued by his bank!

"**HOBO NICKELS**" *Believe It or Not!* AMERICAN HOBOS in the 1930s CARVED COINS WITH FIGURES of CLOWNS, ANIMALS and FRIENDS TO TRADE for FOOD and CLOTHING!

• Banks in Thailand employ monkeys to detect counterfeit money!

SAFEGUARDING AND TRANSPORTING CURRENCY

• The Banco Filipino, at Cubad in the Philippines, hired a group of young girls trained in karate and judo as well as firearms, as guards.

THE **WALKING WALLET** NATIVES of Togo, a W. African REPUBLIC, ONCE USED AS MONEY SHELLS WHICH THEY WORE IN LONG STRINGS

• The first United States treasury, a small iron chest kept by **Robert Morris**, George Washington's superintendent of finances, held all the hard money that financed the American Revolution.

• In the 1850s, American bank vaults frequently contained bottles of skunk oil and gases that were hidden inside the walls to deter thieves!

AUCTIONS, SALES AND EXCHANGES

AUCTIONS

• In 1992, a letter signed by **Abraham Lincoln** sold at an auction for $1.32 million!

• Sheep that trimmed the White House lawns during **Woodrow Wilson**'s presidency contributed ninety-six pounds of wool to the Red Cross that sold at an auction for $100,000.

• A lock of hair from the head of Austrian composer **Franz Schubert** was bought at an auction in New York City for six hundred fifty dollars.

• A 1937 baseball jersey worn by New York Yankees great **Lou Gehrig** sold at an auction in 1992 for $363,000!

• A teapot made in 1743 that was found in a garage in southern England, sold at a 1994 auction in London, England, for $63,000!

IN 1993, THE TOUPEE WORN BY ACTOR *Humphrey Bogart* IN THE FILMS "The African Queen" and "Sabrina" SOLD AT AN AUCTION for $500.—

$500

• In 1994, a three-thousand-year-old Assyrian carving from the palace of **Ashurnasirpal II** at Nimrud, Iraq, which was discovered cemented into the wall of a snack shop in Dorset, England, sold at an auction for $11 million!

• In 1994, a lock of British admiral **Horatio Nelson's** hair sold at auction for $13,700!

• In 1995, a 1933 British penny sold at an auction in London, England, for $40,000!

Believe It or Not! A SINGLE SHEET of HANDWRITTEN LYRICS PENNED BY THE LATE JOHN LENNON for THE SONG "I AM THE WALRUS" SOLD for $129,000 AT AN AUCTION in 1999!

• **"Mr. Chuckie IV,"** a turkey weighing seventy-one pounds, twelve ounces, was sold at an auction in 1977 for nearly $2,000.

• **Zhang Shizhu**, a farmer in Shandong County, China, grew a watermelon weighing 41.25 pounds, which sold at an auction for over $1,000!

• In 1994 a pair of black silk stockings worn by England's **Queen Victoria** sold at an auction for $1,600!

• The world's most expensive fish: In 1992 in Tokyo, Japan, a 352-pound tuna sold at an auction for $69,273.30!

• At a an auction in Las Vegas, Nevada, in 1999, **Elvis Presley**'s sixth-grade report card sold for $8,000, a set of his keys to Graceland went for $23,000 and one of his capes sold for $85,000!

• **Didius Julians** purchased the entire Roman empire—an area of several million square miles—at an auction in Rome! (A.D. 193)

SALES

• **Mark Woolff**, of Vancouver, British Columbia, Canada, sells clothing he has worn in his workout videos, including his underwear, shirts, and socks, on the Internet!

• Beatles fan **Brian Faylor**, of Washington, D.C., paid $18,000 for the birth certificate of Paul McCartney!

• A Barbie doll dressed in a gown covered with 160 diamonds was worth $80,000!

• In the 1940s, the Bank of Mason in Mason, Tennessee, paid five cents cash for every rat tail and every pair of front mole feet sent in by customers.

• Two hundred thousand pounds of human hair, worth $1,000,000, was imported into the United States in 1860!

• An auk's egg sold in London, England, for $700.

• Car dealer **Phil Lenentine** of Calais, Maine, once accepted a cow as a down payment on a new car!

• A rare 3.1-inch-long stag beetle sold in Tokyo for $90,000!

• A Packard automobile bought by **Grace Magee** of Warrensburg, New York, in 1934 for $3,485 was sold in 1979 for $65,000.

EXCHANGES

• Each year, islanders around Papua New Guinea go on trading voyages in which shell-money necklaces and bracelets are passed from one village to another in an elaborate clockwise route!

BANKING

• The bank accounts of people in Port Moresby, Papua New Guinea, are identified by names of fish, birds, and animals instead of numbers!

• The first cash register looked like a clock, with one hand for dollars and the other for cents.

ACCOUNTS

• **"Waterhole Ike,"** a pig owned by a syndicate headed by Mark Cowley of Golconda, Nevada, had his own Social Security number, his own bank account, and actually received a $19.17 refund on his 1977 income tax.

• The Sanwa Bank in Osaka, Japan, allows animals to have their own bank accounts!

• An elm tree in Collins Center, New York, has its own bank account.

BANKS

• The bank of Tekama, Nebraska, in the late 1850s, issued $90,000 in currency backed by total bank assets comprising a shanty, a table, and a stove.

• The earliest known bank in the world was established by the ancient Babylonians during the reign of Nebuchadnessar II (604-562 B.C.)! It also had several branches!

THE "YOUNG PERSONS BANK" in Denver, Colo., is a bank that caters to children only!

• A small calfskin trunk was the sole vault of the New York Bank in the 1800s—and each night the treasurer took it home for safekeeping.

• For more than seven years the Bank of Boulder, in Colorado, has given long-term depositors expensive hunting rifles as an incentive—and estimates that up to forty percent of its deposits were inspired by the guns.

• In the 1800s, the Welsh Bank of the Black Sheep issued banknotes featuring pictures of sheep!

• At the Sanwa Bank in Tokyo, Japan, banknotes are washed and sterilized before being dispensed from automatic teller machines!

• A bank in Winnipeg, Manitoba, Canada, actually ran out of money!

• The World Bank, of Basel, Switzerland, handles no cash!

• The bank of Wickhambrook, England, is open only two hours each week.

BANKERS

• **John W. Richardson** of Suffolk, Virginia, was president of one bank and janitor of another—at the same time.

• **Dan Levalley** (1847-1937) of Garfield County, Montana, given the opportunity to withdraw his savings of $110,000 from a bank on the day before it closed, only took out $50 and left the balance to aid other depositors—explaining that at the age of ninety he didn't need much money.

• **Count Gyula Karolyi** of Hungary, carrying $40,000 in gold to a revolutionary committee in Budapest, learned that he had been denounced to the police, so he passed the money in a railroad station restaurant to a complete stranger. The money was later returned by the stranger—who proved to be Baron Rothschild, head of Vienna's largest bank.

• The human calculator: **Judge Samuel E. Perkins** (1811-1879) while president of the State Bank of Indiana, regularly counted its kegs of silver by merely hefting each barrel. Each keg held $500 in silver coins, yet he once noted a shortage of only twenty-five cents.

• **Oscar Martin Carter** (1842-1928), the founder of Houston, Texas, simultaneously served as president of seven different banks.

• **Stephen Girard** (1750-1831) a Philadelphia, Pennsylvania, banker, started his career as a poor cabin boy, but in 1814 he offered to loan the hard-pressed United States government $5,000,000.

CHECKS

• The Second National Bank of Cincinnati cashed a check written on a bowling pin.

• Employees of Tide Creations, a store in Ocean Shores, Washington, were issued paychecks written on pieces of driftwood!

• **B. V. Lilly**, a hunter and trapper, wrote all his checks on chips of wood. They were all readily accepted.

• In 1906, **Joseph Farmer**, of San Francisco, wrote a check for $28,000 on a shingle with chalk—and it was cashed!

• A paycheck received by photographer **Doug Martin** for a 1985 Hawaiian assignment, and cashed in a Provo, Utah, bank, was a coconut with $1,500 written on it.

CREDIT

• In Wisbech, Cambridgeshire, England, rents and debts were once paid in "sticks" of twenty-five eels, and the town was taxed thirty-two thousand eels a year!

• **Dom Joao de Castro** of Portugal pledged his whiskers for $500,000: "Having no gold or silver, nor anything of value to assure the loan, I am sending you my whiskers as a pledge." He used the money to build the city of Diu.

• **James Henderson** (1849-1940) of South Boston, Virginia, never bought an item on credit in his entire lifetime of ninety-one years.

FINANCIERS

• **Bartholma Welser**, a German merchant prince, loaned Charles V twelve tons of gold (equal to $100,000,000 today) and was given the entire country of Venezuela as a present.

• The queen who was pawned: **Queen Philippa** (1314-1369) of England was left as security by King Edward III to cover a loan of thirty thousand pounds!

• **Friedrich Engels**, a German capitalist, financed the writings of Karl Marx—the first communist!

• French poet **Joseph Chenier** (1764-1811) left his embalmed heart to his sweetheart with written permission to pawn it if necessary. She borrowed $200 on it from a French banker!

• Money lenders regularly visit the golden tomb of **Saint Sidi Abdusalam** in Zlitin, Libya, because they believe that by rubbing its rich exterior, they will be spared financial losses.

• The man who paid an emperor two and a half million dollars to visit his home! In 1542, **Gaspar Ducci**, a wealthy merchant of Antwerp, Belgium, loaned Emperor Charles V of Germany $2,425,000 at twelve percent interest—and canceled the entire debt when the monarch honored him by a brief visit to his residence.

FARES, FINES, AND FEES

• **Richard Dodd** of Winamac, Indiana, returned a book to the University of Cincinnati medical library that had been checked out by his great-grandfather and was one hundred forty-five years overdue. Fines on it totaled $22,646.

• The Church of the Most Holy Damn (Iglesia de la Santisima Caramba) in Guayra, Venezuela, was built with money levied on profanity.

• The highest baby-sitting fee in history: The Sauvegran Palace in Dijon, France, was built as a reward to **Symonne Sauvegrain** who "sat" for several months in 1433

for the infant Charles the Bold.

• **Usteud Muhammad Nae**, famed piper of India, was promised twice his weight in gold for a musical composition honoring Emperor Jehangir. Nae increased his weight by stepping onto the scale with all his pipes—and was paid $140,000.

• **King Philip III** of Spain paid Duke Ranuccio I (1571-1622) of Parma, Italy, a total of $15,750,000 for serving as godfather at the christening of his first-born daughter. The duke collected an annual pension of $750,000 for twenty-one years.

• The royal marriage broker: **King Henry III** (1207-1272) of England arranged the marriage of heiress **Maud de Lacy**, an eight-year-old orphan, to the Earl of Hertford, and then collected $350,000 as commission for acting as a marriage broker!

GOLD AND SILVER

• A goldfish owned by **Clara Cassidy**, of Washington, D.C., turned silver when the United States went off the gold standard.

• The richest spot on Earth is a one-and-a-half-cubic-foot spot in the United States Treasury. It contains forty thousand gold certificates each worth $10,000—totaling $400,000,000!

INSURANCE

• New York's great fires of 1835 and 1845 ruined most of the city's fire insurance companies—yet the claims in both fires totaled less than $15,000,000.

• Entertainer **Jimmy Durante** had an insurance policy for $14,000 on his nose!

• Cross-eyed American comedian **Ben Turpin** bought insurance from Lloyd's of London against his eyes becoming uncrossed!

• Inventor **Charles F. Kettering**'s brain was insured for $4 million.

• An insurance company in London, England, offers policies against being abducted by aliens!

• King Prajadhipok, ruler of Siam from 1925 to 1935, insured himself against loss of his throne, and when he was forced to abdicate, collected handsomely!

LOTTERIES AND WAGERS

• **Thurber Brockband**, of Reno, Nevada, found a needle in a haystack in nine hours—to win a $10 bet!

• **Hermann Neilsen**, of Holstebro, Denmark, rolled a marble five and a half miles in one hour and forty minutes to win a wager of $7.

• Famed French playwright, the **Marquis de Bievre** (1747-1789), made a standing offer of $5,000 to anyone who could ask him a question that he could not answer logically with a quotation from Virgil.

• **Sami Sure**, a construction worker in Beirut, Lebanon, was so broke that he couldn't pay his barber sixty-five cents for a shave. Instead, he gave the barber half of a lottery ticket that later won him $133,000!

• A woman in Haarlem, the Netherlands, found $11,600 on the street and turned it into the police—she then won $41,900 in the Dutch lottery!

• **Charles Wells** broke the bank of the Monaco Gambling Casino three times in one year, yet died broke.

• **Linda McManamon**, of Galveston, Texas, won $3.7 million in a lottery using numbers picked by her cat!

PHILANTHROPY

• The house of strangers, Bromley, England: **Walter Boyd**, manager of a Parisian bank, was given a palatial estate by fifty depositors whose accounts he had saved from confiscation in the French Revolution, and demonstrated his gratitude by sheltering fifty strangers in the house every night for the remaining fifteen years of his life!

• **Queen Matilda** (876-936) of Germany gave so much money to charity that her family eventually restrained her generosity by putting her in handcuffs.

• In 1795, Boston millionaire merchant **James Swan** paid the entire American national debt to France out of his own pocket: $2,024,900. Later, the French jailed him for debt. He spent the last twenty-two years of his life in Saint Pelagie Prison.

• **John Steele**, of Toronto, Canada, gave $125,000 to waitress Tracy Dalton as a tip!

• **Rai Khem Chand**, of Hardoi, India, discovering that he had given his entire fortune to a stranger while drunk, vowed in 1579 that no descendant of his would ever drink an intoxicant. The pledge is still honored by every member of the family, after four hundred twenty-two years.

• The temple that was built by a beggar: The temple of Mahabaleshwar, in India, was in ruins when a passing beggar, **Parshram Narayan Angal**, first viewed it. He vowed that he would some day restore it. When he later found a lost treasure, he became a wealthy banker, and kept his pledge to restore the temple.

• **Mangammal**, Queen Regent of Madure, India (1689-1706), gave $6,488,600 to charity to atone for her unwitting "crime" of putting a betel nut into her mouth with her left hand instead of the right!

• In 1990, **Jim Cirrito**, of Manassas, Virginia, set a bartending record by serving drinks for twelve straight days to raise $10,000 for charity!

• The man who left a daily trail of good deeds: **Chelebi Arditi**, a banker of Ismir, Turkey, placed fifty piasters in small change in his pocket each morning, and allowed the coins to trickle out of a hole as he walked.

• The Church of Our Lady in Hirsau, Germany, received a single donation in 1462 from a parishioner, which defrayed the costs of the weekly service for the next three hundred eighteen years!

• In 1991, the president of an ironworks company in Japan offered a reward of $84,300 to be shared by his seventy employees if they all stopped smoking!

• English pirate **Sir Henry Morgan** donated his pirate loot to a church in Port Royal, Jamaica!

• **"Amber,"** a dog in Sydney, Australia, taught to beg for money on the streets, has collected $130,000 for charity!

• Students in Burnt Lake, New York, raised money for charity by playing Monopoly on a life-size board!

• The strangest act of philanthropy in history: **Rani Bhanwani** of Nator, India, to provide for hungry ants, ordered that honey be poured into every ant hole regularly for a period of fifty-eight years—at a total cost of $2,813,000!

RANSOMS

• The strangest ransom in history! French soldiers captured by the Saracens in the Crusade of 1250 were released unharmed on payment of a ransom of eight onions for each private.

• Hampton Court in Leominster, England, was built by **Sir Rowland Lenthall** with the ransom he collected on six French knights captured in the battle of Agincourt in 1415.

• **George Washington Carver** (1864-1943) was kidnapped as a child and ransomed in exchange for a racehorse!

REAL ESTATE

• The Pot of Gold fortress: **Gatti Mudaliyar** built the Fortress of Attur in Salem, India, in 1549 after he found a buried pot containing $2,428,124 in gold. The iron pot is still on view in the fort.

• The Straw Bridge in Venice, Italy, is so named because it was financed by a tax on all the thatched roofs in the city.

• In 1881, **Hamilton Disston** owned four million acres of land in Florida—a tract equal in size to the states of Connecticut and Rhode Island combined.

• The treasure house of Longford, Wiltshire, England: **Sir Thomas Gorges**, governor of Hurst Castle, exhausted his fortune before finishing the construction of his manor. When a Spanish galleon was wrecked nearby, Queen Elizabeth granted Sir Thomas ownership of the apparently worthless vessel—but it carried $120,000 in silver bars, and enabled Gorges to complete his home!

MRS. PARAHI MATAKATEA of Levin, New Zealand, WAS THE LEGAL OWNER of A PIECE of LAND IN THE Tararua Mt. Range THAT MEASURED ONLY 143 SQ. INCHES!

• **Bartolomeo Moreni**, who built La Rotonda, a circular church in Tortgliano, Italy, saved the money for its construction by skipping one meal a day for forty-one years.

MORTGAGES

• In July 1990, **Anita Persson**, of Mississauga, Ontario, sent her old dentures to a bank as partial payment on her mortgage!

• **Henry David Thoreau**, the Concord, Massachusetts, writer-philosopher (1817-1862), recently has been offered a home-equity loan by a Boston bank for the famed cabin he built near Walden Pond and is on dozens of mailing lists.

• In Japan, housing prices are so high that some companies offer one-hundred-year mortgages so that if necessary the homeowners' grandchildren can pay off the loan!

RENTS

• Aquapolis, a floating community off Okinawa, Japan, offers housing at a lower rental than typical Tokyo apartments.

• A coin minted by **Duke Wolfgang**, of Zweibrucken, Germany, for use in paying taxes and giving alms, bore the Biblical inscription: "Give to Caesar what is Caesar's and to God what is God's."

• The city of Richmond, Yorkshire, England, has been paying rent on the island it occupies for 868 years!

• The Goddard cottages in Eastry, England, bequeathed to the city in 1574, are still occupied by five poor families, each of whom pays a rental of only fourteen cents a year.

REAL ESTATE SALES

• Land in the Florida Everglades in 1881 sold for twenty-five cents an acre.

• **Dennis Hope**, of San Francisco, California, has sold 7,753 pieces of real estate on the moon at $15.99 each!

• **Scott Moger**, of New York City, bought an acre of land in every state and resold them in packages of fifty-one-inch plots!

• White marble mansions, the most beautiful buildings erected in New York City in the nineteenth century, sold for only $25,000.

SAVING AND INVESTING

• If it were possible to invest one penny at one hundred percent interest compounded daily you would have $10,737,418 in just thirty days.

STOCKS AND BONDS

• The stock exchange in Rome, Italy, was originally erected in A.D. 138 as a heathen temple to honor Emperor Hadrian!

• Wall Street clerks in the 1900s signaled brokers in other buildings while perched on narrow window ledges.

• America's Black Fridays: The first was September 24, 1868, when the price of gold fell, causing a financial disaster. The second was September 19, 1873, when business failures reported on the New York Stock Exchange resulted in the Panic of 1873.

• A "bad news" calendar, issued by a publishing firm in San Ramon, California, highlights dates when economies collapsed, banks failed, inflation hit double digits, and the stock market crashed.

• In 1827, the New York Stock Exchange occupied one room in the Merchants' Exchange building, for an annual rental of $500.

• In 1929, a seat on the New York Stock Exchange sold for $625,000!

TREASURE

• The lost treasure of the czar: Thirty-three million dollars in gold was dumped from carts by **Admiral Kolchak** in his flight from the Bolsheviki and laid abandoned by a Siberian roadside for weeks! The treasure finally disappeared and no trace of it has ever been found.

• A woman in Toronto, Canada, had a sculpture her father bought for $2 at a garage sale forty years ago appraised by art experts at $150,000!

• **Oskar Keysell**, of London, England, bit into a hamburger and found a diamond worth $2,000!

• A Doberman pinscher in El Paso, Texas, dug up a buried bag that contained $13,500!

WILLS

• **Eduardo Sierra** of Spain received a million-dollar estate for being the only person to attend the funeral of Jens Svenson. The two men were total strangers!

• When **Henry Budd** died in 1862, he left half his estate to each of his two sons on the condition that neither son would grow a mustache!

• Professor **W. H. Jackson**, of Athens, Georgia, left his estate to an oak tree, including the land it grew on!

• The world's shortest validated will, left in 1995 by **Bimla Risha** of Delhi, India, stated: "All to son."

• In 1990, a hog named **"Mr. Pig"** and a German shepherd named **"Calamity Bob,"** of Iowa City, Iowa, were left an estate of $600,000!

In 1931, Ella Wendel of N.Y. left $30 Million in her will to toby, her pet POODLE!

• **Rosemary Ambler**, of London, England, left $32,000 in her will to the queen's corgi dogs!

• **Susan Munro**, of Fall River, Massachusetts, left $100,000 in her will to "Daisy," a thirty-two-year-old carriage horse!

COST OF LIVING

• Inflation was so high in Bolivia in 1985 that merchants weighed money instead of counting it. Inflation was 40,000 percent, and four pounds of cash was needed to purchase two pounds of fish—and printed money cost more than it was worth.

• During a period of inflation in Germany in the 1920s, one U.S. dollar was worth 4,000,000,000,000,000,000 marks!

• Inflation in the twelfth century: The Chateaux de Voufflens in Switzerland was exchanged in 1175 by Guillelme de Wolflens for a new coat for his wife.

• People in the United States spend $10 million a day on potato chips!

• In 1993, in Tokyo, Japan, musk melons sold for twenty-one thousand yen—or two hundred U.S. dollars each!

• In 1911, French house-wives striking against high food prices became so violent that produce had to be sold by police officers.

POVERTY AND WEALTH

• Rags make paper, paper makes money, money makes banks, banks make loans, loans make poverty—and poverty makes rags.

POVERTY

• A man named "Never Fail" filed for bank-ruptcy in Oklahoma City, Oklahoma!

WEALTH

• A billionaire could not spend all his fortune even if he spent $1,000 a day for 1,980 years.

• The host who burned a fortune to light the way for a guest! In 1619, the seventh **Earl of Crichton**, entertaining King James I

A BEGGAR WITH A SKEWER THROUGH HIS CHEEKS, ROAMED THE STREETS OF PEIPING, CHINA, FOR 23 YEARS COLLECTING FUNDS TO REBUILD A TEMPLE -- BEATING A GONG OUTSIDE EACH HOME UNTIL ITS OCCUPANTS MADE A DONATION

of England at Sanquhar Palace in Scotland, guided the monarch to his bed chamber by using a parchment that recorded a $1,500,000 loan to the king, as a torch.

• The statue that is a multi-millionaire: The statue of Santo Christo, Ponta Delgada, in the Archipelago of the Azores, is adorned with a million dollars worth of jewels,

and is the legal owner of many valuable pieces of real estate.

• **Edith Rockefeller McCormick**, daughter of oil billionaire John D. Rockefeller, bought her dog a diamond collar and tiara for $1,000,000, and ran a houseful of servants, but spoke only to her secretary and chief steward—and saw her children by appointment only.

• Computer software magnate **Bill Gates'** worth is equal to the entire budget of the Israeli government!

• The first billionaire: In 1715, **Manik Chand**, of Murshidabad, India, was so wealthy that the emperor permitted him to change his name to Jagat Seth, meaning "banker of the world."

• The most modest multi-millionaire in history: **Alexander Aguado** (1784-1842), a French banker who died in 1842, left a fortune equivalent today to $120,000,000 yet in his will he apologized to his family for his meager estate.

• **Queen Caroline** (1683-1737) of England, as a reward for persuading her husband King George II to appoint Sir Robert Walpole prime minister in 1721, was given an annual pension of $500,000 by Sir Robert.

• The birthmark that was worth $11,200,000,000: **Ho Shen**, a private in the Chinese army, was made prime minister and given a fortune by Emperor Ch'ien Lung in 1776

because of a red birthmark on Ho Shen's neck. Ma Chia, the emperor's favorite concubine, had a similar mark—and the ruler believed Ho Shen was a reincarnation of Ma Chia.

• The pin that made a man a millionaire! **Jacques Laffitte** (1767-1844) refused employment in a bank, was called back and given a job because he stooped to pick up a common pin! Laffitte later became the wealthiest man in all France.

RAGS TO RICHES

• **Andrew Carnegie** (1835-1919), the multi-millionaire industrialist, began his career working in a cotton factory for $1.20 a week.

• Noted bird painter **John James Audubon** was once so deeply in debt that his creditors took everything he owned—except his bird pictures, which they considered worthless.

• **Aristotle Onassis** (1900-1975), the Greek shipping magnate who amassed a fortune of more than $500,000,000, began with a stake of $60.

MILLIONAIRE FORBES KIDDO BUILT A TROPICAL ISLAND WITH A 14-ROOM MANSION, WATERFALLS and a LIGHTHOUSE ON A 700-TON FLOATING CONCRETE BARGE!

RICHES TO RAGS

• **The Duchess of Devonshire**, who was once described by the Prince of Wales as the "best-bred woman in England," was a gambling addict and died owing one million pounds.

• **Friedrich List** (1789-1846), a German economist who later became a naturalized American citizen, wrote a classic book on the subject, "The National System of Political Economy," yet severe financial reversals and other problems drove him to suicide!

• **Abdallah Es-Zaghal,** Moorish king of Granada (1485-1491) who sold his kingdom for five million golden maravedi ($17 million today), enjoyed his wealth for only a short time. Crossing over to Africa on his way to an anticipated life of luxury and ease, he was arrested by King Benimerin of Fez, who confiscated the former king's wealth, blinded him, and turned him out into the streets. For the next twelve years, Es-Zaghal was reduced to begging, going about the streets with a bit of ragged parchment on his back, reading, "This is the unfortunate king of Andalusia."

• **Arthur Hammerstein**, who made $3 million from his Broadway show *Rose Marie*, later filed a bankruptcy petition, listing a bank balance of $5.77.

• **Frankie Valli**, who became a singing star in his teens, was broke at the age of twenty.

EXTREME WAGERING—THE BET THAT GAVE ONE GAMBLING MAN A SET OF BREASTS!

Englishman Brian Zembick can't resist a bet. He'll accept just about any challenge if there's earnest money behind it. When a friend bet $14,000 that Brian couldn't live for a whole month in his bathroom, Brian spent a full thirty days sleeping in his bathtub.

But the bathroom challenge was nothing compared to the next wager Bill faced. A friend half-jokingly dared him $100,000, to get breast implants. To his friend's surprise, Brian accepted the challenge!

Brian had some trouble finding a surgeon willing to perform the operation. Then he had to come up with $5,000 to cover the cost of the surgery. In typical extreme wagerer's style, Brian won the surgery in a game of backgammon with the doctor!

As he was being prepped for surgery, Brian called his friend and gave him one last chance to back out of the deal. Maybe they could call it all off for $50,000? But Brian's friend, not believing that Brian would go through with it, tried to call his bluff. Brian awoke hours later with a new set of size thirty-two breasts.

Brian keeps his breasts tastefully concealed beneath a sports bra, and although they cause him a fair amount of back and chest pain, they're hardly noticeable. In fact, Brian dated his wife Anita for more than two months before she knew he had breasts. "He wouldn't let me hug him," Anita recalls, "He said he was ticklish."

Now that he's collected his money, why doesn't Brian remove his womanly implants? Brian explains that the surgery to have them put in was so difficult and painful that he'd rather not go through it again. Besides, for every year that he leaves them in, Brian collects another $10,000!

Chapter 45
Music
& Dance

GERMAN DESIGNER David Klavins MADE A 13-ft.- HIGH PIANO THAT WEIGHS TWO TONS and HAS A BUILT-IN STAIRCASE and BALCONY!

Music is the universal human language. Westerners tap their toes to Papuan drum beats. Babies only days old respond to Mozart. It's built into us—we're hard-wired for music. Yet within this universal, there's room for infinite variety. We've collected here a symphony of unusual instruments, amazing musical works, incredible dances, outrageous performances, and little-known facts about a few of your favorite musical performers.

MUSICAL INSTRUMENTS

• Flutes used by Inca chieftains were made from the arms and shinbones of captured foes.

• Drums on the island of Timor, in Malaysia, are carved in the shape of a human torso, because an ancient tribal hero could imitate the sound of a drum by thumping his chest.

• The national instrument of Polynesia, in the Pacific, is the nose flute—played with one nostril.

MUSICIAN Bill Milbrodt HAD HIS CAR DISMANTLED AND MADE INTO MUSICAL INSTRUMENTS— INCLUDING A DOUBLE BASS from the GAS TANK THAT ACTUALLY PLAYS!

Billy Glass, of New York City, constructed a complete orchestra out of Plexiglas.

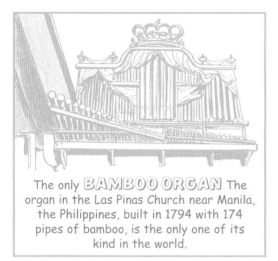

The only **BAMBOO ORGAN** The organ in the Las Pinas Church near Manila, the Philippines, built in 1794 with 174 pipes of bamboo, is the only one of its kind in the world.

THE **HORN** USED BY INDIANS OF PERU FOR COMMUNICATION - AN IMITATION OF THE MEDIEVAL SPANISH HUNTING HORN - IS MADE BY JOINING TOGETHER **6 OXHORNS**

A CELLO PIANO INVENTED IN THE 1890s WAS SUPPOSED TO ASSURE PURER TONES BY HAVING THE MUSICIAN'S LEFT HAND *OPERATE KEYS LIKE THOSE OF A PIANO*

• The Burmese trumpet is carried by one man and played by another.

THE CEREMONIAL DRUMS, USED BY THE LAMBAS of Zambia, Africa, ARE MADE IN THE SHAPE OF. *DUGOUT CANOES*

COMPOSERS

• **Khalil ibn Ahmen** (718-789), a poet and musician in Bassora, Iraq, could only write music and compose poetry when street boilermakers were making noise outside his window.

• **Johann Sebastian Bach** wrote his immortal Saint Matthew's Passion on a piece of wrapping paper.

• **Irving Berlin** received only thirty-seven cents in royalties from his first song—but just one of his other compositions, "God Bless America," has earned more than $650,000.

• **Franz Schubert** (1797-1828), the Austrian composer, once wrote eight songs in a single day.

• **Christoph Gluck** (1714-1787), the German composer, insisted he could only write his music when seated in the middle of a field.

FATS WALLER, the American jazz composer, pianist, and singer, often created the songs he recorded in a taxi on his way to the studio.

"THE PROPHET," A 19th CENTURY OPERA CREATED BY *Giacomo Meyerbeer*, FEATURED A DIVA and BARITONE *WHO SANG WHILE ROLLERSKATING AROUND THE STAGE!*

• Composer **Earle Brown** wrote a piece of music called "25 Pages" that consists of twenty-five pages that can be played in any order, upside down or right-side up!

• **Dezede** (1740-1792), a celebrated French operatic composer, never knew his birthplace, date of birth, the identity of his parents—or the source of a generous pension that was cut off when he attempted to learn its origin.

• The world-famous Austrian composer, **Anton Bruckner** (1824-1896), read daily during the last twenty-six years of his life —but only from the same two books: the Bible and the *History of Emperor Maximilian.*

• **John Philip Sousa** only received ninety dollars for all rights to "The Stars and Stripes Forever," and traded his first song for a dictionary.

• **Wolfgang Amadeus Mozart** (1756-1791), one of the greatest composers ever, memorized and transcribed a long complicated musical composition, copies of which were forbidden to the public—after hearing it only once at the age of fourteen.

• **Ludwig Van Beethoven** was paid a salary for walking! Three Austrian noblemen guaranteed him four thousand gulfen a year if he would walk each day from sunrise until noon, because he composed better while walking!

MUSICAL WORKS

• Instead of being written with notes, medieval music usually had signs called "neumes" above the words to indicate whether the melody went up or down.

• **Faust**, the character about whom fifty-three

operas have been written, was an actual person; Johann Faust was a sixteenth-century doctor of theology at the University of Wittenberg, Germany.

• Composer **Henry Kling** (1842-1918) wrote The Kitchen Symphony to be played on a piano, wineglasses, saucepans, fire irons, milk jugs, and tin pot covers!

MUSICIANS

• The most astounding violinist in all history, **Niccolò Paganini** (1878-1840), often gave concerts before royalty performing his own compositions, and those of others, on a violin with just one string.

• Violinist **Niccolò Paganini** could play eighteen notes a second!

• "The shame flute": Musicians in medieval Germany who played poorly were forced to wear mock instruments with their fingers clamped in position while they made a public apology to the music!

• Roman emperor **Nero** (A.D. 54-68) was an expert bagpipe player!

• The great Russian pianist **Vladimir Horowitz** would perform only on Sundays at 4 P.M., ate nothing but chicken and sole, and taught his students while he lay on the floor.

Billy Beahan, age seventy-eight, played a concertina while doing splits.

Mort Mortensen, of New York, could play two tunes on two pianos at the same time, blindfolded, with a cloth over each keyboard and gloves on his hands!

• **Ignace Paderewski** (1860-1941), the Polish pianist and statesman, once cut short an automobile ride because he feared the "terrific speed" of forty miles per hour would chill his hands.

• At one time, concert violinists believed that handling toads before playing would keep their hands from perspiring!

• Deaf since childhood, Scottish musician **Evelyn Glennie** can play over six hundred musical instruments!

• **Django Reinhart** (1910-1953), of Liverchies, Belgium, became a famed jazz guitarist, despite having lost the use of two fingers of his left hand at the age of eighteen.

LEGENDARY JAZZ TRUMPETER DIZZY GILLESPIE STARTED HIS OWN BAND AT THE AGE of 10!

• **Jascha Heifetz**, the famed violinist, was given his first violin lessons at the age of three.

• American soprano **Geraldine Farrar** starred in a 1915 silent film version of the opera *Carmen*!

PERFORMANCES

• The Pervyi Simfonicheskii Ansambol, a Russian symphony orchestra that made its debut in Moscow in 1922, regularly performed without a conductor!

• "Piano concert for gunshot": **Colonel Borderry**, a French entertainer at the turn of the century, played music on the piano by firing a rifle at the keys!

• **Istvan Kantor**, of Toronto, Canada, wrote and performed an overture played on filing cabinets!

• "The anvil chorus": Ten thousand singers, accompanied by firefighters pounding one hundred anvils, performed Verdi's *Il Trovatore* at the national peace jubilee!

• Former farmer **Roy Gardner**, of Mason City, Illinois, was a star attraction at Ripley's Chicago Odditorium in 1934. He had eighty pipes and strings in his set and claimed to have spent three hours per day just tuning up. Both hands, both feet, and even his head got in on the act while he played all of these instruments simultaneously.

IN 1990, ROCK MUSICIAN *PAUL McCARTNEY* PLAYED BEFORE 180,000 PEOPLE— THE LARGEST PAYING AUDIENCE FOR A SOLO PERFORMER IN HISTORY!

"THE ZOO TV TOUR" IN 1992, THE IRISH ROCK GROUP *U2* PERFORMED ON A CONCERT STAGE *11 STORIES HIGH* THAT WAS SO LARGE IT REQUIRED AIRCRAFT WARNING LIGHTS!

SINGERS

• **Tansen**, the most famous singer in India's history, was paid a fee of $3,245,000 for a single concert at the court of Emperor Akbar the Great.

"FOOD ORCHESTRA"

In 1994 at the Singapore Food Festival, a 25-member band played a selection of tunes on various kitchen utensils!

IN THE 1800s, A WORK OF MUSIC PERFORMED IN FRANCE CALLED *"CONCERT MIAULANT"* OR *"MEOWING CONCERT"* USED CATS TRAINED TO HOWL ON CUE!

• **Jean-Baptiste Solie** (1755-1812), an actor and singer, was the first man in history whose voice was described as a "baritone." For many years every singer with a similar voice was called a "solie."

• Tuvan tribesmen of Siberia sing in tenor and bass simultaneously.

SONGS

• A sixteen-year-old girl named **Euphemia Allen** wrote the tune "Chopsticks" in 1877!

Marjorie Deardorf, of Fort Wayne, Indiana, at age sixteen could pitch her voice nine notes above "high C."

DANCE

• Fire dancers in the Catawba Indian Tribe of South Carolina can hop and whirl for a full hour, barefoot, on blazing coals!

• A dancing girl of Bali starts her training at the age of five—and her career is over before she is fourteen.

• The rain dance of the lamas in the Bonpo Lamasery in Rargya, China, features the waving of a dagger, bell, trumpet, and two hundred strands of hair—one hundred of which come from corpses.

DANCERS

• A dance performed by men of the Guere Tribe, of the Ivory Coast, involves a boy being thrown high in the air while razor-sharp knives are passed under his falling body!

• **Lola Montez** (1824-1861), an Irish dancer, exerted such an influence over King Louis I of Bavaria that his cabinet became known as the "Lolaministerium."

• After a car accident in 1986 shattered her ankle, Broadway dancer **Chita Rivera**, star of *Sweet Charity* and *Kiss Me Kate*, returned to the stage with twelve metal screws implanted in her leg.

A RECORD 5,271 TAP DANCERS PERFORMED A CHOREOGRAPHED ROUTINE AS A TRIBUTE TO THE LATE SAMMY DAVIS JR. IN NEW YORK CITY IN 1990.

ANNA PAVLOVA,

The great Russian ballerina, played poker to relax, and once choreographed a DANCER'S STRIKE during the October Revolution!

THE **BOUNCING** BASQUES!
THE TRADITIONAL DANCE of the Basques of Spain and France REQUIRES ONE MAN TO BE HELD ALOFT ON A FLIMSY CRADLE-- YET HE AND THE DANCERS SUPPORTING HIM MUST KEEP IN PERFECT STEP!

HOW LOW CAN YOU GO? LIMBER LIMBO CHAMP DEFIES ODDS

When Dennis Walston, at the age of thirty-five, told his friends he wanted to become a limbo dancer, their reaction was incredulity. When he told them his goal was to pass his body under a six-inch bar, they dismissed the feat as impossible.

But Dennis Walston proved them wrong.

Growing up, Walston had wanted to become a famous tap dancer. But when he discovered limbo dancing, he knew he'd found his true passion. It took him nearly five years of practice, bringing the bar ever lower, in order to accomplish his goal. Getting his body under such a low obstacle required a special technique. Walston explained that the easy part was from the ankles to the ribcage—from there up, it became a trickier proposition.

After five years of practice, Walston is now able to accomplish the seemingly impossible: working his body under a six-inch limbo bar—without touching the ground.

"Do not let negative friends tell you what you cannot do," Walston advises, "If you believe what they say then you'll never do it. It's all about believing in yourself."

Chapter 46
Names

Signature of
CHARLEMAGNE

Want to guarantee your child success for life? Give him or her the first name "Doctor," "Captain," or "Princess." Why not? Studies have shown that our names affect our destinies— and you don't have to tell that to Iccolo Miccolo, who played the piccolo. Or Nellie May Fly, who married a pilot. We've assembled here a directory of names of people and places—everything from single-letter names to names that cover each letter of the alphabet. It's enough to make "Eggbert" and "Mergatroid" seem commonplace!

• According to studies in England and America, a child's given name can profoundly affect its sex appeal, character, and social and financial success.

BUSINESS NAMES

BAD FOR BUSINESS

• **Mr. Tuf** owned the Tuf Steak Market in Lexington, Oklahoma.

• Lee Kee Boot Factory is the name of a company in Hong Kong!

GOOD FOR BUSINESS

• Workwell and Prosper: a firm of two builders in Surrey, England.

• Take and Take Photos: Photographers' sign in Traverse City, Michigan.

FAMILY NAMES

• The **1792** family lived in Coulomiers, France. At the time Robert Ripley discovered them (in the 1920s) the family had three sons: January 1792, February 1792, and April 1792. A fourth son, March 1792, died in September 1904.

• The Angels live in Paradise, Kansas.

INDIVIDUALS' NAMES

• **Dina Might** kept things bright in Flint, Michigan.

• **A. Fortunat Mann** lived in Indianapolis, Indiana.

• **Annie Rainer Shine** resided in Luverne, Alabama.

• **Ms. B. A. Gentleman** lived in Kendall, Florida.

• **Merry Christmas Day** was born in Bellingham, Washington, on December 5, 1903.

• 100 ~: signature of **Ethyl Hundertmark**, high school teacher, Concordia, Kansas.

• God Love the Plumber: **God Love** was a plumber in Eugene, Oregon.

The hieroglyphic signature of **PETE CATTERMOLE**, a former forest ranger, of Idaho Springs, Colorado, consists of a wildcat track, the letter "R" and the tail-dragging trail of a mole.

SIGNATURE OF
BLANK BLACK,
ITAWAMBA CO.,
MISS.

SIGNATURE of French
poet MAURICE
PHILIP, who evolved
it because Philip, in
Greek, means an
admirer of horses.

Iccolo Miccolo played a piccolo in the Los Angeles Philharmonic Orchestra.

SIGNATURE OF
D. SHARP
RADIO TENOR,
Station KFBK,
Sacramento, Calif.

- **California Poppe** lived in Inglewood, California.

- **Golden Ruel** resided in Milwaukee, Wisconsin.

- **Twinkle Starr** was hit by a car in Portland, Oregon. A newspaper story of the accident brought her name to the attention of the folks at Ripley's.

- **Ms. Cali Fornia** lived in San Pedro, California.

ALPHABETIC NAMES

- **AB C Defghi** lived in Villa Park, Illinois.

- Alphabet Family: **Mr.** and **Mrs. A. W. Bowlin** have thirteen children, who together cover the entire alphabet: Audie Bryant, Curtis Drue, Era Faye, Grady Hampton, Ida Jeannette, Knola Leantha, Millard Nathan, Olivia Penelope, Quincy Ruth, Sarah Thelma, Ulysses Vinson, Wilson Xava, and Yon Zircle.

APTLY NAMED

- **A. Thistle** was president of an Hawaii weed conference.

- **Mattie L. Coffin**, who lived behind a graveyard in Beltsville, Maryland, claimed that her "neighbors" suited her because they were always peaceful and quiet.

- **Eric Gotobed** is the name of a man living in Little Snoring, England!

- **Joseph Guitar** plays the bass fiddle and lives on Music Street.

- **W. E. Towells** was born in Bath, England, and lives in Hot Springs, Arkansas.

- The surname of **Marilyn vos Savant**, a woman with an I.Q. score of 230, means "wise man!"

MISMATCHED NAMES

- **Deep C. Fisher** hated fishing. He was a real estate agent in San Francisco, California.

- **F. E. Male** is a male druggist in San Francisco.

- **Mr. A. Ball Pitcher** of Melrose Park, Illinois, never pitched a ball.

COLORFUL NAMES

- Between February 15 and April 15, 1931, **Judge J. C. Davis** of Dillon County, South Carolina, married the following couples:

Ransome Blue to
    Elizabeth Redd

Russian White to
    Mary Ann Black

Nathaniel Green to
    Amanda Brown

Solomon Gray to
    Josephine Orange

Navy Blue to
    Aurelia Chocolate

Josephus Drab to
    Blanche Walnut

Willie Lemon to
    Juanita Tann

- **Miss Black** married **Mr. Brown**. Their minister's name was Reverend White. Earlier the same day he married Mr. and Mrs. Gray of Rockford, Illinois.

LONG NAMES

• **Abraham K. Kealohu**'s middle name was Kaleialo-hakahohohol-okuakiniokeanuenue-onalanialiikoulana. His middle name means, "The Wreath of Love, Bearing the Colors of the Rainbow of the Heavens, Which a Swift Running Messenger is Carrying from the Great King."

SHORT NAMES

• **Ed Ek**, of Brockton, Massachusetts, once held the record for the shortest name in the United States.

Did she love him for his name? In 1938, Miss Birdie Snyder married C. Canary and became **Birdie Canary**.

MARRIED NAMES

• **Shirley Kinter** married **Robert Shirley**, Iowa City, Iowa.

• Nuptials of Bread and Butter: **Anna Bread** married **John Butter** in Leeds, England, April 22, 1926.

• **John Doe** married **Mary Blank**, Sharon, Pennsylvania, February 18, 1928.

• **Miss Birch** married **Mr. Oaks**! The ceremony was performed by the Reverend Maples. The couple left for Hickory, North Carolina, then boarded with Mrs. Forest on Elm Street.

• **William Gunn** was married to **Emily Pistol** by the Reverend Cannon, in Petersburg, Virginia.

• **Ethel Beard** married **Joe Barber** and now they have two little shavers, in Ogden, Utah.

• In 1949, **Bob Wager**, of Saint Augustine, Florida, married **Bet Dooley**!

• **Miss Caulie** married **Mr. Flower,** Homestead, Florida.

• Girls will be Girls: **Margaret Girls** married **Ivan Girls** in Dubuque, Iowa, 1938.

• Bump became a Dent: **Marjorie Bump** married **Samuel Dent**, in Delaware, Ohio.

WHAT'S IN A NAME?

The **SULTAN** OF **PERAK** - A TINY KINGDOM IN MALAYSIA SIGNS HIS NAME AS FOLLOWS—

KING OF **KINGS** - BROUGHT TO EARTH BY ADAM - THE GOD WHOSE RIGHT EYE IS THE SUN - WHOSE LEFT EYE IS THE MOON - MASTER OF THE BEARDED LANCE AND ARMORED BEETLE - OWNER OF THE SWORD MADE OF THE SOUL OF STEEL AND THE TALKING SABRE WHICH CRIES WHEN SHEATHED AND LAUGHS WHEN DRAWN - LORD OF THE CITY OF ROME - OWNER OF THE AIR - COLLECTOR OF TAXES BY THE BUSHEL BASKET - LORD OF THE BURNING MOUNTAIN WHO MAY SLAY WITHOUT COMMITTING A CRIME - POSSESSOR OF THE TALL COCONUT THAT REQUIRES 10 YEARS TO CLIMB - OWNER OF THE MAN OF 12-CARAT GOLD POSSESSOR OF THE CALAWANG WRAPPED IN AN UNMADE CHINDAY - AND MASTER OF THE OCEAN !

East meets West: **Mr. E. E. East,** of West Virginia, introduces himself to **Mr. E. E. West,** of East Virginia, February 5, 1937.

Washington, D.C., milkman **I. M. Wiser** was married to **May B. Wiser**. Their child was "a little Wiser."

Alexander, Graham, Bell! **Jeanette Alexander, Loretta Graham,** and **Bonnie Bell** were telephone operators for the Newcastle, Indiana, telephone company.

Question: Where do North, South, East, and West come together? Answer: in Eureka, California—over a hand of bridge! Buddies Bill North, Doug South, Ivan East, and Bill West met regularly to play cards.

Les Cool and **Les Hot** worked together at Rabeck Music Company in Olympia, Washington.

Jack Frost sold refrigerators in Washington, D.C.

Howard Cutlip worked as a barber in Spencerville, Ohio.

Lawless lawman! **Greg Lawless** was a police officer with the Bellefontaine Police Department in Bellefontaine, Ohio.

MATCHING NAMES

• **Harde** and **Sharpe** were members of the New York Stock Exchange.

• **Sweet** and **Sauer** were business partners in Chico, California.

NAMES THAT SUIT THE OCCUPATION

• **Mrs. Baker** owned a bakery on Baker Street, in Bakersfield, California.

• **I. Teller** worked as an information clerk at New York City's Hudson Terminal Post Office.

• **A. Fish** was a fish distributor in Oregon.

• **Rene Baton** (1879-1940) became a famed orchestra leader.

• **B. R. Parsons**: a parson who lived in the parsonage on Parson Street in Sarnac, Michigan.

NAMES THAT CONTRADICT THE OCCUPATION

• **A. Sickman** is a doctor.

• **Dr. Chisler** and **Dr. Payne** are dentists in Los Angeles, California.

NUMERICAL NAMES

• **Mr. Ten Million** lived in Seattle, Washington.

• "**108**" is the full name of a Hindu holy man in Amarnath, India, indicating that he has conquered all 108 sins that tempt every Hindu male.

• Frenchman **Quatorze Juillet**, whose first name means "fourteen" and whose last name means "July," was born on July 14, the anniversary of Bastille Day.

PALINDROME NAMES

• **Nilwon Nowlin**, of Coolidge, Texas, can spell her name the same backwards.

REPEATING NAMES

• **Dominique Dominique** married a waitress named **Dominique Dominique**—as did his father!

• **Mrs. Kelley Kelly Kelley Kelley** married three times without changing her name.

PLACE NAMES

• Muck City is the name of a place in Alabama.

• The town of Onoville, New York, was given that name because each time a name was suggested at a town council meeting there was a chorus of "Oh, nos!"

• Accident, a community in Maryland, got that name in 1751 when two teams of unrelated engineers both asked to survey the same plot of six hundred acres of choice land entirely by accident.

• The town of Egg Harbor was named after an egg fight that took place in 1825.

• The city of Liverpool, England, was named after a type of seaweed!

• "Truth or Consequences" is the name of a town in New Mexico!

• In 1961 the town of Hamilton!, Ohio, officially added an exclamation point to its name!

• Knawbone and Birdseye are towns in Indiana!

• "Bucksnort" is the name of a town in Tennessee and "Bald Knob" is the name of a town in Texas!

KING ARTHUR'S COURT IS THE NAME of a CITY in Michigan !

• In Arizona, there are over sixty places with the word "Hell" in their names, including Hell Hole, Hell's Hip Pocket, Hell Zappapin Creek, and Hell's Half-Acre!

William Williams lived on Williams St. in Williamsburg, Kansas.

The TOWN of ELEVA, Wisconsin, GETS ITS NAME FROM THE FACT THAT YEARS AGO PAINTERS LEFT UNFINISHED A SIGN IDENTIFYING A GRAIN ELEVATOR

THEY PAINTED THE LETTERS ELEVA —AND THEN STOPPED WORK UNTIL THE END OF THE WINTER

• "Social Circle" is the name of a town in Georgia.

• "Why" is the name of a town in Arizona!

ADJECTIVE AND ADVERB TOWNS

• "Waterproof" is the name of a town in Louisiana!

• "Droll," "Difficult," and "Defeated" are the names of towns in Tennessee!

• "Uncertain" is the name of a town in Texas!

APTLY NAMED TOWNS

• Nothing!, a town in the arid desert of northwest Arizona, consists of a snack bar, a garage, and a population of only four people.

INAPPROPRIATELY NAMED PLACES

• A drab street in Trier, Germany, completely lined by high masonry walls, is named "Look Around You."

INTERSECTIONS

• A signpost near Hope Road, in Brussels, Wisconsin, reads: Dead End Road and Cemetery Road.

• Ho Hum Road intersects with Easy Street, in Carefree, Arizona.

• In Lake Jackson, Louisiana, there are streets called "This Way" and "That Way," and a road leading to a church called "His Way."

LONG PLACE NAMES

• The official name for Bangkok, Thailand, has one hundred sixty-three letters: Krungthepmahanakornamornratanakosinmahintarayutthayamahadilokphopnopparatrajathaniburiromudomrajaniwesmahasatharnamornphimarnavatarnsathitsakkattiyavisanukamprasit!

• Naromiyocknowhusunkatankshunk is the name of a small brook in the township of Sherman, Connecticut.

• Chargoggagoggmanchaugagoggchaubunagungamaug is the local Native American name for a lake in Massachusetts. Its name translates as, "You fish on your side; I fish on my side; nobody fishes in the middle."

• Slovenskanarodnapodpornajednota, a Pennsylvania town, with one of the longest names in the United States, has only eleven residents, one pay phone, and covers only five hundred acres.

Robert Ripley in Hell: "It had been so often suggested that I go there that I decided to do so. And I liked it very much." Hell, Norway, 1928.

SHORT PLACE NAMES

• T. B. is the name of a town in Prince Georges County, Maryland!

• The river Aa runs through Pas de Calais, France.

• In the Netherlands, there is a bay called "Y" on the Zuyder Zee.

NUMERICAL PLACE NAMES

• A Greek island is named "39," as a reminder that, in 1808, thirty-nine nobles were executed there.

ONOMATOPOETIC PLACE NAMES

• "Zigzag" is the name of a town in Oregon!

• The name of a suburb of Sydney, Australia, called "Woolloomooloo" contains five sets of double letters!

• "Ho Ho Kus" is the name of a town in New Jersey!

PALINDROME PLACE NAMES

• Six towns and islands in Alaska have names that read the same forward or backward: Kanakanak, Kayak, Kamak, Kanak, Kijik, Kak.

TOWNS NAMED AFTER ANIMALS

• In Colorado, there is a town called "Dinosaur," which has streets named after fossils found there!

• The ancient city of Peritas was named after Alexander the Great's dog!

• "Frog Jump" and "Tiger Tail" are the names of towns in Tennessee.

TOWNS NAMED AFTER FOODS

• In Mississippi, there is a town called "Hot Coffee," and in Florida there is a town called "Two Egg."

• "Tomato" and "Artichoke" are the names of towns in Minnesota and South Carolina!

FORMER NAMES

• Portland, Maine, was once called "Quack!"

• "Quizquiz" was the original name of Memphis, Tennessee!

• Cincinnati, Ohio, in the 1800s was the chief pork-packing center of the United States—and was often called "Porkopolis."

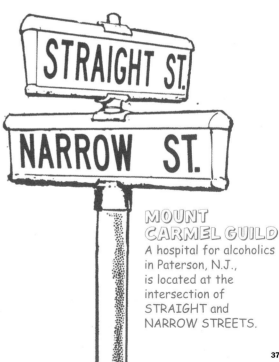

A RURAL POST BOX NEAR BROCKPORT, N.Y.

MOUNT CARMEL GUILD
A hospital for alcoholics in Paterson, N.J., is located at the intersection of STRAIGHT and NARROW STREETS.

Objects

Even the most ordinary objects can harbor extraordinary secrets, as visitors to Ripley's Odditoriums can attest. We've assembled here a collection of seemingly innocent timepieces, toys, furniture, and other familiar items, all of which have an unusual story to tell.

CLOCKS AND TIMEPIECES

• The clock that has hidden its secret for one hundred years: A clock constructed by famed

THE *Lamp* OF THE **HOURS**

OIL CLOCK THAT INDICATES THE TIME AS THE OIL BURNS AWAY

USED IN THE ANCIENT MONASTERIES

A CANDLE CLOCK POPULAR IN THE 19th CENTURY DROPPED METAL PELLETS AT REGULAR INTERVALS AS THE WAX CANDLE BURNED

French magician **Robert-Houdin** is entirely transparent and has no apparent connection to operate the hand by which it keeps accurate time.

• The Great Clock on the old city hall in Prague, in the Czech Republic, has been running continuously since 1490, but has not kept the correct time in over four hundred eighty years!

• A clock built by **August Lehrke** in 1928, in the clock museum at Goslar, Germany, measuring seven feet high and three feet wide, is constructed entirely of straw—including even its tiniest gears and second hand—yet it is still keeping perfect time.

• A wristwatch offered for sale in New York City, with a price tag of nine thousand dollars, is as thin as a credit card.

• An elaborate kitchen clock, including a thermometer, barometer, and calendar, sold in the 1900s for less than five dollars.

• The clock tower of the Chapel of Burghausen, Germany, has two clocks and two sundials, because its builders could not agree whether sundials or clocks were more reliable as timekeepers.

THE GONG BOYS of INDIA
A WATER CLOCK USED IN ANCIENT INDIA CONSISTED OF A LARGE VESSEL OF WATER IN WHICH WAS PLACED A BRONZE DISH WITH A HOLE IN ITS BOTTOM...*A BOY SAT BESIDE THE WATER CLOCK AND WHEN THE INNER DISH SANK HE EMPTIED IT, STRUCK IT LIKE A GONG AND THEN REPLACED IT IN THE WATER*

STEFANO POLETTI, A FASHION DESIGNER IN MILAN, ITALY, HAS CREATED A WRIST-WATCH WITH A *LIVING* **IVY PLANT** AND REAL MOSS THAT MUST BE WATERED DAILY!

PORTABLE WOODEN SUN DIALS ARE STILL CARRIED BY SHEPHERDS IN THE BÉARN REGION OF FRANCE AS *POCKET WATCHES*

SUNDIALS USED AS TIMEPIECES BY BUTCHERS IN MEDIEVAL EUROPE *WERE SHAPED LIKE A SIDE OF BEEF*

A SILVER CUP shaped like a fleur-de-lis was bequeathed to the City of Neuchatel, Switzerland, in 1657 by Henri II to commemorate the fact that 40 years before, its citizens had offered him the cup filled with poisoned wine.

DRINKING CUP made of glass thread, Silesia, Poland.

THE SHOE-SHAPED BATHTUB IN WHICH FRENCH REVOLUTIONARY LEADER PAUL MARAT WAS MURDERED IN 1793, BY CHARLOTTE CORDAY, WAS DESIGNED BY BENJAMIN FRANKLIN

WINE DRINKERS in Zurich, Switzerland, with an intellectual bent, imbibed in the 16th century from cups shaped like books.

THE DRINKING CUP USED FOR CENTURIES BY THE SHOEMAKERS' GUILD OF Salisbury, England *WAS SHAPED LIKE A SHOE*

COOKWARE AND CUTLERY

• There is an exhibition of Tupperware on display at the Wolfsonian Museum in Miami Beach, Florida!

• Stone knives used by the cavemen were more efficient than modern cutlery in cutting the bones of freshly killed animals.

DINNERWARE

• In 1908, **Elmer Walter,** of Harrisburg, Pennsylvania, patented a design for a knife with a mirror in its handle so diners could inspect their teeth after every meal!

• **Saul Freedman,** of Vineland, New Jersey, has designed a biodegradable mug made out of ice, for taking to the beach.

• The skull of **Caligostro,** the famed Italian adventurer who died in 1795, was used by Napoleon Bonaparte as a drinking cup.

• Researchers at Iowa State University have developed a substance, made from corn starch and soy protein, which can be used to make edible plates and utensils!

• In 1855, aluminum forks and spoons were more expensive than cutlery made from gold!

FURNITURE AND DECOR

• In 1866, American **Charles Hess** filed a patent for a one-piece combination bed, piano, sofa, and chest of drawers!

• **William Calderwood,** of Sun City, Arizona, invented furniture that can float in the air for up to six weeks!

• A company in Dysart, Saskatchewan, has developed wooden furniture that is assembled with Velcro instead of nails or nuts and bolts!

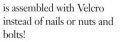

ELABORATE ARMCHAIRS ARE CARVED BY NATIVES of Dahomey, Africa, *FROM A SINGLE BLOCK OF WOOD*

Moose-antler chair, created by **T. Rassmuson** of Victoria, British Columbia.

Ripley's owns an impressive collection of silver-, brass-, and jewel-trimmed Tibetan skull bowls.

WILLIAM HILDERBRAND SR. of Frederick, Md., DECORATES FURNITURE, INCLUDING *LAMP STANDS, CLOTHES TREES* and *WALL PLAQUES,* WITH **WALNUT and HICKORY SHELLS** !

BEDROOMS

• **Ludwig Ederer,** of Omaha, Nebraska, patented an alarm bed, connected to steam pipes, that lowered and dumped the sleeper when the steam pressure fell!

"AROMA SOFA"
A DEPARTMENT STORE in London SELLS SOFAS THAT EMIT FRAGRANCES— INCLUDING ROSE, LAVENDER and VANILLA — WHENEVER THE CUSHIONS ARE PLUMPED!

SNIFF

WOMEN
of the Koniagui Tribe in Gambia, Africa, insist that chairs are not restful, and always relax by sitting in tilted concrete cylinders.

• Over forty thousand mites live in an ounce of mattress dust—that's over two million insects on an ordinary double bed!

• England's **King Richard III** had a bed enclosed in an iron grille that doubled

CONVERTIBLE FURNITURE
such as the chair-tables used in America in the 17th century, originated in the Middle Ages when kings and noblemen used convertible beds and chairs because they traveled with their own silver, furniture, and tapestries.

as a safe—with secret drawers for coins and gems!

DINING ROOMS

• **Richard E. Mahan,** of Houston, Texas, invented an electrified tablecloth

The DEMOISELLE
A wooden "chambermaid" used in France in the 18th century, was a dressmaker's dummy, held a lady's make-up pots, served as a wig stand, and had adjustable arms' holding a mirror and basin.

designed to keep insects from landing near food!

• The **Maharaja of Gwalior** used electric trains on silver rails to bring food from the kitchen to his dining table!

KITCHENS

• An American kitchen design company builds $300,000 "fantasy kitchens," complete with appliances that operate by the sound of human voices!

• In Brazil, early Spanish settlers used large clay termite nests as ovens!

KITCHEN SINKS
on the Island of Corsica ARE ON WINDOW SILLS OUTSIDE EACH HOUSE—PIPES CARRYING WASTE WATER RUN FROM THE WINDOW SILLS TO A CENTRAL DRAINAGE PIPE OUTSIDE THE BUILDING

A WASH BASIN DESIGNED BY VIOLLET-LE-DUC OF FRANCE, IN 1849, FEATURED A MINIATURE GOTHIC CASTLE OF BEATEN COPPER

The WEATHER-VANE on the Church at Sonning, England, shames parishioners by showing the pastor preaching to empty chairs.

Personalized WEATHERVANES were common in America in the 1870s, were often 3½ feet long, 3-dimensional, and made of copper, iron, and zinc.

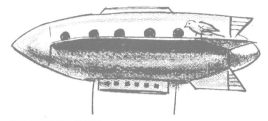

BIRDHOUSE made by blacksmith David L. Schwartz of Berne, Ind., in the shape of a blimp.

LIVING ROOMS

• That's a lot of couch potatoes! A sofa displayed at a furniture fair in Bangkok, Thailand, measured twenty-one feet in length, was ten feet tall, and weighed 1,146 pounds!

• Artist **Willie Cole,** of Newark, New Jersey, created a chair out of high-heeled shoes!

PATIO, PORCH, AND LAWN

• A company in the United States has invented an inflatable sofa, to be used outdoors, that squirts water to keep you cool!

HOUSEHOLD APPLIANCES

• **Abbey Mae Fleck,** age eight, of Saint Paul, Minnesota, invented a kitchen gadget for cooking bacon upright so that all the fat drains away!

• "Big Tex": **Raymond Rodriguez,** of San Diego, California, designed and built a barbecue grill in the shape of a six-shooter gun that stands five feet tall and is ten feet long!

LIGHTING

• Fireflies, or "cucujos," found in the West Indies and South America, emit a glow that is bright enough to read by and are placed in lanterns for use as lights!

• The great chandeliers in the council chamber of the palace of Gwalior, India, which weigh two tons each, were hung only after the building's strength had been tested by leading two elephants across the ceiling.

PERSONAL OBJECTS

• There is enough graphite in a pencil to draw a line thirty-five miles long!

• An eyeglass case owned by **"Diamond" Jim Brady** was adorned with a miniature locomotive made with two hundred and ten diamonds.

• Umbrellas were so expensive in nineteenth-century England that on rainy days most people rented them by the hour rather than buying their own.

TOYS

• Since 1950, over three hundred million "Silly Putty" eggs, with forty-five hundred tons of putty inside, have been sold in North America!

• American jigsaw puzzle-maker **Steve Richardson** often puts into puzzle boxes extra pieces that don't fit anywhere in the puzzle!

• A company in San Francisco, California, created a kite decorated with over one hundred sixty diamonds, rubies, and sapphires, that sells for $100,000!

DURING the 19ᵗʰ CENTURY MINIATURE GUILLOTINES WERE A POPULAR TOY GIVEN TO EUROPEAN CHILDREN!

• A company in Littleton, Colorado, called "My Twinn," will create a doll that looks just like your child, right down to the same hair, eye color, facial features, and clothing!

• Six eight-studded Lego pieces can be connected 102,981,500 different ways!

• The original name for Wham-O's flying saucer toy was the "Pluto Platter"!

Believe It or Not!

THE *HULA-HOOP* WAS FIRST DEVELOPED IN ANCIENT EGYPT AND MADE OUT of *GRAPEVINES!*

A new fad among North American kids is MINI SKATE-BOARDS for the middle and index fingers to ride!

THE WORLD'S ONLY SELF-PROPELLED SUITCASE

In a world full of energy crunches and traffic snarls, it's no wonder we're reaching for bizarre extremes for transportation solutions. Ripley's recently discovered a unique item that solves a number of transportation problems at once.

It's actually two objects in one, both an article of luggage, and a mode of transportation—a suitcase that converts into a go-kart!

The go-kart suitcase, of which only two exist in the world, looks like any other heavy-duty piece of luggage when closed. But this suitcase can do what no other can: within fifteen seconds, it can be opened up, assembled—and driven away!

The go-kart operates on an air-cooled two-stroke engine capable of propelling the odd buggy at more than thirty miles per hour. It features a shallow seat for the driver, insect-like headlights, and a single hand brake.

It might look a bit odd to see somebody driving a piece of luggage down the road. But with the go-kart suitcase, you never need to hunt for a parking space!

The full name of the doll "BARBIE" is actually "BARBIE MILLICENT ROBERTS"!

MISCELLANEOUS OBJECTS

• The weathervane on Saint Martin's Church, Ellisfield, Hampshire, England, was fashioned by **Sir Christopher Wren** in the 1700s in the shape of an insect—to indicate what he thought of the parishioners who were miserly with their payments.

An ANCIENT SWIVEL KEY, the inside of which turns one way in the keyhole while its outer barrel turns in the opposite direction.

• A wooden typewriter in Bayreuth, Germany, manufactured in 1861, was still usable one hundred years later.

• Linen bags imprinted with the owner's name and ready to be stuffed with prized possessions were kept in Colonial American homes in case of fire.

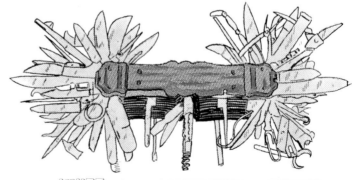

A KNIFE with 384 blades—each blade is different. Made by John Hayes, Limerick, Ireland.

Chapter 48
Occult

Believe It or Not.!
ACCORDING TO THE *VAMPIRE RESEARCH CENTER* in Elmhurst, N.Y., *THERE ARE 550 KNOWN VAMPIRES LIVING IN THE UNITED STATES.!*

Do you believe in creatures of the night? Of course, nearly all of us deny it—in the light of day. But throughout human history enough of us have nourished a healthy respect for ghosts, demons, vampires, and various other species of the undead to keep a spine-tingling tradition of tales and superstitions alive. Read on, but be prepared to sleep with the lights on tonight!

GHOSTS

• The man whose icy grave was revealed by a ghost! **Sir John Franklin** (1786-1847), the British Arctic explorer, perished with one hundred twenty-eight men when his ships were trapped in the Arctic ice. A later expedition located the spot, by using a map revealed to Franklin's widow by the spirit of a four-year-old girl.

• If a member of a Navajo family dies, his family deserts their home, considering it a "haunted house."

WITCHCRAFT

• **Mary Lamont**, of Renfrew, Scotland, was burned as a witch in 1622 on a charge that she planned to throw the feared Witch's Stone of Tower Hill into the sea to cause shipwrecks.

FROM 1984 to 1989, CHESS MASTER and SPIRITUALIST Victor Korchnoi PLAYED A CHESS MATCH THROUGH A MEDIUM WITH Geza Maroczy WHO DIED in 1951.!

"KNIGHT TO PAWN."

"GHOST MONTH"
IN Taiwan, GHOSTS FROM HELL ARE BELIEVED TO WALK THE EARTH EVERY YEAR DURING THE SEVENTH LUNAR MONTH.!

BRAZILIAN WRITER AND SPIRITUAL MEDIUM CHICO XAVIER IS A BEST-SELLING WRITER WITH OVER 380 BOOKS THAT HE CLAIMS WERE ALL WRITTEN BY REAL GHOSTS!

• In western Brittany and some parts of Russia, the rabbit is hated as an associate of witches, who are believed to enter its body at will.

• The Witch's Stone in Dornoch, Scotland, marks the spot where in 1722 **Janet Horne** was burned as a witch because she mispronounced one word in the Gaelic version of the Lord's Prayer.

• In 1471 in Basel, Switzerland, a hen found guilty of laying a brightly colored egg was burned at the stake!

• In 1692, in Salem, Massachusetts, a dog was found guilty of witchcraft and executed!

• "976-Spell": In Los Angeles, California, people can "dial-a-witch" to have a curse put on someone they dislike!

• Sharp probes were used by sixteenth century European witch hunters to search victims for "the devil's mark"—skin areas such as a healed scar that did not bleed.

• In 1881 in Athens, Tennessee, a horse named "Henny" was accused of witchcraft and burned to purge the devil!

• In eighteenth century France, a cow found guilty of sorcery was publicly hanged!

• **Lydia Gilbert**, of Windsor, Connecticut, was held responsible for the death of Henry Stiles in 1654, although she was not even nearby when he was fatally shot! **Thomas Allen** had left a loaded, cocked musket leaning against a tree. He knocked it to the ground, shooting Stiles. He was let off with just a fine and Gilbert was hanged as a witch.

CREATURES OF THE NIGHT

• The world's first "Dracula congress" took place in 1995 in a medieval castle in Bran, Rumania!

BELIEVE IT OR NOT! WITCHCRAFT WAS A CRIME IN THE UNITED KINGDOM *UNTIL 1951!*

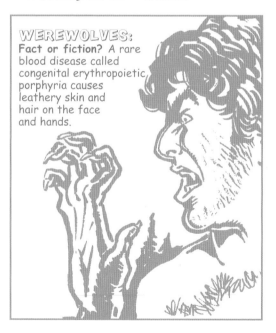

WEREWOLVES: **Fact or fiction?** A rare blood disease called congenital erythropoietic porphyria causes leathery skin and hair on the face and hands.

Since 1984, there have been 519 car accidents on a 40-mile stretch of Alabama highway that locals believe is haunted by the **RESTLESS SPIRITS OF CREEK INDIANS** buried there!

Mary Elizabeth Feldman of Charleston, S.C., has invented **"GHOST AWAY,"** a chamomile-based spray for children to use against ghosts and monsters under the bed!

VAMPIRE HUNTER'S TOOL KIT

Are you prepared for a vampire attack? Many of us in this skeptical modern era are not. But just a century or two ago, the belief in blood-sucking creatures of the night was strong enough that certain individuals felt it necessary to keep a few choice anti-vampire tools on hand. Hence, a small lacquered box that has found its way into Ripley's collection is an eighteenth century vampire extermination kit!

The handsome wooden box, lined with red velvet, contains everything a mortal might need to ward off an attack of the undead: a vial of holy water, a necklace of garlic, and a polished wooden stake for skewering the bloodsucker through the heart. But most effective of all: a small pistol in the shape of a crucifix, designed to shoot—you guessed it—silver bullets!

IT IS CUSTOMARY in Japan for THE FAMILY of A DECEASED PERSON *TO HAND OUT SMALL PACKETS of SALT TO MOURNERS TO PROTECT THEM FROM THE DEAD!*

Chapter 49
Photography

Here in our gallery of phenomenal photographic facts, we'll introduce you to some of photography's most amazing innovations—from the earliest exposures to the remarkable high-tech cameras of the future. You'll also meet photographers with unusual subject matter and astonishing techniques, and discover unusual facts about a few of the world's most famous shutterbugs.

• American photographers, according to the Photo Marketing Association International, take twelve billion photos per year, or almost three hundred eighty pictures per second—stacked up they would form a pile eighteen hundred miles high.

PHOTOGRAPHY'S BEGINNINGS

• Photography was invented simultaneously in 1839 by two men who worked entirely independent of each other, in different countries.

• **Dorothy Catherine Draper,** the subject of a daguerreotype made by her father in 1840, was the first person ever photographed with her eyes open.

THE FIRST PHOTOGRAPH
A PHOTOGRAPH MADE BY NICEPHORE NIEPCE, NEAR CHALON-SUR-SAONE, FRANCE, IN 1826 --USING AN 8-HOUR EXPOSURE AND A POLISHED PEWTER PLATE COATED WITH BITUMEN OF JUDEA

• The world's most expensive photo: A daguerreotype made by Albert Sands Southworth of himself circa 1848, was sold in 1980 for thirty-six thousand dollars.

• Early photographers often put each subject's head in a clamp to keep them still because the exposure time for a photograph was fifteen minutes long.

• The first daguerreotype of a human being: A photograph of a Paris boulevard made by **Louis Jacques Mande Daguerre** in 1839, included in the left foreground an unidentified man getting his boots shined.

• A photograph made by **Robert Cornelius,** of Philadelphia, Pennsylvania, of himself in 1839, is the world's earliest known photographic portrait.

CAMERAS AND PHOTOGRAPHIC EQUIPMENT

• An aerial camera used in 1930 was so large that it used a film roll seventy-five feet long and had to be carried by two men.

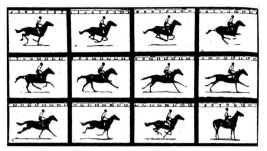

THE FIRST PHOTOGRAPHS OF MOTION
WERE PICTURES OF A HORSE MADE IN THE 1870'S BY
EADWEARD MUYBRIDGE OF SAN FRANCISCO, CALIF.
--WHO USED 24 STILL CAMERAS OPERATED BY
STRINGS STRETCHED ACROSS A RACE TRACK

THE LARGEST CAMERA EVER MADE
A CAMERA MADE IN 1899 TO PHOTOGRAPH AN ENTIRE TRAIN
IN DETAIL, WEIGHED 1,400 POUNDS, WAS 20 FEET LONG, AND
USED A NEGATIVE THAT MEASURED 10 FEET BY 8 FEET

A GUN invented by Rudy
Ortega and Mike Askew
of Jacksonville, Fla.,
has a camera in its butt
which takes a picture
0.25 seconds before it
is fired—giving conclu-
sive evidence whether
or not the person fired
at was armed.

PHOTOGRAPHERS
in the 1870s, using
wet plates, had to
coat them, expose
them, and develop
them immediately—
using portable
equipment often
carried on their backs.

• The world's largest
photographic negative,
measuring one hundred
eighty feet in length and
five inches wide—is of a
coast-to-coast aerial shot
of the United States!

SCIENTIFIC CAMERAS

• Pictures that get under
your skin: The electronic
thermograph, a medical

DETERMINED PHOTOGRAPHERS
OF THE PRIM 1890s BOUGHT DECEPTIVE-ANGLE BOX
CAMERAS THAT MADE IT APPEAR AS IF THEY WERE
SNAPPING PICTURES AHEAD OF THEM BUT, IN FACT,
THEY WERE PHOTOGRAPHING MUCH MORE
INTERESTING SUBJECTS ON THE SIDE

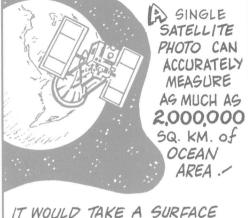

A SINGLE SATELLITE PHOTO CAN ACCURATELY MEASURE AS MUCH AS **2,000,000** SQ. KM. of OCEAN AREA!

IT WOULD TAKE A SURFACE VESSEL TRAVELING 10 KNOTS OVER **10 YEARS** TO MAKE THE SAME MEASUREMENTS!

SURVEILLANCE PHOTOGRAPHY

• A cravat camera invented by **E. Block,** of Paris, France, in 1890 took pictures through a tiny lens that looked like a stickpin.

• The first "spy satellite": In 1909 a tiny automatic camera was attached to a pigeon, enabling the bird to function as a high-flying spy for the military.

WHIMSICAL CAMERAS

• A camera marketed in France in 1882 was shaped like a pistol.

• At the Outlook Tower in Edinburgh, Scotland, visitors can view the city from inside the one-hundred-thirty-one-year-old "camera obscura," a giant version of the first camera invented by **William Talbot**!

A **MINIATURE TV CAMERA** CAN ENABLE A BLIND PERSON TO SEE BY TRANSMITTING IMAGES TO THE BRAIN THROUGH *THE STOMACH NERVES*

diagnose ailments as varied as muscle spasms and migraine headaches!

STATE-OF-THE-ART CAMERAS

• **Henry Abramson,** of Montreal, Canada, has invented a still camera that creates photographs that appear to move!

• A thirty-five-millimeter camera bought by a Saudi Arabian was made of gold covered with blue lizard skin, studded with diamonds—and cost $32,000.

instrument that resembles a television camera, takes infrared pictures of heat variations in as many as sixty-four thousand different parts of the body—helping doctors

"*FLYING CAMS*," DEVELOPED IN BELGIUM, ARE VIDEO CAMERAS MOUNTED ON *FIVE-FOOT-LONG,* RADIO-CONTROLLED HELICOPTERS *THAT CAN FLY UP TO 50 MPH!*

A **LONG-RANGE CAMERA** PERFECTED FOR THE U.S. ARMY AND EQUIPPED WITH 100-INCH TELEPHOTO LENS, PICTURES IMAGES AT A *DISTANCE OF 30 MILES*

PHOTOGRAPHIC SUBJECTS

• The photo-processing department of a British supermarket has a collection of twenty-four thousand photographs of fingers and thumbs that were taken accidentally by amateur photographers!

PHOTOGRAPHS OF CELEBRITIES AND HEADS OF STATE

• Bus driver **Gary Watson** has been photographed with over thirty-eight hundred celebrities, including three Presidents.

• A photo of **Abraham Lincoln** and his youngest son, **Tad**, taken on February 9, 1864, six inches long, and signed by Lincoln himself, sold at an auction in 1985 for $104,500.

• The **Imam Yahia**, the king of Yemen, is the only head of a member country of the United Nations who has never been photographed. He has forbidden his picture being taken under pain of drastic punishment!

• The photograph of American President **Andrew Jackson**, taken shortly before he died by famed photographer Mathew Brady, was denounced by Jackson as making him "look like a monkey."

ANDREW JACKSON AT THE AGE OF 78 BECAME THE FIRST U.S. PRESIDENT *TO HAVE HIS PICTURE TAKEN*

A portrait of LINCOLN made him President of the United States! "It dispelled the opposition base on the rumors of my long, ungainly figure, large feet, clumsy hands, and long, gaunt head; making me into a man of human aspect and dignified bearing." He was nominated 3 months after it was taken and publicly circulated.

The famous photograph of the attempted assassination of New York's Mayor William J. Gaynor in 1910, was made by cameraman William Warnecke only because he arrived too late for the regular photo session and was still trying for a picture after his competitors had left.

PHOTOGRAPHS OF NATURAL PHENOMENA

• The first photograph of a tornado was made in Miner County, South Dakota, August 28, 1884.

• Swiss scientist **Dominique Muller** created the world's first photograph of a memory—the images shows two brain cells touching!

PHOTOGRAPHS OF RARE ANIMALS

• The quagga, a striped donkey exhibited in the London Zoo for twenty-one years, was the only one of its species ever photographed alive. The quagga became extinct in 1878.

• "**Chester**," an eight-hundred-pound Alaskan brown bear raised in California's San Diego Zoo, was so popular that over one hundred million photos of him were taken over the years.

MOTION PICTURE PHOTOGRAPHY

• British photographer **William Friese-Greene** (1855-1921) invented in 1889 the first motion picture camera to use celluloid film.

• **Thomas A. Edison**, after inventing the motion picture camera and projector in the 1880s, refused to spend $150 for an international copyright, insisting, "It's not worth it."

• The **Lumière** brothers of France, widely acclaimed as the first filmmakers in the world, made over two thousand films between 1896 and 1900, most running less than a minute. They invented their own film camera and projection system—but they thought the cinema had no commercial future.

• Motion picture film in the early 1900s was "spliced" by sewing frames together with needle and thread.

• The film "Star Wars Episode I: The Phantom Menace" was the first movie in the world to be distributed in digital format and shown on digital projectors!

• Canadian cartoon animator **Norman McClaren** doesn't use a camera—he draws his cartoons directly on the film!

PHOTOGRAPHERS

THE PHOTOGRAPHY BUSINESS

• Professional photographers in the early 1900s used large papier-maché eggshells and stuffed storks for baby pictures.

• Chocolate Pix, a company in Toronto, Canada, created edible photographs printed on chocolate!

FAMOUS PHOTOGRAPHERS

• **Louis Jacques Mande Daguerre**, inventor of the daguerreotype, the first glass-plate photographs, had an aversion to having his own picture taken.

• The man who was proud to be known as a number: **Alfred Stieglitz** (1864-1946), father of modern photography, was so closely identified with his photo art gallery, which had the street number "291," that he often signed his correspondence "291."

• A new book of photographs by photographer **Helmut Newton** weighs 180.4 pounds and comes with its own coffee table!

• **George Eastman** (1854-1932) who popularized photography by introducing roll film and the box camera, also devised pre-measured packaging of cake and bread mixes.

• **Edward Steichen** (1879-1973), the famed photographer, once spent a full year and took one thousand photos of a white cup and saucer to achieve a perfect print.

• Civil War photographer **Mathew Brady** made many of his famed photos of window panes from shell-wrecked houses. He became a financial success in 1860 when the Prince of Wales crossed the Atlantic specifically to have Brady take his picture, but in 1875 he lost many of his priceless photos because he could not pay a warehouse storage charge.

LOUIS BOUTAN, a Frenchman who was the first underwater photographer, took pictures at a depth of 164 feet in 1893, with his camera supported by a floating barrel.

• **Heartha Bauer**, whose work was the subject of a special exhibition at New York City's New School for Social Research, spent five years traveling around the city shooting twelve thousand photographs of its manhole covers!

PHOTOGRAPHERS WITH UNUSUAL TECHNIQUES

• **Jeremy Lynch**, a photographer in Toronto, Canada, uses only polluted water to develop his photographs—the more polluted the water, the better the images!

• Professor shoots birds with machine gun yet they all live! Professor **E. J. Marey** of Paris, France, invented a photographic machine gun with a lens in its barrel that could take a series of pictures of birds in flight!

• The flip-flop picture: A photograph made at a high school track meet in 1947, by **Roger Williams** of Kingston, Rhode Island, won two prizes when it was published right-side up, three prizes when it was published upside down, and later was published by a national magazine—on its side.

PHOTOGRAPHERS WITH UNUSUAL SUBJECT MATTER

• The lightning hunters: **Larry** and **Stephen Collins**, of Knoxville, Tennessee, who chase and film lightning storms, were in a six-by-six-foot forest tower when a bolt crashed in and struck the compass between the two—leaving them unharmed!

• **Doris Carly** has photographed every one of the 8,828 houses in her hometown of New Weston, Massachusetts.

Photograph made without a camera or lens, by **L. F. Craven.**

FIRE-CHASER RISKS HIS LIFE TO CAPTURE WILDFIRES ON FILM

"I want to fill my lens with fire," says photographer Scott Meadors of his odd obsession with wildfires. "The fire seems alive." For years, Scott has risked life and limb to capture some of the country's deadliest and most unpredictable fires on film.

Scott's fascination with conflagrations began the day his father, a natural disaster photographer, took him to his first fire. Scott was fifteen and from that moment on, he was hooked.

Scott has frequently put his life on the line to get just the right shot. "I've been so close that heat was singeing the hair off my arms." Scott ventures deep inside the kinds of fires other people flee. He knows that once he's inside the borders of a fire, he has to stay on his toes, because conditions can change in an instant. The unpredictable nature of wildfires is one of the things he appreciates most, even though in 1996, that unpredictability nearly cost him his life.

When Scott got the call about a monstrous brush fire in Malibu, he knew instinctively that he was in for a wild ride. Nevertheless, he followed firefighters into the thick of it. Moments after entering the swirling smoke, Scott lost sight of his escort. Soon, he was alone, with fire raging on every side.

At one point, Scott stepped out of his car to get a shot. The heat was almost unbearable. He got back into his truck and drove a few yards further. As he looked back, he saw the spot where he had been standing suddenly vanish in a wall of flames—if he had not moved when he did, he'd have taken his last photo.

He got back out of the truck to shoot some more. Then suddenly, a swirling shower of embers flew up out of nowhere. With his camera rolling, Scott tried to make his way back to his vehicle. All at once, the ground below him vanished in a flurry of hot sparks. Then the wind shifted, allowing Scott to reach the safety of his truck. The incredible footage that resulted netted Scott eighty thousand dollars.

But rather than dampening his enthusiasm, that close call has only fanned the flames of Scott's obsession: "I've never been so scared that I thought that I wouldn't do it anymore. It's a passion, and I can't make that go away."

- **Flo Fox**, a New York photographer whose work has been exhibited in galleries in New York and London, is legally blind.

- **Jose A. Ilgesias**, a photographer blinded during World War II, has published two books of his own photographs!

American photographer ARTHUR S. MOLE, using 18,000 World War I soldiers, created a living Statue of Liberty!

"CAMERA VAN" Harrod Blank of El Cerrito, Calif., COVERED A VAN WITH 1,705 CAMERAS — MANY OF WHICH WORK AND TAKE PHOTOS AS HE DRIVES!

Chapter 50

Plants, Trees, & Fungus

Five tulips on one stem, grown by **Peggy Lilienthal** of San Francisco, California.

What tree is struck by lightning more frequently than any other? What flower blooms exclusively underground? Where can you find a plant that can be lit like a torch, and will burn brightly for days? Welcome to Ripley's compendium of bizarre botanicals, where we'll introduce you to some of the world's most unbelievable plant life.

FLOWERS

• In 1991, botanists in New Zealand accidentally discovered "*Corybas carseii*," a rare orchid that blooms only two days a year, after they sat on the flower while eating lunch!

• The european bee orchid (*Ophrys apifera*) is so named because its blossoms look like bees.

• Hyacinth bulbs, normally costing thirty-five cents, became so popular in France after **King Louis XV** bought $200,000 worth for Madame de Pompadour, that their price soared to $500 for a single bulb.

• *Shortia galacifola*, a rare wild flower first discovered in 1788, was not seen again until 1877, eighty-nine years later.

• Wolffia, only $1/_{25}$th of an inch long, is the smallest flowering plant in all nature.

A TULIP GREW in Rev. C.N. Van Dyke's DRIVEWAY in Shubert, Neb., *THROUGH 10 INCHES of* ROCK and BLACKTOP!

ROSES HAVE BEEN ON EARTH *for* 115 MILLION YEARS!

SNIFF

PLANTS

• The living candles of the Andes: *Puya raimondii*, a plant that grows to a height of thirty-three feet, is so saturated with resin that shepherds use it as a candle—it will burn for days!

• The grass is not always greener! Barnyard grass and love grass are purple, while prairie, three-awn grass is white and northern drop grass is black!

• **Charles Abbott** of Exeter, England, has a collection of over eight thousand cacti that he regularly shampoos and trims!

The CROWN OF THORNS A Madagascar cactus can be trained to grown in a circular shape so it can be worn in holiday festivals.

• A lemon vine, which still flourishes in the West Indies, is the parent plant from which all cacti evolved sixty million years ago.

• The string-of-buttons cactus looks like buttons strung on a thread.

• The sundew plant has hairs on its leaves, which glisten in the sun like drops of dew, luring thirsty insects—which the plants smother and devour.

NATURE'S APARTMENT HOUSE FOR BIRDS
THE SAGUARO, A GIANT CACTUS, SERVES AS THE NESTING PLACE FOR THE GILDED FLICKER, THE GILA WOODPECKER, ARIZONA FLYCATCHER, ELF AND SAGUARO OWLS—*SIMULTANEOUSLY*

• The peuririma palm of the South American Amazon grows to a height of fifteen feet—yet its stem is no thicker than a man's finger.

• *Halostachys caspia*, a desert plant, has roots fifteen times as long as its height above ground.

The OLD MAN'S BEARD, a Brazilian plant that grows without roots on the branches of trees, is used by birds in building their nests—but it spreads so rapidly it drives the birds out of the nest.

• Spanish moss, which grows in gray festoons from trees in the southern United States, is not a moss—it is a member of the pineapple family.

• The seedless water lily of the tropics grows a new plant from the center of its leaf.

VICTORIA REGIA, A GIANT WATER LILY, has 8-ft.-wide leaves that can support the weight of an average-sized person!

THE SILVERSWORD GROWS ONLY IN HAWAII

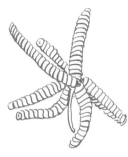

The SCREW BEAN has a pod that looks like spirally twisted wire.

The TURK'S CAP, an edible gourd, looks like a broad-brimmed hat.

• The bladderwort, an aquatic plant that floats in ponds, has trap doors in its leaves through which minute water organisms enter but can never leave. The dead bodies of the organisms help keep the plant afloat.

• The shell of the tungoil fruit, when burned, yields a soot that is used by the Chinese to make ink.

• The ocotilla, which grows in American deserts, sprouts new leaves every time it rains.

• The marimo, a spherical green plant, grows only at the bottom of three lakes—one in Switzerland, one in Japan, and one in Siberia.

• The piggyback plant is so called because new plants grow up from its leaves.

• The canoe palm (*Iriartrea venticosa*), which grows in the Amazon region of South America, has a huge bulge in its trunk which, when cut in half, serves natives as a canoe.

• The seed capsule of the *Pleiospilos bolusii*, a South African plant, can remain closed for years—releasing its seeds only when there is sufficient moisture for them to germinate.

• The chayote, a West Indian herb, bears a fruit that tastes like a pear and has a twenty-pound root that tastes and looks like a sweet potato.

• *Ipomoea pes-caprae*, a tropical vine of India, is eaten as a vegetable—its leaves are considered a treatment for rheumatism, and its juice is regarded as a medicine to cure edema.

• The disc-shaped leaves of the whistling gum tree of Australia tear loose in high winds and spin around their stems while making a loud whistling noise.

• *Carmichaelia petriei*, a desert plant of New Zealand, has no leaves—which enables it to reduce evaporation and preserve moisture.

• The ground creeper (*Rubus parvus*) of New Zealand was once a climbing plant, but now can only creep along the ground.

MUSHROOMS AND OTHER FUNGUS

• The "lady in the veil" mushroom (*Dictypphoria phalloides*) takes only twenty minutes to grow to its full height of eight inches—and makes an audible cracking sound while growing.

• The earth star, a puffball fungus, gets its name from the fact that its outer skin splits into pieces that form a star.

The "OXYPODUS NOBILISSIMUS" FUNGUS, A RARE, GIANT MUSHROOM THAT GROWS TO OVER THREE FEET IN HEIGHT and THREE FEET ACROSS, IS COVERED WITH COARSE HAIR!

THE BOWL FUNGUS HAS BOWL-SHAPED RECEPTACLES FILLED WITH SPORES WHICH IN OLDEN DAYS COULD PORTEND THE COMING SEASON'S HARVEST-- AND THUS PREDICT THE PRICE OF BREAD

TREES

• Today, only a single tree stands in the center of the Tenere Waste—a six-hundred-mile area of the Sahara—yet once the entire desert was covered with luxuriant vegetation.

• Apricot trees were grown in China more than four thousand years ago.

• The Wawona Tree in Yosemite National Park, California, lived two thousand years, from 31 B.C. to A.D. 1969. In 1881 it was the first tree to have a tunnel cut through its trunk!

• In Tule, Mexico, there is a two-thousand-year-old savin tree that stands one hundred thirty-eight feet high, measures one hundred ninety feet around the base, and weighs an estimated seven hundred tons!

• Some kapok trees on the Palau Islands, in the Pacific, have trunks covered with spikes.

• **Hiroshi Utsunomiya,** of Yamaguchi University in Japan, grew a seven-foot-high white magnolia using a seed found inside a two-thousand-year-old tomb!

• The General Sherman, a 272-foot-tall sequoia tree in Sequoia National Park, California, contains enough wood to build forty five-room houses!

• The Curly Redwood Lodge in Crescent City, California, was built entirely from a single redwood tree that measured eighteen feet across and produced fifty-seven thousand board feet of lumber!

• **Peter Jenkins**, a tree surgeon in Atlanta, Georgia, operates a tree-climbing school in a grove of ninety-foot oak trees!

• **Sam Youd**, a gardener, regularly hugs the two hundred fifty thousand trees he tends in Tatton Park, Cheshire, England!

• A coffee tree presented to **King Louis XIV** of France by the Dutch in 1713 was so treasured that it was protected by the first glass "greenhouse" built in the country.

• The Chaulmoogra tree of Burma yields an oil that is used to treat leprosy.

• **Robert Falls,** of Vancouver, British Columbia, designs and grows square trees!

• The baobab tree of Madagascar has wood so sopping wet that it can be wrung out like a damp rag.

• In Milltown, Indiana, there is a forty-foot oak tree covered with over two hundred shoes!

• "The Whistler," a 212-year-old oak tree in Montijo, Portugal, produces 2,640 pounds of cork every nine years—enough to make one hundred thousand wine corks!

The remarkable Erlandson trees, grown by **A. N. Erlandson,** of Santa Cruz, California, were featured in the Ripley collection more than a dozen times.

• Some oak trees in Audubon Park, New Orleans, Louisiana, are more than one thousand years old.

• A cherry tree in Taylorstown, Virginia, is growing from the heart of a black locust tree!

• The leaves of an apple tree in a period of six months can return to the air eighteen hundred gallons of water.

• A medium-size oak tree can draw one hundred forty gallons of water from the earth every day!

• A forest of aspen trees in Utah consists of forty-seven thousand trees with connected stems that all grew from the root of a single tree!

• **Heino Seppi,** of Palloneva, Finland, while cutting timber, split open an aspen log and found a dried perch inside!

The horned tree, Stephenville, Texas: A set of buck horns, with a 7$^1/_2$ foot span, was grafted on an oak tree by **H. B. Keyser.**

A-coco-gone-loco! The crawling tree in Tahiti.

The Grand TRUNK TREE (2,000 years old). A fallen redwood tree was an auto highway. Giant Forest, California.

The lover's knot natural tree formation in Worcester, Massachusetts.

THE **TREE** OF **FEAR** near Palma, Spain WHICH FOR **400** YEARS HAS BORNE FRUIT ONLY WHEN *"FRIGHTENED" IN THE SPRING BY DRUMS AND RATTLES*

Believe It or Not! WHEN LIGHTNING STRIKES TREES IT IS DRAWN MORE OFTEN TO OAK TREES THAN TO ANY OTHER SPECIES.

• The tree that was a royal walking stick: A staff thrust into the ground at Guimares, Portugal in 672 by **King Wamba** was forgotten, took root, and flourished as an olive tree for 1,279 years!

• The indestructible olive tree of Pandroseion, Greece, has been burned more than one hundred times in the last three thousand years—yet it always grows back.

• The tree that grew from a coffin! In Crouch Cemetery, Broen County, Indiana, a huge poplar tree sprang from the grave of a man named Allcorn—who was buried in a coffin made by hollowing out a poplar tree's trunk.

• The tree that must be artificially pollinated: The flowers of the date tree have no scent and are ignored by bees—so they must be pollinated by hand.

• Redwood trees, which grow to heights of three hundred fifty feet, have seeds so tiny that it takes one hundred twenty-three thousand to fill a one-pound bag!

LUMBER AND FORESTRY

• It takes five hundred thousand trees to supply the paper for a week's worth of newspapers in the United States!

• A used bookstore in Tadami, Japan, gave away over twenty-five acres of forestland in exchange for old books!

• Over one million tons of bamboo are harvested every year—enough to go around the Earth two hundred times!

A **FIG TREE** in South Africa HAS ROOTS THAT REACH **394** feet INTO THE EARTH !

KOTZEBUE NATIONAL FOREST in North-Western Alaska HAS ONLY ONE TREE - A BLACK SPRUCE PLANTED in 1958.

Chapter 51

Prophecies

Can human beings foretell the future? Are future events predetermined? Is there some yet undiscovered link between that which has already happened and that which has yet to occur? If not, how do we explain the abilities of individuals who have acurately predicted unforeseen events? What you're about to read may challenge your notion of destiny and, perhaps, of your own fate.

FORESHADOWED EVENTS

• The jewel beyond compare! At the coronation of **George III** the great diamond in his crown fell out. The archbishop of Canterbury picked it up with the remark that "a jewel beyond compare will be lost to the crown" thus prophetically predicting the loss of the American colonies!

BUILT BECAUSE OF A DREAM

• The school that was founded by a dream: Worcester Polytechnic Institute in Worcester, Massachusetts, was created in 1865 by a retired businessman named **John Boynton**, who donated one hundred thousand dollars to build the school after seeing a building with the inscription, "School of Technology" in a dream.

• The dream church: The old Dutch church in North Tarrytown, New York, was built after a dam on the Pocantico River had been demolished three times by floods, and a slave had a dream that no dam would endure unless a church was built beside it. The church was constructed in 1685—and the dam was never again damaged by floods.

• The dream that became reality: Rose Hill College in the Bronx, New York, which later became Fordham University, appeared to **William Hennen** of Bavaria in a dream so vividly that he traveled through Germany, Holland, France, and the United States in search of it. He eventually found it in 1846—thirty-four years after his dream—and became a member of its faculty.

FORESHADOWED VOCATIONS

• On May 28, 1738, an expectant mother who witnessed an execution was so horrified that she went into labor and gave birth prematurely. Her child grew up to become an important part of history for introducing a highly efficient invention to France. He was **Doctor. J. I. Guillotin**, for whom the famous guillotine is named!

• The girl whose prophesy came true twice! **Isabel Despenser** (1400-1439) as a child was told by a fortuneteller that she would marry a man named Richard Beauchamp—and she actually wed two men with that name! She married the first at the age of eleven, and when he was slain in battle, married the second Richard Beauchamp, with whom she lived happily the rest of her life.

FORTUNES REVEALED BY DREAMS

• The girl who won a fortune because she didn't

THE STEEPLE THAT FULFILLED A PROPHECY This prophecy was quoted in Chichester, England, for 800 years: "If Chichester Church Steeple ever falls in England there is no king at all." The Steeple collapsed in February, 1861—and at that time England had no king on its throne, because its ruler was Queen Victoria.

know arithmetic! **Mary Russel Mitford** (1787-1855) the English novelist, at the age of ten dreamed of the number seven on three successive nights, so she multiplied seven by three and bought a lottery ticket on the number 22—and by her error won $100,000.

• The strangest treasure hunt in all history! **John Chapman,** a peddler in Swaffham, England, journeyed to London because he had dreamed the trip would bring him buried treasure! A stranger he asked for direction scoffed at his story, remarking, "If I believed in dreams I would be on my ways to Swaffham because I dreamed there is a treasure buried there in the garden of a man named Chapman." The peddler hurried home and found two treasure crocks buried in his own garden!

• The strangest gamble in history: **Professor Francisco Garrido,** completing a lecture at the School of Physiology and Hygiene in Madrid, Spain, announced he was resigning his post to pursue popular pharmacy with his winnings in a national

lottery—the drawing for which had not yet been held! His ticket won and he became the wealthiest pharmacist in the country (1870).

PROPHESIED
IN FICTION

• In his book, *The New Atlantis,* written in 1626, **Francis Bacon** described people traveling in airplanes and submarines, and using telephones!

• Author **Jules Verne'**s description of the not-yet-invented periscope in *Twenty Thousand Leagues Under the Sea* was so accurate that the actual inventor of the instrument was refused a patent!

PROPHESIED DEATH

• In England's Holland House in London, the poet **Shelley** and others reported meeting apparitions of themselves—and then each died soon afterward.

• The two gate posts of Margamin, Wales, were left standing for centuries because of a prophecy that if they were ever destroyed the noble Mansell family would vanish. In 1744 young **Lord Thomas Mansell** pulled down the pillars, and within the year the entire family was wiped out.

• The monarch who was killed by a prophecy! **King Henry IV** of England was warned that he would die in Jerusalem. In 1413 he suffered an attack of epilepsy in Westminster Abbey and died of fright when he learned he had been carried to a room called Jerusalem.

• **Calchas the Greek** died laughing at a prediction that said he would die that day!

THE STRANGE PROPHECY THAT WAS FULFILLED BY A VIOLENT DEATH!
WALTER INGRAM, of London, England, BROUGHT BACK FROM EGYPT IN 1884 THE MUMMIFIED HAND OF AN ANCIENT EGYPTIAN PRINCESS, WHICH WAS FOUND TO BE CLUTCHING A GOLD PLAQUE INSCRIBED:
"WHOEVER TAKES ME AWAY TO A FOREIGN COUNTRY WILL DIE A VIOLENT DEATH AND HIS BONES WILL NEVER BE FOUND!"
4 YEARS LATER INGRAM WAS TRAMPLED TO DEATH BY A ROGUE ELEPHANT NEAR BERBERA, SOMALILAND, AND HIS REMAINS WERE BURIED IN THE DRY BED OF A RIVER BUT AN EXPEDITION SENT TO RECOVER HIS BODY FOUND A FLOOD HAD WASHED IT AWAY

THE MONARCH WHO WAS FRIGHTENED TO DEATH BY A LETTER

KING GEORGE I (1660-1727) of England kept his wife, Sophia Dorothea, imprisoned for 32 years—until she died in 1726. On January 10, 1727, a note from her was tossed into his coach, summoning him to divine judgment a year after her death—frightened, the king died on the spot!

PROPHETIC PHOBIAS

• **Don Everardo Blasco,** of Barcelona, although well, spent twenty-seven years in bed because a sage had predicted that he would never die in bed. An earthquake, however, tossed him out of bed, and he was killed by a falling beam.

• The phobia that proved prophetic: Famed French aviator **Helene Boucher** (1908-1934) had a superstitious fear of the number thirty, and repeatedly refused to compete in any race on the thirtieth day of a month. Persuaded to fly on November 30, 1934 she was killed in a crash from a height of three hundred feet.

• The monarch who couldn't escape his fate! Emperor **Anastasius I** of Byzance, warned that he would be killed by lightning, always sought shelter during electrical storms—but in 518 he was crushed to death while he cowered in an old house during a thunderstorm.

DEADLY DREAMS

• **Walter Craig**, a hotelier in Ballarat, Australia, during the 1860s, dreamed that his horse, "Nimblefoot," won the Melbourne Cup. He was puzzled, though, as to why the jockey in his dream wore a black armband. A few days before the race, Walter died and at the race, Nimblefoot crossed the line first!

DEATH INESCAPABLE

• The prophecy that frightened a man to death: **Cardinal Thomas Wolsey** (1475-1530), warned by a fortuneteller that Kingston would mark the end of his life, avoided the town of that name for years. When King Henry VIII sent a constable named Kingston after him, Wolsey died of shock.

• **Theodor Zwinger** (1533-1588), a professor of medicine at the University of Switzerland, fearlessly assisted victims of an epidemic in 1588—then told his friends he would be dead in eleven days. Exactly eleven days later he was dead!

FORETOLD OWN DEATH

• The man who foretold his own doom to the hour! **George Thaler,** of Gnadenwald, Austria, predicted in 1643 that he would die five years later at 4 A.M. on September 4. At 4 A.M. on September 4, 1648, he died of natural causes. His prophecy is inscribed on his tombstone.

• Famed author **Mark Twain** was born in 1835 on a day when Halley's Comet was visible. He later predicted he would die when it reappeared. He died in 1910, shortly after Halley's Comet again appeared in the sky!

PROPHETS

• The Prophet of Doom: **Ned Pearson**, gravedigger of Grimsby, England, for a period of twenty-two years, always visited the home of his next client twenty-four hours before the person died!

• The prophet of death! **Aunt Rieka,** a seamstress of Sennel, Germany, made a shroud for every person who died in the community over a period of forty-one years and always appeared at the doomed one's home seventy-two hours before death!

SOOTHSAYING

• Wearing wooden hats with long streamers, the Tarahumaras of Mexico whirl around until they collapse. Tribal soothsayers then predict future events based on the directions in which the various dancers fell.

THE 1784 SPACESHIP
A space station envisioned in France 200 years ago—to be manned by the French Army, was shaped like a balloon-lifted battleship.

DEADLY DREAMS—
CHRIS ROBINSON PROPHESIES
DISASTER WHILE HE SLUMBERS

It began as an ordinary night's sleep.
Chris Robinson, a janitor in Bedfordshire,
England, had just dozed off for a restful
night of slumber, when he began to dream
of a man who urgently needed to show him
something. Robinson followed the man to a
hotel room, where he observed five people
plotting a terrorist attack. When he awoke,
Robinson called the police and reported his
uncanny dream.

The police ignored him—until the dream
came true.

Robinson's prophetic dreams continued.
Time after time, Robinson dreamed of disastrous events before they happened. Finally,
Scotland Yard began to rely on Robinson for
tips, even assigning officer Alex Hall as his
full-time liaison.

At first, Hall had little faith in Robinson's
abilities, but Robinson's uncannily accurate
prediction of a Gloucestershire air show
plane crash changed all that.

This time, Robinson was able to tell
a crowd of people exactly what would
transpire: that two jets would meet in midair,
causing a fiery explosion. The planes did just
that, bursting into flames and pinwheeling
into the ground in what looked like an unsur-
vivable crash. Yet Robinson told the crowd,
"Don't worry. In my dream both pilots came
down in their parachutes." Miraculously,
the two pilots did parachute to the ground,
unharmed.

Robinson admits that at first his strange
ability frightened him, but he now views it as
a useful gift. He no longer minds being the
bearer of disturbing visions. "I'm glad it happens to me because I'm able to help."

• In the 1920s a horse named
"Lucky Wonder" used a
typewriter to spell out its
psychic predictions—includ-
ing the reelection of President
Truman, and the entry of the
United States into World
War II!

VISIONS OF
THE FUTURE

• The famous epitaph of
Kirby, Essex, England: The
following words are taken
from a five-hundred-year-old
tombstone in the church of
Kirby cemetery:
  "When pictures look alive
    with movements free
  when ships like fishes swim
    beneath the sea
  when men outstripping
    birds shall span the sky
  then half the world deep
    drenched in blood shall
    lie!"

• In 1900, the *Ladies' Home
Journal* magazine predicted
that by the year 2000 the
letters "C," "X," and "Q"
would be gone from the
alphabet and strawberries
would be the size of apples!

Predictions are made by
natives of the Cameroons,
Africa, using the burrows
of native GIANT
SPIDERS—the
natives scatter leaves over
11 ribbons around the burrow and the next morning
base their prophecies on
the way the spider has
rearranged the leaves.

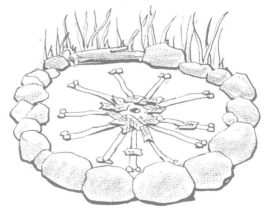

Chapter 52
Puzzles & Riddles

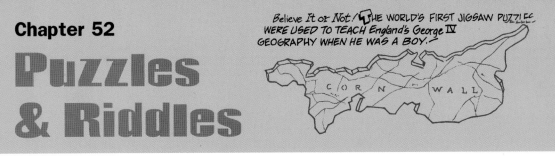

Believe It or Not! THE WORLD'S FIRST JIGSAW PUZZLES WERE USED TO TEACH England's George IV GEOGRAPHY WHEN HE WAS A BOY.

A good puzzle is like a trip to the gym for our brains. Jigsaws, crosswords, anagrams—they keep our minds limber while they keep us entertained. But watch out, some of these mind-bogglers may leave you downright puzzled. . .

CROSSWORD PUZZLES

• **Roger Bouckaert**, of Belgium, worked five hours a day for four years to create a crossword puzzle that had over fifty thousand words and was one hundred feet long!

This could by the WORLD SMALLEST CROSSWORD!

Period is the meaning of the across clue; **Dot** is the clue running down!

During World War II, the Nazis showered England with progaganda in the form of CROSSWORD PUZZLES!

• The *London Times* once included the word "Honorificabilitudinitatibus" in a crossword puzzle!

JIGSAW PUZZLES

• **Anne Williams,** of Maine, has a collection of twenty-five hundred jigsaw puzzles, including the oldest known jigsaw puzzle map, dated 1776!

A GAME COMPANY in Norwich, Conn., MADE A JIGSAW PUZZLE WITH 52,000 PIECES THAT SOLD for $60,000!

• The world's largest 3-D puzzle: A jigsaw puzzle replica of the *Titanic*, assembled in Dusseldorf, Germany, measured 15.4 feet in length and contained 26,500 pieces!

Believe It or Not! In North America during the Depression Era, JIGSAW PUZZLES were so popular that dairies frequently sold and delivered them with the milk!

"THE BIGGEST PUZZLE"

STUDENTS at Gravenvoorde School in Almelo, the Netherlands, ASSEMBLED A JIGSAW PUZZLE CONSISTING of 204,484 PIECES and MEASURING 1,036 SQ. FEET!

WORD PLAY

PALINDROMES

• The phrase "race car" reads the same forward as backward.

RUSSIAN CZAR PETER the GREAT HAD A ROOM IN HIS PALACE WITH WALLS COVERED IN 100,000 PIECES of CARVED AMBER ARRANGED IN A JIGSAW-PUZZLE PATTERN! (1799)

• "Kinnikinnik," a word used to describe a mixture, smoked by Native Americans, that is made of leaves and bark but no tobacco, is the same spelled forward and backward.

• Palindrome sentence: "Ma is as selfless as I am."

CAN YOU MAKE 4 SQUARES OUT OF 5 BY MOVING ONLY 3 MATCHES?

MOVE MATCHES INDICATED BY DOTS AND FORM A NEW SQUARE!

HOW MANY CUBES CAN YOU FIND?

FRANCE'S KING LOUIS XIII, WHO REIGNED from 1610-1643, APPOINTED A ROYAL ANAGRAMIST TO CREATE ANAGRAMS AT A YEARLY SALARY of $1,200!

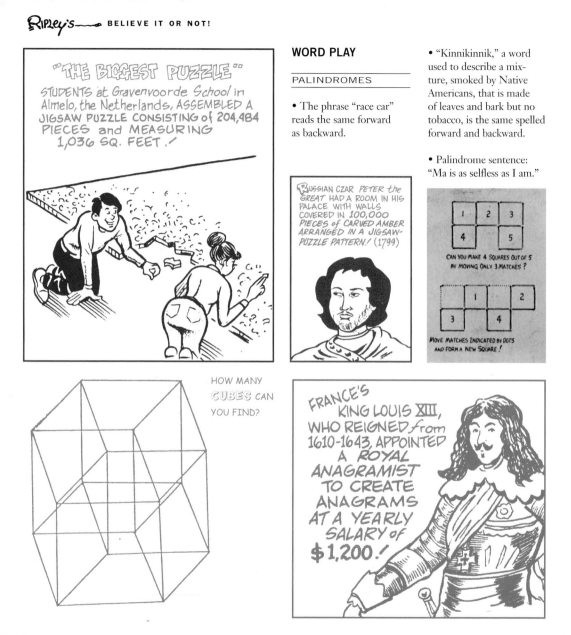

PUNS

• Killer pun: **Napoleon** once killed over a thousand people with a single cough. In 1799, he was in the midst of deciding whether or not to release twelve hundred Turkish prisoners of war. He was just about to give the order to set them all free, when he coughed. He exclaimed, "Ma sacrée toux!" (My darned cough!), which sounded to his officers like "Massacrez tous!" (Kill them all!) So they did.

• A tree has limbs but
cannot walk;
A cave has a mouth but does
    not talk;
A chair has arms it never
    swings;
Without a throat the kettle
    sings;
A rooster's crow is never
    black;
A gun goes off but doesn't
    come back;
A dog has pants but not a
    vest;
And with a lawsuit you're
    not dressed;
A pig of iron never squeals;
Without a knife the thunder
    peals;
A clock does not in deep
    disgrace
Hold up its hands to hide its
    face;
A cat with whiskers never
    shaves;
A gravy boat doesn't ride the
    waves;

A ram its own horn never
    toots;
A fiddle bow no arrow
    shoots;
The needle's eye will never
    see;
Such things are strange, you
    must agree.

• Quizotic!
Where can a man buy a cap
    for his knee?
Or a key to the lock of his
    hair?
Can his eyes be called an
    academy,
Because there are pupils
    there?
In the crown of his head,
    what gems are found?
Who travels the bridge of
    his nose?
Can he use, when shingling
    his house,
The nails on the end of his
    toes?
Can the crook of his elbow
    be sent to jail?
If so, what did it do?
How does he sharpen his
    shoulder blades?
I'll be hanged if I know, do
    you?
Can he sit in the shade of
    the palm of his hand?
Or beat on the drum of his
    ear?
Does the calf of his leg eat
    the corn on his toes?
If so, why not grow corn on
    the ear?

ANAGRAM MAN! NEIL BINES'S UNCANNY UNSCRAMBLING ABILITY

Any Scrabble player can tell you that the big scores come from putting together the longest words. But can you imagine constructing words from as many as twenty-eight scrambled letters? Neil Bines can—and he can do it without even seeing the letters.

Neil has had an uncanny knack for unscrambling anagrams since he was a child. He remembers one day, when he was a boy, looking at the word "mobil," and realizing that the letters could be rearranged to spell "limbo." From that moment, he was hooked. Now, Neil sees anagrams wherever he goes. For instance, if he reads the word "gallery," he automatically scrambles it into "regally," "largely," and "allergy."

How does Neil keep track of all the scrambled letters in his head? By creating mnemonic devices for each, like the one that many people use to remember the names of the Great Lakes. The word "homes" contains each of the letters necessary to begin Huron, Ontario, Michigan, Erie, and Superior. But even with these mnemonic helpers, Neil's ability is astonishing. Even champion Scrabble players acknowledge that Neil Bines's extraordinary mental talent makes him a master of anagrams!

Records

For generations, Ripley's has cultivated a fascination with mosts and firsts, bests and worsts, greatest and smallest. We've assembled here a few of the wildest record-holders in our archives—surely the weirdest collection of its kind!

FIRST

• The first American author, **Domingo Augustin**, in 1568 established a mission on Saint Catherine's Island, off Brunswick, Georgia, and created a grammar of the language of the Guale tribe of Indians—the first book written on American soil.

In 1876, Marshall Jones Brooks of England, who made the FIRST RECORDED HIGH JUMP of six feet, wore a top hat while competing!

• The first escalator in Britain, installed in 1898 in Harrod's department store in London, had a clerk who waited at the top with a glass of brandy for each customer!

Violet Verry, age fourteen, was the first girl to execute a full twisting butterfly somersault.

DEEPEST

• The world's deepest lake: Lake Baykal, in the Siberian region of the former Soviet Union, is 5,315 feet deep in one spot.

HEAVIEST

• **Ivan Sergeyevich Turgenev** (1818-1883), brilliant Russian novelist and poet, had the heaviest brain of any genius ever weighed: four pounds seven ounces.

LARGEST

• The largest American flag ever made, weighing five thousand pounds, with twenty-foot high stripes and sixteen-foot stars, was unfurled in Pottstown, Pennsylvania, in 1992!

• The world's largest yard sale: A yard sale featuring over thirty-two hundred vendors is held annually along a six-hundred-mile-long stretch of Highway 127, from Covington, Kentucky, to Gadsden, Alabama!

• On Red Mountain, near Birmingham, Alabama, there stands a fifty-six-foot-tall statue of Vulcan, the Roman god of fire! It's the largest cast-metal statue in the world and the largest statue ever made in the United States!

• The world's biggest Scrabble game: In 1998 a giant Scrabble game covered the entire soccer field at Wembley Stadium in London, and had letter pieces that required two men each to lift them!

"FOREVERTRON"!
THE WORLD'S LARGEST SCULPTURE, in Baraboo, Wisc., IS A **320-TON** "TIME MACHINE" CREATION BY SCRAP METAL ARTIST *Tom Every!* IT BOASTS *DEATH RAYS* and A *DISINTEGRATION CHAMBER!*

Susan Montgomery Williams of Fresno, Calif., blew a **BUBBLE** that measured 23.2 inches in diameter—a world record!

• The world's largest butterfly farm, in Coconut Creek, Florida, is home to twenty-five hundred butterflies, belonging to eighty different species!

Rory Timmins, a farmer from Oakville, Manitoba, Canada, has made the **WORLD'S LARGEST GARLIC BRAID!** The chain extends 702.9 ft. in length and weighs 3,990 lbs.

• The Rani Ka Naur in the Udayagiri Hill in Orissa, India, is the largest palace in the world located entirely inside a cave.

• The world's largest tuba: A tuba that measures seven feet, six inches tall, and three feet, four inches across the bell, was built for composer John Philip Sousa in 1896!

• The world's largest auto showroom: The Armory Automotive Family in Albany, New York, has a 3,500-foot indoor showroom—the largest in the world—that can display up to two hundred fifty cars at one time!

• The Twinings Tea Shop on the Strand in London has the world's biggest teapot, which serves over thirteen gallons of tea!

• The world's largest library: The Library of Congress, in Washington, D.C., has five hundred thirty-two miles of shelving!

• The world's largest church organ: An organ in the Cadet Chapel of the United States Military Academy at West Point has 18,701 pipes and four keyboards!

"THE WORLD'S BIGGEST BURRITO"
HECTOR PLACENCIA of PHOENIX, ARIZ., PREPARED A
140-YD.-LONG BURRITO USING 900 TORTILLAS
and 198 LBS. OF BEEF.

• The largest ship model in the world, the *Lagfoda*, a half-size replica of an actual whaling ship in the Whaling Museum, New Bedford, Massachusetts, is fifty-nine feet long and has a mast fifty feet high.

• The world's largest potato chip: A potato chip displayed at the World Potato Exposition in Blackfoot, Idaho, measured twenty-five by fourteen inches—equal to eighty regular-sized chips!

• The biggest hot dog of all time was stuffed by the German Butcher's Guild for their celebration in Koenigsberg in 1601. This hot dog was more than half a mile long (exactly 3,001 feet) and required the efforts of one hundred three butchers to carry it on parade. It weighed 885 pounds, and was later distributed among the members of the guild at a banquet table.

• The William Penn statue atop the City Hall of Philadelphia, Pennsylvania, thirty-seven feet high and weighing 53,348 pounds, is the largest sculpture on any building in the world.

"The WORLD'S LARGEST KITE"
A kite resembling a giant blowfish flown in Bangkok, Thailand, was 70 yards long, 26 yards wide, and weighed 551 lbs!

"THE WORLD'S LARGEST PAPER GLIDER"
HIGH SCHOOL STUDENTS in Hampton, Va., BUILT A PAPER AIRPLANE WITH A 30 ft. WINGSPAN THAT FLEW 115 FEET!

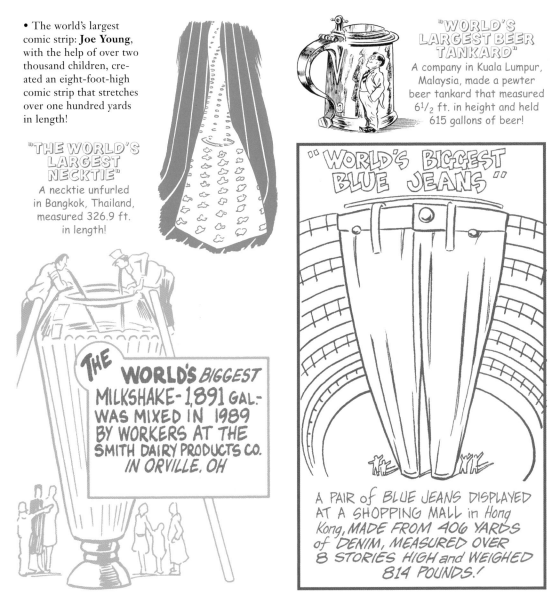

• The world's largest comic strip: **Joe Young**, with the help of over two thousand children, created an eight-foot-high comic strip that stretches over one hundred yards in length!

"THE WORLD'S LARGEST NECKTIE"

A necktie unfurled in Bangkok, Thailand, measured 326.9 ft. in length!

"WORLD'S LARGEST BEER TANKARD"

A company in Kuala Lumpur, Malaysia, made a pewter beer tankard that measured $6\frac{1}{2}$ ft. in height and held 615 gallons of beer!

"WORLD'S BIGGEST BLUE JEANS"

A PAIR of BLUE JEANS DISPLAYED AT A SHOPPING MALL in Hong Kong, MADE FROM 406 YARDS of DENIM, MEASURED OVER 8 STORIES HIGH and WEIGHED 814 POUNDS.!

THE WORLD'S BIGGEST MILKSHAKE-1,891 GAL-WAS MIXED IN 1989 BY WORKERS AT THE SMITH DAIRY PRODUCTS CO. IN ORVILLE, OH

LONGEST

• World's longest paper chain: In 1991, in Dunstone, Devon, England, members of the Interact Club created a twenty-nine-mile-long paper chain with three hundred thousand links!

• The longest speech in Senate history: South Carolina Senator **Strom Thurmond**, on August 28 and 29, 1951, gave a speech that lasted twenty-four hours, eighteen minutes, and filled ninety-six pages in the Congressional record!

• The longest acceptance speech by a winner of an Academy Award was given in 1942 by **Greer Garson**, who talked for over an hour!

• The world's longest drawing: In 1991, students from Lake High School in Union-town, Ohio created a continuous landscape drawing that measured one mile in length!

• **Burhan Montaruddin**, a disk jockey in Kuala Lumpur, Malaysia, set a new world record by staying on the air for one hundred four hours—ten hours longer than the previous record!

• The world's longest cussword! Next time you get mad, say: "Himmelher rgottkreuzmillionendonne rwetter!"

• The longest word ever used by **William Shakespeare** was "honor-ificabilitudinitatibus," in his 1594 play *Love's Labor Lost*!

• The longest known word that can be spelled the same way backwards and forwards is "sailp-puakivikauppias," the Finnish word for a lye merchant!

• The longest word ever used in a movie title is the German word "Schwarzhuhnbraunhunh-nschwarzhunhnweisshunh-nrothuhnweiss"!

• The longest sentence: French author **Marcel Proust** (1871-1922) wrote a sentence in his novel *The Cities of Pain* that contains nine hundred fifty-eight words!

• The world's longest kiss: In September 1985, **Edie Leven** and **Delphine Chra** of Chicago, Illinois, kissed continuously for seventeen days, ten and a half hours!

"The WORLD'S LARGEST DANCING DRAGON" A Chinese paper dragon measuring 5,550 ft. from its nose to its tail, required 610 people to operate it! (Beijing, China, May 1995)

"The LONGEST CAR" IN 1993, AN EXHIBITION of CARS in Barcelona, Spain, FEATURED A 106-FOOT LONG LIMOUSINE EQUIPPED WITH A SWIMMING POOL, HOT TUB and HELICOPTER LANDING PAD!

LOUDEST

• In 1992, **Harry Schuler,** of New Zealand, screamed a record one hundred thirty decibels—thirty decibels louder than the sound of a jet taking off!

MOST

• A record twenty-seven students in Timmins, Ontario, Canada, crammed themselves into a 1999 Volkswagen Beetle!

NORTHERNMOST

• The Hotel Wien, in Kotzebue, Alaska, on the Arctic Ocean, is the northernmost hotel in the world.

OLDEST

• The Oldest Cake: The Alimentarium, a food museum in Vevey, Switzerland, has an Egyptian honey, sesame, and milk cake on display that dates back to 2,200 B.C.!

• The world's oldest map: A map of the village of Mizhirich, Russia, was carved by hunters on mammoth ivory over fifteen thousand years ago!

• The world's oldest dentist's chair was first used in England in the time of King Henry VIII, four hundred fifty years ago.

• **Mario Borradori**, of Lugano, Switzerland, is the world's oldest skydiver. He jumped from a plane for the first time at the age of ninety.

• The world's oldest Avon lady: In 1997, **Rosie Gries**, of Goodrich, North Dakota, was age one hundred and had worked as an Avon lady, selling cosmetics for over fifty years!

SMALLEST

• The smallest house in England: A home on Conway Quai, North Wales, is seventy-two inches wide, one hundred inches deep and one hundred twenty-two inches high.

• The world's smallest police station, in Carrabelle, Florida, is actually just a phone booth!

• The smallest movie set: The only set Alfred Hitchcock used for his 1944 film *Lifeboat* was a lifeboat!

"Little Pumpkin," the world's smallest horse, stood only fourteen inches tall. He was raised by J. C. Williams of Inman, South Carolina.

• World's smallest car: In 1993 **Ola Wallin** of Goteborg, Sweden, built a car that measured only two yards in length, weighed one thousand pounds, and could reach a speed of ninety-two miles per hour!

• The world's smallest book, owned by the Toppan Printing Company of Japan, has fifty pages of verse bound inside .078-inch square covers!

• America's smallest church! The Cross Island Chapel, in Vernon, New York, measures three and a half feet by six feet!

• The world's smallest robot is on display at the world's biggest computer museum, in Germany! "Robotmaus Monsieur Epson" weighs only 0.15 ounces and can reach speeds of almost seven miles per hour!

TALLEST

• The battle monument in Bennington, Vermont, commemorating the 1777 Battle of Bennington, is the tallest battle monument in the world—measuring three hundred two feet.

Willie Camper, of Memphis, Tennessee, was 8 feet 5½ inches tall at age 17, with a shoe size of 33.

Robert Pershing Wadlow, at 8 feet 11 inches, dwarfed his father Harold.

• The lighthouse at Cape Hatteras near Buxton, North Carolina, two hundred eight feet high, is the tallest lighthouse in the United States.

• The world's tallest free-standing dinosaur: A skeleton of a "Barosaurus" on display in New York City, assembled by Peter May of Burlington, Canada, stands as high as a five-story building!

• The tallest stairway in the world: Djebel Musa, Sinai, is 2,100 feet high, with three thousand steps. It leads to the top of the mountain where Moses received the Tablets of the Law. Natives believe this stairway was carved by angels in a single night.

YOUNGEST

• **John Payton,** of Plano, Texas, a justice of the peace, heard over one thousand cases by the time he had reached the age of twenty!

• **Monte Collins**, of New York, twenty months old, was the youngest band leader. He conducted the New York Baby Orchestra.

The world's youngest trick rider! **Roylene Smith**, a member of Roy Knapp's Rough Riders, a trick riding troupe, could perform a 'fender drag' on her pony, "Small Fry," at the age of two and a half!

"ROPE WARRIOR" JUMP-ROPE RECORD HOLDER PUTS ON A SHOW FOR FITNESS

David Fisher is the world's greatest rope-jumper. He holds two rope-jumping records, both for jumping rope—while hopping on his behind! "I call them tush-ups," David explains.

A professional rope-jumper, David calls himself "the Rope Warrior." His mission is to help get people in shape by jumping rope. He advocates jump ropes as an ideal way to get fit: it's inexpensive, portable, and offers a full-body workout. Also, there's an infinite number of things you can do with it: "I'm constantly looking for new ways to challenge myself," says David.

David exhibits his unusual knack for jumping rope at schools across the country. For his big finale, he turns off all the lights and performs a jump-roping routine in the dark, to rock music, with special glow-in-the-dark ropes. David says the kids' cheers are so wild they drown out the music!

Chapter 54

Religion & Philosophy

ON London, England, THERE IS AN ANNUAL "CLOWN SERVICE" at Holy Trinity Church IN WHICH CLOWNS IN FULL COSTUME and MAKEUP GATHER TO COMMEMORATE Joseph Grimaldi, THE FAMOUS 16TH CENTURY CLOWN!

"Strangest is man when he quests after his gods," Robert Ripley quoted upon observing the marvels of India's Hindu mystics. Though perhaps the most exotic to Western eyes, the Hindu ascetics Ripley recorded in various states of self-torture are no less bizarre than any of us in our most pious moments, regardless of our religious affiliation. Humankind, in its thirst for the sacred, in its quest for the divine, weaves an elegant and multicolored tapestry of religious belief and tradition. Not one of us can tell for sure how close we may be to the truth. For all we know, perhaps God appreciates the diversity. As a wise man once put it, "We're all looking out different windows at the same light."

"A LIVING GODDESS" THE ROYAL KUMARI of NEPAL, A FOUR-YEAR-OLD GIRL CHOSEN AS THE REINCARNATION of A POWERFUL VIRGIN GODDESS, IS WORSHIPPED BY 20 MILLION PEOPLE UNTIL SHE REACHES PUBERTY!

• "Raelians," a religious group with twenty-eight thousand members worldwide, believe that aliens created the Earth tens of thousands of years ago, and will return in 2020.

• The temple of all faiths: Birla Temple in New Delhi, India, includes separate areas for worship for every known religion.

BUDDHISM

• A Buddhist monk in China, to achieve the rank of abbot, must remain completely placid while three paper pellets filled with sawdust are ignited one after the other on his shaven skull.

• The patient pilgrims to the Lamasery of Labrang: Tibetans visiting the sacred Lamasery of Labrang, China, circle the entire mountain on which it stands by falling forward on the ground, then rising and falling again—a painful journey that requires seven days. They wear sandals on their hands because of the rocky terrain over which they must drag themselves forward.

THE MOST DEDICATED PILGRIMS IN THE WORLD
Mount Minobu, Japan
BUDDHISTS PAYING HOMAGE AT THE GRAVE OF NICHIREN, FOUNDER OF A JAPANESE SECT, REMAIN MOTIONLESS AND SILENT WHILE 5 CANDLES PLACED ON EACH OUTSTRETCHED ARM *BURN DOWN INTO THEIR FLESH*

IN 1995, A GROUP of 10 TIBETAN MONKS from the Gyuto Monastery in Tibet CURED A SICK SNOW LEOPARD AT THE San Francisco Zoo BY PERFORMING A TRADITIONAL CHANT of HEALING!

AT THE Yokohama, Chuo Cemetery in Japan THERE IS A *LIFELIKE ROBOTIC REPLICA of a BUDDHIST PRIEST* WITH BLINKING EYES THAT CHANTS OVER THE DEAD EACH MORNING.

• Monks of the isolated monastery of Ketho, in the Himalayas, must live for three years, three months, and thirteen days alone in a windowless dark cell. They are then permitted the same period of freedom, but for the remainder of their lives, they must alternate between such spans of meditation and freedom.

CHRISTIANITY

• It was not until the fourth century that the church began to celebrate the feast of Christmas.

• **Billy Sunday** (1862-1935), the American Revival preacher, addressed one hundred million people in his career before the days of radio and television.

• The **Reverend Jonathan Boucher** (1738-1804), of Prince Georges County, Maryland, a fiery Tory, preached for a period of six months in 1775 with a pair of loaded pistols on his pulpit.

• **Robert E. Harris**, a circuit-riding preacher, sermonizes on horseback along Interstate 40 near Asheville, North Carolina!

• **John Henderson** (1686-1758) a ship master of Borrowstounnes, Scotland, attended four public prayer meetings and seven private prayer meetings each Sunday for sixty-two years.

THE BIBLE

• An English Bible printed in 1560 is known as the "Breeches Bible" because it states that Adam and Eve "sewed fig leaves together and made themselves breeches"!

1,400 years ago, a raven saved the life of
ST. BENEDICT
by snatching a poisoned slice of bread
from his hand! As a result, for 14 centuries,
the Benedictine Monastery at Subiaco,
Italy, has never been without a tamed
raven as pet.

"OUR LADY OF THE SEA"
A church in Southport, Queensland,
Australia, that seats 50 people, is actually
a floating church mounted on a flat boat!

• The first Bible printed in America (1663) was a translation into the Algonkian Indian language.

• The word "and" appears 46,277 times in the King James version of the Bible!

CHRIST

• On the basis of our calendar, **Christ** was not born in A.D. 1 but in 5 B.C.

• The Church of the Lord's Prayer, in Jerusalem, stands on the very spot where **Christ** delivered the Lord's Prayer—inside the church are wall tablets displaying the prayer in thirty different languages.

• A thorn from the crown of **Christ**, brought back from the Holy Land by a Crusader in 1185, is

THIS SILVER STAR MARKS THE BIRTHPLACE OF JESUS IN THE GROTTO OF THE NATIVITY –Bethlehem
CHRIST WAS BORN 10 FEET UNDERGROUND IN A ROCK CAVE
"She Brought Forth Her Firstborn Son and Wrapped Him in Swaddling Clothes and Laid Him in a Manger." St. Luke, 2:7
A QUARREL OVER THIS SILVER STAR CAUSED THE CRIMEAN WAR IN WHICH 1,000,000 MEN LOST THEIR LIVES.

preserved in the Church of Chalandry, France, and exhibited each Good Friday.

HINDUISM

• The members of the Shah Dawal Temple in Berar, India, make up the only sect in the world that must attend religious services while wearing iron handcuffs. They are believed to put the wearer in the proper mood for fervent supplications.

• **Ranganatha**, of Allahabad, India, counted each hair on his head every day for thirty-six years! It took nine hours each day—yet he punished himself with a severe fast if he erred by even one hair!

• A double-pronged hook is thrust into the flesh of a sect of Hindu practitioners and they are lifted forty feet into the air and whirled around and around—as a demonstration of their faith!

During a live broadcast in 1938 of Robert Ripley's radio show, Hindu holy man **Kuda Bux** walked barefoot across a blazing 1,220-degree pit of coals, without injury or apparent discomfort.

THE PED SADDHUS AN INDIAN SECT, BARS ANYONE WHO CANNOT RELAX WITH HIS RIGHT FOOT RESTING UPON HIS LEFT SHOULDER

• Hindus have many differences in religion and each group considers a different date to be the beginning of the New Year!

• **Thata**, a fakir of Benares, India, rode astride a sacred cow every waking moment for twenty-eight years!

• **Hijmar**, a holy man of Benares, India, held his left arm in the same position for twelve years.

• Even the shadow of an Untouchable will cause defilement to a high-caste Hindu.

THE **MAN** WHO REPEATED **ONE WORD** NIGHT AND DAY FOR **20** YEARS
MAHARAJA SHEO RAO BHAO
RULER OF JHANSI, INDIA, FOR 21 YEARS, GAVE UP HIS THRONE TO BECOME A SAINT AND SAT ON THE SHORE OF THE GANGES RIVER FOR ALL THE REMAINDER OF HIS LIFE
FOR 2 DECADES HE SPOKE NO WORD BUT "RAMA" (GOD) - AND THAT WORD HE REPEATED WITH EVERY BREATH HE DREW !

ISLAM

• The door of the mosque of Sheik Selim Chisti, in Fatehpur Sikri, India, is studded with horseshoes hung there by owners of ailing horses—who felt this would make their animals well.

• The first book digest: **Dubash Meghji,** of Zanzibar, ate one page of the Koran each day for thirty years!

• Each year, Shia Muslims in Ahmadabad, India, mourn the death of **Imam Husain**, a descendant of the prophet Mohammed, by whipping themselves with knife-tipped chains!

JUDAISM

• The Star of David, the Jewish emblem, consists of a combination of the two D's in the name of King David. In the older Hebrew script the letter D was represented by a triangle.

• Jewish folklore tells of the Sambaytion, a river that flows for six days of the week and stops on the seventh. There is such a river. It is the Nahr el Arus, in Lebanon.

• In 1993, Israel's phone company offered a service for people to fax messages to God, to be placed in Jerusalem's Wailing Wall!

ACTS OF DEVOTION

• **Benjamin Schulze** (1689-1760) copied the Bible in longhand three times—each time in a different Indian language. He knew one hundred foreign alphabets and could recite the Lord's Prayer in two hundred fifteen languages.

• **Saint Simeone Stylites** lived and preached from the top of pillars for thirty-seven years.

• **Dom Benito Zurtuza,** a monk in the monastery of Miraflores, Spain, abstained from all food and drink for twenty-four hours three days each week for twenty-four years.

• **Saint Francis** of Paula (1416-1508) took a vow of perpetual Lent! For seventy-eight years he never ate meat, butter, eggs, or cheese, or drank milk. He ate one meal a day consisting of bread and water—and lived to the age of ninety-one!

PENANCE

• **Señora Salomea Wolf** had the portrait of her husband tattooed on her tongue to atone for nagging him to death in Jerez, Spain, 1927.

THE MAN WHO BURNED HIS TONGUE WITH A RED-HOT IRON **95,000** TIMES!

BAIRAGI GYURI of Badrinath, India, SAID HIS PRAYERS 5 TIMES A DAY FOR NEARLY 52 YEARS AND EACH TIME PLUNGED HIS IRON STAFF INTO A FIRE AND LICKED ITS HOT TIP WITH HIS TONGUE! GYURI WAS CREMATED AT HIS DEATH AT THE AGE OF 62 IN A PURPLE SHROUD WHICH HE HAD WORN THROUGHOUT HIS LIFETIME

• In 1992, thieves who stole $1,400 in collection money from Our Lady of Lourdes Church in Baltimore, Maryland, returned the money with interest and a note of apology.

• The man who wore iron underwear: **Sir William de Lacy**, a Norman baron who became a hermit in 1100, wore his coat of armor as underclothing day and night for twenty-one years.

PRAYER

• **Genku** (1133-1212), a Japanese religious leader who devoted all his waking moments to prayer, pronounced the Japanese name for "Buddha" sixty thousand times each day for thirty years.

PILGRIMAGE

• A Huichol Indian of Mexico once in his lifetime must make a forty-day pilgrimage from his village to bring back "peyote"—a hallucinogenic drug.

• In Esquipulas, Guatemala, devout pilgrims eat clay tablets imprinted with religious symbols as a sign of faith!

• Forty nuns at a convent in Stetyl, the Netherlands, have maintained a continuous prayer in their chapel for ninety-eight years!

• The people who worship a nail: The Maria Gonds of Chanda, India, pray only to a twelve-inch spike.

LITTLE PILGRIMS to the shrine of Our Lady of Fatima, in Portugal, are dressed to look exactly like the church's famed statue of the Madonna

PRAYER STONES addressed to the Egyptian God Ra and sold to worshippers in Ancient Egypt had large ears engraved on them—so Ra would be sure to hear their messages.

THE STRANGEST PRINTER IN ALL THE WORLD!

A LAMA near Ra-gyrya, China, CONSTANTLY DIPS IN THE HWANG HO RIVER A FONT OF INKED TYPE CONTAINING A PRAYER, IN THE BELIEF HE IS INFLUENCING THOUSANDS DOWNSTREAM BY *IMPRINTING HIS PRAYER ON THE RUNNING WATER!*

SACRED OBJECTS AND RELIGIOUS ITEMS

• The begging bowls used by Kailas pilgrims in Tibet are made from human skulls.

• **Apis**, the Egyptian bull who became a god! The bull was worshiped at Memphis by the ancient Egyptians as the soul of Osiris. A temple and a magnificent dwelling were prepared for the bull, and his birthday was elaborately celebrated each year. When he died, he was embalmed with divine honors.

• A pair of eyeglasses worn by **Saint Philip** three hundred seventy-one years ago are preserved in the church of Saint Philip de Neri in Rome, Italy.

THE KEY OF ST. PETER, now in the Church of St. Servatius, in Maastricht, Holland, is said to have been given to St. Servatius in Rome by St. Peter himself.

SACRED SITES

• Pushkar, near Ajmere, India, is considered so sacred that within the town limits it is a sin to kill a fly.

• Myajima, an island in Japan, was once worshipped as a god—and barred to women.

• The sanctuary of Sidi el Yamani, in T'Zenin, Morocco, is covered with gobs of clay because pilgrims whisper their wrongdoing to the walls, then pile wet clay over the spot to modestly hide their sins.

TEMPLES, CHURCHES, AND SHRINES

• At the company headquarters of Wacoal, Japan's top maker of ladies' lingerie, there is a shrine to the underwear deity!

• At the Mango Pir shrine in Karahi, Pakistan, worshipers decorate crocodiles with roses and ritually feed them by hand!

• At the Zenshoji Temple in Japan, there is a statue of "Gorufu Kannon," the golf goddess of mercy, which was erected to protect worshipers from stray balls from a local golf course!

• In April 1990, at Tokyo's Nishichisan Temple, dedicated to the god of fire, one thousand people walked across a bed of burning sticks to rid themselves of evil passions!

• A temple on the Greek island of Tenedos was erected circa 1500 B.C. to celebrate a military victory in which the Greeks were aided by mice that gnawed through the enemy's bowstrings and shields!

• In 1992 a historic church in Melle, France, installed a jukebox that plays Gregorian chants, Tibetan mantras, and Jewish liturgical music!

• Shrines in Ceylon, for the convenience of travelers, are located among the roots of the sacred Banyan tree.

• The temple of Sanju Sangen-Do in Kyoto, Japan, has one thousand and one life-size gilded statues of the goddess Kwannon—yet each has a different face.

• Church of two faiths: In 1908, the village of Keystone, Nebraska, built a church with a Protestant altar at one end and a Catholic altar at the other—and reversible pews!

• The seven bells of Saint Martin de Tours Church, in Saint Martinville, Louisiana, were given names and baptized!

• Ancient Egyptian priests in 450 B.C. trained baboons to sweep out their temples!

• Thousands of temples in India are dedicated to two members of the Hindu trinity, Vishnu and Siva—yet Brahma, the leading figure in the Hindu trinity, has only a single temple.

• The Dhevaraj temple of Ayuthia in Thailand was built to fulfill a monarch's vow. The Thai king in 1880 learned that his queen had drowned in a ship wreck, but swore to build a temple if his son survived. The king kept his vow when the prince was found to have been saved.

• The church of Saint Peter and Saint Paul, in Mautby, England, celebrated its first Christmas service by electric light in December 1999—after ninety years of services using candlelight!

• The temple that honors the memory of a hair: The temple of That Luang near Vientiane, Laos, was built as a shrine for one hair from the head of the Buddha—but before the structure was finished the hair was stolen.

THE CHINESE IMPERIAL ANCESTRAL TABLETS WERE SO SACRED THAT PRIOR TO THE EARLY 1900s ANY COMMONER WHO LOOKED UPON THEM IN PROCESSION WAS PUT TO DEATH

A temple dedicated to the GOD OF BRIDGES AND ROADS stands on a span across the River Kiulung, near Amoy, China, so pedestrians can conveniently pray for a safe journey.

THE PARADE THAT HONORED A TOOTH! A tooth of Gautama Buddha is Ceylon's most sacred relic, and is honored each year by a procession of 50 richly adorned elephants.

• The Ammain Temple, in Bangkok, Thailand, was constructed to shelter a single footprint of the Buddha.

BLESSINGS

• "The Blessing of the Bicycles": At a special service held at the Cathedral Church of Saint John the Divine, in New York City, one hundred cyclists and their bicycles received a special blessing!

• "Blessing of the Motorcycles": For the past seven years, Reverend Lamberty of Mitchell, South Dakota, has performed an annual blessing of a fleet of motorcycles!

• On Saint Hubert's Day, November 3, at Saint Crois Church in Liege, Belgium, bread is blessed, then fed to dogs to protect them from rabies!

CURSES

• In 1685 a church bell from a Protestant chapel in France was whipped and burned after being charged with "inflaming the hearts of heretics"!

• **Egbert**, an early bishop of Trier, Germany, publicly denounced a flock of swallows that chattered during his sermons—and forbade them from entering his church!

PHILOSOPHERS

• **Socrates** (479-399), the Greek moralist and philosopher, was condemned to death on charges of impropriety and corrupting the young, by a jury of two thousand people. He refused to escape from prison as he might have done and died by drinking hemlock!

• The man who never really lived! **Bernard de Fontenelle**, a French philosopher, reached the age of one hundred years—yet he never laughed, never cried, never married, and never had a friend!

• **Thomas Hobbes** (1588-1679), the English philosopher, wrote so boldly that King Charles II forbade publishing his work—yet Hobbes was afraid to sleep in the dark.

• **Peter Abelard** (1079-1142), the French philosopher and theologian, was severely berated for declaring that teachers should be paid for their services.

• **Immanuel Kant** (1724-1804), the German philosopher, for sixty years ate only one meal a day—always at noon and in the same restaurant. He was never ill during his entire lifetime.

In 1989, at New York City's Cathedral of St. John the Divine over 1,000 ANIMALS AND A BOWL OF ALGAE were blessed at the annual Feast of St. Francis of Assisi!

RITUAL CRUCIFIXION—EXCRUCIATING EXPRESSION OF FAITH

Christians throughout the ages have pondered the final agonizing moments of Jesus Christ's life on Earth, when he was crucified and left to die. But every spring in the remote Philippine village of San Pedro Etude, devout followers don't just meditate upon the crucifixion of Christ—they live it.

For more than forty years, a handful of village men—and once, one woman—have commemorated Good Friday as Jesus did: nailed to a cross. The annual ritual attracts thousands of onlookers, both the pious and the merely curious, to this otherwise quiet town.

Cita Sangalong, a local fish seller and family man, has endured the ritual for an agonizing fourteen years in a row. It all began in 1987, when his mother fell ill. He made a promise to God that when his mother recovered, he would perform the ritual. His mother regained her health, and Cita carried out his vow—and has done so every year since.

When Good Friday arrives, Cita spends the hours before dawn in meditation and prayer, holding in a small sterile jar the sharp steel spikes that will soon be hammered into his flesh. At sunrise, Cita dons his robe and crown of thorns. He is bound and led through the city streets, then he must carry the heavy crucifix to a hillside, where he and as many as twelve others are bound hand and foot to their crosses.

Though it never becomes easy, Cita admits that the first time was the most horrible: "I was trembling even before the first nail pierced my skin." The pain is excruciating—almost unbearable. Yet amid the agony, Cita admits he experiences a deeply satisfying spiritual fulfillment.

When it's over, the participants receive immediate medical treatment. Amazingly, their wounds heal speedily. In more than four decades, no one has sustained permanent injury from the ritual.

Even so, the sheer physical agony has taken its toll on Cita. Cita told Ripley's, "Next year will be my last crucifixion."

Chapter 55
Royalty & Nobility

THE ROMAN EMPEROR *NERO* HAD A PAIR of *SUNGLASSES* **WITH CARVED EMERALDS for LENSES!**

Royalty and aristocracy have always held a seductive appeal. We study them, emulate them, admire them. We're fascinated. Ironically, royalty often enjoy an adoration from their subjects that few elected officials receive. Here in the United States, where no national royalty exists, we must content ourselves with following European royalty. And part of what captures our attention is the sheer license, even indulgence, which comes with that wealth, title, and power. For perhaps a host of reasons, life at the pinnacle of society gets downright bizarre. . .

CALIPHS, CHIEFS, KHANS, AND SULTANS

• The royal scepter of chiefs of the Kaonde tribe in Africa is a head covered with human skin topped by real hair.

• The strangest bodyguards in the world! Three wooden monkeys carved out of a single tree in the form of a statue twenty-two feet high guarded the African palace of the Sultan of Fumban—the huge monkeys were commissioned as army commanders and were on the royal payroll as official bodyguards.

• **Dhaffer**, the caliph of all Egypt from 955 to 960, was assassinated by his grand vizier, **Nasr ben Abbas**, because the murderer was incensed at the number of honors, promotions, and awards bestowed upon him by the man he killed.

• **Kublai Khan** (1216-1294), the Asian potentate, presented his important barons, as a symbol of their power and privilege, command of one hundred thousand men with umbrellas.

EMPERORS AND EMPRESSES

• After Roman emperor **Constans II** was assassinated in his bath in Syracuse, his successor, **General Misizi**, was reluctant to ascend the throne. To speed up his decision, Misizi's army commanders dumped the general, fully clothed and armored, into the same bath in which the former emperor had died, informing the soggy general that he would have to stay there until he changed his mind. The water was hot, and the weather was uncomfortably warm—not a nice combination when you're fully armored. Misizi accepted the crown but died after ruling for only one year.

• **Diocletian**, a slave and the son of a slave, became a Roman emperor and lord and master of the

THE **HORSE WHO CAME TO DINNER!** EMPEROR CALIGULA (12-41) of Rome invited his horse, INCITATUS, to every state banquet—feeding it at the table beside the honored guests.

THE **MONARCH** WHO WAS REARED IN AN IRON CAGE **SULTAN ABDUL HAMID I** (1725-1789) of Turkey IMPRISONED IN A SMALL CAGE AT THE AGE OF **6** DID NOT LEAVE IT UNTIL HE WAS ENTHRONED AS RULER OF ONE OF THE MIGHTIEST EMPIRES ON EARTH **-43 YEARS LATER!**

world. He even called himself god and made his subjects prostrate themselves before him.

• The sweetest smelling emperor of them all: Emperor **Augustus Caesar** (63 B.C.-A.D. 14) used different scented oils on his chest, arms, and knees.

• Roman emperor **Augustus** celebrated his birthday every month!

• The Roman epicure, **Apicius**, of the first century A.D., who was financially ruined by his elaborate banquets, poisoned himself in fear of starvation!

• **Tzu Hsi**, an empress of China (1884- 1908), slept on a brick bed that was warmed by a fire burning beneath it!

• The Roman emperor **Tiberius** used relay runners to bring out-of-season fruit from distant lands to his dinner guests in Rome!

• French emperor **Charles IV** had a palace with four rooms, each with four doors, four tables, and four chandeliers. He ate four meals a day, each with four courses and four different kinds of wine, and he was married four times!

KINGS AND CZARS

• Opera singer **Farinelli** (1705-1782) was hired to sing King Philip V of Spain to sleep every night!

• The royal cape worn by Hawaiian **King Kamehameha** was made with the feathers from eighty thousand o'oao birds!

• The gold and jeweled crown of Persia's **King Sapori** (A.D. 244-272) was so heavy that to "wear" it, he had it hung with unseen wires above his head!

• Attila's Throne on the island of Torcello, off Venice, Italy, is a block of marble used as a throne by the King of the Huns over fifteen hundred years ago.

IN THE 1840s, KING KAMEHAMEHA I of Hawaii, ISSUED A ROYAL DECREE STATING THAT ONLY PRIESTS and ROYALTY COULD SURF STANDING UP — **IN ORDER TO BE CLOSER TO GOD!**

LUDWIG II OF BAVARIA (1778 – 1848) HAD AN ARTIFICIAL LAKE BUILT ON THE THIRD FLOOR OF HIS MUNICH APARTMENT, WHERE HE FLOATED IN A SWAN-SHAPED GONDOLA TO THE MUSIC OF A *HIDDEN ORCHESTRA!*

KING HENRY VIII, of England, carried a gold cane with a perfume dispenser in its head.

Egypt's KING FAROUK, a skilled pickpocket, once removed Winston Churchill's watch at a state reception!

• The King of Oyo, southern Nigeria, wears a veil of blue beads in order that his subjects (who believe him to be immortal) cannot tell whether it is the old king or his successor.

• **King Bela II** of Hungary was elected monarch and ruled the country for ten years (1131-1141)—although he was totally blind! His uncle, King Koloman, had blinded Bela in the belief that it would make him incapable of succeeding to the throne.

• The skull of **King Wenceslaus** of Bohemia, who died in 935, was crowned by the people of Czechoslovakia one thousand years after his death.

• In 1800, Russia's **Czar Paul I** ordered a horse formally court-martialed and beaten for having reared beneath him in a parade!

• **King Hugh Capet** (938-996) of France, founder of the Capetian Dynasty, was given the name Capet—meaning cap—because as an exuberant prince he often knocked the caps off passersby.

• **King Henry VI** (1421-1471), last English monarch of the house of Lancaster, held the thrones of both England and France before he was twelve months old.

• **King Louis XIV** (1638-1715), ruler of France for seventy-two years, had such an abhorrence of water that he never washed more than the tip of his nose.

• **King Philip I** (1527-1598) of Spain, fearing that a canal across Panama would endanger Spanish America, made it an offense punishable by death to even mention such a project. The ban was in effect for over two hundred years.

THE JACKAL THAT BECAME A KING! The RAJAH OF PARTABGARH in India AS A GESTURE OF CONTEMPT FOR A DEFEATED MONARCH CROWNED A JACKAL AS RULER OF GARWARA —AND THE ANIMAL REIGNED FOR 12 YEARS!

• **King Louis XIV** of France (1638-1715) was so vain that he could often be heard singing and humming songs written in praise of his rule.

QUEENS

• **Catherine the Great** of Russia had thirty-two lovers! She spent 99,820,000 rubles on them (about a billion dollars in purchasing power today). In addition she gave them 107,800 human beings as slaves.

• **Queen Isabella** of Castile took only two baths during her life-time—one at birth and the other just before her wedding!

• After the death of her husband, King Philip in 1506, **Queen Juana** of Spain had his body embalmed and placed in a jeweled coffin that she kept with her during meals and even when she slept!

• **Elizabeth I** of England (1533-1603) was the first monarch to use a fork for eating—the custom outraged the clergy, but caught on in the New World!

• England's **King Charles II** (1630-1685) rubbed the dust collected from Egyptian mummies onto his skin in the belief that the greatness of the pharaohs would rub off on him!

• "Yeoman Bed Hanger" and "Yeoman Bed Goer" were the titles given to employees of England's Buckingham Palace who searched the royal bedrooms each night for intruders!

• **King Henry IV** of France, on rainy days, had trees, rocks, and grass brought into a corridor of the Louvre to stage indoor fox hunts with his courtiers!

• A haircut or death? The answer—death!: **Clotilde**, Queen of the Franks (474-545), whose grandchildren were heirs to the throne, was issued this ultimatum by her enemies—"Cut off their hair or cut off their heads!" She chose that the children should die!

• The Queen of Hearts: **Queen Marguerite de Valois** (1552-1615), of Navarre, had pockets in the lining of her hoop skirt so she could carry with her always the hearts of her thirty-four successive sweethearts—each embalmed and sealed in a separate box!

• A cannonball that was fired for a ball: The water in the Medici Fountain in Rome, Italy, spouts from a cannonball that was fired by **Queen Christina** of Sweden against the gate of the Villa Medici in 1658 to remind inhabitants of the villa that they were invited to the exiled queen's ball.

PRINCES AND PRINCESSES

• **Averroes** (1120-1198), famed Arabian astronomer and philosopher, translated the writings of Aristotle into Arabic, a project that so delighted Prince Yusuf of Cordoba that he rewarded Averroes with the weight of Aristotle's works—in diamonds!

• England's **Prince Charles** once gave his parents, Queen Elizabeth II and Prince Philip, a gift of plastic noses and fake mustaches wrapped in old socks!

THE BEST KNOWN FACE IN HISTORY
Elizabeth of York
QUEEN of HENRY VII of ENGLAND
HER PORTRAIT HAS APPEARED **8** TIMES IN EVERY DECK of PLAYING CARDS FOR **400** YEARS

YOUNG AND OLD RULERS

• **Isabel** of France, Queen of England, was engaged at the age of two, married at the age of seven, became a widow at the age of eleven, married Charles of Angouleme at the age of sixteen, and died in child-birth at the age of twenty.

• **Joaquin** (1449-1565) became patriarch of Alexandria, Egypt, at the age of ninety-eight, and held that office until his death eighteen years later at age one hundred sixteen.

STRANGE CORONATIONS

• The king that ruled from the womb! **Sapor II**, king of fourth-century Persia, was crowned before his birth. When Shah Hormouz died without an heir, his magi predicted that his widowed queen would give birth to a boy, conceived before Hormouz's death. On his word, the queen was laid upon a royal bed, and the crown of the Sassanids was placed on her belly. A few months later, the queen gave birth to a son, who lived to enjoy a lengthy reign.

• **Kansu el Ghouri** (1441-1516), a freed slave, rejected the throne of Egypt in 1501—accepting it only when warned that he would be assassinated unless he became the country's ruler. As Sultan Melik el Ashraf, he was on the throne for fifteen years before being slain in battle.

NOBILITY AND ARISTOCRACY

• Etruscan aristocrats, as a status symbol, vied to see who could amass the greatest array of shoes.

• **Francis Henry Egerton** (1756-1829), the eighth earl of Bridgewater, England, wore a different pair of shoes every day of the year!

England's
QUEEN VICTORIA
frequently ate peas with a knife!

MARCUS SITTICUS, the 17th-century Prince-Archbishop of Salzburg, Austria, had water jets installed in the stools around his palace courtyard in order to surprise his guests!

THE MEN WHO THREW THEMSELVES UNDER A CARRIAGE TO CUSHION ITS WHEELS! **ALI PASHA** (1741-1822), ruler of Janina, Albania, to prevent his carriage from bouncing, always had a dozen men run ahead of his horses and throw themselves into any deep holes in the road! For allowing the coach and horses to pass over him, each man was paid $3^1/_2$ lbs. of bread each day.

AN ORCHESTRA was employed by the Earl of Portland to entertain his horses.

• Long hair indicated nobility among the ancient Gauls, and when **Julius Caesar** conquered them he ordered their hair cut as a sign of submission.

• The British lord who couldn't read or write: Henry Clifford (1455-1553), an English orphan condemned to death at the age of seven for his father's acts, escaped and was an illiterate shepherd for twenty-three years—but in 1485 he was restored to his rightful place as the two hundred fourteenth Lord Clifford, the tenth Baron Westmoreland, the First Lord Vesvci, and possessor of one of England's greatest fortunes!

• **Lord Dudley** and **Ward** (1781-1833) British foreign secretary in 1827, was convinced that his two titles made him twins. He talked to himself constantly in two voices—using a falsetto voice for Dudley and a bass voice for Ward.

• The **Earl of Lonsdale** (1857-1944) did not once miss a running of the English Derby in sixty-two years.

• The landed gentry of eighteenth century England were so powerful that they could seize public land to enlarge their estates, change the course of a public road, raze and remove villages, dam a stream, or create a lake at will.

• **Sir Gerald Tyrwhitt-Wilson**, of Oxfordshire, England (1883- 1950), had the doves that nested around his home painted in pastel colors!

CHARLEMAGNE FIRST EMPEROR OF THE HOLY ROMAN EMPIRE sat on his throne for 397 years! He was interred on his marble throne in 814 after a reign of 46 years—and his corpse was still seated on it when the tomb was opened in 1165!

In Burma, a **WHITE ELEPHANT** was once given a palace with 30 attendants and the honorary title of "Minister of State"!

"IT'S GOOD TO BE THE KING"—DUTCH TOURIST IS CROWNED TRIBAL KING IN GHANA

The typical vacationer heading off for a few weeks of leisure has visions of sightseeing and suntanning. And these were probably the same kind of activities Hank Oster, of Amsterdam, the Netherlands, had in mind for his recent trip to Africa. But Hank had a special treat awaiting him when he arrived in Ghana—he was crowned as a king!

Forty-three-year-old Hank Oster traveled to Africa with his wife, Patience, after an accident ended his career as a construction worker. While Hank pondered the next direction his life would take, Patience, a native of Ghana, suggested that they visit her tribe, the Ewe.

Immediately upon arrival, Hank felt a mystical connection with the land and the people: "It was my home. I belong here." Soon afterward, a local witch doctor identified Hank as the incarnation of the Ewe's former king, who had died without an heir. The Ewe had been searching for the king's successor for seventeen years.

The witch doctor pointed out several personality traits Hank shared with the departed king. "It is your destiny," the shaman told the former construction worker, "It is your fate." Hank discussed his ascent to the throne with Patience, who was supportive. "It suits you," she told her husband.

Hank was crowned in a traditional ceremony, and has ruled happily for several years. He can remain king as long as he serves the people, a task for which he seems ideally suited. Hank is responsible for approximately two hundred thousand people. He has built schools and public buildings, and has served as a liaison to local government. And he loves it: "It's good to be a king in Ghana."

As king, Hank has the privilege of taking more than one wife, but he doesn't wish to. Of Patience, his devoted queen, he says, "She's all that I need, and all that I can handle." And this time, when the king passes on, the Ewe will not have to search for his reincarnation. Hank has a son who will inherit the throne.

Chapter 56
Science & Technology

Robots in Japan *are being used to construct buildings* as well as paint walls and pour concrete!

Scalding hot ice? A clone of Abraham Lincoln? A plant that grows plastic? All of these marvels and more are under study in our research facilities and places of higher learning. As our scientific knowledge expands exponentially, the objects of our studies just seem to get weirder. Herein we'll offer a glimpse at a few of the most amazing would-be scientific breakthroughs of the future—and some that may already be upon us.

COMPUTING

• The first computer cards: A machine to turn out punch cards was patented by **Doctor Herman Hollerith** for his work with the United States Census Bureau in 1889.

• Niobium wires used in computers are so tiny it would take fifteen hundred to equal the width of a single human hair.

• Employees of Reeve Aleutian Airways received the following notice at the end of the year: "Effective January 1, 1980, we will now be on computer for all employees, therefore it is going to take longer to do the payroll."

GENETICS

• In 1992, scientists at Michigan State University altered the genes of a mustard plant so that it produced plastic!

• Scientists at Johns Hopkins School of Medicine in 1991 tried to clone tissue samples taken from the body of Abraham Lincoln!

PHYSICS

• A ship's weight is lower when the moon is directly above it!

• A column of air one inch square and six hundred miles high weighs only fifteen pounds.

• A person is more buoyant in quicksand than in water!

• At a depth of twelve thousand feet underwater, there is two and a half tons of pressure on every square inch of an object!

• A person weighs less standing at the equator than anywhere else on earth!

• A half dollar laid alongside another and then rolled around it will revolve twice around its own center before returning to its original position.

• A voice being broadcast on the radio will be heard thirteen thousand miles away sooner that it will be heard at the back of the room from which it is being broadcast!

A BALL of SOLID STEEL CAN BE BOUNCED **HIGHER** THAN A RUBBER BALL.

SCIENTISTS AT THE *INDUSTRY RESEARCH CENTER for BIOTECHNOLOGY* IN BERLIN, GERMANY, *HAVE INVENTED BACTERIA* **THAT CAN DIGEST THE CELLULOSE RESINS** OF METAL CAR BODIES.

IN 1990, SCIENTISTS AT CAMBRIDGE UNIVERSITY WORKING ON A CURE FOR BALDNESS, SUCCESSFULLY GREW HUMAN HAIR IN A TEST-TUBE!

PSEUDO-SCIENCE

• Swedish doctor **Nils Olof Jacobson**, after conducting tests on corpses, concluded that the human soul weighed twenty grams!

RESEARCH

• Researchers at Ohio State University have discovered that plastic pot scrubbers inserted in a cow's first stomach aid its digestion!

• Researcher **Catherine Maloney**, of Fairfield, Connecticut, published

• A hit golf ball spins about eighty thousand revolutions a minute!

• A ship weighs less going east than going west.

• Scalding hot ice was made by professor **Percy W. Bridgeman** of Harvard. Water was subjected to six hundred thousand pounds of pressure.

a study she conducted called "Feline Reactions to Bearded Men," in which cats were shown photographs of men with beards!

• Chickens in a laboratory in Cambridge Massachusetts smoked cigarettes to help scientists get a better understanding of their toxic effect.

• **Curtis Ebbesmeyer**, an oceanographer in Seattle, Washington, studies ocean currents by following the path of some eighty thousand running shoes that were accidentally dumped in the pacific!

ROBOTS

• A sheet-iron robot, seven feet tall and weighing two hundred pounds, designed by eighteen-

A ROBOT at Waseda University in Tokyo, Japan, TURNS RED WHEN IT'S ANGRY, GREEN WHEN IT'S HAPPY AND BECOMES SLEEPY WHEN ITS BATTERY IS RUNNING LOW!

year-old James Chisholm, of Portsmouth, Virginia, could walk, talk, add, subtract, and take pictures.

KOMODO DRAGONS—GIANT VENOMOUS LIZARDS MAY HOLD THE ANTIDOTE TO BIOLOGICAL WARFARE

Biological warfare is one of the most dreaded developments of modern times. It is especially feared because at present there are few means of counteracting its deadly effects. But researcher Terry Fredeking is seeking to change that. He hopes to find within the animal kingdom a substance that will act as an antidote to chemical weapons.

Considered the "Indiana Jones" of biological exploration, Fredeking has taken venom from vampire bats, Tasmanian devils, and several species of poisonous snake. But he has now decided to extract a venom sample from the most formidable poisonous animal of all: the Komodo dragon.

These gigantic lizards live only on Indonesia's Komodo Island. Only three thousand survive today. They are ferocious, swift—and venomous. When they attack their prey, they need only to take one healthy bite, and the chase is over. Within seventy-two hours, the bitten animal will die.

Yet Komodo dragons are somehow mysteriously immune to each other's bite. Fredeking suspects that once we unlock the secret of their immunity, we may have a clue to making human beings immune to the deadly effects of biological warfare.

But extracting a sample of a Komodo dragon's deadly saliva is no easy trick. Komodos have been known to devour human beings, and even contact with the secretions on their armored skin can be fatal. Despite the risk, Fredeking and his coworkers have managed to corner and cage the creatures long enough to extract a sample of their venom. Now perhaps this living legacy of the lost age of dinosaurs will someday provide us with a key to our own survival.

"TUMBLING MAN"
In 1991, Americans Chico MacMurtie and Rick Sayre created a robotic sculpture that can contort into several different positions!

• Remote-controlled robots are used by New York City's Police Department to remove bombs. Eighteen inches high and weighing two hundred thirty pounds, they are equipped with television cameras, X-ray equipment, a water cannon, and a shotgun—and can even climb steps!

SCIENTISTS

• **René Descartes** (1596-1650), the father of modern scientific thought, conceived the basic ideas for his work in methodology, physics, and mathematics in 1619 by three separate dreams in a single night.

• An actual finger from the right hand of astronomer **Galileo** is displayed in the Museum of the History of Science, in Florence, Italy—pointing towards the heavens.

• **Nikola Tesla** (1858-1943), an electrical genius offered the Nobel Prize for physics in 1912 jointly with **Thomas Edison**, refused to share the prize because he considered Edison "a mere inventor."

• **Henry Woodward** and **Matthew Evans**, of Toronto, Canada, produced light inside a glass bulb by heating a carbon filament—six years before Thomas Edison!

• **Charles Steinmetz**, the electrical genius, told that he could not smoke in the General Electric plant, stalked out and halted all work in the laboratory for two days until assured that the rule would not apply to him.

• **Albert Einstein** failed his first college entrance exam!

• In 1997, the brain of scientist **Albert Einstein** traveled from Florida to California inside a Tupperware container placed in the trunk of a rental car!

Chapter 57

Sports

Sports are an integral part of our lives. Most of us play a favorite sport, or follow a favorite team. But even in a realm as closely observed as sports, we can uncover an undercurrent of the bizarre and unbelievable. We've brought together a collection of little-known facts about your favorite sports, and we'll introduce you to a few rare athletic pastimes you may never have heard of. Welcome to the world of sports, Ripley's-style.

ARCHAIC SPORTS

• **Kublai Khan**, the Chinese potentate, on his hawking expeditions used five hundred falcons and ten thousand men.

• The ancient Aztecs played "tlachtli," a basketball-like game in which players who scored were allowed to grab clothing and jewelry from spectators!

ARCHERY

• In October of 1970, **Harry Drake**, of Lakeside, California, shot an arrow a distance of one mile, one hundred one yards, and twenty-one inches using a foot bow!

Adolph Topperwein, famous Winchester arms shooter, shot 72,500 small wooden blocks tossed into the air at a distance of 25 feet and missed only nine of them. He broke 14,540 in succession.

THE JOUSTING TOURNAMENT HELD ANNUALLY AT MT. SOLON, VA., SINCE 1821, IS THE OLDEST CONTINUOUSLY HELD SPORTING EVENT IN AMERICA

WADA DAIHACHI A 17th CENTURY JAPANESE ARCHER USING AN 8-FOOT LONGBOW FIRED 8,133 ARROWS IN A PERIOD OF 24 HOURS

A DOUBLE PLAY! IN 1905, JAMES BENNETT INVENTED A **DOUBLE BASEBALL GLOVE!** THE PLAYER WORE ONE PART of THE GLOVE ON EACH HAND AND CAUGHT THE BALL BY CLAPPING HIS HANDS TOGETHER!

I'VE GOT IT!

• **Joe Fries**, a champion American archer, killed a buffalo with a single arrow at a distance of ninety feet.

BASEBALL

• The earliest known reference to organized baseball was found in an 1825 edition of the Delhi, New York, *Gazette*—fourteen years before Abner Doubleday allegedly invented the game!

• **Jay Justin Clarke**, the catcher in a 1902 Texas League game, hit a world-record eight consecutive home runs!

• Until 1859, baseball umpires called games while sitting in rocking chairs behind home plate!

• **George Sisler**, first baseman for the Saint Louis Browns in the 1920s, nailed phonograph needles into his baseball bat to make it heavier!

• In the early 1900s, baseball pitcher **Rube Waddell** signed a contract that included a clause forbidding him from snacking in bed!

• **Babe Ruth,** the famed Yankee home-run slugger, in 1923 was walked one hundred seventy times.

"RADAR BALL"

A NEW BASEBALL DEVELOPED IN THE U.S. HAS A MICROCHIP INSIDE THAT CALCULATES THE SPEED of THE THROW AND DISPLAYS IT ON A TINY WINDOW!

Believe It or Not! BASEBALL GREAT **HANK AARON,** WHO RETIRED WITH **755 CAREER HOME RUNS,** ACTUALLY LOST HIS FIRST PROFESSIONAL HOME RUN in 1952 BECAUSE HE MISSED FIRST BASE!

• **John Parsons**, age ten, of Houston, Texas, has designed a baseball glove for children with no hands that allows them to both throw and catch.

• In 1993 **Chris Looney, Brent DeRiszner, Mark Johns,** and **Mike Casagrande** drove 17,339 miles across the United States in order to watch twenty-eight major league baseball games in twenty-eight days.

• An explosive fastball! In 1897, a pitching gun using real gunpowder was used by coaches for batting practice!

• **Rogers Hornsby** (1896-1963), considered the greatest of all right-handed batters, never went to the movies or read a book for fear they would impair his vision.

• **Ty Cobb** (1886-1961), one of the greatest base runners of all time, walked up to thirty miles a day each winter—with lead in his shoes.

• In 1993, the New York Mets team used over twenty-one thousand baseballs.

• **Walter Carlisle,** center fielder of the Vernon Baseball Club, in the Pacific Coast league, playing against Los Angeles on July 19, 1911, made an unassisted triple play.

• **Fernando Tatis**, a third baseman for the Saint Louis Cardinals, made baseball history in 1999 by becoming the first player to hit two grand slams in one inning!

• **Cliff Carroll**, a baseball player in Pittsburgh, Pennsylvania, during the 1800s, had his pet monkey, the team's mascot, buried under home plate at the team's ballpark!

• **Marv Owen**, a third baseman for the Detroit Tigers, in 1914 set a world series record with thirty-one consecutive hitless times at bat!

• In Olean, New York, **Ted Lesko** hit a high-fly that struck and killed a nighthawk!

• **Larry McPhail**, General Manager of the Brooklyn Dodgers, introduced yellow baseballs to the game in 1938, claiming they would be easier to see.

Pitcher JACK URBAN of the Southern Association in 1954 pitched a no-hitter against New Orleans—yet failed to win the game!

• **Don Larson** and **David Wells**, the only two pitchers ever to throw perfect games in New York's Yankee Stadium, both attended Point Loma High School, in San Diego, California.

• **Joe DiMaggio** had a lifetime batting average of .325 and a fifty-six-game hitting streak (a record that still stands), hit three hundred sixty-one homers, and struck out only three hundred sixty-nine times during his carreer!

• At the Baseball Hall of Fame in Cooperstown, New York, there is a baseball signed by **Pope John Paul II!**

• **Jimmy Johnston**, who played for San Francisco in 1913, stole one hundred twenty-four bases in one season!

• **John "Scissors" McIlvaine** was a baseball pitcher in Pittsburgh, Pennsylvania, for fifty-five years—pitching his eight hundredth game at the age of seventy-one.

• The first pro baseball player, **Lipman E. "Lip" Pike** (1845-1893), in 1866 was paid twenty dollars a week to play third base for the Philadelphia Athletics—becoming the first baseball player to receive a salary.

• **Larry Parrish**, playing third base for the Montreal Expos in a game against Saint Louis, was at bat five times, had five hits, scored five runs, and drove in five runs!

BASKETBALL

• **Geri Grigsby**, a basketball player at the University of Kentucky, set a new record for both women and men by scoring 4,385 points during her high school career—averaging 46.1 points per game.

• **Harold "Bunny" Levitt**, in a basketball exhibition in Chicago, Illinois, in 1935, made four hundred ninety-nine consecutive free throws. He never lost a foul-line contest—yet he never achieved fame in basketball because he was only five feet four inches tall.

• **Tom Diringer** of Norwalk, Ohio, on the basketball court of Shelby High School, in a period of twenty-four hours shot 14,500 free throws and made 13,208 of them for a 91.09 percentage, July 15-16, 1978.

• **Wilt Chamberlain**, the first pro basketball player to score thirty thousand points, scored one hundred points in a single game in 1962.

• Basketball great **Michael Jordan** played wearing his University of North Carolina shorts under his Chicago Bulls uniform to bring good luck!

BOXING

• Boxers in ancient Greece hit only to the head, and a blow to the body was always accidental.

• A fight to the finish: Prize-fighters in ancient Greece and Rome wore metal-studded boxing gloves—and slugged each other until one boxer was dead.

• **Kid Lavigne** of Saginaw, Michigan, knocked out Dick Burge, the British lightweight title-holder, to become the first American lightweight champion of the world, June 1, 1896.

• **Freddie Steele**, who won the world middleweight title in 1936, had fought nine professional paid bouts by the time he was thirteen years old.

• **Jack Dempsey**, in his championship fight with **Luis Firpo**, was knocked down twice and floored forty-seven times in the same round.

MUHAMMAD ALI, who became heavy-weight champion of the world, took up boxing as a boy so he could clobber a thief who stole his bicycle.

THE ROMAN BOXER *MELANCOMAS* ONCE HELD OFF AN OPPONENT WITH A "STRAIGHT ARM" FOR TWO DAYS AND WON *WITHOUT HAVING DEALT A SINGLE BLOW!*

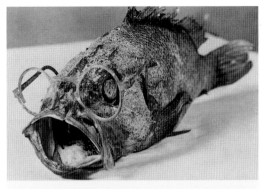

Fisherman **Ira D. Erling** lost his glasses overboard, only to have them returned by this considerate fish, caught a short time later.

Peter Wimbrow caught a shark with his bare hands in Vero Beach, Florida.

CYCLING

• British cyclist **Reg Harris**, who survived being blown up in a tank during World War II and having his neck broken in a car accident, went on to win four world racing titles!

• **Charlie Miller**, competing in a six-day bicycle race in New York's Madison Square Garden in 1898, pedaled 2,093.4 miles.

• The bicyclist who outraced the French fleet: **Charles Terront**, learning that the French fleet was sailing from Paris to Saint Petersburg in 1893 for a courtesy visit, set out in the opposite direction at the same time, covering the one thousand five hundred fifty miles in fourteen days, six hours, thirty-eight minutes—and beating the fleet's time by two days!

FENCING

• **Charles Bothner** of New York City was so expert with the foil, the epee, and saber that in 1897 he won all three American fencing titles.

FISHING

• **Ron Thomas,** of Phoenix, can cast fourteen fly-fishing rods all at the same time.

• A cod caught by **Arthur Smith,** of Cambridge, Massachusetts, hundreds of miles at sea, had inside it a photograph of two girls that was still in perfect condition.

• **Edward F. Spence**, an English angler and author of *The Pike Fisher*, caught eight thousand pike in waters around the world—and threw every one of them back.

• A thirty-three-inch muskie, caught by **Reinhold Elke** of Detroit, Michigan, was found to have in its stomach a pint bottle full of ale!

IN 1959 Alf Dean
LANDED A **2,664 LB.**
WHITE SHARK off
the COAST of South Australia—
*THE HEAVIEST FISH EVER CAUGHT
ON A ROD and REEL!*

One bass's head got caught in the mouth of the other after they both went after the same bait in Herrington Lake, Kentucky, 1933.

Anna Lee Slaughter, at age five, caught and landed a $22\frac{1}{2}$-pound bass by herself.

A record catch for **Bobby Cunningham,** of Belfast, Maine, who caught this speckled trout sporting a 45 R.P.M. record on June 7, 1966.

• **Carl Moore,** of Morgan, Oklahoma, caught an eight-inch-trout—without his hook touching the fish! The trout had been hooked some months before, and the hook had remained in its mouth. Moore's hook went through the eye of the other hook!

FOOTBALL

• The only triple Hall of Famer, **Cal Hubbard,** of Keytesville, Missouri, was elected to the College Football Hall of Fame, the National Football League's Hall of Fame, and the Professional Baseball Hall of Fame.

THE FOOTBALL "HUDDLE" WAS INVENTED BY DEAF PLAYERS AT GAULLADET COLLEGE IN WASHINGTON, D.C., *WHO WANTED TO HIDE THEIR HAND SIGNALS FROM THE OPPOSING TEAM.*

IN NEW YORK AT THE TURN OF THE CENTURY, A GAME OF FOOTBALL, IN WHICH PLAYERS COULD TACKLE WITH ONLY ONE ARM, WAS PLAYED ON HORSEBACK!

• **E. Cook**, an Oklahoma University halfback, on November 6, 1904, swam to a touchdown! A blocked kick fell into a river behind the goal posts—Cook swam the ball back for a touchdown!

• **Galahad Grant,** of New York University, lost twenty-two pounds in a single game of football. The team lost two hundred sixty-seven pounds that day, October 1, 1927.

Dick Crayne punted 102 yards in an Iowa-vs.-Indiana football game.

• **George Musso** was the only NFL Hall of Famer to play against two United States Presidents—Gerald Ford in 1935 and Ronald Reagan in 1929!

• **"Skeeter Bomb,"** a cat owned by Robert Amo of Castro Valley, California, attended Oakland Raider football games on its own season tickets.

GOLF

• **Seymour Fleming,** of Port Saint Lucie, Florida, has scored two holes in one although he is a one-armed golfer.

• The Westward Ho! golf club at Bideford, England, is the oldest course in England located on its original site.

LLAMAS ARE USED AS CADDIES AT THE Talamore Golf Course in Southern Pines, N.C.!

Alex Ednie, golf pro, drove a golf ball through a five-hundred-page phone book. The book was put on end without support.

• In 1992, **Merle Ball,** of Sebring, Florida, hit a golf ball across four states with a single stroke!

• **Doctor R. C. Spangler** of Morgantown, West Virginia, played eighty-three holes of golf and scored an eighty-three on one of the eighteen-hole rounds—on his eighty-third birthday.

• Golf champion **Jack Nicklaus** scored a fifty-one in the first nine holes he ever played—when he was only ten years old!

• **Julian H. Parke,** playing golf at the Ogden Utah C.C., scored a hole-in-one on the ninth hole twice in the same week.

• At the annual Pioneer Pass Golf Challenge, players start at the top of a seven-thousand-foot-high mountain and play golf through mountain passes, snake-filled ravines, an abandoned mine shaft, and a desert!

HOCKEY

• **Bobby Hull**, the Chicago Black Hawks hockey star, skated at a speed of nearly thirty miles per hour, and hit a puck at a record one hundred eighteen miles per hour.

The oldest depiction of a field hockey game was found in the TOMB OF SESOSTRIS II, A 12th Dynasty Egyptian ruler!

• The Dawson City Klondikers hockey team had to travel twenty-three days and four thousand miles by bobsled, train, and boat in order to play the Ottawa Silver Sevens for the 1906 Stanley Cup Game!

OLYMPICS

• For three thousand years, a mirror and an olive branch have been used to light the Olympic flame on Mount Olympus in Greece! A torch that is lit from this fire is used to ignite the flame that burns during the Olympic games!

• How to assure victory: **Emperor Nero** of Rome entered several

Believe It or Not! THE TUG-of-WAR WAS ONCE AN **OLYMPIC EVENT!**

MIRSADA BURIC, A RUNNER WHO COMPETED IN THE 1992 OLYMPIC GAMES, TRAINED IN WAR-TORN Sarajevo and SPENT **13 DAYS AS A PRISONER** of SERBIAN TROOPS BEFORE ATTENDING THE Barcelona COMPETITION!

A POLO MATCH in Jaipur, India, WAS PLAYED ON ELEPHANTS INSTEAD of PONIES! (1976)

Olympic contests in A.D. 66, accompanied by five thousand body-guards—and was declared the winner in every event in which he competed.

• Speed skater **Jaqueline Boerner,** of Germany, unable to skate for more than a year after a serious car accident in 1990, won a gold medal at the 1992 Olympics!

POLO

• Left-handed polo players, unless they competed before 1974, are banned from all matches sanctioned by the United States Polo Association.

• Polo, the oldest equestrian sport, is believed to have been played by the Persians in 2000 B.C.

TENNIS

• Tennis was invented by **Major Walter C. Wingfield** of England in 1873 and patented under the name of "Sphairistike."

• **John Gambuccho,** of Grand Forks, North Dakota, led his high school tennis team to two consecutive state

championships by winning fifty-three consecutive matches.

• **J. Donald Budge**, the tennis champion who won every game he played in 1937, and brought the Davis Cup back to the United States after fourteen years, disliked tennis as a youngster.

• **Pancho Gonzales**, who held the world tennis championship for eight years, never received formal instruction in that sport.

• **Maureen Connoly** (1934-1969), who became the youngest United States girls' tennis champion at age fourteen, won the National Women's Title at sixteen, and ended her fabulous tennis career while still in her teens.

RACING

AUTO RACING

• A racing car built in England in the 1930s, shaped like a turtle and made of aluminum, was so light it cold be dented by a man's fist.

HORSE RACING

• **"Regret"** was the only filly that ever won the Kentucky Derby. She did it in 1915.

• A triple dead heat was rerun in Moorfield, New South Wales, Australia, on October 10, 1903—and ended in another triple dead heat! The three winners were "High Flyer," "Lock Lohie," and "Bardini."

• Jockey **Ray Selkrig** was thrown from his horse, "Hot Chestnut," during a 1973 race at Kembla Grange, New South Wales, Australia. He became tangled as he fell, and crossed the finish line literally dangling from the horse's reins. Judges later decided that the horse had transported Selkrig's weight across the line, and awarded him the victory!

WHEN BILL SHOEMAKER *RETIRED* FROM HORSERACING IN 1990, HE HAD WON 8,833 OF THE 40,349 RACES HE HAD COMPETED IN!

CAMARERO "THE UNDEFEATED CHAMPION"! A horse owned by José Vidal won 55 consecutive races from April 1953 to August 1955!

Three horses at the Laurel Park Race Course, in Maryland, finished in a dead heat for third place on April 6, 1954.

• **"Silver Mint"** won the 1949 jumping event on the White City track in London, England, when the horse was twenty-eight years of age. His rider, Alan Oliver, was only seventeen.

• **"Signorinetta,"** owned by Chevalier Ginistrelli, won the English Derby in 1908—and paid off at odds of one hundred to one.

SHELL RACING

• **Hiram Connibear** revolutionized shell-crew racing with "the Connibear stroke" yet when he first took the job of rowing coach at the University of Washington he hated the water, couldn't swim, and had never even seen a racing shell.

RUNNING

• **Duncan MacClean,** who established himself as one of the world's fastest sprinters by running one hundred yards in 9.9 seconds in 1904, ran that distance in fourteen seconds at the age of eighty-eight.

• **Bill Rodgers,** a repeat winner of the Boston Marathon, trains by running about one hundred thirty miles a week—but before a big race he runs two hundred miles a week.

• **Emil Zatopek,** of Czechoslovakia, who broke eighteen world records for distance runs, once broke the world's time for ten thousand meters after a five- hour train ride in which he stood all the way and had eaten only dry biscuits.

SKIING

• A ski race championship held annually at Sugarloaf, Maine, limits entry to skiers weighing at least two hundred twenty-five-pounds.

AMERICAN SKIER

JEFF HAMILTON HOLDS THE *WORLD RECORD for SPEED SKIING* – HE ONCE SKIED DOWN A MOUNTAIN AT *150.028 MPH !*

SOCCER AND RUGBY

• **Richard Anderson,** a sheep farmer in New Zealand, arranged his entire flock of sheep in a pattern across a field to spell out the name of his favorite rugby team!

• **King Edward II** of England, in 1314, forbade soccer "on pain of imprisonment."

• Soccer has a world governing body (the Federation of International Football Associations) that has more members than the Untied Nations.

WALKING

• **Emile Anthoine,** president of the French Walking Union, won eight hundred professional walking contests—covering a total of six hundred thousand miles.

WATER SPORTS

• **Doctor Christiaan Barnard,** who performed the first heart transplant operation in 1967, at one time put aside his own career in an attempt to make his daughter a world's champion water-skier.

WRESTLING

• **Milo** of Crotona, the most famous Greek wrestler of ancient times, could curl his finger around a pomegranate so that no man could pry open his grip or damage the fruit.

• The Iron Man: **Thomas Nicholson,** famous English wrestler, danced all night at Penrith, England, walked twenty-five miles to Ambleside, and then defeated his opponents in four heavyweight wrestling matches—in succession.

• Modern wrestlers still use more than two hundred holds that were depicted

Underwater runners average 50 yards in 25 seconds, and push 8,900 pounds of water.

Byron Ferguson— Archer Extraordinaire

World-class exhibition archer Byron Ferguson is acknowledged as the best shot in the world, a title anybody who's seen him shoot has to agree he deserves.

He's good.

How good? How about being able to shatter an aspirin in midair? How about being able to spear a gold ring on the way to the target? Or piercing a balloon bobbing along behind a remote-controlled airplane? Or, a shot that many archers admit takes the most precision of all, piercing three balloons in a row in a carefully calculated double bank shot? Ferguson can handle them all—and he makes them look easy.

Archery is Byron Ferguson's lifelong passion. "Archery bit me pretty early," he says. Ferguson perfected his shot by sitting in a dark room and shooting out a lit candle! As he developed his skill, he quickly graduated from stationary targets when he discovered that a moving target was a lot more fun.

Unlike the modern compound bow used by most other pro archers, Ferguson shoots with a simple five-and-a-half-foot-long bow with a seventy-one-pound draw. Today's high-tech compound bow would take most of that seventy-one pounds of strain for him, but with this bow, Ferguson feels every ounce of it!

For the past seventeen years, Ferguson's wife, Wanda, has been the one to toss targets into the air for him, a task she admits took some getting used to. She is literally inches away from the arrow's path as it pierces targets that left her fingers only a fraction of a second before! Yet in nearly two decades, Wanda has never been injured. Her calm confidence in her husband's talent is absolute.

How do you get to be a master archer like Byron Ferguson? Practice. And a certain amount of faith: "You trust your instincts and let the shot happen."

on the wall of the temple tombs of Beni Hasan, in the Nile Valley, nearly five thousand years ago.

CHEERLEADING

• Professor **Robert C. Matthews,** of Fort Lauderdale, Florida, who organized acrobatic cheerleading in 1899 at the University of Illinois—was still an active cheerleader at the age of ninety.

• Cheerleaders for the Sun City, Arizona, Saints, a women's ball club, range in age from fifty-five to seventy-two.

NEW SPORTS

• "Whirly ball," a new North American sport, is played by using a scoop to flick a whiffle ball—while riding in modified bumper cars!

UNUSUAL AND EXOTIC SPORTS

• Face slapping was once a sport in Kiev, U.S.S.R., and in 1931 **Wasyl Bezbordny** and **Michalko Goniusz** slapped each other continuously for thirty hours.

• "Coalball," a game played indoors by two teams of six who try to put a ball into the opposing teams' net, requires all players to wear blindfolds!

• **Julio Aparicio,** a Spanish bullfighter, as a demonstration of his bravery would take a bull's horn in his teeth.

• The man who fought wild bulls for sixty-one years! **Pedro Romero** (1754-1838), famous Spanish bullfighter, killed his five thousandth bull at the age of seventy-six! In his sixty-one years in the ring, not one bull even so much as scratched him.

Believe It or Not!
MANUEL GARCIA,
a Spanish matador, fought a bull while riding a bicycle!

Chapter 58
Time

We tend to think of time as a constant—as a genuine phenomenon that occurs outside ourselves, which we merely observe. But, as you're about to read, time as we know it is a human invention. In many cases, we can even pinpoint the individuals in history who instituted the concepts of time we use to this day. However, we must also remember that there are people still living in the world today who conceive time in a completely different manner than ourselves.

The more we ponder time, the less it can be observed to exist at all. When, for example, is "now"? It's strange that a concept we rely upon as concrete and unchanging in reality has little substance outside our own minds. Prepare yourself to experience time as you never have before. . . .

THE BEGINNING OF TIME

• A hour is divided into sixty minutes, based on a system developed by the ancient Sumerians in 2400 B.C.!

• The first Leap Year was in 46 B.C.!

• **Abul Hassan,** Arabian poet, invented the twenty-four-hour day. He divided the day and night into twenty-four equal parts, in the thirteenth century.

CALENDRICAL TIME

• Each new year comprises 365 days, 5 hours, 48 minutes, and 45 seconds.

• 1896 was a leap year; 1900 was NOT a leap year; 1904 was a leap year, and 2000 was a leap year. Why? Leap years must be divisible by four and centenary years must be divisible by four hundred.

• The last minute of 1998 had sixty-one seconds instead of sixty!

• In 100 years there are: 400 seasons, 1,200 months, 5,218 weeks, 36,521 days, 876,504 hours, 52,590,240 minutes, and 3,155,414,400 seconds.

TRICKS WITH TIME

• It is possible to have a letter delivered the day before it was mailed. How? A plane leaving Wake Island at 12:01 A.M. Sunday arrives at Midway Island at 7:31 A.M. Saturday. You lose a day crossing the eightieth meridian.

• The most amazing time of the twentieth century occurred fifty-six seconds after 12:34 on July 8, 1990, when the time was 12:34:56, 7/8/90.

• The year 1961 was the last time the date could be read right-side up and upside down! It won't occur again until 6009!

• On January 10, 2011, the date will have the same digits backward and forward! The last date to have this feature was September 29, 1929!

• February 2, 2000 (2-2-2000) was the first time in over one thousand years that every digit in a date had even numbers! It last occurred on August 28, 888!

• November 19, 1999, was the last day of the Gregorian calendar to carry all odd numbers! This phenomenon will not happen again until January 1, 3111!

TIME AS IT IS MEASURED ELSEWHERE

• The ancient Incas of Peru measured time by how long it took to cook a potato!

• People of the Thonga tribe of South Africa originally told time according to six positions of the sun: cool-dawn, sun-piercing, sun-burning, sun-middle-of-the-sky, sun-goes-cooler, and sun-at-horizon!

• The ancient Aztec week was twenty days long!

ODD HOURS

• The United States Naval Observatory's master clock, which is the official time keeper for the entire country, experienced a Y2K glitch and posted the date at the stroke of midnight as "19100"!

PASSAGE OF TIME was noted in ancient times, at night when sundials could not function, by burning lengths of rope knotted at regular intervals

A CLOCK THAT GAVE YOU THREE GUESSES. a one-hand clock invented by Benjamin Franklin in 1770, was not marketed until 200 years later. The hand here reads either 3:35, 7:35, or 11:35, but Franklin figured anyone would know about what hour of the day it was.

SPHERICAL CLOCKS IN 17th-CENTURY GERMANY WERE SUSPENDED FROM CHAINS WHICH REWOUND THEM AS THE CLOCKS SLIPPED DOWN

- The unique "magana" clock of the magician **I. Fez**, of Morocco, is the only clock in the world to strike thirteen hours.

- A Japanese company has invented a wristwatch with a 1,100-year calendar, dating from 1400 to the year 2499!

- **Morton Rachofsky**, of Dallas, Texas, has invented a clock with twenty-five hours!

CHANGING TIMES

- In 12,890 years, summer will officially begin on December 21 and the first day of winter will be June 21!

- The madman who changed the French New Year: **Raoul Spifame** (1518-1563), an insane French lawyer who thought he was King Henry II, looked so much like the monarch that the king humored him by giving him a castle and a retinue of servants who always addressed him as "Your Majesty." Although he was mad, Spifame "issued" many laws which were adopted by the French government—the first of which changed the French New Year from March 25 to January 1.

- Until 1883, there were eighty different time zones across North America!

IN 1656, IRISH ARCHBISHOP JAMES USSHER CALCULATED THAT THE EARTH WAS CREATED AT EXACTLY 8 P.M. ON SAT. OCT. 3, 4004, B.C.

4 MEDIEVAL HOURGLASSES bound together and filled with different amounts of sand measured 60 minutes, 45 minutes, 30 minutes, and 15 minutes.

THE **FIRST CALENDAR** WAS THE *GREAT PYRAMID*!

THE *SHADOW* OF THE PYRAMID OF CHEOPS REVEALED TO THE EGYPTIANS THE EXISTENCE OF THE YEAR AND THE FOUR SEASONS AND LED TO THE ESTABLISHMENT OF THE SOLAR YEAR.

Chapter 59

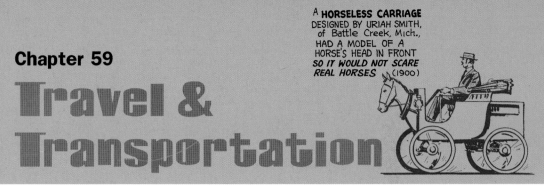

A **HORSELESS CARRIAGE** DESIGNED BY URIAH SMITH, of Battle Creek, Mich., HAD A MODEL OF A HORSE'S HEAD IN FRONT *SO IT WOULD NOT SCARE REAL HORSES* (1900)

Travel & Transportation

Humankind has poured some of its most creative energies into solving the problem of transportation. We've run the gamut of rocket-powered cars, bird-propelled balloons, dog-pedaled tricycles—and still we're inventing. The process that began the day our ancient ancestors recognized the superiority of four hooves over ten toes, has continued into this era of supersonic and space flight, and shows no signs of stopping. Travel is an art that may never be perfected. Ripley's collection of bizarre transportation begins with the quaint and obsolete travel modes of the past; takes us through the days of early motoring, to today's automobiles, trains, planes, and ships; and offers a look at some of the world's most exotic means of getting around.

• At the turn of the century, special uniformed catchers were employed in the Boston and London subway systems to help passengers cope with newly installed escalators.

ANTIQUATED TRAVEL

• The first taxicab in history appeared in Rome two thousand years ago: A horse-drawn carriage was equipped with a meter that dropped pebbles into a drum when a rear wheel revolved! Counting the pebbles determined the fare.

• A wagon with rich bronze inlays, found in pieces at Dejbjerg, Denmark, had been dismantled and thrown into a bog as a sacrifice some two thousand year ago.

• **Robert Valturio** designed a war vehicle, in 1472, that was to be propelled by windmill sails.

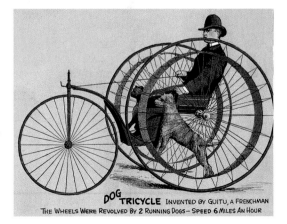

DOG TRICYCLE INVENTED BY GUITU, A FRENCHMAN THE WHEELS WERE REVOLVED BY 2 RUNNING DOGS— SPEED 6 MILES AN HOUR

AIR TRAVEL

EARLY AVIATION

• The world's first human flight: A paper balloon was flown above Paris, France, by **Pilatre de Rozier** and the **Marquis D'Arlandres** on November 21, 1783—and they put out a fire in their paper craft with a large sponge and water.

• The first flight by man in America: **Jean Pierre Blanchard** (1753-1809), a French balloonist, made a forty-six-minute ascension in Philadelphia on January 9, 1793, with George Washington as a spectator.

• A flying machine patented by **Jerome Blanchard** in 1895 required the pilot to pedal the front end of a bicycle.

BALLOONS AND AIRSHIPS

• **Joseph-Michael Mongolfier** created the first hot-air balloon after watching his wife's wedding dress, being dried by the fire, fill with hot air!

BALLOONS in the 18th century were equipped with sails in the mistaken belief they could be maneuvered like a ship at sea.

BIRD-POWERED BALLOON A balloon patented in the U.S. in 1887 by Charles R. E. Wulff of Paris, France, was to be propelled by "living motors," captive eagles, vultures, and condors.

• The first dirigible was constructed in 1785 by **Count D'Artois**, who later became King Charles X of France. It could be steered by shifting vanes with a winch.

• A balloon invented by **Frederick Eshoo,** of Iran, rose to an altitude of 12,500 feet and stayed aloft four hours, ten minutes, seventeen seconds—buoyed only by the heat of the sun's rays.

MODERN AVIATION

• **Brian Milton,** of Britain, is the first person to fly around the world in a bicycle with wings—completing the journey in one hundred twenty days! (1998)

• A plane lands or takes off from O'Hare Airport, in Chicago, Illinois, every forty-five seconds every day of every year.

• A United States defense agency has developed miniature airplanes the size of a person's hand that can fly up to seventy miles per hour for a distance of twelve miles!

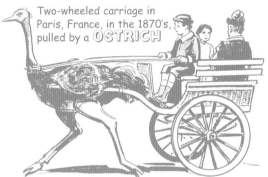

Two-wheeled carriage in Paris, France, in the 1870's, pulled by a OSTRICH

A **MECHANICAL HORSE** OPERATED BY ELECTRICITY— ENVISIONED BY LU SENARENS, AN AUTHOR, IN 1896

• **Henry Langer,** better known as Cloudbuster Hen Langer, went up in an airplane four hundred seventy-nine times, but never landed in one. He parachuted to earth during his first plane ride in 1932, and did so during every plane ride afterwards.

• American space scientists are working on designs for a plane that can fly from New York City to Tokyo in three hours at a speed of four thousand miles per hour!

A COMPANY in Japan HAS DEVELOPED A *PERSONAL HELICOPTER* for ONE RIDER THAT IS EQUIPPED WITH FOUR 125cc TWO-STROKE ENGINES AND CAN FLY for UP TO AN HOUR AT A SPEED of 62 MPH.!

A BUILD-IT-YOURSELF AIRPLANE KIT ADVERTISED BY A KANSAS FIRM, CONSISTED OF 4,155 PARTS --BUT IT COULD ONLY BE ASSEMBLED UNDER SUPERVISION OF AN FAA INSPECTOR

AVIATORS

• England's **Edward Duke of Windsor** had a pair of special glasses made for his favorite dog "Cora" that countered the effects of high-altitude flying!

• **Arthur Ray Smith** (1890-1926), a pioneer Indiana aviator, persuaded his parents to mortgage their home so that he could build his own airplane when he was sixteen.

AUTOMOBILES

• **Mike Tonis,** of Sacramento, California, who bought a 1926 car for five dollars, has always done all repairs himself—and has driven it over six hundred fifty thousand miles.

EARLY MOTORING

• The Cugnot Steam Wagon, the first automobile that ran under its own power, was built in France in 1771—on a cannon carriage.

• A twenty-one-ton amphibious vehicle invented by **Oliver Evand** and operated in Philadelphia, Pennsylvania, in 1805, was the first American road vehicle operated by steam.

FEMALE MOTORISTS IN THE EARLY 1900s, BECAUSE MOST AUTOS HAD NO WINDSHIELDS THEN, SHIELDED THEIR FACE FROM WIND AND DUST BY PORTABLE WINDSCREENS

• The conveyance that was ahead of its time: A steam carriage invented by **Richard Dudgeon,** of New York City, in the 1800s, could travel four miles per hour—fueled by one barrel of anthracite coal.

• A steam carriage built by **Sir Goldsworthy Gurney** so terrified natives on a journey from London, England, to Bath that Gurney and his engineer were attacked by a mob and beaten.

• The first car with a three-speed transmission was patented in England by **W. H. James,** in 1832.

• The London & Birmingham Steam Coach, built in Birmingham, England, in 1833, carried twenty-eight passengers inside and seated twenty-two more outside.

THE FIRST HORSELESS CARRIAGE
A CARRIAGE BUILT BY HANS HAUTSCH of Nürnberg, Germany, IN 1649 COULD BE PEDALED AT A SPEED OF ONE MILE PER HOUR —AND AT THE SAME TIME SPRAY PERFUME ON PASSERSBY THROUGH AN ATOMIZER IN THE DRAGON'S HEAD, WHICH ALSO SERVED AS ITS TILLER

A BICYCLE PATENTED IN THE U·S· IN 1898, WAS ROWED LIKE A BOAT

• An automobile invented in Paris, France, in the nineteenth century needed so much fuel to run its steam engine that bags of soft coal always had to be left along its chosen route.

• A Winton motor car, to show its dependability, was driven eight hundred miles from Cleveland, Ohio, to New York City, in 1897, in seventy-eight hours, forty-three minutes. The fuel was cleaning fluid purchased in hardware stores.

• The first motorized taxis looked like old horse-drawn hansom cabs, and the driver rode outside.

• The first auto race in America: About eighty cars entered a race from Chicago to Waukegan, Illinois, on November 28, 1895—a distance of fifty-two miles. All but six failed to start, and the average speed was seven and a half miles per hour.

ALTERNATIVE AUTOMOTIVE POWER

• A company in Germany has developed a car with an electric motor for driving in the city and a gas engine for highway driving!

IN 1869, THERE WERE OVER 50 SCHOOLS in New York City ORGANIZED TO TEACH PEOPLE HOW TO RIDE PENNY-FARTHING BICYCLES!

The first auto to cross the U.S., piloted by **E. I. Hammond** and **L. L. Whitman**, traveled 900 miles without meeting another automobile.

A tricycle 10 feet high was made by **James P. Glass** of Riverside, California to ride in parades.

An automobile built by Jaap Zwart from a **BATHTUB** Amsterdam, Holland

BICYCLE BUILT FOR 10
THE DECEMTUPLE, BUILT IN 1896, *CARRIED 10 RIDERS*

Joseph Steinlauf, builder of whimsical bicycles, created this brass-bed bicycle, as well as a "gangstercycle," a sewing machine bicycle, and a bicycle built for ten!

AN **8-MAN TRICYCLE** BUILT IN NEW ENGLAND IN 1896 WEIGHED **2,500** POUNDS, WAS **17** FEET IN LENGTH, AND *ITS REAR WHEELS WERE 11 FEET IN DIAMETER*

• The wagon built by **Samuel Peppard,** of Oskaloosa, Kansas, in 1860, powered only by the wind, sailed over five hundred miles across the prairie from Oskaloosa to the Kansas gold fields in less than five weeks.

ODD CONFIGURATION OR CONSTRUCTION

• A Japanese car company has invented a two-seated vehicle that uses optical sensors to read traffic signs and road conditions!

• "The Ultimate Taxi," The world's smallest recording studio is a 1978 Checker taxicab in Denver, Colorado, that contains a theater, toy store, Internet connections, dry ice machine, digital camera, computer, cell phone, digital drums, and a planetarium!

ODD DECORATION

• The one thousand forty-five horsepower car: **Ronald Colt Snow**, of Los Gatos, California, has mounted on his auto one thousand forty-five plastic horses.

Arlene Lambert of Toronto. Ont. Canada drives a car that is covered with hundreds of PLASTIC BABY DOLLS!

Believe It or Not.✓ A CAR WITH *TRIANGULAR WHEELS* WHICH COULD CLIMB STAIRS WAS DISPLAYED at the **ANNUAL IDEA OLYMPICS** in *Toyota, Japan.*✓

The "Hondime," a 1973 Honda covered with hundreds of dimes—and one quarter.

• **Charles Miller** of Portland, Oregon, stretches out on the roomy back porch of his charming clap-board house truck and admires his spacious green lawn. Miller lived in his three-foot-nine inch wide six-foot long vehicle for more than two years and toured the country in it nine times. The chassis had more than 200,000 miles on it when he purchased it, and Miller added 200,000 more.

ANIMAL TRANSPORTATION

• Chariot horses in ancient Rome were shod in leather sandals attached to their feet with cord or leather puttees.

• Wagons traveling the three miles from Lancaster to Ulverston, England—because of sudden shifting in the bay's sandy bottom—often were submerged in water.

• Mounted policemen in Australia, using camels, often patrol an area of 168,000 square miles.

• The six-horse sleigh used by the mother of **Czar Peter the Great** of Russia was always accompanied by twelve grooms—one for each horse, and the other six who pushed the sleigh to increase its speed. All the grooms had to run steadily for miles.

• Sleighs in Iceland, to make them more durable, are made without nails or screws.

ROADS AND HIGHWAYS

• The Appian Way, near Rome, Italy, still in use after two thousand years, is a four-foot-thick highway that would cost more than five hundred thousand dollars a mile to duplicate today.

• The first mileage sign: A Roman pillar listing localities and distances erected at Tongres, Belgium, 2,000 years ago.

"THE LONELIEST HIGHWAY IN AMERICA"
Travelers who journey the length of Northern Nevada's highway 50 through desert and mountains receive a special "Survivor" certificate issued by the governor!

PRINCESS RADZIWILL of Poland AT A MEETING OF THE SKATING CLUB IN ROME, ITALY, IN 1910 DROVE A ROMAN CHARIOT DRAWN BY A LEOPARD AND A LION!

A BABY CARRIAGE pulled by a SHEEP was used by the Menendez Family of Sevilla, Spain, for 140 years!

Hub-a-hubba **Emanuele Damonte**, of San Francisco, used over 3,000-hub caps to decorate his home, garage, shed, fence, driveway—and outhouse!

• Drivers in Trondheim, Norway, have to pay to enter the center of the city between the hours of six A.M. and six P.M.!

SHIPS AND OTHER WATERCRAFT

• In Panama, native Indians trail pepper pods behind their dugout canoes to repel sharks.

• Steerage passengers traveling from Europe to America in the nineteenth century paid approximately thirty dollars for their accommodations.

• Gufas, large round wicker baskets covered with skins, are still used as boats on the Tigris River in Southwest Asia.

A POTTERY BASIN 2¹/₂ feet in diameter and only 15 inches deep serves travelers in Bengal, India, as a boat in which to cross placid rivers and ponds.

The CHINESE JUNK is one of the most aerodynamically efficient sailing ships—yet its simple rig was never adopted by western seamen.

• On ferries traveling to the Hebrides Island, in Scotland, sheep farmers can travel at a reduced rate as long as they are carrying at least one sheep in their car!

• In 210 B.C., the Egyptian leader **Ptolemy** built a trireme ship called "Tessarakonteres" which needed four thousand oarsmen!

• The first workable submarine, the "eel boat," constructed by **Cornelius van Drebbel** of Holland, in the early 1600s, of wood protected by leather soaked in oil, was propelled by twelve oarsmen.

This houseboat off Sauries Island, in Portland, Oregon, was a river steamer that ran aground and became a residence.

ON 1894, H.B. Ogden of Brooklyn, NY, INVENTED THE "MARINE VELOCIPEDE"— A BRASS BOAT PROPELLED BY TWO MEN PEDALING BICYCLES!

"THE TURTLE" First American submarine, used by George Washington in the Revolutionary War. Invented by David Bushnell.

Nature's dry dock. The *Princess May* ran high and dry 30 feet in the air on Sentinel Island, Alaska. At flood tide, the vessel got off undamaged.

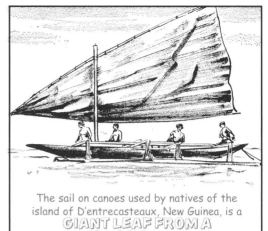

The sail on canoes used by natives of the island of D'entrecasteaux, New Guinea, is a **GIANT LEAF FROM A SAGO PALM**

Tortoise Boat
— INVENTED BY LI SOON SIN —1591

THE FIRST IRONCLAD WARSHIP EVER BUILT!
IT ENABLED KOREA TO INFLICT A MOST DISASTROUS DEFEAT UPON THE JAPANESE
IT COULD MOVE BACKWARDS, FORWARDS AND SIDEWAYS AND SUBMERGED LIKE A SUBMARINE —
ALMOST UNAIDED IT DEFEATED THE JAPANESE NAVY

FISHING BOATS
IN ANDALUSIA, SPAIN, HAVE HUMAN EYES PAINTED ON THE BOW *TO HELP THEM LOCATE SCHOOLS OF FISH*

• The *Beaver*, launched on the Thames River at Blackwell, England, in 1835 and sailed to Fort Vancouver, North America, where it was fitted with paddle wheels, became the first steamboat on the Pacific Ocean.

• Sailing craft can actually travel at a speed that is greater than the wind speed that is propelling them!

• The *Hannah*, a schooner commissioned at Beverly, Massachusetts, in 1775, was the first ship in the American Navy.

• The "intelligent whale," a submarine built by the United States Navy and used experimentally between 1864 and 1872, was propelled by a hand crank.

• Steamboats carried cabin passengers on rivers of the American West, in the 1850s, for a fare of one to one and a half cents a mile.

TRAINS

• The train that rode on invisible rails: The railroad track between Saint-Nazaire and La Roche-Bernard, France, over which passengers and freight were carried for thirty years, was always submerged by water.

• The railroad station in Savona, Italy, constructed in 1962, has no railroad!

• The Celestial Railway, so called because its terminals were the Florida towns of Jupiter and Juno, had no means of turning its engine around—so on the run from Juno to Jupiter the train always backed up the entire seven and a half miles.

• The first electric inclined railway, Echo Mountain Railway, carrying passengers three thousand feet to the top of Echo Mountain in Pasadena, California, was put into service July 4, 1893.

• Rail tracks were created by the ancient Egyptians in the form of grooves in long slabs of stone.

• Railway lines across the Nullarbor Plain bordering South and Western Australia are so straight that on a clear night train travelers can see the lights of an approaching locomotive two hours away!

• Freight trains used by the Oahu Railway of Hawaii, during the seventy-two years from 1889 to 1961, had no cabooses, and the crews had to ride atop the boxcars.

IN 1989 A NEW HIGH-SPEED TRAIN DESIGNED AND BUILT IN FRANCE SET A NEW WORLD RECORD FOR RAIL SPEED OF 289 MPH.!

"TOM THUMB"
The steam locomotive invented by Peter Cooper in Baltimore, MD, raced a horse-drawn carriage on Sept. 18, 1830—and lost!

CRAMPTON LOCOMOTIVES,
used on British railways in 1849, had driving wheels 8 ft. high.

WALKING AND CARRYING

• By the age of fifty, the average person has traveled seventy-four thousand miles on foot!

J. Clark Cullom, of Cincinnati, carried a piano with him wherever he went! He traveled more than 15,000 miles with it.

The INCLINED ELEVATOR linking Johnstown and Westmont, PA., is the steepest in the country—896½ feet long, with a 71% incline, it has been in use for 78 years.

• To get to school for a period of four months, in 1864, **Miss Clara Weston**, a teacher in Pueblo, Colorado, waded the Arkansas river twice each day.

• New Yorkers travel farther up and down than they do on the level: the tall buildings make it necessary to travel more vertically than horizontally.

• Peasant women on the Portuguese island of Madeira carry as many as six wicker chairs to the market on their heads!

UNUSUAL FORMS OF TRANSPORTATION

• Bicycle riders in the Netherlands can ride in a special eight-mile-long tunnel that contains huge electric fans that will push them along at twenty-eight miles per hour!

HIGHER LEARNING

Children on Ou, in the Rukyu Islands, go to and from school each day by traversing a 1,500-foot-wide channel on stilts.

Children in some rural areas of China are still transported to school daily in a WHEELBARROW

- Motor-driven roller skates, invented by **Alphonse Constantitni** in 1906, could travel forty miles an hour.

- Children in Schleswig, Germany, are trained to leap unbridged streams with a vaulting pole known as a "klootstock."

- The Sloan Square station in London, England, is the only tube station in the world located beneath a river.

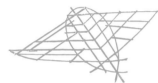

A NAVIGATION CHART used by the Polynesians on long sea journeys was made entirely of wooden sticks.

MAPS AND NAVIGATION

- On a single page, a road map often provides thirty thousand pieces of information.

- In ancient China, maps were drawn with the south at the top of the page!

ROAD MARKERS in the Sahara Desert comprise piles of wafer-thin stones chosen to resist the constant sandstorms.

IN TAI SHAN, CHINA, PORTERS CARRY PEOPLE IN CHAIRS STRAPPED TO THEIR BACKS UP A MOUNTAINSIDE THAT HAS 6,700 STAIRS!

FIVE GENERATIONS ON ONE BICYCLE! A BICYCLE BUILT FOR FIFTY-FIVE

The Dumas family recently celebrated their family reunion in a unique manner: on a bicycle built for fifty-five!

Roger Dumas, the mastermind behind the one-of-a-kind contraption, labored for more than twenty years to create a working bicycle that would transport his entire family. The bicycle went through numerous incarnations over the years, incorporating parts from one hundred fifty other bicycles. Dumas claims the bicycle was built with "absolutely no drafting, no calculations. It was trial and error."

At the Dumas reunion, Roger carefully seated five generations of his family, aged three to seventy-six, on his invention, and helped coordinate the pedaling. The journey was not without mishap, but the bicycle built for fifty-five traveled a total of 3,236 feet, 6 inches with all fifty-five members of the Dumas family aboard!

Family members recall fondly that it was the first time in twenty or more years that they had all gotten together and done something as a family. And the memory of that one-of-a-kind bicycle ride will be passed down among generations of Dumases!

Chapter 60
The Unexplained

Have you ever hoped that when you die, you'll have an opportunity to spend a little time in some great celestial "video room," with an endless library of answers to all the questions that are unanswerable on this side of existence? Along with the whereabouts of the wallet you lost in 1982 and the reason why men have nipples, the following collection of mysterious phenomena may add a few more questions to your list.

FATE UNKNOWN

• Skeleton Crew: "While cruising near the coastline off Punta Arenas, Chile, the British sailing ship *Johnson* sighted what appeared to be a boat with sails floating in the wind. When British signals elicited no response, the craft was approached. The crew noticed that the ship's masts and sails were covered with some kind of green moss, and that the vessel seemed abandoned by its crew. Upon boarding it, the skeleton of a man was discovered beneath the helm. The deck was decayed to such an extent that it gave under the footsteps. Three more skeletons were found near a panel, ten were found in the crew's quarters, and six on the bridge. Upon the ravaged prow of the vessel, the words 'Marlborough Glasgow' could still be discerned. The *Marlborough* left Littleton, New Zealand, in January 1890 with a cargo of wool and frozen mutton, and a crew of twenty-three men under Captain Hird... In April of 1890 an unsuccessful search for the vessel was made..."
–Wellington, New Zealand, *Evening Post*, November 13, 1913 and *Agence Havas*, November 26, 1913.

STONE HEADS

carved by the Olmec Indians of Mexico 3,000 years ago, and weighing 20 tons, were moved miles throught the jungle—yet the Olmecs had no knowl-edge of the wheel.

MYSTERIOUS DISAPPEARANCES

• **Benjamin Bathhurst**, British envoy to the court of Vienna, vanished mys-teriously in 1809 on his way back to England to report to his government, and his disappearance has remained unsolved for one hundred ninety-two years.

• The biggest sailing ship in the world vanished without a trace! The five-masted bark *Kobenhaven* disappeared into the unknown, although she carried radio equipment and auxiliary engines. Seventy cadets—members of the most prominent families in Denmark—vanished with her. Her fate is unknown.

• On June 6, 1810, a lake two miles long in Glover, Vermont, suddenly disappeared.

MYSTERIOUS PLACES

• Wash Basin of the Gods: Peru's Lake Titicaca, nearly the size of Lake Erie, is higher than two Mount Washingtons stacked on top of each other. Its waters are mysterious: iron will not rust in it, eggs will not boil in it, and only one kind of fish can live in it.

• The contrary well: The water of a well near Beresford, Dale, England, becomes warmer when the weather turns colder.

• The Mystery Spot in Santa Cruz, California, has areas in which it is impossible to stand upright.

• The ice mine: a freak of nature. Strange ice formations and mammoth icicles form during hot weather and thaw out in cold weather in Coudersprot, Pennsylvania.

FACES OF THE **PAST** ! – EASTER ISLAND, SOUTH SEAS
GIGANTIC MYSTERIOUS STATUES - BURIED TO THEIR NECKS – WITH THE BACKS TO THE SEA – THAT STAND ON A LONELY ISLAND IN THE SOUTH PACIFIC

A MONKEY that can be clearly seen only from the air in the desert region of Nacza, Peru, that measures 260 feet from head to tail, is one of about 30 baffling huge drawings made by ancient Peruvians between 1000 B.C. and A.D. 1000.

2 ELEPHANTS are portrayed in a Mayan sculpture on the Temple of Copan, Honduras—yet the sculpture pre-dates Columbus' voyages, and elephants were unknown in the New World.

• The path that is always green: The Green Way between Winterbourne and Clarendon, England, is covered with thick green grass even in winter—when the rest of the countryside is buried under snow.

UNEXPLAINED PHENOMENA

• The cow that gave black milk! **Rupert Hansborough,** of Chillicothe, Ohio, in 1891 found that his cow's ink-like milk was entirely palatable, and so was the butter, which resembled coal tar. Chemists could detect nothing to account for its sable color.

• The casket of **Queen Elizabeth I**, while on view in Whitehall Palace, London, on the eve of her interment, mysteriously exploded! The coffin was shattered and had to be replaced—yet the queen's body was unharmed.

• In an area off the coast of Japan known as the Dragon's Triangle, aircraft radio systems suddenly go dead, and hundreds of merchant ships and fishing boats have mysteriously vanished!

• Smoke emanated from a tree on the Isle of Wight, in Britain, without any apparent cause!

• An iron pillar in Qutb Minar, Delhi, India, has not rusted in over sixteen hundred years.

• In the village of Bijori, in India's Mandla district, it once rained beads. All colors. All sizes. Already bored for stringing. The natives collected them and prized them highly. They have been named

"THE HAUNTED CAR" THE ENGINE of A VAN OWNED BY Kevin Wise of New Philadelphia, Ohio, MIRACULOUSLY TURNED ITSELF ON 6 MINUTES AFTER FIREFIGHTERS HAD EXTINGUISHED A FIRE UNDER ITS HOOD!

Sulaimandana, or King Solomon's Rosaries. The mystery of their origin has never been explained. Many of Ripley's readers thought that this was the most unbelievable of all Believe It or Nots. It is comedian Johnny Carson's all-time favorite Believe It or Not cartoon.

• A male dog named "**Zoë**" in Belfast, Ireland, has an audible and persistent humming noise coming from its head!

The **2,300-YEAR-OLD GLIDER** A wood model shaped like a modern glider found at Saggara, Egypt, in 1898, and carved more than 2,300 years ago.

A **TOY DOG** found in the grave of a Mexican child buried in A.D. 1000 moved on wheels—yet the Aztecs constructed no wheeled vehicle for transportation until after the Spanish Conquest.

In 1903, a fishing boat off the coast of Normandy sailed for two days *through a "blizzard" of white butterflies!*

• Rocks weighing up to seven hundred pounds mysteriously move across a lakebed in Death Valley, leaving half-inch-deep tracks!

• A photograph of her father snapped in England in 1920 by **Elizabeth Priestly**, who was then twenty years of age, mysteriously showed in the right background a likeness of Elizabeth herself when she was five years old.

• In 1939, **George Stoflet**, of Reading, Pennsylvania, was struck in the head by a cooked trout that fell from the sky!

• A one hundred watt electric bulb, in the Fort Sanders Baptist Church in Knoxville, Tennessee, was forced through a plywood door when an adjoining structure collapsed—yet the bulb did not break.

• In 1976, two German ministers found $1,130 worth of bills that had floated from the sky to the ground!

• A freestanding garage, with a car inside, disappeared and was found several days later by the owner on a neighboring street!

• **H. H. Getty**, of Edmonton, Alberta, discovered that a match held to his skin caused neither pain nor blistering. Getty visited several prominent physicians in an attempt to discover an explanation for his "asbestos skin." None was found.

• A snake was found in an ordinary hen's egg.

UNIDENTIFIED CREATURES

• Scotland has Nessie, America has Bigfoot, but Australia's most beloved monster is the **Yowie**! Believed to be a holdout from the Ice Age, the hairy primate Australians have named the Yowie has reportedly been sighted three thousand times since 1865. Monster hunter Rex Gilroy, of Katoomba, New South Wales, has plaster casts of the Yowie's footprint, measuring almost eighteen inches long and fourteen inches across the toe.

• **Mokele-Mbembe**, a dinosaur-like beast, has been sighted several times in the African Congo's Lake Telle area. Sightings have been reported by many people, including members of a scientific expedition. According to some scientists, it could be the world's last surviving dinosaur!

UNKNOWN FORCES

• During the Civil War, **Julia Ward Howe** was visiting Washington and saw soldiers returning from the war. She went to sleep for the night, but when she awoke at dawn, she found herself sitting at her desk. She discovered that she had written a poem of five verses entitled, "The Battle Hymn of the Republic." To her death, Julia wondered if she really wrote the masterpiece or was merely an instrument of something bigger.

THE **MISSING LINK?**
A **MONKEY** PHOTOGRAPHED BY FRANÇOIS de LOYS, A SWISS GEOLOGIST, ON THE BORDER BETWEEN COLOMBIA AND VENEZUELA IS AN "UNKNOWN" TYPE NEVER SEEN BEFORE OR SINCE 1917

"DARK DAY"
ON May 19, 1780, TOTAL DARKNESS DESCENDED OVER New England AT MIDDAY— A PHENOMENON THAT SCIENTISTS HAVE NEVER BEEN ABLE TO EXPLAIN .✶

THE **ENTIRE CREW** OF THE ENGLISH WARSHIP, "DAEDALUS," SAILING BETWEEN ST. HELENA AND THE CAPE OF GOOD HOPE REPORTED SIGHTING A **SEA SERPENT 65 FEET LONG AND EXTENDING 4 FEET ABOVE THE SEA** (August 6, 1848)

IN THE 1870s, A GIANT SAILING SHIP WAS FOUND IN THE California DESERT, NEAR THE Arizona BORDER, OVER 100 MILES from THE NEAREST OCEAN!

Chapter 61

Vacation & Tourism

At the **AMSTERDAM HILTON**, guests can rent the suite where John and Yoko staged their "Bed-in for Peace"—their faces are etched on windows and their music is painted on the ceiling!

Planning your next vacation? Looking for something a little different to do this weekend? Ripley's can help! Here you'll find the weirdest and wackiest in dining, lodging, tourism, and leisure time. Bon voyage!

• The first guide book, listing temples, battlefields, and other historical sites, was written in A.D. 22 by the Roman author **Pausanias** for tourists traveling to ancient Greece!

LODGING

• A vacation down below: Jules' Undersea Lodge (named after *Twenty Thousand Leagues Under the Sea* author Jules Verne) is located in a former marine research center off Florida's Key Largo. For $295 a night, guests can enjoy all the comforts of home, thirty feet below the sea while gazing at life underseas.

• The mountain resort that is always in motion: Grossgmein, an Austrian resort village built on a rocky base, is constantly shifting because it rests on a bed of salt one thousand feet thick.

• **Pete Falcione** operates a fifty-tank "fish hotel" in Norwalk, Connecticut, for boarding fish. They are kept in aquariums that match the chemical balance of their home tanks—and fed on either the one-meal-a-day European plan or an American plan providing custom, gourmet diets!

The **Dirty Shame** was the first hotel in Big Beaver, Alaska.

THE *Luxor Hotel* in Las Vegas, Nev., IS A 30-STORY GLASS PYRAMID WITH 2,526 ROOMS, A 10-STORY SPHINX WITH EYES THAT SHOOT LASERS and an ATRIUM BIG ENOUGH TO HOLD NINE 747 JETS!

In Hamilton Township, N.J., there is a tavern called "THE COUNTRY BARREL INN" that is shaped like a large beer barrel!

At Michael Garnier's Bed and Breakfast in Oregon, guests stay in TREEHOUSES!

"THE TREETOPS HOTEL"
In Kenya, Africa, there is a hotel built 40 ft. off the ground-up in—the branches of a giant tree!

DINING

• Restaurant diners in Zahle, a resort town in Lebanon, sit at tables that straddle branches of the Barduni River.

• Maggie Patterson's drive-through restaurant in Niles, Michigan, serves all-natural, fast food for dogs!

• The Opus Restaurant, in Toronto, Canada, provides a selection of reading glasses to customers who have forgotten theirs and cannot read the menu!

The BECKHAM CREEK CAVERN in Jasper, Ark., is a deep mountain crevasse that was once used as a bomb shelter and is now a bed and breakfast!

"THE LARGEST RESTAURANT IN THE WORLD" THE TUMP NAK THAI in Bangkok, Thailand, consists of 65 adjoining houses built on 10 acres, seats over 3,000 people and has 1,000 waiters who serve while wearing roller skates!

At the BBOSS NIGHT CLUB in Tsim Sha Tsui, East Hong Kong, guests ride in a Rolls Royce along a starlit highway to their tables!

A restaurant in San Francisco, Calif., called "CASA SANCHEZ" offers free lunches for life to anyone who will sit and be tattooed with the restaurant's logo!

MUSEUMS

• The Nut Museum, founded by **Elizabeth Tashjian** in Old Lyme, Connecticut, exhibits nuts of every kind from all over the world—including a thirty-five-pound double coconut!

• In Kennet Square, Pennsylvania, there is a museum devoted to mushrooms!

• At the Museum of Improbable Research in Boston, Massachusetts, there is a display of plaster casts of the feet of Nobel Prize-winning scientists!

• In Amsterdam, the Netherlands, there is a museum dedicated to cheese!

• In Onset, Massachusetts, there is a museum dedicated to thermometers—with over 2,460 thermometers on display!

• In Chincoteague, Virginia, there is a museum dedicated to oysters!

• In Tarpon Springs, Florida, there is a museum dedicated to sponges!

• A museum in San Antonio, Texas, features a display of three hundred seventy-five decorated toilet seats!

• In Wichita, Kansas, there is a barbed wire hall of fame!

• The Museonder in Otterlo, the Netherlands, is a museum in a buried building dedicated to things that live underground!

• There is a museum dedicated to kites in Long Beach, Washington!

• There is a museum in Conwy, Wales, dedicated to teapots!

• Fuguay-varinma, North Carolina is home to a museum dedicated to gourds!

IN Keswick, England, THERE IS A MUSEUM DEDICATED TO *PENCILS!*

IN Ise, Japan, THERE IS A MUSEUM DEDICATED TO *PEARLS*, FEATURING A SCALE MODEL OF THE *LIBERTY BELL* MADE OUT OF 12,000 PEARLS.

• In Llansantffraidym-mechain, Wales, there is a museum dedicated to over four hundred breeds of dogs!

• In Chattanooga, Tennessee, there is a museum dedicated to knives!

• In Columbus, Georgia, there is a museum with over three thousand lunch boxes and over two thousand thermos bottles on display!

• In Nima, Japan, there is a museum dedicated to sand!

• In San Jose, California, there is a museum devoted to trash, including a one hundred foot by twenty-foot "wall of garbage" made of old shoes, beer cans, dolls, and disposable diapers!

• At the Mouse House Museum in Scottsdale, Arizona, there are over three thousand replicas of mice and displays including a miniature Victorian mansion with mouse inhabitants!

• In Philadelphia, there is a museum dedicated to pretzels!

• Over one hundred antique human-hair wreaths and over four hundred pieces of human-hair jewelry are on display at Leila Cohoon's Hair Museum in Independence, Missouri!

• In Lawrenceburg, Kentucky, there is a museum of whiskey history with a collection of over two-hundred odd-shaped whiskey bottles!

• In Santa Cruz, California, there is a museum devoted to surfing!

• In Naples, Florida, there is a teddy bear museum that displays over sixteen hundred teddy bears and works of art devoted to teddies!

• The Lock Museum in Terryville, Connecticut, displays over twenty-two thousand locks, including a tumbler lock from Egypt that is four thousand years old!

• There is a museum devoted to helicopters in Westchester, Pennsylvania!

• "Scheider Haus" in Kitchener, Ontario, is a museum devoted to elaborate wood carvings created by hobos in exchange for a meal or a room for the night!

• In Lincoln, Nebraska, there is a museum dedicated to roller skates—with a display of skates made for horses!

• In Guanahuato, Mexico, there is a museum of mummies with over one hundred eighty mummified men, women, and children on display inside glass coffins!

• In Erdenheim, Pennsylvania, there is a museum dedicated to business cards!

• In New Market, Virginia, there is a museum devoted solely to bedrooms!

• Rutland, Vermont, is home to the International Lint Museum!

• In Los Angeles, California there is a museum dedicated to doorknobs!

• In Los Angeles, California, there is a Museum of the Modern Poodle, with over eight hundred objects dedicated to poodles!

• In Mount Horeb, Wisconsin, there is a museum dedicated to mustard—with over twenty-five hundred different kinds on display!

• In Gaellivare, Sweden, there is a museum dedicated to mosquitoes!

- The Nagai Sock Museum, in Japan, has over twenty thousand pairs of socks on display!

- In Manchester, Vermont, there is a museum of fly fishing with over forty thousand fishing flies on display!

- In Verneuil-en-Halatte, France, there is a museum of historic graffiti!

- In Rocksprings, Texas, there is a museum dedicated to Angora goats!

- The Franklin Museum, in New York City, had a display of hundreds of chopsticks, take-out food containers, fortune cookies, and five thousand menus from Chinese restaurants!

TOURIST ATTRACTIONS

- Children can visit Saint Nicholas all year round at Finland's Santa Park!

- In downtown Toronto, there is a "wilderness" park with a seven-hundred-ton slab of granite from the Canadian shield, native fir trees, and posts that emit thick clouds of fog and mist every few hours!

- "Snow Garden," a popular attraction in Hong Kong, allows visitors to rent thermal jackets and boots in order to play in real snow, slide down an ice slide, and experience subzero temperatures!

- An indoor beach park in Yokohama, Japan, has a constant temperature of thirty-two degrees Celsius (ninety-two degrees Fahrenheit) artificial sand, and time-controlled sunlight and sunsets!

- In 1992, a British company offered two-day vacations at an abandoned Royal Air Force Base in Hampshire, England in which people pretended to be prisoners of war and take part in roll calls, work parties, and escapes!

- You could go to jail just for being a tourist! Tourists visiting London's Brixton Prison can stay overnight in a cell and have a typical prisoner's breakfast before they're released in the morning!

- The zoo in Copenhagen, Denmark displayed two live people, Henrik Lehmann and Marlene Botoft, in a plexiglass cage!

"GRAVE LINE," a company in Los Angeles, CA, takes tourists on a tour of the graves of such Hollywood stars as Marilyn Monroe, Montgomery Clift, and Douglas Fairbanks—in a hearse!

IN QUEENSTOWN, NEW ZEALAND, TOURISTS CAN LEAP OFF A WOODEN BRIDGE 45-METERS ABOVE THE KAWARAU RIVER WITH ONLY AN ELASTIC BUNGI ROPE TIED TO THEIR ANKLES — FOR $48 A JUMP!

"MOLAR COASTER" In 1991, workers in Blackpool, England, drained a lake near a roller coaster and found hundreds of sets of false teeth, several wigs, and six glass eyes!

OCEAN DOME A PERFECT DAY AT THE BEACH—GUARANTEED

Dreaming of a perfect day at the beach? Now there's a place you can go where the air is always a balmy eighty-five degrees, the water is a comfortable seventy-five degrees, the sun shines year-round, and the surf is always perfect.

Welcome to Kyoto, Japan's Ocean Dome, the largest water park under one roof. The Ocean Dome features a perfect beach of artificial non-stick sand made of crushed marble, and an "ocean" of synthetic seawater. Visitors can enjoy a perfect day at the beach here any day of the year, with never a raindrop, a jellyfish sting, or a sunburn.

And for surfing aficionados, the Ocean Dome is unparalleled. Serious surfers comb the globe for that perfect "barrel" wave, but at the Ocean Dome, picture-perfect waves roll along one minute apart. Surfing at Ocean Dome is so good that surfer Matthew Pitts packed up and moved to Kyoto to be near the ultimate surfing experience.

Ocean Dome is controlled by a high-tech "brain center" overlooking the beach. From this room, technicians can cue sunsets, manipulate the surf, and even open the dome's enormous seven hundred ton retractable ceiling—but they only open it on the finest of days.

At $24 per person, nearly a million people visit the Ocean Dome each year. Most feel it's a small price to pay for a guaranteed perfect day at the beach!

• England's Windsor Safari Park exports lions to Africa!

• At the San Diego Zoo, the plants are worth more than the animals!

• Nan Mahdol, a seven-hundred-year-old city in the islands of Micronesia, is a popular tourist center with eight thousand visitors a year, yet there are no hotels, and tourists never stay overnight because of an ancient curse!

• The hot springs of Beppu, Japan, used by the Japanese for health bathing, produce more than ten million gallons of scalding water every twenty-four hours.

ON David City, Neb., THERE IS A "DAVE HALL of FAME" DEDICATED TO MEN NAMED DAVE.

LETTERMAN

THE SKY BATHERS
A HOTEL ON HONSHU, JAPAN'S WAKAYAMA PENINSULA, OFFERS HOT-SPRING BATHS IN A CABLE CAR AS IT TRAVERSES A DEEP GORGE

Chapter 62

Weapons & Warfare

A GATLING GUN USED IN EGYPT AND THE ORIENT IN THE 19th CENTURY WAS DESIGNED TO BE FIRED FROM THE *BACK OF A CAMEL*

All's fair in love and war, as they say—which is why the art of warfare is fertile grounds for Ripley's fare. Human beings at war frequently resort to extreme measures in order to survive—and to prevail. On the war front, things are bound to get a little weird. . .

• The most successful military recruiter in history: The **Duchess of Gordon** (1743-1827) recruited the entire Scottish regiment of Gordon Highlanders by placing each recruit's enlistment shilling between her lips and allowing him to collect it with his teeth.

WARFARE

BATTLES AND STRATEGIES

• **Archimedes**, a scientist of ancient Greece, saved the city of Syracuse from attack by Roman ships by burning them—using huge mirrors and the sun!

• The first aerial dogfight took place between **Phil Rader** and **Dean Ivan** during the Mexican Revolution, using pistols!

• At one time, Hungarian soldiers were often accompanied into battle by gypsy violinists!

• In 525 B.C., **King Cambyses** of Persia conquered Egypt using an army of dogs!

• Soldiers in ancient Babylon painted their mouths red before going into battle!

• In the seventh century B.C., the ancient Egyptians assaulted the town of Azotus (now in Israel) for twenty-nine years before the residents surrendered!

THE CITY THAT WAS SAVED BY A GULP! Rothenburg in Bavaria, Germany, was spared from destruction during the Thirty Years' War, in the 17th century, when Count Van Tilly agreed not to sack the city if a member of its council could empty a $3\frac{1}{2}$-quart wine goblet in a single gulp—Burgomaster Nusch accomplished the feat.

• **Napoleon** often drew his battle plans in a sandbox!

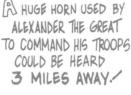

A HUGE HORN USED BY ALEXANDER THE GREAT TO COMMAND HIS TROOPS COULD BE HEARD **3 MILES AWAY!**

THE MOST SENSELESS DUEL IN ALL HISTORY!

BODO von EGISHEIM and RUDOLPH LOSTIER, KNIGHTS IN THE SERVICE OF EMPEROR SIEGMUND of Germany, QUARRELED OVER THE AFFECTIONS OF A GIRL IN 1425 —*BUT WERE ORDERED BY THE EMPEROR TO POSTPONE THEIR DUEL FOR 70 YEARS* THE DUEL WAS ACTUALLY FOUGHT AND BOTH MEN WERE WOUNDED IN 1495 —WHEN THEY WERE 94 YEARS OF AGE

THE FIGHTING MEN WHO WERE CARRIED TO SAFETY BY THEIR WIVES!

KING KONRAD III
HAVING CAPTURED THE BESIEGED TOWN OF WEINSBERG, GERMANY, DECLARED ITS WOMEN COULD DEPART UNHARMED *WITH ANYTHING THEY COULD CARRY!* THE WOMEN LEFT THE TOWN **CARRYING THEIR HUSBANDS** Dec. 21, 1140

DUELS, FEUDS, AND FIGHTS

• In 1817 in Kingston, Jamaica, **Henri D'Edgeville** challenged a Scotsman named **Captain Stewart** to a pistol duel—to be fought in an open grave.

• When **Sainte-Beuve**, a nineteenth-century French literary critic, was challenged to a duel, his weapon of choice was spelling!

• Dueling is still legal in Uruguay!

• A fatal duel was fought in France with billiard balls as the weapons! (1843)

• The Tuaregs of the Sahara Desert still fight duels using medieval weapons and shields.

• **Samuel August Maverick**, who gave us the word "maverick," meaning dissenter, once fought a duel with a man who had interrupted his father at a public meeting, then took his wounded opponent home and nursed him.

THE **RUSE** THAT MADE ENGLAND RULER OF THE SEAS!

AN ENGLISH FLEET
OUTNUMBERED 5 TO ONE BY THE FRENCH, WON BRITANNIA'S FIRST MAJOR NAVAL VICTORY NEAR DOVER ON AUG. 24, 1217, WHEN HUBERT DE BURGH MANEUVERED HIS ENGLISH SHIPS TO WINDWARD — AND MADE USE OF THE FIRST SMOKE SCREEN IN HISTORY BY POURING GREAT MASSES OF QUICKLIME INTO THE SEA!
THE BRITISH CUT DOWN THEIR BLINDED FOES WITH CROSSBOWS — AND CAPTURED 55 FRENCH SHIPS

WILLIAM THE CONQUEROR could leap onto his horse while wearing a full suit of armor!

MILITARY LEADERS

• The great British naval commander **Lord Horatio Nelson** (1758-1805) was constantly seasick even after thirty years at sea!

• The craziest command ever given: While reviewing the troops before the Kremlin in Moscow, **Czar Paul I** became displeased and ordered them to march to Siberia. They did—and were never heard of again.

• **General Lopez de Uyraga**, commander of the Oriental Army of Mexico under President Benito Juarez, fought with a wooden leg.

• **General George Custer** accidentally shot his own horse during a buffalo hunt!

• **Abraham Whipple** (1733-1819), an American naval officer, as a privateer during the Revolution captured ten British ships in ten days.

• **George Armstrong Custer** (1839-1876), known among the Indians for his flowing locks, perished unrecognized in the massacre at Little Big Horn because he had just had a haircut.

• **Count de Fontaine**, Spanish leader of an army that invaded France in 1643, was eighty-two years of age and crippled by gout at the battle of Racoroi, but insisted on directing troops from a litter—he was killed in battle.

• The ruler who gave every robber a license to loot and kill! **Garcia de Avellaneda**, Spanish Viceroy of Naples, facing an enemy invasion in 1654 without means of defense, appealed for aid to the country's numerous bands of highwaymen. The bandits defeated the invading French army—and were given permission for the viceroy's entire seven-year reign to rob and murder without fear of punishment.

• **Baron de Charnace** of France held three military ranks simultaneously: he was a colonel on weekdays, a captain every Sunday, and a field marshal on each birthday.

• **Caliph Omar I** (582-644) of Isla, in a period of twenty-nine years, captured thirty-six thousand castles and fortresses, destroyed four thousand temples, and constructed fourteen hundred mosques.

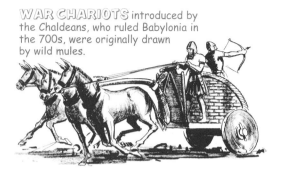

WAR CHARIOTS introduced by the Chaldeans, who ruled Babylonia in the 700s, were originally drawn by wild mules.

A SPECIAL HONOR FEATHER WAS AWARDED BY THE DAKOTA INDIANS of No. America, *TO A BRAVE WHO CUT A FOE'S THROAT*

THE BATTLE TROPHY of the Bamun tribesmen of the Cameroons, IS A GOURD TO WHICH ARE ATTACHED *THE LOWER JAWS OF SLAIN ENEMIES*

• **Captain John Doughty** (1754-1826), for the period from June 20 to August 12, 1784, commanded the entire United States Army—which at that time numbered eighty men.

• **Simón Bolívar** (1783-1830), South America's liberator who raised an army that defeated the Spaniards repeatedly in pitched battles, had no prior military experience or training.

SOLDIERS AND SAILORS

• An officer in the Afghan Army of Mahmud el Ghazni who was charged with cowardice was always paraded past the populace with a mule's feedbag full of oats tied around his neck.

• The soldier who had a charmed life! **Count Augustin Belliard** (1762-1832), a French general, had twelve horses shot from under him during six different battles.

WARRIORS

• In Japan in the four-teenth century, warriors wore a yellow chrysan-themum as a badge of courage!

• The Dellis—a word meaning "crazy" in Turkish— were an eighteenth-century Turkish army unit whose soldiers always wore the wings of an eagle, and fought so daringly that they were considered insane.

• **Brave Chief**, a Pawnee Indian of the 1830s, had hands painted on his chest —indicating a hand-to-hand combat in which he was victorious.

WAR MACHINES

TANKS

• The "Mouse," a German tank built in 1944, weighed one hundred eighty tons, was twenty feet high, and could cross the bottom of a river forty feet deep.

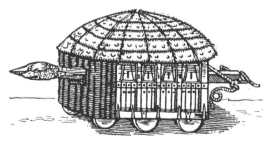

BATTERING RAMS used in the 1500s were often shaped like tortoises.

TROOP TRANSPORT

• The first aircraft carrier, the *George Washington Parke Custis*, a flat-topped vessel built in the Civil War, was the launching platform for a balloon used to observe the Confederate blockade in 1861.

• The army that traveled in barrels! **Duke Guillame** of Aquitaine captured Nimes, France, in 804 by slipping soldiers into the city—secreted in wine barrels!

WARSHIPS

• The Russian Navy in the 1870s built two circular warships, *The Admiral Popov*, and the *Novogrod*, that were designed so that they could swing around and point their guns in any direction!

WEAPONS AND ARMOR

ANCIENT AND TRIBAL

• The oldest known boomerang was carved in Poland twenty-three thousand years ago, from the tusk of a mammoth!

• South Sea Islanders in the nineteenth century once used the inflated skins of porcupine fish as battle helmets!

• An assault tower used by the Chinese and the Tatars against Russia in the thirteenth century was equipped with a battering ram, archery loopholes, wheels, and drop gates.

• The mace, a weapon of the Middle Ages, was called in Spain "matasuegras"—"mother-in-law killer."

ARMOR

• The ancient Greeks lined their helmets and armor with sponges!

• Researchers at the Rajamankala Institute of Technology, in Thailand, have developed a bulletproof vest made of silk!

• Cheese vats were once used as military helmets in Holland!

• A company in Pennsylvania has developed a personal protection system that consists of a bulletproof shield with a radar sensor that activates like an air bag at the first sign of terrorist attack!

EXPLOSIVES

• Children in Highbridge, England, used a live World War I bomb as a toy for fifteen years without knowing what it was!

• In March of 1994, a cook in northern Portugal found a live hand grenade in a sack of potatoes!

• In 1998, a woman in Fairhaven, Massachusetts, discovered that a hand grenade that her husband had brought home after World War II and placed in a drawer was still live!

• A woman raking leaves in her backyard in Truro, Nova Scotia, Canada, discovered a live grenade on her lawn!

FIREARMS

• **Samuel Colt** (1814-1862), inventor of the revolver that bears his name, got the idea for its revolving cylinder as a sixteen-year-old seaman watching the helmsman turn the ship's wheel— each spoke aligning with a clutch that held it fast.

DOGS IN SUITS OF ARMOR FREQUENTLY ACCOMPANIED SOLDIERS INTO BATTLE DURING THE MIDDLE AGES.

IN ANCIENT ETHIOPIA, SOLDIERS WORE HELMETS *MADE from the SKULLS of HORSES.*

• The Pilgrims used muskets, not blunderbusses—the blunderbuss was not developed until 1650, some thirty years after the arrival of the *Mayflower*!

• Firearms issued to British troops, when the Spanish Armada attempted to invade England in 1588, were less accurate than the bow and arrow and had a shorter range—but were considered more effective because of the psychological effect of their flash and explosion.

• In the nineteenth century, warriors in India fired garnets instead of bullets from their guns, believing that the gems would cause bloodier wounds!

• Fifteen hundred soldiers, using matchlock muskets in the 1600s, in a single battle would use up five hundred pounds of matches.

• A flintlock rifle of the type used by colonial Americans took three hundred hours to make by hand.

• Austrian Bader troops in the nineteenth century were required by regulations to carry their rifles under their cloaks—with the barrel inside their right sleeve.

KNIVES, SWORDS, AND BLADES

• In India, the ancient Sikhs used as a weapon a razor-sharp metal disk resembling a Frisbee, which they flung at their enemies!

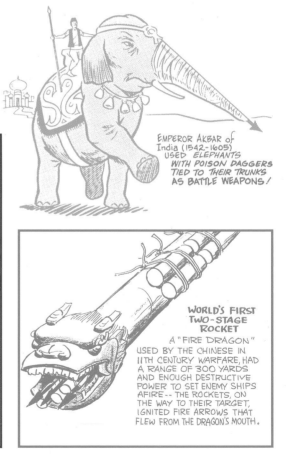

EMPEROR AKBAR of India (1542-1605) USED ELEPHANTS WITH POISON DAGGERS TIED TO THEIR TRUNKS AS BATTLE WEAPONS!

THE **FIRST USE OF BIOLOGICAL AND PSYCHOLOGICAL WARFARE!** HANNIBAL
247-183 B.C. The Carthagian general enabled King Prusias of Bithynia to win a great naval victory over King Eumenes of Pergamum by suggesting that the Bithynians hurl onto the decks of the enemy's ships earthenware jugs filled with venomous snakes!

WORLD'S FIRST TWO-STAGE ROCKET
A "FIRE DRAGON" USED BY THE CHINESE IN 11TH CENTURY WARFARE, HAD A RANGE OF 300 YARDS AND ENOUGH DESTRUCTIVE POWER TO SET ENEMY SHIPS AFIRE -- THE ROCKETS, ON THE WAY TO THEIR TARGET, IGNITED FIRE ARROWS THAT FLEW FROM THE DRAGON'S MOUTH.

PROJECTILES

• A military launch ramp, designed in the sixteenth century to propel rockets, was the forerunner of the World War II bazooka.

• The knifelike teeth of piranhas are used by natives in South America as arrow tips.

• Cannon in the seventeenth century were protected from enemy fire by huge balloons filled with wool.

UNUSUAL AND EXPERIMENTAL WEAPONS

• In the 1800s, marbles were often used as ammunition on warships!

• In the 1940s, the United States National Defense Research Committee considered using bats fitted with tiny incendiary bombs as weapons of war!

• **Albert B. Pratt** of Lyndon, Vermont, filed a patent for a combination gun, helmet, and cooking pan!

NON-LETHAL IS NOT NON-PAINFUL— TOM PINNEY OFFERS HIMSELF AS A TARGET TO TEST PACIFISTS' WEAPONS

Tom Pinney is a human guinea pig—by his own choice. A self-proclaimed pacifist, Pinney has for years encouraged police departments to adopt non-lethal methods of law enforcement. With the streets becoming ever more dangerous, in an era when one officer is killed on America's streets every day, the need for effective weaponry is paramount.

Pinney finds that plenty of police departments would be willing to incorporate non-lethal means of crowd control and suspect apprehension—and there are plenty of such devices on the market—if they had a better idea how these weapons behave when fired at a person. Shooting at paper targets and mannequins are one thing—but how will these non-lethal weapons work against live human beings?

That's where Tom Pinney puts his money where his mouth is. He regularly offers himself to police officers for target practice. Pinney has allowed himself to be painfully shot, shocked and gassed—all in the name of research!

Among the weapons Pinney has had tested on him is a noxious little number called the "Attitude Adjuster." Designed to disperse unruly crowds, this weapon fires an explosive pellet that emits a foul odor on contact—its smell is so awful that it can break up the most determined crowd!

Even more unpleasant is the "Sticky Shocker," a projectile that, when fired, attaches itself to a suspect's clothing, and emits a mild to moderate electric shock. While testing this device on a low setting, Tom was knocked to the ground. On a higher setting, the sticky shocker caused Tom's body to flail uncontrollably.

Perhaps least pleasant of all, Tom has allowed himself to be shot with tiny red marble-like bullets that emit on contact a mix of pepper spray and other painful chemicals. After he was shot with pepper bullets, Tom's nose, throat, and eyes stung so horribly that he could not speak for several minutes.

None of these weapons are particularly pleasant, as Tom can attest. But in spite of all the assaults Tom has endured, not one has harmed him permanently. Tom hopes that with a human test subject, police departments will gain more confidence in these new weapons' effectiveness. But Tom Pinney can tell you, from firsthand experience: non-lethal does NOT necessarily mean non-painful!

Chapter 63

MINERVA BONHAM of Ontario, Canada, struck by lightning, had all of her hairpins pulled out of her hair! (1951)

You've heard the expression "once in a blue moon." But did you know that in Australia, if you're very lucky, you might actually see one? Bizarre weather phenomena and inexplicable atmospheric occurrences have been recorded throughout written history. But there's seldom a way to predict them. It's often a matter of pure chance, of being there at the right place and time. Because the world's weirdest weather only happens. . .once in a blue moon.

ATYPICAL WEATHER

• Snow fell three times during July, in New England in 1816—fulfilling a prediction in that year's edition of the Old Farmer's Almanac—inserted as a prank!

• The day it snowed in the Sahara: Snow fell on Gargaff and Serir Benaffen in the most arid section of the Sahara on January 6, 1913, to a depth of four inches—the area's only snowfall in three thousand years.

• Snow fell on Indiana in July—an eight-inch snowfall covered four hundred square feet of the Rich Valley, July 2, 1924.

• The most destructive hailstorm in all history! Hailstones as large as baseballs smashed Moradabad, India, on April 30, 1888, killing two hundred thirty people.

• In 1995 a snow storm swept through Alexandria, Egypt, for the first time in living memory!

FORECASTING

• The barometer house of Yale, Oklahoma, trembles violently when rain or stormy weather is due.

ONCE A BLUE MOON
APPEARED IN AUSTRALIA
IT WAS CAUSED BY A TREMENDOUS DUST STORM
CONTAINING MYRIADS OF SPECKS OF SILICA OXIDE
WHICH CUT OUT THE RED AND YELLOW RAYS
—LEAVING ONLY THE BLUE

"The Big Wind"

IN 1934, *THE STRONGEST NATURAL WIND EVER RECORDED—223 MILES PER HOUR—OCCURRED ON Mt. Washington, New Hampshire!*

• A cliff in the Tyrrhenian Sea, 287 feet high, is located forty miles from Sicily—yet serves Sicilians as a barometer. If they see the cliff the weather is sure to remain fair.

• The strangest barometer in all England: Saint Catherine's Tower, on the Isle of Wight, is considered an infallible forecaster of rain whenever daylight can be seen through its eight upper windows.

ATMOSPHERIC PHENOMENA

• Green clouds have been seen over Australia.

• The moon rainbow, a multicolored arc of light sighted over Lobenstein, Germany, on May 7, 1947, was formed by the light of the moon.

• The whirling cloud of Mount Jirinaj, Indonesia: A floating cloud hovering over the peak of an extinct volcano, affected by hot air rising from the crater, spins swiftly around and around.

EXTREME TEMPERATURES

• The thermometer registered 158.8 degrees Fahrenheit in the Oasis of the Tuaregs, in Northern Africa, in 1927.

• Guns and harpoons are left outside igloos in the Arctic because heat from stoves would make the weapons unusable when they were returned to the frigid cold.

RAINBOWS VIEWED from AIRPLANES APPEAR AS COMPLETE CIRCLES!

FOR SEVERAL MONTHS in 1883, AFTER THE ERUPTION of Indonesia's Krakatau Volcano, PEOPLE AROUND THE WORLD REPORTED SEEING AN EMERALD GREEN MOON, SET IN A CRIMSON SKY!

EGGS IN NORTHERN ALASKA'S FRIGID TEMPERATURES, WHICH REACH 60° BELOW ZERO, IF LEFT OUTDOORS TOO LONG, CAN BE BOUNCED LIKE RUBBER BALLS

THUNDER AND LIGHTNING

• Two thousand thunderstorms may be above the earth at any one time, generating one hundred lightning bolts every second—equivalent to four billion kilowatts.

• Kampala, Uganda, averages two hundred forty-two days of thunderstorms every year!

• In 1995, seventeen English soccer players were struck by one bolt of lightning! All seventeen survived!

• A thunderstorm on Saint Paul Island, in the Bering Sea, in November 1992 was the first to occur there in forty years!

• During a thunderstorm, the bolted iron door of the Eddystone Lighthouse, in England, burst open from inside due to the pneumatic pull of the waves!

• **Saint Osmund**'s cathedral in Old Sarum, England, which took thirty years to build, was destroyed by lightning only a few hours after its completion.

• Lightning strikes thrice: In 1991, lightning destroyed a house in Maleville, France, for the third time in twenty years!

• **Martin Uman,** of Gainesville, Florida, operates a Museum of Lightning-struck Objects, including charred telephone receivers, melted radios, and fried clotheslines!

In 1959, U.S. Marine pilot WILLIAM RANKIN parachuted out of an airplane at 47,000 ft. during a severe thunderstorm and was trapped in the middle of a strom cloud for 40 minutes!

• The church of Contigny in France was struck by lightning while services were being conducted in it on June 21, 1789. The belfry crashed into the edifice, demolishing the church—yet not one of the 153 worshipers was injured.

• **Mary Clamser,** of Oklahoma City, Oklahoma, confined to a wheelchair with multiple sclerosis, stood up and walked for the first time after being struck by lightning!

HURRICANES

• In 1979, at the Santo Domingo Airport in the Dominican Republic, a cargo plane weighing eight tons was blown into the air by Hurricane David and deposited upside down on the roof of a warehouse!

• Hurricanes are so feared in the United States Virgin Islands that July 30 is celebrated as Supplication Day—when the natives pray for deliverance from such storms.

• It is estimated that Hurricane Mitch, which devastated the Caribbean, contained the equivalent of thirty trillion watts of energy per second—more energy than the entire human race used in 1990!

• Australia weatherman **Clement Wragge** was the first person to name hurricanes after people, using the names of people he had at some time quarreled with!

• In 1989, a swarm of desert locusts caught in a hurricane traveled a distance of twenty-seven hundred miles from Africa to the West Indies!

• During the Florida hurricane of 1926, a twelve-foot alligator was blown out of the water and carried two miles in the air!

• Hurricane Pauline, which devastated parts of Mexico in 1997, swept three people, who had been lost at sea for fifteen days, safely back to shore!

• A concrete shelter anchored to the ground with chains was lifted and split open by two-hundred-mile-per-hour hurricane winds!

FREAK STORMS

• During a freak storm, fifteen million trees were blown down in southern England!

• A single dust storm in 1934 blew away three hundred million tons of topsoil—the same amount of earth dredged from the Panama Canal!

FLOODS

• During World War II, five hundred thousand acres of land in Holland were flooded, drowning an estimated two hundred fifty billion worms!

• During a flood in 1933, a rocking chair owned by **Robert Currey** floated thirty miles down the Ohio River, but was returned unscathed!

• In California's Mojave Desert, a flash flood once swept away a railway locomotive and buried it in mud over a mile away!

• After severe flooding in Orange County, California, a police officer caught a thirty-pound carp swimming in the street and handcuffed it to his bumper!

• Dinner cruise! After a flood in Hunter Valley, New South Wales, Australia, a small pig was found in half a pumpkin floating down the river. It had been gnawing on the pumpkin's flesh as it sailed!

TSUNAMIS AND WILD SEAS

• The U.S.S. *Wateree*, a two-hundred-foot iron gunboat, was swept by a seventy-foot-high wave across the harbor of Arica, Chile, and deposited a quarter of a mile inland!

• **Typhoon John**, which raged in the North Pacific in 1993, lasted thirty-one days!

• A New Years' Day Ice Bowl football game, on King Island, Alaska, scheduled to be played on a giant ice floe, had to be canceled when the playing field was blown away in a storm!

A COTTAGE IN MALAGASH POINT, NOVA SCOTIA, CANADA, WAS LIFTED from ITS FOUNDATION AND SET DOWN ¼ MILE AWAY DURING A FIERCE WINTER STORM—Believe It or Not./ EVERYTHING INSIDE REMAINED INTACT, INCLUDING BOTTLES ON TOP of THE KITCHEN CABINETS./

A tornado carried away the end of this house without disarranging the dishes in the pantry!

• A 278-foot-high tidal wave off Japan's Ishigaki Island flung an 850-ton block of coral a distance of 1.3 miles!

TORNADOES

• A tornado that tore through Illinois and Indiana in 1917 traveled two hundred ninety-three miles in seven hours.

• In 1840 a tornado swept through Natchez Landing, Mississippi, with such force that iron spikes were driven up to their heads in the walls of houses!

• A 1990 tornado in Bakersville Valley, Texas, removed three hundred feet of blacktop from a highway and rolled two ninety-ton oil tanks a distance of three miles, depositing them six hundred feet up the side of a mountain!

• In 1896 in Saint Louis, Missouri, a tornado tore a team of horses from a wagon—but left the wagon and driver unharmed!

• An 1878 tornado in Iowa carried a cow a distance of ten miles through the air!

• The strangest tornadoes in all nature: Huge columns of sand appear suddenly in the Sonora Desert, in Mexico, and mysteriously whirl violently—although there is not the slightest breeze in the area.

• A tornado near Moorhead, Minnesota, lifted from a passenger train eight cars, each weighing eight tons—and dropped one over eighty feet away! (May 27, 1931)

• A pedal organ blown from a home in Georgia in 1932 by a tornado, was found miles away virtually undamaged.

• In 1919 in Fergus Falls, Minnesota, a tornado split open a tree, then blew an automobile off the road into the split!

• A tornado twisted a wire fence into a ball, trapping a chicken inside. The chicken survived—but was plucked bare!

• A cat belonging to **Paul** and **Chris Staton** of Greenfield, Indiana, survived after a tornado sucked it out of its home and dropped it four miles away!

• An 1898 tornado passing over a lake in Australia raised a water spout a mile high!

• In 1994 a tornado in Le Mars, Iowa, picked up a doghouse with a dog inside and set it down several blocks away—without harming the animal!

• **"Sadie,"** a Yorkshire terrier owned by James Davis, was picked up by a tornado in Saginaw, Texas, and set down uninjured two miles away!

• A tornado blew a cloud of canceled checks two hundred miles from a bank in Wichita Falls to Tulsa, Oklahoma!

SNOW

• It is estimated that 10,000,000,000,000,000, 000,000,000,000,000,000 snowflakes have fallen to the Earth since the Earth was formed!

• Seventy feet of snow fell at the Alta Ski Resort, in Utah, during the winter of 1983-1984!

• Santa Fe, New Mexico, averages more snow per year than New Haven, Connecticut!

IN 1887, HUGE SNOWFLAKES MEASURING *15 INCHES ACROSS AND 8 IN. THICK* FELL NEAR FORT KEOGH, MT!

• Chocolate snow! As a result of a dust storm in the Mallee district of Victoria, Australia, and a snow storm over the Victorian Alps, chocolate-colored snow fell at Mount Hotham in July of 1935!

• A single blizzard that hit the western United States in 1942 lasted for seven weeks!

• On October 14, 1775, red snow fell over the Swiss Alps!

• In 1978, 50,000,000,000, 000,000,000 snowflakes fell on Boston, Massachusetts, in one snowstorm!

RAINFALL

• Precipitation falling on the United States every

day totals an average of 4,200,000,000,000 gallons, of which people use only about six percent.

• The average thundercloud holds six trillion raindrops!

• Storms on August 5, 1890, in Adair and Union Counties, Texas, left six-foot-high drifts of hail that stayed on the ground for a month!

• On July 15, 1911, during a rainstorm, every acre in Baguio, the Philippines, received an average of fifty-four hundred tons, or one million three hundred fifty thousand gallons of water.

• Forecast: Rain—For the Next Million Years: There's a small stretch of land near the Parana River in Paraguay where rain has been falling ceaselessly for millions of years.

Believe It or Not! RAINDROPS CONTAIN VITAMIN B12!

LIGHTNING STALKER— A PHOTOGRAPHER RISKS HIS LIFE TO CAPTURE HIGH VOLTAGE ON FILM

When a lightning storm streaks the sky, the prudent individual runs for shelter. But just as you're running towards cover, you might be surprised to see a man with a camera running in the opposite direction.

Photographer David O. Stillings is a lightning-stalker. For the past twenty-five years he has braved the deadly voltage of electrical storms in order to capture those split-second arcs of light as they flash across the sky.

Stillings risks life and limb to get his incredible shots. Not only must he stand outside unprotected in the worst of weather, but his camera, tripod—and nearly every other piece of his equipment—are metal. He literally makes himself a human lightning-rod in order to capture his subject on film.

David has had a few close calls. In his line of work, if you find yourself in trouble, it's too late to do anything about it. David recalls once being too close to a lightning strike: "The next thing I knew I was picking myself up off the ground."

David began his photographic career shooting sunsets and rain clouds. But he forsook this tamer fare the day he accidentally caught a lightning bolt on film. He's been hooked ever since.

Of course, if you're going to photograph lightning, you have to go where the storms are. David lives in Orlando, Florida, where the turbid air from the Gulf and the Atlantic mix into a volatile stew overhead that creates an average of ninety lightning strikes a year.

Photographing lightning is a feat of serendipitous timing. "If you wait for the flash, it's too late," David explains, "You have to photograph it before it happens."

It RAINS FISH in Yoro, Honduras. Each July freak tropical storms shower fish as long as 6 inches over the entire countryside.

IN 1994, A RAIN of GREEN LIQUID FELL ALONG A SINGLE BLOCK of Mission St. in San Francisco, Ca.

• The rainiest spot in the world: Mount Waialeale, Hawaii, has an average rainfall of four hundred sixty inches a year.

ODD RAIN

• A rain of thousands of maggots fell over Acapulco, Mexico, in 1968.

• On October 9, 1892, a yellow cloud hovered over the town of Paddehorn, Germany, then a rain of live mussels poured into the streets!

• A rain of freshwater carp encased in ice fell from the sky in Essen, Germany, 1896.

• In 1876, a shower of fresh meat fell from the sky in southern Kentucky.

• In 1876 during a severe hailstorm in Bovina, Mississippi, a six-inch turtle encased in ice fell to the ground.

• One thousand toads once fell from the sky over a village in France!

Index